U.S. History *as* Women's

U.S. History *as* Women's History

New Feminist Essays

EDITED BY *Linda K. Kerber,*

Alice Kessler-Harris, & Kathryn Kish Sklar

THE UNIVERSITY OF NORTH CAROLINA PRESS *Chapel Hill & London*

Library of Congress Cataloging-in-Publication Data

U.S. history as women's history: new feminist essays /

edited by Linda K. Kerber, Alice Kessler-Harris, and

Kathryn Kish Sklar.

p.   cm.—(Gender and American culture)

Includes bibliographical references and index.

ISBN 0-8078-2185-3 (cloth : alk. paper).—

ISBN 0-8078-4495-0 (pbk. : alk. paper)

1. Women—United States—History. I. Kerber, Linda K.

II. Kessler-Harris, Alice. III. Sklar, Kathryn Kish. IV. Title:

US history as women's history. V. Title: United States

history as women's history. VI. Series: Gender & American

culture.

HQ1410.U17   1995

305.4'0973—dc20   94-27192

CIP

99 98 97 96 95   5 4 3 2 1

TO GERDA LERNER

in admiration for her courage

her leadership

and her pioneering work

CONTENTS

PART 3. KNOWLEDGE

T his book is dedicated to Gerda Lerner, who has been a resolute advocate of the capacity of history to change the course of human events. A historian of women who has transcended the limits of the academy to reach out to a wide audience, she has challenged a generation of scholars and activists to join her. Committed to expanding the possibilities for women to participate fully in society, she has worked to expand knowledge about women's past in ways that will change the consciousness of men and women. This book celebrates Gerda Lerner's intellectual and political energy, her talent for engaged scholarship, her creativity, her persuasive powers, and the combative spirit that has enabled her to give new meaning to the historical enterprise.

The contributors to this volume grew up into a world in which history was rigidly limited. It paid little attention to social relationships, to issues of race, to the concerns of the poor, and virtually none to women. Women figured in history for their ritual status, as wives of presidents like Abigail Adams or Dolly Madison; for their role as spoilers, from the witches of Salem to Mary Todd Lincoln; or for their sacrificial caregiving, like Clara Barton or Dorothea Dix. Even when women like Sojourner Truth, Jane Addams, and Eleanor Roosevelt were named by historians, the radical substance of their work and their lives was routinely ignored. A very few historians of women—Eleanor

Flexner, Julia Cherry Spruill, Caroline Ware—worked on the margins of the profession, their contributions unappreciated and their writing vulnerable to the charge of irrelevance.

The politics of the 1960s sparked a radical change. The civil rights movement, resistance to the Vietnam War, and a new wave of feminism inspired a generation of scholars to explore subjects previously ignored. The feminist assertion that "the personal is political," which unearthed so many hidden injuries, had its own resonance for historians who took up the challenge to interrogate the ways in which the structures and experience of daily life, and women's roles in them, shaped the construction of public culture. If the personal and the private had political implications, then the significance of women, even positioned as private and apolitical beings, also had substantive political implications.

When Gerda Lerner entered graduate school at Columbia University in 1963, she overcame her mentor's resistance and wrote a dissertation on the Grimké sisters. By the time she completed her degree three years later, a generation of graduate students committed to an engaged history was beginning to form. Each of the contributors to this volume found her or his own path to women's history in the years between 1967 and 1972. Trekking through unfamiliar terrain, each of us encountered Gerda Lerner: sometimes it was through something she had written; sometimes it was at a political meeting; sometimes it was on a scholarly panel. She seemed to be everywhere. Her authoritative voice, with its muted Viennese inflection, cajoled, persuaded, encouraged, and demanded changes in the way we wrote history and in the way the profession treated women. We responded because her words resonated with what we were thinking and because she was radical and brave. She took risks: in the subjects she chose to study, in the research and analytic strategies she adopted, in the ways she negotiated the surfaces of the profession. She was older than we were, yet she was more energetic than most of us. She could hold a room with her formidable presence.

For Gerda Kronstein Lerner, history was her third, perhaps even her fourth career. In 1938 she received the "Matura" in her native Vienna just before she was forced by the Nazis to leave the country of her birth. Arriving in the United States, she took a succession of what she later described as "typical women's jobs" while she learned English and then married Carl Lerner and raised two children. Over a twenty-year period, she became an active political organizer around issues of social justice and women's equality, and a creative writer. She collaborated with Eve Merriam on a musical called the *Singing of Women*, which was produced in 1951; published a moving novel, *No Farewell*, in 1955; and wrote an important screenplay, *Black Like Me*, published in 1964. In

1959 she resumed her formal education, earning a B.A. at the New School for Social Research in 1963 before she entered Columbia to start on her Ph.D. By then she already knew that she would make a career of women's history. Her dissertation quickly became, in 1967, her first historical publication, *The Grimké Sisters from South Carolina: Rebels against Slavery.*

In the relatively short space of time since then, Gerda Lerner's talent as a scholar, thinker, practical politician, and organizer has been widely felt. Her scholarly work, which began with a stubborn insistence that sources could be found to study even the poorest and most subordinated of women, has stretched the boundaries of our knowledge about women's lives and encouraged historians to ask questions previously considered impossible.

At first, Lerner focused her attention on the American context, producing articles and books in which she placed women's activities as institution and community builders at the center of political struggle. In order to find the documents that are included in *Black Women in White America* (1972), Lerner traveled throughout the South, visiting African American churches, schools, and families, her own example energizing allies to help her in retrieving written records that many historians had easily assumed had not survived. The book—which, like virtually all of her major publications, remains in print—still offers a warning against the assumption that any people are voiceless. By its example, it has inspired other documentary retrieval projects, notably Darlene Clark Hine's Black Women in the Middle West archive.

Presciently, Lerner recognized that if there were to be a new women's history it would need to organize itself around principles that would illuminate women's lives. She had already begun to do this in her classic article, "The Lady and the Mill Girl: Changes in the Status of Women in the Age of Jackson" (1969), where she demonstrated how differences in class location altered women's relationships to each other and shaped their responses to technological and economic change. In her documentary history, *The Female Experience* (1976), she developed a chronology and periodization that reorganized history around life-cycle categories opening up fresh possibilities of thinking about women in terms of their own experience. She virtually predicted the general outlines of the future historiography of the field in "Placing Women in History: Definitions and Challenges" (1975).[1]

By the end of the 1970s Lerner had already concluded that studying the United States alone —even over the course of its four-hundred-year settlement—was insufficient to provide an authentic understanding of the problematic relations between men and women. Americans had made their own reinterpretations of the patriarchy that they had inherited, but they had not invented it. As fearless as ever, Lerner embraced a more capacious agenda.

Raising some of the same questions that Friedrich Engels had addressed in 1884 in *The Origin of the Family, Private Property, and the State*, she began to seek the origins of patriarchy and of the subordination of women. Though her project moved her out of familiar time, it led her back to the European-centered turf in which she had been steeped as a child. Working with familiar and unfamiliar languages and cultural references, and with a broad sweep of literary sources as well as religious and archaeological artifacts, she painstakingly traced the emergence and development of patriarchy over more than two millennia of Western civilization.

The result has been an astonishing demonstration of virtuosity. In the first of two volumes, *The Creation of Patriarchy* (1986), she challenged traditional conceptions of the emergence of slavery to construct new definitions of class and to reveal new meanings of customary ideas and metaphors about women. The argument forged a new and persuasive synthesis that has revealed patriarchy's vulnerability to social circumstance and historicized its construction. In *The Creation of Feminist Consciousness* (1993), Lerner explored the devastating effects on women of their exclusion from the historical record. She persuasively argued that women's struggle to comprehend their own history lies at the heart of their ability to envision a world in which they are full participants.

This insight pervades every phase of Gerda Lerner's life. At a time when many American academics insisted that good historical practice required that historians distance themselves from the political passions of their time, Lerner taught that one wrote history to save one's own life, indeed one's own sanity. As a person who had been, by Fascist law, racialized into an "Other," she had experienced the significance of racism. As a political activist, she had learned how crucial class relations were to understanding the historical process. As a feminist, she had already concluded that integrating women into history would wholly transform historical and therefore present consciousness.

All the contributors to this volume share some portion of these sensibilities, but Gerda Lerner lives them with an intensity and conviction that leaves us breathless. Convinced that history was "an absolute lifeline to self-recognition and to giving our life meaning," she has dedicated herself both to innovative and resourceful research and to the training and education in women's history not only of young scholars, but also of female activists and the public. Her accomplishments in this area are nothing short of remarkable. As a faculty member in 1972 at Sarah Lawrence, she persuaded the college to invest in what was then the unique idea of a master's program in women's history. With help from the Rockefeller Foundation, this program became a model for graduate education in the field, preceding and inspiring the many Ph.D. programs that followed, including her own expanded work at the University of Wisconsin.

All the while, Gerda Lerner traveled to college campuses to teach truculent colleagues the importance of women's history. With astonishing patience, she helped reluctant historians understand how they might integrate gender issues into American history courses and research. Outside the academy, she played an important role in making women's history visible to the general public. She conceived the notion of an Institute for Women Leaders, which met at Sarah Lawrence in the summer of 1979. There, Molly McGregor brought from Sacramento the idea of a day-long celebration of women's history, and the proposal for a "Women's History Week" was born. When the institute concluded its meetings at a Washington, D.C., press conference, its leaders persuaded Colorado congresswoman Patricia Schroeder to ask for congressional endorsement. Since then, Women's History Week has become a month-long observance, transforming elementary and secondary school curriculums and bringing public programs that celebrate women's past to libraries, trade unions, and civic celebrations across the nation. Other institutes have had an equally startling impact. Gerda Lerner has organized programs for secondary school teachers and for scholars and students of black women's history. In 1988 she helped coordinate a conference on graduate training in U.S. women's history, which marked the maturity of the field by attracting scholars from fifty-two institutions that offered doctoral training in women's history. Each of these activities has spun off a web of activity and created networks of active participants.

We honor Gerda Lerner for her service to the profession and for her capacity to reach audiences far beyond the scholarly community. She continues to inspire us through her own example to think rigorously, systematically, analytically, and globally about women's role in history. We honor her for her success in demonstrating, in her own words, that women's history is a "primary tool for women's emancipation." We are grateful to her for challenging us to think in the ways that are reflected in these essays.

"I read [history] a little as a duty," observes Catherine Morland, the heroine of Jane Austen's *Northanger Abbey*, "it tells me nothing that does not either vex or weary me. The quarrels of popes and kings, with wars or pestilences . . . and hardly any women at all." Much of the work of women's historians has been dedicated to retrieving historical women, respecting their records, describing their lives. In "Placing Women in History," Gerda Lerner in effect predicted a historiography for a field of study that then barely existed. In the first stage historians would be like Diogenes with a lantern, wandering through the past, seeking literal evidence of women's historical existence. It was a stage characterized by productions like biographical dictionaries and documentary collections. That stage—marked in 1971 and 1980 by the publication of *Notable American Women*—continues to retain its vitality, as the publication in 1993 of *Black Women in America: An Historical Encyclopedia* testifies.[2] Once biographical presence was established, Lerner asserted, there would be a second stage, in which historians would easily recognize women's contributions to developments already marked as "important" but thought to have been completely the work of men; in a third stage it would be possible for historians to appreciate those enterprises that women themselves reshaped or reconfigured. Most of the contributions to the explosion of publications in women's history in the last three decades can readily be placed in one or another of these three categories.

Lerner understood, however, that to recognize women's historical agency would ultimately radically unsettle historical narratives as they had been written. To recognize women as historical actors—vulnerable as men are to forces beyond their control, striving as men do to shape the contours of their lives as best they can—is to introduce into historical work the analysis of gender relations. The work of women's history expands to include not only those experiences particular to women but also the complex relations between men and women. Asking questions about how men and women construct meaning for their historical experience, historians now understand that gender itself is socially constructed, a culturally specific system of meaning that—as Alice Kessler-Harris has said in another place—"orders the behavior and expectations of work and family, influences the policies adopted by government and industry, and shapes perceptions of equity and justice."[3] To put it another way, now that Catherine Morland can no longer complain that there are "hardly any women at all," historians are challenged to turn their attention back to "popes and kings, wars and pestilences," that is, to seeking to understand how men and women, in all their abrasive interaction, together construct and transform the world by power and by knowledge.

Women's history began by questioning the claims of the normative. It has intruded upon and destabilized virtually every element of the old narratives. All the standard topics—whether witchcraft, or slavery, or westward expansion, or industrialization, or political change—require reassessment. There is no doubt that the grand narratives that we have inherited, built as they were on the assumption that men's experience is normative and women's experience is trivial, are partial narratives; as Edmund S. Morgan once said in another context, they are "revisions in need of revising."[4] We are challenged to enter into dialogue with them; to reframe their questions; in short, to revise them, with the understanding that our work will be revised in its turn. Women's history has itself not been immune from charges that it has established a new set of norms. As a field, it has been profoundly tested by the challenge of African American scholars that it constructed its own exclusionary assumption that white women are the measure.

The essays in this book reflect the continuing dialogue over what we are as a field as well as how we influence the process of historical understanding. They are in their different ways evidence that the field has reached the fourth stage of development predicted by Lerner nearly two decades ago. Seeking a synthesis of what we know about women and about men, these essays are driven by questions about how power is certified and exercised, and how knowledge is produced and restricted. In this context women's agency sometimes achieves expression, but often it is subordinated. Individually and together these essays seek to discover how gender serves to legitimize particular constructions of power and knowledge, to meld these into accepted practice and state policy. In seeking women's agency, we seek to recapture voices of women in dialogue and in confrontation with men. We trust that these voices will lend depth to our perception of what counts as historically significant and that they will contribute information about women even as they help us comprehend what enables and sustains power for certain groups of men. When we find silences, we seek not simply to hear the still voices, but to discern how it was possible to write history from which women's voices were excluded; when we find spaces that seem empty, we ask how boundaries have been imposed and maintained.

State formation, power, and knowledge have not traditionally been understood to be the subjects of women's history. But they are themes that permeate the essays in this volume. As editors, we did not ask nor intend that this be so. It simply happened. In approaching potential contributors, we sought out historians of our own generation whose lives and work had been touched by Lerner's efforts to expand the impact of women's history. We make no claim to be inclusive; the network of powerful minds reached by Lerner is far more extensive than we could possibly encompass. Nor did we aspire to be fully representative as to field or approach. Rather, we wanted, by means of example, to illustrate how the new work in women's history had provoked an exciting reassessment of what constituted the historical enterprise.

As the essays began to come in, each of them an individual reflection on how current questions merged in or had affected its author's work, the editors discovered just how much the field of women's history had moved from the discovery of women to an evaluation of social process and institutions. The authors have rarely been explicit about problems of method or the theoretical implications of their work. But each, in exploring an element of individual research, has necessarily touched upon one or more ingredients of the linked nexus of power, knowledge, and state formation. The authors share a refusal to concede that the private is necessarily nonpolitical, a refusal that eases the examination of the reciprocity embedded in systems of political agency that empower men and systems that disempower women. It also becomes easier to seek sites of women's agency and power.

As states continue to develop, they continue to construct and reshape gender relations. Rights and obligations are rarely distributed or enforced evenly throughout a society; fissures run along the lines of gender, race, and class. Often race lines intersect with those of gender or of class. In the construction of citizenship, state formation, power, and knowledge merge until the elements are impossible to separate. Gender is implicated in the rights that states make it possible to claim; as Linda Kerber argues in her essay (Chapter 1), gender is also implicated in the obligations that states impose on citizens. What is right, what is obligation is negotiated; who wins these negotiations is determined not only by power relations but also by the confidence with which knowledge of appropriate social relationships can be asserted. In ideological systems that sustain the "knowledge" that women serve the state through serving the men of their family, women's exclusion from both rights and obligations is understood to be rational, realistic, and wise.

Thus in the United States the consent of the governed has been understood to be measured by voting, but for two-thirds of the nation's history, none of its women citizens could vote, and until the last few decades, explicit barriers to African American voters sustained their exclusion. Yet if, instead of assuming that therefore women had no political life we adopt a capacious understanding of the possible ingredients of politics, we discover that they did indeed have a political history, one that involved petitioning, testifying, and mobilizing themselves and others. Kathryn Sklar's essay in this volume (Chapter 2) shows how members of an organization of middle-class women developed their own forms of knowledge, their own view of power, and their own location in the political process, differentiating themselves from an analogous group of men and making it possible for them to accomplish what men could not. By enlarging her story to encompass the male-dominated political process, she shows how fundamental features of state formation in the United States created opportunities for women that were closed to men. In this case we see how women's gender-specific actions served as a surrogate or substitute for what ultimately became class-specific public policies. Part of this outcome arose from women's activism, part from the male-dominated polity in which they maneuvered.

Women can differ among themselves over how to achieve political voice. The particular strategies they choose depend on their assumptions as well as their goals, as Jane De Hart reveals in her astute assessment of more recent political activists (in Chapter 10). In the 1970s, campaigners for ratification of the Equal Rights Amendment, while exhibiting different styles of political behavior, acted on a shared notion of entitlement to equal rights. In the 1980s and early 1990s, practitioners of a feminist-inspired electoral politics mobilized to put women and men in office who supported a feminist agenda. They focused less on rights and more on representation of interests. More effective in their embrace of political power, they are nevertheless dependent on a broadly diffused feminist consciousness among the electorate.

The political history of women involves a narration of their regulation and control as well as of their agency; it involves a continuing struggle to shape political choices in a variety of sites. Power, even political power, has never been completely monopolized by those who were supposed to monopolize it; it has always been contested, always flowed into odd places. Linda Gordon's essay (Chapter 3) indicates how gender is implicated in systems of entitlements that also simultaneously become systems of regulation and control. When diverse coalitions of women attempted over a period of years to protect children, they found that they were most effective when they defined themselves, and the recipients of government aid, as selfless mothers. This reflected knowledge already in place among the middle classes and the elite; adjustment to this knowledge made possible a reshaping of state agencies. But a state that reshaped itself to assist children did so in part as a way of avoiding assisting more diffuse categories of adult women; the strategy of putting children first backfired, Gordon argues, because it required that women conform to a rigid and limited definition of motherhood. "Child-centeredness," writes Gordon, "worked for women primarily when they could get themselves defined as good mothers . . . ; when there was any question about their qualifications or parenting style, they became vulnerable to losing control over their children." Almost no activity in which adults participate is so generally thought to be a matter of private choice as marriage, yet, as Nancy Cott shrewdly points out (in Chapter 5), the context in which these private choices are made has always been rigidly shaped by state power and state policy. Who is eligible to marry, what pairings of individuals will be marked as miscegenation and made illegal, all are defined by the law of domestic relations. This system of law is coterminous with the origins of the state and inseparable from it.

As states develop bureaucracies and state services, these agencies too reflect cultural assumptions about what is fitting for men and what is fitting for women, hardening theory into practice. These assumptions sometimes result in gendered contests of power on sites that we have long understood to be explicitly involved in the exercise of male power, such as courts, schools, and prisons. Most American historians now concede that during the years from

1890 to around 1920, organized women exercised a great deal of influence over the social institutions governing American society. Searching for an explanation of why their influence waned after that date, some historians have pointed to the achievement of the suffrage; others, to the increasing bureaucratization of the state. But Estelle Freedman (in Chapter 8), using the life of prison superintendent Miriam Van Waters as a case in point, shows that separate women's organizations continued to support women who were able to acquire formal political authority. Although women's movements for reform were "smaller, more beleaguered, and more vulnerable after 1920," women continued to organize as women—even without an explicit ideology of gender difference.

The idea that women could construct pockets of public power that can be understood only by understanding the personal influences that moved them provides the model that William Chafe uses (in Chapter 9) to explain Allard Lowenstein's rise to power. Despite his provocative stances on issues of civil rights and social justice, Lowenstein, the child of immigrants, became a well-known congressman. Using Eleanor Roosevelt's life as a touchstone, Chafe demonstrates that in both cases the construction of their political careers can only be fully understood by understanding the personal anxieties that propelled them. But, in turn, the personal becomes a way for historians to understand the twists and turns of state policy in particular periods.

Yet even when it is so understood, maintaining that understanding involves invoking subtle and hidden forms of power. Power involves the controlling of choices and the continuing struggles to shape those choices in a variety of sites. These loci can include the most private spaces of all: we now understand clearly that even the happiest of nuclear families are places in which gendered power is exercised. Nell Painter challenges us (in Chapter 6) to take seriously the point that so long as slavery endured, all American families, white and black, enslaved and free, were necessarily participating in a single social system, one that licensed male heads of households to indulge their wish for power over all dependents. To live as a free person in a society based economically on slave production and characterized by open and unabashed captivity and physical abuse of adults and children had social and psychological implications, both for people who were themselves enslaved and for people who understood themselves to be free. If, as radical abolitionists maintained, all American society was indeed complicit in sustaining "the use of violence to secure obedience and deference," and in maintaining obedience and submission as ideals, then we are forced to reconsider many familiar generalizations about antebellum society, especially the North as a domain of freedom and individual choice.

If the process of state formation is intricately connected to practices of power, it is no less tied to the shaping of knowledge. Men and women know who they are and how they behave, and on the basis of that knowledge, they interpret their own lives. On the basis of that knowledge they seek to intervene in state formations. And on the basis of that knowledge, they lay claim to the shape of public policy, incorporating what they know into the construction of policy. Michel Foucault speaks of many knowledges; what we "know" and how confidently we know it is related to the knower's social place. For more than a century, young women of the middle classes searched in Louisa May Alcott's *Little Women* for what they needed to know in their quest for meaningful adulthood. Barbara Sicherman's subtle examination (in Chapter 11) of the ways in which interpretation of a single book varied by the "social location, interpretive conventions, and perceived needs of disparate communities of readers" is a powerful demonstration of the uses to which a historian can put the analytic strategies of reader-response theory. Read this way, *Little Women* becomes a social text, doing cultural work, not least for the young Jewish women whom Sicherman finds using the novel as a guide to upward mobility and what they understood to be authentic "American" life.

Michel Foucault also identifies a sphere of privileged knowledge, which, claimed by elites, by agents of state power, or by leaders, can be exercised in ways that regulate and control. A superb example of how this works on a small scale occurs in Judith Walzer Leavitt's essay (Chapter 7). For nearly a century, Leavitt reports, "Typhoid Mary" has been an abstraction, conveying the belief that women are associated with pollution, but not conveying anything at all about the real woman, Mary Mallon, or about the historical process that created her. Needing to regulate the disease, authorities had to create a picture of social disorder that the disease exemplified. To do this required them to find a symbol; in the process they constructed an image of a denatured woman. Descxing Mary Mallon, turning her into an Amazon, became the vehicle for enhancing the power of public health officials and advancing the status of the medical profession. When Mary Mallon was jailed, no powerful groups of women noticed the gendered basis of her incarceration and isolation. The "knowledge" of the experts organized in the public sector had overwhelmed the knowledge of nonprofessional, nonorganized friends and acquaintances. The cost was the reinforcement of the public conviction that, uncontrolled by social norms, women posed a threat to social order.

Alice Kessler-Harris suggests (in Chapter 4) some of the more general policy implications of particular constructions of knowledge. Her essay on the 1939 amendment to the Social Security Act explores some of the ways in which gendered assumptions permeated the legislative process. On the basis of who they think they are, men and women lay claim to policy knowledge, which in turn helps them shape a political agenda and construct social policy. In this instance, organized groups of women played an inconspicuous role, yet social policies did not escape the implications of gendered ideas that, in turn, sustained racial agendas. The Advisory Council, justifying a lower social security stipend to aging women, believed that they should live with a child. According to its chairman, "the grandmother helps in the raising of the children and helps in home affairs, whereas the aged grandfather is the man who sits out on the front porch and can't help much." State policies formulated on such a basis clearly had long-range implications for the construction of gender relations and for their uses as well.

Foucault also locates what he calls "subjugated knowledges"—knowledges "disqualified as inadequate to their task or insufficiently elaborated."[5] Women's knowledges, especially when claimed by women understood to be themselves subdued on the grounds of race or class, have often, but not always, been of this latter type. Such knowledge is often regulated by explicit repression, which Gerda Lerner has described in the case of women as the world-historical tendency to deny women access to their own past, even their own recent past. In an elegant illustration of this process, Amy Swerdlow's reconstruction (in Chapter 13) of the Congress of American Women (CAW) laments the process in which, even within a ten-year period, women activists could lose track of their own predecessors. Swerdlow has restored to us the history of the Congress of American Women, a group that once had a quarter of a million members and a wide-ranging program that included virtually every second-wave feminist goal. Repression not only killed the group but also eliminated memory of it. The Emma Lazarus Federation of Jewish Women's Clubs, which paralleled the CAW and lasted for about a decade longer, is the subject of Joyce Antler's essay (Chapter 12). Its much smaller Jewish immigrant membership continued to exercise power and influence by a conscious effort to sustain its cultural roots. But language and culture provided a closed system that did not outlast the generation of women who founded the group.

When young, white middle-class women in the 1960s sought ways to express their discontents, they did not have the experiences of either the Congress of American Women or the Emma Lazarus Federation available to them. Nor, indeed, could their mothers or their teachers provide them with energizing examples of ambition, authenticity, and political effectiveness. Largely ignorant of women's history, young women reacted against the Feminine Mystique of the 1950s. "The invisible ghost haunting their youth," writes Ruth Rosen (in Chapter 14), "wore an apron and lived vicariously through the lives of her husband and children." In their search for a different life, they responded to the criticism and activism of male rebels. Social critics lumped them together with young men and pronounced a "generation gap." But no one noticed that it was a gendered generation gap. For young women, rebellion against tradition turned into a much more complicated journey. Only after a struggle could they perceive that male claims for adventure were grounded in the assumption that women would continue to serve the needs of others. Without knowledge of their own historical situation, neither they nor the larger culture understood that "*two* generation gaps existed . . . each with its own gender-specific fears, dreams, and solutions."

The final essay in this volume movingly demonstrates the tragic example of wiping out historical memory for historians themselves and the efficacy of restoring lost women to us. Darlene Clark Hine describes (in Chapter 15) her painful decision to become involved in the creation of *Black Women in America: An Historical Encyclopedia* and the rewards of having done so. Her project restores to American history a vital culture and a crucially important community. Playing midwife to the reincarnation of the lives of 640 African American women enabled Hine to provide a historical record where none had existed. One can imagine their ghosts waiting for this fine encyclopedia.

Questions about the interrelationship between power and knowledge haunt the essays in this volume. If people understand themselves in a certain way, should we, as historians, take their "knowledge" for our own? When people are denied knowledge, they are usually also simultaneously disempowered. What does it mean to "know"? What does it mean to have, or to resist, power? When people in power or social movements seeking power use their knowledge to shape policy, knowledge and power become synchronous. State formation cannot be separated from the material conditions under which states are formed and constantly reshaped; the knowledge that guides state founders is knowledge of material conditions as well as of theory.

Women's history as traditionally practiced in the United States and elsewhere has situated itself as critique of inherited narrative. In each successive historiographical stage it has implicitly positioned itself as a disconcerting, destabilizing force, its practitioners locating themselves as outsiders who aimed to alter the trajectory of scholarship. In its early phases, practitioners took the risk that their conclusions would not be taken as obvious by historians whose gaze was on traditional measures of power. That risk turned out to be real; whether ignored or admired, women's history has been vulnerable to marginalization. But positions of marginality are frequently fruitful. Protest against marginalization drove Gerda Lerner's volumes on the relationship of patriarchy and feminist consciousness; we suspect that protest against marginalizing tendencies in part accounts for the efforts of the contributors to this volume to intrude into regions of the American historical narrative from which women had been excluded or in which gender relations were not thought to play a part. If the normative U.S. history can no longer be understood to be male, then there must be room for women in its center: room for Miriam Van Waters in the history of prisons, room for the persistent influence of the law of domestic relations in our understanding of the construction of citizenship, room for Typhoid Mary in the definition of disease. Like these essays, the new U.S. women's history of which they are a part provokes us to construct a new normative stance for all of U.S. history. This new history suggests that changes in gender relations in moments of social change have participated in changing power relations. It affirms the likelihood that these changes are central to new configurations of social power. In this sense we end with a vision of U.S. history as women's history quite as much as it is men's history.

"Human beings," Gerda Lerner has written, "have always used history in order to find their direction toward the future: to repeat the past or to depart from it."[6] As historians, including those represented here, seek to develop a more complexly articulated understanding of human relations in the past, they participate in a continuing effort to make power less mysterious and knowledge more accessible. It is, we think, a worthy quest.

Linda K. Kerber
Alice Kessler-Harris
Kathryn Kish Sklar

PART I *State Formation*

CHAPTER 1 : A CONSTITUTIONAL RIGHT TO BE TREATED LIKE AMERICAN LADIES : WOMEN AND THE OBLIGATIONS OF CITIZENSHIP : *LINDA K. KERBER*

The title of this essay comes from the words of Kathleen Teague, who represented the Eagle Forum, a conservative women's organization, in testimony before the House of Representatives Armed Services Committee in March 1980. The Soviet Union had invaded Afghanistan the previous winter; seeking a measured response, President Jimmy Carter had proposed universal mandatory draft registration. Carter recognized that in the event of a draft, current rules required that women be assigned only to noncombat roles; nevertheless, with 150,000 women already serving in the all-volunteer army, he believed that "[t]here is no distinction possible, on the basis of ability or performance, that would allow me to exclude women from an obligation to register." Teague argued against the administration's proposal. She and her colleagues pointed out that the obligation of military service had always been marked by gender. Recognizing the reciprocal relationship between rights and obligations, Teague pointed out that the absence of an obligation to serve in the military was tantamount to the presence of a right; women, she said, had the right "to be treated like . . . ladies. . . . [A right] which every American woman has enjoyed since our country was born."[1]

Teague was not wrong to argue that American tradition and precedent have sustained the practice of defining the ingredients of citizenship differently on the basis of gender. Women have been citizens of the United States from the moment of its origins: they could be naturalized, they were subject to its laws, and they could claim the protection of its courts; as single adult women, they were vulnerable to taxation. But American women's relationship to the state has from the beginning been understood to be different in substantial and important respects from the relationship of their male counterparts and contemporaries. Rights and obligations have generally been stated in generic terms incumbent on all citizens, male and female, but they have been experienced differently by men and by women. Struggle over women's suffrage and, in recent years, over the interpretation of the meaning of the right to the "equal protection of the laws" guaranteed in the Fourteenth Amendment has publicized the extent to which the meaning of rights has been linked to gender. That there is a history of gendered obligation is less well understood.

I suspect that we have not thought much about gendered differences in citizenship because we employ egalitarian language; all citizens, after all, pledge allegiance to the flag, using a capacious rhetoric that ignores differences of gender, race, and ethnicity. Indeed, in recent years the suspicion has been voiced that public understanding of the meaning of citizenship has shifted sharply. It is possible that an older scheme that emphasized conduct—the exercise of rights and the fulfillment of duties—is fading, to be replaced by an emphasis on claims without reciprocal duties, what Mary Ann Glendon has called "rights talk." Lizabeth Cohen and others have pointed out that the meaning itself is changing; in the late twentieth century, citizenship is increasingly treated as a commodity. Instead of being understood as a status that in turn authorizes civic participation, citizenship is increasingly likely to stand for a range of entitlements: to unemployment compensation, to welfare payments.[2]

What did Kathleen Teague mean when she asserted that American women have the "right" to be "treated like ladies"? The context suggests that she understood being a "lady" to involve being *excused* from civic obligation. Most contemporary theorists of citizenship, as well as members of Congress, acknowledged that the power to draft women was implicit in the sovereignty of the state. But many, like Teague though not so explicitly, also took the position that the failure of the state to exercise that power over the long course of the history of the republic had been tantamount to abandoning the claim. Although no one made the explicit analogy, the reasoning was not unlike the logic of the Supreme Court in *Minor v. Happersett* (1875), when the Court had agreed that given the absence of prohibitions against woman suffrage in the original constitutions of the federal government and the states, the original intent of the founding generation might well have encompassed the development of woman suffrage. But in 1875 the Court also maintained that the failure to act on that potential over a long period of time had established a fact. If woman suffrage had not been generated within a century after the ratification of the Constitution, the burden was on suffragists to establish their claim. A century after *Minor*, Teague conveyed that if an obligation of military service had not been developed over the course of nearly two centuries since ratification, a reciprocal right to be free of that obligation had been constructed in its place. She concluded that those who wished to change that status quo carried the burden of persuading women that the change was to their advantage.

In John Locke's classic formulations, claims of rights are generally related to reciprocal duties; the right to self-preservation is linked to the duty to preserve the safety of others.[3] Theorists of the social contract generally connect a duty to obey the law with the power to claim rights under it. The right to invoke the protection of the state is, for example, often tied to the obligation to bear arms in its defense. The relationship of rights and duties is rarely, however, so neatly reciprocal. The obligation to pay taxes has not always brought with it the right to vote, the right to vote does not bring with it the obligation to vote, and until very recently the right to serve on juries did not bring with it the obligation to serve on juries.

In her transformation of an issue of obligation into a problem of rights, Teague was squarely in the American political tradition; constitutional and theoretical debates have generally been focused around claims for *rights*. American political theorists have had relatively little to say about obligation. This emphasis is congruent with English political theory, which has, ever since Magna Carta, stressed claims that subjects can make against the prerogatives of the Crown and in which articulation of obligation has been correspondingly weak.[4] Much American thinking on the subject developed in the late eighteenth century, when the relation of the citizen to the state was theorized by revolutionaries who were asserting claims of rights against the state. Arguments were modeled on those expounded by Whigs during and after the English civil war, and also on those developed by Baptists, Quakers, and other groups in their struggle against compulsory church taxes in colonial Massachusetts and elsewhere. These political and religious rebels pushed the defense of rights in the direction of protecting freedom of thought and conscience and of resisting taxation without representation. The federal Constitution was remarkably silent on obligation. It was restricted to a succinctly outlined set of specified powers; the first ten amendments activated a set of limits on those powers, to be enforced by the act of *claiming* rights. The Civil War amendments continued in the same spirit; the Fourteenth Amendment, for example, describes citizenship in terms of its "privileges and immunities," not its duties or obligations. The strategy continues to infuse American constitutional and legal thinking.

The term *duty* is often informally used interchangeably with *obligation*. But *duty* is a broad term, encompassing behavior understood to be required by systems of morals as well as systems of law. Avoiding the term *obligation*, with its implication of a binding and perhaps transcendent moral duty, American constitutional argument, like liberal political theory in general, has mainly rested on the confidence that individuals can be authentically bound only by rules that they themselves have chosen, and that authentic government is shaped by freely chosen agreements among the ruled. Consent theory makes all obligation in some way an obligation to oneself, "there being," Thomas Hobbes wrote in *Leviathan* (pt. II, chap. 21), "no obligation on any man, which ariseth not from some act of his own." Much American constitutional talk proceeds as though the Revolution had created a state of nature and as though the Constitution were a social contract; having consented to the political order, all obligation becomes individually elected obligation. The burdens of citizenship, in theory, rest on all citizens alike. Once the powers of government are properly framed, a binding obligation, impersonally imposed on all citizens, ensues.

Consent theory, however, brings with it a number of fictive elements. As Edmund S. Morgan has poignantly argued, "government requires make-believe." It requires that an imagined community be called into being, personified "as though it were a single body . . . superior to government, and able to alter or remove a government at will."[5] When the Continental Congress issued a decree "on the authority of the people," and—especially—when the federal convention, exceeding its mandate to revise the Articles of Confederation, issued its Constitution in the name of "We the People," it was, as Michael Warner observes, displaying a "delirious theatricality . . . acting out, through time, the eighteenth century's narrative of legitimation: the social contract." In that context "the People" functioned as "a legitimating signifier," interpolating subjects into a political world; it was "cultural assumptions that allowed the printed constitution to embody the will of all."[6]

Even if the authority of "the people" is conceded, men and women have been differently situated in relation to consent theory. Carole Pateman's searching examination of the theory of social contract reveals that men are imagined as entering the social contract as free agents, but most women enter the social contract already bound by marriage and by antecedent obligations to their husbands.[7] This was certainly true in early America. When revolutionaries challenged laws governing the relations between male subjects and the king, reconstituting men as individuals free of patriarchal constraint, they left intact the law of domestic relations, which systematically merged the civic identity of married women with that of their husbands. Even though coverture, which transferred a woman's civic identity to her husband at marriage, giving him the use and direction of her property throughout the marriage, was theoretically incompatible with revolutionary ideology and with the liberal commercial society developing in the early republic, patriot men carefully sustained it. They even continued to refer to the body of law of coverture by its traditional name, "The law of baron et feme," that is, not the reciprocal "husband and wife" or "man and woman" but "lord and woman."[8]

To examine early American law of the household is an exercise in turning Pateman's theorizing into practice. To put it another way, before the constitutions were constructed as new social contracts, there were marriage contracts and the complex system of subordination and authority that they were understood to embody. If ever there were a site to examine the simultaneity of the personal as the political, it is here. The legal treatises of the early republic describe households as hierarchical as if Locke had never written.

Tapping Reeve, for example, conducted perhaps the most respected legal training in his generation; among his students were his own brother-in-law Aaron Burr and John C. Calhoun; there were also future U.S. congressmen and senators, judges and Supreme Court justices. A full generation after the Revolution (forty years after the Declaration of Independence and twenty-nine years after the Constitutional Convention) Reeve published an authoritative treatise on the law of baron and feme. First published in 1816, it was reprinted with up-to-date annotations in 1846, a testament to its continued vitality.[9]

Reeve began with the forthright statement that "the husband, by marriage, acquires an absolute title to all the personal property of the wife"; in the second chapter he described the husband's control of the wife's real estate. By the third chapter Reeve was asking "what advantages the wife may gain, eventually, by marriage, in point of property" and answering directly, "She gains nothing." Reeve did not stop there, however. Once these asymmetrical property relations were established, personal implications wound their way throughout the law. From the husband's control of all property there logically resulted the wife's inability to resist him; his coercive power over her was so great by blackmail that he was not thought to need to use force. Any legal offense that she did in his presence "if he joins in committing it, or also encourages, or in any way approves thereof, the law presumes, that whatever the wife does, is done by the husband's coercion." A wife could not make a contract, since it would not be reasonable to hold her to its terms, "as it might be effect of coercion."[10]

To follow the law of domestic relations, as Reeve delicately spun out its implications, is to watch the playing out of a stacked deck. Husbands were responsible for crimes committed by their wives in their presence or with their approval—except in the case of treason, a crime so severe that responsibility for it overrode obligation to the husband—or in the event that a wife kept a brothel with the husband's knowledge, since keeping a brothel "is an offense of which the wife is supposed to have the principal management." Because a wife could not make contracts in her own name, a husband was bound "to fulfill the contract of his wife, when it is such an one as wives in her rank of life usually purchase. . . . If, however, she were to purchase a ship or yoke of oxen, no such presumption would arise, for wives do not usually purchase ships or oxen."[11]

The law of domestic relations presupposed the husband's right to sexual access to the wife's body. For example, when Reeve explained why it was logical that wives could not enter into contracts, his reason was not only that wives did not control property that could guarantee their performance of the contract; wives could not enter into contracts involving their own labor. "[T]he right of the husband to the person of his wife," Reeve observed, ". . . is a right guarded by the law with the utmost solicitude; if she could bind herself by her contracts, she would be liable to be arrested, taken in execution, and confined in a prison; and then the husband would be deprived of the company of his wife, which the law will not suffer." However, if a husband were banished from the realm, then his wife "could contract, could sue and be sued in her own name; for in this case, . . . he was already deprived of the company of his wife, and her confinement in prison would not deprive him of his wife to any greater extent than was already the case."[12]

Under coverture, a woman's only freely chosen obligation was to her husband. Once she made that choice, he controlled her body and her property; there were relatively few constraints on what he could do with either, except for the near universal guarantee of the use of one-third of his property during her widowhood. A married woman had no means of acting upon a choice of her own that challenged her husband's; there were too many ways in which he could, by "moderate correction" or by manipulating her property, coerce her into agreement with him. Instead of protecting her against coercion, the law acknowledged that it was embedded in the marriage relationship. The married woman could have no will of her own. The legal system acknowledged her dependency by the practice of holding private examinations of married women before permitting them to sign away their right to any dower property and by not holding married women responsible for crimes committed in the presence of and with the knowledge of their husbands. If married women were permitted to vote, it was understood that husbands could too easily pressure their choices.

American revolutionaries did not change the law of domestic relations at the same time that they radically changed other civic relations; they did not even debate the possibility. They did not need to. Male revolutionaries of different classes and regions were differently situated in regard to slavery; some men benefited enormously, some a little, some not at all. It is not surprising, therefore, that white men debated the system of slavery and made some modifications in it. But all free married men—whatever their class position, whether they were white or black—benefited from a system of law in which husbands controlled the bodies and property of their wives. They felt no need to renegotiate it.

Rights and obligations are reciprocal elements of citizenship; so long as married women were understood to owe all their obligation to their husbands, they could make no claims of rights against the political community. They would have no way to consent or withhold their consent. American political theorists not only recoiled from making voting—the most explicit gesture of consent—an obligation of citizenship; they also refused until very recently to make it a natural right inseparable from citizenship. This hesitancy helped in large measure to sustain the gendered construction of the American citizen. The *feme covert*, asserted one prominent lawyer in the early nineteenth century, "has no *political* relation to the *state* any more than an alien."[13] Not until deep into the twentieth century was this statement prima facie absurd.[14] In the early republic, women were citizens, but they expressed their citizenship derivatively; it was the rare immigrant woman, wealthy with property in her own name to protect, who sought naturalization in her own right.

In effect, the law of domestic relations came down to the husband's property rights in his wife's body and to his position as barrier between her and public obligation.[15] If she could not make a private contract, how could she enter the social contract? The same body of reasoning that governed the relations between husbands and wives monitored all household relations— parent and child, master and servant, guardian and ward. Against that system of law there would be hurled, throughout the nineteenth and twentieth centuries, the complex ideologies of individual rights, fueling a political women's rights movement from the founding generation of the republic to the present. The agenda of second-wave feminism, the women's movement of the late twentieth century, has included many items that responded to elements of the old law of domestic relations inherited from two centuries before. Thus a flyer for the equal rights march in New York City on August 26, 1970, the fiftieth anniversary of the passage of the suffrage amendment, included in its list of grievances, "Women cannot buy property without their husbands' signature (they don't need yours); Women cannot be sterilized without their husbands' signature (again they don't need yours)."[16]

Many historians have traced the history of the claiming of rights by women. But the denial of rights in the old law was accompanied by the exemption from obligations, and we have only rudimentary understanding of the relationships between rights and obligations. There is a history of obligations just as there is a history of rights; like the history of rights, the history of obligations is a gendered history, bordered differently for men and for women. In what follows I want to suggest the persistence of the idea that obligations, first to husbands directly, then to households more generally, was understood to substitute for obligations to the state. In the early republic, these substitute obligations were forthrightly named; a century later the original understanding had faded, and the absence of civic obligation was instead understood to represent privilege. By the time Kathleen Teague spoke, privilege had been transmuted into "rights" that should not be abandoned without a struggle.

As they emerged from the Revolution, American women faced a polity that made little space for them. Although women had long been active in public places—running taverns, making and selling goods, accepting pay for delivering babies and for teaching young children the rudiments of reading—they had also long been excluded from formal civic roles and denied formal political responsibility.[17] Between 1770 and 1800 many writers, both male and female, articulated a new understanding of the civic role of women in a republic. This ideology drew on some old ingredients but rearranged them and added new ones, creating in the process a gendered definition of citizenship. As Carroll Smith-Rosenberg has recently argued, male citizenship was understood to be in conflict with the feminine and racialized other; the political iconography of the early republic subjugated the unruly figures of women, blacks, and Native Americans, using white women to confirm the superiority of the white male citizen of the republic. Susan Juster's examination of evangelical churches in New England shows that the "process by which women came to occupy that position of 'other' " was not simply a semiotic one. Even as the patriarchy of king and lords was overthrown, signs and symbols were embedded in a social and historical process in which "manliness was seen to reside in patriarchal privilege."[18]

In this context the task of claiming space for a woman citizen was formidable. It was attempted most clearly by Judith Sargent Murray in America and Mary Wollstonecraft in England, who stressed women's native "capability" and competence and offered them as preconditions of citizenship.[19] With the claim that women were competent, rational, and independent beings, it finally became possible to attack directly the classical allocation of civic virtue to men and of unsteadiness, vulnerability to *fortuna*, to women. By claiming civic virtue for themselves, women undermined the classical polarities and attacked the republican discourse that created the male citizen out of his contrast to the feminine. The new formulation of citizenship reconstructed gender relations, politicizing women's traditional roles and turning women into monitors of the political behavior of their lovers, husbands, and children. The formulation assumed for women the task of stopping the historical cycle of achievement followed by inevitable degeneration. Women would keep the republic virtuous by maintaining the boundaries of the political community. Lockean child rearing was given a political twist; the bourgeois virtues of autonomy and self-reliance were given extra resonance by the Revolutionary experience. In her role as mother the republican woman entered historical time and republican political theory, implicitly promising to arrest the cycle of inevitable decay by guaranteeing the virtue of subsequent generations, the virtue that alone could sustain the republic, guarding the revolutionary generation against the epigone. The limits of the politics of republican motherhood were obvious; women could claim political participation only so long as they kept their politics in the service of the men of their family, using it to ensure republican authenticity on the part of their husbands and their sons.[20]

The role of the republican mother linked elite and upper-middle class women to the new republic in a political context in which women were denied the privileges of republican citizenship—the vote, the right to hold office, eligibility to serve on juries or as judges, and, if married, the right to independent ownership of property. As Elizabeth Blackmar has argued, the concept provided a language that permitted the wives of upwardly mobile, entrepreneurial men to account for their own household responsibilities as productive, even civic duties requiring them to supervise working-class women as domestic workers.[21] The concept developed in part as a way of deflecting male criticism that the woman who "meddled" in political ideas necessarily desexed herself.[22] In the hostile environment of the early republic, bounded by the unrevised law of domestic relations, to claim the role of the republican mother was to claim a role of expanded scope, to claim powers of mind that most men denied women had, and to claim convictions and resolution of which most men thought women incapable. The ideology of republican motherhood represented an early stage in the development of Western understanding of the role of bourgeois women in the civic culture, a primitive, hesitant, even nostalgic form of connection of the domestic woman with the public world.

Republican motherhood was at its origins an unstable position. It embodied a conservative, stabilizing role, deflecting the radical potential of the revolutionary experience; it also stretched the old boundaries, sustaining a substantial step in the direction of a liberal individualism that recognized the political potential of women.[23] The political generation of Elizabeth Cady

Stanton positioned itself against the first variant and allied itself with the latter. As successive battles over the gendered meaning of citizenship were fought— and some of them were won—positions that had once represented the cutting edge of progress could come to seem retrograde. Exclusions from the political process that had been described as privileged exceptions were increasingly understood as denials of rights. One way of summarizing the course of the political history of women in the United States is to observe the redirection of a series of obligations from husbands and households to oneself as an individual or to the state. The language of republican motherhood, once a progressive language (if ambivalently so), increasingly became a conservative one; by 1980 it was not at all strange for the Eagle Forum to claim that language for its own.

The campaign for suffrage emphasized rights claims and the integrity of women's duties to the state; against these arguments, insistence on the obligations that women owed their husbands and families infused the rhetoric of antisuffragism. Ellen DuBois has traced the defeat of women's rights advocates' efforts to claim rights on the basis of equality and individualism in the years after the Civil War; when this campaign, the "New Departure," failed, DuBois writes, "winning the vote for women was no longer tied to an overall democratic interpretation of the Constitution [or] . . . linked to the general defense of political democracy."[24] Had the New Departure been effective, it would have challenged the law of domestic relations, which, as we have seen, itself repeatedly challenged the Constitution, at least insofar as the Constitution was democratically interpreted. The narrowing of focus, from universal suffrage to woman suffrage in a context in which the rules of the household remained largely unchanged, necessarily set wives' obligations to husbands against their ability to claim rights against the state.[25] "Is there any escape from the conviction that the industrial and political independence of women would be the wreck of our present domestic institutions?" Caroline Corbin, an Illinois antisuffragist, asked in 1887. "May it not be possible that an intuitive sense that woman suffrage is incompatible with the present relations of men and women in the home, has something to do with the fact that . . . an overwhelming majority of women do not desire the ballot?"[26] Corbin did not understand "the present relations of men and women in the home" to be problematic or to involve power relations; but in predicting that woman suffrage, which enacted the claim of women to make civic choices that were different from those their husbands made, was indeed incompatible with "our present domestic institutions" she was on the mark. Carl Degler has argued that not until this concern was deflected, not until arguments from equality and individualism were abandoned and not until arguments made on the basis of women's difference from men and justified on the basis of "extending woman's special sphere to society" were substituted could majority support for suffrage be accomplished.[27] "In sum," Degler writes, "woman suffrage was accepted at long last simply because it was no longer perceived as likely to produce the effects upon women's behavior and the relationships within the family that the suffragists had hoped for."[28]

Degler may overstate the case a bit, but attention to the force of anti-suffrage, and to the compromises that suffragists had to make in order to achieve necessary majorities, will protect us against expecting the accomplishment of suffrage to have resolved all questions of women's citizenship. Gradual but modest revisions of the law of domestic relations had continued throughout the Progressive Era but had not rendered the old system unrecognizable.[29] The argument that duties to husbands and families trump duties to the public and to the state continued to permeate the controversy over civic obligation.

Contest over civic obligation in American history has typically been framed by four issues: the obligation of allegiance (and its corollary, the obligation to refrain from treason), the obligation to pay taxes, the obligation to serve on juries, and the obligation to risk one's life in military service. In each of these, a general obligation that appears at first glance to weigh on all individuals equally turns out to have obligated people of different racial origins differently and also to have constructed different civic obligations for men and for women. At its height, the system of coverture exempted women from virtually all civic obligations except the obligation to refrain from treason and the obligation to pay taxes. As women claimed civic rights, their capacity to perform civic obligations followed. But it did not follow as a matter of course or in clear relationship to rights claims. The substitution of obligation to husbands and family for obligation to the state—understood as privilege if one approved, favoritism if one did not—engendered its own debates on a time-table independent of the timing of debates about the obligations of male citizens.

The test of allegiance is embedded in the status of citizen. The *feme covert*, asserted a Massachusetts attorney in 1805, successfully challenging the seizure of a loyalist wife's property during the Revolution, "has no *political* relation to the *state* any more than an alien."[30] In 1855 Caucasian alien women who married American men were automatically granted citizenship; that is, it was assumed that their allegiance to a new state was contingent on the oath they took to their husbands. The same logic left the status of American-born women who married alien men unclear. Their obligation to their alien husbands was understood to have the potential to override their rights of American citizenship and their obligation of obedience to the state.[31] No doubt was left on this point when a federal statute of 1907, upheld in the Supreme Court in 1915 (*Mackenzie v. Hare*), provided that American women forfeited their citizenship when they married alien men.[32] Debates on married women's nationality perforce became debates on the relationship of women, their husbands, and the state. Between 1855 and 1922 immigrant women received their citizenship along with their marriage license and native-born women risked losing theirs; after 1907 what had been risk turned into standard practice.[33] In the pre–World War I years, in the face of a real threat to American women who had married Germans, and in the presence of a vigorous suffrage movement that understood suffrage to be part of a larger array of women's rights, the disparity between the stability of men's citizenship and the instability of women's citizenship was increasingly problematic. The internationalism that was engendered by World War I drew feminists' attention to the international dimensions of the problem; they came to understand the American situation as part of a larger, international trend, resisted only by Latin American countries and the Soviet Union. After the war and the accomplishment of suffrage, independent citizenship for women was placed high on suffragists' agenda, and the Cable Act of 1922 was the result. But racism saturated the reformist intentions of the Cable Act; a woman citizen who married "an alien ineligible to citizenship"—that is, a Chinese, a Japanese, or an immigrant from India—"shall cease to be a citizen of the United States."[34] This placed a substantial number of American-born women at serious risk of statelessness, a risk that was not theoretical in the dangerous international context of the 1920s and 1930s. Even the final revisions of the Cable Act in 1934 left some important elements open to interpretation.[35] "If she was good enough to be a citizen before marriage," complained Burnita Shelton Matthews, "she is good enough to be a citizen after marriage."[36] Dozens of individual women who discovered that their marriages deprived them of citizenship publicized their situation in the 1920s and 1930s; a pamphlet literature on the theme of "the woman without a country" highlighted the contingent nature of women's citizenship. Feminists worked hard to make problematic the assumption that obligation to husbands overrode obligation to the state; they had modest success, but the old understanding was not erased.[37]

Although Revolutionary-era ideology heavily stressed the reciprocity of taxation and representation, most American women were legally disfranchised until 1920 and African American women and men in many regions were effectively disfranchised until the 1960s, yet they were obligated to pay taxes.[38] Carolyn C. Jones has shown how the development of joint income tax law in the 1940s was shot through with concerns about gender roles. In the aftermath of World War II, as federal income taxes rose, and in an effort to lower the amount of federal taxes their constituents paid, a number of states began to shift from common law to community property systems. Community property systems, however, also entailed acknowledging the wife's direct control of one-half of the family property, whether or not she had contributed it to the family account. Jones quotes the complaint of a Pennsylvania court that "Might he so much, indeed, as buy a cigar or a newspaper with money one-half of which belonged to his wife without at least the technical duty of accounting to her for her portion of the money thus expended?" and newspaper headlines like "Community Property Law Can Aid Wives in Putting Mates Over Barrel."[39] To recognize domestic partnerships could potentially undermine the performance of services to the family business as part of the "wifely duty." In a context in which state laws rarely asserted the obligation of the married woman to support her family (but did establish that obligation for men), a wife's contribution to the family partnership was interpreted as activity that enabled husbands to fulfill their own obligations.[40] Jones quotes *Newsweek*: "In most states, if a husband left his wife or if a wife went home to mother, the best she could hope for was a nominal support allowance. In any community-property state, the woman automatically came out with half the family bankroll."[41] *Newsweek* clearly thought that its readers would regard the second sentence as unfair. The adoption of the joint tax return was a conservative compromise, offering tax reduction comparable to what was available in community property states "without any change in the legal rights between spouses."[42] In effect, the joint tax return accomplished a tax advantage without renegotiating the limited authority that women could claim over family income.

I have already remarked that jury service has posed particular problems of discriminating between rights and obligations. The Constitution treats speedy trial by a jury drawn from the "district wherein the crime shall have been committed" as a right to which defendants are entitled. Throughout the nineteenth century women's rights activists, complaining about their exclusion from the social compact that alone could justify civic obligation, insisted that one of their burdens was that they were not judged by a jury of their peers.[43] When woman suffrage was accomplished, only a few states made women automatically eligible for service on juries.

At first the argument about jury service was made in terms of a claim to the *right* to serve on juries, and at first—that is, within the first three years after the achievement of federal suffrage, the argument from rights was generally successful. But if state courts had not ruled on the subject, or if the legislature had not passed new statutes by 1923, then a difficult and extensive campaign was likely to be required. Until 1922, much had been expected—and feared—from a "woman's vote"; when a clear political bloc did not materialize, state legislators lost their anxieties. "Getting the word 'male' out of jury statutes," observed Gladys Harrison, executive secretary of the League of Women Voters in 1930, "is requiring something very like a second suffrage campaign—laborious, costly and exasperating."[44]

Each state has its own history of the struggle for women's service on juries. Opponents discovered that they could concede the principle of women's eligibility but maintain the practice of virtually all-male juries by eliding the difference between requirement and privilege, between obligation and right. Complexity and a degree of permissiveness were characteristic of women's jury service statutes; most introduced an element of voluntarism and choice. Thus in some states women's names were not added to the jury pool unless they actually went to the county courthouse to register their willingness to be called. In most others, women's names were added to the jury pool but those who were called were permitted a wide range of exemptions. In New York, for example, no women served on any jury until 1937, when they were made *eligible* to serve on the same terms as men but were simultaneously offered the opportunity to be excused from service by filing a simple affidavit.[45]

Feminists opposed permissive jury service because although it acknowledged the right of women to serve on juries, it did not exact an obligation to serve. After the first month or so of the new statutes, when activist women proudly signed up, it became clear that most women happily took advantage of their easy exemptions. But if women charged with crime were to be tried by "a jury of their peers" or, what was more to the point, a jury drawn from a cross section of the entire community, then other women would have to be obligated to serve on those trial juries. The passage of permissive jury service statutes did not resolve the problem. For more than half a century, from 1920 to 1975, when the Supreme Court finally ruled that men's names and women's names should be added to jury pools on the same terms, male opponents of obligatory jury service offered roughly similar arguments. Sometimes they complained that women were too emotional, too easily swayed; sometimes they complained that women were too easily shocked by what they might hear in the courtroom; sometimes they complained that women *should* be shocked by what they might hear in the courtroom and should be protected from obscenity and vulgarity. But always—state after state, decade after decade—the argument against women's obligatory jury service rested on the point that women's obligations to their husbands and children took precedence over their obligations to the state. "I must confess," wrote George Wickersham, appointed by Herbert Hoover as chairman of the National Commission on

Law Observance and Enforcement, "that I am not convinced of the wisdom of making jury service compulsory for women. I think that in many instances women make admirable jurors, but they have other duties that seem to me to rise far beyond the heights of serving on juries, and these I think should not be interfered with."[46] Jennie Loitman Barron, in 1924 a young Boston lawyer, wrote a vigorous response to those who claimed that household obligations should excuse women from juries, emphasizing the large proportion of adult women whose children were grown and no longer needed to be available for the constant care of infants or young children. Pointing to the substantial number of women who worked outside the home, for wages or as volunteers, Barron observed slyly, "Grace and charm have not departed from the American home . . . children have not gone, in greater numbers than before, breakfastless to school. There is no recorded increase in the burning of soups."[47]

Few listened. As late as 1961, when Gwendolyn Hoyt appealed her conviction for second-degree murder, a conviction at the hands of an all-male jury whose names had been drawn from a pool of 3,000 names of which only 10 were the names of women, the U.S. Supreme Court sustained permissive jury service. Hoyt claimed that she had not been tried by a jury drawn from a full cross section of the community. If she were to enjoy her right to a jury of her peers, other women would have to be obligated to serve. Why was it reasonable to offer these other women easy permission to avoid jury service? Because, Justice John Marshall Harlan wrote in his opinion, "women are the home and center of family life." If the state of Florida believed that women's obligations to their families outweighed their obligations to their fellow citizens, that was a decision for the legislature of the state of Florida to make. During the oral argument before the Supreme Court, George Georgieff, the assistant attorney general for Florida, had tried to explain to the justices why it was logical to excuse women from jury service so easily. Caught off guard by a question from Earl Warren, he burst out, "Well, Mr. Chief Justice . . . they have to cook the dinners!"[48]

Exclusion from juries followed from a vision of the female in service to their families, now less as teachers than as providers of food, whether with babies at their breasts or, as Georgieff blurted out in court, "cooking the dinners." In that phrase, Georgieff reached across the bench to claim alliance with the male justices as part of the group of men who expected their dinners to be prepared for them. Georgieff's words highlighted the bond between those whose dinners were cooked and those who were freed from their civic obligation of jury service so that they could cook those dinners. The understanding that the state had an interest in enforcing women's performance of their domestic chores did not die with the *Hoyt* case. In 1964 Congressman Emmanuel Celler promised to support the inclusion of the word "sex" in the Civil Rights Act if he could be reassured that women would continue to perform their household chores: "Frankly, I am caught between the urging of the gentlewoman from Michigan [Martha Griffiths] and a male constituent, who expects a hot meal on the table when he returns from work. Is it the gentlewoman's desire to come between man and wife?" In this peculiar, bizarre, even tawdry way, the old tradition of republican motherhood, which had understood women's service to the state to involve nurturing civic virtue in the men of her own and of the next generation (their husbands and sons), persisted into the cold war era. No one worried about who cooked Gwendolyn Hoyt's dinner.[49]

Criticism of housework was central to the rhetorical attack of the revitalized feminism of the 1970s; it was a criticism not only of domesticity itself but also of a domesticity that was understood to substitute for other competencies. The woman who had devoted her energies to family obligations at the expense of all others discovered herself to be at a great disadvantage should her marriage fail and she need to face the world as an individual: the report of the President's Commission on the Status of Women of 1963 revealed that she would be disadvantaged in seeking credit, disadvantaged on the job market, and disadvantaged were she to count on alimony for support. Second-wave feminism was soaked with suspicion of republican motherhood and maternalist politics, with skepticism that civic credits banked as wives and mothers could be reliably reclaimed, with anxiety to warn young women to distrust the promises of coverture. Central to the agenda of second-wave feminism was a program of legal change that sought to eliminate the legacies of coverture. One at a time, these legacies were attacked by the argument that difference did not equal privilege; that different treatment left women vulnerable, not protected. Exemptions from jobs that involved strenuous physical labor and physical danger—construction work, police work, fire fighting—were attacked on the grounds that women were indeed capable of the work and burdened by exclusion from it. Beginning with the Supreme Court's decision in *Reed v. Reed* (1971) that the tradition of giving automatic primacy to fathers' claims to being the executor for their children denied mothers equal protection under the law, one after another of what were thought to be obsolete distinctions—including exemption from jury service—fell.

By the time Kathleen Teague faced the Senate Armed Services Committee, it could be argued that the only surviving ingredient of the old "right to be treated like American ladies" was continued exemption from obligatory military service. Theodore Roosevelt had captured the relationship nearly a century before: "the woman who has had a child . . . has that claim to regard which we give to the soldier . . . who does a great and indispensable service which involves pain and discomfort, self-abnegation, and the incurring of risk of life. . . . The woman who flinches from childbirth stands on a par with the soldier who drops his rifle and runs in battle."[50] Teague understood that the right to be a lady was saturated with claims of difference, a difference embedded in traditional patterns of "respect, chivalry," and religious culture. Her words in 1980 were firmly in the Roosevelt tradition: "Servicewomen are not fungible with servicemen. . . . Motherhood is not fungible with fatherhood. . . . Our daughters are not fungible with our sons." For Teague, the maintenance of gender difference was a matter of civil rights: "Our young women have the right to be feminine, to get married, to build families and to have homes. Our daughters should not be deprived of rights which every American woman has enjoyed since our country was born."[51] The right to be an American lady, to be a mother in the traditional American polity, involved exemption from the obligation to bear arms.

Teague's testimony expressed the common sense of the matter for most members of Congress. Although few members echoed her words, which already sounded somewhat outmoded, they sustained her argument. The Selective Service Act of 1980 required the registration only of men at their eighteenth birthday. But the assumptions on which that strategy rested had long been weakening. As childbirth became anesthetized and less dangerous, the ancient analogy lost its vitality; its availability as the implicit grounding for exemption from military risk receded. Within a decade, military women would be required to accept postings into the theater of war. Among the women sent into the Gulf War of 1991 were single mothers; in a few families both husbands and wives with small children went to the Gulf. This created a certain amount of wistfulness but only muted public resistance, a moderation that did not change even when ten military women were killed and one was captured and sexually violated.[52] At this writing, the expansion of military roles for women, the development of plans to remove combat exemptions for female pilots, and the creation of a structure for a gender-blind physicians' draft put into question the permanence of female exemption from the obligation of military service.

In the Progressive Era, criticism of war was a major part of the feminist critique of the public order, as the career of Jane Addams attests; it remained part of the feminist critique through the Vietnam War. But although many feminists maintained a pacifist skepticism deep into the 1970s, increasing numbers found that skepticism difficult to maintain in the presence of an all-volunteer army and the campaign for the Equal Rights Amendment.[53] The first removed the threat of a draft; the latter drew them into a rhetoric of equal opportunity and equal obligation. By the late 1980s virtually all liberal women's advocacy organizations were linking military participation to first-class citizenship.[54]

The erosion of the combat exemption in an all-volunteer army does not necessarily or directly measure Americans' understanding of whether *all* women, like all men, have an obligation to bear arms, to put their lives at risk when the commander in chief decides it is appropriate. The use of women in the Gulf War may increase the likelihood, but does not ensure, that women will also be drafted—that is, that all women will be understood to have a military obligation. The relationship of women to state violence challenges us to know considerably more than we do now about the relationship between gender and aggression and to consider more precisely the way this relationship has been, and ought to be, deployed by the state.[55] We live at a time when traditional markings of systems of gender difference are changing. What we are learning—in the enrollment of women into other units of state force and violence, notably police departments and corrections forces, as well as the gradual absorption of women into military roles accompanied by scandals like Tailhook and the vulnerability of gay servicepeople to violent physical attack— is that it is possible to revise even this most traditional system of gender difference while at the same time keeping systems of male domination intact.

If I were to make a prediction, it is that we have already slid into a situation in which the protective exclusion of women from the obligation to enact state-directed violence has eroded. These changes are the perhaps inevitable climax of the slow deterioration of the practices of coverture over the course of the last two centuries; as women's independent rights to property, suffrage, and bodily integrity were slowly established, the complementary practices of sub-stituting family duties for civic obligations crumbled. The role of the republi-can mother, who enacted her civic obligations through her service to her family, merging private choices with public obligations, had been marked as retrograde as early as the 1840s by Elizabeth Cady Stanton and her colleagues. But deep into the twentieth century American law and practice continued to breathe oxygen into the customs of coverture, for all the world as though the republican mother were the Resusci-Annie doll now widely used in cardiopul-monary resuscitation training. Although for the most part feminists of the 1970s, like virtually all American reformers before and since, spoke the lan-guage of expanded rights, they could not help but imply expanded obligations. The ending of coverture has been an extended process, accompanied by the almost willful insistence of historians that coverture and the problems it raised never really existed, or existed so long ago as to be antique.[56] The reexamination of the gendered boundaries of military obligation is likely—as was characteristic of other civic obligations—to be a somewhat extended one. It has been accompanied by hostility against feminists for their complicity in developing an ideology in which it appeared that traditional immunity against military obligation had been traded off for inchoate opportunities that many women do not understand to be an advantage. The end of the ideology of republican motherhood also marks the abandonment of the claim—long since found unreliable—that women as a sex would situate themselves as skeptics, voicing the claims of higher obligations than those that the state would place upon them. Skepticism of the state, however, has never been and should not be limited by gender; if public life is to be an arena of human freedom, men and women will have to find ways to make it so.[57]

CHAPTER 2 : TWO POLITICAL CULTURES
IN THE PROGRESSIVE ERA : THE NATIONAL
CONSUMERS' LEAGUE AND THE AMERICAN
ASSOCIATION FOR LABOR LEGISLATION

KATHRYN KISH SKLAR

T he single most important center of reform activity during the Progressive Era could be found at the Charities Building at Twenty-second Street and Fourth Avenue in New York City. Behind a four-story stately exterior, the structure's spacious offices and corridors housed the national headquarters of many leading reform organizations, including the National Child Labor Committee, the National Consumers' League (NCL), and the staffs of *Survey* and *Outlook*, prominent reform periodicals.[1] There men and women reformers constantly interacted, occasionally worked together as members of the same organization, but more often formed ad hoc coalitions across the boundaries of their gender-specific associations. "What's this bunch call itself today?" the editor of *Outlook* asked in March 1906, pausing by a meeting room filled with many familiar faces.[2] The presence of Florence Kelley, head of the National Consumers' League and one of the era's most active coalition builders, may have prompted his affectionate gibe. Less well known in this New York setting was John R. Commons, who had come from the University of Wisconsin to introduce the newly founded American Association for Labor Legislation (AALL). The March 1906 meeting drew together men and women interested in joining the AALL's efforts.

If we had a snapshot of this gathering we might think that it depicted the growing equality of women and men reformers as they met on common ground to work toward shared goals. Yet if we take a longer view and compare the two chief organizations represented that day—the NCL and the AALL— we find a different story, one that locates more importance in their gender-specific differences than in their cross-gender similarities.

This essay explores those differences and what we can discover from them about the political consequences of the social construction of gender during a major watershed in American history between 1900 and 1920. Because they were differently situated in the polity, women and men reformers in the NCL and the AALL promoted social change in different ways. In many cases women and men reformers accomplished together what could not be done separately, yet these two organizations show that gendered differences in membership, leadership, methods, and agendas could produce conflicting policy results. By comparing the AALL and the NCL, we gain insights into the process by which the gendered construction of politics gave distinct opportunities to women's political activism and at the same time set distinct limits on that activism.

The central dilemma of Progressive Era social justice activism revolved around the need for reformers to embrace many of the values and modes of operation associated with machine production at the same time that they sought to humanize that production. While reformers sought to preserve human agency and other qualities of human individuality from the relentless forces of industrialization, they also had to cooperate with those forces. Otherwise they could not hope to affect them. The NCL and the AALL were both caught in this dilemma. Neither sought to install an alternative to the materially based juggernaut of industrial capitalism. Both sought only to limit its capacity to harm. Through new forms of knowledge and power they tried to discipline the forces of industrial production, but in so doing they borrowed from standardizing ethics induced by machine production. Were workers injured on the job? Systems of compensation could be created as a remedy for missing body parts. Did the division of labor into repetitive, unskilled tasks create opportunities for the exploitation of child labor? Medical inspections and systems of licensing could keep the youngest and least healthy outside the factory door.

Nevertheless, within these parameters of the possible, the NCL and the AALL differed in the degree to which each was willing and able to challenge the dominance of capitalist values. For reasons that have partly to do with Florence Kelley's leadership within the NCL, and partly with the position of middle-class women within the polity and the economic marketplace, the NCL challenged capitalist assumptions in ways that the AALL did not.

Fundamental social, political, and economic changes in American life be-

(*Above*) Florence Kelley, general secretary of the National Consumers' League, 1910; (*opposite*) John B. Andrews, secretary of the American Association of Labor Legislation, ca. 1910. (Courtesy of the Library of Congress)

tween 1890 and 1930 laid the foundation for the modern nation that we know today, but these changes were anything but smooth. By 1890 massive immigration, rapid industrialization, and urbanization had generated the potential for widespread social disorder. Social relationships and values constructed in preindustrial America no longer met the needs of an increasingly diverse and stratified society. Pastoral landscapes gave way to sprawling cities and towering smokestacks. Day laborers and an urban proletariat outnumbered the skilled artisans who previously had dominated working-class life. Great wealth accumulated in the hands of a few, their spacious mansions contrasting grotesquely with the crowded tenements of immigrant neighborhoods.

Native-born middle-class Americans benefited in many ways from the new entrepreneurial opportunities available within the expanding national economy. For example, they moved into the new white-collar jobs created by the managerial revolution that accompanied vertical economic integration, and they had access to a cornucopia of new consumer goods. But the same forces that enhanced middle-class life also threatened to topple middle-class dominance within American political and social institutions. Politically, they were displaced by urban bosses who drew much of their support from recent immigrants. Socially, their authority diminished when, due to the Catholic and Jewish identities of most "new" immigrants from Southern and Eastern Europe, Protestant churches and clergymen became less important arbiters of social and class relations. Clearly, a new America was emerging, but its connections with earlier patterns of life were unclear. Did the grinding poverty of vast numbers of working people imperil the comforts of middle-class life? What did the social classes owe one another? Was democracy compatible with capitalism? These questions grew in urgency during the 1890s, when struggles between capital and labor repeatedly erupted into bloody armed conflict, and a severe depression crippled the economy.

Out of this crucible a multitude of middle-class organizations emerged to address the nation's problems. Women's organizations were prominent among them. "Progressive reform" (as this movement came to be called) developed three basic thrusts—economic, political, and social. Economic reform, expressed in the Sherman Antitrust Act of 1890, sought to protect the competitiveness of small economic units and curb the growing might of large ones. Political reform, seeking changes in governmental structures and the electoral process, tried to increase governmental responsibility and responsiveness by instituting innovations like the referendum, the recall of public officials, and the popular election of U.S. senators. Political reform also sought to rationalize governmental decision making by creating new administrative units, especially city managers, whose decisions were based more on scientifically based expertise and less on purely political considerations. Last, but not least, social reform expressed concern for the nation's social fabric by focusing on the quality of life among working people.

The efforts of middle-class women were concentrated in political and social reform, but their chief impact lay with the latter. Were working-class children attending schools? Or did their families' economic circumstances require them to work? Were wage-earning women and children exploited through long hours and low wages? Did working-class families have adequate food, housing, and health care? Middle-class women, better educated than ever before, posed and answered these questions through expertise acquired in women's organizations.

Historians have offered three explanations for the power of women's organizations in the Progressive Era. One emphasizes the "maternalist" theme in women's reform activism, which focused on policies pertaining to women and children in ways that accentuated gender differences. Paula Baker in 1984 named the fruitful convergence of the needs of raw industrial cities and the interests of women's public culture, "the domestication of American politics." Maureen Flanagan in 1990 speculated that members of the Women's City Club of Chicago pursued more progressive policies than members of the (men's) City Club because of the higher value that women placed on nurturance. In her 1992 book, *Protecting Soldiers and Mothers*, Theda Skocpol elevated this approach into a reigning paradigm by painstakingly documenting the achievements of women's organizations and contrasting them with the failure of "paternalism" before 1930.[3]

Linda Gordon has given us a different interpretation. Writing from the perspective of social provision to Families with Dependent Children (AFDC) in the Social Security Act of 1935, Gordon has analyzed the casework methods that shaped AFDC and the distinctions those methods made between the deserving and nondeserving poor. Calling casework methods a female tradition, both in its providers and its clients, Gordon contrasted them with what she saw as a male tradition that provided social benefits more broadly based on need rather than on other personal qualifications.[4]

My own work has reached a third conclusion—one that emphasizes a "strong state-weak state" paradigm to explain the broad strokes of women's activism and sees class relations as a prominent theme. In this view, women's activism was greater when the state's activism was weaker, and crucial dimensions of women's success were achieved because gendered policies acted as a surrogate for class policies.[5]

My dissatisfaction with both the "maternalist" and "deserving" frameworks arises from their inability to account for important aspects of women's activism, particularly those associated with labor legislation. Campaigns for labor legislation for women and children, which were central to the activism of middle-class women between 1880 and 1930, can be fully explained by neither maternalist nor casework frameworks. Important as these paradigms were in women's public culture, they go only part of the way in accounting for the creation of the most fundamental feature of what we call the "welfare" state— that is, the provision of a "floor" or minimum working or living standards beneath which no one should fall.[6]

To highlight the effects of class and the impact of American traditions of limited government on women's activism, this essay compares two organizations with very similar goals in neighboring niches in the pantheon of Progressive reform, the National Consumers' League and the American Association for Labor Legislation.

Comparisons are more effective when drawn between two entities with many common features. The NCL and the AALL resembled one another in many ways. Both organizations were part of the remarkable surge of social reform in the Progressive Era that sought the passage and enforcement of laws promoting "the conservation of the human resources of the nation."[7] Founded within a decade of one another, the NCL in 1898, the AALL in 1906, each was responding to the problematic qualities of industrial work in the context of the growing power of the American nation-state. Although both forged cross-class coalitions that embraced organized labor, the heart and soul of each was middle-class. Both claimed to speak for the welfare of the whole society, and to rise above "interest group" or "partisan" politics. Both maintained national offices with a paid staff, drew on professional expertise, lobbied for legislation, and forged coalitions with other reform organizations. While they chiefly worked at the state level, each also became involved in federal legislative campaigns. Their shared goal of creating nationwide minimum standards of labor legislation placed them among the progenitors of the American welfare state. These similarities meant that the two organizations frequently interacted and benefited from one another's activities.

More remarkably, perhaps, the two groups functioned relatively independently. By exploring their differences we learn about the gendered construction of American politics and public policies. This essay explores three dimensions of the differences between the National Consumers' League and the American Association for Labor Legislation: the origins of the two groups, their organizational structures, and their legislative agendas. These differences show that an analysis of women's experience sheds new light on fundamental themes in American history, especially the process by which knowledge and power translated into expanded state responsibility.

The National Consumers' League came into being in 1898, when local consumer leagues in New York, Massachusetts, Pennsylvania, Illinois, Minnesota, New Jersey, and Wisconsin decided to form a national office to coordinate their efforts. The movement began in New York City in 1888 in response to protests by wage-earning women against sweatshop working conditions. Leonora O'Reilly, a shirtmaker and later a leader in the New York Women's Trade Union League (WTUL), founded in 1903, called upon the city's most politically prominent woman, Josephine Shaw Lowell, to help her recruit middle-class women to attend a special meeting of the New York Working Women's Society. There O'Reilly and others "made an eloquent appeal for help and sympathy from the wealthy and educated women of New-York for their toiling and down-trodden sisters." The Reverend James Otis Huntington, Episcopalian founder of the Church Association for the Advancement of the Interests of Labor, exhorted the ladies "to feel it their personal duty to go on doing whatever and as much as they could to correct the social evil that permits their unfortunate sisters to be so frightfully overworked and badly paid."[8] In response, members of the audience "left their names and addresses, and expressed a willingness to answer any call upon them for the working girls' cause."[9] Two years later, when wage-earning and middle-class women met again to discuss women's working conditions, an organization emerged. Imitating a group formed in London a few months earlier wherein consumers compiled a register similar to the list of "fair houses" published by trade unions, they hoped to enlist "the sympathy and interest of the shopping public" in a "White List" of retail stores that "treated their employees fairly."[10] In January 1891 the organization named itself the Consumers' League of the City of New York, elected Josephine Shaw Lowell its president, and appointed an exclusively female board of advisers and vice presidents.[11] In later years the New York league remained the most important local voice within the national organization.

With Florence Kelley's appointment as general secretary of the national league in 1899, the NCL assumed leadership of a burgeoning Consumers' League movement. Her early annual reports urged new forms of knowledge and power on league members as a by-product of persisting gender distinctions. "The one great industrial function of women has been that of the purchaser," Kelley wrote in 1899. "All the foods used in private families," as well as furniture, books, and clothing, are "prepared with the direct object in view of being sold to women."[12] To be effective consumers, women had to be organized. "What housewife can detect, alone and unaided, injurious chemicals in her supplies of milk, bread, meat, home remedies?" Goods that women used to make themselves were now produced in unregulated shops and factories. Male experts were not supplying knowledge about the integrity of products made under these new conditions. "Men have devised tests" but only for products like "warships, locomotives, railway bridges and electrical installations." It was up to women to protect themselves and their families from harmful goods. By uniting in the Consumers' League, Kelley promised, women could safeguard their families and at the same time could drive out of the marketplace articles produced under conditions "injurious to human life and health."[13]

The NCL thus held out a dual hope of aiding both consumers and producers. This vital link between consumer and producer generated substantial social power for the NCL. It lent personal meaning to the commitment that members made to the organization and connected that meaning to the lives of working people. The NCL not only supplied its members with knowledge of the relationship between consumer and producer, it also sought to transform that knowledge into a moral force. Far from being passive purchasers, consumers actually constructed production, Kelley insisted. Daily choices "as to the bestowal of our means" determined how others "spend their time in making what we buy." Kelley and the NCL sought to politicize those choices by moralizing them: "It is *the* aim of the National Consumers' League to moralize this decision, to gather and make available information which may enable all to decide in the light of knowledge, and to appeal to the conscience, so that the decision when made shall be a righteous one."[14] This old-fashioned word, "righteous," captured the league's stance as a moral arbiter anchored in an earlier era.

This personal ethical thrust ran against the grain of anonymous market forces, especially those competitive practices that drove down the price of goods with cheaply paid labor. The National Consumers' League did not object to cheapness gained through technological change, Kelley said, but it did oppose that "attained by making children run foot-power machines in tenement kitchens."[15] The league's stance also resisted that recent embodiment of consumer culture—advertisements. As early as 1899, Kelley recognized advertisements as the moral consumer's enemy, since they were "distinctly not meant to educate or instruct, but to stimulate, persuade, incite, entice, and induce the indifferent to purchase."[16] Thus the league purveyed a special kind of knowledge that connected the home and the marketplace in new ways and brought to bear on that connection an older strand of moral agency rooted in neither the discipline of machine production nor the dictates of advertising.

This oppositional stance defined the league's place in consumer culture and required it to proselytize. Since righteously made goods cost more, "there must be numbers of consumers sufficiently large to assure purchases steady and considerable enough to compensate for the expense incurred by humane employers."[17] The league could not expect to achieve its goals without the cooperation of large numbers of purchasers. Women's knowledge could be converted into power only through the power of numbers.

Therefore, in the first five years of the league's existence, Florence Kelley devoted herself to building a grassroots movement of righteously knowledgeable consumers. Between 1900 and 1907 she spent roughly a day on the road for every desk-bound day. Her efforts were rewarded by the spectacular expansion of NCL locals, both in number and location. The NCL's 1901 report mentioned thirty leagues in eleven states; by 1906 they numbered sixty-three in twenty states.[18] The Massachusetts Consumers' League described the effects of Kelley's leadership in 1903: "[She] can travel from one end of the Continent to the other without losing her hold upon local problems in State Leagues the farthest removed from her bodily presence, stirring our zeal and opening new fields for our activity by letters, which are prompt and full as if letter writing were the chief occupation of her day." "Mrs. Kelley," the report concluded, "gives us service which it is impossible to overestimate."[19]

Kelley's goal of thirty thousand members was not met until 1913, but her impressive early gains demonstrated the fertile soil on which the NCL message fell. Local leagues sustained the national's existence, channeling money, ideas, and the support of other local organizations into the national office. At the same time locals served as vehicles for the implementation of the national's agenda at the state level. Most league members were white, urban, middle-class Protestants, but Jewish women held important positions of leadership. Catholic women became more visible after Cardinal James Gibbons of Baltimore consented to serve as a vice president of a Maryland league, and Bishop J. Regis Canevin of Pittsburgh encouraged members of that city's Ladies Catholic Benevolent Association to join. In 1903 the Massachusetts league undertook a systematic effort "to enlist the wives of farmers through the Farmers' Institutes, Granges, etc."[20]

But "righteous" choices by a multitude of consumers were not in themselves strong enough to counter the economic and cultural forces against which they were arrayed. Women's knowledge could be translated into power only if women forced government to act. Florence Kelley persistently channeled the grassroots power of local leagues into political action. For example, in 1901 the Wisconsin league worked especially closely with the state's only woman factory inspector, Ida Jackson, and proved to the state legislature that "the present law regulating the hours of women and youths is a dead letter."[21] The Michigan league secured two women on the Board of Factory Inspectors, one of whom worked closely with the league in Grand Rapids and achieved "splendid obedience to the school attendance law."[22] The New Jersey league employed its own secretary in 1901, making factory inspection part of her duties. With the aid of the state factory inspector, she examined twenty-four factories employing a total of 1,085 women and girl operatives.[23] A year later the New Jersey league hired Helen Marot, author of the *Handbook of Labor Literature*, who in 1899 had investigated the custom tailoring trades in Philadelphia for the U.S. Industrial Commission, to write an assessment of the state's lax enforcement of the law and presented it to the legislature and the governor.[24]

The "Consumers' White Label," devised by Florence Kelley and adopted by the NCL as the chief activity during its first decade, became the tactic that wove together women's knowledge, women's power, and expanded state responsibility.[25] It replaced the White List of stores with a strategy that sought to regulate the conditions under which goods were produced, not only the conditions under which they were sold. Both White List and White Label carefully avoided the appearance of blacklisting or secondary boycotts, which, as a tool tried by organized labor, the courts had declared illegal.[26]

The NCL's White Label campaign focused on the manufacture of white muslin underwear. Seeking to affect the conditions under which these goods were produced throughout the country, the league awarded its White Label to manufacturers who shunned child labor and overtime work and abided by state factory regulations. By limiting its attention to "one narrow field of industry," the NCL shined an investigative spotlight on the production of garments that every middle-class consumer needed. "The finest hand-made goods copied from French models" were excluded from consideration. Included were drawers, chemises, petticoats, "corsets, corset-waists, and substitutes, skirts, and skirt and stocking-supporters, wrappers and flannelette goods."[27]

The goods were intimate, but the goal was political. Throughout the Northeast, Midwest, and Pacific West, the White Label ineluctably carried middle-class women into the nitty-gritty of local factory conditions and law enforcement. Did the manufacturer subcontract to home workers in tenements? Were children employed? Was overtime required? Were working conditions safe and sanitary? Were state factory laws violated? How far below the standard set by the consumers' label were their own state laws?[28] Even more technical questions arose when women's organizations came into contact with factory inspectors, bureaus of labor statistics, state legislatures, and courts.

Should the state issue licenses for home workers? What was the relationship between illiteracy in child workers and the enforcement of effective child labor laws? Was their own state high or low on the NCL's ranked list showing the number of illiterate child workers in each? Should laws prohibit the labor of children at age fourteen or sixteen? Should exceptions be made for the children of widows? Could workers live on their wages or were they forced to augment their pay with relief or charitable donations? How energetically were state factory laws enforced? How could local factory standards be improved? Questions recently quite alien to middle-class women held the interest of thousands of the most politically active among them. This was no small accomplishment. State leagues differed in the degree to which they worked with state officials, but wherever they existed they created new civic space in which women used their new knowledge and power to expand state responsibility.

To some degree the NCL's mobilization of middle-class women against the power of unregulated capitalism derived from Florence Kelley herself. Born into an elite Philadelphia family tied to Quaker and Unitarian reform traditions, Kelley was the daughter of William Darrah Kelley, a radical Republican congressman who served fifteen consecutive terms between 1860 and 1890. From him she learned about the connection between social justice and positive government. On her mother's side she was the grandniece of Sarah Pugh, a leading abolitionist and Lucretia Mott's closest friend. From her she learned the power of women's collective action. Kelley began reading government reports at the age of ten and started using the Library of Congress at age twelve. After graduating from Cornell in 1882, she studied law and government at the University of Zurich. There she married Lazare Wischnewetzky, a Russian socialist medical student, had three children in three years, converted to socialism, and translated classic writings by Friedrich Engels and Karl Marx. Ever after she viewed the world through the lens of "scientific materialism," seeing social relations as the outcome of people's relationship to production and perceiving manufacturers' ownership of the means of production as the origin of a wide range of social problems—especially the exploitative advantage they exercised over women and children industrial workers.

After she, Lazare, and the children moved to New York, Kelley became a self-trained expert in labor legislation for women and children and emerged as one of the fiercest critics of the ineffectiveness of state bureaus of labor statistics. When Lazare began battering her in 1891, she fled with the children to Chicago, where she discovered Hull House, Jane Addams's newly founded social settlement. There she became one of the nation's leading authorities on the passage and enforcement of labor legislation for women and children, drafting, lobbying for, and (as Illinois's chief factory inspector) enforcing pathbreaking eight-hour legislation for women and child workers. A young man who went to live at Hull House in 1894 was awed by the way Kelley "hurled the spears of her thought with such apparent carelessness of what breasts they pierced" but nevertheless felt that she was "full of love." According to him: "[She was] the toughest customer in the reform riot, the finest rough-and-tumble fighter for the good life for others, that Hull House ever knew. Any weapon was a good weapon in her hand—evidence, argument, irony or invective."[29] When she carried her formidable talents into the New York office of the National Consumers' League in 1899, women's political culture gained a warrior with formidable rhetorical and organizational skills.[30]

Yet Kelley's rage for social justice bore fruit because her vision of expanded state responsibility for the welfare of women and children took root within the ranks of "organized womanhood." Her chief means of carrying the NCL's vision to a larger constituency lay through the General Federation of Women's Clubs (GFWC). By 1900 the GFWC had grown to thirty-six state federations of 2,675 clubs with a membership of more than 155,000.[31] At the GFWC biennial meeting that year in Milwaukee, Kelley and others introduced the federation to the work of the Consumers' League at a special evening program, and federation officers "asked the delegates to report favorably to their respective clubs and federations upon the work of the League."[32] The results, Kelley said in 1901, "are still perceptible at our office in the form of invitations for speakers, requests for literature, and a vast increase in correspondence and in the demand for labeled goods in many diverse parts of the country."[33]

Between 1900 and 1902 Kelley chaired the federation's standing committee on "The Industrial Problem as It Affects Women and Children." This committee and its state counterparts were expected "to influence and secure enforcement of labor ordinances and state laws." State federations were asked to "agitate for enforcement of laws, and for amendments to laws, if they were not up to the standard of the Massachusetts labor laws."[34] Her efforts as committee chair were later described as "a campaign of education" during which "a great advance was made in arousing sentiment on behalf of the working child." To individual clubs Kelley sent 2,000 copies of a circular offering a brief but cogent class-based explanation of "the industrial problem as it affects women and children." The very existence of the federation, she said, was "due to the fact that the industries have gone out of the homes of the prosperous, leaving to the women in those homes leisure for study, recreation and philanthropy. But these industries have largely gone into the homes of the poor, ruining the domestic life of the home workers. . . . [and drawing] from the homes of the wage-workers the women and children to work in factories, workshops, stores, offices and public-service employment." The industrial committee's circular also emphasized "the need of encouraging organization among the women who labor" and provided an informative bibliography prepared in cooperation with the League of Working Women's Clubs.[35] Arguing that middle-class and working-class women were related to and affected by the same industrial process, one positively, one adversely, this analysis pricked the consciences of middle-class women about the material basis of their leisure and linked their destinies with working women and children.

State federations of women's clubs in Connecticut, Delaware, Maryland, and Tennessee responded by appointing "standing committees to promote the work of the Consumers' League." Addresses by NCL officers became a regular event at their annual meetings. In such far-flung areas as South Carolina, Utah, and Washington, GFWC members presented papers on league work. Where statewide Consumers' Leagues existed, they worked closely with state federations of women's clubs. In several cases the state federation "inclosed literature of the Consumers' League when sending out the year book of the Federation." In Kelley's words, this gave "the most emphatic evidence of approval and very practical help." Small wonder that the NCL office was inundated with GFWC correspondence. "For a time at least," the federation's chronicler wrote, "the quickened conscience made the average woman . . . a more intelligent purchaser."[36]

By 1903 both the National Congress of Mothers and the National American Woman Suffrage Association had created child labor committees, and Florence Kelley headed both. In these capacities, she said, "it has been possible to secure a hearing for the truth" before audiences who would otherwise not have invited a league lecturer. To these and other groups Kelley urged "that it is we who are the real employers of the children, we who buy the product of their labor."[37] Standing between capital and labor, a grassroots phalanx of consumers became thoroughly implicated in the conditions under which goods were produced.

Having built her constituency, Kelley in 1906 shifted away from the White Label into a campaign for the legal limitation of women's hours. That campaign intensified and focused her use of grassroots constituencies to support the passage of legislation at the same time that it drew on legal expertise to defend hours laws in the courts.

Throughout the industrializing world, reformers and trade unionists alike viewed shorter working hours as the key to the improvement of working-class standards of living; for trade unionists, shorter hours were second in importance only to the right to unionize. Florence Kelley often summarized the significance of shorter hours in gender-neutral terms. Of trade unionists, she wrote in 1905:

The effort of the wage-earners is to establish the right to leisure; to transmute the unemployed time of the full season, with its attendant demoralization and suffering, into regular daily leisure, with salutary opportunity for rest, recreation, education, family life and self-help by means of savings societies and all those agencies administered by working people themselves which depend for their success upon the regular attention of persons free from over-fatigue and irregular pressure.[38]

Yet only a small, well-organized portion of the labor force, mostly skilled men, could achieve the benefits of shorter hours. Others, including most female and child workers and the vast majority of unskilled male workers, were forced to work longer. They endured twelve-hour, fourteen-hour, or even longer working days that imperiled their health and undercut their ability to rise above their impoverished circumstances. Because women were excluded from most and crowded into a few occupations, regardless of their skills, they had to compete with one another for the few jobs available to them. Therefore their long hours were usually accompanied by subsistence or below-subsistence wages, while skilled men worked shorter hours and earned higher wages.

Despite the need that reformers saw for legislative regulation of hours or wages, such statutes were very difficult to achieve in the United States, primarily because American political institutions circumscribed the power of legislatures by investing courts with the power to rule legislative enactments unconstitutional. The power of the American judiciary did much to shape the American labor movement. In the 1890s Samuel Gompers turned the American Federation of Labor (AFL) away from legislative solutions for labor's problems because, in Gompers's words, "the power of the courts to pass upon the constitutionality of the law so complicates reform by legislation as to seriously restrict the effectiveness of that method."[39]

In England, Germany, and France laws designed to benefit working people were passed by central governments that had their own reasons to be concerned about social welfare. Yet in the United States the harsh conditions of laissez-faire capitalism were preserved by political traditions that defended the freedom of employers to devise the terms on which they employed workers.[40] Between 1900 and 1920 the National Consumers' League circumvented those traditions by invoking gender-specific justifications for legislation designed to benefit working women. The league and its supporters argued that gender-specific legislation was constitutional because it utilized the state's police powers to preserve health and morals. First, they asserted, since women workers tended to be young and unskilled and therefore did not have trade unions to represent them in negotiating better working conditions directly with their employers, they were unable to protect themselves, so it fell to the state to safeguard their health and morals through legislation. Second, they contended that because most women workers later became mothers, their injuries through overwork or low wages could produce birth defects or lead to prostitution, each of which affected the welfare of the whole community and should be prevented through legislation. These arguments embodied nineteenth-century notions of gender differences, which women reformers like Kelley shared when it was pragmatically effective for them to do so, but just as easily evaded when it helped their cause. Most important, these assertions earned them the support of constituencies beyond the reach of their own organizations, including judges and working men.

Responding to such arguments, nineteen states passed some form of hours laws for women by 1906. That year the NCL successfully defended an Oregon ten-hour law for women before the state supreme court. After the U.S. Supreme Court upheld the Oregon statute in 1908, the NCL led a campaign that established hours laws for women in twenty-one more states by 1919. In many cases their efforts amended existing legislation to reduce the legal length of the work week and in most they greatly enhanced the enforceability of all state hours statutes.[41] At the crest of this success in 1909, the league added a crusade for minimum wages for women.

By 1917, when the NCL successfully defended the constitutionality of hours laws for men in nonhazardous occupations, it had become clear to friends and enemies alike that the league was using women as an entering wedge for the protection of all workers—that is, it fashioned gender-specific constituencies and gender-specific issues to accomplish class-specific goals.[42] What American political traditions prevented from being achieved in class-specific provisions was obtained through gender-specific terms. The NCL's mobilization of middle-class women made this possible.

The American Association for Labor Legislation offers a compelling contrast to the NCL's rallying of middle-class women. AALL leaders treated knowledge as professional, not personal. They exercised power through the prestige of their position and expertise, not through numbers. And, rather than seeing government as a democratic extension of the popular will, the AALL viewed the state as a vehicle of enlightened administration. This set the association on a different political path from the NCL and made it a frustrating ally.

The AALL grew out of a call by the International Association for Labor Legislation for the creation of an American branch. Founded at the Paris Exposition of 1900 at a congress on labor legislation, the international sought "to serve as a bond of union to those who, in the different industrial countries, believe in the necessity of protective labor legislation."[43] With no grassroots urgency spurring them on, American members of the international were slow to organize a national branch. Carroll Wright, former U.S. commissioner of labor and the nation's most prominent labor-related official, tried "to interest our United States bureaus of labor statistics, business men, and others in giving their adhesion to the international organization" but was "sadly disappointed in the lack of interest displayed."[44]

A second effort under the leadership of John Commons, Richard Ely, and other economists proved more successful. At the 1905 annual meeting of the American Economics Association in Baltimore they called a conference for the following year in New York at which the AALL was launched.[45] The founders tried to reach out to "technical experts in different lines—medical, sanitary, statistical" and sought "a very competent [staff] person" who could "give his or her entire time to the work." Richard Ely thought that "Mrs. Kelley would be a good one, although it might be unfortunate to take her away from her present work."[46] But since the AALL could not yet afford a paid staff, John Commons, Ely's protégé at the University of Wisconsin, agreed to serve as secretary. With the unpaid help of one of Commons's students, Irene Osgood, the AALL operated out of a corner of his office until early 1909, when a few large contributors allowed it to hire John B. Andrews, another Commons student, as a full-time salaried executive secretary.[47]

In 1909 a wealthy AALL member underwrote the cost of moving John Andrews, Irene Osgood, and the AALL office to Manhattan, where they occupied the sixteenth floor of the tower of the Metropolitan Life Insurance Building. This location brought the AALL closer to the nation's philanthropic foundations and to equivalent national organizations, such as the National Child Labor Committee and the National Consumers' League.[48] Until 1909 AALL membership lingered at about 200, but by 1913 it had expanded to 3,348, about a tenth of the membership claimed by the NCL that year.[49] From the start, the AALL was an elite group, "composed of experts and officials as well as public spirited citizens." Article III of the constitution limited membership to those who were "elected by the Executive Committee."[50]

In contrast to the NCL's mass mobilization for direct consumer action, the AALL's mandate was grander but more vague: "the conservation of the human resources of the nation." But for what purpose? An early AALL statement answered this question by declaring its commitment to both labor and capital, to the "conservation of human resources in the mutual interest of employer and employee by non-partisan legislation."[51] Ever "objective," the AALL viewed partisanship as its antithesis. Yet without a political constituency and the partisanship that came with it, the AALL had much greater difficulty than the NCL in forging an effective political agenda.

Whereas the NCL treated local branches as its main arteries of power, the AALL tolerated local branches only briefly. Revealingly, women were active in the creation of most AALL locals, including the first one, formed in Chicago by Irene Osgood, AALL assistant secretary, and Jane Addams.[52] Keenly aware of the potential importance of local branches, Osgood thought that "our first work with the new local" would be to compile a bulletin comparing American and foreign laws on employee health, comfort, safety, and accidents. The newly appointed Illinois commission on the safety of employees "will then take hold of it and prepare such a bill as they think they can get through the Illinois Legislature." She imagined that the local would hold "meetings for the purpose of publicity and rounding up all the support possible by getting different organizations to unite on demanding this one measure." It would also "secure news material to circulate throughout the newspapers of the state, especially those reaching the small towns." Finally, the local might also "bring some pressure to bear on [the governor] to appoint a man as chairman on the Committee on Labor who is not openly antagonistic to the cause of labor," since such hostility "defeated the protective machinery bill last year."[53] Between 1908 and 1912 five local branches of the AALL emerged to accomplish goals similar to those envisioned by Osgood. By 1916, however, they had all lapsed. What happened? How can we explain this very substantial difference between the NCL and the AALL?

The most potent reason for the demise of AALL locals lay with the self-definition of the association's founders as experts who advised others who, in turn, carried their advice forward into the political arena. The AALL's task, as John Commons saw it, was to render judgments about proposed legislation so as to improve it, and only secondarily to advocate particular forms of labor legislation. As early as 1909, Commons wrote to Henry Farnam at Yale, a large contributor to the AALL and a member of the association's Executive Committee, strongly urging "that the organization of state branches be discontinued, and that the Association resolve itself into a scientific bureau to aid other associations in promoting labor legislation."[54] The work of coordinating the locals absorbed too much of the secretary's time, Commons thought. It would be quite enough for John Andrews to respond to calls seeking "information as to what other states and countries have done, how other laws operate, what investigations we have made on the subject, what suggestions or model draft of a bill we have to offer." On nearly every issue there was "an active organization at work endeavoring to promote certain specific labor legislation." That promotional work "is already taken up, or promises to be taken up, and can be better handled by other organizations."[55]

The "work of information" was not being done, however. Bureaus of labor could not do it "because their business is so closely connected with the administration of labor laws." Neither could societies primarily interested in promoting legislation, "because their line is the active work of propaganda and is restricted each to a part of the great field." The AALL, Commons concluded, "occupies the unique position of an organization to promote legislation by means of scientific investigation." Societies "equipped for the work of propaganda and political agitation . . . must necessarily look to us for the scientific basis that will make their agitation effective and keep it on solid ground."[56] This "work of information" did not require local branches.

Yet the association's determination to remain scientifically objective and above the political fray was constantly undercut by the profoundly political character of labor legislation. This was especially apparent at the local level. For example, when the Massachusetts Association for Labor Legislation dedicated itself to the goal of establishing a state department of labor, it needed more than scientific objectivity. "The prospects are excellent," its secretary informed John Andrews, "but there is going to be a fight and a great need for money."[57] Scientific objectivity, unaided, did not win political contests. Nor, apparently, did it even provide local branches with a basis for united action. "Being agreed only upon the desirability of wise legislation in general, there is a great difficulty in getting general agreement on any specific project," Arthur Holcombe, Harvard professor of government, wrote John Andrews about the Massachusetts local.[58]

In its effort to protect "the scientific basis" of labor legislation, the AALL required all locals to obtain the approval of the national's Executive Committee for any legislation they endorsed.[59] This sapped local initiative, created irritating delays, and generated a backlog of paperwork. Even so, locals regularly eluded the national's control. Crystal Eastman, perhaps the nation's leading expert on industrial injuries and the irrepressible organizer of the New York branch, incurred "rather heavy" expenses for that local's first meeting. The national office grudgingly agreed to pay and then resolved that "each section ought to pay all of its own expenses."[60] Enterprising Miss Eastman arranged for the Russell Sage Foundation to provide her with a salary of $1,000 to enable her to serve as secretary of a newly created New York State Employers' Liability Commission at the same time that she continued as secretary of the New York AALL branch.[61] Andrews held his breath in a letter to Commons a year later when he reported, "Miss Eastman has been working for some time toward the organization of a New Jersey branch. . . . I am naturally somewhat surprised to know that she is willing to assume such responsibilities, but I am going ahead with the idea of co-operating just as far as possible."[62] Sometimes local initiative threatened to overwhelm the national organization.

"There is a movement on here in New York to make radical changes in our Constitution," Andrews told Commons just before the annual meeting in 1910, urging his mentor to attend and participate in the discussions.[63]

Yet the worst enemy of AALL branches was local indifference. The number of people willing to act as local labor legislation watchdogs with only scientific rather than political or moral imperatives proved extremely limited. Andrews and Commons were "quite surprised" when the people they had rounded up at the annual meeting of the American Economics Association to form a New York local in 1910 "had really not given any careful thought to the important question of filling the [president's] office until the dinner, an hour and a half before the time set for the meeting."[64]

Ultimately the financial bottom line did the locals in. While the national office received large contributions from a few sources, the branches failed to attract enough money to pay their own way, let alone aid the national. During the years between 1913 and 1916, when the locals were folding, AALL annual income did not decline.[65] The association never relied on the locals as a means of expanding its membership. Membership stayed at its 1913 level of about three thousand until the organization disbanded after John Andrews's death in the early 1940s.[66] The end of the Massachusetts branch was near when Arthur Holcombe wrote to John Andrews in January 1912 on a copy of the local's letterhead on which every name had a line drawn through it. "Can I see you in New York?" Holcombe said, "I want to . . . discuss the ways and means of making ourselves more useful to you."[67] By 1916 the burden of local branches had been shed.

Meanwhile, John Andrews kept busy fielding a constant barrage of requests for information about labor legislation. In 1911 he began to publish a scholarly quarterly, the *American Labor Legislation Review* (*ALLR*), which printed papers from the organization's annual meeting and from special AALL conferences, provided topical criticisms of existing laws, and summarized recent labor legislation by subject and state.[68] Yet at the same time that the AALL cleared its decks for "the work of information," Andrews and Commons recognized the need to engage in more substantive activities and pursue its secondary mandate of recommending particular forms of legislation. Crystal Eastman led the way. Her book, *Work-Accidents and the Law*, one of the most significant of the six-volume *Pittsburgh Survey*, was in press in 1909 when she was appointed secretary of a New York commission on employers' liability.[69] The example of her success was not lost on the AALL leadership. In a 1910 letter to the head of New York's Bureau of Labor Statistics, Irene Osgood Andrews (recently married to John Andrews) noted "the very rapid growth in interest and activity on the subject of workman's compensation"; she concluded, "All eyes seem to be turned toward New York. We receive constant demands for information as to what is being done here."[70]

Responding to this opening, the AALL placed compensation for workplace injuries at the top of its agenda for the next five years. In 1911 ten states passed some form of compensation, and by 1915 the number had grown to thirty-three.[71] Yet the AALL experience with workmen's compensation differed in one crucial respect from the NCL's contemporaneous campaign to reduce hours and raise wages for working women. Although it claimed a leadership position by virtue of its "scientific" superiority, in fact the AALL often took second place to a group that sought to represent the joint interests of workers and employers, the National Civic Federation (NCF).[72] Founded in 1900 to pursue arbitration and mediation between capital and labor, the NCF began working on workmen's compensation in 1908. By 1910 its Department on Compensation attracted the participation of 600 representative employers, attorneys, labor leaders, insurance experts, economists, state officials, and members of state compensation commissions. The NCF's model laws on workmen's compensation, although they often favored employers, became the chief focal point for discussion among state legislatures, employers, and representatives of organized labor because they were seen as efforts to combine the interests of labor and employers. For example, the NCF's model compensation law of 1914 was sent to all the affiliated bodies of the AFL and to 25,000 employers.[73] The AALL lacked this reach into grassroots constituencies and failed to dominate the issue on the basis of scientific expertise alone.

A turf war between the AALL and the NCF in the autumn of 1911 exemplified the AALL's difficulty in exercising political leadership without grounding itself in a political constituency. When Seth Low, former president of Columbia University, former mayor of New York City, and NCF president between 1907 and 1916, suggested that the AALL "follow behind the scheme which the Civic Federation is beginning to send along," Andrews indignantly replied that the federation should "fall in line and cooperate with our committee." He wrote Commons: "from past experience I anticipate that [the] Civic Federation will endeavor to crowd us out of our position and if possible create a sentiment for the purpose of bringing us into line in support of their own program. Personally I feel that our committee should push its work through and not allow itself to be confused or retarded." Andrews felt that the AALL's "hard work" would prepare the way for the "development of friendly sentiment."[74] Nevertheless, the NCF adeptly outmaneuvered Andrews, developing, for example, a uniform accident reporting scheme before the AALL could devise its own and presenting it to the Federal Workmen's Compensation Commission of 1911. In the end both the NCF and the AALL claimed credit for advances in compensation law between 1910 and 1920.[75]

The AALL's ability to shape public policy was severely limited by its failure to form an effective relationship with organized labor—the most obvious group capable of serving as its grassroots equivalent to the NCL's women's organizations. Whereas trade union organizing was an important secondary or indirect goal of the NCL—for example, Kelley thought that shorter hours and higher wages would increase the number of women who joined trade unions, and she worked closely with the WTUL—this was never the case with the AALL. "The active support of organized labor would probably tend to strengthen the work of your association," Morris Hillquit wrote Andrews in 1911, but Andrews explained to an AALL member in 1913, "while I am a firm believer in the necessity for trade unions, yet my conclusion is that the greatest permanent social gains have come and will continue to come from remedial legislation, slow and conservative as this movement sometimes appears and is." He expressed special concern for "the cause of the unskilled worker," which seemed "particularly hopeless" through organization.[76] True, political conditions in the United States, especially the tendency for courts to undo labor-supported legislation, turned Samuel Gompers away from political solutions to labor's problems as early as the 1880s and reduced his interest in cooperating with the AALL.[77] Nevertheless, Gompers served as a vice president of the AALL for some years, and Andrews might have done more to develop labor allies if he had worried less about "non-partisan" appearances. As it was, Gompers never cooperated fully with Andrews, charging him on one occasion with "stupidity" and "arrogance," and when he finally resigned from the AALL in 1915, he called the organization the "American Association for the Assassination of Labor Legislation."[78]

Knowledge, power, and expanding state responsibility meant different things to the NCL and the AALL and flowed in different channels. One practical effect of those differences can be seen in the relationship of each organization to the nation's first minimum wage campaign, 1909–17. Both sought to remedy problems of the wage-earning poor, but their differing understanding of social problems and differing power bases led them to different solutions.

Viewed by one advocate as "the keystone of the arch in labor legislation," minimum wage laws were integrally related to other reform efforts aimed at the working poor, especially to hours legislation, and antisweatshop measures.[79] More explicitly intended as a means of redistributing wealth than any previous labor laws, minimum wage legislation expressed a new form of social justice that aimed to establish a floor beneath which wages could not fall. Reformers hoped that such a floor would end the downward spiral of wages wherein sweatshop employers paid low wages to workers, who then required support from relief or charity, thereby indirectly providing employers with subsidies that enabled them to lower wages further.

What Florence Kelley called "predatory management" and "parasitic manufacturers" had been her enemy since she led Chicago's antisweatshop campaign in the early 1890s.[80] When employers complained that competition forced wages down, and that compliance with her eight-hour law would put them out of business because they could not make enough in that time to compete with factory-produced goods, she replied that they *should* go out of business if they had to adopt parasitical practices. This view was most fully articulated in 1897 by Beatrice and Sidney Webb's *Industrial Democracy* in a section on "Parasitic Trades":

> If the employers in a particular trade are able to take such advantage of the necessities of their workpeople as to hire them for wages actually insufficient to provide enough food, clothing, and shelter to maintain them in average health; if they are able to work them for hours so long as to deprive them of adequate rest and recreation; or if they can subject them to conditions so dangerous or insanitary as positively to shorten their lives, that trade is clearly obtaining a supply of labor-force which it does not pay for.[81]

In 1909 the British Parliament acted on this belief by passing the Trades Boards Act, which created mechanisms to provide minimum wages for all workers in certain poorly paid occupations.[82]

As early as 1899 Kelley hoped "to include a requirement as to minimal wages" in the NCL's White Label.[83] Australia and New Zealand had already organized wage boards as part of compulsory arbitration, but the path to an American equivalent did not seem clear until she and other Consumers' League leaders in 1908 attended the First International Conference of Consumers' Leagues, in Geneva, where they learned about the proposed British wage boards.[84]

Almost immediately on her return Kelley established her leadership in what became an enormously successful campaign. First she raided the languishing AALL branches for male supporters. Reverend John Ryan, professor of economics at St. Paul Seminary, founder of the AALL Minnesota local and the leading advocate of minimum wage legislation in the United States other than Florence Kelley, spoke at the NCL's annual meeting in 1910. In 1911 Kelley organized a "special Committee on Minimum Wage Boards" in the NCL with Arthur Holcombe, president of the Massachusetts Association for Labor Legislation, as its chair, and including John Ryan (who by then had quit his membership in the AALL) and Henry Seager, Columbia economics professor and AALL president.

Also in 1911 the Massachusetts Consumers' League, the Women's Trade Union League, the United Textile Workers, and the Massachusetts Association for Labor Legislation all lobbied for the creation of a state commission to investigate minimum wage legislation. But the power to shape the proposal fell to the NCL when Mary Dewson, a Consumers' League activist, was appointed the commission's secretary, and Elizabeth Glendower, one of the commission's five members and a close friend of Kelley (with whom her daughter had boarded), funded much of the commission's work.[85] The high point of the campaign occurred in 1913, when eight additional states passed minimum wage laws for women: California, Colorado, Minnesota, Nebraska, Oregon, Utah, Washington, and Wisconsin.[86]

Relying on grassroots support from women's organizations, the NCL's leadership in this campaign was augmented by organized labor and conscientious employers who sought to eliminate unscrupulous competition. Although the NCL could not count on universal backing from women or men trade unionists, cooperation with the Women's Trade Union League and with many state federations of labor produced a much smoother alliance than the relationship the AALL had forged with the national American Federation of Labor.[87] The political stance of organized labor varied from state to state, but whereas the AFL officially opposed wage legislation (arguing that the minimum could become the maximum), the NCL promoted minimum wage as an agent of both class and gender realignment.

Florence Kelley saw low wages as a simple matter of class exploitation. She freely denounced her enemies in three industries at the heart of the NCL campaign—retail stores, the tenement house garment making, and cotton mills. "These industries are what they are by the deliberate, determined policy of the men who conduct them," she insisted, detailing the large profits made by "merchant princes," "shoddy millionnaries," and textile manufacturers. Against these men, "persuasion has failed as a means of improving wages." They responded by forming employer associations "for the purpose of fighting all encroachment upon their freedom of exploitation." Yet, Kelley insisted, "Low wages produce more poverty than all other causes together"; she urged that "goods and profits are not ends in themselves to which human welfare may continue to be sacrificed."[88]

These class-specific goals were achieved through gender-specific means. In some respects the wage campaign reinforced the gendered status quo. A much higher proportion of women workers were young, unskilled, and poorly paid compared to working men, and the NCL moralized their plight, often referring to the temptation of young working women to drift into prostitution because they could not support themselves on their wages. Nevertheless, her sensationalism was contained within a vision that endorsed young women's independence: "So long as women's wages rest upon the assumption that every woman has a husband, father, brother or lover contributing to her support, so long these sinister incidents of women's industrial employment (tuberculosis, insanity, vice) are inevitable." Kelley urged that "society itself must build the floor beneath their feet."[89] A minimum wage would free daughters from dependency on their families and create more stability in the lives of the approximately 20 percent of working women who lived separately from their families around 1910.[90] This group was a permanent part of the labor force, she believed, and deserved better treatment from employers and reformers alike. What they needed most was a better wage.

Kelley also argued that minimum wages would give women workers more negotiating power with their employers. In the NCL's model law, wages were set by a board consisting of "the employers, the workers, and representatives of the consuming public."[91] Thus minimum wage boards gave working women an equal voice with their employers: "[A minimum wage board] gives effect to the will of those who have in the past been mere pawns in the hands of masters who have played the game on terms laid down by themselves alone. It gives votes to women in a field in which women most sorely need them, in the determination of their wages."[92] In this way wage legislation could have civic as well as economic effects.

Yet gratifying as the minimum wage campaign was—in Elizabeth Glendower Evans's words, it "pierces to the heart the classic claim that industry is a purely private affair"—legal complications made it enormously frustrating.[93] Reformers had to squeeze their arguments through the only constitutional loophole through which the courts might sustain wage laws—that low wages affected the health and morals of (young) women and therefore were properly subject to intervention under the police powers of the state. Kelley decried legislators who focused on "the meanest consideration on which such a discussion could conceivably have been carried forward"—the "contemptible" question: " 'What is the least sum on which an honest working girl can keep soul and body together and escape disgrace?' "[94] But to establish the need for a nine-dollar weekly wage, she and her allies were constantly forced to justify small expenditures—twenty-five cents for carfare and fifty cents for clothes.[95]

During this arduous campaign Kelley received almost no help from the AALL. At the campaign's outset a Milwaukee member wrote to Andrews hoping that the AALL could "give us some aid in some shape or other" in support of the minimum wage campaign in Wisconsin, concluding, "I shall be only too pleased to keep in touch with you because I am always seeking help from experts." Andrews loftily replied: "I question very seriously the wisdom of injecting the minimum wage proposition into the legislative campaign of this year, because I do not believe our courts would at the present time uphold such legislation, and I am afraid it would seriously jeopardize the splendid progress now being made in legislation to establish maximum working hours."[96] Two years later the AALL still opposed minimum wage legislation as premature.

In January 1912 Arthur Holcombe wrote from Cambridge, Massachusetts, twitting Andrews that he was being left behind: "Are you yet prepared to endorse minimum wage? that is, the principle? The Massachusetts Commission will soon."[97] When Henry Seager, AALL president and a member of the NCL's Minimum Wage Committee, sent Seth Low a pamphlet about the AALL's "program of work," he added an embarrassed reference to the backwardness of the national AALL: "the Massachusetts Association is . . . likely to approve the Minimum Wage Board Bill. . . . I speak of this part of our work because I do not wish to give the impression that the items referred to in the enclosed printed statement are the only phases of labor legislation in connection with which we are active."[98] In a 1915 article in the *American Labor Legislation Review*, Irene Andrews offered a half-hearted endorsement of minimum wages that emphasized the need to link wage laws with solutions to the problem of the seasonality in women's occupations.[99] Three years later Andrews told an Indiana member, "This Association . . . as you know is not concerned primarily with wages. We are trying to raise the standards of health and safety."[100] By that time several states already had legislation in place, but the campaign was stalled. Between 1909 and 1915 the NCL had led the movement to obtain pathbreaking wage laws. Now they needed forceful, not lukewarm allies.

Until the passage of the Fair Labor Standards Act (FLSA) of 1938, all state minimum wage laws and many state laws regulating working hours in the United States applied only to women. Not until 1942, when the U.S. Supreme Court approved the constitutionality of the FLSA, did the eight-hour day and the minimum wage become part of the social contract for most American workers.[101] The class-bridging activism of middle-class women forged the way with these fundamental reforms.

In some ways their activism signaled the dawn of modern America. New forms of knowledge, power, and state responsibility emerged to frame a new social contract that became embodied in the New Deal of the 1930s and continues in our time to shape political debate about the welfare of working people. Nevertheless, the same traditions of limited government that made it so difficult for the NCL and other Progressive reformers to enact social legislation in the early decades of this century seem stronger than ever today. And the direction of change has shifted: the working day is growing longer and wages are diminishing. Some organizations still try to use the welfare of children as a lever to raise the standard of living of all working people, but they now seem to be working against rather than with the flow of public opinion. The possibility that middle-class women could be mobilized today to intervene in public life on behalf of working people seems remote.

In some ways, therefore, the activism of NCL members can best be seen as the culmination of nineteenth-century trends, many of which have not survived into the late twentieth century. Moral notions about public responsibility for the welfare of women and children rank high among these. Because they accentuated gender differences, today these notions seem outdated and ineffective. Yet as this comparison between the NCL and the AALL shows, through grassroots mobilization women's organizations succeeded in accomplishing reforms that male expertise and power could not initiate. Women did not reside at the margins of progressive social reform; they occupied its center.

The agency of women and the agency of men were shaped by the gendered definitions of their opportunities for political activism in the Progressive Era. Ultimately, this comparison suggests that no corner of American political life was unconnected to the system of gendered meanings that informed the ongoing process by which civic activity was molded. The more we understand about American women, the more we understand about American history.

CHAPTER 3 : PUTTING CHILDREN FIRST :
WOMEN, MATERNALISM, AND WELFARE
IN THE EARLY TWENTIETH CENTURY
LINDA GORDON

> *I think it is unquestionably true that if a person wishes to do any*
> *constructive social work in a community that the confidence of the people . . .*
> *can best be secured by beginning with work for the children.*
> *— Emma Duke, Children's Bureau, 1919*

> *Children are not safe and happy if their parents are miserable. . . . The*
> *power to maintain a decent family living standard is a primary essential*
> *of child welfare.*
> *— Julia Lathrop, 1919*

A strategy of putting children first has indelibly marked the U.S. welfare state.[1] This strategy created, for example, the program to which most people refer when they say "welfare" or Aid to Families with Dependent Children (AFDC) and has been basic to the most prominent welfare advocacy for over a century. Women were influential in formulating and popularizing the view that promoting the welfare of the nation should begin with children. Thus, as men and women welfare reformers championed the well-being of children, they expressed and acted out a major concern of the world's most powerful women's movement and in turn shaped that movement. In this essay I sketch the historical development of "putting children first" and examine its meanings and consequences. I want to suggest that it was a strategy expressive of some of the conditions and assumptions of nineteenth-century and Progressive Era women reformers, always containing contradictions and limitations, and that more recently its defects may have outweighed its advantages.

The strategy contains both modern and traditional elements. The ethical and political notion that children should be the best treated of us all is quintessentially modern; in premodern, patriarchal societies children were often expected to make do with the worst food, with little attention, and with scant opportunity to express their preferences. Although putting children first

"A Woman's Work Is Never Done," from the *New York Telegram*, 1918.

is by no means exclusively a women's or a feminist point of view, its development was nevertheless closely associated with women's increased cultural and political power, and organized women were influential disproportionately to their formal political power in the creation of a modern child-welfare consciousness and movement. This consciousness, paradoxically, derived from the traditional: women's responsibility for children is a transhistorical, transcultural pattern, so it is hardly surprising that women carried that sense of responsibility into organized political activity. The identification of women with children was shared by feminists and antifeminists.

Historically, putting children first arose with putting forward motherhood as women's claim to respect and power. The dominant form of this construction among activist women was what some called "maternalism,"[2] and this too took a variety of historical and political forms. Nevertheless, maternalism had several common ingredients. First was the conviction that women reformers should function in a motherly role toward the poor because the poor needed moral and spiritual as well as economic help. The second shared belief was that women's work, experience, and/or destiny as mothers made them uniquely able to lead the campaign for public social provision while it made poor mothers uniquely deserving of help. This argument was sometimes biological, sometimes social, but it always expressed a commitment to gender differentiation. Maternalists almost always accepted the family-wage principle—that men, husbands and fathers, should ideally be able to earn enough to support their families, freeing wives and mothers to devote themselves to homemaking. Yet some maternalism also served to subvert that premise, for a third aspect was a commitment to giving aid directly to women, not through their husbands, thereby challenging women's economic and political dependency on men as precisely unfitting them for their best possible work as mothers. Most renditions of maternalism led women to give priority to the needs of children in their reform campaigns.

I approach this material on the basis of previous work about family violence, poverty, and welfare. I have been interested in bringing children into social history, not only as the objects of reformers but also as subjects, to the extent that we can find the sources that allow us to do so. However, to study children without a gender analysis is to miss a great deal, because historically childhood was constructed in relation to motherhood, and vice versa. In the late twentieth century, that relation is changing in several respects: women so often parent children without a man's support that single motherhood can no longer be called exceptional; widespread male parenting and nonmaternal women are ordinary. This vantage point makes possible a new view of the maternalist welfare tradition.

The welfare strategy of putting children first produced a series of contradictions, always present but recently intensified. Most vivid today, and unavoidably influencing any scholarly discussion, is the deepening poverty of children in the United States. Children have been entering poverty at rates higher than other sectors of the U.S. population. The usual comparison is with the elderly who, at least in the middle and upper working class, were the beneficiaries of the New Deal's Social Security Act: in 1949, 60 percent of the elderly were in poverty; in 1990, 12 percent. Children also benefited at first from Social Security provisions (as well as economic gains in the mid-twentieth century): in 1949, 48 percent were in poverty; in 1979, 17 percent. But more recently children have fared decidedly worse, their poverty rate rising to 21 percent by 1990 and still higher since then.[3] And the children of the poor never benefited relative to other age groups. Today half of all African American children, for example, are classified as poor (by government figures that consistently understate impoverishment).[4] Several of the concerns most specific to the contemporary welfare crisis—drugs, teenage pregnancy, gangs—are about the young. Forty percent of the homeless—1.8 million—are children. The United States has become notorious in the world for its poor showing with respect to certain basic child welfare indices: infant mortality rates, educational attainment, teenage pregnancy incidence, and poverty among children. It is difficult to reconcile these circumstances with the fact that we have a welfare system that was supposed to benefit children particularly.

Another contradiction of the maternalist welfare strategy is that, while it reflected the unusual power of women in welfare agitation in the United States in comparison to the power of women in comparable industrial countries, it may have ended by disadvantaging women. Ironically, the putting-children-first strategy, to the degree that it identified the interests of children as separate from those of their mothers, justified policies that made it more difficult for women to mother, especially when mothers were employed or without male financial support. Of course, the increasing powers of the state to intervene in parent-child relations also weakened paternal power, but since mothers were held responsible for children's welfare, the state's policies impinged on them more directly.

Still another contradiction is that, while the child-centered strategy provided the basis for a strong reform alliance, which from the 1870s through the 1940s pushed some welfare programs through Congress against the resistance of powerful interests, the strategy may at the same time have limited the welfare state. Finally, the child-centered programs built by this alliance became in the end, paradoxically, weaker than more adult-centered programs.

By focusing on these contradictions, I do not mean to imply that the putting-children-first strategy was exclusively responsible for the limitations of our welfare state; as will become clear below, various constitutional, political, and economic factors were more important. Nor am I belittling the efforts of the remarkable welfare activists who worked so hard against the grain of a culture steeped in individualism. What follows is a critique, not a criticism: the choices made by reformers at any given time may have been the only practicable ones. Historians can rarely collect enough evidence to prove the viability of paths that were not taken. I want merely to tell a historical story in such a way as to illuminate the implications of the paths that *were* taken. After a brief introduction to the history of the putting-children-first strategy, this essay discusscs thc mcanings of this priority for the women's movement and offers an analytic description of the resultant overall structure of the U.S. welfare system; it then focuses on two examples of putting children first: the rise of child-protection, or anti-child-abuse, work; and the development of AFDC.

The putting-children-first strategy might be traced to a reorientation in women's reform activity in the mid-nineteenth century.[5] Lori Ginzburg locates in the 1850s a shift from moral suasion as the primary mode of organized female reform discourse to a more pragmatic "political" discourse that emphasized what women could contribute to others. Particularly relevant in her analysis is a shift from autonomous women's organizations to male/female groups in which women sometimes functioned as auxiliaries but often did most of the work, allowing men to retain leadership roles; and from attacking societal injustice to creating institutions for victims of these injustices, children prominent among them.[6] Ginzburg's distinction is an improvement on, but related to, Aileen Kraditor's older one between "justice" and "expediency" arguments for women's rights. Kraditor's was a moralistic and misleading distinction because, on the one hand, women activists of most varieties were concerned with creating more justice in the world, and, on the other hand, most were willing to make compromises, gestures, and tactical decisions for the sake of expediency. But certainly the move to emphasize women's proclivities and abilities to help others was a move away from natural-rights arguments for women's empowerment to a more pragmatic one.[7] Anne Firor Scott has identified four stages of women's philanthropic work, and her analysis produces a slightly different but by no means contradictory periodization: first, "benevolence" at the turn of the nineteenth century; second, social reform in the antebellum period; third, an interlude of union patriotism and aid to the armed forces during the Civil War; and fourth, a great expansion of activism stimulated by radical class and demographic changes in the society that produced in particular new kinds of urban poverty and its consequences. Scott's interpretation is the more discerning because it is based on an examination of a variety of different groups of women activists—black and white, northern and southern, middle-class and working-class.[8]

This historic turn in the nineteenth-century women's movement prefigured in some ways the split over the Equal Rights Amendment in the twentieth century; the split is best seen as characterizing two aspects of a feminist (as it later came to be called) outlook that have existed in varying proportional strengths since the beginning of organized women's reform.[9] One aspect emphasized the common humanity of women and men and criticized the "artificial" imposition of a division of labor and sensibility that produced "exaggerated" feminine and masculine types. Although close in some respects to the late-twentieth-century concept of gender, this critique differed because it was in its way essentialist, postulating an authentic humanity (which, some have charged, remained in many ways modeled on the masculine). Some but not all feminists of this orientation favored absolute legal sameness in the treatment of men and women, thus supporting an Equal Rights Amendment, not because they denied social difference but because they thought that the best way to erase it was with complete formal equality. The second stream of feminist thought accepted in various degrees male/female social and psychological differences as desirable and sought means of raising women's status and power without denying the appropriateness of a large-scale sexual division of labor. Understanding *both* these perspectives as feminist is important to our appraisal of the woman-dominated child welfare movement: the maternalists were (generically) feminist. Moreover, the distinction between equal-rights and maternalist thought is often rendered as too absolute by historians, especially as it concerns children. Few feminists challenged women's unique responsibility, and internalization of this responsibility, for children.[10] But the second perspective gave much more priority, obviously, to women's maternal role as important in itself and as a basis for women's social and political power.

In the second half of the nineteenth century these two perspectives had been united, if not unified, within a hegemonic "woman movement" broad enough to encompass politically and socially different causes. These causes included temperance, suffrage, protection for working women, unions for working women, reproduction control (called then "voluntary motherhood"), divorce, married women's property rights, and many others. One such cause, the struggle for maternal custody of children in cases of marital separation, was important in the development of a maternalist feminism and the putting-children-first strategy. Women's victories in achieving preference in custody disputes illustrate the ambiguous meaning of these gains for women and children. As was typical of most U.S. family-law reform, the campaign for maternal custody took place on many smaller sites rather than one central locus, due both to the federalism of the United States and its weak central government, and to the separation of powers that left family law so much to the discretion of the judiciary for so long. And it was a reform with many meanings. For one, most women wanted their children badly and were unwilling to leave even the most abusive husbands if doing so meant losing their children, so that child custody also gave women greater self-confidence in standing up to dominating husbands. Moreover, maternal custody was a reform that helped build the state, through building the power of the courts, undercutting a traditional patriarchal power invested in husbands and fathers;

it was the courts, not women, that gained ultimate control over the disposition of children. Yet it was a reform that simultaneously created the expectation that the state had a responsibility to look after the "best interests of the child" as against the interests not only of fathers but equally against the more fragile respect for mothers' claims.[11] As one judge said in 1902, in the context of upholding a piece of protective legislation, "Women and children have always, to a certain extent, been wards of the State."[12] Thus there was an ambiguity at the heart of maternal custody victories: that gains in women's power over children—which may well have been in most cases benefits for children—also strengthened state control over the family and gave it the potential to intercede against women's interests as well. But the consequences of this ambiguity would not be fully evident for a long time to come. At this time the campaign for maternal custody in the name of the best interests of the child was a women's-rights issue and produced one of the great women's victories of the nineteenth century. Later, in the early twentieth century, Edith Howe entitled an article "Our Right to the Lives of Babies"; she meant it in the context of lobbying for work against infant mortality, but it was also a symbolic expression of her concept of women's rights.

In the 1890s maternalist reformers developed a more coherent approach to social betterment that became known as "social work." It grew from traditional charity, largely religious and denominational, in the early nineteenth century, through "friendly visiting" and charity organization at the turn of the century. Religiously motivated "friendly visitors" for, say, a Provident Association felt themselves part of a community, albeit a conflictual one, with prison matrons, temperance activists, and advocates of tenement laws. All this social reform impetus had a female character in the Progressive Era. It was commonplace for men as well as women to speak of the emerging welfare state in the feminine gender: "Only thus will our great state fulfill her present duty to her citizens in the making,—those in whom are rightly centered her most minute solicitude and her largest hope," commented Minneapolis District Court judge Edward Waite in 1914.[13]

This feminized reform community began to divide into clearly defined sectors in the 1920s. A professional social work developed, still female-dominated but increasingly with a male hierarchy. "Amateur" women's charity and service organizations continued to be strong. Starting in the 1890s black women's welfare activism became nationally organized, its importance suggesting that African Americans shared with whites the view that such activism was a "natural" extension of women's familial nurturing work. And women agitated for public welfare provision. Some of the white women attained footholds in new government welfare agencies, while others rejected the idea of public responsibility and defended private charity. Over time the children-first approach had been pioneered by the more conservative charity women, who felt comfortable with motherhood as the reason and justification for women's activism, but by the late Progressive Era that approach was adopted by many public welfare advocates as well. This was one of the factors that allowed the white groups—black women were excluded—to overcome their differences and at times form lobbying coalitions.

The turn toward putting children first was by no means identical among all class, ethnic, religious, and racial groups of women. But it was a general trend. Two examples may suffice here. Catholic charities, partly because of the unique Catholic sisterhoods, were even more woman-dominated than were the Protestant charities. In New York City, Irish Catholics from the mid-nineteenth century on, led by nuns, were developing their own welfare services. In the first few decades after the famine immigration these Sisters had emphasized care for unwed mothers and "fallen" women, as Protestant elite women had done in earlier decades; after the Civil War the Sisters, partly under pressure from the hierarchy, began to concentrate on schools, orphanages, and foster care.[14] African American orientation toward children can be seen in the emphasis placed on building educational institutions, a necessity because of the refusal of the state governments of the South to provide schools for black children. (Not enough research has yet been done about other nonwhite minority groups to allow us to know how different or similar their welfare views were to those of whites.)

By the early twentieth century the woman-dominated social-work networks had gained substantial coherence and even created national organizations, such as the National Consumers' League, the National Association of Colored Women, the National Council of Jewish Women, and the National Council of Catholic Women. The most influential network, mainly Protestant and entirely white, was acquiring considerable influence on government, even without the vote, particularly at local levels. Its biggest legislative achievement in the Progressive Era was the mothers' aid, or mothers' "pension," laws passed in most of the states between 1910 and 1920. The discourse about these small public aid enactments was largely about children. The laws were designed to remedy two kinds of damages to children: removal from their parents, particularly from single mothers,[15] because of their mothers' poverty; and child labor. Other reforms for which women lobbied were also aimed at child welfare: for example, protective labor legislation, the Pure Food and Drug Act of 1906, and juvenile courts.

Early in the twentieth century, leaders of the maternalist reform network generated a plan to gain a foothold in the federal government, the success of which was extremely consequential for the formation of welfare in the United States. In an extraordinary development unique to this nation, women welfare reformers established a federal enclave: the Children's Bureau, created in the Department of Labor (DOL) in 1912. The fact that this agency, which was devoted to investigating child welfare, antedated the Women's Bureau, established also in the DOL in 1918, reflects several aspects of the putting-children-first strategy: the women's own child-centered priorities, the greater legitimacy of women's work for children than for women, and women's manipulation of the symbolic meanings of children in order to force politicians to support welfare initiatives. Nevertheless, the Children's Bureau was as much a (generic) women's bureau as the Women's Bureau; the two agencies achieved a practical and for the most part amicable division of labor, with the latter focusing on employment issues while the former ranged widely into other areas, despite its location in the DOL. Indeed, the founders of the Children's Bureau hoped that it would become a kind of department of health, education, and welfare within the DOL.[16] The Children's Bureau served as a hub of a national woman-dominated welfare network and helped coordinate campaigns for many reforms not at all limited to or focused on children. Immediately after its establishment, the Children's Bureau's first chief, Julia Lathrop, called a conference of her informal social-feminist network, thus signaling what was to be the agency's continuing pattern of ignoring the boundary between governmental and civic organization; it was understandable that when women were so rare in government, their main lines of responsibility and consultation would tie them to their community of women reformers. By the 1920s, the Children's Bureau was the conduit used by many civic organizations pressuring for virtually any kind of social legislation.

Putting children first was not a mirror of women's mothering, neither an instinct nor a transparent internalization of social responsibility. It was a strategy and a vision, complexly reached, internally ambiguous. Its meanings are not obvious but require interpretation and may be contested.

The uniqueness of the female commitment to children becomes clearest when we note another fissure in the welfare-reform community, that between women and men. Among elite, white eastern reformers after World War I there developed two relatively separate streams of thought: the social-work tendency, which remained woman-dominated and child-centered, and a new social-insurance tendency, which was overwhelmingly male and virtually ignored children. A brief comparison vividly illustrates the putting-children-first strategy.

The social-work strain of welfare thought, maintaining the nineteenth-century charity tradition, continued to assume that an effective program of public aid required distinguishing between the "deserving" and the "undeserving" poor and treating them differently. Social workers feared, even well into the Great Depression of the 1930s, that their own aid-giving practices might create "pauperism" by undermining the work ethic. Good social work required more than material relief; it demanded character reform. Aid to the poor must be preceded by careful investigation and accompanied by guidance toward prevention of or rehabilitation from pauperism. Thus welfare called for supervision of a personal nature—of home, family, and neighborhood life, of work and school records—an approach that came to be called *casework*. Effective casework required individual treatment of each client, not simply across-the-board relief, and such treatment was more easily given in programs designed for particular categories of the needy. Categorical assistance, as this approach became known, produced special programs for children, the blind, the disabled, and the unemployed, among others.

The social-insurance perspective grew up outside the charity tradition. Its proponents were mainly male academics, from a similarly elite class position as the largely female social workers.[17] Learning from European programs, particularly German and British, they introduced at the turn of the century a new approach to welfare, whose basic principles were government provision, based on compulsory participation, and automatic (that is, not means- or morals-tested) benefits among covered groups. Social-insurance programs were not particularly directed at the poor; one of their selling points was that they benefited all classes. While the social workers focused on treating poverty so as to prevent pauperism, the social-insurance proponents aimed to prevent poverty itself, by aiding workers as soon as there was a loss of earnings, as in the case of workmen's compensation, or by providing incentives for employers to maintain steady employment and safe working conditions, as for example through the use of tax incentives. The social-insurance advocates had great confidence that poverty could be prevented, but this by no means made them necessarily more Left or democratic than the women's social-work network. Some of them leaned toward the Socialist Party, whereas others were quite conservative. Despite different motives, socialist and capitalist, they shared the mission of altering economic structures, whether by radical transformation or by tinkering, to reduce poverty.[18]

Social-insurance advocates ignored children almost entirely. Focusing on what they saw as the core of the economy, the capital/labor exchange, these reformers aimed their plans at wage earners. They believed that all welfare needs could be met by maintenance of the male family wage, thus allowing men to support their dependents and eliminating the need for any substantial programs for women or children. Their concerns excluded nonemployed women and children, except in their positions as dependents of wage earners. (They also tended to ignore women wage earners.)

By contrast, to the female-welfare advocates, children were central; they did not concentrate on wage earners. Some were socialists but not much influenced by Marxism and not much given to a class-conflict analysis. (Despite Florence Kelley's European socialist education, she quickly assimilated to the American reform community.) Rather, many were what we might call "socialists of the heart," such as Jane Addams with her noble disdain for greed and exploitation and her longing for higher forms of community than the market could produce. They inherited the charity legacy, with its direction toward the "helpless" and "innocent victims," and the "rescue" tradition of nineteenth-century moral reform, with its interest in control and regeneration. Children fit all these categories: helpless, "innocent," controllable, malleable. At the same time children were a connection to other women, perhaps the most universalizing of connectors. Women's own lives were inextricably involved with children, their identities and claim to respect strongly founded on motherhood. This was as true of childless women as of mothers, for the female relational, nurturant ego is formed long before women reach maturity and become parents. Girls were raised in large part as little mothers, trained in the skills of domestic economy and nurture, socialized to look out for the needs of others. (Indeed, the women—especially but not exclusively the white women—who poured their energies into these welfare campaigns were disproportionately unmarried and childless.)[19] Moreover, all experienced the greater respect that women acquired through motherhood. In their predominantly liberal, as opposed to Calvinist, Protestantism, children were born innocent and thus quintessentially deserving among the poor. Children were helpless and thus ipso facto in need of help. Children were plastic and thus could be influenced by guidance and reform efforts. And these women activists saw their own plight in that of children; we will see this vividly in their approach to family violence, below, but we can also see it in their approach to welfare for adults.

The focus on children was, of course, not exclusive. On the one hand, women social workers fought for many welfare reforms only indirectly related to children, such as industrial health and safety, protective legislation for women, and adult education. On the other hand, reformers and politicians of all perspectives used the rhetoric of "helpless" children to justify and gain support for their proposals. But the women's arguments had a particular feminist meaning: anything of benefit to mothers (or sometimes women in general, as potential mothers) benefited children. Putting children first implied and strengthened a particular construction of femininity. In 1909 Edith Howe wrote: "One, and only one, great power can stem the tide [of infant mortality]—mothers' love, informed, organized, militant. . . . Any step toward the emancipation of woman that does not register itself in a lower infant mortality is a step backward."[20] Emphasizing the unique connection between the well-being of mothers and that of their children must have played a role in their inability to think of men as capable of parenthood. Woman suffragists claimed the vote itself on those grounds; several of them, such as Harriot Stanton Blatch, grounded this claim biologically: "What chiefly distinguishes the human being from the lower animals is the increase in the former of cerebral surface and organization, and the necessary accompaniment . . . a lengthened period of infancy. . . . this increased time of immaturity is a direct tax upon the mother . . . natural selection has carefully fostered the maternal instinct. . . . The paternal instinct is not a factor in evolution. . . . Ever since the patriarchate was established there has been a tendency to cramp the mother in her maternal rights; so we see no race improvement comparable with our advance in material science."[21] Only through bettering women's conditions, then, could the race be improved. Since early-twentieth-century thinkers did not know Mendelian genetics and believed firmly and imaginatively in the inheritance of acquired traits, they could use the eugenical thought fashionable at that time to argue that welfare provision would improve the children of the future.[22]

There were substantial differences in maternalist welfare politics as in maternal experience. Class, race, and wealth affected parenting in every way, from the quality of nutrition one could offer to the aspirations one had for one's children. The richest women transferred parenting work to nurses, nannies, and governesses; most upper-middle-class women hired domestic help, and many women *were* domestic help. While all aimed to support mothering, the emphasis on children in the hands of the most influential social workers involved a greater romanticization of motherhood, concentrating on its symbolic, domestic arrangements. Black women, for example, more often combined mothering with remunerative labor, both working-class and professional, and within their own race won more respect as economic and professional achievers than did comparable whites. Their motherhood did not, could not, emphasize and romanticize motherly domesticity as white women's did. Yet the rhetoric of black women reformers could sound remarkably similar. Consider: "Yes, it is the great mother-heart reaching out to save her children from war, famine and pestilence; from death, degradation and destruction, that induces her to demand 'Votes for Women,' knowing well that fundamentally it is really a campaign for 'Votes for Children.' "[23] This was the voice not of a white suffragist leader but of Carrie Clifford of the Ohio Federation of

Colored Women's Clubs. Organized black women in this period concentrated much of their welfare activism on day nurseries, protecting girls' purity, and education in motherhood. But this motherhood emphasis had considerably different meanings and would, had it been more influential, have resulted in very different policies. For African Americans, motherhood rhetoric was in the vanguard of race uplift and civil-rights activity, and it involved refuting the charges of impurity and incompetence so often directed by whites against blacks. Indeed, motherhood assumed an oppositional meaning, directed against the racism of white women reformers as well as government domination by whites.

White women activists used arguments from motherhood, for children, in their own racialized way. Their definitions of good mothers and children were highly culturally specific, based on the conditions and aspirations of prosperous urban white Protestants. In the Progressive period, the white women's reform network saw non-WASP immigrants as racially different. They believed that children were crucial in the Americanization process precisely because of the greater resistance of adults to cultural reformation.[24] Many of these reformers joined the "race suicide" panic of the turn of the century, worrying that overly high birth rates among the immigrants would overwhelm Anglo-Saxon civilized values. In a variety of policies they advocated, from mothers' aid to tenement housing codes, they sought simultaneously to use xenophobic fears and hostilities to gather support for social reform and to use social reform to remake minorities in their own image.[25]

Yet women's welfare focus on children did not emerge from a chute directly connecting women's private "experience" to public activism. The strategy to garner support for public social provision by organizing around children's needs was a *political* decision and a *political* tradition. Their focus on children represented a thoughtful appropriation of a sphere in which the politically disfranchised could claim power.[26]

The error of interpreting their emphasis on children as an unexamined emotional reaction to "experience" is apparent when we consider the variety of political meanings women have given to child-centered reform. Women from diverse political positions have used motherhood as a base for activism and influence in the public sphere. Today, motherhood is claimed by antinuclear activists, antiabortionists, the La Leche League, even nudists. These multiple possible political constructions of motherhood and childhood have been visible at least since the late eighteenth century, with the birth of what might be considered modern feminism. Mary Wollstonecraft swung back and forth from natural-rights theory to motherhood in grounding her claims for women's equal access to education and political participation. Linda Kerber showed how women in the American Revolutionary era used a notion of republican motherhood to justify "absorption and participation in the civic culture."[27] Fifty years later Catharine Beecher, as Kathryn Sklar has so vividly shown, tried to reconstruct motherhood and domesticity as rationalized, socially respected labor, presenting a contradictory message: earning her living largely by public speaking and writing about the virtues of women's domesticity.[28] In the early twentieth century Ellen Key's version of politicized motherhood drew "new women," as they were called, to free love and disdain for marriage, while in New York mothers banded together to introduce film censorship to protect children.[29]

The choice of child-centered politics was not always conscious, but at times it was, even manipulatively so. By the second decade of the century activists like Florence Kelley, Julia Lathrop, and Grace Abbott argued that public provision for children could become an opening wedge for a broadly conceived, even universal, welfare state. The Children's Bureau urged this strategy upon others. Emma Duke, for example, director of the Children's Bureau's Industrial Division, responded to an inquiry about how to do community organizing this way: "When you called at the office recently and spoke of the difficulty of . . . welfare work in a mill community . . . I think it is unquestionably true that . . . the confidence of the people who live in the community can best be secured by beginning with . . . the children. Work for children is so disinterested and must make an appeal to all classes of people."[30] Sophonisba Breckinridge and Edith Abbott secured federal funding for the first national study of women workers by adding women as a rider, so to speak, to a bill authorizing a study of child labor.[31] The campaign against child labor influenced the campaign for regulation of women's labor, and both were intended by their major advocates to prepare the way for regulation of all labor. Members of this women's network even used children as an excuse for not-so-covert strike support. In the 1912 Lawrence, Massachusetts, textile strike, strikers and their support organizations arranged to send scores of children out of town to be cared for in safer places and publicized their actions to win public support for the strike. In 1928 settlement worker Mary Dreier used child welfare concerns to organize a committee to help bituminous coal strikers and unemployed textile workers obtain $75 million in federal relief.[32]

Putting children first was not only a moral stance but also a posture in which, as I imagine it, women held up children in front of them, plump little legs and adorable wide eyes inducing a suspicious gatekeeper to open a door to the public treasury. Stephen Jay Gould has argued that the protective response to the childlike physique and countenance is universal and powerful. No doubt there are market researchers who work for the large charities today who can tell us whether it is still true that the proportions of a child's body are the most effective device for opening pocketbooks.

The relation between pity for the suffering child and other goals, however, has shifted considerably over time. This was particularly true for those social-work activists who hoped to advance women's rights as part of the promotion of the general welfare. For feminists in certain periods the appeal for women's empowerment on the basis of its benefits for children had a powerful attraction as a standpoint from which to criticize male dominance within the family, opening the family to scrutiny. Through rhetorical moves that positioned children as the culturally accepted victims, women were able to bring into view male behaviors that had been rendered literally unspeakable when women were the object of concern. This was the case, for example, when to speak of wife beating was to bring ignominy onto the *victim*—a shame arguably greater than that of the accused. By speaking of child abuse instead, the same culprit could be ostracized and the long-suffering wife turned into a moral hero. In such a situation the focus on childhood became close to irresistible.

In that kind of situation children symbolized *all* the victims of male dominance, young and old. By the twentieth century, however, the meanings had narrowed. Children were less often used as rhetorical surrogates for women. Indeed, in the 1920s putting children first became part of the receding of feminism, the reburying of the particular welfare needs of women. In 1919 Julia Lathrop, head of the Children's Bureau, argued that "children are not safe and happy if their parents are miserable. . . . The power to maintain a decent family living standard is a primary essential of child welfare."[33] But in 1935, despite the opportunity presented by the depression and the newly positive attitude toward federal welfare provision, her friends and successors did not try to use this logic to develop basic income security for parents.[34] Instead, the emphasis on children began to set up an antagonistic relationship between women's rights and children's welfare. Two historical narratives will show some of the contradictory consequences of the ostensibly chivalric deferring to children.[35]

In the last quarter of the nineteenth century a new reform movement swept the country: the discovery of child abuse and the rise of child-protection agencies, usually called Societies for the Prevention of Cruelty to Children (SPCCs). This campaign was conditioned by women's reform influence, too. In most states men led these agencies, the exclusion of women legitimated by the fact that ferreting out cruelty to children—which, it was widely understood, occurred mainly in the lower classes—required entry into dangerous neighborhoods and exposure to unseemly behaviors. Nevertheless, the child-protection movement arose from woman-influenced streams of child saving, such as the creation of separate asylums for children, campaigns against corporal punishment, and agitation for age-of-consent laws.

In raising the level of public outrage about child mistreatment, the women's rights movement strengthened its critique of male domination in the private sphere. As in temperance before it, the anti-child-abuse movement made male violence a powerful subtext. The anti-child-abuse campaign was in an important way antipatriarchal.[36] The acknowledgment that there was parenting so bad that the state needed to protect children, and that parental rights should sometimes be severed, changed the culture toward much greater acceptance of *formal* public responsibility for child welfare, which in modern society meant greater governmental responsibility.

Yet the record of the anti-child-abuse programs is mixed, and it is a record about which we should think critically as we appraise child-protection work today. Antipatriarchal, yes, but the anti-child-abuse movement also had class and cultural meanings that were by no means so homogeneously progressive. Agencies like the SPCCs were attempting to impose on their largely working-class immigrant "clients" norms of proper parenting that not only were alien but also sometimes created obstacles to their family welfare. Putting children first did not make sense to everyone. For instance, SPCC agents prosecuted cases in which cruelty to children was caused, in their view, by children's labor: girls doing housework and child care, often required to stay home from school by their parents; boys and girls working in shops, peddling on the streets; boys working for organ grinders or lying about their age to enlist in the navy. The SPCCs worked with truant officers and even raised the ante, defining nonattendance at school as child neglect. But poor parents often needed their children at home or work; to the poor, frequently from farm or peasant backgrounds, it seemed irrational and disrespectful that adult women should work while able-bodied children remained idle. The SPCCs were opposed to the common practice of leaving children unattended and allowing them to play and wander in the streets. This violated the norm of domesticity for women and children; proper urban middle-class children in those days were not supposed to play outside without supervision. But working-class children lived in tiny crowded homes, and their mothers had no leisure to take them to parks.

Thus some cases of alleged cruelty to children arose from class and cultural disagreement about proper child raising, and others from the inevitable cruelties of poverty, experienced by parents as well—such as disease and malnutrition, children left unsupervised while their parents worked, children not warmly dressed, houses without heat, bedding crawling with vermin, unchanged diapers, injuries and illnesses left without medical treatment. But child abuse was most definitely not merely a figment of cultural bias or an inevitable result of poverty. On the contrary, child abuse was identified as a problem even by its perpetrators, many of whom, despite their awareness of the discrimination they might encounter at the hands of the SPCCs, sought the help of these agencies.[37] For women and children, the biases of the SPCCs were often preferable to the oppressiveness of the discrimination they experienced at home. Children sought help against their parents. Women manipulated agencies concerned with child abuse to get help against wife abuse. Mothers also sought help in their own child raising, often going to agencies because they perceived themselves as inadequate parents. Child-protection agencies saw themselves as teaching good standards to poor and ignorant parents, but in fact they were encountering people with their own views about good family life who tried to use these agencies in their own interest.

The SPCCs' paradigm for understanding and intervening in domestic violence nevertheless remained, until the 1970s revival of feminism, one of protecting children from their parents. The SPCCs imagined children as innocent victims and parents as suspect, at least potentially noninnocent. The greater the emphasis on the innocent child, the harder it was to avoid a presumption of parental guilt. It is remarkable how little concern there was with nonfamilial cruelty to children. A few token cases against employers of child labor, concerning industrial and chemical hazards to children, were investigated in the first decade of the anti-child-abuse movement but not pursued thereafter. Physical punishment in the schools was not addressed.

Increasingly the parents against whom children needed protection were specifically mothers. For example, the Progressive Era child-saving discourse de-emphasized child abuse and sexual abuse, often male crimes, and featured child neglect, by definition a crime of mothers (fathers were not held responsible for children and accordingly were never cited for child neglect). Mothers were often double-binded—blamed for children's failures but rarely credited for their successes. Child-protection agencies did not often recognize the actual conditions of mothering, which so often included not only poverty but also women's own subordination and frequent victimization. Family-violence agencies tried—unsuccessfully—to ignore wife beating.[38] There was never a Society for the Prevention of Cruelty to Women.

Thus child protection, although influenced by maternalist feminism, tended to oppose mothers' to children's interests. Yet, ironically, the child protectors had few tools with which to aid children who were being abused or neglected. Certainly they had no preventive program, for their model was one of crime and punishment, and luckily a residual civil-liberties tradition in the courts held back some of the most egregious invasions of privacy attempted by these agencies. When courts found that child abuse or neglect was taking place, social work still had little to contribute.[39] The sad history was that abused and neglected children almost always suffered more if removed from their parents because of poor institutional and foster care.[40] The poverty of public provision for children resulted not only from cultural and economic individualism and political exploitation of hostility to taxes. It also revealed that the put-children-first policy orientation was never strong enough to alter the cultural commitment to nuclear family child raising, and when such families failed children, no decent alternative was provided.

Child protectors recognized their failure to help abused and neglected children. At several points in the now 120-year history of child protection, reformers acknowledged that prosecuting parents rarely helped children and urged rehabilitation of parents. But child protection always ran up against a miserly welfare policy. Child protection was enfeebled by the paradox that in focusing on children, and thereby gaining widespread rhetorical support, protective efforts failed because of social and political stinginess toward needy adults, a miserliness in part created by the focus on children.

The children-first orientation in the development of public assistance programs similarly ended badly for children as well as women.[41] The state mothers' aid laws, passed between 1910 and 1920, took a step toward helping mothers as well as children. Then the depression of the 1930s created a crisis and an opportunity to expand the welfare state. It was during the New Deal that the social-work network's commitment to putting children first most indelibly marked the American welfare state. When Franklin D. Roosevelt agreed to support a permanent program of social provision, both the social-work and social-insurance networks tried to influence its design. The resulting omnibus law, the Social Security Act, was created through a mutually agreed-upon division of labor: social-insurance men designed the two biggest programs, Old Age Insurance (OAI, later OASI) and Unemployment Insurance (UI); the social-work network designed other provisions called the public assistance programs, including Aid to Dependent Children (ADC), aid to the blind, old age assistance (for those not covered by OAI), and a small child and maternal health program ($7 million was asked for this). The social-insurance programs became well funded and widely respected, not included under the pejorative rubric "welfare"; the social-work programs became stingy and deeply stigmatized.[42] Today, the inferiority of the public assistance as compared to the social-insurance programs is vivid and much analyzed. Indeed, some feminist critics have mistakenly attributed their inferiority to a transhistorical patriarchy, implying that men made them substandard out of contempt for women. This was not the case. What contributed to the stratification among welfare programs was, first, a common commitment to the family wage and, second, the particular dedication among elite women welfare activists to putting children first.

Family-wage assumptions led virtually all welfare reformers to assume that women's and children's poverty would usually be corrected by supporting husbands' and fathers' incomes. That is, the social-insurance programs for men would take care of men's dependents. Not even the most feminist welfare advocates expected single-mother families, for example, to be a significant or enduring fraction of the population. The needy that were to be served by the public assistance programs were expected to be few and, except for the permanently disabled, temporary. And they were to receive casework along with their stipends to make sure that they were not pauperized and to correct any character problems they already had.

The women designers of Aid to Dependent Children did not intend it to be an inferior program. In fact, some would have liked to do away with a two-track welfare system altogether. Edith Abbott, often spokesperson for her sister Grace, then chief of the Children's Bureau, spoke for many when she argued for one universal program for all public provision. She believed it possible to abolish poverty through public aid—not social insurance—available to all without stigmatizing qualifications. She argued for a policy that would abolish the "pauper laws," the private and public charity programs, as "disgracefully opprobrious and un-American" and perpetuating inequality, and called for bringing all forms of public assistance together in one welfare statute, to which federal, state, and local government would all contribute.[43] The Abbotts did not like the "insurance" programs because their policies of "contribution" represented regressive taxation, and in this respect the two sisters can be characterized as more left-wing than the insurance proponents. They were also strongly committed to the view that just giving out money was neither sufficient nor safe, and that the poor required supervision, counseling, and reeducation—casework by trained social workers.[44] In this respect they can be considered more conservative than the insurance proponents.

Continuing the old strategy of putting children first, ADC provided stipends *only* for children, not for their caretakers.[45] There were several reasons for this. The women lacked the confidence and self-importance to make demands on behalf of women; indeed, they were by now accustomed to getting things for women through their role as mothers. Moreover, by the 1930s social workers had come to understand that the single-mother families who needed this help were composed not only of widows—who qualified as the deserving poor—but increasingly of divorced and separated women and sometimes even of never-married women. Wishing to avoid the hostility such women provoked, the designers of ADC accepted the odd fiction that children's support could somehow be separated from their parents'. They built on and strengthened the rhetoric about "innocent" children, arguing that they should not be burdened by the sins of their parents.[46] While children had once served as a surrogate for mothers, a means of increasing women's power, as in the campaign for maternal custody, they now received aid despite their mothers. During the campaign to "sell" Social Security, both before and after its passage, there was a complete silence about single mothers. In a memo to the drafters of the Social Security Act, Katherine Ward Fisher wrote, "People too young for self-support have properly a *direct* claim upon the national (or social) income . . . at least as strong as their claim for free education."[47] No one agitated for single mothers' own distinct needs for help. Thus Grace Abbott, in discussing the sufferings caused by the inadequacy of local mothers' aid, noted: "Waiting lists have grown longer . . . many thousands of children have been removed from their own homes or are living from day to day in uncertainty as to their future."[48]

The design of ADC was not only a matter of compromise and the politics of judging what was possible. It also represented the social-work network's views about proper family life.[49] The activists' "maternalism" presupposed the male family wage as the basis of family life. They did not want to encourage single-mother families, and their insistence on casework reflected, in part, their concern that such families usually represented and created social pathology. They were nervous about mothers' employment, an anxiety that becomes particularly striking when compared to black women's much greater acceptance of it, and of the day-care needs it created. After the beginnings of a small movement to establish day nurseries in the nineteenth century, white women activists became more negative in the Progressive Era, worrying that such child care might "tempt" mothers to "attempt the impossible" (that is, combine family and work) in Jane Addams's view, or encourage family desertion, in Lillian Wald's.[50] Grace Abbott remained negative about day care during the New Deal.[51] These reformers were not advocating maternal bonding ideas, that children needed full-time mothering, which appeared much later, but they hesitated, precisely out of their feminist perspective, to burden women with what they conceived to be too heavy a load of work and responsibility. To these social-work leaders, day care seemed to undercut women's claims as mothers.

One result was a very small program, with an original request for $25 million, intended to serve fewer than 300,000 families, because the designers, assuming the family wage to be a norm, expected that most children would be supported by fathers. Another result was the pegging of stipends at an extremely low level, $18 per month for the first child and $12 for each additional child, as compared to old age assistance stipends of $30 per month per individual.[52] Still another was the premise that since child welfare was the issue, the government should have the responsibility to ascertain that the child was being raised in a suitable environment. Known as the "suitable home" requirement,[53] this provision became the basis for a great deal of snooping into the lives of "welfare mothers," as ADC recipients came to be pejoratively called several decades later: did they have boyfriends? were they buying clothes for themselves instead of for their children? did they have disallowed resources such as automobiles, telephones, or savings accounts?[54] The investigation and the means testing were, of course, contradictory: the aid was supposed to be only for the child and was rarely sufficient to support the mother too, but it was the mother's means that were tested. One justification was obviously that an immoral or cheating mother was not good for children. The problem was that the punishment of the immoral mother cut off support for the children. (Meanwhile, public provision for children without a parent was so stingy that no matter how bad the parental home—morally, economically, or in terms of abuse—institutional or foster-home placements were on average always worse.)

Another justification, recently revived in the new social contract theory of various 1990s welfare reform proposals, was that the ADC stipend involved some kind of exchange. This was actually a complex idea, interpreted differently by different participants in the discourse—and sometimes by the same participant at different times. At least four distinct meanings are identifiable. One interpretation rephrased the old deserving/undeserving distinction, assuming that an ADC grant was a charitable gift for which recipients should prove themselves worthy. Another, more state-centered version assumed that recipients should contribute to society, in this case by raising children well. The quintessentially social-work view was that state and mother formed a partnership to improve the race by improving child raising. Katharine Lenroot of the Children's Bureau liked to tell a story about a mothers' aid recipient speaking knowledgeably to a caseworker about child development. The worker asked, "Where did you learn all this?," to which the recipient replied, "Oh, I'm a state mother. I have to know these things."[55] When a welfare-rights movement formed much later, it became clear that ADC recipients had their own interpretation of this exchange, similar to the wages for housework demanded by some feminists in the 1970s. But this interpretation had older roots. During the original campaign for mothers' aid, some of its advocates had already argued that the stipends should be considered payment for services to society—hence the popularity of the term *pension*, fashioned after veterans' pensions. In a more moderate variant Grace Abbott argued that the program rested on "recognition . . . that the contribution of the unskilled or semiskilled mothers in their own homes exceeded their earnings outside of the home and that it was in the public interest to conserve their child-caring functions."[56]

Yet these contractarian views implied that the mother was the recipient and participant in the exchange.[57] They all contradicted the official policy that ADC stipends were for children only.

Of course, the flaws in today's public assistance programs do not only or even primarily derive from their design by the Children's Bureau network.[58] Race was the major factor influencing the exclusions of the Social Security Act.[59] But it is hard to disentangle race from gender systems: for example, which system was it that made so many prosperous southern whites in the 1930s feel entitled to cheap domestic servants? Race and gender became connected further as AFDC expanded to include many unmarried, even never-married, mothers and their children. Older assumptions about the immorality of blacks combined with new patterns. Urban conditions of poverty and unemployment increased the proportion of single-mother families among blacks, and at the same time black migration northward took an existing family form and moved it into visibility among the prosperous in northern urban centers.[60] Thus the fear that "welfare" would destroy a "work ethic," making AFDC recipients unwilling to take low-wage jobs, spread from southern agricultural and domestic employers throughout the nation, affecting particularly service-sector employers, and became combined with the anxiety that welfare actually encouraged high fertility and unmarried motherhood. It remains difficult to separate racial from gendered content in these attitudes.

Nevertheless, it is fair to say that promoting the "innocence" and deservingness of children did not get them much material help and that the women's hope that kids could open the door to a maternal welfare state was disappointed. Children do not thrive when their caretakers are impoverished, depressed, or hopeless. Giving to children while those around them do without has proved unworkable. Depriving women does not maximize their effectiveness as mothers. Defining the interests of mothers as against those of children does not often help children.

Moreover, because AFDC is a program not for all children but particularly for single-mother children, the emphasis on "innocent" children made sense only in contrast to the noninnocence of their mothers. (There is a striking similarity here to antiabortion rhetoric about the "innocent" unborn.) The justification for aid to children argued equal opportunity in childhood: no child should be held back by her or his parents' poverty. The silence here is quite articulate: adults did not have an equal right not to be held back by poverty, presumably because their poverty was their own fault, their punishment for various crimes or failures of character. This rhetorical strategy supported the general suspicion of adults who needed public help. That suspicion then turned back against children: given a modern psychology that assumed that children were deeply influenced by their parenting, it became difficult to maintain public hopefulness about children with poor parents, particularly single mothers, and this in turn undermined public support for the children's programs.

Beginning even in the nineteenth century, the putting-children-first strategy ran into several contradictions. First, it proved difficult to "deliver" services to children except through parents. But, second, the very identification of children as uniquely deserving tended to undercut the claims of adults to public help, which then made it more difficult to help children. Child-centeredness worked for women primarily when they could get themselves defined as good mothers, an ability that poor and minority mothers often lacked; when there was any question about their qualifications or parenting style, they became vulnerable to losing control over their children. Putting children first also tended to impose a set of maternalist assumptions upon women that undermined their struggle for freedom in other arenas.

This essay is not a historical argument against special benefits for children. It is a reading of a particular history—of children raised in a culture that strongly legitimated individualism and nuclear families, of a feminist reform strategy worked out in the context of that culture. In trying to help children, there are of course many ways in which adults can construct children's "needs." I am discussing one such construction that romanticized mother-child bonding and women's and children's joint domesticity. It occurred in an era in which influential female activists felt comfortable using children as their surrogates, secure (albeit constrained) in their identity as mothers, and confident in their power as mothers in charge of children. Some of the more privileged activists imagined mothers as regents preparing future dynasties and ruling in the name of their charges; yet many who knew the poor and tried to speak for them also cherished such visions of maternal importance, confident in the mobility provided by U.S. democracy. In such a context it was reasonable to conclude that any gain for children would be a gain for women.

Whatever merit this approach had a century ago, it deserves close scrutiny today. In a society of increasing inequality and cultural diversity, where single mothering is commonplace and motherhood is by no means the major definer of women's identity, it is not clear that this strategy is good for women or children, or that identifying any particular groups as especially "deserving" benefits the whole society.

CHAPTER 4 : DESIGNING WOMEN
AND OLD FOOLS : THE CONSTRUCTION
OF THE SOCIAL SECURITY AMENDMENTS
OF 1939 : *ALICE KESSLER-HARRIS*

> *[W]hen you begin to help the family to attain some security you are at the same time beginning to erect a National structure for the same purpose. Through the well-being of the family, we create the well-being of the Nation. Through our constructive contributions to the one, we help the other to flourish.*[1]
> *– Mary W. Dewson, 1937*

On March 19, 1975, in the landmark decision of *Weinberger v. Wiesenfeld*, eight justices of the U.S. Supreme Court (the ninth abstaining) agreed that Stephen Wiesenfeld, a widower and the lone parent of an infant child, was entitled to Social Security benefits. Wiesenfeld claimed the benefits on the basis of contributions made by his wife Paula, who had been a schoolteacher before she died in childbirth. But the Social Security Administration (SSA) had turned him down: widows' benefits were available only to women. Now the Supreme Court demurred. "A father no less than a mother," said the Court, "has a constitutionally protected right to the companionship, care, custody and management of children he has sired and raised."[2] On this basis, the Court struck down forty years of "archaic and overbroad generalizations," accepting the argument put forth in Wiesenfeld's defense that such generalizations unfairly discriminated against women because their contributions to Social Security did not buy as much as the contributions of men. Wiesenfeld's lawyer, Ruth Bader Ginsburg, had done her part to historicize gender—to turn it from a descriptive characterization of the social organization of the sexes to a potentially powerful cudgel.

The decision in Wiesenfeld was followed by others. An aged widower was entitled to benefits on his wife's earnings just as a widow was entitled to benefits earned by her husband, the Court declared two years later.[3] It was legal, said the justices, for the Social Security system to attempt to remedy some of the discrimination of low earnings for women by excluding their lowest paid quarters from benefit calculations.[4] With the Department of Health, Education, and Welfare and the Social Security Administration fighting every step, the Court methodically undermined a carefully structured set of assumptions about women's roles in the family. Henceforth, the Court concluded, classifications by gender "must serve important governmental objectives."[5]

But, the earlier classifications had served extremely important governmental as well as popular objectives. They were merely different from the ones the Court now chose to protect. Those first objectives had been suggested nearly forty years before, when the U.S. Senate set up a Federal Advisory Council to propose ways of revising the Social Security system—then only two years old. They are explicit in the debates within the council and in the legislation that resulted from its recommendations. For example, halfway through its eighteen months of deliberations, the Advisory Council confronted the question of how much to give aged widows who (like other dependents) had been excluded from the original act. Should it be half of what their provider-husbands would have received? two thirds? three-quarters? After several hours of debate, one member thought to ask a question that had escaped scrutiny. "Why should you pay the widow less than the individual himself gets if unmarried?"[6] "She can look after herself better than he can," shot back the group's actuary.[7]

The question would not die. A couple of months later the Advisory Council returned to the issue. This time, the chairman, prodded by one of the council's three female members, took up the defense. "A single woman," he suggested, can "adjust herself to a lower budget on account of the fact that she is used to doing her own housework whereas the single man has to go out to a restaurant."[8] By now, others had joined the fray. When the argument resumed at the next meeting, distinguished economist J. Douglas Brown, Wisconsin trained, a Princeton professor, and chair of an appointed congressional committee, tried to end it. Lower rates for women made sense, he said, his patience clearly worn thin, "on the principle that it is more costly for the single man to live than for the single woman if she is able to avail herself of the home of the child. A woman is able to fit herself into the economy of the home of the child much better than the single man, that is, the grandmother helps in the raising of the children and helps in home affairs, whereas the aged grandfather is the man who sits out on the front porch and can't help much in the home."[9]

With those homely and persuasive words, Brown laid out the assumptions that, a long generation later, led Stephen Wiesenfeld to court. In this and other ways the Advisory Council constructed "men" and "women" each after particular gendered patterns. It provided definitions of appropriate behavior for each that sustained independent bread-winning status for husbands, while discouraging wives from that option. Insofar as these patterns were out of reach for the most disadvantaged families, they sustained and perpetuated discrimination rooted in racial constructions.

Rarely are we privileged to observe influential people create the mechanisms that sustain notions of male dignity and female virtue—to watch how casual characterization and appeals to consensus participate in molding ideas of equity and fairness. Even more rarely do we observe how easily generalizations about male/female behavior are embedded in public policies, turning an informal politics of behavior into an authoritative weapon. The possibility of observing this process exists in the case of the Federal Advisory Council, which produced what became the language and substance of the 1939 amendments to the Social Security Act, because the council left verbatim accounts of all of its meetings. Its minutes reveal something about the political work done by gender, opening up the ways that commonly held understandings of male/female relationships can infuse policies and yield formal change. Because their focus on gender is explicitly racialized, the minutes also tell us how council members helped to sidestep pressures for racial equality. The history of the adoption of the 1939 amendments thus sheds a powerful light on a process that has often seemed elusive. It illuminates how the racially specific meanings assigned to gender provided implicit and explicit messages that, inscribed into government programs, shaped the relationship of citizens to the state.

My explorations of the meaning of gender in shaping the content of policy diverge sharply from recent efforts to explain the sources of state policy, though they do not necessarily contradict them. I share with Swedish political scientist Gosta Esping-Anderson the assumption that the welfare state is an "active force in the ordering of social relations."[10] But I do not believe that exploring the sources of social policy at the level of either social struggle or state structures can reveal very much about the meaning of the policies adopted. Rather, I want to elucidate those meanings by exploring the effects of deeply gendered understandings on state policies. Thus, my approach diverges from those who suggest that the operation of state variables (including previous state policy, the interests of entrenched bureaucracy, and the structures of political parties), even when they are seen in interactive relationships with societal structures, can explain the content of particular policies.[11] While, in their most complex rendering, these theories provide a diagram of how and why certain kinds of policies are adopted, their failure to explore the content of legislation renders them too schematic to account for how policies worked.[12] Theories that reverse the emphasis, and assign priority to class and social struggle, offer an explanatory framework that I want to supplement by restoring an ideological dimension.[13] My own concern is with how the sometimes unwitting legislative incorporation of ideologies of gender shape policy outcomes for different kinds of men and women as each is differently constituted in relation to the state. I hope, in so doing, to enrich and extend explanations of social policy to accommodate the ways embedded conceptions of gender contributed to understanding the particular expansion of the state's role. By gender, I refer not to the organized activities of women (or of men and women) on behalf of women, but to the ways in which the sometimes unconscious and generally unquestioned acceptance of the normative and ideational patterns by which the sexes are organized are transcribed into politics and behavior.[14] I suggest that these understandings shaped and limited state intervention, providing a blueprint for the American welfare state that was imprinted with gender.

I use the 1939 amendments to the Social Security Act partly because the discussions around them provide enormously juicy evidence and partly because few could dispute their influence. As a central pillar of the American version of the welfare state, the Social Security Act, adopted in 1935, consolidated a haphazard array of state and federal provisions for individual economic security. But it was by no means universally popular. Fiercely challenged for many years after its passage, it was subject to attack because it restricted individual autonomy and assumed that government intervention was necessary to preserve the economic security of citizens. The Social Security Act survived in large measure because of the amendments adopted in 1939.[15] These amendments reconfigured the system from its bent toward the principles of private insurance toward a greater capacity to accommodate those of social insurance. They provided, in the words of a former commissioner of Social Security, "the kind of Social Security Program we have today."[16] The Social Security Act and its successor amendments have done far more than create the current framework for state-regulated benefits. They have shaped popular attitudes toward the appropriate role of the state in providing financial support to families and enhancing the security of many individuals. These amendments have also helped to construct a complicated conception of dependency that is closely linked to gender, class, and race.

Signed into law by President Franklin Delano Roosevelt on June 19, 1935, the original Social Security Act incorporated two kinds of programs. One provided matching funds to the states for means-tested welfare for the poor and aged and allowed states to impose restrictions and conditions on recipients. This program was governed by the principle of adequacy. It was to be paid for out of general revenues and the relief or assistance it provided were to go only to the needy. This category included maternal-infant care, public health services, and the program called Aid to Dependent Children (ADC), which was later transformed into Aid to Families with Dependent Children (AFDC) and is now commonly called "welfare." It also included Old Age Assistance (OAA)—a state-matched, means-tested program for the very poor. The second set of programs in the original act was characterized as insurance and meant to be paid for, not out of general revenues, but out of a reserve fund built by the contributions of beneficiaries and their employers. Based on the principle of "equity" because benefits were to be based not on need but on the level of contribution, it included unemployment compensation, which would be administered by the states, as well as Old Age Insurance (OAI) and an associated death benefit.[17] We now tend to reserve the label *Social Security* for the Old Age Insurance program, which provided for the first direct federal grants to individuals who were not veterans or their families. To avoid undermining the work ethic and to sustain the cherished American value of self-reliance, Old Age Insurance benefits were closely tied to contributions. Every contributor could expect to receive back at least the amount invested plus $3\frac{1}{2}$ percent interest. The death benefit guaranteed that survivors would receive as a lump-sum legacy any sums not yet used by contributors who died before receiving any or all of the funds due them. The program, warned the president and others, ought not to be "allowed to become a dole through the mingling of insurance and relief." It was "not charity. It must be financed by contributions, not taxes."[18] The Social Security Act did not provide for health insurance, though Roosevelt badly wanted it, and its architects debated it at length.

From its conception, the architects of the Social Security system attempted to preserve the line between the two kinds of programs. Insurance was designed to be more or less equitable, to provide benefits earned as a right, and to reward thrift and a disciplined lifetime of work. It would cushion the vagaries of the marketplace for those who normally earned wages. Old Age Assistance and other relief carried the opprobrium of means testing. They required a demonstration of destitution and the absence of a family willing and able to provide support. No effort was made by the federal government to ensure that states would offer "a reasonable subsistence compatible with decency and health." Indeed, that language was excised by the House Ways and Means Committee to meet the objections of southern congressmen who feared excessive costs for supporting poor African Americans in their districts.[19]

Despite the sharp and purposeful distinctions between adequacy and equity, the principle was violated by the very first set of amendments, which added Old Age Insurance benefits for wives and widows who had not paid for them. No charitable impulse toward women motivated this act; no concern for their poverty inspired it. Rather, Congress added dependent wives and aged widows in order to shore up the legitimacy of a system in trouble. It did this by making the benefits of already-covered (mostly white) males more adequate by granting extra benefits to those who had aged wives to support and extra insurance to those with young children who survived them. Thus, it reinforced the prerogatives and self-images of some males while reaffirming racialized conceptions of gender. In effect, therefore, it redefined equity to incorporate more adequate and appropriate provision for the male, infusing the American system of entitlements with the peculiar imbalance that has governed it ever since.[20]

By 1937 the Old Age Insurance provisions of the Social Security Act had achieved only fragile support. They faced three major problems. First, though a 1 percent payroll tax was instituted in 1936, no benefits were scheduled to be paid until January 1942. Contributions were rapidly building up a surplus that, in a depression economy, threatened to exercise a deflationary effect. Second, powerful popular support had built for the state-run, noncontributory Old Age Assistance programs that provided more generous benefits to the aged than those envisioned by the Old Age Insurance program for most contributors. Seventeen states had already legislated such benefits, and California's generous assistance had drawn widespread national attention.[21] Most important, the Old Age Insurance provisions of the Social Security Act excluded nearly half the working population, including farmworkers, casual laborers, domestic servants, and laundry workers, as well as seamen, the self-employed, government employees, and those who worked for nonprofit groups.[22] Because the program did not provide benefits to those who worked in covered occupations intermittently or for only a few years, more than three-fifths of fully employed African Americans were denied coverage.[23] Sixty percent of the excluded workers were female—in a labor force where less than 30 percent of women were employed. Probably as many as 80 percent of wage-earning black women were deprived of participation and benefits.

Clearly there were good reasons for the popularity of Old Age Assistance. But if that program succeeded in undermining Old Age Insurance, many feared that the damage to the principle of equity would bring the work ethic tumbling down with it. What was to be done? Could the surplus be spent? If so, on whom? In the spring of 1937 the Senate Finance Committee pressured the Social Security Board (SSB) into jointly creating a Federal Advisory Council to suggest remedies. In May, when the new Advisory Council was announced, it consisted of twenty-four members: six from the labor movement, six representing employers, and twelve "public" participants, most of them academics and businessmen. In the event, the six labor representatives were only marginally involved, frequently missing meetings and rarely speaking when they did attend.[24] On the employers' side, two—Albert Linton, president of the Provident Mutual Life Insurance Company of Philadelphia, and Gerard Swope, president of the General Electric Company—had a long history of involvement with Social Security and continued to play active roles. All of the business representatives attended regularly and contributed at least occasionally to discussions. The public members were a mixed batch. In addition to J. Douglas Brown, Josephine Roche, A. L. Mowbray, and Edwin Witte had been active in the Committee on Economic Security, which drafted the original act. Several members were connected with John Commons and the University of Wisconsin. In addition to Brown and Witte, they included Alvin Hansen, Social Security Board chair Arthur Altmeyer, and its actuary, William Williamson. Among the public members were three women. Originally, they were Theresa McMahon, Elizabeth Wisner, and Lucy Randolph Mason, all of them social reformers by profession or commitment and all more or less connected with the network of social work professionals identified by Linda Gordon.[25] When Mason resigned before the council actually met, she was replaced by Josephine Roche, an old friend of Frances Perkins, a National Consumers' League activist, and an assistant secretary in the U.S. Treasury Department at the time of her appointment. Consistent with the Senate's instructions, the Advisory Council worked closely with members of the Social Security Board, one of whose members was Mary W. Dewson. The only other woman actively involved in the Advisory Council's deliberations, Dewson was a committed social reformer and a longtime defender of the minimum wage for women who resigned as vice chair of the Democratic National Committee to join the Social Security Board in the summer of 1937.

Together with the Social Security Board and several congressional committees, the Advisory Council, led by J. Douglas Brown, worked through the following year and a half to recommend basic changes. Their charge from Congress was clear: they had to recommend a permanent way of dealing with ballooning reserves.[26] They were to do this by beginning Old Age Insurance benefits earlier than the currently mandated January 1942 start-up date and by making them larger. They were to explore the possibility of extending benefits to the disabled, to survivors, and to excluded groups. In the end, the council sidestepped the challenge of significantly extending insurance to most of the excluded groups, including the disabled, domestic servants, and agricultural workers and chose to rely on expenditures for aged wives and survivors to reduce the surplus.[27]

The discussions over these alternatives tell us something about how invisible assumptions about men and women informed an entire network of social policy. For when the Advisory Council moved to expand the benefits of those already covered, it utilized gender to mediate the conflict between adequacy and equity—a conflict in which women played little role, but issues of masculinity and womanliness assumed paramount importance. The council's set of proposals served congressional purposes well: relieving budgetary pressures, undermining challenges to the legitimacy of the Old Age Insurance program, and providing more adequate subsistence for some of the aged, while sidestepping the politics of southern racism. It did so by renegotiating "equity" to include male dignity. Incorporating the family needs of men into the principle of contributory insurance provided additional benefits for covered men while finessing the demands of some groups for an income for the aged based on their needs rather than on equity. "The Council," as its chairman, Douglas Brown, put it, had adopted "the principle of family protection."[28]

What was meant by family? Whose families should be protected and how? Without debate, the council agreed on pensions for fatherless children—an idea that already had popular support.[29] The Advisory Council adopted the notion rapidly because it promised to significantly reduce the numbers receiving means-tested assistance under both Title I (OAA) and Title IV (ADC) and strengthen the entire Social Security program by providing the illusion that their support was a product of insurance, the provenance of thoughtful and thrifty fathers.[30] Benefits to children, Advisory Council members agreed, should be a matter of right in order to "avoid the growth of a habit of dependency among its youth" and to sustain "the concept that a child is supported through the efforts of the parent."[31]

What about his widow? The Advisory Council used the same concept of equity for covered men to provide insurance for the widowed mothers of young children. The sums granted, and the restrictions on them, suggest that insurance for widowed mothers was conceived of as a matter of peace of mind for the husband. The widowed mother was to get three-fourths of what her husband's pension would have been. The pension was granted as a matter of need, to enable "the widow to remain at home and care for the children."[32] It was to be reduced or eliminated if her earnings exceeded $15 a month (a tiny sum, even in 1939), and in the likely event that a widow's children reached eighteen before she turned sixty-five, the council recommended that all support end. Survivor's insurance was intended to protect minor children and the aged.[33]

The conversations within the council and the provisions finally adopted negated any possibility that the pension might be considered a question of fair treatment to women—a product of the joint efforts of a marriage partnership. Consistent with the notion of sustaining male provision for the family, in clear violation of insurance principles and over the objections of some members of the Social Security Board, the council voted to eliminate any annuity to a widow who remarried lest it construct a system that, in the words of one member, constituted widows "a prize for the fellow that has looked for it."[34] Research director Isadore Falk pointed out that this denial violated the notion that the widow, "during the years when she was married to the insured person, was also accumulating certain rights because the basic rights of the insured person come to her by reason of earnings of which she was a partner." But the council overrode his objection, and Falk backed off. Once a woman was no longer dependent on the earnings of a particular male (dead or alive), the council contended that his support for her should cease, "rendering the woman ineligible whether she is the widow of an annuitant or the widow of a worker who dies before 65."[35] As long as she remained dependent on him, the level of the surviving widow's benefits, like the level of children's benefits, would be tied to the earnings of the deceased male, feeding the illusion that families deprived of a father or husband would nevertheless conceive him in the abstract as a continuing provider.

Tying the dignity of men (defined as their capacity to provide) to the virtue of women (their willingness to remain dependent on men and to rear children) proved to be a continuing problem for young and old widows alike. We have already glimpsed the arbitrary assumptions about dissimilar levels of adequacy for grandmothers and grandfathers that led to differential benefits for men and women. These assumptions underlined other decisions as well. The Advisory Council voted against giving a widow a lump-sum death payment because "such settlements are likely to be used for many other purposes long before her old age." It deferred the annuity of an under-sixty-five-year-old widow until she reached that age on the grounds that "there is some likelihood that the widow may re-enter covered employment."[36] Under that circumstance, her own contribution or that of her husband would simply be swallowed up. To avoid what it referred to as "deathbed marriages," the council adopted a clause requiring a pair to have been married and living together for at least a year before the husband died or reached sixty for his widow to be eligible for benefits on his account.[37]

The degree to which equity for men was at issue emerges most poignantly in the treatment of aged, dependent wives. On what grounds should a man get extra income to support his wife? Bruited about in the fall of 1937 by Wilbur Cohen, and half suggested by Falk in a November 1937 memo, a successful proposal was formulated by Albert Linton, president of the Provident Mutual Insurance Company of Philadelphia, and offered to the December meeting.[38] "We should arrange our benefit schedule in Title 2," he suggested, "so that you will get one amount if you are single and alone and another amount if you have a wife living with you."[39] Drawing on the British system, in which each member of a married couple received the same basic benefit, Linton went on to suggest the basic outline of a new and dramatic set of proposals. "If you were married and had a wife aged 60 or over—because the average figures show that the wife is usually 5 years younger than the man—you would receive an additional 50 percent of the primary benefit." If one partner died, the pension would revert to the individual level.

Reactions ranged from puzzled to skeptical. "Why isn't it a contributory group?" asked one. "I didn't quite get that," said another; "It makes no difference whether the wife has earned or not?" Many expressed distress at the degree to which the proposal bent toward adequacy. What about adding a means test for those whose insurance was inadequate? asked several. Linton stood his ground. Conceding that a wife "may have picked up some credits along the way" and that she might therefore be entitled to benefits on her own account, he held firmly to the principle that "it makes no difference" whether a wife had earned or not. "If she has not been in industry at all and is married to a man who has been in industry the double benefit is paid just the same as though she had been in industry. It is a scheme by which you assure a certain figure when you are 65."

The minutes do not indicate that anyone responded in terms of the advantages the proposal offered to wives, or widows, or even families. Nor do the minutes indicate that external pressure from any women's groups played a role in these deliberations. None of the three women on the Advisory Council (Theresa McMahon, Elizabeth Wisner, or Josephine Roche, who seems to have been there only rarely) or Mary Dewson, who attended meetings as a member of the Social Security Board, raised a question about gender equity or the rights of women. The letters and papers of the three women on the council and of Mary Dewson, who actively served on the Social Security Board during nine crucial months from September 1937 to June 1938, provide no clues as to their silence on these issues.[40] In the several speeches that Dewson gave in the early days of the debate, there is no more than passing mention of extending benefits to wives.[41] We can speculate that under the historical circumstances the proposals of the Advisory Council offered far more security to the families of covered workers than most women then had. Since influential women social reformers had long since accepted that providing security for the family was the most likely way to safeguard women, giving them independent benefits would have been an unlikely strategy. All the women on the Advisory Council had been involved in some part of the effort to develop state-run welfare systems, and all were more or less hostile to the efforts of more radical feminists to place women's rights at the top of the agenda. Had the Old Age

Insurance program become a battleground for that issue, the rights of married women would certainly have come under scrutiny.[42] But they did not. In fact, the idea that women could be subsumed within the family might well have been enhanced by the tendency of at least some elements of the women's reform network (including perhaps Dewson herself) to abandon an earlier strategy of seeking benefits for women only and to focus instead on an integrated system of security.[43]

Extending benefits to men with aged wives appealed to some because it recognized the family responsibilities of men, it appealed to others because it retained equity among covered men—a piece that was essential to overcome southern racism.[44] When Dewson challenged the variable, contribution-related benefit figure, comparing it to the flat entitlement adopted by the British, Linton's response indicated that deference to current racial divisions and to the opinions of southern legislators had led him to adopt a strategy that reinforced gendered roles. "It is impractical to have a level benefit in this country because of the differences between the colored workers of the south and the skilled workers of the north. A single flat figure for everybody would not work."[45] By establishing the earnings level of the husband first and then calculating the additional sum as 50 percent of his benefit, whatever that was, the system preserved the contributory relationship and yielded a more adequate income for elderly married beneficiaries without transgressing relative expectations of income based on occupation or race.

There were other options to the white, male standpoint that dominated the discussion, but these attracted little attention. For example, Gerard Swope's plan for earnings sharing received scarcely a hearing. Provision for wives might readily be made, argued Swope, president of the General Electric Company, an old friend of Brown's and a business representative to the Advisory Council,

> by providing that of the total wages earned by any married person, one half would be credited to his (or her) account, and that the other half would be credited to the spouse's account. Benefit payments correspondingly would be based upon the earnings of each person who has passed age 65. When both husband and wife have passed age 65, the income would be approximately the same as at present (except as each would profit from the liberal percentages in the regressive scale) and when husband or wife dies, the income would be reduced, but a substantial income would be available to the survivor.[46]

The suggestion was never pursued by the Advisory Council. Though the discussion that followed lasted many months, and ultimately resulted in including a wife's benefit in the Advisory Council's proposals, neither female security nor justice to women was at issue. In the council's deliberations, the achievement of benefits for wives and widows seems to have been neither the object of female struggle nor the source of conflict between men and women. Rather, once the council determined that the surplus was to be spent, questions were raised only within specified boundaries. To what extent would a benefit to men on behalf of their wives provide them with equity with regard to each other as well as with regard to family life? The language is quite explicit: "whether the enhancement of early benefits shall be by method of the wives' allowance or whether by the method of enhancing the individual, whether man or woman, the individual benefits regardless of marital status."[47] Neither the Social Security Board nor the Advisory Council indicated receiving any pressure from outside groups to enhance women's benefits per se.

From its first introduction, the plan to offer men benefits for their wives used language that mingled the rights of men with their control over women. Linton, for example, defended the popular appeal of his plan "in that you are doing something real for the man,"[48] who would enjoy the security of the additional income. Concern for manhood persisted throughout the debate. For instance, in the first discussions of the wife's benefits, as they were incorporated into a new proposal (AC-12) placed before the Advisory Council, Douglas Brown used the following language: "First of all, the plan has in it the idea that a wife of a beneficiary should receive in her behalf in the form of an addition to her husband's benefit an allowance up to 50%. That means that the base benefit is augmented by 50% in the case of a married man whose wife is 60 years of age or over. Should the man die, his wife receives a widow's benefit equivalent to ½ of the total, or 75% of the base . . . of her husband's benefit. If the man is married, instead of getting the base pension he gets 150%. If the man dies the benefit drops to ½ of that 150% or 75% of the original base."[49] Whatever the negotiated amount, the check was to go to the man, a request for his wife's signature being included only to ensure that she was in fact still alive when he cashed the check. Crucially, public perception seems to have confirmed the council's sense of an adequacy that did not disturb the appearance of male provision. The *New York Times*, commenting editorially on the bill under consideration, noted approvingly that "benefits to married men are supplemented by 50 per cent where there is an aged wife."[50]

If benefiting the male-centered family was the object of the legislation, then retaining some sense of normalcy in the power relations that operated within the family was crucial. The most hotly contested issue was whether it would be possible to give wives secondary benefits that sustained their husbands' sense of well-being without providing a basis for wage-earning women to make additional claims. Albert Linton's original proposal contemplated benefits for wives when they reached age sixty, five years earlier than men. "This is necessary and desirable" noted the Advisory Council, "because it is recognized that women do not remain in gainful employment as long as men do." At issue here was not women's needs, but the expectations of their spouses. The council feared that retired men would be disadvantaged if their wives did not receive benefits at an earlier age. "It is the normal situation where the wife is younger than the husband," remarked one council member, affirming a preliminary proposal that justified an age differential as "particularly necessary since the male annuitant at age 65 usually has a wife about five years his junior."[51] The question of women's physiology, their capacity to work as long as men, was only marginally introduced. The real concern was for "the strange situation where the man of 65 who quits is going to get his pension and who has a wife two or three years under 60, where she has to keep on working for a couple of years."[52] "What we are saying here," commented Douglas Brown, "is not whether women should retire at 55 or 60 but whether the play allowed as between the husband and the wife should be not more than five years."[53] Brown could not have made the underlying concern clearer: "If a married man reaches 65 and his wife is 61, let's say, and you don't give him the wife's allowance until the wife becomes 65, you have virtually reduced his benefit during the years when he is 65 to 69."[54]

The idea that a sixty-five-year-old husband would be allowed to claim a benefit on behalf of his sixty-year-old wife quickly ran into trouble. The council could not find a way to compensate men who had younger wives without giving the same benefit to independent wage-earning women. The problem, as Brown posed it, was simply that of "giving the married women an allowance at a certain age but. . . . requiring the single women to continue to age 65."[55] Such a policy would create an "essential discrimination between the fact that women earning their own benefits entirely would have to wait until they were 65 to get benefits, while their sisters, who are married, were getting the wives' allowance as of age 60."[56] The council played vainly with the idea of reducing retirement for working wives to age sixty and even to fifty-five, then dropped it. Still, in its final report, it took a moment to regret that the wives' allowances payable to aged men whose wives were several years younger than themselves "will be delayed some time after possible retirement of the husband."[57]

If the conversation suggested ambivalence about married women earning wages, it also contained apprehension that women might choose to marry for the purpose of gaining support. "Designing women," the committee feared, would marry aging men simply to participate in Social Security benefits. To forestall such a possibility, the Advisory Council agreed that a wife's benefit would be payable only if a couple had married five years before the husband turned sixty-five. The provision was hotly contested because it also discriminated against men who married after they passed their sixtieth birthdays.[58] But the restriction raised once again the question of whether Social Security was an insurance system or a moral policeman. "A two year period was long enough in a life insurance policy," thought one participant, who "was not at all sure" that even a five-year period would be an adequate "defense against a designing woman." To which Brown wondered, "How far should those in need be kept in need to protect the system against designing women and old fools?"[59]

To an outside observer, the most disturbing thing about the construction of the 1939 amendments is not that its architects operated from such a white, male field of vision, nor that many women did not benefit. Rather, what is problematic is that in order to preserve the appearance of equity for some men, they incorporated an essentially passive, and even sacrificial, role for women, for whom the consequences of the legislation were barely considered. In hindsight we see how the assumptions embedded in the language produced a continuing tension in the expectations of married women and in the relationships of the married to the unmarried. On the one hand, "a married woman whether she works or no will receive an allowance because of her husband's earning, whereas a single woman earns her own benefit rights." On the other, it was evident that "a married woman who works will not get advantage . . . of her own earnings, as in any case she will receive the 50% allowance for her husband."[60]

The actual situation was much worse. The Advisory Council fully expected that married women would work occasionally and that their contributions, as well as the early contributions of single women who then married, would both be absorbed by the system and help to sustain its financial health without necessarily yielding any direct benefit to the female contributor. There is no question that this was intentional, done, as Brown told the House Ways and Means Committee, which approved the council's recommendations, "in order to control the cost of the system. . . . women, as time passes, will more and more have had industrial or other employment in their early or middle years. They will have more and more credits in their own right, so as they approach 65 they will help build up the financing of these wives' allowances . . . so that they are not a net addition to the cost of the plan."[61] If a wife's own credits as a member of the labor force exceeded those to which she was entitled as a family member, then her family advantage was forfeit. Put another way, if a woman did not function as a stay-at-home wife most of the time, her husband would get no benefit on her behalf.

The effect of this policy on women was unclear, but the hopeful anticipation of the architects was not: it might, thought Brown, have the advantage of discouraging wives from returning to industry.[62] It would "take away the urge to go back and compete with the single women." And yet the availability of Social Security in their own right could also have the opposite effect, stimulating "more of them to come back in industry." While some members of the council deplored its failure to provide equitable treatment to wives who earned wages, suggesting for example that "women who work all their lives should have a larger return than those who don't," most sided with Paul Douglas, who declared, "Of course, wives work too."[63]

In the final analysis, inequitable treatments of differently positioned women drew less public attention than the inequities the council's proposal generated among differently positioned men. An early version of the final plan contemplated that allowances for wives, widows, and children would be paid for by slightly reducing benefits to single people whose accumulated taxed incomes exceeded $15,000 over a lifetime's work. The proposal raised questions as to whether the system would unfairly disadvantage the single man in comparison with his married peer and thus threaten the equity principle so carefully built into Old Age Insurance. To resolve the dilemma, one council member suggested that the tax rate for single men be cut to compensate for his reduced benefits.[64] But skeptics feared that the cut in rates might encourage more highly paid workers to try to exclude themselves from Social Security.[65] Consensus was achieved, finally, by capping benefits for highly paid single male and female retirees. After all, actuary Williamson argued, a single man "doesn't know what he will be in the future, and if . . . each man has his right to marriage and the money that goes with it, it will be all right."[66] The argument did not apply to single women, whose benefits were likely to be reduced on marriage, who would be entitled to no additional compensation for aged spouses, and whose compensatory family insurance was less extensive than that offered to men. Nevertheless, public attention focused on rationalizing the unfairness to single men. Press reports pointed out that the new benefits would be paid for by "a reduction in the eventual rates of benefit to be paid to single men as compared with the present law" and occasionally tacked on the marginal disadvantages to women, such as a reduction in the lump-sum death payment.[67]

The economic feasibility of the Social Security program as it was designed in 1935 rested on forms of behavior traditionally associated with white male lifestyles and population. But this was not the worst of it. The conversations around the 1939 amendments reveal that some conscious sense of preserving an appropriate gender balance went into constructing the system. Although rules of the program punished and discouraged dependency in general, its economic viability rested on the occasional contributions of women and the poor who would never earn enough to collect any benefits. In so doing, it punished poor women several times over. It failed to cover the occupations in which most poor women worked. It extracted contributions from those who worked occasionally in covered occupations, instead of exempting them.[68] It relegated women who had no male partners, or whose partners had been uncovered, to relief and the means-testing apparatus. It thus assigned women who belonged to an economy, culture, and race that discouraged independent female breadwinning or consigned them to marginal jobs to a distinctly disadvantaged role. Women could escape if they acted sufficiently like men to earn the rewards offered to men or if they married men with secure, well-paying, and covered jobs.

Whatever its difficulties, the power of the gender dynamic fostered change while other proposals for spending the surplus took second place in the council's agenda. For example, no one on the Advisory Council disputed the virtue of extending coverage to the disabled, but its members could not agree as to how to do it and so remanded the issue for further study. While self-employed workers were ambivalent about whether they wished to be covered, and the operators of nonprofit groups were negative about having their employees participate, both groups were recommended for inclusion as soon as feasible.

The recommendations on behalf of domestic workers and farm laborers were far more ambivalent. The Advisory Council debated coverage for domestic workers, agricultural laborers, and casual laborers at length, conceding that incorporating 5 million mostly nonwhite, poor, and female workers would create popular loyalty to the whole Social Security program. Their original exclusion (which contravened the recommendation of the Committee on Economic Security) had been based partly on the assumption that their low wages would not permit them to contribute enough to an annuity-based scheme to warrant the administrative difficulties of covering them. But as it became clear in the deliberations over the 1939 amendments that adopting a pay-as-you-go formula would ultimately require extending coverage as broadly as possible, the wisdom of continuing to bar some workers came into question. Paul Douglas argued the case for an "all-inclusive universal system" succinctly: "If everybody is in from the standpoint of benefits, then everybody is in from the standpoint of contributions, and if there is to be a government subsidy . . . for only the industrial part of the population, it is going to be difficult to have the entire population pay taxes for benefits designed for only half of the population."[69] Still, the Social Security Board raised objections on both administrative and political grounds. A payroll tax, it argued, could not be efficiently collected from a transient group of workers, and Congress in any event would oppose additional coverage. The Advisory Council ducked the issue by conceding the abstract need to include these groups without recommending that they be immediately involved.[70]

Not even an organized political struggle succeeded in covering African Americans. As early as 1937, the Social Security Board knew that domestic workers sought to be allowed into the insurance program, and it had already received many letters from African American constituencies.[71] "As you know," wrote Adam Clayton Powell Jr., "the Farmer and Domestic Worker is not taken care of under the present set up. This vitally affects our people, for most Negroes are employed along these two lines."[72] By August 1938, a campaign was in full swing. Roy Wilkins, then assistant secretary of the NAACP, wrote a public letter to FDR in which he placed the issue of exclusion on racial grounds. "The great bulk of negro wage earners in this country is now excluded from the benefits of the Social Security Act because they are occupied in agriculture and domestic service. Of the five million colored people normally gainfully employed, some three and a quarter million are engaged in agriculture and domestic service, so that you can realize how important to colored Americans is the contemplated revision of the Social Security Act."[73] Discussion of the issue continued when the Advisory Council's recommendations went to Congress, but the resistance of southern congressmen prevailed.

Comparing the negligible results of the pressure to make the Old Age Insurance system more racially inclusive with the minimal efforts required to extend the system to wives and widows points up the racial and gender issues involved. For all of its inconsistencies, it was still easier to deploy gender in a way that extended the system than to transcend barriers of class and race. While everyone recognized that ultimately this would have to be done, no one wanted to pay the political price of doing it too quickly. Thus the Social Security Board and the Advisory Council made public statements indicating how necessary it was to include these groups without moving an inch toward doing so. For all of the new plan's inconsistencies, it was still easier to shore up the system by deploying gender in a way that sustained adequacy for certain groups of white male workers than it was to transcend barriers of race in order to extend the system to provide adequate coverage to all. If anything, the force of the gendered argument, and the capacity of a gendered solution to resolve the issue of the surplus, reduced pressure on the council to find a solution for the poorest workers. Including the wives and widows of relatively privileged white male workers as dependents legitimized the system without conceding to race.

Intentionally, consciously, even eagerly, those who redesigned the Old Age

Insurance provisions of the Social Security Act utilized gendered understandings to reinforce a system in trouble. By June 1938 the council had agreed on the preliminary outlines of the proposal it would send to Congress. The proposal provided a "supplementary allowance on behalf of an aged wife" that clearly defined gender roles. The document used the terms *annuitant* and *married annuitant* to refer to men. It justified the additional benefit to women by the marked inadequacy of benefits that "must support not only the annuitant himself but also his wife" with data indicating the degree of need: "in 1930, 63.8 percent of men aged 65 and over were married."[74]

Nowhere in the document, as it was submitted by the Advisory Council to Congress and passed into law with minimal attention to these issues, is mention made of dependent husbands, or of wives with older husbands, or even of wives whose own jobs were covered by Social Security but whose husbands' jobs were not. Rather, the document brilliantly conveys a set of messages about how people should live. Women would be well advised to marry older men and to stay married for at least five years. Those who chose to live under another roof without the support of husbands lost their pensions. It did not matter if a woman contributed her bit to the household: she was unlikely to earn enough more than his annuity would provide anyway. Men could expect little benefit from sending their wives out to work, and women who earned wages would have to work mighty hard to exceed the pensions offered them for being stay-at-home wives. The more dependents, the more a man's Social Security contributions bought. But though a wage-earning woman could expect that her Social Security would protect her aged parents when they depended on her for support, her insurance bought no protection for her spouse. Regardless of the father's ability to support his children, a mother's insurance provided for children only if she were their sole support. A surviving widow without children might be entitled to a death benefit payment; but one with minor children lost that right in return for an annuity that would enable her to remain at home with the children. If she earned more than $15 a month or remarried, her annuity disappeared.

The impact on women was the least of it. The achievement of the 1939 amendments that have since provided the outlines of the American system of economic security is that they managed to extend adequacy within narrowly defined gender boundaries. They avoided generosity to many of the poor; reinforced traditional, white definitions of masculinity; and preserved the values of regular, consistent work about which most policymakers cared. The debates around the origins of these amendments illuminate the series of ideological tropes that governed their conception and implementation—among them prevailing beliefs about the importance of the work ethic, the value of self-reliance, the virtue of thrift, the possibility of achieving success by individual effort, and above all the validity of the traditional family and the naturally ordained quality of current gender boundaries. Not all of these were internally consistent. In particular, traditional family expectations and gender boundaries were sharply at odds with success and self-reliance for women, a contradiction not at first apparent to the majority of men or women who operated within familial constraints.

The policymakers and legislators who crafted the amendments shared a sense of gendered understandings that enabled them to preserve the sense that the system as a whole remained equitable while flagrantly violating its own decrees against adequacy. The House Ways and Means Committee, applauding the achievement of the Advisory Council, took the measure of its success: "By relating benefits to contributions or earnings, contributory old age insurance preserves individual thrift and incentive; by granting benefits as a matter of right it preserves individual dignity. Contributory insurance therefore strengthens democratic principles and avoids paternalistic methods of providing old age security."[75] The distinctions built into the system for men and women tell us less about injustice and inequities than they do about the ways in which men and women conceived the relationship between national values and the role of the state in preserving the family in its traditional form. "At the base of American civilization," Douglas Brown told the House Ways and Means Committee, "is the concept of the family and the perpetuation of that concept is highly important."[76] Mary Dewson did not disagree. The primary object of Social Security, she argued, was to "establish a greater measure of security in the life of the family. . . . Through the well-being of the family, we create the well-being of the Nation. Through our constructive contributions to the one, we help the other to flourish."[77]

For more than fifty years the United States has struggled with the effects of the Social Security system—a system whose program of entitlements delivered biting messages to ordinary working- and middle-class men and women about how they should live and provided boundaries around what most people might properly expect from the state. Social scientists and welfare activists have repeatedly deplored the effects of constructing categories of dependency in the Social Security legislation, arguing that the existence of means-tested welfare, meanly enforced, has, at least in part, been responsible for the creation of a two-tier society and for some of the consequences in the form of alienation, disrupted families, perpetual joblessness, and urban decay. At the heart of this division and crucial in its construction is the role played not so much by individual men and women as by a gendered meaning system. If gender can act, as it did in this instance, as a mechanism for enhancing the legitimacy of the Old Age Insurance program without threatening the boundaries of race, it can also play other social roles. My own reading of the debates suggests that no capitalist conspiracy, no structural predisposition can provide a sufficient explanation for why the system emerged as it did. Rather, the embedded nature of patriarchy; the existence of knowledge and belief systems inscribed into efforts to retain stability and direction and justified by ideological claims to truth; and the failure, quite simply, to see—these acted as powerful shaping devices in the emergence of a social welfare system.

That, essentially, is what Stephen Wiesenfeld discovered when he asked the Supreme Court to spell out the "important governmental objectives" served by denying support for his role as a father. In the space between the adoption of the original amendments and the time Wiesenfeld went to court, the implicit gendered assumptions that governed social policy had changed dramatically. In giving him the right to collect the insurance paid for by his wife, the Supreme Court acknowledged these changes and confronted and altered a set of governmental objectives around men's breadwinning roles that had never formally been recognized.

CHAPTER 5 : GIVING CHARACTER TO
OUR WHOLE CIVIL POLITY : MARRIAGE
AND THE PUBLIC ORDER IN THE LATE
NINETEENTH CENTURY : *NANCY F. COTT*

Marriage is commonly thought to lie in the realm of private decision making, but I want to emphasize, alternatively, in this essay, that the institution of marriage is and has been a public institution and a building block of public policy. Marriage is public in the sense that a condition of its existence (with rare exception) is its being known or publicized; just as important, the institution called "marriage" is a *legal* institution, its form and obligations created and regulated by public authority. Presumptions about and provisions for the obligations and benefits of marriage have always been built into many legal and governmental structures in the United States, from property-holding to citizenship and from immigration to military service and tax policy. Marriage operates as a systematic public sanction, enforcing privileges along with obligations.

This may be obvious, even tautological to stress. It "goes without saying" until some of those excluded from the benefits—homosexual couples are the prime recent example—bring it up. Unmarried couples, straight or gay, do not get the tax advantages, social security benefits, veterans' survivors' benefits, intestate succession rights, hospital and jail visitation privileges, favorable immigration laws, and property and support rights upon divorce that legally married couples do.[1] Their protests about exclusion from marriage have brought out the extent to which government actions (at local, state, and federal levels in the United States) are not extrinsic but intrinsic to the marriage institution.

The state is actively involved in creating social and civic statuses for both men and women through legal marriages—therefore actively involved in forming and sustaining gender itself. But if marriage is not examined as a public institution, this configuration of state power remains invisible. So far, U.S. historians have barely looked at the ways that public authority has been served by marriage. Social historians' innovative investigations into marriage and family in past times have fully succeeded in showing that these are socially constructed—not merely "natural"—institutions, subject to change in tandem with economic and intellectual shifts, but their work has focused on marriage as a demographic regulator, community shaper, or private experience, rather than as a vehicle of public policy.[2] I mean to take up the neglected perspective.

For as long as the past millennium in the Christian West, the exercise of formal power over marriage has been a prime means of exerting and manifesting public authority in general. In the early Middle Ages in Europe, marriages were dependent on public repute but made largely by private arrangement, outside formal law; a major way that the late medieval Catholic Church then asserted and consolidated its power over the populace was by bringing marriage formally under ecclesiastical authority and regulating it through the church courts.[3] Subsequently, a principal means and symbol of early modern European nation-building was the state's wresting of authority to regulate marriage from the church and vesting it in secular authorities. Largely completed by the eighteenth century, that process signaled the rise of the modern nation-state.[4]

Wielders of public authority in the Christian West since the early modern period have seen monogamous marriage as the most crucial precondition of public order—as a "pillar of the state." The evolution of monarchical rule depended on the patriarchal model and metaphor, of course. Beginning with the early modern period, state authority was seen as patterned on the male-headed family, its legitimacy dependent on the same source. It was the genius of the founders of modern political theory, the seventeenth-century contractualists who deserted monarchy in favor of representative parliamentary government, to sever that connection between the husband/father and the monarch: that is, to deny that the form of the legitimate state followed the form of the family (created by marriage and generations), to see it as sui generis, formed by consenting (male) adults. Yet as Carole Pateman has brilliantly argued, a presumption of a "sexual contract," by which men dominated and represented women, preceded and was incorporated as a foundation of the contractual theorists' polity.[5]

One might go so far as to say that the institution of marriage and the modern state have been mutually constitutive. As much as (legal) marriage does not exist without being authorized by the state, one of the principal means that the state can use to prove its existence—to announce its sovereignty and its hold on the populace—is its authority over marriage. This relationship between marriage and the state is so accepted or normalized among modern populations as to be virtually invisible or unexamined. My point here is to attempt to make it visible, to examine it, so that marriage can be better understood as a constitutive part of public order in a given time and place, in a relation subject to change.

To insist on marriage as a public institution as I am doing does not mean that marriage does not also signify a private relationship between two people. Marriage inspires the private realm of familial intimacy, being the precondition for its (legitimate) founding. Marriage also anchors private property by establishing lineage for its transmission. The institution of marriage may have even older and stronger links to private property than to public authority—the husband's property in his wife being the archetype of the connection.[6]

In the historical emergence and ideological recognition of a realm of private life, marriage has been central. Prior to the Revolutionary era in Anglo-America, "private" had two principal inflections: one, etymologically related to "privilege," meant reserved for a select few (as in "the Privy Council"); the other meant covert, shameful (as in "the privy").[7] There was no strong sense of privacy attached to the family life created by marriage: family residences hardly afforded seclusion or private spaces. The households of the rich were highly populated locations for both business and pleasure where individuals of all ages, genders, and social strata were likely to interact, while the households of the poor were small, cramped, and thin-walled. The material preconditions for creating a "private world" at home did not appear for the largest proportion of the population. As late as 1775 only half of the middling households in Massachusetts, for example, even had forks and knives, much less chairs, tables, beds, pillows, tea sets, books, musical instruments, and other accoutrements. Sociability and surveillance, not privacy, marked the household.[8]

By the late eighteenth century, however, social and economic change as well as political philosophy began to make possible a firmer, more elaborated definition of privacy centered around marriage and the domestic site of the household. Along with greater emphasis on individualism and a rise in the proportion of middle-class households with more space and comfortable trappings, a third and more positive valuation of privacy began to emerge, combining withdrawal from the world with privileged status. In the nineteenth century, with the ascendancy of marketplace relationships and partisan politics, the private domestic arena created by marriage was positively valued as an alternative to the competitive, turbulent, and soul-withering world of business and politics outside.[9]

By that time two different constructions of the public/private divide were visible, as they still are today. In one reading, the public included business and politics—all the doings of men—and the private was the family arena, formed by marriage, where men got involved with women. In that reading the polarities between public and private, work and home, man and woman, were all parallel and mutually reinforcing. But in another and also prevalent reading— the reading enshrined in law—the public was more strictly the commonweal, or, in short, the state, and the private was a larger category, including the market (private property transactions) along with the domestic marital realm.[10]

In either of these readings, the differentiation of public from private was incomprehensible without marriage, which created couples who made homes and families that amassed and transmitted property. Because marriage bears a formative relation to both private property and domestic intimacy, it not only inhabits but undergirds the domain of privacy. The performance of obligations and duties and rewards of the marriage institution is assumed to be insulated from public scrutiny unless visible deviations occur or one of the spouses speaks out to complain. In hard fact, however, privacy in marriage and family choice and practice exists as the privilege of those who conform to— whether or not they consciously acknowledge—the public and legal order. In the matter of marriage regulation, most people do not "feel" the law; already having been formed by the same preconceptions that dictate it, they go along with its expectations.[11] But state structuring and public enforcement of such norms, with penalties for deviations, are essential to the marriage system; those who do *not* conform feel the coercive power of the state. Therefore privacy in marriage is rather a reward than an absolute right.[12]

Perhaps no institution is simultaneously so private and so public as marriage is. Marriage both establishes the boundaries that mark off private from public and confounds by crossing those boundaries. Public and private aspects are linked in the impact of marriage on an individual's civic responsibility. Marital status has, traditionally, not only defined individuals' household and sexual relationships but also has shaped their civil and even political status. As feminist political theorists have pointed out, in the Western political tradition a man's headship of a family, his responsibility for dependent wife and children, is what qualified him to be a participating member of a state.[13] In the republican theory behind the American Revolution, independence for the citizen (as well as for the former colonies) was a key term: it implied economic independence (as opposed to vassalage) along with, and as the underpinning for, freedom of judgment. Economic independence for men was associated, unquestionably, with age and marital status—with the succession to (inherited) property or livelihood that came along with establishing one's own marriage and household. The founders assumed that marriage and property-holding and heading a family were closely related as attributes of citizen-voters. In a discussion of political participation in 1776, for instance, Thomas Jefferson wrote to a friend that he favored "extending the right of suffrage (or in other words the rights of a citizen) to all who had a permanent intention of living in the country. Take what circumstances you please as evidence of this, either the having resided a certain time, or having a family, or having property, any or all of them."[14] Married status did not literally become a requirement for men's voting, but the age of twenty-one and property-holding did, and these denoted marriageability if not marriage itself.

Men's civil and political status grew, then, from being independent heads of units that included dependents, from heading household units that deserved representation in the civil world. In corollary, women's citizenship was compromised by their marital position, by being dependents, by presumably lacking the potential to be economically and civilly independent since they would be married. It may be more common to stress the impact of the common law regarding marriage on the civil and political status of women, since it so clearly deprived them of legal personhood or individuality (merging wives' legal identities in their husbands'), but it is just as important to recognize the impact of marriage in endowing men with the fullness of their civil status as independent individuals. By stipulating civic and political statuses of husbands and wives, as much as by enforcing a sexual division of labor (requiring the husband to be the economic provider and, under the Anglo-American common law, awarding the wife's property and earnings to him), marriage has been a cardinal—arguably the cardinal—agent of gender formation and has institutionalized gender roles.[15]

To look at marriage as a public and civil institution is to acknowledge that marriage is less a natural than a civil right, a right selectively denied or withheld. Consider, in this light, the nonrecognition—the lack of legal existence or protection—of slaves' marriages. State courts during the years that slavery was an American institution agreed that slaves could not be validly married because their status as someone else's property prevented them from being able to consent freely—a crucial requisite for marriage. Moreover, slaves could not carry out the obligations of marriage because their duties to their masters came first. Slaves' inability to marry was one form—a definitive form—of their inability to contract.[16] Slaveholders' promotion of private ceremonies for slave unions, always breakable by masters' whims—*not* upheld by the state—quintessentially marked slaves as without civil rights, as lacking in the basic civil status of persons, whatever provisions might be made for "the rule of law" in the slave-holding system. Since marriage institutionalized gender roles, being deprived of marriage also de-gendered slaves in the eyes of the law: male slaves were denied the privileges and female slaves the protections (so to speak) of coverture. In their eagerness to remarry legally during Reconstruction, ex-slave couples exercised newly awarded civil rights and asserted their own legitimacy as civil beings.[17]

The link between marital status and civil/political status is also visible in the federal government's campaign to eliminate the Church of Jesus Christ of the Latter-Day Saints, mainly because its members practiced polygamy. In a major step taken in 1882, the U.S. Congress enacted new restrictions in the territory of Utah, where most Mormons lived, including the disfranchisement of polygamists. A man was required to swear that he was not a polygamist and a woman to swear that she was not the wife of a polygamist before either could cast a ballot. (Utah had enfranchised women a dozen years earlier.) A number of Mormons sued the registrar who refused to register them to vote in the 1882 election. The U.S. Supreme Court, to which the case eventually went, found no fault with Congress's enacting a marital qualification for voting. "It is precisely similar to an inquiry into the fact of nativity, of age, or of any other status made necessary by law as a condition of the elective franchise," the Court announced, going on to state that the sovereign power could legitimately "declare that no one but a married person shall be entitled to vote." Since monogamy was "wholesome and necessary" to a "free, self-governing commonwealth," Congress was exercising its authority suitably in withdrawing political power from those who appeared hostile to monogamy.[18]

Every state made bigamy a crime and prescribed penalties for it (although in the wide open spaces of mid-nineteenth-century America, certain forms of bigamy were not much hindered: that is, a man's leaving one wife, going to a new location, and marrying another; or a woman's assuming her long-gone husband was dead and remarrying).[19] Since bigamy was a crime, the disfranchisement of Mormon polygamists could be assimilated to the practice of depriving convicted criminals of the vote, as many states did during the nineteenth century. But the purpose here seemed more similar to the disfranchisement imposed on the leaders of the Confederacy after the Civil War than that imposed on ordinary criminals; the crime in polygamy appeared to be a form of treason, given that the state was committed to the principles and practice of monogamy.

Legislators, jurists, and a budding crop of social scientists in the last third of the nineteenth century, the period I want to focus on, took for granted that

Innocent kids vs. un-innocent kids.

Blacks of status / class (456

(457) very had mothers active

∴ social reform.

(70) social insurance vs. social workers

Women saw their own plight in that of children.

(75) - strategy to further support for public sec. provision by org. around mothers' needs — was a polit. decision ✓

polit. tradition —

Well removed ⌐ nat-right
       └ motherhood

(77) Easier to talk of child-beating than wife-beating because in latter woman was shamed.

AFDC — abolist gave $ to mothers.

monogamous marriage and the state were closely intertwined, which accounted for the fact that marital and civil/political status were also. As the Supreme Court of Washington put it in a 1892 decision, the institution of marriage was "closely and thoroughly related to the state."[20]

Yet these same parties interested in defining and maintaining monogamy as a pillar of the state were also committed to regarding marriage as the linchpin of private relationships. To begin with, marriage had always been defined as a contract in America. The ability to make a contract—to consent—was the basic capacity that an individual had to have in order to marry, as the slave counterexample illustrates.[21] In the initial English settlements in America, marriage was regarded as a civil contract rather than a sacrament. Since the Anglican Church never managed to set up ecclesiastical courts in the colonies, secular magistrates, legislatures, and courts from very early on claimed the power to create, regulate, and end marriages and to judge and punish infractions such as fornication, adultery, and bigamy.[22] The strong tradition declaring marriage a civil contract underlay the innovation of divorce in the American colonies and the early republic; it was essential to the widespread acceptance of "common-law" marriage—marriage without valid ceremony—which was amazingly frequent in the eighteenth and nineteenth centuries, especially in southern and sparsely populated areas.[23]

Contracts between consenting adults were supposed to be private matters.[24] It was contracts that gave lifeblood to the regime of private property, and the state was not to interfere in them. The founding fathers valued this principle so highly that they included in the U.S. Constitution the insistence that "no State shall . . . pass any . . . law impairing the obligation of contracts." But if contracts were private and marriage was "closely and thoroughly related to the state," then marriage had to be more than or different from a contract. Joseph Story, who sat on the U.S. Supreme Court from 1812 to 1845 and was also extremely influential as a treatise writer, treated marriage as a contract in his *Conflict of Laws* because it was commonly spoken of thus, but he admitted that "it appears to me to be something more than a mere contract. It is rather to be deemed an institution of society, founded upon consent and contract of the parties, and in this view it has some peculiarities in its nature, character, operation and extent of obligation, different from what belong to ordinary contracts."

Such awareness resounded and intensified through the nineteenth century. The difficulty of pinning down an institution that was neither simply private nor simply public surfaced in the dual characterization of marriage as a contract and a status. Most tellingly, jurists pointed out that marriage, while formed by consent, could not be changed, modified, or ended thereby: once marriage was entered, its "rights, duties, and obligations" were "of law, not of contract," "the creation of the law itself," as the Maine Supreme Court declared in 1866. The Indiana Supreme Court, in an 1857 decision, commented: "At common law, marriage as a *status* had few elements of contract about it. For instance, no other contract merged the legal existence of the parties into one." Considering the "distinctive elements" of marriage, this court pronounced it "more than a contract": it was the result of "public ordination" as much as private agreement, "a great public institution, giving character to our whole civil polity."[25]

If in its contractual aspect, then, marriage was conceded to be—even celebrated as—private, in its status aspect it was public. Although marriage is in many respects unique, this condition of dual belonging to private and public was not unique to it in the last third of the nineteenth century, when the possibly competing meanings of the contract and status definitions of marriage came increasingly to be decided by courts. The great burden of legal/constitutional struggles of this period had to do with defining economic activities as private and/or public in order to judge whether and how far the federal or state government could intervene. The "obsession" of the law of government-business relations of this period (in the words of one historian) was defining the boundary between public and private.[26] The ideological distinction between public and private and the social relations on which it appeared to be based were challenged in a host of ways: by—to name but a few—the increasing number and complexity of government-sponsored initiatives at both state and federal levels (including tariffs, taxes, social service, and educational institutions); the larger scale and reach of manufacturing and transportation industries—especially railroads—that seemed to occupy a middle ground between private and public; the demands of workers for working-class legislation that would limit employers' control over the hours of labor; and women activists' campaign to emerge from the "private sphere" into full civil and political status via economic independence and the ballot.[27]

On both marital and economic questions, courts repeatedly had to admit that the divide between private and public did not hold. In the economic arena an important turning point was reached in 1877 in a U.S. Supreme Court decision, *Munn v. Illinois*. There a majority of the justices recognized an intermediate term between private and public, a concept of private business "affected with a public interest." Even though such a business was privately owned, the Court said, it could justifiably be regulated by a state legislature.[28] As the ultimate legal arbiter in a land where lawyers were the principal public men and courts were the most numerous and visible state apparatus, the Supreme Court symbolized and represented public authority.[29] At the same time, court decisions are never removed from the cultural and social matrix of the time but rather are an intertwining and constitutive part, and the high court's step in *Munn* indicated that consensus about the distinguishability of private from public was no longer solid.[30]

Yet courts were eager to retain the categories—to distinguish "private rights" from "the public interest"—because without rights of private contract, all was public domain and all market transactions might be subject to government claims. An understanding of property ownership and marital privileges as analogous archetypes of private rights was implicit in much legal deliberation. Occasionally the analogy became explicit, as it did in a U.S. Supreme Court decision in 1875. The immediate question was whether the city of Topeka could default on municipal bonds, pledged to be paid back by tax money, when the bonds had been issued to aid a private manufacturing corporation. The Supreme Court found that the bonds had been invalid from the beginning: in issuing them, Topeka had invaded the private right of taxpayers. To emphasize the "implied reservations of individual rights" that prevented a city or state from taxing its people to support anything but the public interest, Justice Samuel Miller proposed the analogy that a court would, of course, declare void a statute "which enacted that A. and B. who were husband and wife to each other should be so no longer, but that A. should thereafter be the husband of C., and B., the wife of D. Or [a statute] that should enact that the homestead now owned by A. should no longer be his, but should henceforth be the property of B."[31] Whatever general subconscious fears or specific contemporary referents inspired Miller to invent this hyperbolic example—perhaps the utopian experiment in "complex marriage" coming under siege at the Oneida community, agitation about "free love," or the passage of homestead exemption laws or married women's property rights acts—the example suggests that the public/private divide was a central ideological instability that dogged legal approaches to both property questions and marital ones.[32]

Courts sustained a double characterization of marriage (as private *and* public, contract *and* status) rather than inventing an intermediary term as they did in *Munn* with respect to business. Four U.S. Supreme Court decisions of the 1870s and 1880s illustrate that double characterization. Two of the four decisions affirmed that marriage was a private contract. In both of these the question was the validity of a common-law marriage. The other two decisions—one declaring the practice of polygamy unprotected by constitutional guarantees of religious freedom, the other supporting a state legislature's power over divorce—affirmed that marriage was intimately related to the state or a creature of the state.

The timing of the two decisions validating common-law marriage (by which I mean a continuing heterosexual union unauthorized by formal ceremonies) is especially interesting. While informal or self-marriage was widespread in the first half of the nineteenth century, there was a reaction against it by the 1860s and 1870s among reformers (concerned also about the rising incidence of divorce) who believed that marriages were being hastily or thoughtlessly made. These reformers, led by ministers, lawyers, and academics, wished common-law marriage to be undermined by state pronouncements.[33] Dampening their hopes, the U.S. Supreme Court in 1877 confirmed what it regarded as "the settled doctrine of the American courts," namely, that marriage was "everywhere regarded as a civil contract" that could be joined by the consent of a man and a woman. While state statutes could certainly regulate it, informal marriage was valid unless it was specifically prohibited. Even state laws indicating how marriages were to be solemnized were to be seen as directory, not mandatory, in the absence of specific prohibitions, "because marriage is a thing of common right, because it is the policy of the State to encourage it, and because . . . any other construction would compel holding illegitimate the offspring of many parents conscious of no violation of law."[34] The lower courts most often claimed, as did the Texas Supreme Court in 1864, that it was "upon the highest considerations of public policy" that they saw a valid marriage where "the consent of the parties and the intention to enter into the state of matrimony, and to assume its duties and obligations, is clearly shown."[35] In a second U.S. Supreme Court decision, in 1884, Justice Stephen Field delivered a ringing affirmation of this view, saying that a couple's known consent to marry and general repute as married were sufficient, while also stressing that "public policy" required "public recognition" as a necessary ingredient.[36]

These decisions, which seemed to grant great latitude to individuals to contract marriage, silently incorporated specific assumptions about what constituted the "state of matrimony" and its "duties and obligations." With no sense of contradiction, the same Supreme Court in 1879 denied members of the Mormon Church the religious freedom to engage in what they called "plural marriage." While the campaign against the Mormon practice of polygamy was waged by Protestant churchgoers and unruly mobs as well as by Congress, U.S. presidents, and the Supreme Court, it most certainly was a campaign of the nation-state—carried on from the Civil War years to victory in 1890—and dramatically illustrated the U.S. government's shaping of public policy around a specific model of marriage.[37]

The Latter-Day Saints had been persecuted ever since rumors circulated in Illinois, where they lived in the 1840s, that they were practicing polygamy. Leader Joseph Smith indeed was. The church publicly declared its practice of "plural marriage" for leaders in 1852, by which time the community had moved to Utah. The U.S. Congress first explicitly challenged plural marriage by pointedly restating the illegality of bigamy in the Morrill Act, a federal statute of 1862 dealing with the territories (of which Utah was one).[38] When a test case, in which a Mormon leader who was charged with bigamy defended himself on the basis of religious duty, reached the U.S. Supreme Court late in 1878, the decision made plain that polygamy was not protected by the First Amendment's guarantee of religious freedom.[39] The nation's perceived obligation to monogamy won out. Following various Enlightenment authors, Chief Justice Morrison R. Waite called polygamy "always . . . odious" to northern and western Europeans, and only characteristic of "Asiatic and of African people." Waite affirmed that "it is within the legitimate scope of the power of every civil government to determine whether polygamy or monogamy shall be the law of social life under its dominion," for he saw forms of marriage as generative of forms of state. "According as monogamous or polygamous marriages are allowed do we find the principles on which the government of the people, to a greater or less extent, rests," he contended. Only monogamy could give rise to democratic government.[40]

In this decision, *Reynolds v. the United States*, the Supreme Court endorsed congressional power to prohibit bigamy in Utah and emphasized that religious claims exempted no one, since "actions in violation of social duties or subversive of good order" were not protected by constitutional guarantees of religious freedom. Laws could not interfere with religious *belief* but they could police *actions*. To make the point unmistakable the Court asked rhetorically whether anyone would seriously contend that the state would not step in to prevent human sacrifice proposed as religious ritual. If plural marriage were allowed on the claim of religious freedom, then religion would become "superior to the law of the land," every citizen would become "in effect . . . a law unto himself," and "Government could exist only in name." In other words, polygamy was as threatening to the state as anarchism.[41] Indeed, in immigration policy, polygamists were among the first groups declared excludable and deportable, along with the insane, paupers, felons, and those with a loathsome or dangerous disease (1891). In early twentieth-century immigration and naturalization acts, polygamists were listed as excludable and deportable right next to anarchists, as if (following Waite's logic) those who would overthrow the institution of monogamy were dangerously similar to those who would overthrow the state. The two groups together were declared ineligible for citizenship.[42]

The fourth decision I will mention, an 1888 case in which the U.S. Supreme Court vigorously upheld the Oregon territorial legislature's (as distinct from a court's) power to decree a divorce, repeated the strong sense in the *Reynolds* decision that monogamy was crucial to orderly government and that having and exercising power over marriage was essential to government functioning. In this case Justice Stephen Field declared that "marriage, as creating the most important relation in life, as having more to do with the morals and civilization of a people than any other institution, has always been subject to the control of the legislature." To vindicate legislative divorce Field had to prove that the constitutional provision cited earlier, that no state should pass any law impairing the obligation of contracts, did not apply to the contract of marriage. He did so handily by citing numerous nineteenth-century legal authorities and decisions to the resounding effect that marriage, while a civil contract, was also a status defined by law.[43]

Field's definitive statement that states could regulate marriages without being guilty of impairing contracts answered a question not directly presented to him at the time, but circulating in state courts since 1866, about laws prohibiting interracial marriages. His opinion thus had impact far beyond vindicating legislative divorce; it addressed the issue of racial ordering through marriage regulation. The most striking marriage restrictions in American law have had to do with race. Laws making marriages between whites and blacks illegal or void first appeared in the English colonies in the seventeenth century, an American innovation having no basis in the common law.[44] The very first act criminalizing interracial marriage, passed by the Maryland assembly in 1664, singled out for punishment "freeborn English women" who made "shamefull Matches" with "Negro slaves." The act stipulated that such women would serve their slave-husbands' masters for the duration of the marriage and that their progeny would be slaves. (The same statute first instituted lifelong bondage for blacks.) Later bans on marriage between blacks and whites used gender-neutral language—their defense typically resting in "natural law" and the taboo of "corruption of races"—but the echo of the first Maryland statute hung around them; the subtext of these laws, all designed and implemented by white men, drew boundaries around their "own" women, white women.[45]

Initiated in six colonies, these bans and punishments multiplied in many states during the nineteenth and into the early twentieth century and were not declared unconstitutional until 1967. This was not simply a southern phenomenon. Forty-one states at some time in their histories criminalized or nullified marriage of whites to nonwhites, fifteen of them (mainly in the West) extending the proscription beyond "Negroes" and mulattoes to Native Americans and/or Asians.[46] Such laws—like the protests of homosexual couples today—show that prohibition or absence of some kinds of marriages is as important as encouragement of others in defining marriage policy. The laws forbidding marriages "across the color line" (like the denial of legal marriage to slaves) should be seen not as exceptions to marriage policy in the nineteenth-century United States but as intrinsic to, indeed defining, it.[47] They are powerful evidences of public authority using marriage policy to create a social order of racial separation and hierarchy. In these examples one can see that constructions of race have been central in public policies of marriage in U.S. history. Notions of race depend on a biologistic or familial formulation in which sexual reproduction is essential, while marriage rules (including penalties for incest, fornication, adultery, and bigamy) are the state's main method of regulating sexual reproduction.[48] Sexual reproduction not only secures a population to the state—which is certainly crucial!—but also creates the qualities and characteristics of the "body politic."

More legislation punishing interracial marriage and making it void or null was passed by states during and immediately after the Civil War—when the "body politic" was being reconstituted—than in any other sixteen-year period of U.S. history. Ten states passed new laws; eight others reiterated or refined their bans and punishments; an additional six kept antebellum strictures on the books.[49] But proscribed couples were emboldened to challenge such restrictions, because the Civil Rights Act of 1866 reiterated rights of free contract and because the Fourteenth Amendment to the U.S. Constitution (adopted in 1868) emphasized that states could not abridge citizens' privileges or deny them equal protection of the law or due process of law. In fifteen appellate cases in nine states between 1869 and 1895, challenges to interracial marriage bans were raised. These were met and denied with the answer that marriage was not simply a contract but was a status or relation appropriately regulated by the state. No racial discrimination was seen in the marriage bans because they applied to whites as well as to people of color.[50]

Thus when Justice Field of the U.S Supreme Court said, in the 1888 case regarding the Oregon territorial legislature's right to implement a divorce, that marriage was "an institution, in the maintenance of which *in its purity* the public is deeply interested, for it is the foundation of the family and of society, without which there would be neither civilization nor progress," he supported state legislators and jurists who wanted to retain or add interracial marriage proscriptions.[51] Although no case on the constitutionality of interracial marriage bans came before the U.S. Supreme Court during the nineteenth century, the high court showed that it accepted the reasoning about marriage as a public institution on which such statutes rested. In the now-infamous *Plessy v. Ferguson* decision of 1896, which justified racial segregation in public places, the Court mentioned that intermarriage prohibitions were "universally recognized as within the police power of the State"—that is, the power of each state to protect the public health, safety, and welfare.[52]

Public policy in the United States, at both the federal and state levels, strongly encouraged marriage. Many states had moved in the early nineteenth century to empower more diverse personnel to perform marriages and had eliminated hurdles or fees associated with banns or licenses; and the Supreme Court had affirmed that even without valid ceremonies having taken place, a union that looked like a marriage for all intents and purposes would be taken as one.[53] Such a policy had advantages for the state, putting women and children under the control of male heads who had political representation and making men obliged to their dependents; it made the sexual division of labor operational and clarified private property transmission.

The four Supreme Court decisions discussed here indicate, however tersely, that the United States as a polity was not endorsing and enforcing *any and every* type of marriage, but a particular model of monogamous, intraracial, and, I think one can accurately say, Christian marriage. To the founders of the American republic, as Carol Weisbrod has emphasized, separation of church and state never meant that the United States was not a (Protestant) Christian nation.[54] Nineteenth-century marriage policy made an obvious and positive connection between Christian morals and stable government. The Supreme Court decisions on Mormon polygamy, for instance, embraced the idea, firmly rooted in missionary rhetoric and happily adopted by social Darwinians, that Christianity and civilization were inextricably intertwined. Supreme Court Justice Joseph Bradley called Mormon polygamy "a return to barbarism. . . . contrary to the spirit of Christianity and of the civilization which Christianity has produced in the Western world." The name of God appears a great deal in court decisions on interracial marriage bans too, his aims conveniently dovetailing with temporal concerns. The Virginia Supreme Court, for example, defended that state's ban in 1878 by declaring it derived from the "laws of God and the laws of property, morality and social order . . . [that] have been exercised by all civilized governments in all ages of the world."[55]

Neither state nor federal government was willing to leave marriage to the general workings of Christianity and civilization, however: both moved toward more extensive and intensive "hands-on" policies in the late nineteenth century. Even the Supreme Court validation of common-law marriage can be seen in this light. Although state authority seemed to back away in the acceptance of common-law marriage, the result of this acceptance was to widen the ambit of the state's enforcement of marital obligations, duties, and rewards and to reinforce state support for monogamous marriage as an institution.[56] Courts' approach to common-law marriage underlined the double characterization of marriage as simultaneously private and public, contract and status. By crediting couples' private consent, it drew them into a set of duties and obligations set and enforced by the state.

What I have given here is a sketch, based on very specific material of limited chronological and geographical bounds, of the way that historians might treat the institution of heterosexual marriage as the most direct link of public authority to gender formation, as the primary institution that makes the public order a gendered order. By this I mean to implicate male as well as female gender. Furthermore, marriage norms and laws may be deployed as important and powerful tools of class hegemony and cultural regulation, as well as of racial formation as has been so evident in the United States. To denaturalize marriage, to enable it to appear not as an inevitable, little-changing feature of social organization but rather as a site where public authority and private initiative join, which is constantly being rebuilt—thus reinforcing or reshaping the gendered public order—is my aim here, and one that I hope will have application beyond this limited sketch.

PART 2 *Power*

CHAPTER 6 : SOUL MURDER

AND SLAVERY : TOWARD A FULLY

LOADED COST ACCOUNTING

NELL IRVIN PAINTER

T he Sojourner Truth whom we know walks out of the dust jacket of
Gerda Lerner's *Creation of Feminist Consciousness*, an eloquent black
feminist abolitionist. But this figure did not come ready-made;
Truth's was the kind of past that had to be transcended. A poor,
despised slave and freedwoman, Truth defeated tremendous personal odds to
remake herself into an embodiment of power. Lerner in her own life did not
have to repair anything as deep as the wounds of slavery, but she, like Truth,
had her injuries, and, like Truth, she is a powerful woman.

Sojourner Truth, the ex-slave, has long held an attraction for Gerda Lerner,
the historian. In 1972 Truth appeared in one of Lerner's early books on
women's history, *Black Women in White America*. More than twenty years later,
Lerner returned to Truth to emblematize something larger than the essence of
black women: In 1993 Lerner situated Truth within a millennium-long tradition of women who reinterpreted the Bible. These women forged a Christ-
centered manifesto of respect for the humanity of all people—women as well
as men—out of the book that seemed mostly to convey the Pauline caution
against women's speaking in public. In Judeo-Christian culture, in which con-
secrated writing supplied the main epistemological framework, this reinterpre-
tation became a crucial first step into women's thinking for themselves, into
what we now term "empowerment."

Sojourner Truth, who is so useful to Lerner as the embodiment of a woman who unfettered her own intellect, had not always been self-confident. Born a slave in Ulster County, New York, at the end of the eighteenth century, she was Isabella Van Wagener (or Van Wagner) in the mid-1830s, when she spent three years in a commune headed by a tyrant. The leader of Truth's community was a man who had been born Robert Matthews and who had changed his name to the "Prophet Matthias." Within what he called his "kingdom," Matthias made all the rules and broke them at will; he flew into hour-long rages and ranted at his followers whenever the spirit moved him. He made them call him "Father" and appropriated the best of everything for himself, from houses and furniture and carpets and silver to the richest white woman in the community, even though she was married to someone else. As is so often the case in movements built around a charismatic leader who sets himself above worldly laws and common decency, the Matthias kingdom came to ruin over unorthodox conjugal arrangements and allegations of murder. Isabella Van Wagener was his devoted follower until he left her. She did not leave him.[1]

Why are people (even people like Sojourner Truth) continually attracted to communities headed by autocrats who abuse their followers verbally, physically, and sexually? One answer is to be found in the psychological scars that disfigure so many adherents. Leaders who emerge from emotionally trying backgrounds wield power aggressively, and they hold a singular appeal to people who were abused, especially sexually, as children. Such was the case with Sojourner Truth, who was a slave for the first thirty years of her life and who dictated and published in 1850 her recollections of bondage in the Hudson Valley of New York. The *Narrative of Sojourner Truth* has taught me a great deal about how crucial slavery was to the formation of identity, whether the subject was a northerner or a southerner. As a historian of the American South, I might have been tempted before writing about Sojourner Truth to equate slave society with southern society and to speak only of southerners in the relation between slavery and psychology. This, after all, has been the habit in American historiography since the mid-nineteenth century, a habit that I have now broken in my own work. Having evaded the regional snare, I write a good deal nonetheless about the South, for the historical scholarship on slavery is mainly southern. Even so, this regional tilt should not obscure the prevalence of the institution: In the seventeenth and eighteenth centuries, slavery was a national phenomenon, and its effects were by no means limited to the South.

We all know on a certain, almost intuitive level that violence is inseparable from slavery, but historians rarely trace the descent of that conjunction. In this essay I accept that unhappy task. My aim is to examine the implications of soul murder (a phrase to which I will return momentarily) and use them to question the lacunae in historians' descriptions of American society during the era of slavery. My hope is that a more complete accounting—what bookkeepers would term a "fully loaded cost accounting"—of the costs of slavery, most notably the tragic overhead costs that were reckoned in the currency of physical abuse and family violence, will yield a fuller comprehension of our national experience. With the broad geography of American slavery in mind, I take as my theme "Soul Murder and Slavery," which does not stop at the borders of the South.

This work is interdisciplinary, drawing on the history of American slavery, feminist scholarship on women, the family, and the workplace, and on the thought of sociologists and psychologists regarding children. My questions have their roots in second-wave feminism of the 1960s, which inspired Gerda Lerner and, with her crucial contributions, influenced the rewriting of history generally. By focusing attention on women's lives, feminist scholarship has made women visible rather than taken for granted and queried the means by which societies forge gender out of the physical apparatus of sex. While some feminist thinkers have analyzed women's writing and gender, recently other intellectuals and activists have turned a spotlight on a protected, potent social institution: the family. Even though families, as the site of identity formation, shape the elaboration of politics, and even though public policy profoundly influences families, family dynamics have generally been treated as private and separate from the public realm and have not traditionally figured prominently in the writing of history.

Historiographical blindness toward families still persists, even though the source material is abundant. Turning new eyes on evidence that has been at hand forever, feminist historians are able to hear subaltern voices and recognize phenomena that had not previously been investigated seriously.[2] What were long termed "discipline" and "seduction" of the young and powerless, who were described as feckless and oversexed, we can now call by their own names: child abuse, sexual abuse, sexual harassment, rape, battering. Psychologists aggregate the effects of these all-too-familiar practices in the phrase *soul murder*, which may be summed up as depression, lowered self-esteem, and anger.

Soul murder has a long genealogy, going back to folk beliefs in Europe and Africa about the possibility of stealing or killing another person's soul. Soul murder appeared in connection with the 1828 story of Kaspar Hauser, who, having spent his childhood imprisoned alone in a dark cellar, emerged as an emotionally crippled young adult unable to talk or walk. Before emerging into the light, Hauser had glimpsed only one other person, his jailer, to whom he wished to return. Within psychoanalytic literature, the classic, anguished phrasing of soul murder as the violation of one's inner being, the extinguishing of one's identity, including sexual identity, comes initially from Anselm von Feuerbach's 1832 account of Hauser and from Daniel Paul Schreber's 1903 *Memoirs of My Nervous Illness,* inspired by Feuerbach and commented on, in turn, by Sigmund Freud and Jacques Lacan. Schreber's memoir made him the world's most famous paranoid.[3] More recently, soul murder appears in the title of a book by a professor of psychiatry at the New York University School of Medicine, Leonard Shengold, *Soul Murder: The Effects of Child Abuse and Deprivation* (New Haven: Yale University Press, 1989). The "abuse" in the subtitle can be violent and/or sexual, which presents children with too much sensation to bear. "Deprivation," as in the case of Kaspar Hauser, refers to neglect that deprives children of enough attention to meet their psychic needs.

Sexual abuse, emotional deprivation, and physical and mental torture can lead to soul murder, and soul-murdered children's identity is compromised; they cannot register what it is that they want and what it is that they feel. Like Kaspar Hauser, they often identify with the person who has abused them, and they may express anger toward themselves and others. Abused persons are more at risk for the development of an array of psychological problems that include depression, anxiety, self-mutilation, suicide attempts, sexual problems, and drug and alcohol abuse.[4] Victims of soul murder do not inevitably turn into abusers—there is no direct or predictable line of cause and effect—but people who have been abused or deprived as children grow up at risk psychologically.

We surely cannot translate twentieth-century psychology directly into the mentalities of eighteenth- and nineteenth-century societies, because many aspects of life that we regard as psychological were, in earlier times, connected to religion. Spirituality then, as now, varied considerably from person to person and from group to group; with the passage of time, religious sensibilities were subject to fundamental alterations. American religion generally changed in the aftermath of the Great Awakening of the early eighteenth century and the Second Great Awakening of the early nineteenth century. The various evangelicals, especially Methodists and Baptists, deeply influenced what we would call the psychology of Americans, as well as the terms in which they envisioned and communicated with their gods.

Despite differences of mentality wrought by greater or lesser religiosity, psychology—when used carefully, perhaps gingerly—provides a valuable means of understanding people and families who cannot be brought to the analyst's couch. Ideally historians could enter a kind of "Star Trek" realm of virtual reality in which we could hold intelligent conversations with the dead, then remand them to their various hells, purgatories, and heavens and return to our computers. Lacking this facility, we can only read twentieth-century practitioners and enter the archives with our eyes wide open.

Even without the benefit of an esoteric knowledge of psychology, we readily acknowledge the existence of certain conventions associated with slavery: the use of physical violence to make slaves obedient and submissive, the unquestioned right of owners to use the people they owned in whatever ways they wished. But we may need to be reminded that these habits also translate into a set of ideals that were associated with white women in middle- and upper-class families and into another set of ideals identified with evangelical religion. Submission and obedience, the core values of slavery, were also the key words of patriarchy and piety.

Because the standard of slavery calibrated values in other core institutions, slavery deserves recognition as one of the fundamental influences on American family mores and, by extension, on American society as a whole. Religion, democracy, the frontier, patriarchy, and mobility are all recognized as having played their part in the making of American families and American history. Slavery also counted, and not merely for Americans who experienced it as captive, unpaid laborers.

No matter how much American convention exempts whites from paying any costs for the enslavement of blacks, the implications of slavery did not stop at the color line; rather, slavery's theory and praxis permeated the whole of slave-holding society. Without seeking to establish one-to-one relationships or direct lines of causality, I will pose questions and suggest answers that may foster more comprehensive and feminist thinking about American history. Ironically, perhaps, names that have only recently been coined help reinterpret the past.

The fields of study focusing on child abuse, sexual harassment, and sexual abuse were born in the 1960s and 1970s. In the last decade or so these fields have grown and supplied therapists, medical doctors, recovering victims, lawyers, and feminists, some of whom were looking for the roots of women's impaired self-esteem, others of whom were seeking to right the wrongs that women have suffered in patriarchal families and in the workplace. Perhaps the appearance of professionals who profit from suits over child abuse, sexual abuse, and sexual harassment is inevitable in a capitalist society. Nonetheless, the profit-making aspect of the phenomenon of recall has provoked a good deal of commentary about suppressed memory and false memory. The debate now centers mainly on women who can afford therapists and lawyers and whose family mores and career chances have encouraged the suppression rather than the reporting of unacceptable memories. Much commentary on child sexual abuse—currently the most discussed form of violence against the young—involves what the skeptical philosopher, Ian Hacking, terms "memoro-politics." His and psychologist Carol Tavris's doubts are institutionalized in the False Memory Syndrome Foundation, founded in Philadelphia in 1992.[5] This controversy obscures the subjectivity of enslaved people, whose victimization is well documented and uncontested.

American habits of thought—what Marxist philosopher and critic Louis Althusser and Pierre Macherey call "ideology"—have rendered the experience of slaves utterly invisible in the literature of child abuse. No one at all disputes the fact that these children and women endured hurts that they did not forget, yet these victims do not currently figure in the consideration of the effects of child abuse and sexual harassment. An example is to be found in the widely acclaimed work of Judith Herman, one of the premier analysts of sexual abuse, who includes a chapter entitled "Captivity" in her second book, *Trauma and Recovery*. Here the captivity in question is figurative rather than literal, as was the detention of millions of American slaves over several generations.[6]

For most scholars of child abuse and sexual abuse, slavery possesses neither a literal meaning nor consequences; it serves only as a potent, negative metaphor. As a historian familiar with the institution that existed throughout most of American territory into the early nineteenth century, I *do* want to think literally: I want to investigate the consequences of child abuse and sexual abuse on an entire society in which the beating and raping of enslaved people was neither secret nor metaphorical.

The first step is to think about slaves as people with all the psychological characteristics of human beings, with childhoods and adult identities formed during youthful interaction with others. As ordinary as is the assumption that white people evolve psychologically from childhood to adulthood, to speak of black people in psychological terms can be problematical, for this history has a history. Much of scholars' and readers' reluctance to deal with black people's psychology goes back to the 1960s debate over Stanley Elkins's *Slavery: A Problem in American Institutional and Intellectual Life* (Chicago: University of Chicago Press, 1959), which provoked extensive criticism and revision.

Acknowledging the "spiritual agony" inherent in American slavery, Elkins compared slavery in the American South with Nazi concentration camps, in which, he thought, an all-encompassing system of repression infantilized people who had been psychologically healthy. Elkins wrote that on southern plantations and in Nazi concentration camps, inmates *"internalized"* their masters' attitudes. Drawing a flawed analogy between concentration camps, which existed for a few years, and slavery, which persisted over many generations and was psychologically more porous, Elkins argued that the closed system of slavery produced psychologically crippled adults who were docile, irresponsible, loyal, lazy, humble, and deceitful, in short, who were Sambos. With regard to both slavery and concentration camps, Elkins's methodology was more psychological than archival, and he also overlooked resistance in both contexts. In the American South, Elkins ignored the significance of slave families and communities and the long tradition of resistance and revolt, as chronicled in Herbert Aptheker's *American Negro Slave Revolts* (New York: International Publishers, 1943).[7]

The scholarship that appeared in the 1970s and 1980s provided a more complete view of slaves and slave families than Elkins had presented in the broken-up character of Sambo. Yet since the thunder and lightning of the Elkins controversy—even after the appearance of extensive revisionist writing—scholars and lay people have avoided, sometimes positively resisted, the whole calculation of slavery's psychological costs. The Sambo problem was solved through the pretense that black people do not have psyches.

The prevailing wisdom says that strong black people functioned as members of a group, "the black community," as though black people shared a collective psyche whose only perception was racial, as if race obviated the need to discuss black people's subjective development. Within this black community, the institution of "the black family" appeared preternaturally immune to the brutality inherent in slavery. Black patriarchy with a human face appears in much of this post-Elkins writing, particularly in the case of the well-intentioned work of Herbert Gutman, which refuted a 1965 report by Daniel Patrick Moynihan that blamed poverty and criminality on black families.[8] In family groups or as individuals, slaves emerged from historians' pages in the pose of lofty transcendence over racist adversity. Any analysis hinting that black people suffered psychological trauma as a result of the vicious physical and emotional practices that slavery entailed seemed tantamount to recapitulating Elkins and admitting the defeat of the race at the hands of bigots.

Rejecting that reasoning is imperative, because denying slaves psychological personhood impoverishes the study of everyone in slave-holding society. Historians already realize that including enslaved workers as part of the American working classes recasts the labor history of the United States; similarly, envisioning slaves as people who developed psychologically sheds new light on the culture of violence in which they matured.

Societies whose economic basis rested on slave production were built on violence, and the calculus of slavery configured society as a whole, as nineteenth-century analysts realized. When proslavery apologists spoke of owners and slaves as belonging to the same family, they were acknowledging the relationship between modes of production, politics, family, and society that three other nineteenth-century commentators, Karl Marx, Friedrich Engels, and Alexis de Tocqueville, also perceived. From very different vantage points and with quite different emphases, Tocqueville in *Democracy in America* and Marx and Engels in *The German Ideology* recognized the influence of the political economy on civil society. For Marx and Engels, "the production of ideas, of conceptions, of consciousness, is at first directly interwoven with the material activity and the material intercourse of men," which they totaled up as "the language of real life." Material existence, they said, shapes the relationships between husbands and wives and between parents and children that we term "*family*" and that they underlined in the original.[9]

Peering through the lens of political economy, Marx and Engels spoke in the interest of workers, but Tocqueville, who was more comfortable with people of his own privileged class, unabashedly admired what he called the democracy of the United States. Moving among Americans who had flourished since the American Revolution, Tocqueville in his appraisal of the consequences of American institutions was generally positive. He credited American political arrangements with the creation of more democratic relationships within American families, but he also traced democracy's limits. Where there was slavery, he noted, democracy could not do its salutary work. Slavery was "so cruel to the slave," but it was "fatal to the master," for it attacked American society through opinions, character, and style and devalued the ideals that undergird democratic society.[10]

Marx and Engels may have overestimated the ramifications of the dominant mode of production, and Tocqueville may have held too sanguine a view of the potential of political democracy within the household, but all three remind us that political and economic life shape families and households. This point has been rephrased by authorities of our own time. Twentieth-century commentators like Louis Althusser modify Marx and Engels's analysis of relations between the economic base and the social superstructure but nonetheless relate the institutions of civil society, including the family, to the political economy. Psychoanalyst Jacques Lacan indicates the crucial role of the family—the role of the father, in particular—in reproducing on a subjective level the power relations of the political economy.[11] When the household was also a work site, the influence of labor relations within families would have been magnified.

CHILD ABUSE AND SLAVERY

Slave owners, slaves, jurists, abolitionists, and historians all have recognized personal violence as a component of the regulation of owned labor; as Charles

Pettigrew, a slaveholder, wrote to his son: "It is a pity that . . . Slavery and Tyranny must go together and that there is no such thing as having an obedient and useful Slave, without the painful exercise of undue and tyrannical authority." Tyrannical authority there was in abundance, and slave children's parents, even when they were present, could not save their babies. It was as though a slave mother's children were not her own, a former slave recalled: "Many a day my old mamma has stood by an' watched massa beat her chillun 'till dey bled an' she couldn' open her mouf."[12] From an entirely different vantage point, southern judiciaries acknowledged that owners needed and should lawfully exercise total power over their slaves. The central legal tenet of slavery was summed up by a southern judge: "The power of the master must be absolute, to render the submission of the slave perfect." Kenneth Stampp entitled the fourth chapter of *The Peculiar Institution*, "To Make Them Stand in Fear."[13]

On the personal level, the evidence of this kind of discipline is heartbreaking, whether between master and slave, slave parent and child, or across the generations. When he was a child, fugitive slave narrator William Wells Brown witnessed the harrowing scene of his mother being flogged for going late into the fields. Years later Brown recalled that "the cold chills ran over me, and I wept aloud." Sojourner Truth, who was beaten as a slave in New York's Hudson Valley in the early nineteenth century, beat her own children—to make them obedient and to stop their hungry cries when her work prevented her from feeding them.[14] One of the most vivid testimonies of the intergenerational effect of child beating in slavery appears in oral testimony gathered one hundred years after the abolition of slavery. In Theodore Rosengarten's *All God's Dangers*, an old black Alabamian, Ned Cobb (alias Nate Shaw), laments that his father, Hayes, who had been a slave for his first fifteen years, beat his children and his wives as he himself had been beaten.[15] Cobb testifies to two kinds of hurt, for in addition to himself having been flogged, he was haunted by his father's brutal attacks on his mother and stepmother.

Masters beat slave children to make them into good slaves. Slave parents beat children to make them regard obedience as an automatic component of their personal makeup that was necessary for survival in a cruel world, a world in which they were to be first and always submissive. In other words, slave parents beat slave children to make them into good slaves. Their motives differed radically, but the aims of masters and parents coincided.

Parents and owners taught slave children to quash their anger when they were beaten, for anger was a forbidden emotion for slaves to display before owners. A Virginia owner summed up the prevailing wisdom among his peers in these phrases: "They Must obey at all times, and under all circumstances, cheerfully and with alacrity." Suppression of this kind of anger is one of the characteristics of what psychologist Alice Miller terms the "poisonous peda-gogy" of child abuse, and it has certain fairly predictable effects on its victims: feelings of degradation and humiliation, impaired identity formation, suppres-sion of vitality and creativity, deadening of feeling of self, anger, hatred, and self-hatred on the individual level and violence on the social level.[16]

Slave children, particularly those whose mothers worked in the fields, were also very likely to suffer physical and emotional neglect, because their mothers were rarely allowed much time off the job to spend with their children. Child care by people other than mothers could be adequate, as in the case of the young Frederick Douglass, who began his life in the custody of his maternal grandmother. But in other situations, the caretakers of children might be too old, too young, or too infirm to provide adequate supervision. Ex-slave narra-tives illustrate child-rearing patterns that forced hardworking parents to ne-glect their children and that, as a consequence, often denied babies the oppor-tunity to attach to a parent or parental figure securely.[17]

The slave trade, which disrupted an estimated one-third of all slave families in the antebellum South, also took a devastating emotional toll, as antislavery writing and iconography illustrated.[18] As a young child in New York State, Sojourner Truth lived with her own parents, but they were chronically de-pressed as a result of having sacrificed their children to the market, one after the other. Such forfeiture would have been tantamount to having one's child die, and Truth's grieving parents lost ten children to this callous trade.

In slave societies, neglect was routine, abuse was rampant, and anger was to be suppressed. The question regarding the neglect and physical abuse of slave children is not whether they took place—everyone agreed that they did—but rather, what they meant to the children and adults who experienced them. Did the whipping that was so central a part of child rearing and the enforcement of discipline among slaves affect them and their families as child abuse trauma-tizes twentieth-century victims?

There is evidence that the child abuse of slavery imposed enormous costs. The relationship between abuse and repercussion is not simple or predeter-mined, but the damage is frequent enough to be recognizable. For countless women and children, these injuries were magnified by the intimate nature of the abuse.

SEXUAL ABUSE AND SEXUAL HARASSMENT

Like child beating in slavery, the sexual torment of slave women and children has been evident for more than a century. Some of this mistreatment occurred in situations that we now recognize as sexual harassment on the job, and some occurred within households—which were work sites for hundreds of thousands of slave women—and with overtones of incest. One well-known figure exemplifies both patterns.

While many ex-slave narratives mention master-slave sexuality, the most extended commentary on the sexual harassment of slave women comes from Harriet Jacobs, who was a slave in Edenton, North Carolina. Writing under the pseudonym Linda Brent, Jacobs published a narrative in 1861, entitled *Incidents in the Life of a Slave Girl*. Jacobs's character, Linda, becomes the literal embodiment of the slave as sexual quarry in the testimony of slaves. We know from the work of critic Jean Yellin that *Incidents in the Life of a Slave Girl* is autobiography, and that Jacobs's master harassed her sexually from the time she was thirteen. Her narrative is a story of pursuit, evasion, and, ultimately, escape, although in order to evade her owner Jacobs had to spend seven years closed up in her grandmother's tiny attic crawl space, unable to stand up straight, sweltering in the summer, cold in the winter. As portrayed in *Incidents in the Life of a Slave Girl*, much of Jacobs's life in North Carolina revolved around avoiding her master's advances.

Jacobs says that without her master's having succeeded in raping her, he inflicted injuries that young female slaves frequently suffered and that we would consider psychological. As she became nubile, she says, her master began to whisper "foul words in my ear," which robbed her of her innocence and purity, a phenomenon that psychologists call inappropriate sexualization, which encourages a child to interpret her own value primarily in sexual terms. Describing the effect of her master's "foul words" and the angry and jealous outbreaks from her mistress, Jacobs says she became, like any slave girl in her position, "prematurely knowing in evil things," including life in a household cum work site that was suffused with predation, infidelity, and rage.[19]

Jacobs commits an entire, highly charged chapter of *Incidents in the Life of a Slave Girl* to "The Jealous Mistress." The angry figure of the jealous mistress, frequently ridiculed, never seriously investigated, is so common in the literature of slavery as to have become a southern trope. Perhaps because I have my own jealous mistress, so to speak, I am certain that the figure deserves a longer, much longer look. My jealous mistress is Gertrude Thomas, of Augusta, Georgia, who kept a journal from the time she was fourteen years old in 1848 until 1889, when she was fifty-five. I helped edit and wrote the introduction to the publication of her journal: *The Secret Eye: The Journal of Ella Gertrude Clanton Thomas, 1848–1889*, edited by Virginia Burr and published by the University of North Carolina Press in 1990.

Although she was a jealous mistress, Gertrude Thomas becomes more easily understandable as the victim of adultery. According to the ostensible mores of her community, she stood near the pinnacle of society (as a woman, she was denied space at the very top). She was a plantation mistress in a society dominated by the minuscule proportion of white families that qualified as planters by owning twenty or more slaves; she was an educated woman at a time when only elite men could take higher education for granted; and she was white in a profoundly racist culture. Yet neither Gertrude Thomas's economic or educational advantages nor her social status protected her from what she saw as sexual competition from inferior women. She knew, as Mary Chesnut and her friends knew, that they were supposed to pretend not to see "what is as plain before their eyes as the sunlight."[20] The deception did not ease the discomfort, for Thomas knew and wrote that white men saw women—whether slave or free, wealthy or impoverished, cultured or untutored, black or white—as interchangeable. She and other plantation mistresses failed to elevate themselves sufficiently as women to avoid the pain of sharing their husbands with their slaves.

Preoccupied by the issue of competition between women, Thomas realized and recorded with tortuous indirection a central fact of her emotional life: that female slaves and female slaveholders were in the same sexual marketplace and that in this competition, free women circulated at a discount due to the ready availability of women who could be forced to obey. The existence in the same market for sex of women who were literally property lowered the value of Gertrude Thomas and her mother as sexual partners. The concept of women as property has long been evident to feminists as a powerful means of keeping women subjected.

The traffic in women, a phrase coined by the early twentieth-century American anarchist, Emma Goldman, is shorthand for cultural practices that anthropologists (such as Claude Lévi-Strauss) and psychoanalysts (such as Jacques Lacan) have seen as basic to human nature but that feminists have identified with patriarchy and considered devastating to women. The phrase reappears in a classic 1975 essay by feminist anthropologist Gayle Rubin, who analyzes the sex/gender system of several different cultures.[21] Although Rubin uses the concept of the traffic in women allegorically when she turns to American society, the notion of such a traffic is useful both literally and metaphorically with regard to American society during its nearly three centuries of slavery. Over the course of those ten or more generations, rich white women saw themselves in competition for the attention of husbands whose black partners were ideal women: Slave women had to come when summoned and were conceded no will of their own. Gertrude Thomas knew moments of despair over her husband's infidelities, but if she contemplated suicide, she censored the thought. Testimony from Kentucky captures marital strife more vividly.

Andrew Jackson, an ex-slave narrator, had belonged to a fiery preacher he called a "right down blower." Though the owner's preaching moved his congregation to tears, at home he and his wife quarreled bitterly over his attraction to their enslaved cook, Hannah. Jackson recalled hearing the wife accuse the preacher of having gone into the kitchen to see Hannah, which the preacher denied. "I know you have, you brute," Jackson quotes the wife crying, "I have a great mind to cut my own throat!" To this, Jackson says, the preacher replied, "I really wish you would." The wife understood his meaning: "Yes I presume you do, so that you could run to the kitchen, as much as you please, to see Hannah." Andrew Jackson concluded that slaveholders "had such bad hearts toward one another" because they treated their slaves so brutally.[22]

At the same time that jealous mistresses were angry over their husbands' adulterous conduct, slave women like Harriet Jacobs who were the husbands' prey realized fully that mistresses saw themselves (not the slaves) as the victims in these triangles. Slave women resented what they envisioned as their mistresses' narcissistic self-pity, and they returned their mistresses' anger in kind. Jacobs's outrage at her mistress is part of a larger phenomenon, for other ex-slave narrators, like Sojourner Truth, and historians, like Kenneth Stampp, Elizabeth Fox-Genovese, and Eugene Genovese, corroborate the existence of a good deal of resentment at jealous mistresses on the part of slave women. Slave women's anger has etched yet more deeply the unsympathetic portrait of women who held slaves. Today we can see that more was at stake than contention over the ultimate title of victim.

What slaves could seldom acknowledge and historians did not see is that attachment often lay at the core of slave women's resentment. With slave families constantly subject to disruption, mistresses often functioned as mothers—good or bad—to their young female slaves. In this sense, the bitterness that Linda Brent felt as the prey of her master emerged against her mistress, just as victims of incest often hate their mothers for not saving them from the sexual advances of fathers and stepfathers. Psychiatrist Judith Herman says that many sexually abused children feel deeply betrayed because their mothers or mother figures are not able to protect them. Victims who do not display anger at their abusers may displace their rage on to nonabusing but impotent parental figures: mothers.[23] The psychological dynamics of the heterogeneous households of slavery explicate attitudes and behaviors that cannot be explained if we deny to slaves the personhood that we grant to our own contemporaries.

It has been difficult for historians to view interracial households as families and slaves as workers and as people, but such understanding places the sexual abuse of slave women and children (including boys) within categories that are now familiar and that we now term sexual harassment. One of the founders of the field, Catharine A. MacKinnon, noted in the 1970s that poorer women seem more likely to suffer physical harassment than middle-class and career women, whose abuse is more often verbal.[24] This should alert us to the triple vulnerability of slave women; they were among the poorest of working women and members of a race considered inherently inferior, and, if they were domestic servants like Harriet Jacobs, they spent long hours in the company of the men who had power over them.

Psychologists say that children and young women who are sexually abused, like children who are beaten, tend to blame themselves for their victimization and consequently have very poor self-esteem. They may also see their sexuality as their only means of binding other people to them as friends or allies. Recent scholarship outlines a series of long-term psychological repercussions of sexual abuse and incest: depression, difficulty sleeping, feelings of isolation, poor self-esteem, difficulty relating to other people, contempt for all women including oneself, revictimization, and impaired sexuality that may manifest itself in behaviors that can appear as frigidity or promiscuity.[25] It is doubtful that slaves possessed an immunity that victims lack today.

While it is tempting to see all slaves as strong people who were able to transcend the savagery to which they were subjected from very early ages, ex-slave narratives also bear witness to much psychological hurt. What today's psychologists call anger, depression, and problems of self-esteem come through ex-slave narratives and attest to slaves' difficulty in securing unqualified trust. Theologian Benjamin Mays discerned the theme of personal isolation that pervaded black slave religion and that is movingly emblemized in spiritual songs. Their titles are embedded in American memory: "Sometimes I Feel Like a Motherless Child," "Nobody Knows the Trouble I've Seen," "I'm a Long Way from Home."[26] We are used to hearing such sentiments as poignant artistry, but they are also testimonies of desolation. Slaves' situation within a system built on violence, disfranchisement, and white supremacy was analogous to that of twentieth-century victims of abuse, and some slaves, like people today, responded with self-hatred, anger, and identification with the aggressor. As understandable as such responses would have been, they are not all there is to the story.

Were this analysis to stop here, it might seem to invite a rerun of the controversy over Stanley Elkins's *Slavery*, for I might seem to be saying, like Elkins, that slavery inflicted psychic wounds so severe that slaves were massively disabled psychologically. This is *not* a recapitulation of Stanley Elkins, because my arguments exceed Elkins's in two important ways: I insist, first, that slaves had two crucial means of support that helped them resist being damaged permanently by the assaults of their owners and their fellows; and second, that owners also inflicted the psychic damage of slavery upon themselves, their white families, and, ultimately, on their whole society.

BLACK PEOPLE'S MEANS OF SURVIVAL

Since the 1959 publication of Elkins's *Slavery*, historians such as John Hope Franklin and Earl E. Thorpe have presented evidence of the ways in which slaves seized the initiative and found "elbow-room" within a system that was meant to dehumanize them.[27] Once historians began to seek it, confirmation of slaves' resistance and survival appeared in abundance. The testimony comes from slaves and from owners, and it affirms that most slave women and men were able to survive slavery in a human and humane manner, particularly if they lived where they were surrounded by other blacks who were actual or fictive kin. Historians have concentrated their attention on the half or so of slaves in the antebellum South who lived on plantations with twenty or more bondspeople, and those were the people more likely to belong to a community of slaves. They did not, however, represent the totality of Americans who were enslaved. So far, unfortunately, the other half of southern slaves and virtually all northern slaves, who were surrounded by mostly white people, have received little scrutiny.[28] Slaves living in isolation would hardly have benefited from the psychological support that a slave community could provide.

Historians like Deborah White and John Blassingame show that plantation slaves' psychic health depended largely on two essential emotional counterweights to owners' physical and psychological assaults: the slaves' own families and a system of evangelical religious beliefs that repudiated the masters' religious and social ideology of white supremacy and black inferiority. Blassingame sees slave families as a source of psychic protection from slavery's onslaught and considers families "an important survival mechanism." (Had he been critiquing Elkins's whole argument, Blassingame might have extended this insight to concentration camps, where actual and fictive kin and comrades helped inmates resist their dehumanization.) Deborah White, writing as a feminist, is more explicit, and she explores slave women's own community in far more detail. White entitles one chapter of her book on plantation slave women "The Female Slave Network," in which she shows how slave women working together created their own internal rank ordering. Although their owners and other whites might dishonor and mistreat them, slave women forged "their own independent definition of womanhood" through their own web of women's relationships, which functioned as an antidote to slavery's degradation.[29]

White and Blassingame are supported by psychologists such as Gail Wyatt and M. Ray Mickey, who explain that the existence of a countervailing value system helps people who are abused resist internalizing their oppressors' devaluation of their worth.[30] Ex-slave narratives from the nineteenth and twentieth centuries make it clear that slaves could reject their masters' assumptions that slaves were constitutionally inferior as a people and that they deserved to be enslaved.

Slave religion also buttressed a countervailing belief system by promising that equity would ultimately prevail in God's world. During and after slavery, religion was an important means through which powerless people preserved their identity, as in the case of Sojourner Truth. Scholars such as Albert Raboteau, Gayraud S. Wilmore, and James Cone have shown how black people forged their own evangelical religion, which could be apocalyptic and reassuring. Wilmore, especially, indicates that a belief in the impending apocalypse, a perennial theme in American evangelicalism, served the particular needs of the black poor by promising that there would soon come a time when God would judge all people, that he would punish the wicked, who were the slaveholders, and reward the good, who were the slaves. Cone stresses slaves' identification with the crucifixion, which symbolizes Jesus' concern for the oppressed and his repudiation of the hierarchies of this world.[31]

Psychologists have noted that in situations where the individual is totally powerless, faith in a greater power than the self becomes a potent means of survival. Slaves with a firm religious belief were able to benefit from this nonmaterial source of support, which we recognize today in the methodology of twelve-step programs for overcoming addiction that begin by putting one's fate in the hands of a greater power than the self.[32]

In their appeal to countervailing ideologies, supportive communities, and spirituality, slaves were, in a sense, behaving like good feminists seeking means of lessening the power of oppression and sexual abuse in their lives. Having been identified and set apart as a despised race, slaves found it easier to create alternative ideologies than the white people—including women—who owned them and who told them what to do. There is no denying that white ladies were able to oppress slaves, but even so, the ladies lacked access to much of their society's other kinds of power. Of all the people living in slave-holding societies who might have benefited from an alternative system of values, rich white women were least likely to forge one. In the words of Catherine Clinton, plantation mistresses, unlike plantation slaves, "had no comparable sense of community."[33]

Owning as well as owned families paid a high psychological and physical cost for the child and sexual abuse that was so integral with slavery. First, despite what black and white scholars assume about the rigidity of the color bar, attachment and loss often transcended the barriers of race and class and flowed in both directions. The abuse of slaves pained and damaged nonslaves, particularly children, and forced those witnessing slave abuse to identify with the victim or the perpetrator.

Second, the values and practices of slavery, in particular the use of violence to secure obedience and deference, prevailed within white families as well. The ideals of slavery—obedience and submission—were concurrently and not accidentally the prototype of white womanhood and of evangelical piety, which intensified the prestige and reinforced the attraction of these ideals. Nineteenth-century evangelical religion meant various things to its many believers, and it could compel them toward startlingly different ideological conclusions, as exemplified in the North in the Jacksonian era. After the abolition of slavery in the North, evangelicalism fostered a profusion of convictions, including abolitionism and feminism; in the region still committed to slavery, however, evangelicalism produced no reforming offshoots that were allowed to flourish. Instead, unquestioning evangelical piety was more valued, and piety was another word for submission and obedience, terms that also figured prominently in the language of the family.

The imageries of religion and family have much in common, rhetorically and structurally, and scholars have repeatedly stressed the crucial role of human families as structural models both in religion and in slavery. Christians speak of God the Father, the Son, and the Holy Ghost, and Christians, Jews, and Muslims trace the origin of humankind to the family of Adam and Eve. Religions routinely evoke the language of kinship when sketching out holy relationships between gods and people.

Slavery and the family are just as inextricably intertwined, for the etymology of the word *family* reaches back to the Latin words *familia*, meaning a household, and *famulus/famula*, meaning servant or slave, deeply embedding the notion of servitude within our concept of family. As the ideals and practices of servitude, family, and religion are so firmly linked in this cultural system, a search for cause and effect is bound to prove frustrating. Even without recourse to relations of causality, however, the confluence of values is noteworthy.[34]

Slavery accentuated the hierarchical rather than the egalitarian and democratic strains in American culture, thereby shaping relations within and without families and polities. Patriarchal families, slavery, and evangelical religion further reinforced one another's emphasis on submission and obedience in civil society, particularly concerning people in subaltern positions.

Despite the existence of a wide spectrum of opinion on slavery and feminism, agreement exists on the close relationship between the concepts of the white woman and slavery. Proslavery apologists often insisted that the maintenance of slavery depended on the preservation of patriarchy within white families, arguing that white women, especially rich women, must remain in their places and be submissive to their fathers and husbands so that slaves would not conceive notions of equality. Similar motives prohibited white men from acknowledging publicly that white women commonly labored in southern fields at tasks that the culture reserved rhetorically for women who were enslaved.[35] The reasoning of proslavery apologia ran from women's honor to gender roles to black men–white women sex, skipping over the reality of white men's sexual use and abuse of black women in a manner that twentieth-century readers find remarkable: for its silences, its intertextuality, and its unabashed patriarchy. Of course, there is nothing at all contradictory between family feeling and hierarchy, between attachment and the conviction that some people absolutely must obey others.

Hierarchy by no means precludes attachment. Just as young slaves attached to the adults closest to them, white as well as black, so the white children and adults in slave-owning households became psychologically entangled with the slaves they came to know well. When Sojourner Truth's son, Peter, was beaten by his owner in Alabama, his mistress (who was Sojourner's mistress's cousin) salved his wounds and cried over his injuries. That story concluded with Peter's mistress's murder by the very same man, her husband, who had previously abused Peter. Like Peter's murdered mistress, other slave owners, especially women, grieved at the sight of slaves who had been beaten.

Abolitionist Angelina Grimké recalled scenes from her life as a privileged young woman in Charleston, South Carolina. When Grimké was about thirteen and attending a seminary for wealthy girls, a slave boy who had been severely battered was called into her classroom to open a window. The sight of his wounds was so painful to Grimké that she fainted. Her school was located near the workhouse where slaves were sent to be reprimanded. One of her friends who lived near it complained to Grimké that the screams of the slaves being whipped often reached her house. These awful cries from the workhouse terrified Grimké whenever she had to walk nearby.[36]

As slave-owning children grew into adults, their identification with victims or victimizers often accorded to gender. Elizabeth Fox-Genovese shows that mistresses could be cruel tormentors of their slaves.[37] But in comparison with masters, white women were more likely to take the side of the slaves, while white men nearly unanimously identified with the aggressor as a requisite of manhood. Becoming such a man did not happen automatically or painlessly. Playing on the patriarchy inherent in Western cultural institutions, which are also rooted in Christian religion, Jacques Lacan terms this socialization "the name-of-the-father."

Fathers ordinarily did the work of inculcating manhood, which included snuffing out white children's identification with slaves. In 1839 a Virginian named John M. Nelson described his shift from painful childhood sympathy to manly callousness. As a child, he would try to stop the beating of slave children and, he said, "mingle my cries with theirs, and feel almost willing to take a part of the punishment." After his father severely rebuked him several times for this kind of compassion, he "became so blunted that I could not only witness their stripes with composure, but *myself* inflict them, and that without remorse."[38] The comments of Thomas Jefferson on this whole subject are revealingly oblique.

Thomas Jefferson, Founding Father, slave owner, author of the Declaration of Independence, and acknowledged expert on his own state of Virginia and the United States generally, wrote *Notes on the State of Virginia* in response to a questionnaire from François Marbois, the secretary of the French legation at Philadelphia. Between 1780 and 1785 Jefferson codified his social, political, scientific, and ethical convictions. Jefferson did not have a very high opinion of Africans, though American Indians, he thought, would display their real and substantial worth when afforded decent opportunities. Jefferson found African Americans stupid and ugly, a people more or less well suited to the low estate they occupied in eighteenth-century Virginia. Contrary to facile assumption, Jefferson's appraisal of the capacities of Africans did not make him an unequivocal supporter of slavery. Nonetheless, as a gentleman whose entire material existence depended on the produce of his slaves, he was never an abolitionist. In fact, his reluctance to interfere with slavery hardened as he aged. By 1819, as the Missouri Compromise was being forged, Jefferson was warning American politicians not, under any circumstances, to tamper with slavery, even though he realized that by preserving slavery, the United States was holding "a wolf by the ears."[39]

Jefferson's reservations about slavery pertained to the owners of slaves, not to the slaves themselves. Being the property of other people was not noxious to blacks, he thought, but owning slaves entailed great drawbacks for whites. Jefferson recognized that the requirements of slave ownership "nursed, educated, and daily exercised" habits of tyranny, and he observed that "[t]he man must be a prodigy who can retain his manners and morals undepraved by such circumstances." In this part of his discussion, Jefferson's customary verbal talent and intellectual suppleness turned into obfuscation. He veiled his explanation of the bad things that slavery did to slaveholders and was only able to write, intriguingly, of slavery's breeding "odious peculiarities."

Jefferson's phrasing does not appeal to today's family systems theorists and psychoanalysts, who use instead the language of triangles to explain family relationships, including those that are violent. Children who are observers of abuse are likely to assume the position of the other members of the triangle: either by becoming victims themselves or by abusing others, especially younger siblings or children in positions of relative weakness.[40] This is the kind of repercussion that eighteenth- and nineteenth-century observers like Thomas Jefferson were deploring through euphemism.

So far in this discussion, only slaves have figured as the victims of physical and psychological abuse. But the ideals of slavery affected families quite apart from the toll they exacted from the bodies and psyches of blacks. Thanks to the abundance of historical scholarship that concentrates on antebellum southern society, it is possible to reach some generalizations regarding whites. But even in the slave South, historians have been much less aware of the abuse of white women than of the oppression of black slaves. Abuse there was, as the diary of Baltimorean Madge Preston indicates.[41]

Petitions for divorce and church records show that wife beating was a common motive for the attempted dissolution of marriages and the expulsion of men and women from church membership. Doubtless this was true in nonslave-holding regions as well. What is noteworthy in this context, as Stephanie McCurry shows for the South Carolina low country, is that legislators and church leaders routinely urged women to remain in abusive unions and to bear abuse in a spirit of submission.[42] In the hard-drinking antebellum South, which was well known for rampant violence against slaves and between white men, white women had little recourse when their husbands beat them, for, in general, the southern states were slow to grant women the legal right to divorce or to custody of their children in cases of separation. Until the 1830s, southern states lacked divorce laws, and state legislatures heard divorce petitions on a case-by-case basis. The result was a small number of divorces granted inconsistently and according to the social and economic status of the petitioner in her community.

The disposal of the small number of cases of incest that came before judges also illuminates the reasoning of the men who exercised power in the slave South. As in instances of wife beating, so in cases of incest, judges preferred to investigate the flaws of the female petitioner, who, even despite extreme youth, usually came to be seen as consenting. Not surprisingly, incest seldom became public, but when it entered the criminal justice system, the girls in question were likely as not seen as accomplices in their own ravishment.

In the interests of preserving patriarchy, victims of incest, like victims of wife abuse, were abandoned by law and sacrificed to the ideal of submission. Legal historians like A. Leon Higginbotham and Peter Bardaglio have discovered that the southern lawmakers and judges who were anxious to regulate racialized sexuality were loathe to punish white men for sexual violence against white or black women and children.[43]

Incest and wife beating do not usually appear in general studies of the antebellum South, where the received wisdom, as in histories like Daniel Blake Smith's study of eighteenth-century planter society in the Chesapeake, is that planter families came to be child-centered and companionate.[44] Such a vision fails even to allow for the level of familial abuse that psychologists see as usual in twentieth-century households, where, according to the American Medical Association, one-quarter of married women will be abused by a current or former partner at some point during their lives.[45] Were planter families more straightforwardly loving than we? I think not.

KEEPING SECRETS FROM HISTORIANS

Aristocrats were skilled at keeping secrets and preserving appearances, as I know from experience with Gertrude Thomas. Only by reading her 1,380-page journal repeatedly was I able to discover her secrecy and self-deception. In this case, the secret I discovered was adultery, for both her father and her husband had outside wives and children. Her journal never reveals her other family secret, her husband's drunkenness, which was only preserved orally in family lore.

Then and now, family violence and child sexual abuse are usually concealed, and the people with the most privacy, the wealthy, are better at preserving their secrets than poor people, who live their lives in full view of the rest of the world. Scholars have connived with wealthy families to hide child sexual abuse among people of privilege, which one psychologist concludes is "most conspicuous for its presumed absence."[46] This is an old, old story.

In the 1890s Sigmund Freud discovered the prevalence of incest as a cause of hysteria; when his professional colleagues objected to what he had found, he reworked his theory into fantasy and the oedipal complex. In 1932 Freud's friend and protégé, Sandor Ferenczi, reestablished the facts that childhood sexual trauma was common in the best of families and that it was devastating to emotional development. A few months after he presented his paper,

"Confusion of Tongues between Adults and the Child," to the International Psycho-Analytic Congress in Wiesbaden, Ferenczi died, and his theory died with him. In the 1980s Jeffrey Masson revealed Freud's about-face and was drummed out of psychoanalysis.[47] Historians who have taken their sources at face value have missed the family secrets of slave-owning households, but in their unwillingness to see, they find themselves in distinguished psychological company.

Some historians are ready to examine their sources more critically. Recent books by Richard Bushman and critic Jay Fliegelman alert us that by the late eighteenth and early nineteenth centuries, wealthy Americans had come to prize gentility so highly that they spent enormous amounts of time and energy creating pleasing appearances. Bushman and Fliegelman say, and I concur, that the letters, speeches, and journals that historians have used as the means of uncovering reality and gauging consciousness ought more properly to be considered self-conscious performances intended to create beautiful tableaux. People with sufficient time, space, and money modeled themselves on characters in novels and acted out what they saw as appropriate parts. What was actually taking place at home was another story entirely, which was not necessarily preserved for our easy investigation.[48] If historians are to understand the less attractive and deeply buried aspects of slave society, the scales will have to fall from their eyes. They will have to see beyond the beauty of performance and probe slavery's family romance more skeptically.

Once we transcend complete reliance on the written record, deception clues are not hard to see: The eloquent violence, alcoholism, and invalidism of eighteenth- and nineteenth-century America (and especially of the nineteenth-century South) could not be concealed, and they point to the existence of compelling family secrets. In the 1940s southern author Lillian Smith summed up the society in which she lived in a phrase that applies to slave societies. Smith said that her thoroughly segregated South, with its myriad instances of bad faith, was "pathological."[49]

Historians need to heed the wisdom of psychologists, take Lillian Smith to heart, look beneath the gorgeous surface that cultured slave owners presented to the world, and pursue the hidden truths of slavery, including soul murder and patriarchy. The task is essential, for our mental health as a society depends on the ability to see our interrelatedness across lines of class and race, in the past, as in the present.

Two women stood before judges in the early twentieth century, both having been accused of transmitting typhoid fever as they carried out their work of cooking for other people. Ostensibly they were in court because public health officials thought that they endangered the health of people around them. Indeed, both had been found to harbor typhoid bacilli and were capable of infecting others through food contaminated with the pathogenic bacteria from their urine or feces. In addition to the laboratory findings and the public health threat, another factor stands out as also prominent in determining the fate of these women before the bench: ideas about proper womanly behavior. The authorities concerned with these cases believed not just that the bacilli and food handling made the women dangerous, but that women were more dangerous than men because cooking was a traditional and necessary female activity. One woman was a New Yorker, Mary Mallon, known to the world as "Typhoid Mary." The other was Chicagoan Jennie Barmore, defended before the Illinois Supreme Court by Clarence Darrow. The stories of these two women can be told as episodes in early twentieth-century public health, whereby science, demonstrating new ways to control the spread of infectious disease, triumphs over sickness. Such a telling would mark the gendered words of the public health officials or the court (if it noticed them at all) as unimportant to the larger story of the healing

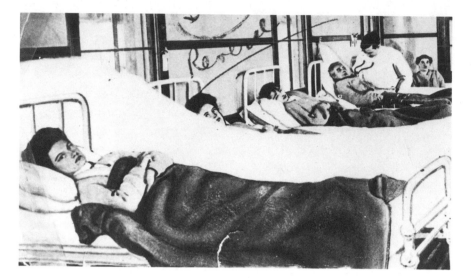

Mary Mallon in bed at Willard Parker Hospital. The photograph was presumably taken when she was first admitted to the hospital in March 1907, but it did not appear in print until the time of the habeas corpus hearing in June 1909. (Courtesy UPI/Bettmann)

potential and march of progress of medical science. But by centering the women as well as the science, we can demonstrate that cultural gendered expectations about who women were and what they did formed important elements in determining the activities of early twentieth-century public health. The progress of science was not the only factor affecting public health actions. As women's historians have demonstrated over and over again in the last twenty-five years, we can enrich and make more complex our understanding of the past; indeed, we can often completely transform our understanding of the past, by including gender considerations as part of our analysis.[1]

In emphasizing the gendered significance of the cases in this essay, I do not in any way mean to diminish the importance of other elements. Elsewhere I have explored the Mary Mallon episode as an illustration of early bacteriological practices, and I am working on other aspects of the civil dilemma she posed for health officials who were trying to protect the public's health and at the same time not infringe on the rights of individual citizens.[2] Yet in studying the documents left to us, I have been struck by the prominence of the gendered language used to describe the experiences and fate of Mallon and Barmore; I am convinced that this language reveals an important determinant of the public officials' and the courts' actions. Public health officials employed gender stereotyping to support and uphold their activities and thereby to gain public acceptance of them. Both informal utterances and more formal legal discourse divulge some deeper meanings for some of the health officials' actions. Early twentieth-century public health texts provide insight into social views about women and how those views affected the treatment women received in medical and legal contexts.

The specific words chosen by the people who pushed Mallon and Barmore to seek legal redress reveal gendered meanings that historians cannot ignore. New York health officials portrayed Mary Mallon as "masculine" in her walk and her thinking. Chicago public health physicians insisted that Jennie Barmore, if freed, would immediately go and cook for her friends. Neither of these perceptions was a necessary part of the scientific indictment against these women (which could have been phrased in laboratory and scientific language alone), yet health officials used them nonetheless in framing their case. What impact did the gendered expectations embedded in these descriptions of behavior have on the outcome for the two women? Why did officials find it necessary to add gendered arguments to their indictment of Mallon and Barmore when establishing that their bodies were infectious? These questions must be explored in order to understand the full nature of public health activities and public policy during that period. Gendered subjective sentiments were woven into the fabric of public health even during the very years when the new science of bacteriology seemed to be pushing the field in the direction of greater objectivity.

Before examining the specific events in Mary Mallon's and Jennie Barmore's stories, it is necessary to explain the medical context in which they took place. The turn of the twentieth century was one of the most exciting and dramatic periods in all of medical history. At the end of the nineteenth century, medical scientists had come to accept germ theory, a new theory of disease causation brought to medicine through basic science research. Laboratory experiments established that microorganisms could cause disease, a conceptualization that radically altered previous views and seemed to make unnecessary the widescale urban cleanups and social welfare programs that had characterized activity under the older filth theory of disease.

Formerly, people's whole lives came under the purview of health officials who were trying to stem the tides of disease; in future, officials would need to concentrate only on the microbes. Because microbes could not distinguish between rich and poor, black and white, men and women, many people engaged in public health at the new century's debut believed that the new bacteriologically based public health would be more evenhanded than its predecessors. The reduction of public health science to the microbe would narrow public health activity and make it more equitable. While few cures had emerged from the study of microorganisms by the beginning of the century, bacteriology was brimming over with assurances for the future. The optimism led public health physicians—those in the front-line confrontation with infectious disease in the cities where death rates soared along with the population—to search out answers from the new science and from the laboratory whenever possible.[3]

Typhoid fever had been one of the nineteenth century's major killers. A water- and food-borne systemic bacterial infection, typhoid caused sustained fever, headache, malaise, and gastrointestinal problems in its victims. Although many mild cases occurred, typhoid carried a case fatality rate of about 10 percent.[4] It struck most harshly those cities that sent untreated lake or river water through the pipes; thus it responded well to water filtration systems and sanitation efforts instituted during the last third of the nineteenth century or in the early years of the twentieth century.[5] Urban sanitation campaigns brought significant reductions in death rates from typhoid fever, but the disease did not disappear as a public health problem. Early twentieth-century bacteriologists tried to understand how this bacterial infection continued to thrive in relatively clean city environments. In 1902 bacteriological studies in Europe finally led to the realization that typhoid, along with diphtheria and a few other diseases, could be transmitted by healthy people. Mary Mallon was the first healthy carrier to be carefully traced in North America. The excitement about her case, as well as some of the confusions surrounding it, must be seen within this context of the scientific breakthrough that she represented. She was the first of hundreds of New Yorkers whom the health department accused of sheltering typhoid bacilli in their gallbladders and, through their urine and feces via unwashed hands, transmitting the germs to susceptible and unsuspecting people and making them sick.

Mary Mallon provided the nation's first publicized test case of how to stop healthy people from transmitting typhoid fever to others; thus, this essay concentrates on her story. Jennie Barmore's situation offered an important adjunct to Mallon's and was more important as legal precedent. Although the sagas of these two women represent one extreme of what was possible in public efforts to protect the public health and welfare, and not the norm, they are instructive to study nonetheless, because they reveal the broad spectrum of factors that could and did influence public health policy. In this early twentieth-century period of medical breakthroughs and scientific excitement, public health officials brought more than laboratory findings to bear in their decisions about how to best protect the public.

Mary Mallon was a peripatetic Irish-born cook living in New York City at the turn of the twentieth century. She hired herself out to wealthy families, finding most of her placements through an employment agency. Some of her assignments lasted for years; often she stayed a few weeks or months before moving to a different family. Reputedly, she was a good cook; she did not have difficulty finding work. Her career pattern was completely ordinary, following the limited opportunities available to single women of her ethnicity and class.[6] During the fine summer days of August 1906, she cooked meals in the household of a New York banker, Charles Henry Warren, at the family's rented summer residence in Oyster Bay, Long Island. Within weeks of her arrival, six persons in the household of eleven were attacked by typhoid fever. Those stricken included Warren's wife and two daughters, two domestic workers, one white and one black, and the gardener. The initial investigation revealed that this particular household epidemic had not been caused by contaminated water or milk (frequent sources of typhoid infection); nor had the family consumed any infected clams from the bay. The owner of the house hired George Soper, a sanitary engineer trained at Columbia University and known for his epidemiological work on typhoid fever, to investigate.[7]

Having read the latest literature out of Europe positing healthy people as carriers of typhoid fever, and ruling out family members and other servants, Soper focused on trying to find the cook who had been employed by the family only three weeks before the outbreak and who left the family three weeks after it. By tracing the cook's job history before her arrival in Oyster Bay, with the help of her employment agency, he identified eight families who had employed her; in seven of them typhoid fever had followed her stay. Soper became convinced that if Mary Mallon could be found, and her feces and urine tested, he could prove in the laboratory what his epidemiological study had already shown: that she, although healthy, had transmitted typhoid fever to those who unsuspectingly ate the food she prepared.

It took Soper until March 1907 to trace Mallon to her current employment in a home on New York's Park Avenue. He later described what happened: "I had my first talk with Mary in the kitchen of this house.... I was as diplomatic as possible, but I had to say I suspected her of making people sick and that I wanted specimens of her urine, feces and blood. It did not take Mary long to react to this suggestion. She seized a carving fork and advanced in my direction. I passed rapidly down the long narrow hall, through the tall iron gate, ... and so to the sidewalk. I felt rather lucky to escape."[8] Unable to obtain Mallon's cooperation in the investigation and thinking the epidemiological evidence sufficiently compelling, Soper reported his findings to Hermann M. Biggs, medical officer of the New York City Department of Health, with the recommendation that Mary Mallon be apprehended.

The health department did not find it any easier to get Mallon's cooperation. Possibly thinking that a woman could most easily approach another woman, Biggs sent Dr. S. Josephine Baker, a medical inspector in the department (later director of the Bureau of Child Hygiene), to collect specimens of urine, feces, and blood. Dr. Baker's first visit with Mallon in the East Side brownstone yielded nothing: she, too, was summarily dismissed. Interpreting this as a case of "blind, panicky distrust of doctors and all their works which crops up so often among the uneducated," Baker returned the next day, this time accompanied by three police officers and an ambulance. The young physician was again overpowered by the resistant cook: "Mary was on the lookout and peered out, a long kitchen fork in her hand like a rapier. As she lunged at me with the fork, I stepped back, recoiled on the policeman and so confused matters that, by the time we got through the door, Mary had disappeared. 'Disappear' is too matter-of-fact a word; she had completely vanished."[9]

Baker enlisted more police, and the search continued for five hours. The servants, showing what Baker recognized as "class solidarity," denied any knowledge of her whereabouts. Finally, one of the police officers saw a bit of calico showing in the doorway of the space under the outside steps, where they had not looked because of the dozens of filled ashcans heaped up in front of it (more evidence of her colleagues' support). Again Baker described the scene:

> She came out fighting and swearing, both of which she could do with appalling efficiency and vigor. I made another effort to talk to her sensibly and asked her again to let me have the specimens, but it was of no use. By that time she was convinced that the law was wantonly persecuting her, when she had done nothing wrong. She knew she had never had typhoid fever; she was maniacal in her integrity. There was nothing I could do but take her with us. The policemen lifted her into the ambulance and I literally sat on her all the way to the hospital; it was like being in a cage with an angry lion.[10]

Examination of Mallon's feces showed a high concentration of typhoid bacilli, proving in the laboratory that Soper's epidemiological study had been correct in its target: Mary Mallon was, in the press's words, a walking "human culture tube."[11] With active *salmonella typhi* bacilli in her feces, when she did not wash her hands thoroughly after using the bathroom, she transferred the germs to others for whom she cooked. She was held, against her will, in the Willard Parker Hospital and later moved to North Brother Island in the East River.

Although presumably proud of its discovery of the first healthy carrier in the country, the health department did not publicize the capture of Mary Mallon. Probably, it did not want to cause public panic. Moreover, the health officials were uncertain about the legal ramifications of their actions. Never before had the department faced the issue of locking up a healthy individual on the basis of laboratory reports. William Park, the health department bacteriologist, voiced the worry about the potentially long-term incarceration of healthy persons—the carrier state might last a lifetime—when he asked in his first paper on Mary Mallon: "Has the city a right to deprive her of her liberty for perhaps her whole life?"[12] Did police powers stretch that far?

While this question percolated, Mary Mallon remained in quarantine. Obviously bitter about her incarceration, she spent her days alone in a cottage on the grounds of Riverside Hospital, the isolation facility on North Brother Island. A hospital attendant brought her meals to the door and left; she saw no one. She wrote "violently threatening letters" to Hermann Biggs (none of which seems to have survived) and kept up with events by reading the daily newspaper.[13] Ultimately, the press discovered her whereabouts and publicized her story, although without using her name, which reporters were unable to learn from the health officials.[14] In the wake of public notice, and with a lawyer hired possibly through the Hearst newspaper, the *New York American*, which actively pursued the story, Mary Mallon decided to sue for release. On June 28, 1909, she and her lawyer filed a writ of habeas corpus with the New York Supreme Court, claiming that she was in perfect health and that she was being held "forcibly and without warrant or order of any character" and "that she is not in any way or any degree a menace to the community or any part thereof."[15] The *American* quoted Mallon as saying in court: "I never had typhoid in my life, and have always been healthy. Why should I be banished like a leper and compelled to live in solitary confinement with only a dog for a companion? . . . I am an innocent human being. I have committed no crime and I am treated like an outcast—a criminal. It is unjust, outrageous, uncivilized. It seems incredible that in a Christian community a defenseless woman can be treated in this manner." The newspaper voiced sympathy with Mallon's plight.[16]

The court decision came on July 16, 1909: the judge ruled that indeed Mary Mallon was a menace to the public health and that she must remain in health department custody. Newspapers quoted the judge as saying, "While the court deeply sympathizes with this unfortunate woman, it must protect the community against a recurrence of spreading the disease."[17]

The one remaining letter in Mary Mallon's hand is from this period, probably written in July 1909 during the legal proceedings, and it is the only direct source we have for understanding her perspective on the events. She was angry, and she directed her emotion against William Park, who had presented her case before medical audiences. She insisted that she was being kept a "prisoner without been sick nor needing medical treatment." The laboratory may have proved that her medical history included a case of typhoid fever, but she herself denied that she had ever been ill with the disease. She was aware of her situation and the stigma society attached to her. There had been, she said, a "visiting Doctor who came here in October he did take quite an interest in me he really thought I liked it here[,] that I did not care for my freedom." Mallon saw the situation clearly as one of lost liberty. She concluded her letter perceptively: "I have been in fact a peep show for Every body[;] even the Internes had to come to see me & ask about the facts alredy Known to the whole wide World[.] the Tuberculosis men would say there she is the Kidnapped woman[.] Dr. Parks [*sic*] has had me Illustrated in Chicago[.] I wonder how the Said Dr. Wm. H. Park would like to be insulted and put in the Journal & call him or his wife Typhoid William Park."[18]

After the court rejected her petition, Mary Mallon returned to North Brother Island, where she remained until a new health commissioner in 1910 decided to let her go. Ernst J. Lederle recognized that such a total isolation as Mallon had been subjected to was not medically indicated for typhoid fever carriers who were dangerous only when they cooked the food that others ate. He told the press, "She has been released because she has been shut up long enough to learn the precautions that she ought to take."[19] Lederle's compassion for Mallon was duly noted by the *American*, which quoted him as saying: "For Heaven's sake, can't the poor creature be given a chance to live? An opportunity to make her living, and have her past forgotten? She is to blame for nothing—and look at the life she led!"[20]

The health commissioner apparently helped Mary Mallon find employment in a laundry and did keep track of her for some time. But Mallon was not happy in another occupation and could not earn a good living away from the kitchen. She tried unsuccessfully to sue the city for damages and then faded from public view; in time, the health department also lost sight of Mary Mallon.

She did not hide for long, however. In early 1915 an outbreak of typhoid fever occurred at the Sloane Maternity Hospital in New York City. Twenty-five doctors, nurses, and hospital staff were stricken, and two died. A new cook, a Mrs. Brown, had been employed three months before the outbreak. Another dramatic arrest followed, as health department inspectors followed "a veiled woman," recognized by inspectors as Mary Mallon, to a Corona apartment, where, refused admission through the door, they pursued her with a ladder to the upper window. The health officers brought her back to the hospital, and Health Commissioner S. S. Goldwater promised that "she would never endanger the public health again."[21]

Indeed, she did not. This time Mary Mallon did not contest her quarantine, and she remained on North Brother Island for the rest of her life. Sometime in 1933 she suffered a stroke, and, paralyzed and unable to care for herself, she was hospitalized until her death on November 11, 1938. She had been in health department custody for a total of more than twenty-six years; at least forty-seven cases of typhoid fever had been traced to her, and three people had died. Nine mourners, three men, three women, and three girls, who would not identify themselves to reporters, paid her final tribute at her funeral in the Bronx. She was, it was estimated, seventy years old.[22]

The second arrest and proposed lifetime isolation of Mary Mallon evoked more newspaper copy and less sympathy than previous events. George Soper wrote sentiments that were echoed in the press: "Whatever rights she once possessed as the innocent victim of an infected condition . . . were now lost. She was now a woman who could not claim innocence. She was known wilfully and deliberately to have taken desperate chances with human life. . . . She had abused her privilege; she had broken her parole. She was a dangerous character and must be treated accordingly."[23]

At the time of Mary Mallon's second incarceration, Soper declared to the *New York Times*: "Liberty is an impossible privilege to allow her."[24] At that moment, in 1915, after Mary Mallon had persisted in cooking with the knowledge of three years of incarceration behind her, Soper did not see any conflict or dilemma in his statement. Liberty was not a right of citizenship, it was a privilege to be earned, and Mallon had abused the privilege. She knowingly continued to infect unsuspecting others. Earlier she may have been an innocent offender (although Soper had supported her isolation from the first), in 1915 she became a guilty one. Soper's explanation seemed to fit previous legal decisions: a minority need not be allowed to define the health standards of a whole community in its disinclination to cooperate with health authorities.[25]

Previous police power quarantine rulings had applied to sick people for a delimited amount of time.[26] In this instance, however, with the penalty applied to a healthy person and for an indefinite period, the case for quarantine was considerably more shaky. When Mallon had been isolated the first time, in March 1907, she was not sick nor was she yet a repeat offender. Furthermore, it had not been demonstrated that total isolation was necessary for healthy carriers of typhoid fever. If such people could be instructed in strict personal hygiene and if they would not cook for anybody other than themselves, they could walk the city streets without endangering anyone. George Soper himself conceded in 1915 that while "proper precautions" ought to be taught to healthy carriers, "this does not mean isolation, nor anything drastic. There is only one way that the germs can be transmitted, and that is through contact with the waste products of the body."[27] In retrospect, it seems that the health authorities acted very quickly in taking away Mallon's liberty without exploring other options that may have been available.[28]

Mary Mallon herself provided some of the earliest answers to the medical questions about the carrier state. While she was in isolation between 1907 and 1909, physicians tried various drug regimens, hoping to kill off the *salmonella typhi* bacilli in her body. They offered to excise her gallbladder, the organ harboring the bacilli, a surgical procedure that many physicians advised against as too dangerous. They carefully observed the vicissitudes of Mallon's bacteria counts, monitoring them three times a week.[29] They were learning, and Mary Mallon's body was their laboratory.

Mallon's personal liberty became expendable in the name of science and as insurance against the future. Practical considerations, most explicitly the limits of the state's ability to handle large numbers of noncooperative carriers, created the need to encourage others to go along with health department policies. As the *Medical Record* put it: "It is evident that [healthy carriers] cannot all be segregated and kept prisoners. . . . It would be difficult to obtain popular sanction to such interference with the liberty of apparently healthy individuals, and even if the measure were recognized as justifiable the number of bacilli carriers would render it difficult of execution."[30] If for practical reasons the state could only constrain a few, officials needed convincing arguments that would resonate widely. They built a case against Mallon in their efforts to provide an example, presumably believing her to be expendable in the larger battle to contain the disease. The question for historians is why Mallon became the example and what she was thought to exemplify. Was she isolated for life because she was the first healthy carrier in the nation to be carefully traced? Or was it that she personified other characteristics in the minds of the health officials?

There were many other healthy carriers found in New York City after 1907 who remained free, regulated by new department rules established just for them. Once apprised of the dangers that healthy people who handled food could pose, the health department in 1916 initiated a system of inspection of food handlers in the city.[31] In 1924, when a second healthy carrier went before New York courts, 150 healthy carriers were under health department observation; by the time of Mallon's death in 1938, there were 394 healthy carriers under surveillance in New York City. They were not permitted to handle food; Mallon was the only one held in long-term forced custody.[32]

Examination of the second healthy carrier court case in New York helps us to understand some of the dynamics at work in Mallon's situation. Under the systematic regulation of food handlers begun in 1916 and based on what was learned from Mallon, Alphonse Cotils had been identified as a healthy carrier of typhoid fever and had been denied a food handler's license. In March 1924 Cotils, a bakery and restaurant owner, was found preparing a strawberry shortcake in his restaurant despite his previous banishment from such an occupation. He defied health department rules, his physician said, because officials were " 'annoying' him about working in his own bakery." Cotils knew that he was a typhoid carrier, and he knew that he was not allowed to prepare food for other people. But he, like Mary Mallon before him, refused to cooperate with the regulation and continued his work. When his case came before the court, the judge found Cotils guilty of violating the section of the sanitary code that prohibited food handling by typhoid carriers. Yet, in his case, the judge suspended sentence "after Cotils had promised to remain away from his restaurant and keep out of kitchens. He intends to conduct his business by telephone, he said." According to the *New York Times*, the judge reasoned: "I am thoroughly impressed with the extreme danger from these typhoid carriers, particularly when they are handling food. I could not legally sentence this man to jail on account of his health."[33] At the very moment the judge said that he could not legally imprison Cotils because he was not sick, a healthy Mary Mallon was securely held in her isolation on North Brother Island. Both had violated a previously imposed quarantine; only one was physically detained for it.

What were the reasons for the discrepancy? In which case, Mallon's or Cotils's, did the health department and the court more adequately protect the public health? Why did authorities see the need for denying personal liberty in one case and only restricting it in the other?

Both Alphonse Cotils and Mary Mallon were proven carriers of typhoid fever. Their work involved handling the food of others, and thus they endangered the health of those unsuspecting people whose food they prepared. Most important, they persisted in cooking, thus putting other people at risk. As the *New York Tribune* editorialized, those carriers who would not voluntarily give up their activities that spread typhoid were a menace to the public and needed to be locked up: "The plain and obvious fact is that we have no way of dealing with these unlucky persons except by keeping them where they cannot do harm to others. . . . when the danger has been so clearly demonstrated as in the case of "typhoid Mary" there can be little doubt as to the right course to follow."[34] Previous public health experience taught that forcible incarceration could become part of normal procedures as a last resort in those cases deemed otherwise intractable. The question remains why health officials and the court deemed Mary Mallon intractable, and thus deserving of being denied her personal liberty, and why Alphonse Cotils, also a cook repeater whose case went to court, although restricted, was allowed his liberty.

One acknowledged justification for the denial of liberty in Mary Mallon's case was her recalcitrance, her "perversity" as some called it. Soper claimed that if only Mallon had cooperated, her freedom could have been saved. Dr. Josephine Baker wrote, too, that Mallon "might have been a free woman all her life. It was her own bad behavior that inevitably led to her doom."[35] Because of the different and less restrictive treatment of other recalcitrant carriers, we know that other factors in addition to her refusal to cooperate must have existed. Indeed, we find in the health officials' words and deeds evidence with regard to class, ethnicity, and gender that bears closer scrutiny.

First, health officers gave much importance to Mary Mallon's social condition. Before her case, social differences had affected policy execution. People with no home or family had been particularly vulnerable to official control, because they did not have the social and physical supports to convince authorities that they could care for themselves and not endanger others. Alphonse Cotils owned his own restaurant; while we know comparatively little about his social situation, that fact alone put him in a class apart from Mallon. Health officials repeatedly called attention to Mallon's lifestyle. As Soper wrote:

> I found that Mary was in the habit of going, when her work for the day was finished, to a rooming house on Third Avenue below Thirty-third Street, where she was spending the evenings with a disreputable looking man who had a room on the top floor and to whom she was taking food. His headquarters during the day was in a saloon on the corner. . . . He took me to see the room. I should not care to see another like it. It was a place of dirt and disorder. It was not improved by the presence of a large dog of which Mary was said to be very fond.[36]

These unsavory and disordered conditions, in addition, no doubt, to the unspoken judgment on out-of-wedlock cohabitation, became part of the justification for keeping careful watch over Mallon: it was obvious that she could not care properly for herself.

The rules adopted by the New York City Department of Health for typhoid carriers bore out this sentiment: "Typhoid fever carriers need not be retained in hospitals or institutions if not desired. They will be sent home *if home conditions are satisfactory.*"[37] People without homes and families, or, presumably, with unacceptable homes and families, thus became more vulnerable to detention because of the perception that they could not take care of themselves. Public health officials found it necessary to describe not just the bacillus-carrying nature of those deemed dangerous to the public health, but also their social condition, even if that social condition was immaterial to describing the health dangers they posed.

Soper was concerned not just with Mallon's living conditions, but with her personal hygiene as well, since she transmitted the typhoid bacilli in large part because she did not keep her hands clean. But the engineer epidemiologist did not limit himself to cleanliness in his observation: "She was careless in her personal habits, but so are most cooks."[38] Soper underscored his belief that Mallon needed to be under strict observation by placing her as part of a group, which he, and society, denigrated. The stigma attached to healthy carriers could be linked to the inferior status of domestic workers and together help justify Mallon's incarceration.[39]

Perhaps if Mary Mallon had had a home to shelter her, one authorities might have recognized as safe, and family to take care of her, she might have been released despite her refusal to cooperate with health department guidelines. Perhaps if she had been a housewife and not a domestic laborer, no matter how hot her temper, health authorities may have found reason to liberate her. Certainly Cotils gained liberty, if we can read meaning into the judge's decision in his case, in part because he had some of these social options in his life: he could promise to carry out his business from his home on the telephone, for example. Perhaps if Mallon had not been Irish, with a stereotypical hot temper, she might have received less coercive responses to her actions. Although not often overtly a factor, her ethnic background lurked behind the scenes in many comments about her temper and lack of cooperation with health officials.[40] We can never know what would have happened if Mallon had been someone else, if the first healthy carrier followed so carefully in this country had been someone, even if uncooperative, who represented more respectable middle-class America. We can know that some class- and possibly ethnic-related perceptions were evident in the official and public thinking about Mallon's situation and that they affected attitudes about her and seem to have affected the treatment she received from the health authorities.[41]

The social class difference between Mary Mallon and the people she served also was a factor in how health officials regarded the dangers she posed. As a newspaper reported, "[A] well-known member of the Board of Health [revealed] that this human culture tube has worked for prominent families in this city and communicated the disease to some of its members."[42] Working-class domestics entered the private spheres of the rich; those who carried disease threatened the city's most powerful in their most vulnerable settings, the sanctity of their homes.

In addition to class and ethnicity, gender considerations played an important role in this story. Authorities used Mallon's case to illustrate the dangers all women, society's main food preparers, posed as potential typhoid fever carriers; they also used gendered language to single her out as unique and deserving of particularly harsh treatment.

Mary Mallon spread typhoid not just because she harbored the bacteria in her bowel movements, but also because she was a cook. This predominantly female occupation made women especially dangerous. Health officers noted repeatedly that more women were identified as carriers because more women were in occupations, paid or not, that made it easy for them to spread germs to unsuspecting others.[43] Being a carrier was a gendered condition, one in part defined by sex-role expectations. As cooks, all women food handlers were potentially dangerous to the public health, whether they were employed outside the home or within it. In a fascinating passage, quoted in the *New York Times Sunday Magazine*, Soper blamed upper-class women, who hired cooks, for not being more careful to make sure they were not bringing danger into their homes. He blamed middle-class women, especially mothers, who went from the sick room to the kitchen to prepare the family's meals, thereby spreading typhoid fever. And he blamed working-class domestics who entered the homes of others as cooks, bringing their germs with them and spreading them to unsuspecting people. Women of all social classes, by virtue of their culturally defined tasks, were potentially dangerous.[44]

While all women thus became suspect for spreading typhoid fever, health officials could not for a moment have considered locking up all women identified as typhoid carriers. It was not sex alone or cooking per se that made Mallon a candidate for incarceration. Nonetheless, there are clear indications that cultural ideology about sex-appropriate behavior did affect her case. By contrasting Mary Mallon with a male working-class carrier followed by the health department in these years, it is possible to see how social prejudices of the health officials affected their decisions about healthy carriers. In 1922 a New York City carrier, a man who had reportedly caused an outbreak of eighty-seven cases of typhoid fever and two deaths and whom the health department had been following, absconded from its purview and was found by New Jersey health authorities, who blamed him for still another outbreak that had resulted in thirty-five cases and three deaths. Rather than incarcerating this healthy carrier for repeated violations and breaking parole, the health officers instead added him to the list of carriers and concluded the case with the remark, "This carrier is now employed in this City as a laborer in building construction work and is required to report to us weekly."[45] From all indications, this man was as dangerous to the public as was Mallon. In fact, he had already been identified with more typhoid fever cases and more deaths than Mallon. He had disobeyed the law in two states with repeated violations, certainly showing perversity and lack of respect; yet health officials allowed him his freedom to find construction work and continue at liberty. One reading of this incident, which unfortunately cannot be followed more closely with extant documentation, could conclude that as a male wage earner, he was viewed as a family breadwinner and therefore as necessary to the family economy. Despite his recalcitrance and his record as a menace to the public health, he was not locked up; Mary Mallon, in parallel circumstances, was denied her freedom and not retrained for a different job.[46]

There was precedent for finding other means of support for healthy typhoid carriers instead of isolating them. At the Pasteur Institute in Paris, bacteriologist Ilya Metchnikoff had found employment in a library for a healthy carrier whose case interested him. In 1918 New York State began subsidizing the incomes of those carriers who were having difficulty finding adequate employment outside the food industry. The absence of a record of attempts to find funding or alternate employment for Mallon is notable.[47]

Another indication of how gendered expectations affected Mary Mallon can be seen in the language Soper, Baker, and others used to describe her. Soper noted that Mallon had "a somewhat determined mouth and jaw." He thought, "Nothing was so distinctive about her as her walk, unless it was her mind. The two had a peculiarity in common. . . . Mary walked more like a man than a woman and . . . her mind had a distinctly masculine character also."[48] These comments leap out of the page as we read them today because they are so obviously not connected to the health dangers that Mallon posed. Her walk or the character of her mind in no way influenced the bacilli lodged in her gallbladder. Yet Soper could not refrain from calling attention to them in his characterization of the stigmatized woman. The *Medical Record*, with similar disregard for relevance, described Mallon as "a perfect Amazon, weighing over 200 pounds." Josephine Baker emphasized Mallon's fierceness—she was like an angry lion, she was maniacal, she fought and swore.[49] Mallon was set apart in these accounts as different, deviant, unfeminine. The *World-Telegram* noticed, too, that she "was not imbued with that sweet reasonableness which would have allowed her to listen to the explanations of learned men about her particular case."[50]

None of these characteristics was relevant to Mallon's public health case. Her weight, her strength, her energy level, her lack of deference, and her degree of femininity were all extraneous to the health dangers she posed. Even more startling, the one early photograph I have been able to find of Mary Mallon, as well as line drawings in newspapers, indicate that the physical description of Mallon was not only immaterial, it was false. She looks to the camera's eye as a distinctly "feminine" woman. The robust, physically imposing, masculinized woman seems to have existed only in the eyes of the anxious beholders, in the vision of those who needed to see in her an aberrant "other" in order to justify their actions against her. The description of Mallon as deviant and masculine was part of building a comprehensive explanation to establish the new principle of healthy carriers as dangerous to the public health.

Health officials helped to justify Mallon's incarceration and bolster public support through this negative portrayal. They did not want the public to become too sympathetic to Mallon's plight, or people might not support the general policies instituted to regulate healthy carriers. Reflecting commonly held social values about proper class, ethnic, and female behavior, the portrayal of Mallon as a social pariah and an unnatural woman thus became as important a part of the case as notifying the public of her bacilli-carrying feces. Gender stereotyping bolstered the public health policy.

Mary Mallon's case thus functioned as a vehicle for public education. From the early newspaper accounts, the public learned about the incarceration of this unfortunate, unlucky woman. When the public showed some sympathy with her plight, officials worked to re-create her image as a social undesirable, as a frightening and dangerous person, in order to discourage others from following her ways and to encourage public distance. The medical dangers could best be portrayed through building a specific, individual case of social disorder. Chronic bacillus carrying itself was not sufficient. Health officials needed social as well as medical arguments to help shape public knowledge and discourse about healthy carriers. They constructed an image of a deviant and physically unappealing "Typhoid Mary" out of the story of Mary Mallon.

Health officials brought to bear the full strength of the state against Mary Mallon. In the name of protecting the public health of all citizens, they took away her liberty for more than twenty-six years, more than (as far as I can determine) any other healthy typhoid fever carrier in U.S. public health history. They made no concerted effort to try to teach her another skill, one that would not have endangered the public, until her productive years were almost over. Not until the later years of her incarceration did she work in a hospital laboratory. Mallon became, in reality and in symbol, as she characterized herself, a social "leper." She evoked some sympathy in the early years of her isolation, but she came to represent the worst in human behavior. Embodying the fullest extent of the law's ability to deny individual liberty, Mallon became an example for others, a reason to cooperate with health officials when they came knocking. Her name, her epithetical "Typhoid Mary," stood—and stands—for the ultimate stigma, someone to be feared, to be avoided, to be maligned.

By the beginning third of the twentieth century, health departments had forged for themselves wide powers to prevent the spread of infectious diseases by curtailing or denying the liberty of a few individuals, sick and healthy, and using them as examples to shape the thinking and behavior of the majority. They did not often explore the full reaches of their power, but the potential existed for significant denial of personal freedoms in the cause of protecting the public health. The role women played in forming the answers to the dilemmas posed in the new century bears witness to the limited and sex-defined expectations of the culture and illustrates how social prejudices affected public health history even during the period when scientific advances were most prominent.

In 1910, the year Mary Mallon was released from her initial quarantine, Jennie Barmore, then fifty-six years old, and her husband George opened a rooming house at 100 West 113th Place in Chicago. They had grown children and a big mortgage. George Barmore had been invalided, and the family's sole means of support was the income collected from their lodgers for their rooms and the meals Jennie cooked for them.

In November 1919 the Barmores' economic security ended. An alert health department officer had noticed that during the previous few months at least five single men and women, who were receiving treatment in different hospitals around the city for typhoid fever, all gave 100 West 113th Place as their address. One subsequently died. In July 1919 David Barmore visited his parents and became ill soon after returning home. His physician also diagnosed typhoid fever, although David later denied any knowledge of this. Because of these cases, a health department nurse visited the Barmore residence and informed the family of the sickness traced to them. Since Jennie Barmore had always prepared the food the roomers ate, the nurse took her to the hospital in November and December 1919 to obtain specimens of her feces and urine. Three specimens collected tested positive for typhoid.[51] As a result of these tests, the health department, following its own guidelines for the management of healthy carriers, required Barmore to stop cooking for others and keeping boarders. Probably out of economic necessity and because she denied ever having typhoid fever, she did not comply. As a result of Jennie Barmore's lack of cooperation, Dr. Herman Bundesen of the Chicago Health Department, on December 15, 1919, knocked on the door of the Barmore home and proceeded to take the sixty-five-year-old woman to Cook County Hospital as a suspected typhoid fever carrier.[52] At the hospital, Barmore, "against her will," was "compelled" once again to submit excreta for examination. The health department ultimately released her to her home under a rigid house quarantine.

Barmore's house was placarded with a large red sign declaring that a typhoid fever carrier lived within:

DEPARTMENT OF HEALTH　CITY OF CHICAGO
TYPHOID FEVER CARRIER
REMOVE NO MILK BOTTLES

All persons, not occupants of this apartment, are hereby notified of the presence of Typhoid Fever within, and are warned not to enter. The person having Typhoid Fever must not leave the apartment without permission of the Commissioner of Health, until this warning sign has been removed by the Department of Health. The Milkman must not enter the house. The family will set the vessels outside, into which the milk or cream may be poured by the Milkman, who MUST NOT HANDLE THE VESSELS. Milk or cream may be delivered in bottles, provided the bottles received are not returned to the Milkman, until this notice is removed by the Department of Health.

This warning card must not be concealed from public view, must not be mutilated or defaced and MUST REMAIN POSTED ON THESE PREMISES UNTIL REMOVED BY THE DEPARTMENT OF HEALTH.

PENALTY FOR VIOLATION OF THE RULES OF QUARANTINE; A fine of up to $200, or imprisonment not to exceed six months, or both.

By order of John Dill Robertson, M.D.,
Commissioner of Health[53]

In addition to having to submit to the sign on her house, a stigmatic symbol of governmental intrusion, Barmore was prohibited from keeping boarders unless they had been inoculated against typhoid fever. She was not to cook for anyone other than her husband, not even her visiting children. She was not to shop in any stores, go into crowds, use public toilets, or in any way endanger the health of the citizens of Chicago. She was, as one health department official later testified in court, "not allowed to leave her house and go out for a walk. . . . After she was quarantined she was not allowed to have any communication with the outside world at all."[54] This "modified" quarantine carried with it the constant threat of arrest and hospital confinement if its orders were violated.

Apparently right from the beginning of her house quarantine, Jennie Barmore resisted its terms, which her lawyers' brief later termed "arbitrary and absolute."[55] Repeatedly, according to the health officials (although this point was contested in court by the defense), she tore down the sign and continued to take in unvaccinated boarders. Herman Bundesen threatened to put her back in the hospital if she continued to disobey the quarantine. Indeed, he told the court that he would "cause her to be seized and hospitalized, and in so doing, he would not apply to any court for any writ or process or warrant of any kind for her arrest or detention."[56] Before Bundesen could rehospitalize Barmore, however, she filed suit for her release from the quarantine. The American Medical Liberty League provided financial support for the case, and the firm of Clarence Darrow represented Barmore. The writ stated: "Dr. Bundesen went to the home of your petitioner, Jennie Barmore . . . and confessedly, without any warrant, paper, document or process of law . . . forcibly took and seized the body of your petitioner without her consent and against her will, and took her into custody and detained her in the Cook County Hospital and other places and did then and there extract and take blood from her body and her bowel contents for examination."[57]

Darrow built his defense around three issues: that Jennie Barmore had been forcibly denied her liberty and her right of immunity from compulsory self-incrimination without due process, points that the health department never disputed; that she had never been sick with typhoid and had not been the cause of any epidemic or illness in any other person, a point answered by the use of laboratory evidence; and that the imposed quarantine was too rigid and oppressive in that it went beyond merely constraining her from handling food and serving food to others, an interpretation that engaged the court and respondents for most of the proceedings.

Judge Joseph Sabath heard the case in the Superior Court of Cook County, taking testimony from medical experts, health department officers, and nurses, and from Barmore and her son. On November 23, 1920, Sabath determined that Barmore was indeed a menace to the health of Chicago and could be held indefinitely:

> I am satisfied that to permit the relatrix free intercourse with the public, and particularly to continue in her business of preparing and serving food to others, would menace the health and safety of those with whom she would come in contact. . . . It is true that . . . her isolation is an apparent denial of her liberty, but . . . liberty of the individual may be restrained when the failure to do so would threaten the health and happiness of the community.[58]

The judge admitted that his decision would cause the Barmores "great hardship, loss and inconvenience," but he believed that "the present mental attitude of the relatrix is such that she clearly shows a lack of cooperation," and that it was therefore necessary to keep her under quarantine.[59]

Darrow appealed to the Illinois Supreme Court, where, again, the harshness of the terms of the quarantine were at issue. The health department insisted that "the relatrix in this case is not a prisoner. She has not been arrested in the meaning of the word 'arrested.'" Rather, the health officials insisted, the quarantine was imposed in order to protect the health of Chicagoans and only because of Barmore's refusal to obey orders. The printed testimony showed that there was no ambiguity about the meaning of Barmore's quarantine:

> *Bundesen:* These cases very seldom recover, your Honor.
> *Darrow:* Has she got to be taken care of all her life?
> *Bundesen:* Yes, sir; they are usually typhoid carriers all their lives.
> *The Court:* You don't contend that the city would have a right to detain her all her life, do you?
> *Bundesen:* . . . I will say that it is our experience with typhoid carriers that they very seldom recover.[60]

The defense tried to argue that Barmore, as the family breadwinner, should not be deprived of her ability to earn a living. One of Darrow's colleagues stated, "Her husband has been injured in an accident, and she wants to be free to take people in there and help take care of him, and with that sign on the house, she can't do it." By the end of the court proceedings, however, it was clear that the most the defense could argue was for leniency in the quarantine. Jennie Barmore showed her weariness and resignation. She told the court, "If my children want to come home, I want them to have the privilege of coming home, and very frequently." Even that was too much for the health department: "No; her children can go there if they don't eat food prepared by her, and if they do, we will take her back."[61] Judge J. Thompson filed the opinion on February 22, 1922: the Illinois Supreme Court remanded Barmore to the custody of the Chicago Department of Health, allowing the house quarantine to continue.

In March, Darrow applied for a rehearing. The application stated that the court's opinion assumed "that Jennie Barmore is an abnormal person" and that the medical theory upon which her quarantine was based was unproven. "If Jennie Barmore is to be quarantined, she is made a life prisoner not because of anything she has done, but because the medical men have evolved a theory which, so far, is not based upon any recorded facts."[62] Darrow rejected the laboratory evidence used to condemn Barmore as unimpressive. In light of the Mary Mallon precedent, not cited anywhere in this case, Darrow's last argument was even more interesting. The lawyer posited that the quarantine law was arbitrary in that it allowed health officials to "discriminate between individuals" who might be equally dangerous to the public's health:

> They may permit one carrier complete liberty to go about in his usual manner, transacting his ordinary business, while another may be confined under the strictest quarantine. Or one may be allowed his freedom upon merely giving his word that he would sterilize his discharges and another

denied that privilege. If there is any reason for different treatment of typhoid carriers, the conditions under which the quarantine will be relaxed or modified should be set forth in the rule. . . . At present the Board assumes the right to arbitrarily discriminate between persons of the same class.[63]

The court did not allow the rehearing, and Barmore remained under virtual house arrest, as far as I can determine, for the rest of her life.[64]

Especially in light of Darrow's last argument about arbitrary discrimination between healthy carriers, it is important to scrutinize the arguments of the Chicago health officers. Much of their testimony centered on their perception that Barmore would not stop cooking if she were released from her quarantine. Despite this belief, they never discussed training her for another occupation, subsidizing her income, or helping to find alternatives to what was, at the time, her family's only support, even though all of these possibilities had been utilized with healthy carriers elsewhere in the country. Rather, they repeated the accusation that, no matter what, she would persist in her cooking. There is a clue to what undergirded the officials' belief that a rigid quarantine was necessary to constrain Jennie Barmore, and we see it in the discussion before the court about why she could not be released from her house quarantine:

If relatrix is released from the present quarantine and isolation, she undoubtedly will have a big dinner party, inviting all her friends to partake of the food, which she has gone to the store for, purchased, brought home and prepared. While the relatrix is in the store handling food, she may there leave some deadly germs. While she is preparing the food, she may leave some deadly germs in the food. While she is serving the food, the same may happen. We believe the court can readily see that a great many persons could thus become afflicted with typhoid fever through no fault of their own.[65]

In their vision of how to prevent the spread of illness, health officials could not see beyond traditional female domestic activity. The very job definitions of cooks, mothers, wives, and nurses implicated them as carriers of food- and water-borne disease and justified strong measures of control. Not only did sex roles define Barmore's activities; the authorities could recognize in her no ability to change her ways. Physicians argued that Barmore needed the strict quarantine by definition of her gender roles that would automatically come into play if she were released. She "undoubtedly will have a big dinner party," they claimed. Apparently there was no way to stop such behavior in a woman; therefore it was necessary to keep her rigidly confined.

Accepted societal ideas about gender roles thus influenced public health policy. If women could not be expected to change their traditional duties, they would have to undergo the most severe penalties. Under this thinking, it would not be so necessary to lock up a recalcitrant male healthy carrier, even one working in food preparation; such a person could change his job. But health officials seem to have had difficulty imagining women giving up their domestic duties, which were, supposedly, inherent in their being.

The distinction in public health treatment of men and women was underscored in Chicago's policy restraining the spread of venereal diseases. At the same time as Chicago health officials determined Barmore's fate, the same officers forcibly isolated only female sufferers of venereal disease even though they identified many male victims. They sequestered only women, "realizing that the application of the [isolation] rule [to men] may lead to interference in the business affairs of men involved and perhaps to trouble in their family affairs." This informal application of the law only to women remained policy in Chicago through these years, although women's groups in the city publicly objected to this particular form of the double standard. Health officials, too, declared that "adequate hospital facilities should be available for the retention and quarantine of males, the same as is provided for females." But regulation of female prostitutes continued to be the main focus of Chicago's venereal disease control program throughout the decade. When detained women filed writs of habeas corpus to try to gain their release from detention, as many did during the 1920s, they were all remanded to the health department's control.[66]

The stories of Mary Mallon and Jennie Barmore are instructive for historians because they open to scrutiny the underlying beliefs and social norms that, along with medical and scientific advances, influenced public health policy. Science was not impartially applied in the public arena in the early part of the century, and our reading of the triumph of science must be tempered by the knowledge that social prejudices entered into the determination of legal and medical decisions about the people's health.

Without denying the health dangers Mallon and Barmore posed, it is possible to understand that these two women received particularly harsh treatment at a time when most other healthy carriers retained their freedom. Although Clarence Darrow might not have recognized it as such, gendered expectations for women influenced their cases, and in his words they became the victims of "arbitrary discrimination." Mallon and Barmore both resisted the characterizations of themselves and their lives and fought back through the courts, and thus we know about them and can analyze their situations; we do not know how many other women healthy carriers were similarly affected by gendered stereotypes. Certainly there were hundreds, nationwide, thousands, of healthy typhoid fever carriers, male and female, who did not suffer the stings of this particular public health arrow. Most of them no doubt cooperated with health officials enough to disappear from public view. There were other recalcitrant, perverse, uncooperative, and difficult healthy carriers who somehow managed to continue with their lives outside of isolation. If the arguments of this essay are transferable to their cases, most of them were male. But the argument here does not depend on that possibility. Historians can recognize that Mary Mallon and Jennie Barmore, regardless of what happened to anyone else, bore the brunt of health department authority, arbitrarily imposed. A lifetime of institutional isolation, to a healthy woman in the prime of life, and the lifetime house arrest of another older healthy woman were harsh penalties indeed, penalties informed by ideas of women's proper behavior and roles as much as by scientific evidence, penalties imposed in both cases before all options had been explored.

CHAPTER 8 : SEPARATISM REVISITED : WOMEN'S INSTITUTIONS, SOCIAL REFORM, AND THE CAREER OF MIRIAM VAN WATERS : *ESTELLE B. FREEDMAN*

I n November 1945 a group of college students who were conducting research on women and social reform paid a visit to the Framingham, Massachusetts, women's prison. They went to meet with the superintendent, Miriam Van Waters, a prominent juvenile justice and prison reformer. In 1927 Van Waters had served as president of the National Conference on Social Work, and she currently presided over the American League to Abolish Capital Punishment. Talking with the students about their projects gave Van Waters a chance to reflect back upon her career. That night, writing in her journal, she posed an intriguing historical question: Why, she wondered, were there no longer any great women leaders in social work, women of the stature of Florence Kelley, Jane Addams, and Julia Lathrop?[1]

Van Waters's sense that the golden age of women and reform had passed by the 1940s has been echoed by historians, who generally date the ascendance of American women's public moral authority in the mid-nineteenth century and its decline sometime after the enactment of suffrage in 1920. Yet both Van Waters's own career and recent scholarship on the twentieth century suggest the persistence of women's contributions to social reform in the postsuffrage era. Even during the rise of professionalized social work and the provision of welfare by state and national governments, women's local, voluntary associations continued to play an important role in sustaining progressive reform. To explore this premise, I would like to look more closely at continuities in women's contributions to social reform after 1920. I draw particularly on the career of Miriam Van Waters to do so, placing her life within a larger historical landscape.

The role of women in American social reform has a long and complex history. In the antebellum period, religiously motivated middle-class women began to provide the impetus for local and national reform movements. White women formed associations to achieve temperance and prison reform, while black and white female antislavery societies appealed to women to work for abolition. At the turn of the century African American women's clubs crusaded against lynching and provided critical local social services such as health, education, and day care in southern black communities. In the North, elite and working-class white women cooperated in movements for protective legislation for workers, while white middle-class women's clubs sponsored a variety of "child-saving" measures, including local juvenile courts and state child labor laws. Women's voluntarism and reform campaigns not only filled a significant gap in American political life but they also gave disfranchised women a degree of public authority. In the settlement houses, through the National Consumers' League, and in the U.S. Children's Bureau, reformers like Addams, Kelley, and Lathrop brought women's maternal vision of social justice into the mainstream of American life and helped lay the groundwork for a welfare state.[2]

After the waning of progressivism, however, and coincident with the attainment of suffrage in 1920, organized womanhood seemed to play a less influential role in social reform. Women's clubs, which had once led the movement for juvenile justice, now gained a reputation as mere recreational groups. Rescue homes founded by nineteenth-century Protestant women missionaries closed or were taken over by male authorities during the 1920s and 1930s. Even as women entered the new profession of social work, they lost a measure of their older moral authority. Among professional social workers, male domination began to "insinuate itself" in the 1920s and it deepened during the depression.[3] What one historian has termed the "Female Dominion in American Reform" may have culminated in the New Deal steps toward a welfare state, but, in the process, male officials attained increasing state authority over concerns once left largely in the hands of women volunteers. According to another historian, women "surrendered to government functions that had belonged to the woman's sphere" and so lost their separate political culture.[4]

The explanations for this shift from female to male authority in reform vary, from the personal—for example, a decline in women's interest in serving

Eleanor Roosevelt provided political support for Miriam Van Waters's innovative programs at the Framingham reformatory. Roosevelt let Democratic officials in Massachusetts know that she took a special interest in Van Waters's work by writing to them in praise of the superintendent and visiting the reformatory to address the inmates. In this 1945 picture, Roosevelt and Van Waters share a laugh during a photo session with state officials. (Courtesy of The Schlesinger Library, Radcliffe College)

others—to the structural—such as economic competition for social work jobs during the depression. I have previously argued that women's postsuffrage efforts to integrate into male organizational structures undermined their autonomous political base, since separate women's networks and institutions are critical to the survival of the women's movement.[5] New historical research, however, has shown the ways that separatism, or female institution building, did, in fact, survive as a reform strategy after 1920. Indeed, where separatism in some form persisted, women continued to influence social reform and politics to an extent that earlier histories have underestimated. The persistence of women organized for reform complicates and challenges a monolithic interpretation of the decline of women's moral and political authority after the suffrage victory.

As historians have shifted attention from the private, female sphere of the nineteenth century to the public, political activities of women in the twentieth century, they have clarified the contours of that amorphous term, the *women's movement*. We now recognize the coexistence of many social movements led by women—some to protect women and children in the family or workplace, some to benefit larger social groups (such as workers or African Americans), and others committed solely to the goal of equal political rights for women.[6] Given this broadly defined women's movement with overlapping memberships, the suffrage victory in 1920 seems like a narrow and inappropriate benchmark for periodizing women's history.

Continuity as much as change characterized the pre- and postsuffrage decades for African American women, for example. In the South, suffrage did not usher in a new era, for political, economic, and social discrimination persisted, necessitating local social service and self-help programs that continued to rely on female leadership. After World War I, in response to the northern migration, middle-class black women formed new clubs that provided service to urban communities, and in several cities working-class women organized Housewives Leagues to support black-owned businesses. In addition, educated black women worked within interracial groups, such as the Consumers' League, the local juvenile courts, and the League of Women Voters; in the Young Women's Christian Association (YWCA), black women waged a fervent though largely unsuccessful campaign for racial equality.[7]

Among privileged white women, a variety of postsuffrage organizations continued to influence reform. Some groups—such as women's clubs and the Consumers' League—drew upon an older ideology of female difference, using maternalism as a basis for their contributions to politics and social reform. Others, such as the National Woman's Party, embraced the newer ideology of "feminism," which claimed that women merited political authority because they were equal to, not different from, men. Despite their ideological differences, however, both groups of women frequently relied on the separatist institutions of the earlier women's movement to achieve their goals.[8]

The legacy of separatism can be seen, for example, where women reformers continued to draw upon the kinds of close personal networks that had long nurtured activists such as Jane Addams and Florence Kelley. The "emotional anchor" of friendship helped buttress women's social service efforts within African American communities. Personal networks advanced women's political goals in the 1920s and especially during the New Deal, when middle-class reformers such as Molly Dewson and Frances Perkins worked to extend the benefits of the welfare state to working women. In addition, formal women's institutions, such as the Children's Bureau in the Department of Labor and the Women's Joint Congressional Committee, maintained the "female dominion" of reform through the New Deal era. At the other end of the ideological spectrum from these "social feminists," the National Woman's Party also drew on close personal networks and separate female organizing to support its lobbying efforts for the passage of the Equal Rights Amendment, providing a critical link to the reemergence of liberal feminist politics in the 1960s.[9]

Separate networks and institutions also sustained women's quests for economic opportunities in the postsuffrage era. The National Federation of Business and Professional Women's Clubs, founded after World War I, sought equality at work through a separate women's organization. Among working-class women, recent scholarship suggests, separate women's locals best served the interests of unionized women, such as waitresses. Among California cannery workers, the continuing sexual segregation of labor helped create a female workplace culture of predominantly Mexican and Jewish women, which in turn facilitated union organizing during the 1930s and 1940s.[10]

Women's social service and social reform organizations provide another example of continuity in separatist institution building after suffrage. Although the YWCA had nineteenth-century origins as a separate women's organization, it flourished after 1920, resisting efforts by the Young Men's Christian Association to subsume it and adopting more explicitly political goals. In the 1920s the college division of the YWCA took the lead in opposing racial segregation in the South, and by the 1940s and 1950s black and white leaders struggled over how to integrate the segregated YWCAs without inadvertently taking autonomy away from important black community institutions.[11]

A final legacy of separatism is the survival of women's intimate relationships in the twentieth century. Historians once argued that the emergence of a medical and psychiatric definition of lesbianism as a sexual perversion served to suppress the loving friendships that once flourished among white, middle-class women.[12] Although prescriptive literature may have stigmatized homosexuality in the early twentieth century, the naming of lesbianism simultaneously granted to women the capacity to have sexual relations with members of their own sex. More important than labels, when opportunities for economic self-support freed women from dependence on marriage, female couples proliferated. In settlement houses, during the Harlem Renaissance, among political activists of the New Deal, in the women's armed forces during World War II, and in the lesbian bars of the 1950s, lesbian subcultures gradually emerged, laying the groundwork for the homophile and lesbian-feminist political movements. Although female couples did not necessarily claim a lesbian identity, particularly before 1950, intimate relationships between women nonetheless continued to provide one means of support for activists, including social reformers.[13]

These examples of women's networks and female institution building in the postsuffrage era, along with the women's peace movement and the southern white women's antilynching movement, force a revision of the modern history of women and reform.[14] Rather than portraying only decline or erosion of women's organizations and their role in social reform after 1920, we may need to tell a story that includes pockets of quiet persistence. Understanding where and why separate women's organizations did survive may help explain the contours of reform in the twentieth century as well as the reemergence of feminism in the 1960s.

The career of Miriam Van Waters (1887–1974) illustrates the continuing importance of women's networks and women's institutions in modern American social reform. A nationally known juvenile justice reformer in the 1920s, Van Waters made headlines in 1949, when she successfully defended herself from dismissal as superintendent of the Massachusetts Reformatory for Women in Framingham. A series of dramatic public hearings inspired both a popular biography and the classic women's prison film, *Caged* (1950), in which Agnes Moorhead created a remarkable facsimile of the high-minded superintendent. Miriam Van Waters continued to direct Framingham until her retirement in 1957.[15] Throughout her career she chose to work with and for women, and female institutions provided critical support for her reforms. An examination of separatism in her life suggests that historians may need to rethink the periodization of modern women's history by looking more closely at women's voluntary and political institutions between 1920 and 1960.

Like that of other middle-class women activists of the nineteenth and twentieth centuries, Miriam Van Waters's commitment to serve women and children originated within the broader context of liberal Protestantism. Growing up in the rectory of her father's Episcopal church in Portland, Oregon, Van Waters was exposed to both the late-nineteenth-century social gospel and support for the rights of women. In 1904 she graduated from an Episcopal girls' school and entered the University of Oregon. Suffrage activism was gathering strength in Oregon, and as editor of the campus literary magazine Van Waters urged more women to participate in student government lest they be unprepared to vote.[16] A strong dean of women may have provided a model for Oregon students, for in addition to Van Waters and several of her women friends, a disproportionate number of the university's female graduates pursued advanced degrees.[17] After completing her M.A. in psychology at Oregon in 1910, Van Waters entered Clark University to study with the country's leading psychologist, G. Stanley Hall.

Three years later, disillusioned with Hall's scientific methods and dismayed by the second-class status accorded academic women, Miriam Van Waters completed her doctorate in anthropology. She joined a small but growing elite of highly educated American women. Like other early women social scientists, Van Waters wanted to put her academic expertise to "constructive" use.[18] Inspired by Jane Addams, the suffrage movement, and juvenile court reformers, she began a lifetime career working with delinquent women. After an internship at Boston Children's Aid, she returned to the West in 1914 to direct the Frazer Detention Home in Portland, Oregon. There she implemented sweeping reforms in education, recreation, and self-government. After 1917 Van Waters worked at the Los Angeles Juvenile Court, which, like its predecessor in Chicago, was the product of a reform campaign led by local women's clubs. She directed Juvenile Hall and, as one historian has written, "quickly transformed this institution into one of the leading progressive detention centers in the country."[19] From 1920 to 1930 she served as court "referee," a quasi-judicial position. In her capacity of recommending the disposition of cases of girls and young boys brought to court, she favored probation rather than incarceration.

At Juvenile Hall, Van Waters worked with both girls and boys, but the project dearest to her was El Retiro, an experimental school for adolescent girls brought to the juvenile court. In 1919 she helped transform this former sanitarium into an unenclosed, rural, residential high school for girls, operated on a system of student self-government. El Retiro stressed education and economic self-sufficiency for its residents. Van Waters served as a surrogate mother to many of its students and as their advocate in juvenile court. She proselytized the El Retiro model nationally through the liberal press and in her influential studies of delinquency, *Youth in Conflict* (1925) and *Parents on Proba-*

tion (1927). Van Waters also investigated girls' reformatories around the country, exposing punitive conditions and calling for improvements.[20]

As did reformers of an earlier generation, Miriam Van Waters found support for her work within a network of like-minded women. For over a decade she operated within a circle of women lawyers, judges, and social workers who staffed the juvenile court and participated in an elaborate community of professional women in Los Angeles. Van Waters herself belonged to the Professional Women's Club, the Women's Athletic Club, and the Los Angeles Business Women's Club. She shared a communal house with former juvenile court referee Orfa Jean Shontz and two classmates from Clark University, UCLA psychology professor Sara Fisher and Los Angeles school psychologist Elizabeth Woods. When Van Waters adopted a daughter, members of the household helped raise her. All supporters of the presuffrage "woman movement," the housemates continued to seek greater public authority for women in the criminal justice system and more equal treatment of female delinquents.[21] In the 1920s their suburban home, "The Colony," served as a latter-day salon for women reformers from around the world, such as Chicago philanthropist Ethel Sturges Dummer, who visited The Colony whenever she went to Los Angeles. Similarly, when Van Waters traveled around the country, she stopped at Hull House to stay with her colleague Jessie Binford and meet with Jane Addams, Edith Abbott, and other reformers. In Los Angeles or Chicago, these women exchanged information on the juvenile court movement and social legislation to improve the conditions of women and children.

The community of women reformers in Los Angeles during the 1920s extended beyond paid, professional workers like Shontz, Fisher, Woods, and Van Waters. An extensive network of women's clubs, whose members came from both elite and middle class families, took up the cause of the female juvenile delinquent, largely at the urging of Miriam Van Waters in her frequent addresses to local women's organizations. For example, the Friday Morning Club—with 1,000 members the largest women's club on the West Coast—offered political support for her efforts to improve conditions at Juvenile Hall. Van Waters chaired the juvenile court division of the California Federation of Women's Clubs and took special pride in her relationship with the Colored Women's Federation, which sought to establish a training school for "colored girls."[22] Church-affiliated women's auxiliaries sustained both the social gospel and the moral authority of Protestant women when they brought pressure to bear during recurrent conservative attacks on the El Retiro experiment. Van Waters also made allies of the local Council of Jewish Women, which funded a court social worker. In her most effective use of women's professional networks in the 1920s, she helped convince the Los Angeles Business Women's

Club to fund a residential home where young women released from El Retiro could live on their own while they began to be self-supporting, thus preventing their return to hostile or abusive families. Through such efforts, separate women's organizations in Los Angeles supported both the professional and political advancement of women like Miriam Van Waters and maintained a female voice within social reform efforts.

However supportive the Los Angeles women's community, local politics ultimately impinged on Van Waters's reform efforts, destroying the El Retiro experiment in 1927. Frustrated by the failures she witnessed in the juvenile court movement and drawn into national service on both President Herbert Hoover's crime commission and a Harvard Law School crime survey, Van Waters shifted her career in two directions: from California to Massachusetts and from juvenile to adult corrections. In 1932, at the age of forty-four, she accepted the position of superintendent at the Massachusetts Reformatory for Women in Framingham. For the next twenty-five years she made Framingham a testing ground for her reform philosophies and innovative social work methods. Van Waters vowed "to bring our neighbors into our planning, to have the community flow into us, and our institution into the community."[23] She drew local students, college faculty, clergy, and women's groups into the prison as volunteers; introduced psychological counseling and therapeutic recreational groups for inmates; and established intensely close familial relations with the women whom she called "students" and in whom she invested unusual trust and responsibility for their daily lives. Her efforts to create an alternative correctional institution at Framingham echoed the visions of the nineteenth-century women prison reformers who had founded the reformatory, but her methods contrasted sharply with the disciplinary style of prison administration that prevailed during the 1930s and 1940s. Critics accused Van Waters of coddling prisoners and defying state authority. Even some supporters marveled at the extent of her regal command over the Framingham reformatory. Repeatedly Van Waters conflicted with the parole board and the Massachusetts Department of Corrections, and, as in Los Angeles, she often mobilized women's networks to support her reforms.

Although the Framingham prison was an involuntary women's institution, under Miriam Van Waters it often resembled a voluntary community as well. Hundreds of women, imbued with a mission to rehabilitate incarcerated women, chose to work there as interns and staff members. In many ways, Van Waters modeled Framingham as much on Hull House as she did on El Retiro. Indeed, over the years residents of various settlement houses visited or interned at Framingham. So did women college students in search of meaningful work. One such woman, a recent graduate of Cornell, recalled her first impression of Framingham in the mid 1930s: "I think from the moment I walked in there was something about the atmosphere. I just thought . . . 'This is wonderful.' . . . It was more like a progressive school. There was no prison atmosphere whatsoever. . . . the whole atmosphere was one of growth and excitement and new experience, you know, and people coming in and out."[24] This woman stayed as an intern, then joined the staff, and after receiving a social work degree, spent the rest of her career as a devoted employee of Van Waters at Framingham. Similarly, interns from Vassar, Smith, Wellesley, Simmons, and other colleges went to the reformatory to teach classes on current events, ceramics, art, and psychology. Van Waters herself enjoyed the opportunity to lead weekly literary study groups. Like progressive educators, she tried to make the entire institution a learning experience. The nursery, which housed children born in prison, became a training ground for teachers and health workers. The nearby woods provided an incentive for well-behaved and trusted inmates who aspired to join the nature study club that took weekend hikes. In the 1940s and 1950s Van Waters incorporated elements of group therapy and the self-help model of Alcoholics Anonymous into her programs for inmates. "Only delinquents can solve the problems of delinquents," she wrote, and so Van Waters offered jobs to former "students," some of whom chose to return to the institution as staff members.[25]

As much as it was like a school, Framingham was also a social welfare institution in the broadest sense. Many of the women committed by the courts were simply homeless, pregnant, or alcoholic. Van Waters and other staff members preferred to view them as women in need of supportive services, not punishment. "Framingham presents all the problems of the modern world," Van Waters once reflected, noting that its residents shared with other women the dilemma of finding adequate child care to enable them to go to work.[26] Since poverty and inadequate health care plagued the residents, Van Waters pressed for both medical and mental health personnel to address their problems. Job training became a central goal, and she developed a "furlough system" that allowed many "students" to work for pay on the outside.

Material support was only part of Van Waters's program. A deeply spiritual woman, she spoke of her mission as "Christian Penology." As she recorded in her journal: "here I intend to build—'a kingdom of heaven on earth'—that is to say—a world of order, protection, fluid understanding, where both spontaneity and discipline—express the service of justice."[27] Central to achieving her goal of "The Framingham Symphony" was the personal charisma of conductor Miriam Van Waters. As one observer noted, the "faith and friendship of the superintendent" was key to the "informal rehabilitation" that characterized Framingham. In the words of one inmate, "The Superintendent has so much faith in me that I can't ever let her down."[28] Van Waters maintained a sincere respect for "the child of God" in each woman in the institution. In many cases, her charges responded to this personal approach with extreme loyalty, deep adoration, and idealization of their saintly superintendent.

Personal charisma alone could not have maintained so unusual an institution. Van Waters repeatedly relied on a variety of middle-class women's networks and organizations to support her earthly kingdom. Smith, Wellesley, and other women's college graduates, who often worked for room and board plus a small stipend, made possible the educational programs at Framingham. Outside the institution, club women offered support. In 1947 the Altrusa Club of Boston, consisting of fifty-four prominent businesswomen, raised money to hire women workers from the reformatory, since, as one club member wrote, "men in institutions have the privileges of earning and saving money through their labors while such privileges are not given to women."[29] Similarly, the Massachusetts League of Women Voters protested both the injustice of heavier penalties for women offenders (for crimes such as adultery and cohabitation) and the fact that "only poor women are prosecuted for these crimes," many of whom were "foreign speaking."[30] Van Waters also mobilized church women to support her reforms, as she had learned to do in Los Angeles. In a state with long-standing tensions between Catholics and Protestants, she won the respect of every denomination. A striking example of how club women's networks operated appears in a letter to Van Waters from Mrs. Willa W. Brown, who had once heard the superintendent give a college commencement address. Learning that Van Waters might lose her job in 1949, Brown wrote to offer help. "You do not know me," she began. "I am a member of the Boston Wheelock Club, the Florence Crittendon League, the Women's Charity Club, the Bright and Helmstone Women's Club, & the Women's Association of the Brighton Congregational Church. So you see I would be able to obtain a great many signatures in your behalf."[31]

Aside from relying on community support, Van Waters turned to religious, personal, and political networks to bolster her efforts. At the invitation of settlement worker Vida Scudder, she joined the Society of the Companions of the Holy Cross, a select group of reform-minded Episcopalian women who nurtured a spiritual commitment to social justice and class reconciliation.[32] Professionally she remained in touch with her former Los Angeles colleagues and with her first benefactor, Ethel Sturges Dummer, who funded small research projects at Framingham. After 1930, however, Van Waters's main emotional and political sustenance came from her "dearest love," Geraldine Morgan Thompson (1872–1967).

A former suffragist and an activist in the New Jersey women's club movement, Geraldine Thompson devoted her life and her considerable wealth to the cause of charitable institutions. She helped found the Monmouth County Organization for Social Services in 1912 and served on its board until 1952. Thompson took a special interest in the care and cure of tuberculosis and in juvenile justice and women's prisons. As a member of the Board of Control of the State Department of Institutions and Agencies (the first woman appointed to a state board in New Jersey), she helped oversee the women's reformatory at Clinton Farms. Although a lifelong Republican and a national committee-woman during the 1920s, Thompson had intimate ties to the New Deal White House, for she had grown up near Hyde Park and remained a warm friend of Eleanor and Franklin Roosevelt.[33]

Geraldine Thompson met Miriam Van Waters in the mid 1920s, and the two women gradually became intimate friends as well as reform allies. Thompson supported Van Waters's reform efforts at Framingham. She often visited the institution and addressed staff meetings and student assemblies, speaking about politics and public service. Thanks to Thompson, Eleanor Roosevelt also spoke at the institution. Geraldine Thompson's philanthropy provided stipends for interns, funded a part-time psychiatrist, and supplemented the educational and nursery budgets.

In addition to involving herself in the life of the institution through contributions and visits, Thompson provided a physical and emotional refuge for Van Waters. When the superintendent felt overwhelmed by institutional responsibilities and the stress of providing for the close relatives who lived with or near her, she could recuperate at Brookdale, the Thompson estate near Red Bank, New Jersey. The two friends would take early morning horseback rides and long walks, talk of their work and their spiritual beliefs, and take comfort in each other's love. Thus, after a day at Brookdale, Van Waters wrote in her journal: "I am deeply at peace, cherished and blessed beyond words by Geraldine's love and care."[34] After Thompson's husband died in 1936, the two women regularly vacationed together, and they continued to attend conferences throughout the United States and in Europe. Through letters and telephone calls, Thompson provided a well of "strength" for Van Waters. As they aged in the 1950s, Van Waters and Thompson, along with close women friends from the reformatory staff, spent weekends at Audubon Camps in New England and delighted in the company of nature and each other.

Thompson also provided a link to larger women's political networks. Van Waters met Eleanor Roosevelt when the couple dined at the White House in 1940. When Massachusetts politics threatened to undermine the mission at Framingham, Thompson would remind Mrs. Roosevelt of Van Waters's good works and ask her to intervene. In 1945, for example, Thompson feared that the governor might remove Van Waters from office, so she wrote to Roosevelt. "Miriam," Thompson explained, "is not only a liberal, but a radical, and a fighting radical, at that. . . . She is, and has always been, an ardent supporter of yours and Franklin." A brief note to the governor, Thompson suggested, could let him know how much Mrs. Roosevelt appreciated "the type of philosophy and administration which has made Framingham the outstanding Women's Reformatory in this country."[35] Van Waters remained in office, at least partially due to Roosevelt's intervention.

Although Miriam Van Waters staved off political attack through the 1940s, her methods had long infuriated conservatives in the Department of Corrections. From 1947 to 1949, critics of the reformatory made her the subject of state investigations, newspaper exposés, and a series of three public hearings at which she defended her administration. The attack began in 1947, when state officials charged that Van Waters had exceeded her authority by indenturing women in jobs outside the reformatory and allowing some of them privileges such as occasional dinners and movies in town. They also attacked the superintendent for hiring former inmates and for allowing released students to visit friends at the reformatory. The most controversial charge was that she condoned homosexual relationships between inmates, a practice that, opponents claimed, had led to the suicide of one inmate. In January 1949 the commissioner of corrections dismissed her from office.

Van Waters defended herself against these charges effectively, standing up in public hearings for her principles of educational, rather than punitive, treatment and gaining national attention for her work at Framingham. Meanwhile, influential friends throughout the country rallied to stand by her. Testimonials and contributions arrived from women active in reform and politics, including Geraldine Thompson, Ethel Sturges Dummer, Eleanor Roosevelt, and Frances Perkins. Both men and women in the field of social welfare mobilized on her behalf, as did dozens of Boston area Episcopal, Catholic, and Jewish clergy and local college faculty and students. Organizational endorsements included those of the Massachusetts State Federation of Women's Clubs, the National Council of Jewish Women, the Massachusetts Society for Social Hygiene, the YWCA, the Massachusetts Council of Churches, and the Americans for Democratic Action. Outpourings of faith and admiration arrived daily—in handwritten notes from former inmates, on engraved stationery from the wives of prominent men, and in typed letters from professional women. When Van Waters won reinstatement as superintendent in March 1949, letters from supporters around the country poured into her office. Her close friend Felix Frankfurter claimed that the cause of democracy was served through her reinstatement. Having withstood the attack by conservative politicians, Van Waters became a symbol of "progressive penology." Along with her prominent liberal supporters, dozens of former prisoners, local housewives, and complete strangers wrote to congratulate the superintendent on the "vindication of your principles."[36]

At Framingham, Van Waters continued to mobilize local middle-class women's organizations to support her reforms. In the 1950s, for example, members of the Friends of Framingham not only volunteered at the prison but also lobbied the state legislature to preserve the day work system. But hostile state officials, resentful of Van Waters's victory, monitored the prison closely and tried to impede her most innovative reforms. Like other cold war politicians, her critics repeatedly raised the specter of sexual deviance, claiming that homosexuality was rampant at Framingham in order to sensationalize their charges. In 1957, just two months before Van Waters retired, Boston newspaper headlines charged: "Sex Fiends, Boozers Run Wild in Women's Prison." A state legislative investigation soon condemned "aggressive homosexuals" at the facility and led to the resignation of the deputy superintendent, a protégé of Van Waters.[37] These attacks reflected a new climate for women reformers, for the opposition to Van Waters was in many ways symptomatic of a larger postwar critique of women's work outside the home, women's sexual independence, and female political authority. The Van Waters case and its aftermath left a public image that conflated wage-earning women, lesbians, and the specter that strong female leaders encouraged both.

Each stage in Miriam Van Waters's dramatic career—first her life as an influential figure in the juvenile justice movement, then as a champion of women's prison reform, and finally as a reformer under attack—illuminates the history of women and social reform in modern America. Van Waters's decision to apply her education to the provision of social services, and in particular her work with female clients, made sense in terms of the tradition of women's reform. By the time Van Waters came of age professionally, however, the relationship between women reformers and the state had begun to change in critical ways. Women like Florence Kelley and Julia Lathrop had moved beyond the voluntarism and outsider politics of the past, while the expansion of state social services during the Progressive Era, and later during the New Deal, drew women into paid, professional, and often highly politicized roles. As voluntary reformers, settlement workers such as Jane Addams or Vida Scudder had enjoyed a measure of immunity to male political authority. With the professionalization of social work and its centralization within state agencies, a younger generation of reformers, including Miriam Van Waters, entered administrative hierarchies, usually headed by men, under the watchful eyes of state legislators. As a result, women not only expanded their public authority through integration into the male political culture but they also lost some of the administrative autonomy that earlier, voluntary reformers had enjoyed. Thus new obstacles confronted Van Waters at critical points in her career, in the 1920s and the 1940s, when state officials attempted to undermine her reforms or oust her from office because of her sympathies toward prisoners and her innovative methods.

The career of Miriam Van Waters illuminates not only new obstacles, but also certain continuities in women's reform strategies. Van Waters repeatedly relied on women's personal and political networks to advance her programs. Before suffrage, she both created and was supported by strong ties to women— in her family, in school, and in the juvenile court movement. After 1920 she continued to draw on both close personal ties to women and extensive out- reach to women in churches and in social service organizations. That Van Waters could bring such an array of women's community-based organizations into a prison reminds us of the rich yet still largely untapped history of middle- class women's voluntary associations in the twentieth century.[38] Among the women in these organizations—many of whom joined neither the expanding female paid labor force nor the small feminist movement—separate institution building persisted, as did support for women's social reform efforts.

Van Waters's individual character, the nature of women's prison reform, and the local contexts in which she operated might account for the continuing influence of separatism throughout her career. But the fact that she could mobilize so many women's voluntary, religious, and political organizations from the 1920s through the 1950s suggests that Van Waters's story may not be entirely unique. Rather, her life may reveal larger patterns that require at least two kinds of further historical inquiry: first, to learn what common experi- ences inspired and sustained the work of this cohort of reformers; and second, to compare the approaches of pre- and postsuffrage women reformers.

Van Waters belonged to a generation of women reformers that followed in the shadow of Addams, Kelley, and Lathrop. These activists continued to work for women's interests, often based in women's institutions, though con- stantly maneuvering through the obstacles of male political authority. In the labor movement, this generation included women who came out of the work- ers' education movement of the 1920s, such as organizer Rose Pesotta and researcher Theresa Wolfson, as well as Women's Bureau director Esther Peter- son. In civil rights, it encompassed the careers of Mary McLeod Bethune and Charlotte Hawkins Brown, each of whom remained rooted in African Ameri- can women's clubs as they worked through the 1940s to achieve racial equality. In criminal justice, Edna Mahon, a protégé of Van Waters, drew on women's organizations to protect her reforms at the New Jersey women's reformatory; the career of Dorothy Kenyon, a feminist lawyer and public official, illustrates the devastating impact McCarthyism could have on this generation.[39]

Common dilemmas and common survival strategies characterized members of this generation of reformers. Despite the decline of the old social gospel, religious values continued to inspire and sustain reform efforts for Van Waters, as it did for others, such as another minister's daughter, labor activist Mary Van Kleeck, who also belonged to the Society of the Companions of the Holy Cross. Intimate female partnerships among white, middle-class women survived the modern "lesbian taboo" to nourish reformers—as did the Van Waters–Thompson relationship and the partnerships of Lillian Smith and Paula Snelling, Mary Dreier and Frances Kellor, and psychologists Jessie Taft and Virginia Robinson.[40] Whatever degree of consciousness these women had about their sexual identity, like Van Waters they could become vulnerable to veiled accusations of lesbianism, especially during the antigay atmosphere of the McCarthy era.[41] Whether in couples or alone, some women of Van Waters's generation resolved the family-career dilemma by raising adopted children, often with the support of women friends, as did, for instance, Assistant Attorney General Mabel Walker Willebrandt.[42] Whatever personal strategies supported them, I suspect that the members of this generation provided an unrecognized legacy for the founding mothers of the new feminism. How often do the YWCA, Haddasah, black women's church clubs, the Women's Bureau, and the League of Women Voters appear in the genealogies of later activists, inspired, as was historian Ann Scott during the 1940s, by "women of such force and power"?[43]

In addition to appreciating the survival of women's networks and institutions in the twentieth century, turning our historical attention to the generation of postsuffrage women social reformers that included Miriam Van Waters may revise our understanding of continuity and discontinuity in reform strategy from the Progressive Era to the cold war. To compare pre- and postsuffrage reform movements requires at least three kinds of historical analyses: of institutions, of ideology, and of political authority. The clearest evidence of continuity in women's reform is the survival of separate women's networks, clubs, and formal institutions. Despite the emphasis on political integration in the 1920s and the professionalization of women's reform, particularly through social work, older forms of voluntary associations continued. While many professional women worked within male institutions after 1920, nonemployed and nonprofessional women kept up local, voluntary, and often church-based female institutions. In addition, national institutions, such as the Women's Bureau, the Children's Bureau, the League of Women Voters, the National

Woman's Party, and the Business and Professional Women's Clubs, suggest that not all politically active or professional women were willing to turn over the tasks of social service and policy making to men.

The ideology underlying these women's institutions, however, did not necessarily resemble that of their predecessors. In the nineteenth century, women's reform rested in large part on ideals of female difference from and moral superiority to men, as well as on a social authority based on the common experience of motherhood. Within a modern gender system that no longer rested solidly on an ideology of separate spheres, women's moral authority had to derive from more than gender. As Nancy Cott has shown, the idea of a unitary female identity gradually disintegrated after 1910 as feminists both claimed equality with men and recognized diversities among women.[44] The rhetoric of both professional and voluntary women's groups reflected this shift. Although Van Waters and others continued to focus on service to women and children, they were less likely to invoke their own womanhood as a justification for their efforts. Even as Van Waters drew women's groups to her aid, she called on their humanitarian (or, in her terms, Christian) sympathies; an earlier generation would have called on Christian *womanhood*. Privately, however, gender consciousness did not disappear; in her journal, for example, Van Waters compared her minority status as "an isolated female Penologist" to the status of a racial minority, and she once—but only once—requested that a public official testify on her behalf by invoking his support for "the rights of women."[45] Her public rhetoric often played down gender and spoke in neutral terms of the parenthood of the state and the importance of scientific insight into delinquency. I suspect that other reformers similarly mixed their strategies in order to survive in the climate in which they operated. At a time when female bonding was suspect rather than esteemed, reformers relied on women's separate support systems even as they denied the significance of gender in their reforms. Perhaps women's institutions seemed to disappear in the post-suffrage era because separatism had disappeared from women's rhetoric, if not always from their sustenance.

Women's institutions survived, their rhetoric modified, but what kind of political authority did they wield, especially in comparison with the era of Addams, Kelley, and Lathrop? Historians have suggested that red-baiting undermined women's political authority during the early 1920s and that by the end of the decade, the national women's lobby failed to maintain its gains, as evidenced by the loss of state support for maternal health care with the defeat of the Shephard-Towner Act in 1927. Even the New Deal, which can be seen as a culmination of women's social welfare goals, fell far short of meeting the needs of working and poor women. Whether through the success of welfare politics or their shortcomings, women's political authority on the national level suffered serious blows.

Nonetheless, two important questions about the persistence of women's reform influence are suggested by the career of Van Waters. First, to what extent did women maintain legislative influence and administrative authority at the state and local levels after 1930? Only further case studies will reveal how many women like Van Waters remained in office, how they did so, and against what obstacles. Recent revisionist histories suggest that separate institutions did support women who were able to maintain formal political authority. Susan Hartmann has pointed out that many female legislators who sponsored bills to advance women's opportunities in the 1940s (such as Representative Chase Going Woodhouse of Connecticut and Senator Margaret Chase Smith of Maine) gained their political expertise in the League of Women Voters, the Women's International League for Peace and Freedom, the women's colleges, or the Business and Professional Women's Clubs.[46] For them, postsuffrage women's institutions fueled female political authority. The second question concerns women's power outside traditional political institutions. When did women wield authority in neighborhoods, communities, unions, churches, and nascent social movements, and did their power derive in part from separate women's institutions? Again, historical inquiries have just begun, but, as Sara Evans notes, during the 1950s diverse groups of women mobilized their private networks for political ends, ranging from New Mexico Chicanas who took leadership in the miners' strike depicted in *Salt of the Earth*, to San Francisco lesbians whose social network formed the basis for the Daughters of Bilitis, to southern black members of the local Women's Political Council that became critical to the Montgomery bus boycott.[47]

As in the past, separate women's institutions did not have a unified politics, nor did they always work to promote the interests of women and children. Women's organizations, informal or formal, could support class or race supremacy and gender inequality, and they could be used by either conservative or progressive politicians.[48] My focus here, however, is the role that separate women's institutions have continued to play in the service of social reform. In this essay, drawing on the career of Miriam Van Waters, I have tried to suggest that where women continued to organize as women—even without an explicit ideology of gender difference—they had the power to facilitate social reform in their local communities and even in state and national politics. Although women's movements for reform were smaller, more beleaguered, and more vulnerable after 1920, they developed new strategies for navigating within male political cultures, strategies that in turn helped lay the groundwork for yet another surge of women's political activity after 1960.

In 1945, when Miriam Van Waters lamented the passing of great women leaders in social reform, she was at least partially correct in her historical assessment. Gone were Addams, Kelley, and Lathrop, the nationally visible leaders of movements to protect women and children through state-sponsored reforms. Yet Van Waters may have overlooked an equally important historical phenomenon that flourished in her own backyard: grassroots, local, and voluntary women's institutions. These separate organizations continued to nurture an American women's reform tradition well into the twentieth century.

CHAPTER 9 : THE PERSONAL
AND THE POLITICAL : TWO CASE
STUDIES : *WILLIAM H. CHAFE*

P erhaps no phrase is more identified with the scholarship of women's history or the feminist movement from which it sprang than the simple but revolutionary statement, "the personal is political." In her book *Personal Politics*, Sara Evans traces the emergence of the women's liberation movement in the late 1960s to the realization among women civil rights activists that their political activity on behalf of racial equality could not be compartmentalized from their private lives. Justice must be present in personal relationships as well as in public policies regarding race. Indeed, there quickly developed the credo that freedom and autonomy did not exist as external objects or goals to be achieved but had to begin at the very core of one's life—in the family, at home, with lovers and partners, in friendships as well as business and professional relationships. What happened in the bedroom and the kitchen connected directly to what transpired at the office or on the assembly line. Gender roles and sexuality were linked to power and how it was exercised.[1]

From the moment consciousness-raising groups emerged as a central organizing mechanism for the new feminism, this fundamental insight about personal politics came to encapsulate and exemplify the transformative power of the women's liberation message. Having shared information and knowledge about what it means to grow up a woman in American culture, participants in consciousness-raising groups went back to their homes and work situations armed with a collective determination to demand change. Whether that change involved an equal sharing of household and child-care responsibilities, an end to sex-role stereotyping in books, movies, and toys, or the enactment of laws to protect reproductive freedom, there remained the essential animating principle that private and public spheres could not be treated as unrelated; on the contrary, they existed on a single continuum, uniformly susceptible to judgment on the criteria of justice and equality.[2]

The phrase "the personal is political" soon took on additional meanings, however, some of which are more problematic or at least controversial. Presumably, if life is a continuum that does not permit the segregation of private and public spheres, then what transpires in private life helps to shape and inform what goes on publicly, and vice versa. The logical implication of that assumption is that public activity cannot be comprehended or assessed without examination as well of private activity that may help to motivate or structure public actions. But how does that linkage play itself out when the public act being examined is in truth a political act, and the subject of assessment is a political figure's behavior on issues of state and public policy? Does the "personal is political" mean that the historian must delve as much as possible into a public figure's private life in order to understand and explain why that figure behaves in a given way? And if so, how far should the probe go? Is there anything off limits? Does information about a politician's sex life, patterns of toilet training, or treatment of family or lovers become a sine qua non for assessing public policy performance or a person's qualifications to be president, mayor, or cabinet member?

Such questions highlight some of the pragmatic dilemmas that emerge from a sound theoretical insight. Presumably, most historians as well as ordinary citizens believe in some rights of privacy. Commitment to the idea that a direct connection exists between how one acts and is treated in private and how one behaves under the gaze of public surveillance runs counter, at some point, to the competing principle that what people do in their own bedrooms, and with whom, is no one's business but their own. How then can one reconcile these concerns? Does the private always shape the public? What are the shadings of difference? Is there a cause-and-effect relationship between the personal and political or simply one of reciprocal reinforcement?

There are no simple answers to these queries, but in seeking to understand the problem better, it might be useful to look more closely at two examples of public figures whose private lives have been the topic of considerable attention and controversy. One is Eleanor Roosevelt, a legendary heroine for millions whose private love relationships have recently become a focal point

Allard Lowenstein first met Eleanor Roosevelt when he was a student at the University of North Carolina. Subsequently they became devoted friends. (Courtesy of the Southern Historical Collection, University of North Carolina at Chapel Hill)

for public discussion. The other is Allard Lowenstein, congressman from Long Island in 1968–70, a different kind of legendary figure, but someone with the same capacity for galvanizing thousands of people, and with a personal life also a subject of controversy. Each individual's experience dramatizes the issue of how much personal and private matters are essential to understand political and public behavior. Roosevelt and Lowenstein were very different people. Although they knew one another well and played important roles in each other's lives, that fact simply adds an extra fillip of interest and intrigue to their stories. In most ways, their life histories do not lead to the conclusion that there is only one way of answering the questions raised above. Yet their experiences may help us to understand the questions more, as well as the benefits and impediments of continuing to explore how the personal and the political shape each other and must be understood in tandem.

ELEANOR ROOSEVELT

Much of the recent discussion about Eleanor Roosevelt has revolved around Blanche Wiesen Cook's powerful biography covering Roosevelt's first fifty years. In that volume, Cook details with precision and passion the extent to which understanding Eleanor Roosevelt's private life is pivotal to understanding her public life. Although other Roosevelt biographers and essayists had addressed some issues that were primarily private in nature—Joseph Lash, for example, suggested that Eleanor Roosevelt's marital unhappiness helped explain her turn toward a more public role in the 1920s and thereafter—Blanche Cook has explored the private side of Roosevelt with far greater intensity. In the process, she has interwoven accounts of Roosevelt's public activity with discussions of previously obscured personal issues, including Roosevelt's love relationships with other women and men.[3]

The story of Eleanor Roosevelt is one of some sadness and much triumph. Her childhood up to about fourteen years of age and a significant part of her late twenties and early thirties were times of turbulence. Emotional rejection and pain went hand in hand with self-doubt and a struggle to find a place and an identity of her own, where love and self-esteem could flourish. Yet it would be wrong to think of Roosevelt's private life as without joy, because she often—indeed, more often than not—triumphed in her search for personal happiness. Customarily, Roosevelt's public life is described as one of epic achievements on the one hand and of bitter personal unhappiness on the other. But as Blanche Cook and others have shown, that depiction of a dichotomized existence fails to address the complexities of Eleanor Roosevelt's experience. The private and public were part of a continuum.

By virtually everyone's account, Eleanor Roosevelt's early years were miserable. "I was a solemn child," she later wrote, "without beauty. I seemed like a little old woman entirely lacking in the spontaneous joy and mirth of youth." Although her mother—an aristocrat and debutante—warmly embraced Eleanor's brother, she seemed only "kindly and indifferent" to her little girl, calling her "Granny" and, in Eleanor's memory, conveying to her the message that she was plain and old-fashioned. Eleanor's cousin Corinne said, "It was the grimmest childhood I had ever known. Who did she have? Nobody."[4]

That was not quite true, because for a brief period, perhaps magnified in intensity and dimension by the memories of childhood, Eleanor had her father Elliott. "He was the one great love of my life as a child," she observed in her autobiography, "and like . . . many children, I have lived a dream life with him." Charming, generous, and debonair, Elliott had the capacity to make those he loved feel very special, as though no one else counted. Eleanor recalled responding to his attentions with an almost magical sense of wonder. "As soon as I could talk," she said, "I went into his dressing room every morning and chattered to him . . . I even danced with him, intoxicated by the pure joy of motion . . . until he would pick me up and throw me into the air." He called her "father's own little Nell" and wrote her about the "wonderful long rides" they would take "through the grand, snow-clad forests, over the white hills" with their horse and sleigh. Because these visions were so intense, she dreamed of the time they could be together—"always he and I . . . and someday [we] would have a life of our own together."[5]

Tragically, the realities of Elliott's life made such reveries exactly what they appear to be in retrospect—fantasies of intimacy and joy. Although Eleanor knew little about the truths of her parents' relationship at the time, she later learned some of the secrets that made her childhood so emotionally turbulent. Despite their apparent love for each other, Eleanor's mother and father separated by the time she was six. The other side of Elliott's charm and ebullience was a penchant for irresponsibility, recklessness, and alcoholism. Banished from the household until he could show he was cured, Elliott became a figure of exile. Even when his long-awaited visits occurred, they frequently ended in disaster, as when Elliott left Eleanor with the doorman at his New York club and then went off on a drunken spree. When she was eight, her mother died from diphtheria which she contracted after an operation. Two years later, still captive to his alcoholism, Elliott passed away as well. Eleanor was not permitted to go to either funeral. Looking back later in life for an explanation of her difficulty in expressing emotions spontaneously, Eleanor concluded that the traumas of her childhood were the main cause. "Something locked me up," she said.[6]

Yet within five years, Eleanor had recovered her spirits sufficiently that by the time she attended Allenwood, a girls' school outside of London, she became one of the most popular, admired, and loved students in the community. Presided over by Marie Souvestre, an inspirational, strong-minded woman who vigorously defended the cause of the Boers in South Africa and Alfred Dreyfuss in France, Allenwood served as the touchstone for most of the positive things that occurred during the rest of Eleanor Roosevelt's life. She described her stay there as "the happiest years of my life" and declared that "whatever I have become since had its seeds in those three years of contact with a liberal mind and strong personality."[7] Souvestre took Roosevelt with her on tours of the Continent, gave her the place of honor next to her at dinner, and provided a constant source of intellectual and emotional reinforcement. With a strong sense of both self-esteem and purposefulness, Eleanor returned to New York in 1901 for her "coming out" season in society as a very different person than she had been just a few short years before.

Marie Souvestre's imprint on Roosevelt remained clear even in the midst of her becoming a debutante. "Bear in mind," Souvestre had written her, "that there are more quiet and enviable joys than to be among the most sought-after women at a ball."[8] In turn-of-the-century New York, with its new settlement houses and reform crusades, Eleanor Roosevelt heeded the injunction and became an active member of a network of women social reformers. Only eighteen, she joined the National Consumers' League, headed by Florence Kelley and committed to improving health and safety conditions for women workers. Roosevelt also started to teach calisthenics and dance at the Rivington Street Settlement House, where she witnessed both the deprivation that surrounded the lives of the poor and the courage of people responding to the opportunity to change their lives. Unlike other teachers from the upper class who volunteered their services, Roosevelt insisted on taking public transportation to the settlement house, walking through the garbage-filled, raucous streets full of tenements so that she could see firsthand the world her students came from. Although Roosevelt pursued her settlement work for only a relatively brief period prior to her marriage to her cousin Franklin in 1905, her involvement with social reform, together with her years at Allenwood, provided the foundation for much of what would occur politically in the rest of her life. The same years demonstrated the personal rewards that could come from being committed to a community of women who shared common goals and values.

Eleanor's marriage reactivated some of her self-doubts, not so much because of her relationship with Franklin, with whom she shared a delightful sense of romance, as because of her mother-in-law, Sara Roosevelt, who seemed intent on controlling her life. Although Eleanor bore six children in eleven years and ran a complicated household, she never was allowed to feel in charge. Sara purchased and furnished a duplex house in New York City where she could reign supreme, and at Hyde Park, the family estate, she continued to preside. At dinner, Franklin sat at one end of the table, Sara at the other. In front of the fireplace there were two wing chairs, one for her, one for her son. Worst of all, Sara sought to control the rearing of the children, giving them presents, cultivating their allegiance, and eventually even taking them on their grand tours of Europe. At one point, she referred to the children as "my children. . . . Your mother only bore you." Understandably, Eleanor Roosevelt's sense of comfort and identity in this family configuration was less than ideal. Her daughter Anna recalled that she was "always stiff, never relaxed enough to romp," and Eleanor herself regretted her inability to relate naturally and freely to her children and their environment. Only when she was able to set up her own household after Franklin was elected to the state senate in Albany could she begin to regain her own voice and sense of self.[9]

The critical years, however, were the ones spent in Washington during World War I when Franklin was assistant secretary of the navy and then during the 1920s back in New York City when Eleanor took control of her own life. The war provided an opportunity for the social activist side of Eleanor Roosevelt's personality to reassert itself. As a volunteer and wife of a subcabinet officer, she helped organize hospitality centers for soldiers on their way to training camps, supervised knitting rooms at the Navy Department, and devoted herself to improving the conditions at St. Elizabeth's mental hospital. As biographer Joseph Lash observed, "the war gave her a reason acceptable to her conscience . . . to concentrate less on her household and to plunge into work that fitted her aptitude."[10] From that point forward, Eleanor Roosevelt was an active social reformer, publicly championing those causes and issues that meant the most to her.

Also during World War I, Eleanor discovered that her husband had been unfaithful and was carrying on a love affair with her social secretary, Lucy Mercer. Franklin had always been a "gay cavalier"—somewhat like her father—and loved having a good time, whether that involved drinking too much (from her point of view), playing cards with the "boys," or flirting with women. But never before, to Eleanor's knowledge, had he crossed the boundary and violated his marriage vows. Now in 1918, as Eleanor unpacked Franklin's luggage after he was stricken with pneumonia while on a mission to Europe, she discovered a packet of letters between Lucy and Franklin describing their affair. Once again, she was devastated by a personal betrayal. Although she agreed to stay married if Franklin would break off the affair, the magic of their earlier relationship had disappeared forever. As James Roosevelt, the eldest son, later wrote, his parents "agreed to go on for the sake of appearances, the children and the future, but as business partners, not as husband and wife. . . . After that, father and mother had an armed truce that endured until the day he died."[11]

Some have speculated that Eleanor Roosevelt's reemergence as a public figure was caused directly by her private bitterness at Franklin's treachery. But it makes more sense to see her public involvements in the years after World

War I as a continuation and resurfacing of the same interests that had motivated her to join the Consumers' League and teach at Rivington Street in the early 1900s. Eleanor's renewed activism *predated* her discovery of the Mercer affair and could be traced back, ultimately, to the sense of self-esteem, pride, and direction that she had developed first in her relationship with Marie Souvestre at Allenwood.

It would be more accurate to say that the affair, and Franklin's subsequent illness with polio in 1922, created circumstances that propelled Eleanor more quickly into a life of her own. Before the polio attack, Eleanor had already accepted the role of coordinating the legislative program of the League of Women Voters in Albany and had joined the Women's Trade Union League, then viewed as one of the more progressive labor and women's groups. After Franklin contracted polio, she broadened her interests even further, oftentimes saying that she was acting in Franklin's stead, but in fact pursuing her own political and social reform interests as well. She organized the Democratic women throughout the state, lobbied for equal pay and child labor legislation, edited the *Women's Democratic News*, and became widely respected among men and women politicians alike as a powerful figure in her own right. Her distinctive ability to combine partisan politics with a commitment to social welfare placed her at the center of an ever-growing female reform network, providing a model for others to follow. When Franklin was elected governor of New York in 1928, and then president in 1932, Eleanor continued her activist ways, promoting the appointment of people like Frances Perkins to Franklin's state and then federal cabinet, working with close reform associates like Mary Dewson to build support for women in politics, and lobbying Franklin in private and others in public for passage of progressive legislation. Through her efforts, scores of women reformers flocked to Washington to take administration positions. Formerly, Mary Anderson of the Women's Bureau said, women officials had gotten together periodically to dine in a small university club. "Now," she said, "there are so many of [us] that we need a hall."[12]

As First Lady, Eleanor Roosevelt helped to transform the role of women in politics. Women friends such as Ellen Woodward, Hilda Smith, and Florence Kerr played a major role in crafting and implementing the New Deal's social welfare programs in the Works Progress Administration and in the Social Security field. To encourage both these women and the female press corps assigned to Washington, Eleanor Roosevelt initiated a series of press conferences to which *only* women reporters were admitted, and where the First Lady insisted on making "hard" news. By introducing her friends to talk about "their" programs, she underlined the importance of women-related issues as well as providing new status and prestige to women reporters. Roosevelt herself, meanwhile, pressed her husband to do more on issues of civil rights for blacks (the antilynching bill), farm reform, the creation of greenbelt communities through the Resettlement Administration, and the plight of low-paid garment and textile workers. "No one who ever saw Eleanor Roosevelt sit down facing her husband," Rexford Tugwell wrote, "and holding his eyes firmly, [say] to him, 'Franklin, I think you should [do this]'. . . will ever forget the experience. It would be impossible to say how often and to what extent American governmental processes have been turned in a direction because of her determination."[13] And all of this came as much from the lessons she imbibed from Marie Souvestre and her years with the Consumers' League as from bitterness over Franklin's marital infidelity.

If the private disappointments in Eleanor Roosevelt's life did not cause her to assume this new public role, what the Mercer affair did lead to was a gradual reallocation of emotional energy away from Franklin and toward others who became much more important sources of emotional gratification for her than her own immediate family. To an ever increasing extent, Eleanor found her closest personal and political camaraderie in her own community of friends, most of them women who shared her reform concerns but also a powerful affectionate linkage. During the 1920s she spent one night a week with Esther Lape and Elizabeth Read, two women who lived together and were devoted to some of the same political interests as Eleanor, particularly in the League of Women Voters. She also became friends with Women's Trade Union League members like Rose Schneiderman, a person of remarkably different background from herself. Molly Dewson of the Women's City Club and the Consumers' League was another intimate companion. Eleanor became particularly close to Nancy Cook and Marian Dickerman, and in 1926 she moved with them into Val-Kill, a newly constructed cottage at Hyde Park that was Eleanor's very own. The three women managed a furniture crafts factory at Val-Kill, and Dickerman and Roosevelt purchased Todhunter, a private school in New York where Eleanor Roosevelt taught three days a week even in the midst of her hectic political schedule. The linen and towels at Val-Kill were monogrammed "EMN," and the three women very much constituted a family. Val-Kill became the site of many wonderful weekends where Roosevelt's extended network of friends would gather for companionship as well as political discussion. A large number of these women were engaged in lifelong partnerships, then called "Boston marriages." By the 1970s these would be considered lesbian couples in most cases.

Eleanor Roosevelt herself appears to have been romantically attached to at least two people during these years. The first was Earl Miller, a former state trooper in New York who was assigned to be Eleanor's bodyguard when Franklin was elected governor. Miller became Roosevelt's "boon companion" and perhaps more. Described by friends of Mrs. Roosevelt's as "a man's man," he encouraged her to drive her own car, take up horseback riding again, and feel confident in her own instincts and wishes. She went frequently to his home for visits and had him stay at Val-Kill or her New York apartment. They went on long walks together and enjoyed late-evening suppers alone. Although some of her friends disliked his tendency to "manhandle" Eleanor by putting his arms on her shoulders and legs, photographs show that she casually and naturally laid her hand on his knee as well. The two had an extraordinarily close relationship, and James Roosevelt later observed that his mother's ties to Miller "may have been the one real romance in [her] life outside of marriage."[14]

In fact, that statement was only partly true. Eleanor was also in love with Lorena Hickok, a talented and feisty reporter who was assigned to cover her during the 1932 presidential campaign. In close proximity to Mrs. Roosevelt on numerous occasions, Hickok once observed, "that woman is unhappy about something." Eleanor had not wanted Franklin to become president and feared that life in the White House would destroy her independence and cast her in an empty role as hostess and figurehead. As the two women talked about their respective lives, they developed an intimacy and affection so close that Hickok felt obliged to resign her post covering Roosevelt because she could no longer write "objectively" about her.[15]

Within a short time, the two women were exchanging daily letters and phone calls, the contents of which suggested that each woman was deeply in love with the other. "Hick darling," Eleanor wrote on March 6, 1933, "how good it was to hear your voice. It was so inadequate to try to tell you what it meant. Jimmy was near and I could not say, *je t'aime et je t'adore* as I long to do, but always remember that I am saying it." The next night Eleanor wrote again. "All day," she said, "I thought of you, and another birthday, I *will* be with you and yet tonight you sounded so far away and formal. Oh! I want to put my arms around you. I ache to hold you close. Your ring is a great comfort. I look at it and think she does love me, or I wouldn't be wearing it." The two women plotted ways to be together, to steal a few days in the country, to bridge the gap of physical separation that so often stood between them:

> Only eight more days [Hickok wrote]. Twenty-four hours from now it will be only seven more—just a week! I've been trying today to bring back your face—to remember just *how* you looked. . . . Most clearly, I remember your eyes, with the kind of teasing smile in them, and the feeling of that soft spot just northeast of the corner of your mouth against my lips. I wonder

what we will do when we meet—what we will say when we meet. Well—I'm rather proud of us, aren't you? I think we have done rather well.

Over time, Roosevelt's relationship with Hickok cooled somewhat. When Hickok expressed jealousy of Eleanor's other friends, even her children, Roosevelt wrote: "Darling, the love one has for one's children is different, and not even Anna could be to me what you are." From her point of view, the two were like a married couple whose relationship had to "flower." "Dearest," she wrote, "strong relationships have to grow deep roots. We are growing them now, partly because we are separated. The foliage and the flowers will come somehow, I'm sure of it."

Still, Roosevelt could not seem to satisfy Hickok's desire for her total commitment. "I know you often have a feeling for me which for one reason or another I may not return in kind," Eleanor wrote, "but I feel I love you just the same." Hickok had to understand, Roosevelt said, "that I love other people the same way or differently, but each one has their place and one cannot compare them." But in the end, Roosevelt concluded that she had failed Hickok. "I never meant to hurt you in any way," she wrote, "but that is no excuse for having done it. It won't help you any, but I'll never do to anyone else what I did to you. . . . I am pulling myself back in all my contacts now. I have always done it with the children, and why I didn't know I couldn't give you (or anyone else who wanted or needed what you did) any real food, I can't now understand. Such cruelty and stupidity is unpardonable when you reach my age." Obviously, something had gone wrong in the relationship. Yet Roosevelt and Hickok remained close during the rest of the 1930s and 1940s, continuing to share the "special Christmases" that Eleanor reserved for her most intimate friends like Earl Miller, Nan Cook, and Lorena Hickok.[16]

It seems clear that Roosevelt's relationship with Hickok, and perhaps with Miller, was erotic as well as affectionate in nature. As Blanche Cook has noted, "Sigmund Freud notwithstanding: A cigar may not always be a cigar, but the 'north-east corner of your mouth against my lips' is always the northeast corner."[17]

Where either relationship would fall on the continuum of full sexual expression remains uncertain, largely due to the destruction or disappearance of important correspondence. Most significant is what Roosevelt's relationship to these women and men meant about her total life experience. It would seem that she was sustained throughout the most critical periods of her public life by enormously rewarding relationships in her private life. Without these she might well have found it difficult to have been as effective and powerful a personage as she was. In some ways, the nature of these relationships—and who they were with—reinforced and strengthened the particular kinds of public activities she engaged in.

Indeed, throughout her political journey in the late 1930s, 1940s, and 1950s, a strong link seemed to persist between the causes Eleanor Roosevelt embraced and the individuals she found it most attractive and rewarding to be with. In 1939 Roosevelt attended the opening meeting of the Southern Conference on Human Welfare (SCHW) in Birmingham, Alabama, at least partly because she cared so much for Frank Porter Graham, Aubrey Williams, and Mary McLeod Bethune, organizers of the meeting. The SCHW, then and later, was pilloried as a "leftwing" group because of its commitment to civil rights for blacks and progressive economic policies that would address the needs of the poor and disenfranchised. When local police commissioner Bull Connor ordered the black and white delegates to occupy different sides of the room in compliance with local segregation ordinances, Mrs. Roosevelt placed her chair in the middle so that it straddled both the black and white sides of the aisle, dramatically demonstrating her commitment both to the principle and the people who made civil rights important.

During the same period, she became deeply identified with the student movement of America, especially the American Student Union (ASU) and the American Youth Congress, both of which also bore the scars of being called "communist." In this instance, too, she had personal ties that reinforced her political commitments. Joseph Lash, an organizer and leader of the ASU, became an intimate friend. He and his young associates were invited to stay at the White House when they went to Washington to conduct protests and rallies. Attacked for her support of such "questionable" people, she responded: "I have never said anywhere that I would rather see young people sympathetic with communism. But I have said that I would rather see young people actively at work, even if I considered they were doing things that were a mistake."[18]

Eleanor Roosevelt's activism on behalf of civil rights, young people, unorganized workers, and world peace always had a personal dimension. After Franklin Roosevelt's death in 1945, world peace took on a special significance. "The weight of human misery here in Europe," she declared after a visit to Germany and its concentration camps, "is something one can't get out of one's heart." She had driven through England in 1928 noting the names of all the young men who had died during World War I, and now she had completed the same kind of journey through Germany. "There is a feeling that spreads over the land," she said, "the feel of [a] civilization that of itself might have a hard time coming back" if people did not find a way to come together and cooperate.[19] It was to further that end that she became a U.S. delegate to the United Nations in 1945 and helped shape the Universal Declaration of Human

Rights that was approved in 1948; she continued to advocate the civil rights movement through the 1950s and early 1960s and became chair of President John F. Kennedy's Commission on the Status of Women in 1961. It was all of a piece and all connected in some ways to the people who had given her the strength, the self-esteem, and the emotional support to be who she was— Marie Souvestre, Molly Dewson, Rose Schneiderman, Elizabeth Read, Lorena Hickok, Earl Miller.

Toward the end of her life, Roosevelt seemed increasingly drawn to friends and companions who were very young, almost like surrogate children. Joe Lash was one of these. "I love to be with you dear boy," she wrote him. "I never want to be alone when I'm with people I love." She bought him presents, corresponded with him almost daily, and looked forward eagerly to when they could be together so she could express her affection, kiss and hug him, and "tuck [him] in" on his birthday. She developed a similar relationship with David Gurewitsch, another young man who subsequently became her physician and traveled with her through much of the world during her international trips of the 1950s. Finally, there was a young man named Allard Lowenstein whom she met at an Ethical Culture conference in 1947 when he was just eighteen and subsequently befriended throughout the 1950s, getting him a leave from his army post in Germany so he could meet her in Paris and see the city, sharing automobile rides and lengthy conversations about the idealism Lowenstein felt about the younger generation and its chances of transforming the world.[20]

In all these ways, the personal and the political were part and parcel of each other. Contrary to some interpretations, there does not appear in Eleanor Roosevelt's life to have been a cause-and-effect relationship between personal unhappiness and political engagement. In fact, the opposite seems to have been more true. Roosevelt's fundamental political involvement grew out of her positive personal relationship with Marie Souvestre and a community of New York reformers at the turn of the century. Subsequently, those bonds were renewed and strengthened during the 1920s and 1930s, accompanied this time by deeper personal and emotional connections that took the place of the family ties that had been frayed and broken by Franklin's affair with Lucy Mercer. Conceivably, Eleanor Roosevelt's life could be appreciated without any reference to her father, the women and men she loved, and the way she experienced personal tragedy and triumph. But the artistic result of such a venture would seem more analogous to a stick figure than to a richly textured, multifaceted portrait. In this instance at least, it seems that the political approach alone would be insufficient—without the personal—to give depth and substance to the person being portrayed.

The same could be said of Allard Lowenstein—perhaps even more so. A pivotal figure of post–World War II American politics, Lowenstein helped form the National Student Association (NSA) and inspired its anticommunist campaign against international Marxist student groups. He became one of the first Americans to dramatize the evils of apartheid in South Africa and to rally public opinion against it. During the early 1960s he played a critical role in spurring countless white college students to join the civil rights struggle in the American South. And more than any other single person, he helped design, orchestrate, and implement the Dump Johnson campaign that resulted in Eugene McCarthy's antiwar candidacy in 1968 and the decision of Lyndon Johnson not to seek reelection.

All of this is dramatic in its own right. Yet little of what transpired in Lowenstein's life is fully comprehensible without realizing the degree to which his public activities were informed and driven by personal issues he was struggling to resolve, among them his ethnicity, his relationship to his father and mother, and his sexuality.[21]

Allard Lowenstein was born in Newark, New Jersey, in January 1929, the third son of Gabriel and Augusta Lowenstein. Gabriel was a Lithuanian Jew who came to America during the 1905 revolution after being arrested for helping to organize a general strike. After learning English, Gabriel earned a B.S. and then a Ph.D. in biochemistry at Columbia, but he subsequently chose to join his brothers in the restaurant business rather than pursue a career in academia. By all accounts he and Augusta (the daughter of immigrants) were devoted to each other, but shortly after Allard was born, Augusta was diagnosed with breast cancer and died within the year. Devastated, Gabriel remarried within a few months and moved the family to New York, committed, in the words of his second son Larry, to "wiping out the past." As part of that process, he forbade anyone to acknowledge or mention to Allard or his new sister Dorothy that Augusta had lived, or that Florence, his new wife, was not Allard's real mother.

The situation in the Lowenstein home was not easy. Gabriel had little respect for Florence ("Dad and I are hitting it off very well," she once wrote Allard. "I say nothing!"), and the parents quarreled incessantly. On the other hand, Allard—nine years younger than Bert, the eldest, and seven years younger than Larry—quickly became the focus of parental attention, the one male child who treated Florence like a mother and the intellectual genius who offered the vehicle through which Gabriel could realize the ambitions he had never fully pursued in academic life. Allard bore the intense pressure of trying to please two unhappy parents, for both of whom he became a special, almost heroic figure. He was asked to perform at dinner parties (naming all the state capitals or presidents), do brilliantly at school, and in every other way provide the tangible evidence that this family had a reason for being.

As though such pressures were not enough, Allard also had to deal with being treated as different because he was Jewish. The family moved to the Westchester suburbs when Allard was ten, and there he was beaten up and ridiculed by Gentiles. "That's such an important part of Al's identity conflicts," according to his former wife Jennifer Littlefield, "the sense of isolation out there where all the neighbors were Christians [and] they were the only car in miles with a Roosevelt bumper sticker." Later in his life he would make jokes about being "a little Jewish boy from the West Side," but the experience of feeling like an outsider was almost palpable to those who knew him best. "He felt a very powerful sense of inferiority," one childhood friend said, directly connected to his being Jewish. Already self-conscious about his appearance— Lowenstein wore thick, Coca-Cola lens glasses and thought of himself as an "ugly duckling"—he seemed especially sensitive about those physical features associated in the popular culture with being Jewish. "His most characteristic posture," his best friend observed, "was to sit there with his finger pressed against the tip of his nose [as if] he was trying to do away with about half an inch [of it]." Lowenstein told one friend that he had gone to college in faraway Chapel Hill in order to eliminate all vestiges of Jewish behavior and mannerisms, so that he could be accepted once and for all as a real American.

During Lowenstein's adolescence, the sense of difference and marginality that plagued his early years came to a head when he was forced to confront two secrets, both of them about subjects totally taboo. The first had to do with his real mother Augusta. Although Gabriel had tried to obliterate her presence from the family's life, Allard eventually discovered the truth. Looking at a photograph in a relative's home ("people from the old country," he was told— in fact, his grandparents), he saw a picture of his father, another woman (not Florence), and a small baby (himself). Eventually he put the puzzle together. Two years later when he was fifteen, Allard wrote his Aunt Ruth that he knew but did not want anyone else to know that *he knew* because "if my father and everybody else didn't want to talk about it, [it must be] . . . very painful." Never could Allard raise the issue with his father—in many ways the most important figure in his life, the man who lived through him, exhorted him endlessly to excel, was never satisfied ("Where are the extra two points?" he once asked Larry when he got a 98 on a math test), yet a person who one could never confront on an issue that went to the heart of the entire family's identity.

The second secret was even more taboo. Although Lowenstein participated in all the boy-girl parties and games of his friends, he confided in his diary at age fourteen that "the urge I get when I see certain boys is getting out-of-control. God, God, what will I do?" He could at least share the truth about his mother with his aunt and a friend, but he could tell no one about this. It was a time in America when same-sex relationships could not even be talked about. Lowenstein's friend Sanford Friedman, himself in the process of dealing with his own homosexuality, recalled it as a "source of tremendous shame, . . . feeling like the pariah or outcast." Allard must have felt the same. Not for another three decades would it be possible to deal more openly with such issues of sexual identity. In the meantime, Allard conformed with prevailing heterosexual patterns, repressed his unacceptable "urges," and tried to find another way to solve the problem. "This can't go on," he wrote. "I can see only one solution, very good friendships."

That solution offers one clue to Allard Lowenstein's public life in politics, just as his desire to escape the insecurity and inferiority he associated with his family secrets and ethnicity offers another.

By the time he was six or seven, Lowenstein was enchanted and intrigued by politics. His father had been a socialist, an organizer for the garment workers in the 1910s, and a campaigner for Morris Hilquit and Eugene Debs. Political issues were a frequent topic of conversation at Lowenstein dinners. By 1936 Al was handing out Roosevelt literature on his Central Park West block. A year later he had become obsessed with the Spanish civil war, raising money at his school for the Republican cause and plotting on a map in his room the latest news from the battlefield. The day the fascists won, he said, was the saddest of his life.

From that point forward, Allard would identify with causes and crusades that reflected the same high moral purpose as the fight against fascism in Spain. Lowenstein found in such issues the clarity, nobility, and transcendent appeal that erased all sense of ambiguity and conferred, by their righteousness, a sense of empowerment and self-confidence. In his fantasy life, Lowenstein's friend Sanford Friedman said, Al entertained a "Hallmark card" vision of America, where white steepled churches surrounded village greens, bursting fields of wheat swayed in the wind, there was no ethnicity or urban blight, and everyone lived a life of civic virtue. It was an image that recurred throughout Lowenstein's life when he dreamed of a place he might go to find peace. It was also a residential counterpart to the kind of pure politics of morality he embraced throughout his life. Both visions were compelling. If you identified with the poor, the oppressed, and the victims of discrimination, you were not only on the side of right and purity. You were also defended against the need to see yourself as vulnerable, open to question, or suspect because you were different. It was possible to achieve on behalf of others goals that were noble and simultaneously to achieve for oneself a sense of security and purposefulness.

That helps to explain, at least in part, the course of Lowenstein's political career in the 1940s, 1950s, and 1960s. At Chapel Hill where he went to college—a classic "Hallmark card" community—the sixteen-year-old Lowenstein quickly became identified with the battle to abolish Jim Crow in the state student legislature and in student government affairs generally. He also became a campus student leader on behalf of fraternity reform and the creation of regional and national student associations to fight for racial justice at home and support for democracy abroad. Lowenstein always took the morally courageous side on issues, yet he frequently was unwilling to stand for election himself lest he become the issue—and hence subject to acceptance or rejection on his own merits—instead of the cause he wished to support. On the other hand, Lowenstein welcomed the prospect of being "drafted" to serve in a given cause because then he was not placing himself in contention but rather was the recipient of a "call" to serve on behalf of a higher cause.

It was in those circumstances that he was chosen president of the recently established National Student Association in 1950. Calling on his generation of students to accept responsibility for making progress on moral issues that would match the technological breakthroughs of the atomic age, Lowenstein supported student programs embracing civil rights and educational reform. But his major thrust was to make the NSA a leader in world student politics against the international menace of communism. In Lowenstein's view, the Stalinists had been as responsible for the loss of the Spanish civil war as anyone, and now he saw world communism trying to take control of student associations throughout the world as well. "The world," he told a Stockholm student meeting that he had initiated, "[is being] pushed to the brink of tragedy by the willful scheming of evil men bent on world domination." Only a union of Western students committed to fighting communism at every stage could defend freedom against these Marxist student groups, "the greatest menace to civilization, to the timeless truths preached by all religions . . . that have evolved over the centuries." With such transcendent rhetoric, Lowenstein succeeded brilliantly in forging an international anticommunist student movement, in the process becoming so identified as a quintessential leader of student politics that for two decades thereafter, he more than any other single individual was synonymous with NSA activism.

Lowenstein's affinity for crusades that were inherently moral and righteous continued to be the distinguishing feature of his public life. At the end of the 1950s he journeyed to South Africa with two friends under the guise of doing research, but in fact to conduct a detailed survey of conditions in South-West Africa (now Namibia), a territory governed under an international mandate by South Africa. No United Nations observers had been allowed in the territory for years. Now, Lowenstein and his friends used tape recordings, photographs, and first-person description to document vividly and dramatically the brutalization of Africans in the southwest by the Johannesburg regime. An extraordinary venture, the expedition involved distant journeys into barren wastelands where tribal chiefs had been sent into exile and hairline escapes from capture by security police. When the Americans returned to New York, their testimony before the United Nations was so sensational that the U.N. decided to take South Africa to the World Court to force it to alter its trusteeship. Lowenstein himself wrote a colorful and shocking book about the venture, *Brutal Mandate* (1962), that alerted a larger audience to the horror of apartheid.

Not surprisingly, the civil rights struggle in America became the next focus for Lowenstein's political energies. Long committed to the fight against segregation, Lowenstein became involved in the early 1960s in supporting the sit-in movement, helping to inspire demonstrations in New York and North Carolina. But it was in Mississippi, where he first journeyed in July 1963 after Medgar Evers's assassination, that Lowenstein made his greatest mark. "When I first got [there]," he told one audience, "everything was finished. The whites had won. . . . [Black] people had no hope." Lowenstein had expected to find Mississippi like North Carolina, "but after . . . I spent a little time . . . I realized the difference—I think it is Marx who once said that 'if the degree of difference gets big enough, the spark jumps the gap and you get a difference in principle'—well Mississippi was different in principle from the rest of the South." It was as bad as—maybe worse than—South Africa.

Pursuing that analogy, Lowenstein wondered what would happen if Mississippians used some techniques borrowed from black South Africans to dramatize their quest for the ballot and equal protection under the laws. In South Africa, blacks made election day a time of official mourning to commemorate their sadness at not being allowed to vote. Why not use the same principle in Mississippi, Lowenstein asked, only this time have blacks cast real ballots in their own communities—in churches, lodges, and barber shops—to prove that they wanted to vote and *would* vote if only given the chance. The Mississippi "Freedom Vote" campaign became the organizing vehicle for trying to transform civil rights in that state. Mississippi blacks founded their own party, spearheaded by Fannie Lou Hamer, and nominated candidates; Lowenstein volunteered to raise money and recruit white students from Stanford and Yale to come join the campaign; and on election day almost 90,000 Mississippi blacks cast "Freedom Votes," proving once and for all their dedication and desire to be part of the political process.

With the Freedom Vote's success as a foundation, Lowenstein and Bob Moses, a leader of the Student Nonviolent Coordinating Committee in Mississippi, came up with the idea of recruiting another thousand white students to come to Mississippi in 1964 for "Freedom Summer." As much as any other event in the civil rights struggle, Freedom Summer focused national and international attention on the terrorism of white supremacy and the need to outlaw racism. Three students were lynched, churches were burned down at will, and cars and houses were fired on. Lowenstein helped to recruit many of the thousand white students who were part of the summer, and although he eventually became disaffected from the project because of his suspicion that it was being infiltrated by communist-front organizations, he was instrumental in having made the summer possible.

Within two years, Lowenstein was back once more as a political agitator, this time leading a crusade within mainstream politics to end the Vietnam War. Using his links to the National Student Association as a base, Lowenstein proposed that one hundred student body presidents write a letter to President Johnson demanding a review of the nation's policy in Vietnam. As Lowenstein probably expected, the president and Secretary of State Dean Rusk fanned the flames of antiwar protest by responding with condescension to the student letter. Resistance to the war multiplied exponentially as Johnson and others turned their backs on peaceful petitions and university teach-ins. By the spring of 1967, Lowenstein was ready to reveal his own secret strategy for ending the war. Students and adult dissenters would reverse this immoral policy by toppling Lyndon Johnson from the presidency. It was a crusade as pure and righteous as one could find. An evil policy was being implemented by a president who did not understand the will of the people or the power of morality. If the ruler were dethroned, the policy would follow. No one believed that such a crazy idea could work, but Allard Lowenstein and his army of volunteers brought it to fruition.

In all of these ventures, two themes were clear. First, Lowenstein almost always acted as a prophet speaking within the American system of politics and due process, seeking to perfect and save that system by recruiting people to make it work better through reform. He was not a revolutionary. Second, the instrument for his political mission turned out almost invariably to be young people—the kinds of students he recruited first when he headed the NSA, then when he sought companions to go to South Africa, after that in his mobilization of support from students at Yale, Stanford, Harvard, and other schools to go to Mississippi, and finally in the young people's crusade to bring a peaceful end to the Vietnam War by finding a candidate who could defeat or depose Lyndon Johnson. Not by accident, those students who went to New Hampshire and elsewhere to promote the candidacy of Eugene McCarthy canvassed voters under the banner, "Be Clean for Gene." Lowenstein was literally a pied piper, parading through campus after campus, inspiring young idealists with his rhetoric of commitment to take up the cause of morality and justice and follow Al Lowenstein in the crusade to make American democracy work.

It was a method of recruitment that became most explicable in light of Lowenstein's continuing struggle to resolve his private agenda of concerns. If enlisting people in moral crusades provided a means of enhancing Lowenstein's own sense of self, focusing on young people—and especially young men—offered a way of dealing with his continuing ambivalence about his own sexual identity and his desire to find a best friend, or a series of best friends, who might satisfy his need for intimacy. As a rule, Lowenstein had two kinds of relationships. One was with a series of elder heroes or mentors whom he idealized. These individuals were embodiments of near-saintliness, morally pure, clear in their convictions, people to be venerated. They included Frank Porter Graham, Eleanor Roosevelt, and Norman Thomas. The second kind of relationship was with young disciples who became devoted to this moral figure, who would follow him wherever he led, and who readily embraced the chance to share their own hopes and dreams with this charismatic reformer who had allowed them to enter into his world. Lowenstein was their mentor. These individuals called themselves disciples or acolytes—particularly after they gained some distance on their experience. Most often Lowenstein demanded and received from them a kind of unwavering loyalty that some equated with fealty. They were the foot soldiers who helped make his political battles both possible and rewarding. Significantly, Lowenstein had very few relationships with peers.

At times, Lowenstein's emotional ties to these young followers became very personal. He would arrive on a college campus on one of his ceaseless speech-making tours on behalf of one cause or another. After addressing a large throng of students, he might go off for a bull session at some residential house with twenty-five or thirty potential activists. After talking through half the night, the group would dwindle to a few. Frequently, Lowenstein ended up with just two or three people—those who would drop everything to drive him to the airport, pick him up after an appearance, go with him on a trip back to North Carolina. There were hundreds of these people. Most remained ardent followers for only a brief time. Although Lowenstein spoke fondly of wanting to be a "best friend," all too often he treated a new disciple like an aide, failing to provide sustained intimacy or the shared confidence of equals. As one follower said, becoming a Lowenstein disciple was too much like a moth getting close to a flame. It was easy to be consumed. For self-preservation, if nothing else, separation soon came. Yet these young people provided one of the key reasons that Al Lowenstein became the kind of political leader he was, offering him—even if only on a temporary basis—the kind of devotion and reassurance he so deeply needed and so much feared he would never find.

Often, these relationships took on another dimension as well. With certain young men—almost all handsome, preppy, and non-Jewish—Lowenstein initiated or invited conversations that dealt with more vulnerable issues like sexuality, self-doubt, and the meaning of human affection. Sometimes these discussions occurred with students trying to find themselves, sometimes with young men troubled about issues like the draft and the war in Vietnam. Frequently, they led to verbal explorations of what male friendship meant and why in American society and culture greater physical affection was not permitted between men. On numerous occasions, these conversations ended with Lowenstein suggesting that he would like to share such affection with the person by sleeping with him. Usually, that meant lying together and hugging, but the sexual overtones were sufficient to cause most of the young men Lowenstein approached to feel uneasy and distraught.

For most of his life after adolescence, Allard Lowenstein had followed his own prescription as a fourteen-year-old writing in his diary. He would try to solve the problem of his "out-of-control" urges toward other males through the process of seeking "best friends." By the time he reached the age of thirty-five, most of those "best friends" were also at least ten years younger than he and more vulnerable, themselves displaying some of the same insecurity and inadequacy that Lowenstein had felt growing up. Lowenstein cultivated these young friends wherever he went, but he was never willing or able to stop long enough to develop a more permanent or equal relationship with them. He had to keep going at least in part because the problem he could not confront drove him to run from place to place in order to avoid being discovered. David Mixner, a student who worked with Lowenstein in the antiwar movement and eventually "came out," described what it was like to be gay and "in the closet" during the 1950s and 1960s. "You lived in constant and perpetual fear," he said, "always afraid of being exposed or being discovered. . . . You would try to leave . . . a trail that no one could track you on. . . . If you moved fast enough, if you changed people quick enough, they couldn't catch you."[22]

Because of those realities, through most of Al Lowenstein's life, the possibility of dealing openly with the issue of homosexuality remained small, especially if one were a public figure or wanted to exercise influence over a mainstream audience. The culture of cold war America permitted no space for openness about sexual preference. "If you're found out," Mixner noted, "it's not trouble; you were *destroyed*. I mean destroyed, family, career, friends—everything gone . . . forever." In addition, Lowenstein remained unsure of just what his sexual identity was. He fell in love with at least two women, proposed to many, and eventually married and raised a family. He remained a devoted father after he and his wife divorced and never ceased being in love with her.

In many respects, the relationship between the personal and the political in Allard Lowenstein's life was a reflection of the times he lived in. Until the late 1970s it was nearly impossible to deal openly and honestly with issues of sexual identity. Even then, it was not clear that a person could survive, especially in political life. Yet Lowenstein appears to have been ready to explore the possibility. During the last years of his life, he more openly associated himself with the gay rights movement, and in Ted Kennedy's 1980 presidential bid he was especially effective in recruiting support in gay Democratic clubs in Florida and California. Indeed, one of the tragedies of Lowenstein's death that year is that it came during a period when he appeared to be exploring new ways to discover who he was and how he might integrate his personal and political sides.

The other tragedy is the way that his death brought full circle the relationship between the personal and the political in Lowenstein's life. One of the young men he had recruited at Stanford for the civil rights movement was Dennis Sweeney, a bright, handsome, deeply committed student. Sweeney became a Lowenstein disciple, devoted to his causes. The feeling was reciprocal. Lowenstein was devoted to Sweeney as well and on at least one occasion made what Sweeney took to be a sexual advance toward him. Eventually, Sweeney came to distrust Lowenstein and to view him as an agent of the state seeking to subvert the revolutionary aims of the civil rights movement and later the student left. Over the years, Lowenstein's former protégé developed symptoms of clinical paranoia, hearing voices that he believed Lowenstein had caused to be in his head. In the end, he became convinced that the only way to stop the voices was to kill their source, and on a March day in 1980 he walked into the office of the man he had once worshipped and shot him dead.

With Allard Lowenstein, as with Eleanor Roosevelt, it would be possible to write a political history without delving into personal agendas and private conflicts. Yet how much richer such a history is because we know about some of the family, ethnic, and sexual demons that drove this man to be what he was and to act on the public stage as he did. Without that information, our historical understanding of Lowenstein—and the tragedies and triumphs of his life—would be woefully incomplete.

REFLECTIONS

Critics who are concerned about placing too much emphasis on the relation of the personal and the political ordinarily focus on the right of privacy, the dangers of sensationalism, and the threat of reductionism. There is some merit in these concerns. The presidential election campaigns of Gary Hart in 1988 and of Bill Clinton in 1992 illustrate how an obsession with the personal and private—especially when salacious details are involved—can potentially undermine and subvert more appropriate attention to issues of public policy. In 1988 Gary Hart was removed from contention for the Democratic nomination because two reporters alleged—without proof—that he was having an affair with a Florida model and had entertained her, overnight, in his Washington home. For a period of time in 1992, it seemed likely that Clinton would be removed from contention as well because all eyes turned to charges that he was a womanizer and was so obsessed with sexual conquests that he lacked the perspective, time, and maturity to be president. As it turned out, Clinton survived the cause célèbre over his sex life. While admitting to marital problems, he and Hillary Rodham Clinton succeeded in convincing the voters that these were private matters that a husband and wife should be able to handle outside the glare of public exposure. In the meantime, Clinton was able to show that his grasp of public policy issues was sufficiently great to obviate any fear that he was driven solely by sexual appetite. Nevertheless, it is clear that a political life of some importance to the nation could have been destroyed through invasion of the right of privacy.

What does that then say to the argument, strongly supported by women's history, that the political must be seen as connected to the personal, and that a continuum unites and informs our understanding of the private and public parts of existence?

One key variable in sorting out these competing positions is context. Historians are not contemporary journalists. The questions we ask and the information we seek result from trying to understand a total life and to explain how one or more parts of that life fit together in such a way as to make sense. It is important to inquire about Abraham Lincoln's melancholia in trying to fathom the way he perceived and formulated the issues in contention during the Civil War. It is equally important not to view the entire Lincoln presidency as a product of his melancholia. Historical context provides a perspective for seeing the interplay of numerous personal, social, economic, and cultural influences, countering the temptation that a totally presentist framework offers of zeroing in on one issue only and ignoring the rest.

A second important variable, flowing from the first, is balance. Readers of history books are usually expert at detecting when historians overemphasize a particular theme, fail to do justice to alternative explanations, or set out to skew the record by distorting or misreading evidence. Precisely because historians write for an audience larger and more long term than today's consumer of newspaper journalism, they have the opportunity and responsibility to make their conclusions measure up to higher standards. Balance and proportion comprise part of these standards, making it highly unlikely that a book that sounds only one theme will long survive.

A third variable is the commitment of historians to multifaceted analysis. This quality reflects the degree to which history stands between the humanities and the social sciences. From the humanities we learn a sense of the frailty, complexity, and anguish of human striving—the everyday struggle of people to make sense of their own lives, to fashion some means of keeping on, and to seek a formula that will enable a life to achieve direction and purpose. From the social sciences, in turn, we gain respect for the need to separate out different causal forces, explore their interaction with each other, and do justice to their relative strengths and weaknesses as explanations for what people do.

Within this framework of safeguards, there is far less reason to worry about the dangers of treating the personal and the political as intertwined. Because of their concern with context, historians are unlikely to invade areas of privacy that are not pertinent to the larger historical patterns they seek to explain. Even where we know about such details, we are unlikely to write about them unless there seems an overriding need to do so.

For the same reason, it is unwise and therefore not in the historian's professional interest to resort to sensationalism in exploring the relationship between the personal and the political. Not only is such sensationalism a violation of the standards of the historians' guild. It also endangers historians' achieving their ultimate goal—respect and attention from student and fellow scholars.

Finally, historians fall prey to the temptations of reductionism at the peril of their credibility. The historian can only benefit from uncovering new information about an important personage. But it is a risk of considerable proportions for the same historian to say that one thing and one thing only can explain a person's life course. We go back to the debt we owe the humanities and our humility before the realization that all lives are tortured, valiant, and ultimately flawed attempts to make things fit together and work. For us to make them work too easily flies in the face of everything we have been taught about human experience.

We return then to Eleanor Roosevelt and Allard Lowenstein, two individuals whose complexities and painful journeys toward finding a meaning for themselves were certainly as great if not greater than most. In each case, it could be argued that historians have invaded their privacy, that there has been sensationalism about their sex lives, and that the results of exploring that side of their personalities is to oversimplify and reduce the complexity of the motivating forces in their lives. Yet it seems to me that has not happened. In each case, discussion of what transpired in their personal lives is so indispensable to understanding their public lives that *not to explore* the personal is to distort and *misunderstand* the political. It would be bad history—indeed, woefully inaccurate and contrived history—to write about these individuals as though all that mattered were what appears on the public record. Nor is the focus on sexuality as a primary life force a resort to sensationalism. It might become so if historians spent most of their time seeking to describe in detail the actual sexual activities of their subjects. But to recognize the centrality of the issue is not to pander to prurient tastes. Interestingly, Allard Lowenstein was asked, as a close friend of Eleanor Roosevelt, how he thought the Roosevelt library should handle the correspondence between Eleanor Roosevelt and Lorena Hickok describing in erotic terms their affection for each other. Lowenstein responded that if Mrs. Roosevelt had not wanted people to see the correspondence, she would have destroyed it. Lowenstein's own dedication to preserving the historical record by keeping all his diary entries and correspondence suggests that he might have well responded the same way if the question were asked about him. Lastly, historians have not attempted to explain the lives of Allard Lowenstein and Eleanor Roosevelt by focusing on single causes. The personal/political continuum represents an ongoing dialectic where experience in one arena helps shape that in another, and the process is endlessly complicated. The historian's greatest joy is to contemplate and become immersed in that complexity.

Eleanor Roosevelt and Allard Lowenstein were very different people. They do not lend support for, or justify, a simplistic cause-and-effect formula for how the personal and the political are related to each other. But what each of their lives does show is how impoverished our historical understanding of them would be were we not to explore and seek to comprehend the ways their private and public lives were connected.

CHAPTER 10 : RIGHTS AND REPRESENTATION : WOMEN, POLITICS, AND POWER IN THE CONTEMPORARY UNITED STATES

JANE SHERRON DE HART

"Are you going to run as a woman?" The question, a favorite of journalists interviewing female candidates, reveals Americans' fascination with the new woman politician. That the question is being asked in the 1990s rather than in the 1910s and 1920s, when newly enfranchised women first filed for office, suggests how gendered politics and power remain over a half century since suffragists celebrated their hard-won victory. The belief that politics is a male prerogative and government a men's club is an old and persistent one, slow to give way to women's claims for full citizenship. Such assumptions inhibited women's ability to work through traditional political channels throughout the nineteenth century. Those same assumptions have continued in the twentieth century to shape distinctive political styles and strategies employed by women even after they achieved formal access to the political system.

As we approach a new century in which gender, politics, and power will continue to mix in problematic ways, generating new possibilities as well as recurrent problems, it is useful to reexamine those styles and strategies. Scrutinizing how they functioned in the very recent past can reveal elements of continuity and incipient change, inviting us to think afresh about female agency and power.

The political participation of two groups of women provides that opportunity: pro-ERA (Equal Rights Amendment) activists of the 1970s and female political candidates of the 1980s and early 1990s. Both were elite groups influenced in varying measure by the feminist movement of the 1960s, and both sought to end gender-based inequities in American society. While not all activists or candidates chose to call themselves "feminist"—fearing the radical, sectarian connotations often associated with the label—both groups shared a common commitment to equality. Their approaches to politics and power, however, differed significantly.[1]

For pro-ERA activists of the 1970s, as for suffragists, the key to equality was *entitlement*: the belief that all citizens, irrespective of sex, race, and other categories of difference, are entitled to certain basic rights and responsibilities—in this case, equal treatment under the law. For female candidates and officeholders of the 1980s, on the other hand, the central avenue to equality was *representation*: the presumption that women themselves, as direct participants in the policy-making process, can best ensure an end to gender-based inequities. As officeholders they would be responsive not only to the needs of their constituents but also, more significantly, to the needs of women as a group, whenever possible advancing feminist-oriented policies that would benefit women collectively. Functioning as advocates rather than as claimants, the most effective among them would seek not only to embrace power on behalf of women but also, as women, to redefine political power.

The behavior (and ideology) of these pro-ERA activists and women candidates is by no means suggestive of the full range of female political activity in the United States. (Ideology, if not behavior, distinguishes them from their sisters on the Right, for example, about whom I have written elsewhere.)[2] Nor do I mean sequential treatment of the two groups to imply that electoral politics has supplanted other forms of political activism, even among this particular subset of women. Despite media fascination with practitioners of electoral politics, women's political behavior continues to assume many forms. Rather, what makes the experiences of ratificationists and politicians so instructive for historians and activists alike are several factors: first, remarkable congruence with dominant themes in women's political history and that of other groups seeking change; and second, relevance to current efforts to ensure the gender parity in law and politics that is essential to gender justice and democratic praxis.

First, a word about organization. The first section of this essay describes the female political styles and strategies demonstrated in ratification politics of the 1970s, the second assesses the problems and progress of female candidates of the 1980s and early 1990s, and the third integrates the first two with each other and with the more distant past, noting continuity and change as well as the challenges posed by the heightened emphasis on electoral politics in the 1990s.

To understand fully the historical experience of ERA activists requires an appreciation of how compelling the long-sought goal of equality of individual rights became in the early years of feminism's second wave. A constitutional amendment banning gender-based discrimination in the law had languished in Congress for decades, held hostage by fears about its adverse impact on protective legislation for working women and hopes that constitutional guarantees of equality could be achieved through extension of judicial interpretation of the Fifth and Fourteenth Amendments. By the late 1960s, those fears and hopes had dissipated; classification by sex had not. If women, like men, were to be treated for legal purposes as individuals rather than as a sex-defined group, passage of ERA, liberal feminists concluded, was imperative.

Responding to a highly effective lobbying effort, Congress voted overwhelmingly in 1972 to submit the amendment to the states. As they did so, few in the nation's capital suspected that the drive to ratify would generate opponents, many of them female, who would transform this simple guarantee of legal equality into an absolute assurance of gender revolution. Fewer still envisioned a decade-long struggle that would mobilize women politically as had no issue since suffrage. Yet by 1982, when the deadline for ratification expired, the battle had assumed epic proportions, especially in those pivotal states considered most likely to supply the remaining three votes of the thirty-eight required to secure an amendment to the Constitution.[3]

The women whom ERA enlisted into the ranks of ratificationists, organized in coalition, and in some measure transformed were not all feminists, although most aligned themselves with the goals of "the women's movement." In North Carolina, Texas, and Massachusetts (the three states for which data are available), they were predominantly white, middle-class, well educated, cosmopolitan in outlook, liberal in politics, and, if religious, affiliated with churches and synagogues that were either liberal or "mainstream." Married for the most part, they were likely to have held professional or managerial jobs if they worked outside the home. Socialized in families where parents tended to be college-educated and politically active, supporters had continued their own political education in professional associations, women's organizations, and liberal groups. In North Carolina, one of the three critical states targeted by both sides as essential to ratification and the state from which many of my examples will be drawn, the women who became ERA partisans had frequently joined forces to fight racism and the Vietnam War, to free political prisoners, and to oppose capital punishment. In short, they were citizens who believed in the values of equality, justice, liberty, and individual rights—not as familiar abstractions of civic life, but as promises to be fulfilled. Activism was part of their self-definition.[4]

How that activism was expressed politically in a broadly inclusive coalition of feminists and self-styled nonfeminists varied considerably. Variations, which were of loyalties and assumptions as well as behavior, were manifested in three distinct political styles. These may be described respectively as "the politics of citizenship," "the politics of movement," and "the politics of realism." Since style shaped strategy, sometimes merging so as to be virtually indistinguishable, differences between the three often sparked tensions. But tensions did not generate factions. Individuals and organizations could and did embrace more than one style in sequence—and even simultaneously. Distinctions among the three, however, were sufficiently sharp to permit careful examination of each.[5]

Of the three, *the politics of citizenship* best characterized the ratification coalition. Identified with the voluntaristic politics of traditional women's groups, it reflected a history of both female participation in politics and exclusion from power. Organizations such as the American Association of University Women (AAUW), the National Federation of Business and Professional Women's Clubs (BPW), the League of Women Voters, and church women's societies were but a few of the many voluntary associations through which women for over a century had pursued political issues ranging from health, safety, and welfare to moral reform and disarmament. As key components in pro-ERA coalitions, such groups had a long history of involvement with ERA. BPW, founded in 1919, had supported an Equal Rights Amendment when it was first introduced in 1920 as the logical extension of suffrage; the League of Women Voters, founded a year earlier, had not, believing the amendment would jeopardize protective legislation. The presence of traditional women's organizations in the ratification coalition thus embodied continuity: continuity between the first women's movement and the second, between suffrage and ERA. There was continuity too—and this was most important—in a mode of political behavior in which political efficacy resided in influencing those who held power rather than wielding it directly. Traditional women's organizations also signaled respectability and, within limits, inclusivity: respectability as contrasted with the broader, radical implications of making the law gender neutral; inclusivity implied in the coalition motto "ERA IS FOR EVERYBODY." Taken as a whole, such organizations represented not only their own members but also, by extension, women in general as such groups conceived them. In practical terms, they provided access to large membership lists, trusted channels of communication, and established structures for getting things done.

As long as getting things done meant collection and dissemination of information, these practitioners of the politics of citizenship excelled. Members of the League of Women Voters were in their element, trained as they were in a nonpartisan organization that had been created expressly to educate newly enfranchised women about the political system. Together with other activists, they compiled information on legislators: their party district, base of support, campaign financing, voting record on ERA, spouse's position on ERA, pro-ERA political figures by whom they might be influenced, and so on. They collected evidence of sex discrimination in law, academe, politics, the economy, and the military. They learned about the Supreme Court and the Fourteenth Amendment, "suspect classification," protection of privacy, and congressional intent. They armed coalition members with packets containing detailed instructions on legislative lobbying through letter writing and one-on-one contacts. They disseminated information kits to newspapers, prepared newsletters, staged debates—until convinced, as a result of their opponents' angry accusations, that anti-ERA women simply would not respect "the facts." How else could one explain alarmist charges that ratification would result in sexual integration of public restrooms, decriminalization of rape, legitimation of homosexuality, further entrenchment of abortion as an option, the loss of legal privileges for women, and the destruction of the American family?[6]

For practitioners of the politics of citizenship, respect for "the facts" was basic. League and AAUW members especially had a long tradition of examining issues carefully and dispassionately. Acknowledging how "deeply satisfying" it was to be able "to make a *factual* statement in support of equality," they issued fact sheets—"cool facts for the hotheaded opposition." These were women who had faith in expertise and relevant data and in themselves as authoritative informants. Reliance on facts was a way to differentiate themselves from the emotionalism and misinformation of their antagonists and establish the dialectic of debate. Convinced that facts also had the power to persuade, practitioners of the politics of citizenship presented legislators with relevant cases, examples, and corrections of erroneous arguments concerning legal implications of the amendment. That "the facts" inherent in legislative history, clear intent, and authoritative interpretation might not have been "the facts" about ERA most relevant for politicians was an assumption they could not comfortably entertain—at least not initially.[7]

Frustration with those for whom ERA implied different facts, different logic, or alternative meanings was understandable. It was not easy talking about sexual equality in the law to conservative male legislators whose previous experience with racial equality had convinced them that implementation of ERA could mean yet further intrusion of federal power inhibiting their ability to govern. Conveying the necessity for removing legal classification by sex to women who believed that classification by sex actually *protected* women was equally trying. And it was harder still to understand why traditional gender categories known to be at odds with American ideals of equality and freedom still elicited loyalty from women who saw ERA as a threat to those categories. What rankled most, however, was that, as partisans of the amendment, practitioners of the politics of citizenship found their own credibility at issue.

These difficulties point to the limitations as well as the strengths of a political style that carried with it the assumptions and behavior of traditional women's organizations. Bridging differences of culture, class, and race had always proved difficult for women's groups. The problem, however, was not merely one of communication but of the very meaning of action itself. For practitioners of the politics of citizenship, political organizing, in effect, meant study rather than action; informing each other rather than recruiting outsiders, even when those outsiders, as was true of blacks, overwhelmingly endorsed ERA.[8] Political organizing also meant creating and re-creating an array of offices, committees, task forces, and flow charts—creating a "hierarchy," opponents charged; creating the illusion of "doing something," an astute ratificationist noted. Lobbying provided a case in point. Told by ratificationist leaders of the governor's urgent request for four thousand letters from a particular legislative district, the local contact failed to follow through, responding instead with promises to "send a memo." Ratificationists invariably cited the incident as an example of political naïveté during their periodic bouts of self-criticism. That they kept returning to the incident suggests that they sensed a deficiency not so much of knowledge—women's organizations presumably understood the importance of constituent mail—but of will to move through, around, or beyond organizational channels to effect results.

Making the transition from mobilizational politics to electoral politics was even more difficult for those practicing the politics of citizenship. It meant engaging in the "nitty gritty" of electioneering—a change in personality as well as tactics. It meant moving beyond the bounds of a sorority where nonpartisanship cloaked an inability to exert real influence on those in power. As long as practitioners of the politics of citizenship stayed within those bounds, they could evade the reality of politics, consoling themselves in defeat by emphasizing how much they had learned about playing the political game. Learning meant self-development. Losing implied powerlessness. Coming to terms with male power and female powerlessness was, for many practitioners of the politics of citizenship, the ultimate political lesson.

Practitioners of *the politics of movement* "knew" that lesson. Women who had come of age politically in a decade of dissent, they were part of the movement culture generated by the civil rights revolution, the antiwar movement, the student movement, the New Left, and women's liberation. Convinced that justice deferred was justice denied, they understood the limitations of education as a tactic to achieve equality as well as the price of compromise. Comfortable with protest and insurgency, they appreciated the rhetoric of public display, the importance of solidarity and confrontation, the value of symbolic action, and the need to mobilize women outside the organizational networks of traditional women's groups. The result was a style that mobilized and polarized, bonded and divided. The "struggle"—and that is what they called the ratification effort—created a strategic framework within which women devised tactics and performed tasks necessary for ratification. In the process of doing so, new recruits discovered a sense of belonging and meaning—in a word, feminism. The logic of the struggle, therefore, demanded public display: confrontation of patriarchical authority in legislative halls; resistance to male-defined politics; affirmation of solidarity and sisterhood in vigils, marches, and rallies in which ratificationists pledged themselves to equality and to each other. "I did not realize," exclaimed one woman, "that there were that many dynamic, talented, committed, and interesting people that I could trust, and who would really just go full tilt!"

Going "full tilt" implied defiance as well as solidarity. From the outset, practitioners of the politics of movement were true to form. At the first legislative hearings held on ERA, they hissed and booed a witness who undercut his credentials as a legal expert with the patronizing remark that laws were already more favorable to women than to men and that women would not have the legal rights they currently possessed if men had not chosen to release them. "We were rowdy . . . and we acted out too much," recalled one woman, recalling the dress and demeanor that had tagged them as "libbers." Sobered by unexpected defeat, they modified their clothing—but not their sense of injustice, their disdain for compromise, or their zest for symbolic action. In a subsequent session, legislators voting against ratification received a white glove. A symbol of the shift from ladylike lobbying to electoral politics— "removing the gloves," in effect—the gesture promised ultimate retaliation at the polls. Illinois activists went further. Reviving a tactic pioneered by militant suffragists, they chained themselves to the railings before the senate chamber until carried out of the capitol four days later by the secretary of state's police. Returning for sit-ins at the governor's office and on the floor of the house itself, they wrote in blood on the marble floors of the capitol the names of ERA opponents. Much less dramatic, but equally unequivocal messages reached opponent legislators in North Carolina who opened their mail after the final vote on ERA to find chicken droppings—"shit for shits." The politics of movement yielded pleasures even in defeat.[9]

The politics of movement also had its limitations. Within the political culture of state legislatures, confrontation could exact a price. Demanding a vote when the votes for ERA were not there put legislators "on record." It would also produce needless "bloodying" that the ratification bill's sponsors were eager to spare their supporters. Sending provocative packages to well-entrenched antiratificationists who might be persuaded to support other women's issues, such as domestic violence legislation or pay equity, antagonized needlessly. Coalition partners also found the politics of movement counterproductive when fellow ratificationists made ideological purity a higher priority than winning. Early debates about the propriety of hiring a male lobbyist to promote a women's issue seemed, in retrospect, a charming example of political naïveté to veteran ratificationists who had come to prefer feminist victories to feminist symbols. Such tolerance proved harder to muster in 1982, when purists discounted the expertise of the most politically prominent woman in the state because she was "only a politician, not a feminist." Practitioners of the politics of movement seemed to assume that it was feminist women, not (mostly) male legislators, who would ultimately determine the fate of ERA.

That assumption was not shared by practitioners of *the politics of realism.* Some of these women were party activists who had found their party, usually Democratic, after a stint in women's organizations. For others, the route was more direct. One ratificationist wryly noted that she had been "in politics" since the age of ten, when she handed out campaign literature during her father's mayoralty campaign.[10] Still others had cut their political teeth in the ratification campaign, often as members of a fledgling Women's Political Caucus. Many were self-conscious feminists; others, declining the label, staunchly supported feminist issues. All agreed with the assessment of a perceptive ratificationist who, after two defeats of ERA in the state legislature, emphatically concluded: "Idealistic sisterhood has gotten us nowhere. We must play the game of politics the way it is played."

Playing the game of politics assumed a continuing relationship with people with whom one disagreed. It implied compromise, caution, and avoidance of actions that needlessly antagonized. On a superficial level, it dictated adjustments in dress and demeanor. On a more substantive level, it demanded foregoing movement drama and ideological compatibility in the pursuit of political results. It meant acknowledging the expertise of a powerful house speaker who believed that the few conservative legislators whose votes were needed for a pro ERA majority would not be won over by threats of retaliation at the polls, ads in their district prominently displaying the NOW (National Organization for Women) label, or an influx of high-profile, out-of-state feminists. Above all, it meant keeping one's word when promises had been made to forego such actions: understanding that loyalty was not merely a virtue, but the glue of politics.

Style shaped tactics. Playing the game of politics meant rejecting a trusted liberal ally as sponsor of the ratification bill and going instead for an insider whose close ties to the anti-ERA senate leadership might enable him to neutralize powerful opponents. Playing the game meant sacrificing movement priorities, at least temporarily, in order to win at the polls—for example, supporting a pro-ERA male incumbent over a feminist challenger or designing an electoral campaign in which ratificationists privately supplied money and workers while publicly downplaying ERA as an issue. For women legislators, it meant "playing hardball." Defined by an observer of the Washington power game as "clean, aggressive Machiavellian politics," hardball in the context of ratification meant crafty, aggressive bargaining and trading for pro-ERA votes.[11]

A male-defined style, the politics of realism was perfected in a male ethos of wheeling and dealing where ambition, aggressiveness, toughness, and even ruthlessness were privileged over the qualities of connectedness, nurturance, and selflessness traditionally associated with women. As such, it was a style that had limitations, especially in the context of ratification politics. In situations where victory was elusive and motivation required reinforcement, the importance of marches and other activities that might sustain the commitment of volunteers could not be discounted. There was also the risk that a more authoritarian style of leadership could alienate women for whom the ERA struggle had meant sisterhood and participatory democracy.

Far more alienating, however, were the frustrations generated among many politically inexperienced ratificationists who simply did not know *how* to do what their female mentors told them they *had* to do to win. To the uninitiated there seemed to be mysteries withheld; to seasoned politicians there seemed to be an inability to act. Recalling an exchange with women in the administration and legislature, one discomfited woman admitted, "I felt like a little girl." Knowing how it felt to be a little girl politically, she had resolved to grow up.

Learning how to act politically and, more important, the acting itself were constant concerns of ratificationists, whatever their political styles. At first the challenge had seemed merely a matter of learning the rules. But learning how the game was played did not ensure winning. Defeat taught other lessons. In the midst of a struggle that was personally empowering, it underscored the limits of women's political power.

Defeat also dramatized the extent to which female political cultures, nourished in a separate sphere and couched in the rhetoric of disinterested service, had skewed women's political development. This legacy was not limited to those women whom one ratificationist dismissed as "the little church ladies" and the "little BPW ladies." Her characterization of genteel nonpartisanship identified the limitations of a political style that functioned with maximum effectiveness only within a matrix of like-minded women (and sympathetic men). But her remarks ignored the quantum leap in political sophistication and feminist consciousness that had occurred among many such women engaged in ratification politics, as well as the speed with which some practitioners of the politics of citizenship had embraced the politics of realism.

Such criticism also ignored the extent to which even the most politically knowledgeable ratificationists were constrained in their ability to act. The insistence with which women in the legislature talked about "playing hardball" made it no mere tactical refrain. As a metaphor for male politics and power, playing hardball became a kind of mantra, an affirmation of willingness to embrace the substance as well as the style of male politics and power on behalf of other women. That many women legislators had difficulty doing so was a function of their own socialization, marginality, and, in the case of ERA, the nature of the issue. Few in number and denied the key committee appointments that provide real political leverage, they were novice poker players with too few chips.[12]

The varying styles of political activism displayed in ratification politics point to a number of issues familiar to historians: the dynamics of tokenism; the inhibiting effect of class, racial, and ethnic differences on gender-based activism; and tensions between female separatism and male-defined integration, between mobilizational politics and electoral politics, between the "disorderly" transformational politics of social movements and the pragmatism, incrementalism, and hierarchy of conventional politics. Most striking, however, is what this recent example of political mobilization reveals about the persistent gendering of politics and power. To understand the extent to which the political effectiveness of women at the time was still constrained by the sorority, nonpartisanship, and marginality characteristic of earlier generations of activists is to understand the extent to which women's political development, despite undoubted gains, continued to be stunted. "We have been obliged to use the indirect methods too long," complained a politically active New Jersey Republican fed up with a tradition of surrogacy in which women relied on male legislators to represent their interests and needs. As a result, she continued, we "stand on the sidelines" unable to follow through on "the measures we believe in." Her comment is disconcerting, not because it is inappropriate—quite the contrary—but because of the date it was made: January 17, 1921.[13]

To blame the victim for her own marginality, however, is an exercise in futility for activist and historian alike. In the wake of ERA's defeat, strategists struggled to come to terms with unwelcome realities. Although at least one nationally known ERA stalwart continued to insist that it was male legislators who had killed the amendment, not accusations in public quarters from alarmist women, there was no denying the divisiveness of the gender equality issue among women themselves. The ratification struggle had clearly politicized antifeminists as well as feminists, prompting anti-ERA women to move from mobilizational politics to electoral politics in tandem with their adversaries. As staunch opponents of abortion as well as ERA, these newly politicized women on the Right were not likely to abandon campaign headquarters and go home. Even if their efficacy was questioned, there was no denying the mounting disenchantment in the wider body politic with a pragmatic liberalism that rested on faith in government agency.[14]

In sum, defeat of the amendment demonstrated that political efforts by various subsets of feminist-oriented women representing different styles and strategies were a necessary, but not sufficient, condition for policy gains. However, if the ratification struggle had revealed the limits of feminist political activism in an era of conservative ascendancy, it also paved the way for new initiatives.

TOWARD A FEMINIST-INSPIRED ELECTORAL POLITICS

As the most visible and widely accepted single issue identified with liberal feminism, the fight for ERA's ratification had provided supporting organizations with an ideal vehicle for growth. None had used the stalled campaign to better advantage than the National Organization for Women. With carefully worded appeals that underscored the danger posed to women's rights by the antifeminist politics and policies of the Reagan administration, NOW doubled its membership between 1980 and 1982. Funds quickly followed. In the final six months before the 1982 deadline for ratification expired on June 30, NOW alone raised $1 million a month. Gains for other women's rights organizations were less dramatic, but most emerged from the ratification struggle, at least temporarily, with enhanced resources.[15]

The place to apply those resources, many activists now argued, was electoral politics. The intense and overwhelming commitment to ERA among women legislators was seen as evidence that putting the right women in office in sufficient numbers could determine the fate of a whole range of issues of concern to women: pay equity, child care, sexual violence, reproductive rights. The lesson of the 1970s seemed clear: representation, not entitlement, was the key to gender equality. The task of electing women to public office would not be easy, of course. But no matter how formidable, it had been made easier by structural changes affecting electoral politics and party governance. The Democratic Party was more receptive to feminist influence in the wake of gender-based reforms and the ideological realignment of the GOP. Blacks and Chicanos, politically invigorated by the Voting Rights Act, were likely to be receptive to female candidates who demonstrated greater responsiveness to minority interests and more skill at coalition building than did their white male competitors.[16]

And there was the much-touted gender gap. In 1980, 54 percent of male voters, but only 46 percent of female voters, had supported Ronald Reagan, creating the biggest gender gap on record. Analysts pointed to policy differences: women, more dependent than men on social programs, feared proposed cuts in domestic spending; they also opposed Reagan's militaristic posture on defense and foreign policy. Whether, in future elections, they would translate policy preferences into candidate preferences in numbers large enough to elect feminists remained to be seen. While women in 1980 had reversed a long-term trend by voting in greater numbers than men (proportionate to their percentage of the adult population), they continued to be less interested in and knowledgeable about politics and consequently less likely to use their vote to reward candidates whose policies would best advance their collective interests. Still, the possibilities for political sisterhood had not seemed so tantalizing since the 1920s.[17]

Whatever the future prospects of female candidates, advocates argued, electoral politics need not be an exclusionary strategy. Legislative lobbying, litigation, and protest—tactics of choice in the 1970s—could not be abandoned. Grassroots movements (which fostered a politics of movement) and women's voluntary organizations (which nourished the politics of citizenship) also had a role to play. Both, it was understood, brought important resources to electoral politics as well as to pressure politics and the policy process. But the key to gains for women, strategists now insisted, was the woman in office who knew how to use the resources of office on behalf of other women. Female officeholders would simply be more likely to respond to problems arising out of differences in the objective social situation of the sexes, even if particular individuals did not see themselves as representatives of women's interests per se.[18]

Moreover, in the current political climate, electoral politics had to be thought of as a defensive strategy. Conservatives in the White House had already recast the Commission on Civil Rights with conservatives, transformed the Equal Employment Opportunity Commission, and made the attorney general the point man for an attack on affirmative action in the courts. With the Supreme Court the administration's next target, putting progressive women (and men) into elective office at the congressional and state levels was an imperative if the egalitarian policy gains achieved thus far were to be preserved.[19]

This pursuit of office would, in turn, require the professionalization of a feminist-inspired electoral politics. At the very least, new initiatives would have to be devised to deal with old problems. Obstacles to gender parity at courthouse and statehouse had become painfully apparent throughout the 1970s and early 1980s as women in increasing numbers made the transition from such organizations as the PTA, League of Women Voters, or Junior League to school board or hospital board and then on to city council or the mayoralty. Many, still more comfortable with the politics of citizenship than with the politics of realism, lacked the taste or talent for statewide office or the voracious appetite for politics required to win it. Others balked at the high cost to personal and family life, the loss of privacy, the incessant demands on one's time. Some, no doubt, remembered Lady Bird Johnson's apt remark that politicians should be born orphans and remain single. For those who were willing to plunge ahead, money and expertise were essential in an electoral process increasingly dominated by technicians adept at fund-raising, polling, media relations, and advertising. Yet traditional donors often perceived women who came to political office with different résumés as less credentialed and therefore less credible as candidates than their male competitors. Women of color found the obstacles compounded. Challenged within their own racial or ethnic community by minority men eager for office, they were marginalized within the larger community and, therefore, less likely to have the contacts necessary to break into the "money loop." For women who wanted to move from high-level appointive or elective state positions into the governor's office or on to Washington, the range of needs expanded. Spouses, as Geraldine Ferraro would learn in 1984, not only had to provide their blessing, but also bank balances and income tax returns.[20]

Even when family, funding, and strategy were under control, the contradictory expectations of candidates as women and as leaders posed problems in a world in which public perceptions *were* political reality. Not only did the print media pay less attention to female candidates in statewide races, but also the coverage they provided was frequently negative: articles often emphasized these office seekers' unlikely chances of victory. The issue agenda of male candidates was also better represented. Candidates' positions on "hard" (male) issues such as defense, foreign policy, and the economy received more coverage than did candidates' positions on "soft" issues in which female candidates were presumed to have greater expertise such as education, health care, and the environment.

Gender stereotypes loomed large in the minds of voters as well as reporters. It took adroit manipulation of conventional gender images for a woman candidate to be perceived as a family person, but not just a mother—and certainly not a neglectful one; an honest, caring candidate, but not a naive, soft novice; a team player, but not one of the boys; a tough, confident, decisive politician, but not a shrill, strident, abrasive woman. Above all, she had to avoid appearing ambitious. For male office seekers, service to others could be a rhetorical convention; for women, it must seem a motivational bedrock. Feminist stereotypes posed additional problems, generating intense debates among advisers as to how to calibrate the degree of feminist identity that could be safely displaced to various groups of voters.[21]

For young women and for women of color in predominantly white districts, image was even more complicated. Accents underscored "foreignness," transforming the speaker into an "outsider," as Shirley Chisholm, who had spent her childhood in Barbados, discovered in her first congressional race in New York. Black women's assertiveness also posed problems. But so did the soft voice and small, slight stature so often characteristic of Asian American women. The latter conveyed inexperience and lack of authority unless that image was offset—a booming voice and expansive personality would work for Hawaii's congresswoman Patsy Mink. Yet personal expansiveness, combined with youth, signaled sexuality. Voters in predominantly white districts wanted their female candidates to be not only white but also plain looking and older— "de-sexed and safer." Attention to dress and demeanor was no insurance against the sexual innuendo and mudslinging that has long been the lot of female trespassers who disrupt the hierarchies of the public sphere, whatever their background or appearance. As Ferraro would discreetly observe of the charges hurled at her during the vice presidential race, "in a national election the stakes get higher while the tactics get lower." A Texas mayoralty candidate put the problem more bluntly: "if you are in politics, you're either a lesbian or a slut."[22]

Even if the woman politician of a certain age succeeded in draping lace over steel in precisely the right places, there was no assurance that other women (and men) would rally behind her at the polls. Indeed, she risked losing "the women's vote" if she downplayed gender and sisterhood, creating an impression of indifference to women's issues; yet if she emphasized a "women's agenda," she risked reinforcing an image of marginality among voters of both sexes.

Undaunted by the complexity of the task, political activists plunged ahead.

With the recruitment, training, and funding of effective candidates now a top priority, they utilized old organizations and strategies as well as new. NOW revived its demand for gender balance in appointive office, insisting that appointments to boards and commissions be divided equally between men and women. Such positions provided visibility, experience, and contacts that helped to integrate women into traditionally male networks of influence. They also whetted the appetite for higher office. But moving up the political ladder required early money, training programs for candidates and staff, and help with budgeting, press, media, field organization, and fund-raising. To meet these needs organizations such as the National Women's Political Caucus (NWPC), NOW, and the Women's Campaign Fund, which had begun coordinating strategy as early as 1982, were joined by new Political Action Committees (PACs) such as the Black Women's Political Caucus, Hollywood Women's Political Committee, and Emily's List (Early Money Is Like Yeast). State and local PACs quickly followed, especially in California, where Chicana women organized to fund their own, as did Democratic and Republican women. For most, a prochoice position on abortion was an essential criterion for funding.[23]

Other organizations addressed different needs. The National Conference for Women Executives in State Government (NCWESG) emphasized skill building. Restricted to women holding high elective and appointive positions at the state level, the NCWESG provided an array of seminars, briefings, and other activities designed to help its members move between corporate and government worlds and better qualify themselves for gubernatorial or national office. To counteract the loneliness and isolation prevalent among those breaking into all-male bastions, trust-building and friendship-enhancing activities were designed to ease the discomfort of tokenism. The Organization of Women State Legislators also concentrated on skill enhancement with workshops ranging from press relations and reelection funding to model legislation on gender discrimination, family law, and violence against women. Feminist-oriented policy groups, better funded and better connected than in the 1970s, helped prepare the way for new initiatives from this potentially growing cadre of woman officeholders. As part of the effort to increase their numbers and effectiveness, the Rutgers University Center for the American Woman and Politics (CAWP) began systematically examining factors that inhibited or facilitated women seeking public office. By the mid-1980s, scholars working under CAWP auspices were ready to test the premise at the heart of the whole electoral strategy: that having women in office actually makes a difference. The validity of that premise was an article of faith; on this issue, however, practitioners of the politics of realism no less than practitioners of the politics of citizenship needed "facts" that would provide objective confirmation of core assumptions.[24]

As the 1990 elections approached, these varied initiatives began to produce results, albeit slowly and incrementally. To be sure, women candidates still had to "start earlier, run harder, and raise more money" just to be taken seriously, noted the head of an influential women's PAC. And, if they were taken seriously, there was "the Ferraro factor"—that blend of intense scrutiny, sexual innuendo, and relentless attack that had dogged Geraldine Ferraro and her husband John Zaccaro throughout the 1984 campaign. Yet female candidates and activists persisted, seeing obstacles as hurdles to be jumped rather than as insurmountable barriers.[25]

In Texas the hurdles were becoming a bit easier to clear throughout the 1980s as women took over the mayoralties of the state's major cities. The votes of Latinos and African Americans helped. So did hard times—male entrepreneurial elites hesitated to put businesses on hold for a time-consuming political office during the Texas recession. But the women who seized the moment and forged the alliances in the mayoralty contests as well as in other races were strong candidates, none more so than Ann Richards.[26]

A direct, blunt-speaking mother of four with strong liberal and feminist credentials, Richards was also a divorcée and a recovering alcoholic—hardly auspicious credentials for public office in a conservative state where politics has long been a contact sport. An active Democrat, Richards had served as a campaign manager and administrative assistant for Texas legislator Sarah Weddington, the young Austin lawyer who prepared the landmark abortion rights case, *Roe v. Wade*. At Weddington's office, "the epicenter" of the Texas women's political movement in the 1970s, Richards networked with other women while absorbing the political mentoring of Lieutenant Governor William P. Hobby Jr., whom she would later describe as "the first man who talked to me about politics as an equal." (Hobby grew up taking women seriously: his mother, Oveta Culp Hobby, had served in the Eisenhower cabinet in the 1950s, and, as governor, William P. Hobby Sr. had pushed the woman suffrage bill through the Texas legislature.) Running on her own in 1976, Richards had won the race for county commissioner. Elected state treasurer six years later and subsequently reelected without opposition, the silver-haired Texan had acquired a statewide reputation as a hugely popular and highly efficient administrator. By 1988, when she electrified the Democratic National Convention with her keynote address characterizing Vice President George Bush as having been born "with a silver foot in his mouth," she had her eye on the governor's office. She also had in place a grassroots women's network that would prove essential in getting her there. "We'd have crawled to the polls on ground glass if it had been necessary," Richards's longtime friend Liz Carpenter would later observe with minimum overstatement.[27]

Texas women were not the only ones moving up the ladder. San Francisco boasted what one journalist described as a veritable "political matriarchy"— women who had "paid their dues" at lower-level local and party positions and moved on, sometimes after political defeats, to the board of supervisors, the mayoralty, and Congress. Wholehearted practitioners of the politics of realism, "these girls" played "old-boy politics . . . very, very well," commented a San Franciscan whose own old-boy credentials lent credence to his characterization. And they were poised for "the next stage," according to Dianne Feinstein, the former mayor of San Francisco and a future gubernatorial candidate in 1990. Her determination to push through "the glass ceiling" was shared with equal intensity by her passionate colleague, Congresswoman Barbara Boxer.[28]

Other cities provided their own versions of the Dianne Feinsteins and Barbara Boxers. Los Angeles's fiery, charismatic Maxine Waters and Gloria Molina, both aggressive, controversial champions of their minority constituencies, would seek and win higher offices in which to pursue their particular blend of politics. So would Detroit's Barbara-Rose Collins, another woman of color and champion of the urban poor. St. Louis's Joan Kelly Horn and New Haven's Rosa De Lauro also had their eyes on Congress. Unlike Collins and Waters who had served as state legislators, neither Horn nor De Lauro had held elective office. Leaders in feminist political organizations (NWPC and Emily's List) and married to political pollsters, they both had acquired Potomac fever and, more important, considerable political expertise in other jobs. For women already in Congress, such as Illinois's Lynn Martin, Rhode Island's Claudine Schneider, and Hawaii's Patricia Saiki, a seat in the House of Representatives would serve as launch pad for a try for the Senate in 1990.

With a record number of women contending for office at every level of government, optimists predicted that 1990 would indeed be the year—perhaps even the decade—of the woman candidate. The prediction carried even greater force two years later when women ran in unprecedented numbers. With the end of the cold war, "women's issues" had acquired greater importance as the nation turned its attention to the environment, education, health care, and child care. "Kinder, gentler is in," quipped Congresswoman Pat Schroeder (D-Colo.)—and women candidates were likely beneficiaries. Being an outsider could also be an advantage at a time when political corruption, staggering federal deficits, a sluggish economy, the savings and loan debacle, nuclear waste dumps, and other political disasters had left voters angry and disillusioned about politics-as-usual: "cleaning up messes" had long been "women's work." Poll data now indicated that Americans thought women in high office would do as good a job as men, if not better, in every area except the military. Another plus was the inevitable redistricting that would occur in the wake of the 1990 census. The creation of new districts would make it possible for more women to run against an opponent who lacked the advantage of incumbency.[29]

Finally, there was the Anita Hill factor. The treatment of the Oklahoma University law professor during the 1991 confirmation hearings for Supreme Court Justice Clarence Thomas had outraged women throughout the nation who witnessed the hostile grilling of Hill by the Senate Judiciary Committee. Whether or not one believed Hill's charges—and many did—the failure of the all-male committee to comprehend the dynamics of sexual harassment seemed to many women to dramatize the folly of relying on male legislators to protect and promote women's interests. The decision to run for the Senate on the part of Illinois's Carol Mosley Braun, Washington's Patty Murray, and Pennsylvania's Lynn Yaekel and the willingness of women across the country to support them heralded an anger-fed activism that would surely pay off at the polls.[30]

Skeptics counseled caution. Survey data confirmed that female candidates did indeed have greater credibility on "soft issues"; they were also perceived by voters to have greater honesty and integrity. But there were other, more telling factors: the power of incumbency even in an era of anti-incumbency sentiment, the increasing use of negative campaigning, and the gender disparity in campaign funds. Analysts also pointed to the often chimerical character of "the women's vote," even in Democratic circles where polls indicated that women prefer to vote for candidates of their own sex. The gender gap of the 1980s, skeptics cautioned, was really about partisan and issue—not necessarily candidate—preferences. As for the impact of the abortion issue, the Supreme Court's *Webster* decision, which opened the way for state restrictions on abortion, had infused women on both sides of the issue with new political energy much as had ERA a decade earlier. It remained to be seen whether voters cared enough to cross party lines on behalf of "choice" or whether younger women, the group most strongly prochoice and least likely to vote, would respond at the polls. Whether there would be a direct line from Anita Hill to Capitol Hill was also problematic. National polls indicated that many women did not believe Hill's allegations against Thomas. Moreover, a candidate who made the hearings a primary focus of her campaign might find that voters considered other issues more important.[31]

Both optimists and skeptics could find vindication in election returns of the early 1990s. The glass ceiling cracked first at the gubernatorial level. Three of the eight women with major party nominations emerged winners in 1990—all Democrats. California's Dianne Feinstein (who narrowly lost) and Texas's

Congresswomen led by Barbara Boxer march up the steps of the Capitol building in Washington, D.C., to demand that the Senate Judiciary Committee hear Anita Hill. (Courtesy Paul Hosefros/NYT Pictures)

Ann Richards (who won) also demonstrated that women candidates need not run bargain basement campaigns, although both were outspent by their opponents. (Feinstein raised $17 million and Richards $12 million.) Indeed, it took $21 million and all the resources of the opposing party to deny Feinstein the scant 180,000 votes that would have made her governor of the largest, most populous state in the Union. That Richards emerged victorious from two brutal, hard-hitting campaigns suffused with personal attacks and innuendo earned the savvy Texan the characterization "tougher than a $2.00 steak." More important, she had proved that advocates of "kinder, gentler" policies could also "take the heat." The Texas gubernatorial race further demonstrated that abortion was an issue that affected votes, especially when the call for restrictions came from a candidate who became infamous for his sexist remarks. Confronted with such a clear alternative, large numbers of prochoice Republican women—an unheard-of 25 percent—had crossed party lines to support Richards—a phenomenon that occurred, although less dramatically, elsewhere as well.[32]

Comparable breakthroughs occurred at the congressional level in 1992, when the number of women in the Senate tripled while doubling in the House of Representatives. Of the eleven candidates for the Senate, five (including incumbent Barbara Mikulski of Maryland) won—all of them Democrats. Dianne Feinstein and Barbara Boxer made history in California, as did Carol Mosley Braun, of Illinois, who became the first African American woman elected to the Senate in the nation's history. Washington's Patty Murray was the fourth member of what journalists promptly dubbed "the Anita Hill class." Of the 106 candidates for the House—an increase of 64 percent over 1990—24 newcomers, most of them Democrats, joined 23 incumbents, giving the 103d Congress a total of 48 women in the House (including one nonvoting delegate from the District of Columbia) and 6 in the Senate.[33]

Gains, although far less spectacular, continued to occur at the state level. A record number of women—2,375 in 1992—sought legislative seats, many of them in open districts. When the votes were counted, women made up about one-fifth of all state legislatures, as compared to under 5 percent in the early 1970s. Perhaps more surprising than the legislative victories was the number of women elected to top financial and law enforcement positions—state treasurer, auditor, comptroller, and attorney general. Still few, such victories challenged stereotypes and helped to push the number of women holding statewide elected office at the executive level to a record 72 by 1993. At the local level, there were also gains. Among the one hundred largest cities in the United States, the top official in eighteen would now have to be addressed as "Madam Mayor."[34]

Women of color were among the victors, not just in the District of Columbia, which elected its first African American woman mayor in 1990, but in Congress. When the 103d Congress convened, eight African American women, three Latinas, and one Asian American woman sat in the House of Representatives. Minority women also made gains in state legislatures, bringing their number to over two hundred by 1993.[35]

Women contributed to these victories with dollars and votes as well as other forms of support. Women's PACs, which provided 85 percent of their funds to women candidates in 1990, found contributions up dramatically in 1992. The bipartisan National Women's Caucus raised $61,000 from a single newspaper ad depicting a fantasy scene of Clarence Thomas being interrogated by a panel of female senators. Emily's List saw its resources quadruple to an estimated $6 million war chest for prochoice Democratic women. The Hollywood Women's Political Committee wrote checks of nearly $200,000 to its own U.S. Senate candidates Dianne Feinstein and Barbara Boxer. Check writing was not the only form of activism. As campaign workers, female volunteers made possible what U.S. Senator Barbara Mikulski called "sweat-equity campaigns," compensating with time logged at phone banks and door-to-door canvases what they could not provide in money.[36]

Sisterhood was also evident at the polls. In the 1990 gubernatorial races, the number of women voting for California's Dianne Feinstein and for Oregon's Barbara Roberts pushed the gender gap for those two candidates to 16 percentage points. Texas women also provided Ann Richards the margin of victory. In 1992 women voters were no less supportive of women candidates for the U.S. Senate. Female voters also provided the margin of victory for a few liberal, prochoice men such as New Jersey's Senator Bill Bradley, who narrowly escaped an upset at the hands of Republican Christine Todd Whitman in 1990. Feminists were equally discerning in Illinois, using their votes to reward veteran Democratic senator Paul Simon, whose record, many women concluded, indicated that he was the better feminist than his female opponent. Even skeptics sensed a shift in the making. "There is something different out there," a veteran fund-raiser for women candidates had observed. Women "want to get involved. They want to give money. Trust me, it's like night and day." If 1990 was not yet the "year of the woman," then 1992 was coming closer. The "year of the feminist women" would be the more precise characterization Phyllis Schlafly tartly observed as she surveyed the 1992 election results. It was a critical distinction.[37]

Breakthroughs there certainly were, and they should not be discounted. Nor should we minimize the importance of the steady increase in the number of women holding elective office at all levels over the past decade and a half, especially since having women in office does indeed make a difference. Female state legislators from across the nation who gathered at their quadrennial forum in San Diego in 1991 got scholarly confirmation of what many already knew. According to a three-year study undertaken by the Center for the American Woman and Politics, while party affiliation and political ideology matter, women legislators, irrespective of party affiliation, do indeed place a higher priority than do their male counterparts on women's rights issues such as domestic violence, pay equity, and abortion rights as well as on traditional female concerns such as family, children, education, and health care. (Black women are even more likely than white women to make women's rights bills a top legislative priority.) Moreover, women were just as adept as men in getting their bills passed and far more concerned with including citizens in the legislative process, concluded the CAWP study. Other researchers concurred, noting that even when variations between the sexes in terms of voting behavior were small, women legislators were more likely to initiate and promote women's issues. Differences involved intensity of commitment and deeper understanding of what was at stake, noted U.S. Senator Barbara Boxer (D-Calif.)[38]

Although women in office can and do make a difference, their potential to reshape the political agenda is directly related to numbers as well as priorities. Studies of female legislators show that the proportion of women in the state house directly affects the degree to which they take the lead on issues related to women, children, and family. Women representatives, concludes political scientist Susan Gluck Mezey, are simply "more willing to 'act for' women when they are in the presence of other women." It is equally clear, however, that the rate of growth for women in public office during the 1980s had been both low and slow. It had also been uneven. While women made up 40 percent of the state's legislators in Washington, they held only 12 percent in New Jersey and a mere 4 percent in Kentucky. Extrapolating from past results, including the election of 1992, it would be the year 2054 before half of all state legislators would be female. Estimates as to when women might reach parity in Congress and in governorships range from the year 2400 to many centuries beyond. Whether and to what extent these projections would be affected by the even larger numbers of women running for public office throughout the 1990s remains to be seen.[39]

Numbers do not tell the whole story, moreover, especially where power is concerned. Consider those women mayors of Texas who numbered one hundred in 1990. A closer look at the largest cities reveals that only in Houston was the position of mayor one of real power. Dallas, by contrast, had a weak mayor and a strong city manager. Legislatures also varied. The Pennsylvania legislature ranked forty-sixth in terms of the percent of its seats held by women—an overall 6.7 percent in both houses. The New Hampshire legislature, on the other hand, was one-third female, putting it among the top ten in terms of gender balance. But the General Court of New Hampshire was also a citizens' legislature; as such, its members were less well paid and had less power than did their counterparts in Pennsylvania and other states with professional legislatures, where a seat also held the greater promise of upward political mobility. As one New Hampshire lawmaker observed, "men can no longer afford to [serve]." Another explained the presence of women more bluntly: "it's just a continuation of the volunteer bullshit."[40]

Even if the legislative arena in which many women operate is a relatively powerful one, simply being there and doing one's homework is no guarantee of effectiveness. Political scientists noted that women legislators, especially in the 1970s, seemed more comfortable with solving constituent problems than participating in the legislative process. Initially less likely to speak in committee or from the floor, they were also more reluctant to negotiate with fellow legislators and lobbyists. As their numbers and experience increased and as discrimination lessened during the 1980s, their level of participation rose sharply. Old attitudes toward power, however, were slower to disappear.

"In politics, to have power, you have to be perceived as having power," observed Martha McKay, a veteran legislative watcher, echoing Hobbes's famous dictum, "the reputation of power is power." "Some of these women," she lamented, "are so uncomfortable with power, they can't even act as if they had it." And the women themselves often admitted as much. "Power is something I was always very afraid of," confessed a Connecticut congresswoman. "It is a word I don't like." That women who are highly effective legislators also share this discomfort at owning power and incorporating it into their self-image is something the Martha McKay understood. As a consultant on women and management, she had read the literature on socialization and on the gendered perceptions and uses of power. She was also aware of the difference between power and leadership. But she remained convinced that in the stubbornly male arena of politics, every woman in office must understand that power has to be owned and wielded before it can be used on behalf of others (an insight more fully appreciated by the female politicians of the 1990s).[41]

The eagerness of women officeholders to get things done for others, especially women, McKay observed, was itself a source of vulnerability inasmuch as female legislators tended to be clustered on committees where they dealt with "women's concerns." Her observation was suffused with ambivalence. As a feminist, she knew that women's concerns, whether traditional or feminist, were important and must be championed by women. As the founder of a state

Women's Political Caucus and of a feminist PAC, McKay had worked to elect politically talented women to the legislature precisely because their support of women's issues could make a difference. But she was also aware of the ways in which marginalization is perpetuated.

Automatically assigning women to legislative committees dealing with such issues is a kind of ghettoizing of both issues and women. Many women legislators, she acknowledged, get their start in politics as members of local boards concerned with child care, education, health, human services, reproductive rights, or domestic violence; such areas are, therefore, ones in which they have policy expertise. Nevertheless, she was convinced that legislative typecasting tends to stereotype female legislators who have expertise in other areas. It also obscures the extent to which female constituents have interests that are affected by other committees. Even more objectionable, she insisted, is the extent to which the practice allows male legislators (and special interest groups) to retain control over areas in which they perceive real power to reside: taxes and budgets, for example.

She was not alone in her concerns. Women legislators themselves devoted a full session to the problem at their 1991 meeting. In doing so, they served notice that even as legislative bodies sexually integrate and even as women legislators extend their range of committee involvement, the old nineteenth-century concept of separate male and female spheres holds sway. Whether by choice or default, women in office, as in private life, continue to bear primary responsibility for matters dealing with women, children, and family. That reality is not likely to change until such time as women in legislative bodies reach a sufficient mass—around 25 percent or more, some experts suggest; others predict 35 to 40 percent—at which point individual women lawmakers may no longer feel such a strong personal responsibility to make "women's issues" their central legislative effort. (Increased numbers of women office-holders also enhance the likelihood that a greater percentage of male legislators will come to share the views and priorities of their female colleagues.)[42]

Viewed from this perspective, it seems possible that the influx of female politicians may thus far have had less impact on the degendering of both public policy and political power than feminists in both parties would wish. Indeed, what we may be seeing at the municipal level, where women have won elective office in the greatest numbers, is an early stage in the feminization of those offices. In effect, politically ambitious men may be conceding positions that are perceived for whatever reasons to have relatively little impact or political payoff while holding on to those that really matter. Long a phenomenon in the labor market, where the transition from male to female workers is accompanied by significant loss of pay and prestige in the job categories concerned, the feminization of politics is already under way in other nations. In Norway in 1991, for example, a female prime minister was in her third administration and women headed the two major parties and a small, but influential third party. A Norwegian think-tank report entitled *Scenario 2000* predicted that in Norway women would move from a "marginal minority" to a "marginal majority" as men vacated politics for higher-paying, higher-status jobs in business.[43]

Whether women who understand power and its uses can take positions conceded them and devise ways to invest them with new vigor and authority remains to be seen. Whether as members of legislative bodies they can win leadership positions still infused with power is also uncertain, as least in the short term. No less problematic is whether power itself can be redefined, its meaning enlarged to include responsibility, altruism, and nurturance: tough *and* caring—to borrow the tag line from Dianne Feinstein's gubernatorial campaign. Yet many female politicians seem determined to try, clinging to goals of transformation even as they seek integration in institutions whose policies and procedures they also wish to change. In the meantime, male politicians in the United States continue to grasp higher office with a tenacity that suggests that the much-discussed glass ceiling is cracked, but still in place. It is significant that, as of 1990, only three states (Delaware, Iowa, and North Dakota) had passed laws mandating gender parity for appointive positions on state boards and commissions. No less telling was the paucity of women holding leadership positions in state legislatures—in 1990, a grand total of four out of a pool of over one thousand. Nowhere has the gender barrier proved harder to break than in the U.S. Congress, where the power of incumbency is strongest; as of 1994, a woman had not chaired a formal standing committee since 1977.[44]

CONTINUITY AND CHANGE

What, then, are we to make of these developments? First are the obvious continuities. The politics of the last quarter century provide striking examples of the variety of forms in which female political activism has been expressed over time. The politics of citizenship was honed in the political culture of nineteenth-century, single-sex voluntary associations at a time when women's ability to affect public policy rested on their ability to influence those in power through education and lobbying. Still practiced in many of the original organizations in which it was perfected, both style and strategy remain a part of pressure group politics. The politics of movement is also embedded in a rich tradition. Women active on behalf of temperance, suffrage, peace, and civil rights used consciousness as a political tool and struggled with the tension between transformational and incremental change.

The politics of realism seems at first glance to have a shorter and thinner history if we focus only on electoral politics. But here, too, continuities are striking. Consider the constraints, internal as well as external, that contemporary women politicians face. Their greater vulnerability to sexual innuendo, for example, is a reminder of how relatively recently the term *public woman* was synonymous with prostitute. Even the description of electoral politics as "today's medium for helping people" or "social work with power" is freighted with history. This understanding of public office, like the policy preferences of many women in state legislatures, has roots in a venerable tradition of female altruism and civic improvement that helped both to legitimate the entry of women into public life and to create the welfare state.[45] Consider also the assumptions about gender-based disparities in voting behavior, about the importance of women electing women to represent women's interests, about the very existence of special gender-defined interests that require representation on the part of a group divided by race, class, and culture. Debatable assumptions at the beginning of this century, they remain no less debatable at the end.

Just as there is continuity in each of these political styles, so too there is a tradition of moving back and forth among them. For individual women, the transition from League of Women Voters activist to partisan political candidate has been a familiar one for much of this century. The movement, however, is not always toward electoral politics, nor does involvement in electoral politics automatically mean a shift to the politics of realism. Elected officials, particularly at the local level, may continue to practice the politics of citizenship. Nor are these shifts confined to individuals. Organizations can also embrace different styles and strategies sequentially and, to some degree, even simultaneously. The National Organization for Women provides a case in point.

Originating as a voluntary organization during the second wave of feminism, NOW moved from the politics of citizenship in the 1970s to the politics of movement during the ERA ratification struggle to the politics of realism in the 1980s as a player in big-time politics. However, "playing with the boys in the Democratic party" proved to be a short-lived enthusiasm. Angered by the antifeminist backlash among party leaders in the wake of the Mondale-Ferraro defeat and frustrated by the behavior of a Democratic Congress that repeatedly confirmed Supreme Court justices likely to overturn *Roe v. Wade*, the organization has continued to flirt with third-party possibilities. (Eleanor Smeal, NOW's former president, officially announced the formation of the

21st Century Party at a massive prochoice march in Washington, D.C., in April 1992.) A measure of the alienation that pollsters reported a majority of American women felt toward both parties prior to the 1992 elections, the third-party proposal was not without historical precedent. Judged by other women's rights organizations as likely to have no more impact than did the narrowly based National Woman's Party of the 1920s, that initiative coexisted with others ranging from proposed economic boycotts to civil disobedience. Although NOW's current agenda requires multiple strategies, the organization in terms of style still seems more comfortable with a militant outsider stance associated with the politics of movement.[46]

While flexibility is essential to any group seeking social change, especially when confronted with a shift in strategy by opponents, it is not always clear to what extent short-term shifts like NOW's enhance the political agency of women or even of a specific group of women. What has become clear over the past two decades is a growing conviction that gender equality and justice require political power that is gender based and feminist inspired—in a word, representation. Madeleine Kunin, the former governor of Vermont, spoke to the point when she noted that "as much as we have relied basically on a surrogate system, letting men represent our views and our needs, that surrogate system has limitations." Others are more blunt about the need to act directly on behalf of self-defined interests. They cite the threat to reproductive rights, which has diverted attention from other health care problems; the lack of adequate, comprehensive national policies on maternity leave, family leave, and child care; job and pay inequities; welfare reform; domestic violence; sexual harassment; and other grievances. They conclude, in the words of one candidate: "We cannot afford to reelect the problem." Or as Dianne Feinstein put it in her 1992 Senate race, 2 percent may be the right percent of fat in milk, but 2 percent of women in the Senate is bad for the women of America.[47]

Even discounting campaign rhetoric, there seems to be a new reality in the 1990s. Individuals and organizations firmly committed to traditional electoral politics as a vehicle for social change have succeeded in professionalizing feminist electoral participation. They have done so during a decade in which a gender gap in policy preferences became a gender gap in candidate preferences as well. Both reflect a growing gender consciousness among women that is, in part, a result of the diffusion of feminist attitudes. This gender consciousness, the recognition that "one's relationship to the political world is at least partly but nonetheless particularly shaped by being male and female," is not a new phenomenon. Nor is it synonymous with feminism: some women who cling to traditional gender roles also display a high level of gender consciousness. What is new is the extent of the politicization. There are now more women in office who are comfortable with both feminism and power, more female candidates who are credentialed and credible, and more women who are prepared to support them than ever before. Herein lies the potential for change.[48]

Whether that change will develop into a gender-based politics of representation that truly delivers on women's concerns remains problematic. Certainly, the ready identification of the new women in Congress with the bipartisan Congressional Caucus on Women's Issues is a start. But even if the weak party system that facilitates such issue-oriented bipartisanship persists, the women (men also belong) who provide caucus leadership on these issues remain few. Their numbers, while increasing in the future, will continue to be low so long as the current system of barriers remains intact. While the major culprit is the single-member electoral district, political scientists also point to the high rates of incumbency, the huge cost of campaigns, a state legislative environment that limits the number of women on the recruitment ladder, and the dominance in some states of a single party.[49]

The game, moreover, is not merely one of catch-up. (If numbers were all that mattered, it would make no difference whether Barbara Jordans or Phyllis Schlaflys were elected.) Even if the rate at which female officeholders approach parity is accelerated, there are no assurances that women moving into positions of public authority in the twenty-first century will see women's interests as legitimate interests requiring representation or that they will embrace a transformative vision of feminism that is both deeply radical and broadly humanistic. Texas Republican Kay Bailey Hutchinson's victory in 1993 provides a case in point. It brought the number of women in the U.S. Senate to seven. Yet, despite her moderate stance on abortion, many of the feminist groups that had worked so hard to elect women to the Senate in 1992 did not support her candidacy, believing her male opponent to be the better representative of women's interests.[50]

Although preliminary empirical evidence suggests that woman politicians do not lose their gendered perspective and values in order to gain and retain office, some may find it either ideologically uncomfortable or politically inexpedient to embrace publicly feminism, women's collective distinctiveness, or even the outsider status that finally proved in 1992 to be an asset. More important than how they choose to package their candidacies or agenda is what they do in office. Individual consciousness is inevitably transmuted as elected officials interact with institutional circumstances and oppositional forces. Even if those women who consider themselves feminists manage to resist the pressures for acculturation and accommodation on "outsiders" seeking full "membership in the club," female officeholders will continue to have to answer to the same constituencies that men do if they want to stay in power. Moreover, their ability to represent women substantively as well as descriptively will surely be further complicated by the conflicted sense among women themselves as to what their interests objectively involve. Antifeminist women, it is worth noting, were among the voters who rejected an Iowa Equal Rights Amendment and a Colorado gay rights law in 1992. Antifeminist women were also among the candidates of the Religious Right who successfully captured numerous state and local offices, unseating liberal women (and men) and positioning themselves to run for higher office in future elections.[51]

If women are to develop a clear understanding of women's interests that obscures neither their own differences from each other nor their commonalities with men, feminists will have much to do. They will have to develop a political consciousness and activism that takes into account the ways in which differences of race and class as well as gender are intertwined, perpetuated, and effectively challenged. At the very least, they will need a politics that addresses the concerns of other women with differing viewpoints—those who see white, middle-class feminists as privileging gender and ignoring burdens imposed by class and race; those who reject feminism in the name of family; and those who discount women's collective power and the possibilities of electoral politics. In the meantime, they will need to define their issues, establish their priorities, and build their coalitions so that men as well as women will be able to represent them more effectively.[52]

However the task is defined, women will continue to employ the strategies and styles of political activism developed over the course of a century. What is imperative is that they do so both with a keener appreciation of the strengths and limitations associated with each and a far better understanding of power and its uses.

"We are in for a very, very long haul," an eloquent feminist and Republican told a NWPC convention in 1977. "You will lose your youth, your sleep, your patience, your sense of humor and occasionally . . . the understanding and support of people that you love very much." In return, she continued, "I have nothing to offer you but . . . your pride in being a woman, and all your dreams you've ever had for your daughters, and nieces, and granddaughters . . . your future and the certain knowledge that at the end of your days you will be able to look back and say that once in your life you gave everything you had for justice." Her message, initially intended to reinvigorate efforts on behalf of the ratification of ERA, is now prominently displayed on NWPC calendars as feminist political organizations repeatedly gear up for the next election. The words continue to inspire those convinced that the degendering of politics and power is a continuing struggle and that substantive equality requires both rights and representation.[53]

PART 3 *Knowledge*

CHAPTER 11 : READING *LITTLE WOMEN* : THE MANY LIVES OF A TEXT : *BARBARA SICHERMAN*

"I have read and re-read 'Little Women' and *it* never seems to grow old," fifteen-year-old Jane Addams confided to a friend.[1] Writing in 1876, Addams did not say why she liked *Little Women*. But her partiality was by no means unusual among women, and even some men, of her generation. Louisa May Alcott's tale of growing up female was an unexpected success when it appeared in the fall of 1868. Already a classic when Addams wrote, the book has been called "the most popular girls' story in American literature"; a century and a quarter after publication, there are twenty editions in print.[2]

The early history of this publishing phenomenon is full of ironies. Not the least of them is the author's expressed distaste for the project. When Thomas Niles Jr., literary editor of the respected Boston firm of Roberts Brothers, asked Alcott to write a *"girls' story,"* the author tartly observed in her journal: "I plod away, though I don't enjoy this sort of thing. Never liked girls or knew many, except my sisters, but our queer plays and experiences may prove interesting, though I doubt it."[3] After delivering twelve chapters in June 1868, she claimed that both she and her editor found them *"dull."*[4] Niles assured her that he was "pleased—I ought to be more emphatic & say delighted,—so *please* to consider 'judgement' as favorable"; the following month he predicted that the book would " 'hit.' "[5] Influenced perhaps by the verdict of "some girls" who had pronounced the manuscript " 'splendid!' " Alcott reconsidered while

Lithograph by Lizbeth B. Comins, used as a frontispiece in Ednah Dow Cheney, *Louisa May Alcott: The Children's Friend*, 1888. (Courtesy of the American Antiquarian Society)

correcting proof: "It reads better than I expected. Not a bit sensational, but simple and true, for we really lived most of it." Of the youngsters who liked it, she observed: "As it is for them, they are the best critics, so I should be satisfied."[6]

The informal "readers' report" was right on target. Published in early October 1868, the first printing (2,000 copies) of *Little Women, or, Meg, Jo, Beth and Amy* sold out within the month. A sequel appeared the following April, with only the designation *Part Second* differentiating it from the original. By the end of the year some 38,000 copies (of both parts) were in print, with another 32,000 in 1870. Nearly 200,000 copies had been printed by Roberts Brothers by January 1888, two months before Alcott's death.[7] Like it or not, with this book Alcott established her niche in the expanding market for juvenile literature.

Perhaps even more remarkable than *Little Women*'s initial success has been its longevity. It topped a list of forty books compiled by the Federal Bureau of Education in 1925 that "all children should read before they are sixteen."[8] Two years later—in response to the question "What book has influenced you most?"—high school students ranked it first, ahead of the Bible and *Pilgrim's Progress*.[9] On a bicentennial list of the best eleven American children's books,

Little Women, The Adventures of Tom Sawyer, and *The Adventures of Huckleberry Finn* were the only nineteenth-century titles. Like most iconic works, *Little Women* has been transmuted into other media, into song and opera, theater, radio, and film. A comic strip even surfaced briefly in 1988 in the revamped *Ms.*[10]

Polls and statistics do not begin to do justice to the *Little Women* phenomenon. Reading the book has been a rite of passage for generations of adolescent and preadolescent females of the comfortable classes. It still elicits powerful narratives of love and passion.[11] In a 1982 essay on how she became a writer, Cynthia Ozick declared: "I read 'Little Women' a thousand times. Ten thousand. I am no longer incognito, not even to myself. I am Jo in her 'vortex'; not Jo exactly, but some Jo-of-the-future. I am under an enchantment: Who I truly am must be deferred, waited for and waited for."[12] Ozick's avowal encapsulates recurrent themes in readers' accounts: the deep, almost inexplicable emotions engendered by the novel; the passionate identification with Jo March, the feisty tomboy heroine who publishes stories in her teens; and—allowing for exaggeration—a pattern of multiple readings. Numerous women who grew up in the 1940s and 1950s report that they read the book yearly or more during their teens or earlier; some confide that they continue to read it as adults, though less frequently. Presumably for them, as for Jane Addams, the story did not grow old.

One of many intriguing questions about *Little Women* is how and why the "dull" book, the girls' story by a woman who claimed she never liked girls, captivated so many readers. An added irony is that Alcott, the product of an unconventional upbringing, whose eccentric transcendentalist father self-consciously tested his child-rearing theories on his daughters, took them to live in a commune, and failed utterly as a breadwinner, should write what many contemporaries considered the definitive story of American family life.[13]

My concern here, however, is with *Little Women* as a cultural phenomenon and what it can tell us about the relationship between reading and female identity. A cultural profile of the book and its readers casts light on *Little Women*'s emergence as the classic story of American girlhood and why, in the words of a recent critic, it has remained "a kind of miracle of preservation" when most other works of its era have long since disappeared from the juvenile canon.[14] Building on recent work in cultural criticism and history, this study also examines the "cultural work" *Little Women* performed for diverse reading communities.[15] Such an approach challenges traditional assumptions about the universality of texts. It also demonstrates the importance of reading for the construction of female identity.

Little Women was commissioned because the publisher believed a market existed for a "girls' story," a relatively new genre still in the process of being defined. The book's success suggests that this assumption was correct, although there is also evidence that its readership extended beyond the targeted group. Two unusual features affected the book's production and early reception. First, its two-stage publication gave readers unusual influence in constructing the plot, an important element in its long-term appeal. Second, the book was marketed in ways that elicited reader identification with author as well as heroine, an author, moreover, who was not only astonishingly successful but whose connections with Ralph Waldo Emerson (her intellectual mentor) and Nathaniel Hawthorne (her neighbor) were widely known. Enjoying considerable popularity from the outset, *Little Women* became part of the prescribed reading of an American girlhood, as did Alcott's own life.

Knowing how a book is promoted is not the same as knowing how it is read, however. *Little Women* has been interpreted in many ways, by ordinary readers as well as critics.[16] Initially praised by readers and reviewers as a realistic story of family life, by the time of its successful stage adaptation in 1912–14 it seemed "quaint" to some.[17] In the twentieth century, Jo, always the most admired sister, was for many the only one who mattered.

With its origin as a girls' story—by definition a domestic story—and a plot in which the sisters overcome their personal failings as they move from adolescence to womanhood, *Little Women* has been viewed by some recent critics as exacting discipline from its readers as well as its heroines.[18] This interpretative line recognizes only one way of reading the story—a conservative one. Feminist explications have for the most part focused on Jo, who has been variously read as "the one young woman in 19th-century fiction who maintains her individual independence, who gives up no part of her autonomy as payment for being born a woman—and who gets away with it" and as a character who is betrayed and even murdered by her creator, who allows her to be tamed and married.[19]

Whether they discern negative or positive messages, critics agree on the importance of the story. *Little Women* has been called "*the* American female myth," Jo "the most influential figure of the independent and creative American woman."[20] To read the book in this way, even as a failed bildungsroman, as do critics who view Jo's marriage as a surrender of autonomy and a capitulation to traditional femininity, assumes an individualistic outlook on the part of readers, a belief that a woman could aspire to and even attain personal success outside the family claim.

The formulation of *Little Women* as "*the* American female myth" is a distinctly middle-class reading, one that assumes both a universality of female experience and a single mode of reading Alcott's text that transcends class, race, ethnicity, and historical era. While adolescents from diverse backgrounds *can* interpret *Little Women* as a search for personal autonomy—and have in fact done so—this is by no means a universal reading. The female quest plot is inflected by class and culture as well as gender. The story has appealed primarily to an audience that is white and middle class. Historical evidence from working-class sources is scarce and is often filtered through middle-class observers. What we have suggests that working-class women did not necessarily have access to "the simple, every-day classics that the school-boy and -girl are supposed to have read," among them *Little Women*, and that many had a penchant for less "realistic" fiction of the sort usually dismissed as "escapist."[21] For some Jewish working-class immigrant women early in the twentieth century, Alcott's story provided a model for becoming American and middle-class rather than for removing themselves from women's domestic lot, as was the case with the native-born writers and intellectuals to whom *Little Women*'s appeal is better known. In this reading, *Little Women* was still a success story—but of a different kind.

Dissimilar though they are, in both interpretations women readers found in *Little Women* a sense of future possibility. Gerda Lerner has demonstrated that access to learning has been central to the creation of feminist consciousness over the centuries.[22] I would add that literature in general and fiction in particular have been critically important in the construction of female identity, although not always a feminist one. The scarcity in life of models for nontraditional womanhood has prompted women more often than men to turn to fiction for self-authorization.[23]

Little Women's long-lived popularity permits examination of the ways in which adolescent girls of diverse class, culture, and historical era have read the text. Where critics have debated the meaning of the novel, in particular whether Jo is a symbol of independent or resigned womanhood, I hope to show that meaning resides in the social location, interpretive conventions, and perceived needs of disparate communities of readers.[24] But the story of *Little Women* is one of continuity as well as difference, particularly in the common interpretive stance of white, middle-class women readers for more than a century. This persistence can perhaps best be understood as a consequence of the snail-like pace of change for women and the dearth of models for such a quest—in fiction and in life. In this context, Jo March was unique.[25]

EARLY PUBLISHING AND MARKETING HISTORY

Alcott claimed that she kept on with *Little Women* because "lively, simple books are very much needed for girls, and perhaps I can supply the need."[26] She subsequently redirected her energies as a writer away from adult fiction—

some of it considered sensational and published anonymously or pseudony-mously—to become not only a successful author of "juveniles," but one of the most popular writers of the era. Alcott may have regretted being channeled into one type of literature, but she was extremely well paid for her efforts, a source of considerable pride to a woman whose father was so feckless about money.[27]

Juvenile literature was entering a new phase in the 1860s at the very time Alcott was refashioning her career. This literature was more secular and on the whole less pietistic than its antebellum precursors, the characterizations more apt; children, even "bad boys," might be basically good, whatever mischievous stages they went through.[28] An expanding middle class, eager to provide its young with cultural as well as moral training, underwrote the new juvenile market that included genteel literary magazines paralleling those read by adults. So seriously was this literature taken that even journals that embraced "high culture" devoted as much space to reviewing children's as adult fiction; thus the seeming anomaly of a review of Alcott's *Eight Cousins* in the *Nation* by the young Henry James.[29]

In contrast to the overtly religious antebellum stories, in which both sexes were expected to be good and domesticated, the new juvenile market was becoming increasingly segmented by gender. An exciting new adventure litera-ture for boys developed after 1850, featuring escape from domesticity and female authority. Seeking to tap into a new market, Niles asked Alcott to write a "girls' story" after he observed the hefty sales of boys' adventure stories by "Oliver Optic," pseudonym of William Taylor Adams.[30] Since prevailing gen-der ideology defined tales for girls as domestic, it is understandable why Alcott, who idolized her Concord mentor Emerson, adored Goethe, and loved to run with boys, would be disinclined to write one. The designation "girls' story" connoted classification by age as well as gender. Although people of all ages and both sexes read *Little Women*, the book evolved for the emerging female youth market, the "young adults" in the transitional period between childhood and adulthood that would soon be labeled adolescence.[31]

These readers had an unusual say in determining Jo's fate. Eager to capital-ize on his experiment, Niles urged Alcott to add a chapter "in which allusions might be made to something in the future."[32] Employing a metaphor well suited to a writer who engaged in theatrical performances most of her life, the volume concludes: "So grouped the curtain falls upon Meg, Jo, Beth and Amy. Whether it ever rises again, depends upon the reception given to the first act of the domestic drama, called 'LITTLE WOMEN.'"[33] Reader response to Al-cott's floater was positive but complicated her task. Reluctant to depart from autobiography, Alcott insisted that by rights Jo should remain a "literary spinster." But she felt pressured by readers to imagine a different fate for her heroine. The day she began work on the sequel, she observed: "Girls write to ask who the little women marry, as if that was the only end and aim of a woman's life. I *won't* marry Jo to Laurie to please anyone." To foil her readers, she created a "funny match" for Jo—the middle-aged, bumbling German professor, Friedrich Bhaer.[34]

The aspect of the book that has frustrated generations of readers—the foreclosing of marriage between Jo and Laurie—thus represents a compromise between Alcott and her initial audience. Paradoxically, this seeming misstep has probably been a major factor in the story's enduring success. If Jo had remained a spinster, as Alcott wished, or if she had married the attractive and wealthy hero, as readers hoped, it is unlikely that the book would have had such a wide appeal. Rather, the problematic ending contributed to *Little Women*'s popularity, the lack of satisfying closure helping to keep the story alive, something to ponder, return to, reread, perhaps with the hope of a different resolution. Alcott's refusal of the conventionally happy ending represented by a pairing of Jo and Laurie and her insistence on a "funny match" to the rumpled and much older professor effectively subvert adolescent romantic ideals. The absence of a compelling love plot has also made it easier for generations of readers to ignore the novel's ending when Jo becomes Mother Bhaer and to retain the image of Jo as the questing teenage tomboy.[35]

At the same time, an adolescent reader, struggling with her appearance and unruly impulses while contemplating the burdens of future womanhood, might find it reassuring that her fictional counterpart emerges happily, if not perhaps ideally, from similar circumstances. For Jo is loved. And she has choices. She turns down the charming but erratic hero, who consoles himself by marrying her pretty and vain younger sister, Amy. Professor Bhaer is no schoolgirl's hero, but Jo believes that he is better suited to her than Laurie. The crucial point is that the choice is hers, its quirkiness another sign of her much-prized individuality.[36] Jo gives up writing sensation stories because her prospective husband considers them unworthy, but she makes it clear that she intends to contribute to the support of their future family.

By marrying off the sisters in the second part, Alcott bowed to young women's interest in romance. The addition of the marriage to the quest plot enabled *Little Women* to touch the essential bases for middle-class female readers in the late nineteenth century. In this regard, it was unusual for its time. In adult fiction, marriage and quest plots were rarely combined; success in the former precluded attainment of the latter.[37] The inclusion of a marriage plot in a book for a nonadult audience was also unusual. Even though critics noted the need for literature for the in-between stage, variously designated as eight to eighteen and fourteen to twenty, *Harper's New Monthly Magazine* judged the sequel "a rather mature book for the little women, but a capital one for their elders."[38] The conjunction of quest and marriage plots helps to account for the book's staying power: it is difficult to imagine large numbers of adolescent female readers in the twentieth century gravitating to a book in which the heroine remained single.[39]

Little Women took off with the publication of the second part in April 1869. A Concord neighbor called it "the rage in '69 as 'Pinafore' was in '68."[40] A savvy judge of the market, Niles urged Alcott to "'Make hay while the Sun-shines'" and did everything he could to keep her name before the public.[41] Shortly after the appearance of *Little Women, Part Second*, Roberts Brothers brought out an augmented edition of her first critical success under the title, *Hospital Sketches and Camp and Fireside Stories*, and in succeeding years published *An Old-Fashioned Girl* (1870) and *Little Men* (1871), a sequel to *Little Women*. Niles encouraged publicity about books and author, whom he kept informed about her extensive press coverage while she traveled abroad. Alcott was then at the peak of her popularity; between October 1868 and July 1871 Roberts Brothers sold some 166,000 volumes of her juvenile fiction.[42]

The well-publicized autobiographical status of *Little Women*, together with Alcott's realistic subject matter and direct style, encouraged identification by middle-class readers.[43] Reviewers stressed the realism of her characters and scenes; readers recognized themselves in her work. Thirteen-year-old Annie Adams of Fair Haven, Vermont, wrote *St. Nicholas*, the most prestigious of the new children's magazines, that she and her three sisters each resembled one of the March sisters (she was Jo): "So, you see, I was greatly interested in 'Little Women,' as I could appreciate it so well; and it seemed to me as if Miss Alcott must have seen us four girls before she wrote the story."[44] Girls not only read themselves into *Little Women*, they elaborated on it and incorporated the story into their lives. In 1872 the five Lukens sisters from Brinton, Pennsylvania, sent Alcott a copy of their home newspaper, "Little Things," which was modeled after "The Pickwick Portfolio" produced by the March sisters. Alcott responded with encouragement, asked for further details, and subscribed to the paper; subsequently she offered advice about reading, writing, and religion and even sent a story for publication. She took their aspirations seriously, providing frank, practical advice about magazines, publishers, and authors' fees to these budding literary women.[45]

There was, then, a reciprocal relationship between the characters and home life depicted in *Little Women* and the lives of middle-class American girls. An unusual feature of this identification was the perception that author and heroine were interchangeable. Alcott's work was marketed to encourage the illusion not only that Jo was Alcott but that Alcott was Jo. When Alcott traveled in Europe in 1870, Niles encouraged her to send for publication " 'Jo's Letters from Abroad to the March's [*sic*] at Home' "; the following year he asked her to select "from the million or less letters" some that could be published in a volume entitled "Little Women and Little Men Letters or Letters to 'Jo' by 'Little Women' and 'Little Men.' "[46] Neither book materialized, but *Shawl-Straps*, a humorous account of Alcott's European trip, appeared in 1872 as the second volume in the *Aunt Jo's Scrap-Bag* series. Niles sometimes addressed his leading author as "Jo," "Jo March," or "Aunt Jo." Alcott often substituted the names of the March sisters for her own when she answered fans; on occasion, she inserted them into her journal. The equation of author and character continued after Alcott's death. When her sister Anna Pratt supervised publication of *Comic Tragedies* (1893), a volume of childhood plays, she wrote the foreword as "Meg," and the title page read "Written By 'Jo' and 'Meg' and Acted by the 'Little Women.' "

Readers responded in kind. An ad for *Little Women* quotes a letter written by "Nelly" addressed to "Dear Jo, or Miss Alcott": "We have all been reading 'Little Women,' and we liked it so much I could not help wanting to write to you. We think *you* are perfectly splendid; I like you better every time I read it. We were all so disappointed about your not marrying Laurie; I cried over that part,—I could not help it. We all liked Laurie ever so much, and almost killed ourselves laughing over the funny things you and he said." Blurring the lines between author and character, the writer also requested a picture, wished the recipient improved health, and invited her to visit.[47]

The illusion that she was the youthful and unconventional Jo made Alcott a more approachable author. But the conflation of author and character had its risks. Young readers who formed an image of the author as Jo, a teenager for most of the novel, were startled by Alcott's appearance. When the Lukens sisters informed her that some "friends" had been disappointed in her picture, Alcott replied that she could not understand why people insisted Jo was young "when she is said to be 30 at the end of the book . . . After seeing the photograph it is hardly necessary to say that Jo and L.M.A. are *not* one, & that the latter is a tired out old lady of 42."[48]

With the publication of *Little Women, Part Second*, Alcott became a celebrity. Correspondents demanded her photograph and autograph seekers descended on her home while she "dodge[d] into the woods *à la* Hawthorne."[49] Customarily shunning the limelight, she was mobbed by fans on her rare public appearances. After a meeting of the Woman's Congress in 1875, she reported, "the stage filled . . . with beaming girls all armed with Albums and cards and begging to speak to Miss A. . . . 'Do put up your veil so we can see how you really look' said one. 'Will you kiss me please,' said another. . . . I finally had to run for my life with more girls all along the way, and Ma's clawing me as I went." Things were somewhat more decorous at Vassar, but even college students insisted on kissing Alcott and obtaining her autograph.[50] She avenged herself with a devastating portrait of celebrity hounds in *Jo's Boys* (1886), the sequel to *Little Men.*[51]

Alcott also drew more serious admirers, some of whom, like the Lukens sisters, sought her literary advice. In the 1860s and 1870s authorship was the most respected female vocation—and the best paid. Before the consolidation of the American literary canon later in the century, women writers had an acknowledged, though not unchallenged, place in the world of letters. Feminist critics and historians have recently been documenting women's presence, but Alcott has been largely left out of this reassessment, in large part because of her status as a writer of "juvenile fiction."[52]

Alcott was a well-respected writer during her lifetime, an era of relatively inclusive and nonhierarchical definitions of literature. An American literature course taken by Jane Addams at Rockford Female Seminary in 1878–79 covered authors of domestic fiction, Alcott among them.[53] But her literary reputation transcended the category. A review of *Little Men* pronounced: "Even thus early in her brief history as a country and a nation, America can boast a long list of classics—Prescott, Irving, Hawthorne, Longfellow—and Time, the great sculptor will one day carve Miss Alcott's name among them."[54] Alcott received nearly a page to Hawthorne's page and a half in James S. Hart's *A Manual of American Literature: A Text-Book for Schools and Colleges* (1873); both were listed under the category "Novels and Tales." She was compared with her former neighbor on more than one occasion; a younger Concord resident proclaimed: "In American fiction 'Little Women' holds the next place to the 'Scarlet Letter' and 'Marble Faun.' " Since Hawthorne stood at the pinnacle of American literature, this was high praise.[55]

A teenage girl contemplating a literary career could dream of becoming a published author who, like Alcott, might produce a beloved and immortal work. At a time when young women were encouraged, even expected, to take part in the literary activities that suffused middle-class domestic life, such success was not beyond imagining. From Hart's manual a reader could learn that Alcott began writing for publication at sixteen and, by hard work and perseverance, became both famous and self-supporting by her pen in her late thirties.[56] The real female American success story was Alcott's, not Jo's.

There were, then, many reasons why a young woman seeking a literary career in the 1870s and early 1880s would look to Alcott as a model. Most important was the story that brought pleasure to so many. Despite claims that

Little Women is a text about disciplining girls into proper womanhood, a comparison with other "girls' books" marks it as a text that opened up new avenues of experience for readers.[57] The contrast with Martha Finley's *Elsie Dinsmore* (1867), a story in which strict obedience is exacted from children—to the point of whipping—is striking. In this first of many volumes, the lachrymose and devoutly religious heroine is put upon by relatives and by her father, who punishes her for refusing to play the piano on the Sabbath. Elsie holds fast to her principles but is otherwise self-abnegating in the extreme: it is difficult to imagine her even trying to have fun.[58] *Faith Gartney's Girlhood* (1863) by Mrs. A. D. T. Whitney, a forgotten but once highly acclaimed writer with whom Alcott was often compared, was the story of a girl's emergence into serious and self-affirming womanhood. Written for a female audience between fourteen and twenty to show "what is noblest and truest," the book is more complex than *Elsie Dinsmore*, the tone less charged. But Whitney relies heavily on didactic narrative and fails to exploit the emotional potential of her plot: the authorial voice is moralistic and the religion conspicuous.[59]

The fictional world of *Little Women* is strikingly different. Despite the use of John Bunyan's *Pilgrim's Progress* as a framing device, an older Calvinist worldview that emphasized sin and obedience to the deity has been replaced by a moral outlook in which self-discipline and doing good to others come first.[60] Consonant with *Little Women*'s new moral tone, so congenial to an expanding middle class, are its informal style and rollicking escapades. Aided by her love of the theater and influenced as well by her youthful idol, Charles Dickens, Alcott was a wonderful painter of dramatic scenes; some were heartbreaking, but many were high-spirited depictions of frolics, games, and theatrical productions.[61] She also had an ear for young people's language: her substitution of dialogue for the long passages of moralizing narrative that characterized most girls' books gave her story a compelling sense of immediacy. So did her use of slang, for which critics often faulted her, but which must have endeared her to young readers. Finally, the beautifully realized portrait of Jo March as tomboy, one of the first of its kind, spoke to changing standards of girlhood. Beginning in the 1860s, tomboys were not only tolerated but even admired—up to a point, the point at which they were expected to become women.[62] Perhaps it was fitting after all that it was Alcott, writing of her idiosyncratic childhood in the 1840s, who identified a new type of American girlhood for the 1870s.[63]

Why Alcott? Why *Little Women*? The questions were asked during the author's lifetime and after. *Little Women* was strategically placed within the new market for secular juvenile books as well as the more specialized category of "girls' books." A fortuitous combination of author, heroine, subject, and style, along with shrewd marketing, helped propel the book to popularity and its author to celebrity. Alcott, neighbor and friend of writers who were increasingly enshrined in the nation's literary pantheon, partook of their glory. But she had a luster of her own. Although often considered a "New England writer," she was also praised as a quintessentially "American" writer, a sign both of New England's dominance in the American literary tradition and of Alcott's prominent place within it.[64]

JO AS A LITERARY AND INTELLECTUAL MODEL

Reading Alcott became a necessary ritual for children of the comfortable classes. Growing up at a time and in a class that conferred leisure on its young, children devoted considerable time and energy to literary pursuits. *Little Women* was a way station en route to more adult books. But it was also a text that acquired its own cachet. Alcott was such an accepted part of childhood that even Theodore Roosevelt declared, "at the cost of being deemed effeminate," that he "worshiped" *Little Men, Little Women*, and *An Old-Fashioned Girl*.[65]

Readers' explanations of their fondness for Alcott constitute a trope for personal preferences. Not all of Alcott's early readers focused on Jo; some were taken with the saga of the entire March family, which invited comparisons with their own. Charlotte Perkins Gilman, for example, who grew up in genteel poverty after her father abandoned the family, liked the fact that in Alcott, as in Whitney, "the heroes and heroines were almost always poor, and good, while the rich people were generally bad."[66] S. Josephine Baker, for her part, considered Alcott "the unattainable ideal of a great woman." A tomboy who became a prominent physician and wore ties to downplay her gender, "Jo" Baker not only claimed Jo March as her "favorite character in all fiction" but pointedly dissociated herself from Elsie Dinsmore.[67]

Jo March also fueled the literary aspirations of M. Carey Thomas, one of Alcott's early readers, during the critical years of early adolescence. In the fall of 1869, the year of *Little Women*'s great success, Thomas and her cousin Frank Smith adopted the personae of Jo and Laurie, although as Quakers they should not have been reading fiction at all. At the ages of twelve and fifteen respectively, Thomas and Smith began addressing each other and signing their letters as Jo and Laurie; they meted out other roles to friends and relatives. When Bessie King, Thomas's closest female companion, made a bid to be Jo, Frank wrote his cousin that Bessie must choose another part "if she won't be Jo 2., or Meg, or Beth, or Amy; or Daisy, or anybody besides Jo 1. since *thou will* be the latter." Since Jo was the only acceptable heroine of *Little Women*, Bessie chose Polly, heroine of *An Old-Fashioned Girl*, Alcott's latest.[68]

When Thomas began a journal in 1870 at age thirteen, she did so in Jo's name. Declaring at the outset: "Ain't going to be sentimental / 'No no not for Jo' (not Joe)," she had much in common with Alcott's heroine.[69] Both were "bookworms" and tomboys; both desired independence. Like Jo, Thomas wished to do something "splendid." In early adolescence her ambitions were still diffuse, but they centered on becoming a famous writer, a famous *woman* writer—"Jo (not Joe)." Her life was suffused with literature, with writing as well as reading: in addition to keeping a journal, she wrote poetry, kept a commonplace book, and compiled lists of favorite books and poems, some of them annotated. As she gravitated to such champions of aestheticism as Algernon Charles Swinburne and Dante Gabriel Rossetti, by her early twenties she had outgrown Alcott and other writers who upheld morality in their art. But Bessie King acknowledged the importance of their childhood play in 1879, when Thomas took the audacious step of starting graduate study in Germany: "Somehow today I went back to those early days when our horizon was so limited yet so full of light & our path lay as plain before us. It all came of reading over Miss Alcott's books now the quintescence [sic] of Philistinism then a Bible. . . . Doesn't thee remember when to turn out a 'Jo' was the height of ambition"?[70]

At the time Thomas was so engaged with *Little Women*, she was already a feminist. Sensitive to any gender restriction or slight, whether from people she knew or from biblical or scientific sources, she resolved at fifteen to disprove female inferiority by advancing her own education.[71] Despite its inception as a domestic story, then, Thomas read *Little Women* as a female bildungsroman, as did many women after her. This has in many ways been the most important reading, the one that has made the book such a phenomenon for so many years.

With its secular recasting of *Pilgrim's Progress*, *Little Women* transforms Christian's allegorical search for the Celestial City into the quintessential female quest plot. In a chapter entitled "Castles in the Air," each of the March sisters reveals her deepest ambition. In its loving depictions of the sisters' struggles to attain their goals (Jo to be a famous writer, Amy an artist, and Meg mistress of a lovely house), *Little Women* succeeds in authorizing female vocation and individuality. Nor did Alcott rule out the possibility of future artistic creativity: although married and managing a large household and school, Jo has not entirely given up her literary dreams, nor Amy her artistic ones. Beth, who has no ambition other than "to stay at home safe with father and mother, and help take care of the family," dies because she can find no way of growing up; her mysterious illness may be read as a failure of imagination, her inability to build castles in the air.[72]

In Jo, Alcott creates a portrait of female creativity that was not traditionally available to women:

> Every few weeks she would shut herself up in her room, put on her scribbling suit, and "fall into a vortex," as she expressed it, writing away at her novel with all her heart and soul, for till that was finished she could find no peace. . . .
>
> She did not think herself a genius by any means; but when the writing fit came on, she gave herself up to it with entire abandon, and led a blissful life, unconscious of want, care, or bad weather, while she sat safe and happy in an imaginary world, full of friends almost as real and dear to her as any in the flesh. Sleep forsook her eyes, meals stood untasted, day and night were all too short to enjoy the happiness which blessed her only at such times, and made these hours worth living, even if they bore no other fruit. The divine afflatus usually lasted a week or two, and then she emerged from her "vortex" hungry, sleepy, cross, or despondent.[73]

Alcott's portrait of concentrated purpose—which describes her own creative practice—is as far removed as it could be from the ordinary lot of women, at least any adult woman. Jo not only has a room of her own; she also has the leisure—and the license—to remove herself from all obligation to others. Jo was important to young women like Thomas because there were so few of her—in literature or in life. One need only recall the example of Margaret Fuller, a generation older than Alcott, who suffered nightmares and delirium from her hothouse education and often felt isolated as the exceptional woman. By contrast, Jo is enmeshed in a family that constitutes a sustaining community of women.[74]

More conventional readers of Thomas's era could find in *Little Women* practical advice on two subjects of growing concern to women: economic opportunities and marriage. Alcott was well qualified to advise on the former because of her long years of struggle in the marketplace. Though portrayed more starkly in *Work* (1873), an autobiographical novel for the adult market, middle-class women's need to be able to earn a living is a central motif in *Little Women*, as it was in Alcott's life. The novel can be read as a defining text on this subject, at a time when even conservative critics were beginning to concede the point. Mr. March's economic setback, like Bronson Alcott's, forces his daughters into the labor market. Their jobs (as governess and companion) are depicted as mainly unrewarding, although Jo's literary career is described with loving particularity. As we have seen, to please her readers, Alcott compromised her belief that "liberty [was] a better husband." But although the March sisters marry, Marmee March, who wishes no greater joy for her daughters than a happy marriage, declares that it is better to remain single than to marry without love. Opportunities for self-respecting singlehood and women's employment went hand in hand, as Alcott knew.[75]

If Alcott articulated issues highly pertinent to young women of her era, Jo's continued appeal suggests not only the dearth of fictional heroines to foster dreams of glory but the continued absence of real-life models. Perhaps that is why Simone de Beauvoir was so attracted to *Little Women*, in which she thought she "caught a glimpse of my future self":

> I identified passionately with Jo, the intellectual. . . . She wrote: in order to imitate her more completely, I composed two or three short stories. . . . [T]he relationship between Jo and Laurie touched me to the heart. Later, I had no doubt, they would marry one another; so it was possible for maturity to bring the promises made in childhood to fruition instead of denying them: this thought filled me with renewed hope. But the thing that delighted me most of all was the marked partiality which Louisa Alcott manifested for Jo. . . . [I]n *Little Women* Jo was superior to her sisters, who were either more virtuous or more beautiful than she, because of her passion for knowledge and the vigor of her thinking; her superiority was as outstanding as that of certain adults, and guaranteed that she would have an unusual life: she was marked by fate. I, too, felt I was entitled to consider my taste in reading and my scholastic success as tokens of a personal superiority which would be borne out by the future. I became in my own eyes a character out of a novel.[76]

De Beauvoir found in Jo a model of authentic selfhood, someone she could emulate in the present and through whom she could read—and invent—her own destiny. It was a future full of possibility, open rather than closed, intellectual and literary rather than domestic. By fictionalizing her own life, de Beauvoir could more readily contemplate a career as a writer and an intellectual, no matter how improbable such an outcome seemed to her family. She could also rationalize her sense of superiority to her environment and to her own sister. Although de Beauvoir later claimed that she first learned from *Little Women* that "marriage was not necessary," she responded to the romance as well as the quest plot.[77] Far from interfering with her enjoyment, her disappointment that Jo did not marry Laurie prompted her to rework the story to her own satisfaction. Her conviction that Jo and Laurie would marry some day and the "renewed hope" this belief gave her suggest the power of wish fulfillment and the reader's capacity to create her own text. There is no textual basis for this belief: Jo and Laurie each marry someone else; each is a parent by the end of the story. De Beauvoir's reading is therefore not just a matter of filling in gaps but of rewriting the text. Her powerful commentary suggests the creativity of the reading experience and the permeability of boundaries between life and art: lives can be fictionalized, texts can be rewritten, art can become life and life art.

Not all women read with the intensity of Thomas or de Beauvoir. But there is considerable evidence that, from the time of her creation until the recent past, Jo March provided for young women of the comfortable classes a model of female independence and of intellectual and literary achievement. This is not the only way of reading *Little Women*, but it constitutes a major interpretive strand, particularly in the twentieth century. Testimony on this point began as soon as the book was published and persists today among women who grew up in the 1940s and 1950s.[78] Thomas, whose love relations were with women, never mentions the marriage plot, but for de Beauvoir, writing in the twentieth century, it was both important and compatible with a quest plot.

INFLECTIONS OF CLASS AND CULTURE

Not everyone has access to the same cultural resources, wishes to engage the same texts, or interprets them in identical ways. Although class is by no means the sole determinant of what or how much is read, it is a critical variable in determining basic literacy and educational levels. These in turn, in conjunction with the aspirations of group, family, or individual, influence reading practices and preferences.[79]

For African American women, in the nineteenth century at least, class rather than race was probably the primary determinant of reading practices. Both Mary Church Terrell, a graduate of Oberlin College, and Ida B. Wells, the slave-born daughter of a carpenter and "a famous cook" who became a journalist and reformer, read Alcott. Terrell claimed that her books "were received with an acclaim among the young people of this country which has rarely if ever been equaled and never surpassed," while Wells observed: "I had formed my ideals on the best of Dickens's stories, Louisa May Alcott's, Mrs. A.D.T. Whitney's, and Charlotte Brontë's books, and Oliver Optic's stories for boys." Neither singled out *Little Women*; both seem to have read Alcott as part of the standard fare of an American middle-class childhood.[80]

For African American writer Ann Petry, now in her eighties, *Little Women* was much more than that. On the occasion of her induction into the Connecticut Women's Hall of Fame, she noted her admiration for women writers who had preceded and set the stage for her—" 'Think of Louisa May Alcott.' " *Little Women* was the first book Petry "read on her own as a child." Her comments are reminiscent of those of de Beauvoir and other writers: "I couldn't stop reading because I had encountered Jo March. I felt as though I was part of Jo and she was part of me. I, too, was a tomboy and a misfit and kept a secret diary. . . . She said things like 'I wish I was a horse, then I could run for miles in this splendid air and not lose my breath.' I found myself wishing the same thing whenever I ran for the sheer joy of running. She was a would-be writer—and so was I."[81]

Two contrasting responses to *Little Women* from up and down the class ladder suggest the essentially middle-class and perhaps also middle-brow nature of the book's appeal. Edith Wharton, who drops the names of famous books and authors in an autobiography dominated by upper-class and high-culture values, noted that her mother would not let her read popular American children's books because "the children spoke bad English *without the author's knowing it.*" She claimed that when she was finally permitted to read *Little Women* and *Little Men* because everyone else did, "[M]y ears, trained to the fresh racy English of 'Alice in Wonderland,' 'The Water Babies' and 'The Princess and the Goblin,' were exasperated by the laxities of the great Louisa."[82]

Like Wharton, though for different reasons, some working-class women also found *Little Women* too banal. Dorothy Richardson, a journalist, suggests as much in *The Long Day*, an account of her life among the working class. In an arresting episode, Richardson ridicules the reading preferences of her fellow workers in a paper box factory. The plot of a favorite novel, Laura Jean Libbey's *Little Rosebud's Lovers; or, A Cruel Revenge*, is recounted by one of the workers as a tale of a woman's triumph over all sorts of adversity, including abductions and a false marriage to one of the villains. When Richardson summarizes *Little Women*, a coworker dismisses it: " '[T]hat's no story—that's just everyday happenings. I don't see what's the use of putting things like that in books. I'll bet any money that lady what wrote it knew all them boys and girls. They just sound like real, live people; and when you was telling about them I could just see them as plain as plain could be. . . . I suppose farmer folks likes them kind of stories. . . . They ain't used to the same styles of anything that us city folks are.' "[83]

The box makers found the characters in *Little Women* "real"—an interesting point in itself—but did not care to enter its narrative framework. Though they were not class conscious in a political sense, their awareness of their class position may account at least in part for their disinterest in a story whose heroines, despite economic reverses, had the leisure to pursue their interests in art, music, and literature and could expect to live in suburban cottages, conditions out of reach for most working-class women. Since *their* "everyday happenings" were poverty and exhausting work, the attraction of fictions about working girls who preserved their virtue and came into great wealth, either through marriage or disclosure of their middle- or upper-class origins, is understandable. Such denouements would have seemed just as likely—or unlikely—as a future in a suburban cottage. In the absence, in story or in life, of a female success tradition of moving up the occupational ladder, the "Cinderella tale" of marrying up was the nearest thing to a Horatio Alger story for working-class women.[84]

Reading practices depend on cultural as well as class location. It is a telling commentary on class in America that some Jewish immigrant women, who would be defined as working class on the basis of family income and occupation, not only enjoyed *Little Women* but also found in it a vehicle for envisioning a new and higher status.[85] For them, Alcott's classic provided a model for transcending their status as ethnic outsiders and for gaining access to American life and culture. It was a first step into the kind of middle-class family life rejected by Thomas and de Beauvoir. These immigrants found the book liberating and read it as a success story—but of a different kind.

In *My Mother and I*, Elizabeth G. Stern (1889–1954) charts the cultural distance a Jewish immigrant woman traveled from Russia and a midwestern urban ghetto to the American mainstream: she graduates from college, studies social work, marries a professional man, and becomes a social worker and writer.[86] *Little Women* occupies a crucial place in the story. After the narrator comes across it in a stack of newspapers in a rag shop, the book utterly engrosses her: "I sat in the dim light of the rag shop and read the browned pages of that ragged copy of 'Little Women.' . . . [N]o book I have opened has meant as much to me as did that small volume telling in simple words such as I myself spoke, the story of an American childhood in New England. I had found a new literature, the literature of childhood." She had also found the literature of America: "I no longer read the little paper-bound Yiddish novelettes which father then sold. In the old rag shop loft I devoured the English magazines and newspapers." Of the books her teachers brought her from the public library, she writes:

> Far more marvellous than the fairy stories were to me in the ghetto street the stories of American child life, all the Alcott and the Pepper books. The pretty mothers, the childish ideals, the open gardens, the homes of many rooms were as unreal to me as the fairy stories. But reading of them made my aspirations beautiful.
>
> My books were doors that gave me entrance into another world. Often I think that I did not grow up in the ghetto but in the books I read as a child in the ghetto. The life in Soho passed me by and did not touch me, once I began to read.[87]

Stern's testimony to the importance of reading in reconfiguring aspiration is not unlike de Beauvoir's, although the context is entirely different, as is the nature of the desire elicited by her reading. In American books, the ghetto fell away and the protagonist discovered both childhood and beauty. Far from being realistic, *Little Women* was an American fairy tale. Indeed, some of the narrator's "precocious" thirteen-year-old school friends "scoffingly averred that there were 'no such peoples like Jo and Beth.'" As she climbs the educational ladder, she discovers that such people do exist and that a life of beauty is possible, even for those of humble origin. With its emphasis on middle-class domesticity, *My Mother and I* is a story of Americanization with a female twist.[88]

Stern was not unique in reading *Little Women* as a vehicle for assimilation into American middle-class life or in conflating "American" and "middle class." More than half a century later, a Jewish male writer explored the novel's appeal as an "American" book:

> [T]o me, a first generation American, raised in an Orthodox Jewish household where more Yiddish was spoken than English, everything about *Little Women* was exotic. It was all so American, so full of a life I did not know but desperately hoped to be part of, an America full of promises, hopes, optimisms, an America where everyone had a chance to become somebody wonderful like Jo March—Louisa May Alcott who (I had discovered that the Marches and the Alcotts were almost identical) did become, with this story book that I adored, world famous."[89]

What had been realistic to the early middle- and upper-middle-class WASP readers of *Little Women* was "exotic" to Jewish immigrants a generation or two later. Could there be a better illustration of the importance of historical location in determining meaning?

Teachers, librarians, and other cultural mediators encouraged Jewish immigrant women to read what many viewed as the archetypal American female story. Book and author became enshrined in popular legend, especially after publication of *Louisa May Alcott: Her Life, Letters, and Journals* (1889), the year after the author's death, by her friend Ednah Dow Cheney. Interest in Alcott remained high in the early twentieth century. There was a 1909 biography by Belle Moses and a dramatization in 1912 that received rave reviews and toured the country. Alcott's books were sometimes assigned in public schools.[90] Jews themselves often served as cultural intermediaries between native and immigrant communities. When Rose Cohen, an immigrant affiliated with the Nurses' (later Henry Street) Settlement, found *Julius Caesar* too difficult, she asked the librarian at the Educational Alliance, a Jewish agency that assisted recent Eastern European immigrants, for a book "any book—like for a child. She brought me 'Little Women.'"[91]

Cohen was offered *Little Women* as a less taxing vehicle for learning English than Shakespeare. But Alcott was often prescribed as a safe and even salutary writer. Librarians had long debated the effects of reading on those who were young, female, and impressionable. They were echoed by some members of the working class, including Rose Pastor Stokes, an immigrant from Eastern Europe via England. Contending that "*all* girls are what they read," Stokes, writing as "Zelda" for the English page of the *Yiddishes Tageblatt*, admonished her readers to avoid "crazy phantasies from the imbecile brains" of writers like Laura Jean Libbey. She urged those sixteen and under to read Alcott, a writer known for her "excellent teachings" and one from whom "discriminating or indiscriminating" readers alike derived pleasure. Zelda also recommended Cheney, claiming that "the biographies of some writers are far more interesting, even, than the stories they have written."[92]

One of the Jewish immigrants for whom Alcott's success proved inspiring was Mary Antin, a fervent advocate of assimilation into American life. Alcott's were the children's books she "remember[ed] with the greatest delight" (followed by boys' adventure books, especially Alger's). Antin, who published poems in English in her teens and contemplated a literary career, lingered over the biographical entries she found in an encyclopedia. She "could not resist the temptation to study out the exact place . . . where my name would belong. I saw that it would come not far from 'Alcott, Louisa M.'; and I covered my face with my hands, to hide the silly, baseless joy in it."[93] We have come full circle. Eager to assimilate, Antin responded in ways reminiscent of Alcott's early native-born and middle-class readers who admired her success as an author. Antin, too, could imagine a successful American career for herself, a career for which Alcott was still the model.

CONCLUSION

Not all readers of *Little Women* read the same text. This is literally the case, since the story went through many editions. Not until 1880 did it appear in one volume, illustrated in this case and purged of some of its slang.[94] Since then there have been numerous editions and many publishers. I have been concerned here with the changing meaning of the story for different audiences and with historical continuities as well. For many middle-class readers, early and later, *Little Women* provided a model of womanhood that deviated from conventional gender norms, a continuity that suggests how little these norms changed in their essentials from the late 1860s to the 1960s. Reading individualistically, they viewed Jo as an intellectual and a writer, the liberated woman they sought to become. No matter that Jo marries and raises a family; such readers remember the young Jo, the teenager who is far from beautiful, struggles with her temper, is both a bookworm and the center of action, and dreams of literary glory while helping to support her family with her pen. These readers for the most part took for granted their right to a long and privileged childhood, largely exempt from the labor market. Jewish women who immigrated to the United States in their youth could not assume such a childhood. Nor were those raised in Orthodox Jewish households brought up on an individualistic philosophy. Their school experiences and reading—American books like *Little Women*—made them aware of different standards of decorum and material life that we tend to associate with class, but that are cultural as well. For some of these readers, *Little Women* offered a fascinating glimpse into an American world. Of course we know, as they did not, that the world Alcott depicted was vanishing, even as she wrote. Nevertheless, that fictional world, along with their school encounters, provided a vision of what life, American life, could be.

Can readers do whatever they like with texts? Yes and no. As we have seen, *Little Women* has been read in many ways, depending not only on when and by whom it was read but also on readers' experiences and aspirations. It has been read as a romance or as a quest, or both. It has been read as a family drama that validates virtue over wealth. It has been read as a how-to manual by immigrants who wanted to assimilate into American, middle-class life and as a means of escaping that life by women who knew its gender constraints too well. For many, especially in the early years, *Little Women* was read through the life of the author, whose literary success exceeded that of her fictional persona.

At the same time, both the passion *Little Women* has engendered in diverse readers and its ability to survive its era and transcend its genre point to a text of unusual permeability. The compromise Alcott effected with her readers in constructing a more problematic plot than is usual in fiction for the young has enhanced the story's appeal. If *Little Women* is not exactly a "problem novel," it is a work that lingers in readers' minds in ways that allow for imaginative elaboration. The frequent rereadings reported by women in their fifties also hint at nostalgia for lost youth and for a past that seems more secure than the present, perhaps even an imagined re-creation of idealized love between mothers and daughters.[95] Most important, readers' testimony in the nineteenth and twentieth centuries points to *Little Women* as a text that opens up possibilities rather than foreclosing them. With its multiple reference points and voices (four sisters, each distinct and recognizable), its depictions of joy as well as sorrow, its fresh and unlabored speech, Alcott's classic has something for almost everyone. For readers on the threshold of adulthood, the text's authorizing of female ambition has been a significant counterweight to more habitual gender prescriptions.

Little Women is such a harbinger of modern life, of consumer culture and new freedom for middle-class children, it is easy to forget that it was written just a few years after the Civil War, in the midst of Reconstruction and at a time of economic dislocation. For the most part, Alcott left such contemporary markers out of her story, another sign of the text's openness. The Civil War provides an important backdrop and a spur to heroism at home as well as on the battlefield, but it is primarily a plot device to remove Mr. March from the scene. Despite her family's support of John Brown, Alcott does not press a particular interpretation of the war. A final reason *Little Women* has survived so well, despite the chasm that separates Alcott's era from ours, is the virtual absence of references to outside events that would date her story and make it grow old.[96] That way each generation can invent it anew.

CHAPTER 12 : BETWEEN CULTURE

AND POLITICS : THE EMMA LAZARUS

FEDERATION OF JEWISH WOMEN'S CLUBS

AND THE PROMULGATION OF WOMEN'S

HISTORY, 1944–1989 : *JOYCE ANTLER*

On November 22, 1909, over 2,000 New York women's garment workers, many of them already out on strike, crowded into Cooper Union to vote on an industrywide action. In the ensuing hours of debate, speakers repeatedly urged caution in deciding whether to take the dramatic step of calling a general strike. Although the audience was more than half female, the only woman speaker was Mary Dreier, president of the New York Women's Trade Union League.

Then a worker called from the floor to be heard; despite complaints, she was permitted to speak. The woman was Clara Lemlich, a twenty-three-year-old who looked so slight that she was described in the next day's press as a teenage "girl." Yet Lemlich, a worker from the Leiserson shop, had been arrested seventeen times and was then recovering from a beating she had received two days earlier. In Yiddish, Lemlich proclaimed: "I am a working girl, one of those who are on strike against intolerable conditions. I am tired of listening to speakers who talk in general terms. What we are here for is to decide whether we shall or shall not strike. I offer a resolution that a general strike be declared—now."[1] As the delegates roared their approval, Benjamin Feigenbaum, the chairman of the meeting, sprang to Lemlich's side and thrust her right arm into the air.[2] "Will you take the old Hebrew oath?" he asked. According to a newspaper account of the strike, "Two and a half thousand

Members of the Emma Lazarus Federation of Jewish Women's Clubs at the March on Washington, 1963. (Courtesy of the American Jewish Archives, Cincinnati, Ohio)

right arms shot up. Two and a half thousand voices repeated the Yiddish words: 'May my right [hand] wither from [my] arm if I betray the cause I now pledge.' "[3] By the next evening over 20,000 workers had walked out; the strike thereafter became known as the Uprising of the 20,000. When the strike ended fourteen weeks later, 354 shirtwaist shop owners had signed union agreements. Although not all the workers' demands were met, the agreements generally raised wages, limited weekly work hours, and capped the amount of night work employers could demand. The strike also dispelled the myth that women wage earners could not be organized and, by promoting unionization of the garment industry, helped shape the course of labor organizing in the twentieth century.

For her role in these events, Clara Lemlich has been allotted a place in the annals of labor history and in the history of women workers.[4] What has been ignored, however, is the emblematic quality of her actions in the strike as a female *Jewish* activist, an identity that she would claim all her life and that was particularly represented in the organization she helped to found in the 1940s: the Emma Lazarus Federation of Jewish Women's Clubs (ELF). For forty-five years the ELF stood at the forefront of Jewish women's cultural and political activism, staking out progressive stands on a variety of issues, including the fight against anti-Semitism and racial discrimination, and the promotion of women's rights. In their unflinching efforts to reconcile the female, radical, and Jewish components of their identity, Clara Lemlich Shavelson and the Emma Lazarus Federation illustrate the multiple, layered, and shifting amalgam of gender and ethnicity revealed on that momentous occasion in 1909 when Lemlich rose at Cooper Union. Lemlich had stood as a woman, a "girl" striker, speaking from the experience, and abuse, of women's work; as a radical labor movement activist, eager to create working-class unity and push the movement forward; and as a Jew, addressing in Yiddish an assembly of Jews who took a Jewish oath to affirm commitment to the radical cause of women. The search to join these three elements would occupy her and many colleagues throughout their lives; together they would create a new kind of American cultural Jewishness, embodied in the Emma Lazarus Federation, which fostered Jewish, feminist, and radical causes.

Although historians have recognized the importance of ethnic ties to the formation of Jewish women's working-class consciousness in the years prior to 1920, they have ignored the continuing cultural and political activities of these women, especially the primary importance to these activities of Jewish content.[5] The paradigm of assimilation has reigned supreme, with scholarly attention focused on the colorful immigrant period and the seeming denial of ethnic consciousness as Jews moved into the mainstream.[6] But the meaning of Clara Shavelson's life, and that of many of her allies, is that she managed to create a bridge that enabled her and others both to maintain their Jewish identity and to use it in a way that built (and built upon) their social and political commitments. In a world in which to be both radical and Jewish meant to be attacked in different ways and to be divided by ideological fissures (that between religion and communism, for example, or between nationalism and working-class unity), this was no small accomplishment. Even more unusual is the fact that it was built upon a foundation of knowledge in women's history during a period when the subject held little interest even for formally trained academicians. Creating new heroines out of women's experience and promulgating these figures to primarily working-class audiences, the

ELF developed an agenda for collective action that linked women's rights and human rights to historical models. In this cultural work the "Emmas" fashioned a Jewish womanhood sensitive not only to issues of class but also to anti-Semitism and racism. Their post-Holocaust political identity sprang, then, both from a newly invigorated gender consciousness and an increasingly salient sense of themselves as Jewish Americans who were proud possessors of a unique cultural heritage.

Examining the federation's multiple interests—including women's history, Jewish culture, civil rights, peace, Israel, the women's movement, and working-class, consumer, and immigrant issues—this essay will suggest that the federation illuminates a model of what I call "linked" identity, combining elements of gender, culture, politics, race, and ethnicity in a flexible, yet unusually engaged, fashion. The federation's simultaneous commitment to creating consciousness and to activism—another example of its "betweenness"—will also be explored.

FROM TRADE UNIONISM TO JEWISH CULTURE: CLARA LEMLICH
SHAVELSON AND THE EMERGENCE OF THE EMMA LAZARUS
FEDERATION OF JEWISH WOMEN'S CLUBS

Clara Lemlich Shavelson was born in 1886 in the town of Gorodok in the Ukraine, the daughter of an orthodox Jewish scholar and grocery storekeeper. The Lemlichs left their home in 1903, fleeing the Kishinev pogrom. After a few months in England, the family arrived in the United States: two weeks later, Clara found a job in the garment shops. In 1906 she became one of the founding members of Waistmakers Local 25, affiliated with the fledgling International Ladies' Garment Workers Union (ILGWU), then largely an organization of male cloak makers. Clara took part in a succession of bitter strikes: in 1907 at Welsen and Goldstein, in 1908 at the Gotham plant, and in 1909 at the Leiserson shop, where she was beaten up while walking the picket line. She was a seasoned strike veteran when the waist makers gathered at Cooper Union in November 1909.

After the waist makers' strike, Clara served as a delegate to union conventions, a member of the executive boards of Local 25 and of the Women's Trade Union League, an outspoken socialist, and a tireless organizer of women workers. As a working-class proponent of woman suffrage, she spoke frequently on the importance of the vote and its relationship to the labor movement.

In 1913 Lemlich married Joseph Shavelson, a printer and union activist. The couple had three children, a son and two daughters. Struggling to make ends meet on Joseph's $17-a-week salary, they shared a home with his sister and her family on DeKalb Avenue in Brownsville, Brooklyn, then a Jewish immigrant community with an activist tradition; Clara Shavelson returned to work in a tie shop on the ground floor of her own sister's building when her oldest child was two. She also resumed her organizing activities, becoming a familiar figure on neighborhood street corners. Shavelson's goal was to mobilize housewives around consumer and housing issues that affected the quality of working-class life. In 1917 she participated in a series of citywide riots and a boycott against the high price of Kosher meat. In 1919 she helped organize tenants in a rent strike against high housing costs; that same year, she became a charter member of the U.S. Communist Party. In 1926 she helped found the United Council of Working-Class Women, a consumer-based group organized to supplement the party's industrial organizing.

In the early 1930s the Shavelsons moved to the working-class community of Brighton Beach, where Clara established the area's first Unemployment Council and organized hunger marches, rent and food strikes, and kitchens for the jobless. She also participated in a neighborhood tenant council named after the Jewish essayist and poet, Emma Lazarus. In 1935 the United Council of Working-Class Women became the Progressive Women's Council. Though the council never intended to become exclusively Jewish, most members were Jewish immigrants; like Shavelson, many had been involved in the garment union before marriage. During the Great Depression, the council organized housewives to bring down food and housing costs; a 1935 meat boycott organized by Shavelson and Rose Nelson (Raynes) brought Shavelson to Washington to confront Secretary of Agriculture Henry Wallace and spread to dozens of cities.[7]

In the early 1930s Shavelson ran unsuccessfully for the State Assembly as a member of the Communist Party; she was the only female candidate. It was one of the rare times, her daughter recalled, that her mother purchased a new dress.[8] In 1944, with her husband's health in decline, Shavelson returned to the garment industry as a hand finisher in a cloak shop on Thirty-eighth Street in New York, joining Local 9. She remained there for almost a decade.

Shavelson was an activist in the fight against fascism as well. In 1934 she attended the first International Women's Congress against War and Fascism in Paris, traveling afterward to the Soviet Union. After her return, she lectured on the Soviet Union to the Progressive Women's Council, which she served as educational director, giving courses on fascism, war, and peace. She became a familiar figure on Brighton Beach street corners, rallying workers against Hitlerism.

At the time of World War II, the Progressive Women's Council, of which Shavelson was then president, merged with the women's clubs of the Jewish

People's Fraternal Order (JPFO) of the International Workers Order (IWO), a fraternal benefit insurance company formed after a split in the Workmen's Circle (the Arbeiter Ring) between the centrist "*Forward* socialists" and the left-wing, "progressive" radicals friendly to the Soviet Union; nearly 8,000 of the latter left the Workmen's Circle in 1930 to form the IWO as a "proletarian" fraternal organization.[9] After 1936, aided by the encouragement of the Communist Party, now in its popular front phase, the IWO launched a massive recruitment effort among immigrant workers. The party's support of ethnic awareness and pride, coupled with its active campaign against domestic anti-Semitism, made it attractive to Jews; by 1939 they constituted between 40 to 50 percent of party membership.[10]

Although not a political or labor organization, the IWO assisted the CIO's organizing drives and campaigned for unemployment insurance and for aid to Spain. With its health and insurance benefits and its sponsorship of ethnic language schools, summer camps, theater, dance, and other cultural programs, it became the fastest growing fraternal order in the country. By the end of World War II, the IWO counted almost 200,000 members in thirteen nationality societies, white and black; the JPFO, with 50,000 members, was the largest. In addition to its wide variety of benefit programs, many members were attracted by the IWO's multinational, multiracial character and its cutting-edge positions in racial relations and antidiscrimination matters. Even though the majority of rank-and-file members did not belong to the Communist Party (in contrast to major IWO leaders, who did), IWO politics generally mirrored those of the Communist Party.[11]

Clara Shavelson became New York City secretary of the IWO's Women's Division; during the war she organized its knitting circles, first aid clubs, aluminum-collecting campaigns, and bond rallies. In March 1944 the IWO-JPFO gave birth to an Emma Lazarus Division: that year, the IWO published *Emma Lazarus: Selections from Her Poetry and Prose*, edited by Morris U. Schappes, the first collection of Lazarus's work in fifty years.[12] Schappes highlighted Lazarus's dual consciousness as a Jew and an American, a focus that the division adopted. Although earlier women's organizations, including the Brooklyn tenants' group established by Clara Shavelson, had been named after Lazarus, they did not focus on Lazarus's intellectual contributions as an American Jew, as the new division set out to do. Advertising itself as the "home of progressive Jewish women," the division attracted a membership of left-wing, largely Yiddish-speaking women, many of the immigrant generation.[13] Over the next five decades, though she was also an antiwar activist, campaigning against the proliferation of nuclear weapons and for improved international relations, Clara Lemlich Shavelson devoted much of her energy to the "Emmas."

In its broad strokes, Shavelson's biography does not differ greatly from those of other women who were instrumental in organizing and leading the Emma Lazarus Division and the ELF. June Croll Gordon, a founder and longtime executive director of the group, was born in Odessa in 1901; after immigrating to the United States at the age of three, she began working in New York City's needle trades. Gordon became a prominent trade unionist, leading strikes in the textile and millinery unions. By 1935 she was secretary of the Anti-Nazi Federation, helping to arouse public opinion against the Nazis' territorial ambitions. Rose Raynes, who became the ELF's executive director after Gordon's death, came to the United States from Russia when she was ten. Soon employed in garment and millinery shops, Raynes became active in the textile and millinery unions. Like Lemlich, Raynes and Gordon were Communist Party members and officers of the United Council of Working-Class Women and the Progressive Women's Council. All three became targets of McCarthyism. An unsuccessful attempt was made to deport Gordon; Shavelson had her passport revoked. All were called before the House Un-American Activities Committee and harassed by the Federal Bureau of Investigation (FBI).[14]

The Emma Lazarus Division of the JPFO was established by these three women and others with similar backgrounds to combat anti-Semitism and racism, provide relief to wartime victims, and nurture positive Jewish identification through a broad program of Jewish education and women's rights. Founders believed that because of the Holocaust, thousands of women had become "newly aware of themselves as Jewish women," but they urgently needed "history, self-knowledge as Jews, and cultural products" that could sustain the fight against fascism. "Since the attack by Hitler against the Jewish people," Rose Raynes recalled, "we felt that [anti-Semitism] was not only an issue for Europe but for the U.S. as well. We felt that a progressive Jewish woman's organization was the order of the day."[15] Beginning in 1945, the division offered fellowships for works of fiction and history on Jewish themes; it was the first of its many efforts to heighten Jewish identity as a weapon against bigotry. It also supported a home for French war orphans and a day nursery in Israel and championed a broad range of women's issues: full employment for men and women; equal pay for equal work; maternity, unemployment, old age, health, and housing benefits; day nurseries and after-school care; and the inclusion of greater numbers of women in government.

FROM DIVISION TO FEDERATION:
PROMOTING JEWISH WOMEN'S HISTORY

In 1951 the division became the Emma Lazarus Federation of Jewish Women's Clubs, an independent organization. Although links to the progressive Left remained, the shift from division to federation marked an important transformation in the group's focus. The change in status was influenced by attacks against the Communist Party and the IWO. In 1951 the New York State attorney general initiated proceedings against the IWO as a subversive institution formed and directed under Communist Party auspices. Although the IWO denied that it used members' funds to support the Communist Party, New York State, aided by J. Edgar Hoover and the FBI, successfully prosecuted the order and forced it to liquidate in 1954. A much-reduced JPFO, without the financial advantages of a fraternal benefit society, reorganized as the Jewish Cultural Clubs and Societies, retaining several thousand members interested in cultural programs in Yiddish and English.[16] While Communist Party leaders played a part in reorganizing IWO constituencies, the Emma Lazarus Division had been moving toward a more independent, woman-centered stance in the 1940s in any case; cold war necessities further advanced its autonomy.

During the politically charged fifties, the ELF did not relinquish its radical commitments, although some leaders broke with the Communist Party. As an organization, the ELF vigorously protested against McCarthyism. The trial of Julius and Ethel Rosenberg, which frequently focused on their left-wing Jewish associations, especially alarmed federation leaders, who believed in the Rosenbergs' innocence.[17] Although she never met Ethel Rosenberg, Clara Lemlich Shavelson spent two years working on her defense committee, recognizing in the accused woman's labor activism and ethnic associations a replica of her own background. As individuals and in some cases, as chapters, many ELF members rallied to the Rosenbergs' (especially Ethel's) support. After their deaths, the Rosenberg sons were adopted by Ann Meeropol, who was herself a member of the ELF, and her husband.[18]

Throughout the 1950s the federation emphasized the progressive voice of labor as the hallmark of democracy and called for coexistence with the Soviet Union. While Nikita Khrushchev's startling 1956 revelations about Stalinist terrors, and later information about the country's virulent anti-Semitism, left ELF members "shocked" and "grieved," publicly its leaders continued to hope that the USSR would return to its earlier encouragement of ethnic minorities. On at least one occasion, a branch delegate protested that the executive board did not condemn anti-Semitism within the Soviet Union as vigorously as it opposed domestic bigotry; the group remained split for many years between those who wanted to break all ties with the USSR and those who continued to support communism.[19]

Yet the division's unity around cultural work outweighed political differences. By the time the group called its first constitutional convention in 1951 to inaugurate the federation, the Emmas had decided that in the wake of Nazism's terrors, nothing was more important than integrating Jewish heritage into contemporary life. The terrors of McCarthyism, which stigmatized many Jewish radicals as "un-American" Communists, also contributed to the Emmas' desire to claim their own Jewish identity by promoting a progressive, secular Jewish heritage. "Our purpose was to add to the fabric of American culture and democracy by advancing all that is most humane and forward looking in Jewish culture," remarked ELF president Leah Nelson at its third convention in 1959.[20] If Jews were to survive as a people and contribute to world problems in morally responsible ways, they could not be isolated from the social mainstream.

The federation's emphasis on creating a "culturally enlightened American Jewry" coincided with the increasing acceptance of cultural pluralism in postwar life. Even as Jews moved ever more forcefully into the American mainstream, many seemed eager not to obliterate but to identify with their heritage. A so-called Jewish revival, indicated by the construction of synagogues and Jewish social centers, the enrollment of a new generation of youth in Jewish educational programs, and the proclamations of Jewish book, music, and history "months" revealed the desire of many Jews to connect to Jewish roots as well as the increasing acceptability of such expressions of "Americanized" ethnicity.[21]

Yet the ELF believed that this Jewish revival lacked depth and vision. Arguing that knowledge of Jewish tradition should extend beyond holidays and artifacts to an understanding of vital Jewish contributions to American history and democracy, the federation sought to promulgate the neglected history of American Jewish women—their contributions to American arts and letters, to abolition and the trade union movements, and to immigration policy—in order to create a framework for positive identification with Jewish culture and for understanding and acting on present problems. This did not mean assimilation, the Emmas believed, but its opposite: a reaffirmation of the long history of Jewish participation in American democracy *as Jews* and a recommitment to Jews' moral values and humanistic culture. Both the focus on women and the linkage of women's history to activism distinguished this goal from that of the Jewish Cultural Clubs and Societies, the reorganized JPFO group, whose emphasis lay in encouraging Yiddish culture while also supporting progressive Jewish culture in English (for example, aid to *Jewish Currents* magazine).[22]

In promulgating a secular progressive Judaism without relying on the special qualities of *yiddishkeit,* the Emmas resolved a paradox that had long troubled the immigrant Jewish Left. Jewish fraternal organizations had offered cultural programs, sports leagues, and medical services to members in an attempt to serve the interests of an increasingly assimilated Jewish immigrant population and their descendants; Yiddish newspapers began inserting English pages for similar reasons. But the Emmas were unusual in emphasizing a Jewish intellectual tradition that was both militantly secular and progressively American as the best appeal to the post–Yiddish-speaking generation.

In the early 1950s the ELF commissioned biographies of two Jewish women whose achievements they believed symbolized different, though compatible, directions in progressive American Jewish history. The first subject, writer Emma Lazarus (1849–87), the group's major inspiration, had concentrated on Jewish themes within a broad universalistic setting. The other, Ernestine Rose (1810–92), social reformer, abolitionist, and suffragist, had focused her energies on many important problems of the day, not especially Jewish ones. Although they had been radicals in their own time, both women's protests were clearly within the American democratic tradition; thus the Emmas selected models who helped ensure their own legitimacy as political and cultural dissenters.

Lazarus was, of course, the writer whose poem, "The New Colossus," engraved on a plaque on the Statue of Liberty in May 1903, has helped welcome generations of immigrants to the United States. In the 1950s, however (and, it can be argued, even today), neither Lazarus's Jewish or woman's consciousness had been widely recognized. The standard belief was that Lazarus had become concerned with her Jewishness belatedly, only after the Russian pogroms of the 1880s; her contributions to the cause of women were even less commonly understood.

ELF members believed that Lazarus was an inspiration both for Jewish culture and women's rights. Though not associated with the women's rights movement, Lazarus had helped remove the "veils and screens" of women's life, with which the "woman-souled poet," as she called herself, had to grope. In the biography of Lazarus that the federation commissioned Eve Merriam to write (to celebrate the anniversary of the Jews' tercentennial in America in 1954), the author comments that "the figure representing work is a woman to Emma Lazarus, not the conventional symbol of a man."[23]

The federation also portrayed Lazarus as a woman who had spoken out forcefully and consistently against anti-Semitism and assimilation, and as a Jew who was concerned not only with what she called a narrow, "tribal" Judaism but also with oppressed peoples the world over. "Until we are all free, we are none of us free," was the Lazarus line most often quoted by the ELF to demonstrate the poet's concern for all humanity.[24]

Lazarus had originally used the line to refer to solidarity with the Jewish people. "When the life and property of a Jew in the uttermost provinces of the Caucasus are attacked," she wrote, "the dignity of a Jew in free America is humiliated. . . . Until we are all free, we are none of us free." Her universalism appeared in a line that stated that Jews should not "become too 'tribal' and narrow and Judaic rather than humane and cosmopolitan." Instead they must concern themselves with the misfortunes of "our unhappy brethren."[25] To the ELF, this "universal scope" coupled with Lazarus's support for Jewish culture and women's freedom made her an admirable symbol of secular, humanistic values.

Ironically, the federation ignored one element in Lazarus's background that, as a left-wing organization, it might have been expected to highlight: her Jewish-based socialism. Lazarus argued, for example, that the root of the "modern theory of socialism" lay in the "Mosaic Code," which established the "principle of the rights of labor" and denied the "right of private property in land . . . we find the fathers of modern socialism to be three Jews—Ferdinand Lassalle, Karl Marx, and Johann Jacoby."[26] The federation also ignored another major Lazarus theme—her support for a Jewish homeland in Palestine. While the ELF endorsed both formulations, it found Lazarus's leadership in the campaign to promote Jewish culture, aid new immigrants, and fight anti-Semitism both more compelling and more characteristic.

For almost fifty years federation members never tired of presenting Lazarus's ideas to whichever group would listen. Every year the Emmas celebrated her birthday with a trip to Liberty Island; they succeeded in having the mayors of New York and Miami declare an Emma Lazarus Day, and later they arranged a commemorative stamp. The true meaning of Lazarus for the federation, however, lay less in these occasions than in the model of action, authority, and leadership that she claimed as a woman, a Jew, and an American. Basing their program on her work, the Emmas hoped to give "leadership to women in Jewish communities in our own time in the same spirit as Emma Lazarus did in hers."[27]

In 1954 the ELF published a biography of Ernestine Rose that it had commissioned Yuri Suhl to write. To the Emmas, Rose represented a model of activism even more than Lazarus, who spoke with her pen. They cited the fact that Susan B. Anthony had named Rose, along with Mary Wollstonecraft and Frances Wright, as the most important leader of the women's movement, praising her activism on behalf of women's property rights and suffrage.

Unlike Lazarus's, Rose's work did not have a Jewish orientation, yet the federation claimed her as the first Jewish woman reformer in the United States. Born in the ghetto of Piotrkow, in Russian Poland, Rose, the daughter of a rabbi, refused to accept the traditional destiny of young Jewish women. While still a teenager, she took her father to court, protesting his determination to marry her against her will and suing to obtain possession of the dowry her mother had left her. Rose won the lawsuit but returned most of the property to her father. Then, at age seventeen, she left the country, eventually settling in the United States.

Although Rose abandoned the formal practice of religion, she took a "fighting stand" against anti-Semitism, publicly disavowing its presence in her own circle of freethinkers. According to the Emmas, her work on behalf of abolition and women's rights and against anti-Semitism demonstrated the "interrelationships between Jew and non-Jew, Negro and white, men and women." Like Lazarus, she was seen to combine Jewish patriotism with a broader humanism. "Emancipation from every kind of bondage is my principle," they recalled her words. "I go for the recognition of human rights, without distinction of sect, party, sex or color." As she wrote to President Abraham Lincoln during the Civil War, "So long as one slave breathes in this Republic, we drag the chain with him."[28]

The Emmas considered Rose a model for her work in the peace movement; an activist for the Universal Peace Society, founded in Rhode Island, she was a delegate to several international peace congresses. To Rose, women had a special stake in peace crusades: "War is a terrible enemy of man," she observed, "a terrible school. . . . I trust that if every woman touched the sword it would be to sheath it in its scabbard forever."[29] The ELF often quoted these words to legitimate its own work for peace.

Though none received the attention given to Lazarus and Rose, the federation remembered other American Jewish women in its cultural work, spreading biographical reminiscences of Rebecca Gratz, Lillian Wald, Sophie Loeb, Penina Moise, and others. In the early 1950s it commissioned a history of Jewish women in the United States to be published in Yiddish and English but canceled the volume when the draft failed to meet its standards. The ELF debated publishing such a work into the late 1970s.

The federation documented the experience of Jewish women outside the United States as well. In commemorating the anniversary of the uprising of the Warsaw Ghetto, it paid tribute to those who had taken part in the resistance and who had fought for freedom in partisan groups, women like Niuta Teitelboim, Dora Goldkorn, Zofia Yamalka, Rosa Robota, Mala Zimmetbaum, Regina Fuden, Zivia Lubetkin, Hana Senish, Vitka Kempner, and Frumke and Hentche Platnitksy. To federation members, the courageous stand of the "Mothers" of the Warsaw Ghetto merged with the traditions of women trailblazers in the United States—"Ernestine Rose, Sojourner Truth, Susan B. Anthony, Emma Lazarus, and the women from the shops and mills like Esther Greenleaf, a shoe worker, and the later immigrants like those of the Triangle

Shirt and Waist shop who fought against sweatshop conditions."[30] Moreover, the ELF cited women's heroism in the fight for Israeli independence.

The federation also issued study outlines on themes in general Jewish and Yiddish history and culture, writing on such subjects as bigotry in school textbooks, the Jewish contribution to American law and letters, and Yiddish prose and poetry. In praising the work of Sholom Aleichem and I. L. Peretz, the Emmas singled out these writers' forward-looking, empathic treatment of women in the shtetls of Eastern Europe.

TOWARD AN INCLUSIVE WOMEN'S HISTORY: DISSIDENTS, WORKING WOMEN, WHITE WOMEN REFORMERS, AND BLACK WOMEN

Interested in the broader history of American women, the federation developed curricula on such subjects as the contributions of dissident women from Anne Hutchinson to Ethel Rosenberg and the role of America's working women in the Lowell mills and garment sweatshops. In 1954 it commissioned artist Philip Reisman to do a mural of the 1909 mass meeting at Cooper Union, depicting Clara Lemlich at the center; the five-foot-by-seven-foot painting was donated to the International Ladies' Garment Workers Union in 1982.

The link between the women's rights and abolitionist movements was of vital interest. In the 1950s and 1960s the ELF prepared study guides on Sojourner Truth, Ida B. Wells, and Harriet Tubman and paid tribute to the leadership of Sarah Douglass, Mary Bibb, Grace Mapps, and Francis Ellen Harper. The federation also called attention to the contemporary achievements of Rosa Parks, Autherine Lucy, and other black women involved in the civil rights struggle.

Its most important contribution in this area was the pamphlet, "Women in the Life and Time of Abraham Lincoln," a reprint of the proceedings of a conference held by the National Women's Loyal League. Formed at a mass rally called by women's rights leaders (including Ernestine Rose) on May 14, 1863, at Cooper Union in New York City, the league assembled over one thousand northern white women abolitionists who pledged to rally women in their states to obtain one million signatures on a petition to endorse the Thirteenth Amendment. Though the league disbanded after the legislation passed, the Emmas believed that it had activated white women and advanced the women's rights movement. They hoped that its work for abolition would challenge contemporary white women (particularly Jewish women) to work for civil rights.

The ELF pamphlet about the Loyal League contained an introduction by

Daisy Bates, leader of the desegregation struggle at Little Rock High School. Bates was also the principal speaker at a celebration held at Cooper Union by the federation's New York club in December 1963 to commemorate the one-hundredth anniversary of the national league's founding. Thirteen hundred people joined the Emmas on that occasion to celebrate the unity of white and black women in the common struggle for civil rights.

"THINKING . . . EXPRESSED IN ACTION": THE FEDERATION'S CAMPAIGNS FOR HUMAN RIGHTS

For federation members, there was nothing pedantic or merely academic in its cultural work. The ELF believed that women's and Jewish history could inspire contemporary thought and policy by providing models of commitment and activism. "Thinking is expressed in action; culture is . . . promoted by projects," remarked Leah Nelson at the ELF's 1959 convention. Executive Director June Gordon used to say that the federation served the Jewish community as a true "university for women"; later she preferred to point to the ELF's work as a "Veker" and a "Wegweiser"—a pathfinder and awakener—involving members of other Jewish women's groups, as well as the community at large, in vital actions.[31]

The federation's practical work covered a wide spectrum. Its five-point program, adopted in 1951, established lasting goals. In addition to the promotion of Jewish culture (the "number one project"), these included the elimination of anti-Semitism and racism, the campaign for women's rights, support for the state of Israel, and world peace and consumers' issues.[32]

With the legacy of Emma Lazarus, Ernestine Rose, and the National Women's Loyal League pointing the way, the federation dedicated much of its efforts over four decades to work on behalf of civil rights. The "Negro question is ours," as one club member put it in 1955.[33] The Emmas acknowledged that while anti-Semitism and racism sprang from common roots and that American Jews and minorities shared the same dangerous enemy—the ultra-Right—oppression in the black community was not only significantly greater than that of Jews but also could be fueled by Jews' own racism. Consciousness of the impact of racial difference on women's roles and opportunities led the federation to focus on the needs of black women and racial minorities long before the white women's movement turned to these issues in the 1970s.

Its most important leaders, including Clara Shavelson, June Gordon, and Rose Raynes, had been members of the Communist Party at a time when interest in black culture and the promotion of civil rights was actively encouraged; June Gordon herself had married an African American artist, Eugene Gordon. For these reasons, and because of their guiding belief that discrimination in the form of anti-Semitism and that based on racism were deeply linked, the Emmas took on the challenge of promoting racial justice by engaging Jewish women in a joint campaign with blacks. "America's white women have been in semi-hibernation ever since the abolitionist movement," an Emma wrote in the first edition of the group's bulletin, *The Lamp*, in 1952.[34] Through concrete actions, it was time to wake them.

Shortly after its founding, the federation joined in a common statement of principle with the Sojourners for Truth and Justice, a black women's civil rights group. The Emmas made a regular financial contribution to the Sojourners, and the groups met at an annual luncheon.[35] The Los Angeles Emma Lazarus club established a similar relationship with the Southern Region of the California State Association of Colored Women's Clubs, jointly sponsoring an Interracial Mothers' Day event and other programs; in Miami, Emmas joined with black women in an Interracial Mothers' Association that worked on civil rights projects. In 1953 several Emmas traveled to Georgia as part of a delegation of black and white women to plead with the governor against the imprisonment of a black woman for the murder of a white man who had attacked her. (Two decades later they would defend black professor Angela Davis against what they considered unjust imprisonment.) By 1956 the Emmas were sending truckloads of food and clothing to Mississippi and joining boycotts and sit-ins. By the 1960s they were working with civil rights groups throughout the country, supporting the Freedom Rides and Freedom Summer, participating in civil rights marches in Washington, D.C., and organizing local demonstrations, rallies, and picket lines.

The Emmas fought segregation in housing and schools in their own communities, lobbying legislators, presenting petitions, and holding forums. They observed Negro History Week with readings, lectures, and joint programs with black organizations, often highlighting the contributions of black and Jewish women to the building of the country.[36] At annual Mother's Day celebrations, they typically honored a black woman active in civil rights. Black women's associations in some regions honored the Emma Lazarus clubs at their own meetings and made contributions to the Emma Lazarus nursery in Israel.

The Emmas believed, however, that more was needed than occasional meetings with African American groups and ceremonial events; they called for "constant contact" and intensive, rather than token, support of black rights. To this end they established ongoing affiliations not only with the Sojourners but also with the NAACP, the National Association of Colored Women, and other groups, and they urged immediate and varied measures to end discrimination and increase opportunities in all arenas. But they warned against a "humanitarian" approach—whites "helping" blacks—rather than a "joint struggle." Jewish women's special task, modeled by the National Women's Loyal League, was to engage white women and Jews in the civil rights movement.[37]

The federation urged its own members to support equality for blacks by eliminating white supremacist attitudes they might unwittingly hold. In a 1951 position paper on "Racism, Enemy of the Jewish People," the ELF established two principles: first, that blacks suffered greater oppression in the United States than any other people, including Jews, whatever their experience with anti-Semitism; and second, that the main fight against discrimination was the responsibility of whites. While Jews were especially affected by discrimination, since anti-Semitism and racism derived from common white supremacist roots, the ELF argued that "every Jewish worker who wants to fight for peace and against fascism is hurting that struggle when he doesn't root out . . . every bit of racism in himself."[38]

The Emmas gave examples of how "Jewish nationalism and chauvinism" could feed the idea that Jews were superior to non-Jews—for example, the use of the terms *goyim* and *shikseh*. Such superior attitudes applied with double intensity to blacks: Jews who knew the derogatory meaning of anti-Semitic terms were cautioned against the use of *schvartse* and other stereotypical expressions about blacks. The Emmas voiced special concern for Negro women, who suffered "triple oppression, as women, as women-workers, and as Negroes": discriminated against in industry, they were forced to take menial jobs as houseworkers only to suffer from exploitation by white housewives.

The Emmas considered the campaign to secure passage of the United Nations (U.N.) Genocide Convention their most important political crusade. In 1963 the ELF initiated a petition campaign for the United States to ratify the Genocide Convention, which had been adopted by the U.N. General Assembly in 1948 and subsequently signed by seventy-five nations. ELF presented the first 4,000 signatures on the petitions to U.N. ambassador Adlai Stevenson in December 1963. Two years later, when the twentieth session of the General Assembly signed a new treaty to eliminate all forms of racism, it issued a new petition calling upon the United States to ratify both treaties. In 1966 the federation delivered 7,000 signatures to Ambassador Arthur Goldberg; in 1969 it sent a delegation (including three black women) to present 60,000 signatures to Senator William Fulbright of the Senate Foreign Relations Committee. The Senate finally ratified the Genocide Convention on February 19, 1986.[39]

The Emmas never abandoned their faith in the potential of culture, and especially history itself, as an agent of change in the battle for human rights. In 1964 a member of the Emma Lazarus Boston club told the ELF national convention of an incident that confirmed this belief:

> At a panel discussion on the relationship of the Jew to the Negro in Roxbury, where there is considerable racial strife, the Jew did not fare so well. One Negro speaker bluntly said that he considered the Jews and the landlord and storekeeper as one who exploits him. The Jew on the panel, a representative of one of our big organizations, didn't elevate the level of the discussion. He started out, "No matter what," facing the Negro, "you still should be grateful that you live in America. You are still better off than if you lived in Russia."
>
> In the general discussion that followed Elizabeth Stern [president of the Boston Emma Lazarus club] took the floor and directed the attention of the audience to our Panel on the wall of that room and said in effect: "Let me show you a different relationship between Negro and Jew during our Civil War period," and she pointed to Ernestine Rose, Sojourner Truth and all the other characters depicted on the panel. One by one the audience came up to look at the Panel. It was closely scrutinized, discussed, admired by all. Our organization was commended for bringing to light this historical data and for the fashion in which it was presented, and the whole tone of the meeting was changed."[10]

Nor did the federation abandon its conviction that by working for social equality for blacks, its members were expressing their identity as good Jews and good Americans, as Emma Lazarus herself had proclaimed when she highlighted the harmony between America's multiple nationalities and its civic culture. For the Emmas, the civil rights crusade in which they played an early, vigorous, and continuous role was a perfect example of democratic pluralism at its best. Here, for example, is June Gordon's account of the Emmas demonstrating with thousands of black and white women during the historic March on Washington on August 18, 1963:

> At one point in the line of March, as we approached a spot where Lincoln Rockwell's brown-shirted bullies were on the lookout for an opportunity to jeer and make trouble, two young Episcopalian Ministers sprinted up in front of us and declared: "Ladies, pictures are being taken. We want our Bishop to see us leading the Emma Lazarus Contingent." At the same time a fellow Negro marcher chose to walk with us. He moved up front and said to one of our banner bearers: "You must be tired, let me carry it for a while." And so our contingent was headed by Episcopalians; one end of the banner—*on the side where the Nazi hoodlums were lined up*—was carried by a

Negro marcher. Looking for Leah Nelson [the ELF president] to call her attention to the gloriously symbolic sight of unity we represented, we spotted her marching behind a banner of a *Catholic* organization. This truly was America.[41]

Because the Emmas believed that anti-Semitism and racism were inherently linked, they recognized that in working for civil rights, they were "not doing something for the black people, but . . . doing something for ourselves."[42] When in the late 1960s relations between blacks and Jews grew strained, the ELF affirmed the historic relationship between the two groups and insisted that differences on specific issues, which they felt had been inflamed by extremists on both sides, not be allowed to tamper with the groups' common interests. In contrast to many Jewish organizations, the Emmas supported affirmative action, community control of schools, and decentralization. Yet occasionally, when they found evidences of black anti-Semitism, they spoke out in protest: in 1967, for example, they called upon the Student Nonviolent Coordinating Committee (SNCC) to revise its "shocking and disturbing" position on Jewish organizations.[43]

From its inception, the federation was vigilant about anti-Semitism. It tracked, and opposed, the resurgence of Nazism through letters, telegrams, resolutions, pickets, and mass meetings; targets for its attacks included neo-Nazi movements in Germany, England, France, Italy, Argentina, and dozens of cities in the United States. The federation also protested the ominous spread of anti-Semitism among the general population; too often, it noted, Jews were discriminated against at public resorts, at schools and colleges, and in the workplace. Quoting Emma Lazarus's protest against anti-Semitism that the word *Jew* was used constantly "even among so-called refined Christians" as a term of opprobrium and was increasingly employed as a verb "to denote the meanest tricks," the Emmas called for actions to protest pernicious stereotyping as well as discriminatory quota systems.[44] But they persistently argued that groups most guilty of anti-Semitic bigotry—at various times, the Ku Klux Klan, the American Nazi Party, the Liberty Lobby, or the Moral Majority— also posed the greatest danger to the rights of minorities.[45]

The blind spot in the federation's campaign against anti-Semitism remained the Soviet Union. The absence of a committed campaign against Soviet anti-Semitism was a consequence of the continuing political attachment of a significant number of federation members to the Communist Party; others within the leadership had broken with the party, or had become critical of its actions, because of revelations about Stalinist terror and Soviet anti-Semitism. The last president of the ELF, Rose Raynes, for example, was anti-Stalinist, whereas her second-in-command, Gertrude Decker, remained loyal to the

USSR. This split prevented the executive board from taking a vigorous stand against Soviet brutality and harassment of Jews.[46]

The federation was involved in other issues outlined in its five-point program. From its inception, the ELF supported the cause of peace. At the Emmas' first annual Mothers' Day luncheon in 1951, members read poems of peace commemorating the struggles of women written by Gerda Lerner. Yet ELF leaders made clear to members that the role of the federation, as a cultural group, was to support existing peace organizations rather than create its own initiatives. ELF clubs cooperated with the Committee for a Sane Nuclear Policy (SANE), the Women's International League for Peace and Freedom (WILPF), and the Committee for World Development and World Disarmament. Within these groups the Emmas endeavored to help make policy as well as support petition drives and fund collections. As in the civil rights arena, they sought to become liaisons to Jewish women's organizations so as to bring these groups into the peace movement.[47]

While ELF shared a common agenda with SANE and other peace organizations, it criticized the minimal involvement of workers and their families in these groups. Here, too, the Emmas claimed a special role: "With our participating in the communities, we reach women from wage-earning families. Through work in the shops and raising this greatly important question in the union, where many of our sisters and their husbands belong, we can help strengthen and expand the peace organizations."[48] From their early interest in the elimination of nuclear weapons to their activities to end the Vietnam War, the Emmas remained involved in questions of war and peace, militarism, and foreign policy.[49]

As a Jewish women's organization, the federation was greatly concerned with the fate of Israel. The ELF was the first Jewish group to establish a day-care center in the new state (for the Jewish and Arab children of working mothers). The Emma Lazarus Nursery in Jaffa, later moved to Tel Aviv, was administered by the women's division of the Agudath Tarbuth L'Am (the Association for Peoples Culture), which worked mainly with families of immigrants and workers. The federation was the sole support of the nursery, which it considered its "pet project," until 1988, when the facility was forced to close because of the lack of funds. Many members journeyed to Israel specifically to visit the nursery; others knit sweaters for its children. The ELF also raised considerable sums of money for Israel at the time of the 1967 and Yom Kippur wars, and it regularly supported the Red Mogon Dovid.

In addition to holding forums and publishing study guides on Israel, the ELF attempted to focus the attention of peace groups on the need for a constructive stand on U.S. foreign policy in regard to Israel and peace in the

Middle East. The federation distinguished its identification with Israel, however, from that of many other Jewish organizations. Its own positions were based on "kinship with the Israeli people and not on Israel as the core of Jewish life," as it understood was the case with other groups; the most vital service the ELF thought it could render to Israel was to heighten cultural identification among American Jews.

Concern for Israel, in any event, reflected the Emmas' class analysis of the Middle Eastern politics of oil, which it believed threatened the security of Israel and its Arab neighbors. The Emmas questioned whether the success of Arab national liberation movements might not benefit Israel in the long run and worried about the second-class treatment of Arabs within Israel. After the Six-Day War, the federation questioned whether Israel needed all the territory it had won but demanded that Arab neighbors accept Israel's right to exist without qualification.[50]

In November 1975 the federation adopted a resolution condemning the U.N. resolution equating "Zionism with racism" as "vicious anti-Semitism . . . directed against all Jews." But controversy erupted when ELF vice president Gertrude Decker declared in a public speech that she was "for the existence of Israel as a progressive State, not a Zionist state in the service of imperialism" and could not support the Israeli government's "discriminatory and *racist* policies." Board members condemned her remarks, and members of one local chapter circulated a petition opposing them.[51]

Promoting the rights and culture of immigrants and supporting consumer interests were also of deep concern. In the 1950s the federation engaged in a vigorous campaign for a statute of limitation against the deportation of foreign-born Americans; it was the only Jewish group to become a founder of the Museum of Immigration on Liberty Island. The ELF spoke out consistently against the high cost of living and for senior citizens' rights and entitlements; many local groups gave substantial support to the farm workers' union.

Women's issues, finally, were always central to federation interests. The ELF worked continuously to bring women's history to a wide public so that the lessons of the past might help shape the present. In 1956 it inaugurated a year of celebration for the thirty-fifth anniversary of woman suffrage, focusing on women's history. (Twenty years later, Congresswoman Bella Abzug addressed another large ELF-sponsored meeting honoring the achievement of suffrage.) After the advent of the new feminist movement in the 1960s, ELF members worked with women's rights organizations on myriad issues (including the Equal Rights Amendment); its International Women's Day celebration was an annual highlight.

The federation identified a host of economic and social problems that affected the lives of women, particularly working women. Far in advance of the times, its 1955 discussion guide, for example, focused on the lack of equal pay for equal work, "double" wage discrimination faced by black women, occupational segregation, unequal job security and promotional opportunities, lack of representation in trade union and management, and problems of working mothers (day nurseries and after-school care). Issues of educational access and the representation of women in politics, government, and the professions were also highlighted. Here, too, the ELF believed that it could play an important role by representing the needs of working women and implementing programs developed by union members. In addition, the federation hoped to bring a greater consciousness of black women's work, educational, and political situations to women's groups and other organizations to which it was affiliated. It supported these varied goals not only by raising its own members' consciousness through the production of study guides, dramatic presentations, lectures, exhibits, and other cultural programs but also through a continuing series of demonstrations, marches, picket lines, petition campaigns, celebrations and convocations, and other actions.

"JEWISH CULTURE DOES NOT LIMIT ONE": THE ELF AND PROBLEMS OF OUTREACH

Spanning the country, with chapters in New York (Brooklyn, the Bronx, Rochester), New Jersey (Newark, Jersey City, Lakewood, Toms River), California (Los Angeles, San Francisco), and Boston, Chicago, Philadelphia, Detroit, and Miami, the Emma Lazarus Federation maintained its educational and political activities for close to forty years. Yet almost from the outset, questions of expanding its outreach had been raised. At their peak, some of the largest chapters in New York, Chicago, and Los Angeles had more than a dozen branches, with several hundred members each; other groups were much smaller. Though the organization kept no membership records, the best estimate is that the federation attracted approximately 4,000 to 5,000 members in one hundred clubs during the 1950s; membership remained fairly stable in the 1960s but fell in later years.

Though no match for Hadassah, with its hundreds of thousands of middle-class members, the ELF boasted an unusually active, committed membership. Like Clara Lemlich Shavelson, June Croll Gordon, and Rose Raynes, most of the original federation members were working-class women who had been associated with the IWO or other progressive labor-oriented groups. Many had worked in industry and had participated in the trade union movement; others had been radicalized as housewives and consumers. Most longtime members were Yiddish speaking; even when the balance began to shift with increasing numbers of members speaking only English, leaders advocated the bilingual approach: "The sisters [should] use the language which lends itself with greater ease to [their] verbal or written expression. Never, under any circumstances, should one be preferred over the other."[52] *The Lamp*, the monthly newsletter of the federation, appeared in both languages; meetings were usually conducted in English.

Leaders wondered, however, whether the ELF's relatively narrow membership base was sufficient to support the broad scope of its five-point program. Over the years they urged chapters to reach out to a wider circle of Jewish women. "We must be among women and unite on issues of concern to all women," the Newark club president declared.[53] From the beginning, the federation program appealed to a broader constituency than was reflected in its membership: regular presentations to Hadassah, B'nai Brith, synagogue sisterhoods, and similar groups enlarged the ELF's audiences by many thousands. Brooklyn and Los Angeles chapters were proud of their relationships with Jewish women's assemblies; several clubs enrolled non-Jewish, nonwhite members as well.

Although some ELF members did not want to lose their identity by doing "leg work for other organizations" or adjust their message to suit organizational partners, they realized that because new members were needed to keep the federation growing, so were new methods. "Know parliamentary procedures," advised the Philadelphia delegate to the 1955 ELF convention: "Learn to compromise our old methods without compromising our principles. Find new language—i.e., forward-looking people instead of the word 'progressive.' Use language that is acceptable to others . . . so they will come to listen to us. . . . Emphasize the issues that unite and bring with warmth and friendship our message to others."[54]

While some in the Jewish community dismissed the Emmas as "embittered women" with "heavy Yiddish accents," a number of prominent leaders were pleased to be publicly associated with them.[55] In 1947, when the Emma Lazarus Division was an IWO affiliate, Louise Waterman Wise, wife of eminent reform rabbi Stephen Wise and herself president of the Women's Division of the American Jewish Congress, took the podium to introduce a public session ("An Evening of Jewish Culture") at the division's First Constitutional Convention, held at Hunter College.[56] Illinois state legislator Esther Saperstein, impressed with the ELF-sponsored biography of Ernestine Rose by Yuri Suhl, joined the Chicago chapter in the 1950s and memorialized Rose's name in the legislature. New York congresswomen Bella Abzug and Elizabeth Holtzman also honored Rose and Lazarus and participated in federation events.[57]

The question of whether the ideas of the federation were too progressive to attract the support of more mainstream Jewish women—or whether subtle changes in language and procedure might win new members—frequently surfaced. At the 1964 ELF convention, June Gordon denied that the Emmas could not comfortably speak to a broad audience. "Many, all too many members think we are so far in advance of all other Jewish women in our progressive outlook that it is useless to approach them as prospective members and cultivate their interest in joining the club. This attitude is a disservice."[58] Though some members felt that other women's groups were too "reactionary," Gordon insisted that the federation offered a place for women of varied opinions.

Although new members joined Emma Lazarus clubs primarily for their educational programs, opportunities for sociability and friendship were important. "Even more precious than learning," recalled one Chicago member, was "a warm sisterly relation in the club, sisters we can share our joys and sorrows with—in short you feel a part of a great big noisy family." But most important was the connection to Jewish heritage this member (and many others) made as an Emma. She recalled her initiation to the Emmas at her first club meeting, where she had listened to a program about Chanukah and Emma Lazarus:

I suddenly became aware that I was part of the struggles and triumphs of the Jewish people. How was it that I could not see it before? Perhaps because I wanted to forget I was a Jew, and thereby avoid facing the grim facts of my people not being accepted as equals even in our country. . . . I have always been interested in culture generally, and I thought at the time that pursuing Jewish culture only, is too narrow and limited. . . . My interest was aroused, and I joined the club at the following meeting. Since then, having participated in cultural as well as other projects, it became clear to me that Jewish culture does not limit one, but on the contrary, broadens one's horizon. I became conscious of a feeling of pride in my origin, particularly after reading the works of Emma Lazarus.[59]

Attracting young women who had been uprooted from their Jewish heritage was a continuing source of pride for the ELF.

While certain sections were able to attract new members, including young mothers, the graying of the membership became a major problem. Even though attendance at meetings was high, the ability of aging members to take on demanding campaigns diminished. Still, many ELF women remained vigorous well into their seventies and eighties. Here, too, Clara Shavelson led the way: as she aged along with the federation, Shavelson regularly attended its meetings and participated in its activities. In her seventies, she collected 1,500 signatures for the federation's Genocide Convention; the ELF gratefully acknowledged her contributions. Shavelson admitted that although she had been proud of the youthful Clara Lemlich, she thought that Clara Shavelson, a lifetime activist, had accomplished much more. When asked by a student interviewer to talk about the famous 1909 strike, she responded, at age eighty, that "I[n] so far as I am concerned, I am still at it."[60]

After 1968 Shavelson resided at the Hebrew Home for the Aged in Los Angeles, where she participated in political discussions and forums. She died in 1982 at the age of ninety-six. Like Shavelson, many federation members moved to suburban neighborhoods or retirement communities, at a distance from former comrades and Emma clubs. The federation tried to meet the problem by encouraging the formation of chapters in new communities; although Los Angeles was successful in starting suburban clubs, other regions could not adapt as readily to changing residence patterns.

The transformation of women's work, and the women's movement itself, also affected the federation's longevity. By midcentury, most Jewish working women did not share a trade union background with the original Emmas, though they might encounter gender discrimination at work and home. While many Jewish women were drawn to the women's movement, it was not as Jewishly identified women that they joined new feminist ranks. Sexism, although a major ELF concern, was not an exclusive one; women liberationists no doubt found it difficult to identify with the pantheon of federation causes. And while there was an incipient Jewish women's movement in the 1970s, it did not share the Emmas' secularism but rather focused on issues of religious patriarchy.

Despite their lack of progeny, federation members were not discouraged. Indeed, they were delighted that ideas they had promoted for a quarter of a century were attracting the attention of young feminists. "We did our small part," Rose Raynes commented; now it was time for others to take the lead.[61]

By the end of the 1980s ELF leaders like Clara Shavelson and June Gordon had passed on, and elderly members could not be replaced. Though some individual clubs in Chicago, Los Angeles, and the Bronx remained, the Emma Lazarus Federation of Jewish Women's Clubs disbanded in 1989.

THE FEDERATION AND "BETWEENNESS": "A PART OF THE WHOLE MULTI-NATIONAL CULTURE OF AMERICAN LIFE"

For nearly four decades, the federation played a distinct role in Jewish women's organizational life. It was, according to its leaders, the "only Jewish women's organization that encourages mass action, the movement of people," a "progressive organization . . . which meets the needs of those women who are on the move."[62] It had also, over this period, taken its message regarding the significance of Jewish women's history, culture, and ideals to a broad audience of women in more traditional Jewish organizations. At the same time, the Emmas joined successfully with black women and other minorities to work for an end to racism. Though not a peace group, the federation dedicated its energies to programs and education for peace.

All of its varied projects sprang, the Emmas believed, from a dedicated core of Jewish identity. As distinct from Hadassah or synagogue sisterhoods, whose identity focused on Israel or the religious aspects of Judaism, the ELF proudly asserted itself as a secular Jewish group centered in the culture of America and its Jewish population. Much as their ancestors turned to Judaic religious emblems, the Emmas selected a heroine compatible with their own multi-faceted identities as secular Jews, women, and Americans. Their primary identification with Emma Lazarus arose from her secularism, which the Emmas associated with a universalist humanism that they argued reflected the essence of Jewish values.

While the Emmas were a Jewish organization, their proud ethnicity did not hamper, but, in fact, promoted, their identification as women, as workers, and as Americans. As proclaimed in the ELF's first constitution in January 1951, the enhancement of Jewish culture was proposed "as a part of the whole multi-national culture of American life." To be Jewish and American was not a contradiction but an interrelationship; as Lazarus's life had implied, "to be a good Jew was to be a better American."[63] Furthermore, gender was as funda-mental to the group's identity as were ethnicity and nationality: as we have seen, women's issues and history were woven into all activities of the federa-tion over the course of nearly forty years. Class consciousness was also deeply ingrained within the federation: like Shavelson, Gordon, and Raynes, most leaders and members came from trade union backgrounds or had married men who were active in workers' movements. Working-class consciousness distinguished the federation from middle-class Jewish women's organizations and helped shape its theory and practice.

The history of the Emma Lazarus Federation also raises provocative ques-tions about racial identity and sensitivities. From the creation of the Emma Lazarus Division in 1944 to the demise of the federation forty-five years later, members consistently spoke to the necessity of eliminating white racism as well as anti-Semitism. In a series of continuing projects, they directed their efforts practically as well as rhetorically to the support of civil rights, par-ticularly to the task of awakening white women (especially Jewish women) to the cause and allying themselves with black women to improve their situation.

In view of the ways in which the Emma Lazarus Federation amalgamated rather than separated the traditional markers of group identity—class, gender, nationality, ethnicity, and race—the experience of this group sheds light not only on Jewish women's activism in the twentieth century, but also on broader theoretical questions of feminism.[64] As feminists examine the various ways in which race, class, gender, and ethnicity interact and compete for the allegiance of individuals, organizations, and communities, the history of the Emma Lazarus Federation cautions us about the pitfalls of naming "discrete, coherent and absolutely separate" measures of identity.[65] For the Emmas, there was no dichotomy between class and gender, race and ethnicity. In one respect, the group itself represented a "racialized ethnicity," a people with a common ethnic past who came to regard itself as a "race" because of the traumatic experience of the Holocaust, recognizing connections with other victims of genocide and racism.[66]

Like Clara Shavelson, most members of the ELF had begun their organizational lives as trade union members. Yet while Shavelson in 1909 had spoken her famous words as a worker, the delegates to the Cooper Union meeting offered a Jewish prayer before voting on her strike resolution. Jewish solidarity supported workers' consciousness on that occasion, as it did for all the years in which Shavelson, Gordon, Raynes, and their friends took part in the Jewish People's Fraternal Order of the IWO. These women's participation in the United Council of Working-Class Women, the Progressive Women's Council, and the Women's Division of the IWO illustrates their early recognition of the importance of gender as well as class and ethnic consciousness.

Not, however, until the Holocaust had accomplished its unspeakable horrors did the Jewish component of their identity become most salient. Remembering the women victims who "sang lullabies to console their children while facing the open graves before them," Clara Shavelson and her progressive friends made themselves over into "Emmas," dedicating themselves to promote Jewish culture—albeit a woman-centered "people's" culture—as a "shield" against fascism and genocide. "We dare not forget or forgive . . . the crimes of Nazism," they repeatedly exclaimed.

The coming to consciousness of the Emmas as "racialized" Jews in a way that fully incorporated their identities as women, trade unionists, and Americans illuminates the importance of the Holocaust in shaping Jewish women's experience. Yet it was the microcosmic context of these women's lives over a long period of time—their roles and relationships as comrades in the sweatshops and unions, as housewives in their neighborhoods, on bread and meat picket lines, and as associates in the JPFO and Progressive Women's clubs— that provided the fulcrum for their gender-specific response to the Holocaust.

At its twentieth anniversary convention in 1971, the Emma Lazarus Federation reconsidered its organizational roots. "Why are we calling ourselves a Jewish women's organization?" one delegate asked. "Since we are progressive with our ideology and program to benefit all people, why the separation? Why emphasize our Jewishness?" "Why a woman's organization?" Rose Raynes repeated. "Why the Hadassah, the Pioneer Women, the Council of Jewish Women, the Women's Division of the American Jewish Congress, the Women Strike for Peace, the National Council of Negro Women, the Emma Lazarus Federation?"

In response, the ELF president reaffirmed the importance both of "unity as Jews, unity in variety" and the "special approach" needed to solve women's problems because of pervasive attitudes of "male superiority": "We are a part of American life generally, and of the Jewish community in particular," she reaffirmed, as well as a member of the "family" of women's organizations.[67] In pursuing this aim, the ELF created linkages with groups that complemented its purposes yet did not hesitate to criticize allies when they fell short of the mark—peace and women's groups for failure to represent working-class interests; minority organizations for anti-Semitism; "progressive" male Jewish clubs for ignoring the contributions of Jewish women.

Another "unity" in the federation's approach was its elimination of standard dualities between thought and action, history and policy. A cultural organization, the federation was deeply involved in politics: knowledge isolated from activity had little meaning. The Emmas repeatedly pointed out that culture was a "weapon" in the hard battle against bigotry and complacency. History, put forward on the first line of advance, would shape the present and the future.

Ironically, these dualities were bridged almost effortlessly not by feminist theorists but by the working-class women of the federation—both housewives and paid laborers—women who through their self-styled cultural work made themselves into intellectual activists. Here, too, Clara Shavelson had been a prototype. Growing up in the Ukraine, Clara read late at night after her housework and sewing were done, hiding her books to prevent her father's wrath. In New York, following a full day's work in the garment factory, she studied at the free night school, dreaming of becoming a doctor; when she had time, the public library was a favorite haunt. After Clara married and was busy with children, job, and community organizing, she still made time for several newspapers a day and a book "for dessert."[68]

Such hunger for learning was common to the Emmas, even though they belittled their skills and acknowledged the difficulty of being truly informed on the many issues that concerned them. "Sisters, believe me, it is not an easy task to do research, sit up nights and write outlines," confessed Miriam Silver, of the Bronx Coops, ELF's last cultural director. "I am not a professional writer, but I am willing and happy to do my job as long as I know that the material is being utilized."[69]

As demonstrated by these bridgings between theory and practice, Jewishness and universalism, and class, gender, ethnicity, race, and nationality more broadly, the women of the Emma Lazarus Federation cannot easily be ascribed with a fixed identity that framed them as a group apart—coherent, unitary, singular, and unchanging. Identity for the Emmas was neither linear nor static, but rather multiple, loose, fluid, and "linked." As anthropologist James Clifford suggests, when identity is conceived "not as a boundary to be maintained but as a nexus of relations and transactions actively engaging a subject," ethnicity becomes "more complex, less . . . teleological."[70]

Although the group consciousness of the Emmas grew and changed in interaction with historical events, the ability to unite conflicting values, bringing together disparate axes of experience in a new synthesis, remained constant. In many ways, the Emmas resembled the *mestiza* consciousness described by Gloria Anzaldua as a "consciousness of the borderland" that arises from constantly "crossing over" and thereby "uniting all that is separate . . . breaking down the unitary aspect of each new paradigm." Like the mestiza, the Emmas' struggle to live "between ways," between different cultures, developed into a "tolerance for contradictions [and] ambiguity" and the ability to transcend painfully limiting dualities.[71]

The quality of "betweenness" has long been ascribed to Jewish identity as well. Georg Simmel described the Jew as the perpetual "stranger" who combines "nearness and distance" in "reciprocal tension"; more recently, Daniel and Jonathan Boyarin have spoken of Jewishness as a "diasporic" identity, a living apart from and among others, "disrupt[ing] the very categories of identity because it is not national, not genealogical, not religious, but all of these in dialectical tension with one another."[72] The same kind of "disaggregated" identity—one that is partial and fluid rather than whole and linear—may apply to gender; the writers suggest the parallel notion of a "diasporized gender identity" that combines difference and sameness, specialness and universalism, in contradictory, yet positive and empowering, ways.

The Emma Lazarus Federation of Jewish Women's Clubs demonstrates the simultaneity—rather than the dispersion—of the components of American Jewish female identity in ways that exemplify these creative tensions. As women, as Jews, as proud members of the working class, as radical activists, and as Americans sensitive to the horrors of race prejudice, they fought anti-Semitism and pursued their mission of social justice in ways that drew on the many strengths, as well as the weaknesses, of their shared background and experiences. Their lack of sustained attention to Soviet anti-Semitism was ironic, given how often they quoted Lazarus's line, "Until we are all free, none of us is free"—a reference to the plight of Russian Jews—and unfortunate.

The Emmas' response to domestic anti-Semitism after the Holocaust and their commitment to antiracist work was, however, continuing and vigorous; both efforts underscore the varied ways in which they joined cultural and political means to reaffirm Jewish identity even as the pull of assimilation grew ever more powerful. During a period when few others evidenced interest in women's historical consciousness, moreover, the Emmas supported innovative research in many areas of women's history, focusing on subjects that were Jewish and black, working-class and intellectual, American and international; they linked the production of this knowledge to active involvement in a variety of human rights campaigns. The contributions of the federation in these arenas helped transform our knowledge of Jewish culture and politics, and of women's lives, in postwar America.

Rather than accepting the generational trope that posits the denial of ethnic consciousness after the first generation as normative, women's historians would do well to probe the various patterns, exemplified by the Emma Lazarus Federation, by which ethnic, gender, class, racial, and national identities were linked in innovative and flexible ways across the generations. Crossing unsettled boundaries between these markers, the Emma Lazarus Federation struck out for new frontiers that, we, their feminist heirs, are still traversing.

CHAPTER 13 : THE CONGRESS OF AMERICAN WOMEN : LEFT-FEMINIST PEACE POLITICS IN THE COLD WAR

AMY SWERDLOW

his essay is about the fate of Left feminism and peace activism in the aftermath of World War II. It is about political hope and failed opportunity, about cold war repression, the loss of historical memory, and the waning of feminist and class consciousness. It is the story of the Congress of American Women (CAW), a short-lived popular front women's organization (1946–50) that united in its demands the causes of peace, social justice, and women's rights. It is also the history of CAW's demise at the hands of the House Un-American Activities Committee (HUAC) and the U.S. Department of Justice.

The Congress of American Women came to my attention while I was researching the forerunners of Women Strike for Peace (WSP) for a history of this early 1960s maternalist women's peace movement.[1] I had been an active participant in WSP since its inception, so when I encountered the short-lived, long-forgotten CAW, I was puzzled. WSP literature and internal documents revealed no mention of CAW, and I had no personal recollection of ever hearing it mentioned at the dozens of local and national WSP meetings that I attended. How was it possible, I wondered, that the women of WSP seemed never to have heard of this women's peace organization that had preceded it by only eleven years? I did recall that occasionally women who had left the Communist Party of the United States of America (CPUSA) would warn us in ominous whispers to avoid visits to Soviet-controlled international peace meetings and not to affiliate with women's organizations directed by the pro-Soviet Left because such contacts could lead to political suicide. This was the fate, we were told, of an earlier women's peace group, known for its support of U.S.-Soviet friendship, its opposition to the Truman Doctrine, and its protests against the Korean War. When I heard these rumors in the early 1960s I assumed that the women's organization in question was a doctrinaire Communist front, one that had nothing to offer WSP. When I began to study the history of CAW I discovered that I was wrong, not about CAW's consistent support of Soviet foreign policy, but about its historical relevance to WSP, to the women's peace movement in general, and to feminist politics today.

My purpose in this essay is to restore the Congress of American Women to the historical record. I will examine its origins, program, and goals; begin to assess its achievements; and explore the reasons for its collapse in the context of popular front politics and culture, cold war repression of foreign policy dissent, and postwar sexual politics. In so doing, I hope to identify one historic moment when the link between feminism, social justice, and peace protest, which was a political assumption of the postsuffrage interwar peace movement, was severed.

CAW was the U.S. branch of the Women's International Democratic Federation (WIDF), an organization of tens of millions of women in forty one countries. WIDF was founded in Paris shortly after the end of World War II at an international gathering of women leaders of the antifascist, pro-Soviet Left.[2] The thirteen U.S. representatives at the Paris conference, a biracial group of women of diverse ethnic, social, and political backgrounds, were enormously impressed by the achievements and the stature of the other women delegates they met and inspired by their rising power and status in their own countries.[3] A number of the WIDF leaders were heroes of the armed resistance to fascism in Europe and Asia, others were distinguished parliamentarians or jurists in the newly established eastern bloc socialist countries and in liberated Western Europe, and still others were distinguished scientists, artists, and writers in the West as well as in the East. Eager to endorse the WIDF call for world peace through the achievement of full political, economic, social, and legal rights for women, and proud to establish an organization affiliated with an international sisterhood fighting for peace, the returning delegates founded the Congress of American Women on International Woman's Day, March 8, 1946.[4] It was the global aspect of WIDF that held the greatest appeal for its founders and, not surprisingly, it was its international connection, particularly with women of the communist bloc countries, that became CAW's greatest liability.[5]

Left to right: Ada B. Jackson, African American churchwoman and racial affairs activist; Mary Jane Melish, churchwoman and president of the Brooklyn chapter of CAW; Elinor Gimbel, member of the national board. The three were meeting for dinner at Mammy's Pantry Restaurant in the fall of 1947 to make final plans for a CAW mass rally to be held later that evening. (From the collection of Mary Jane Melish)

In its founding years the congress developed a broad constituency of the kind of women Ellen DuBois has accurately identified as "left feminists," women who believed that the attainment of genuine equality for women required the mobilization of "the masses"—for equality and social justice for all.[6] Liberal women's rights proponents who saw the economic and employment gains made by women during World War II being snatched away in the postwar period also found CAW's public policy program attractive, as did New Deal supporters seeking to maintain prewar social gains. In 1948 Elinor Gimbel, a CAW board member, whose family owned Gimbels Department Store and Saks Fifth Avenue in New York City, told a WIDF conference in Budapest that the goal of CAW was to attain the type of world that President Franklin D. Roosevelt had hoped for.[7]

Trade union women were attracted to the organization for its pro-labor, pro-woman program, and CAW recruited a large number of African American women because of its strongly articulated, and frequently implemented, stand against racism. Neighborhood women found a place in CAW chapters because the organization worked at the grassroots level in coalition with ethnic groups, churches, and synagogues, recruiting in housing projects and tabling at supermarket entrances. By the end of its first year, CAW claimed a substantial membership of 250,000 and seemed to have the potential to mobilize hundreds of thousands more for peace and a progressive interracial feminist social agenda unlike that of any previous women's peace organization.

Yet, four years after its birth, CAW was forced to disband because it could not withstand governmental repression of foreign policy dissent and the shift to the right manifested in mainstream and liberal support for the containment of communism as articulated in the Truman Doctrine launched in 1947. By 1950, when CAW was ordered by the U.S. Department of Justice to register as a foreign agent, thousands of its constituents, particularly the ethnic women affiliated with Communist front workers' fraternal orders, had already left the movement because they were disenchanted by Soviet expansion in their home countries in Eastern Europe. And most of the prominent white liberal women, who were either alarmed by Soviet policies or becoming politically cautious in response to government and media red-baiting, withdrew from leadership roles on the national and local levels.

CAW, which was founded as an outspokenly feminist organization, was further isolated by the public acceptance of a conservative, antifeminist domestic ideology that, Elaine Tyler May points out, was an essential component of cold war policies in that it sought to contain not only the spread of communism and the unleashed atomic bomb, but also the potential power of women, one of the most potentially explosive forces of the postwar era.[8]

The political program and tactics of CAW grew out of several strands of interwar political consciousness and activism. Its gender ideology was influenced by the relationship of a segment of its leadership to the postsuffrage, interwar women's movement for peace and progressive reform. Its class consciousness was based in depression-era radicalism and trade unionism, as well as from New Deal liberalism. Its racial awareness may be attributed partly to the racial agenda of the CPUSA and partly to the strong influence of the African American women CAW attracted into its leadership. Some African American women undoubtedly joined CAW because of the growing interest on the part of African American organizations in postwar foreign policy issues, such as the U.S. attitude toward the anticolonial struggles in Africa.[9] It should be noted that CAW had a larger number of black women among its officers than any other feminist or mixed-gender peace organization before the 1940s or since.[10]

The CPUSA's support of an independent broad-based separatist women's movement, not a women's auxiliary of a labor union or a women's division of a party-controlled mass organization, was something new. The acceptance of such a women's group with a women's rights agenda came, no doubt, from Moscow's support of the WIDF, but also from the party's World War II focus on the recruitment of women for war work and party membership to fill the gap left by the thousands of male cadres who were serving in the armed forces.[11] Writing on Marxism and the woman question in 1943, A. Landy, the CPUSA expert on the woman question, stated: "How to help win the war against Hitler slavery: how to release the vast reservoir of women's creative energies in the service of victory . . . in short, how to open wide all the gates especially of production to full and equal participation in the common effort for our nation's survival. This is the real question posed by the war as far as women are concerned."[12] Elizabeth Gurley Flynn, the most prominent woman in the Communist Party leadership, declared in 1942 that women had special reasons, as women, "to destroy the hateful Fascist-Nazi ideology at its deepest deadliest roots" because "Hirohito, Hitler and Mussolini are agreed on the inferiority of women." [13] In a subsequent *Daily Worker* article, Flynn argued that "problems of health and housing, care and feeding of children, juvenile delinquency, high cost of living cannot be solved in the home." She urged housewives to act publicly as members of the working class and as *citizens.* [14] Yet a number of historians studying the Communist Party and the woman question have pointed out that while the party supported the *notion* of woman's equality, its views on sex roles and the family were conservative. This did not prevent the CPUSA, however, from making programmatic efforts to encourage the recruitment of women.[15]

While it is not difficult to recognize the influence, if not the direct hand, of the CPUSA in shaping the foreign policy goals and many of the domestic policies and tactics of CAW particularly after 1948, it is critical to recognize the ways in which its women leaders surpassed the party not only in their focus on practical, concrete improvements in the quality of working-class women's lives, but also in the fight for specifically women's rights, and in the projection of feminist consciousness, at a time when they were under heavy attack.[16] This was undoubtedly due to the strong feminist presence in the organization in its early years and what I suspect was a relatively laissez-faire policy on the part of the CPUSA in relation to CAW. Theodore Draper, in a recent article published in the *New York Review*, argues that the National Student League was the least controlled Communist front because the party was not terribly concerned with middle-class students; "as a result, the Young Communist League left the National Student League largely alone in its formative period."[17] This, I assume, was also true of CAW, which was not a high priority for the CPUSA because not only was it largely middle-class, but also it was female. Margaret Cowl, head of the Women's Commission of the CPUSA, stated in 1974 that in the party "there was indifference to the mass women's movements and that they were not really accepted as part of the working-class movement of the United States."[18] This is confirmed by my conversations with Dorothy Healey, a top party labor organizer and strategist in Los Angeles who was never involved with CAW, despite the fact that one of its largest chapters was in that city. To this day Healey knows very little about CAW, indicating that she heard few discussions of the organization at the highest levels of party leadership.

CAW was truly a popular front mass organization in that it included among its leadership and founders women of varied social, racial, and political backgrounds. Among its founders were Cornelia Bryce Pinchot, an upper-class suffrage leader and wife of the former governor of Pennsylvania, and Jacqueline Cochran, a prize-winning aviator and prominent businesswoman. Cochran was known for breaking speed and altitude records, piloting bombers across the Atlantic Ocean in the early years of World War II, founding the Women Pilot Training program of the army air force, and fighting for the admission of women into the official ranks of the air force. Other founders were actress Faye Emerson, then married to Elliott Roosevelt, a son of FDR; and actress Florence Eldridge, who was identified as Mrs. Frederick March. Gene Weltfish, a lecturer in anthropology at Columbia University, known for her study with Ruth Benedict of *The Races of Man* and for her left-wing politics, was a leading figure in the organization, as was Anna Center Schneiderman, a national vice president of the American Jewish Congress. Schneiderman was executive director of American ORT (Organization for Rehabilitation and Training) and had been chairperson of the American Jewish Congress's Committee on Israel and World Jewish Affairs.[19] Dr. Mildred Fairchild, who had been a member of the State Advisory Council of the Pennsylvania Bureau of Employment Services and Unemployment Compensation of the Department of Labor and Industry and chairperson of the subcommittee on Women Power of the War Manpower Commission of Philadelphia in 1944, was a vice president of CAW. Fairchild had coauthored a book on the factory, family, and women in Soviet Russia. These were obviously women of stature who reached out beyond the influence of the Communist Party. However, CAW did not hide the fact that Communist Party leaders were among its officers, as the party was not yet illegal nor as discredited among liberals and trade unionists as it would later become. The two CAW officers who were known Communists were Elizabeth Gurley Flynn, chairperson of the Women's Commission, and Claudia Jones, both of working-class backgrounds. Claudia Jones, who had been born in the British West Indies and brought to Harlem as a child, was one of the top CPUSA leaders in Harlem in the popular front period. She was a member of the Women's Commission and is reputed to have been "a relentless critic of male chauvinism and a leading party advocate of women's rights."[20]

The most prominent spokesperson for CAW was Muriel Draper, chairperson of the women's division of the National Council of American-Soviet Friendship. Described by *Time* magazine, at the time of her death in 1952, as an "Edwardian Pink," Draper was born into a "Plymouth Rock" family and brought up in "genteel comfort." At the age of twenty-two she married aspiring singer Paul Draper, the grandson of Charles A. Dana, owner of the *New York Sun*, and the brother of the monologuist Ruth Draper. Muriel Draper spent her early married life in Italy, then in England, where she conducted a celebrated salon frequented by the likes of Bernard Berenson, Gertrude Stein, Henry James, Pablo Cassals, Mabel Dodge, and John Reed. In 1915 Draper came back to the United States and divorced her husband, who had lost the last of his money at the racetrack. She was forced into paid employment as an interior decorator and achieved sufficient financial success to resume her role as cislunar. In 1934 Draper made her first visit to the Soviet Union, which so impressed her that she became a passionate advocate of friendship with the USSR, working politically in its defense until her death. As the cold war accelerated, Draper's support of Soviet foreign policy grew stronger and louder. Her son, dancer Paul Draper, who himself fell afoul of the House Un-American Activities Committee, told a *Time* magazine reporter in 1950: "She makes statements that are not so. They are not lies. . . . They are things that she sees and exaggerates to fit what her heart very much wants."[21]

Enlisting affiliates and building coalitions was an organizational technique employed successfully by popular front groups in the 1930s and 1940s to maximize the power of Left-liberal activism. CAW did this very well, adding a substantial number of organizational affiliates with tens of thousands of members. However, the technique of an umbrella group enlisting the support of other mass organizations in peace and women's rights projects did not originate with the CPUSA. Coalition building was used as an organizational tool not only by the women's club movement in the nineteenth century, but also most notably by the interwar National Committee on the Cause and Cure of War (NCCCW), led by suffrage leader Carrie Chapman Catt. In 1924 Catt brought together a coalition of eleven national women's organizations representing millions of women to march, write, and petition for such legal peace-keeping measures as the World Court and the Kellogg-Briand Pact.[22] CAW claimed twelve affiliates in 1949. They included the National Association of Colored Women; ethnic women's organizations associated with the communist Left, such as the women's divisions of the Polish, Russian, Hungarian, and Jewish sections of the International Workers Order; the Emma Lazarus Federation of Jewish Women's Clubs (see Joyce Antler's essay—Chapter 12—in this volume); a number of CIO Women's Auxiliaries and unions, such as the United Office and Professional Workers and the Teachers Union Local 5 of New York City; and the Henry Street Settlement Adult Council. Among the organizations that cooperated with CAW in its various programs were groups such as the Child Study Association of Cleveland, the Henry Street Settlement Adult Council in New York City, and the Illinois Parents' Council for Nursery Schools. The report to the First National Constitutional Convention in 1949 acknowledged that CAW's relationship with affiliates had been loose and nominal in character, and that the leadership was aware that "if we are to maintain our present affiliates, and enlist new ones, we have to develop an active interest in and support of the campaigns of our affiliates so that we may develop in them the same kind of response to our campaigns."[23] This is a lesson few contemporary feminist groups have learned.

CAW grew rapidly under the slogan "Ten women anywhere can organize anything." The motto of the contemporary ecology movement, "Think globally, work locally," could easily have been applied to CAW's multidimensional program. Chapters were organized in most of the large industrial cities and effective working coalitions were created on the grassroots level in a comparatively open political atmosphere. In 1948, when Detroit CAW members sparked a citywide consumer protest against the 122 percent rise in meat prices, they were able to enlist church groups, trade unions, and retailer organizations in support of a "50-cent meat week." They even secured the sponsorship of the mayor and the city council, thus spearheading what they claimed to be "the biggest organized movement against high prices ever seen in Detroit!"[24] Several CAW chapters enlisted nonpolitical neighborhood women's leagues to campaign for recreation facilities for children. The Kansas City chapter was able to work on foreign policy and class issues simultaneously, combining a campaign for the impeachment of President Harry S. Truman with a fight against local loan sharks. The Chicago chapter sent a delegation to the United Nations with 40,000 peace pledges, and the Los Angeles chapter supported a strike in the film studios while at the same time organizing tenants in a housing project against eviction and establishing a baby-sitting coop, a direct service reminiscent of those of the settlement house movement.[25]

One of the founding decisions made by CAW was to establish a Commission on the Status of Women, chaired first by Susan B. Anthony II and later by Betty Millard, a writer for the Communist *New Masses*. CAW laid out a woman's agenda almost fifty years ago that foreshadowed the contemporary feminist agenda; it demanded full equality with men "in all fields of human enterprise," equal pay for equal work, a 65-cent Minimum-Wage Bill, the inclusion of the word *sex* in the Fair Employment Practices Bill, a federal job training program for women in industry, and equal access to professional schools for black and white women.[26] CAW even eclipsed the contemporary feminist movement by calling in 1946 for national health insurance and the organization of twelve million unorganized women into trade unions. What was particularly gender based, and not class motivated, was CAW's protest against negative images of women, which were on the rise in the postwar period, and its recognition of "the importance of such misrepresentation in influencing public opinion against women's right to a free and equal place in America." It resolved that the organization "act as a watchdog of these misrepresentations and take proper action to correct them." CAW called on its members to work against discrimination against women in federal grand jury selections, also not a class demand.[27]

At its founding CAW had established a commission on child care. It was concerned, however, not only with children but also with their mothers, particularly working mothers. The organization lobbied to continue wartime day care, and for hot lunch programs in schools as well as low-cost carry-home dinners for working women and low-cost in-plant feeding for industrial workers, which had already been initiated at some war plants. Recalling the ideas of Melusina Faye Peirce, who in the nineteenth century proposed cooperative housework, CAW raised the feminist demand for large-scale kitchens and dining halls in every public housing project, as well as laundries and infirmaries.[28] Nor did CAW ignore the problems of professional women, demanding an end to all forms of discrimination, including quotas for the admission of women into medical schools.[29] Muriel Draper reported to the International Council of WIDF, at a meeting in Moscow in November 1949, that the Cleveland chapter of CAW was engaged in a fight to save the jobs of women bus and streetcar drivers who faced being replaced by men. According to Draper, CAW was "considering calling for a special session of the Ohio state legislature to consider the problems of these women, most of whom are Negro women and the sole breadwinners for their families."[30]

In a real sense, CAW was the successor to the feminist peace and social reform movements of the interwar period in that it made the issue of women's equality and empowerment central to the fight for peace and social justice. The linear connection of CAW to the suffrage and post–World War I feminist movement was made manifest in two of CAW's prominent members, Susan Anthony II, the grandniece of Susan B. Anthony, and Nora Stanton Blatch Barney, the granddaughter of Elizabeth Cady Stanton and the daughter of Stanton's daughter, Harriot Blatch. There was, however, a critical difference between CAW and earlier women's rights groups. The CAW program and rhetoric showed a much deeper awareness of class and race issues than had any of the nineteenth- and early-twentieth-century women's rights or social reform groups, including the National Woman's Party (NWP), whose campaign for the Equal Rights Amendment (ERA) CAW opposed.[31] CAW did not merely reject the Equal Rights Amendment as the CPUSA did. It offered an equal rights bill of its own, the Women's Status Bill, drafted to "wipe out discrimination against women without doing away with protective legislation." CAW campaigned to get broad support for its Women's Status Bill and claimed it as a model for other bills developed by trade union and consumers' organizations.[32]

With a sense of women's history rare for its time, CAW consciously identified itself with the earlier women's rights movement and women's labor struggles in the United States. This awareness of women's history and CAW's appreciation of its importance for contemporary politics can be attributed in part to the legacy of the suffrage struggle, in part to the pubic romance with America's democratic heritage, which had been evoked by both the government and the media in their attempts to build popular support for the war against totalitarianism, and to a great degree to the influence of the Communist Party. In projecting the popular front line, the CPUSA had sought to identify with radical struggles in American life. It encouraged research by left-wing intellectuals on little known, or forgotten, class, race, and gender conflicts, raising the slogan, "Communism is Twentieth Century Americanism."

Thus, CAW called upon the nineteenth-century women's rights movement's radical history to counter cold war red-baiting of peace protest. "In the past the fight for women's rights was part of the fight against slavery and economic exploitation," CAW declared; "today it is also part of the fight for peace and security everywhere."[33]

The preamble to CAW's constitution invoked the memory of such historic women as Anne Hutchinson, "pioneer in the fight for the Free Will of Man"; Betsy Ross, "whose needle sewed the stars into our flag"; and Harriet Tubman and Sojourner Truth, "who wrote a page in the history of freedom." The preamble also praised Harriet Beecher Stowe, Susan B. Anthony, Elizabeth Cady Stanton, and Lucretia Mott for launching "the long battle for Women's Rights." Honoring working-class women as well as middle-class reformers, CAW recalled the Lowell Mill girls and "the women garment workers of the early 20th century who struck for economic justice."[34] These historical references came at a time when U.S. history textbooks included nothing about women's social, political, or economic role, and young women educated after suffrage had been achieved knew nothing of the suffrage movement or its roots in abolitionism. It is interesting to note that this historical awareness was not totally wiped out with CAW's demise. Two of the pioneering works in the second wave of women's history, recognized for their early focus on issues of race and class, Gerda Lerner's "The Lady and the Mill Girl" and Eleanor Flexner's *Century of Struggle*, are legacies of CAW. Both authors were actively involved in the organization. Lerner was one of the leaders of the Los Angeles chapter, which in 1949 offered its members a seminar in women's history.[35]

More than any other feminist organization before or since, CAW made racial equality a central plank in its program and incorporated African American women in its leadership. This was not accomplished without difficulties, despite the fact that a number of black women's political organizations were CAW affiliates. CAW was represented at the Convention of the National Association of Colored Women in Washington, D.C., celebrated the birthday of Mary McLeod Bethune, participated in an antilynching demonstration at the White House, and picketed to integrate swimming pools. The congress also insisted that the right to work apply equally to "our Negro sisters who suffer a double burden as women and as Negroes." Racial and class inclusiveness were not merely slogans for CAW. It not only organized black and white women around civil rights issues, but also consciously crossed class and race lines by developing services for working-class and poor women such as used clothing exchanges and welfare counseling. This conscious identification with the cause of black and poor women paralleled the CPUSA line and tactics, but the way in which CAW worked on the grassroots level was more typical of the white and black women's club movements and of settlement house work.

In 1949 the bulletin of the Los Angeles chapter of CAW reported that its national council had declared, "Our greatest hindrance to building unity between Negro and white women is the remnants of prejudice to be found in CAW and in our affiliated organizations." These manifestations, it was suggested, "may be subtle or unconscious but they are nevertheless there. Of one thing we may be sure: if there is no social mixing there is bound to be prejudice."[36] The CAW council recommended that each affiliate hold a discussion on this matter and offer lectures on the anthropology and history of the Negro people.[37] The Los Angeles CAW rejoiced that a Chicana and a black woman had been hired at a bank in Watts, where CAW had picketed with other organizations demanding the hiring of members of minority groups.

A number of leading African American women, the pride of their own black community, were prominent in the leadership of CAW. Among them were Dr. Charlotte Hawkins Brown, Vivian Carter Mason, Thelma Dale, Ada B. Jackson, and Irene McCoy Gaines. Charlotte Hawkins Brown was a distinguished black educator and officer of the National Council of Negro Women. She had served as president of the North Carolina Teachers Association from 1935 to 1937 and sat on the national board of the YWCA. She was the first black woman appointed to the North Carolina Council of Defense in 1940.[38] Social worker Vivian Carter Mason was third national vice president of the National Council of Negro Women; Thelma Dale was an organizer for the Office and Professional Workers Union. Ada B. Jackson was a Brooklyn community church and racial affairs activist. In 1945 the *Brooklyn Eagle* named her one of Brooklyn's "three fighting ladies." She was an active member of the Bethany Baptist Church and of the Education and Family Life Division of the Protestant council. Jackson chaired the Committee for Interracial Education of the YWCA, was an executive board member of the Brooklyn branch of the NAACP, and served as treasurer of the Brooklyn chapter of the National Council of Negro Women.[39] The African American *California Eagle*, a weekly newspaper published in Los Angeles, reported in June 1949 that Myrtle Pitts, who had been a delegate to the first national convention of CAW, would be the featured speaker at a meeting at the Bethel African Methodist Church. The article also reported that Pitts had taken part in the presentation of one million signatures for *peace* to the United Nations.[40] This is an example of rare interracial peace activism that bears further study. It is difficult to assess from internal documents and newspaper stories how many rank-and-file African American women were actually active in CAW, and to what extent the prominent black women leaders of racial, church, and community organizations played a decisive role in making CAW policy.[41] Three New York City CAW activists interviewed by Kathy Moos Campbell in connection with her research on her Communist peace activist grandmother, Elizabeth Moos, received a rather negative response when asked about the participation of African American women in CAW in New York City.[42] The three women, Stella Allen, Harriet Magil, and Betty Millard, all members of the CPUSA, recalled that there was never real integration in the New York City chapters. They remembered that "we sort of nursed along a group in Harlem" and that Claudia Jones "ripped into the New York chapter for not having a larger number of black women."[43] However, an interview I conducted on July 6, 1994, with Mary Jane Melish, president of the Brooklyn chapter of CAW, revealed that there was active and successful recruitment of African American women conducted mostly by white CAW activists in that borough of New York City. Melish, the wife of a prominent Anglican minister, visited black churches to recruit black women church leaders, appealing to them on the issue of both peace and racial discrimination. Melish explained that when the CAW women went into neighborhoods where the women were mostly black, there was a good response to the CAW program. But, according to Melish, the African American women in the community rarely attended mass rallies in New York or the marches on Washington because they did not have the resources to leave home or were too occupied with work and children.

As the cold war escalated, friendship with the Soviet Union and outlawry of the atom bomb became the central focus of CAW. The Officers' Report of 1949 states, "It is significant to note that of the three commissions [Peace and Democracy, State of Women, and Child Care] . . . the women themselves have chosen to be most active in the Peace and Democracy Commission."[44] This may have been due to the fact that after the 1948 attack on CAW by the House Un-American Activities Committee, which hounded Susan Anthony and Nora Barney out of the movement and scared off liberal supporters, the majority of those who remained were those who identified cold war attacks on the Soviet Union as the principle issue they wished to address. The list of officers of CAW reveals that the prominent liberal women and the theatrical celebrities had dropped out. Betty Millard recalled in 1981 that by 1950 the CPUSA was directly involved in the decision-making process of CAW, insisting that Claudia Jones be appointed to the steering committee, "and she became the ideologue of the movement."[45]

As Communist women filled in or took over CAW leadership roles, the Congress of American Women focused its energy and considerable vigor on protesting every escalation of the cold war. Together with its mother organization WIDF, CAW opposed the Truman Doctrine, the Marshall Plan, U.S. intervention in Greece, and American support for Chiang Kai-shek in China. These were positions already being conflated with anti-Americanism by the press, the pulpit, the academy, and organized labor. The continued participation of CAW leaders in WIDF conferences in Soviet bloc countries, where the U.S. women received heros' welcomes from the anti-American delegations, provoked anger and ridicule in the U.S. press. The Paris edition of the *Herald Tribune* reported that some thirty American women at a WIDF conference in Budapest in 1949 supported resolutions that made the Soviet Union seem as "pure as the driven snow," whereas America was depicted as "simply dreadful."[46] The *New York Times* reported that at a meeting of the WIDF council held in Moscow in November 1949, Muriel Draper, vice president of CAW, attacked the United States, charging that "because of the absence of social legislation for women the children of some millions of working mothers in the U.S. roam the streets, and fatal accidents to them are multiplying." She stated that U.S. industrialists "are discharging married workers and apparently, it is a crime to work if you love."[47]

The *Christian Science Monitor* stated flatly that CAW was part of the Kremlin's front against American democracy and reported that Eleanor Roosevelt, a liberal cold warrior, had stated, "I wouldn't say they're all Communists or pro-Communists, but they are somewhat foolish, if they don't know they're playing a dangerous game for themselves and their country."[48] Its opposition to the Truman Doctrine and its fight to hold on to wartime initiatives such as price controls and day-care centers made CAW an obvious target for the House Un-American Activities Committee. HUAC declared that its purpose was to expose the fraudulent connection between CAW and the legitimate women's rights movement, and to warn idealistically minded but politically gullible women that CAW's real goal was simply "to disarm and demobilize the U.S."[49] There is an interesting twist in political discourse here. In the 1920s the governmental red hunters sought, through the spiderweb chart and other local lists of feminist leaders, to connect the women's peace movement, along with the struggle for suffrage, to an international communist network, and thus to render all feminist groups suspect of subversion.[50] In 1948 the agenda of the anticommunist House Un-American Activities Committee was to separate Left feminism from a now respectable but fossilized historical memory of its militant activists symbolized by the unfinished statues of Susan Anthony, Elizabeth Cady Stanton, and Lucretia Mott residing in the basement of the Capitol rotunda.

A *Report on the Congress of American Women* published by HUAC singled out for political annihilation the two CAW women whose names connected the organization directly to the suffragists: Nora Stanton Blatch Barney, who was a newcomer to CAW and was also active in the anticommunist National Woman's Party, and Susan B. Anthony II, an outspoken supporter of trade unionism as well as feminism and a participant in the Henry Wallace campaign for the presidency in 1948.

To undermine Nora Barney's credentials as a patriotic American, descended from an elite family with abolitionist and women's rights connections, HUAC pointed to her membership in the National Council of American-Soviet Friendship and her statement on her return from a WIDF conference in Budapest that non-Communists in Hungary enjoyed greater freedom than Communists in the United States. Barney was not, in fact, a communist. The fact that CAW was not tightly controlled by the CPUSA is illustrated by the inclusion of Barney, who opposed the CPUSA stand on the ERA and criticized the United States for copying Russia's faults while inveighing against her.[51] She also spoke publicly of the demands of the civil rights movement in racist terms similar to those of her grandmother, which would have led to serious consequences for party members. Despite the fact that Barney was a member of the National Woman's Party, HUAC attempted to tie her to the CPUSA by reprinting a *Daily Worker* news story that placed her at a CAW celebration of the centennial of Seneca Falls. The *Daily Worker* had reported:

> The granddaughter of Elizabeth Cady Stanton placed a large floral wreath on the grave of her famous grandmother for the Congress of American Women . . . centennial commemorative ceremony. . . . Present also at the services was the nephew of Frederick Douglass. . . . It was Frederick Douglass who seconded Elizabeth Cady Stanton's first resolution in 1848 declaring it was the duty of all women to secure the franchise. Susan B. Anthony II, grandniece of Susan B. Anthony[,] a pioneer along with Elizabeth Cady Stanton . . . [was] present at the ceremonies. . . . [A] message was received from Alice Stone Blackwell, daughter of Lucy Stone.[52]

While this *Daily Worker* story reveals little about Barney except for her appearance at a centennial celebration of Seneca Falls, it tells us a great deal about CAW's inventive efforts to bring past and present, gender and race together. In honoring its feminist foremothers and radical forefathers, it managed to connect successfully with their offspring. Mayor Haley G. Douglass of Highland Beach, Maryland, the grandson of Frederick Douglass, told those assembled at Stanton's grave that he was "very happy to address CAW because it was the only women's organization that had asked him to speak in recognition of his grandfather's role and the close connection between the women's and Negro's fight for freedom in the last century."[53] In the McCarthyite atmosphere of 1948–49, the HUAC charges against Nora Stanton Barney undoubtedly drove away some of the women who joined the organization because of its stand for women's rights. It even moved some women to threaten to quit the National Woman's Party because Barney was a member of CAW as well as NWP.[54]

Using information provided by paid informers, HUAC charged Susan Anthony with wide-ranging associations with Left causes, including Writers for Wallace and the National Council of American-Soviet Friendship. Particularly damaging was the unsubstantiated accusation by an FBI informer that he had seen a picture of Lenin in Anthony's apartment. Anthony refused to discuss these charges with me, stating in a telephone conversation in 1977 that she had been subjected to incredibly unjust persecution, but that she was writing her own book in which she would detail all the false charges. So far the book has not been published. The HUAC charges drove Susan Anthony II out of feminist and peace politics and out of the country, not to reappear in public until 1977, when she marched into the National Women's Conference in Houston hand in hand with Betty Friedan, Gloria Steinem, and Bella Abzug to a thunderous ovation. She then rose to speak in favor of the ERA, which she had opposed in the late 1940s.[55]

The HUAC hearing paved the way for CAW to be cited as subversive by the attorney general in 1948, but it continued to function. While the national office ceased publishing its newsletter in 1949, fourteen chapters remained in existence and continued to campaign against the cold war until 1950, when the membership was estimated by *Newsweek* at 3,000.[56] If the original figure of 250,000 claimed by Gene Weltfish in 1947 was anywhere near the mark, the decrease to 3,000 indicated a devastating decline in acceptance and influence. At that point, in 1950, the U.S. Justice Department ordered the Congress of American Women to register as an enemy agent. With McCarthyism at its zenith, there was little public sympathy for CAW and its right of dissent. A hostile and condescending editorial in *Newsweek* (titled "Women's Club or Agent?") made it clear that if CAW insisted on staying in business, it would incur a $10,000 fine and five-year prison sentences for each of its officers.

Stella Allen, executive secretary of CAW in 1950 and a self-identified former Communist, remembered: "When we did get the notice that we were on the list, we did go through a very painful process. . . . It went on for a long, long time because . . . there were some of us who felt that the organization should exist, and that we should make a strong stand, to fight and say we are not foreign agents."[57] Lawyers consulted by the CAW leadership warned that theirs would be a very expensive legal battle. Kathy Moos Campbell reminded me that when she had interviewed her grandmother, Elizabeth Moos, in 1981, she had asked her if she thought that the women in CAW should have fought harder for the survival of their own unique peace and women's rights group. Campbell reported that Moos told her, confidentially, "I did not think the CAW was worth the time, effort and expense of a court fight since it had such a small, predominantly middle class base and there were other causes more deserving of the limited resources of progressives." Moos also assured Campbell that hers was the official CPUSA position.[58] Harriet Magil, an active Communist in the 1940s, married to a top party leader, A. B. Magil, but bitterly anticommunist when she was interviewed by Kathy Campbell, gave her assessment of the demise of CAW: "We were done in first by McCarthyism and second by the Party constantly giving us hell for not organizing working class women."

Stella Allen recalled in hindsight: "The pattern was basically one of the base narrowing and becoming more political, the pressure in this country to take positions . . . against the so-called Eastern bloc, or the Russians, and the pressure internationally [presumably from WIDF] to reverse the whole thing and be anti-American. . . . This put CAW in a bind."[59] CAW eventually decided, reluctantly but with the concurrence of most of the members, that the fight to save the organization would be prohibitively expensive and probably doomed in the political climate of the day.

The death of the Congress of American Women effectively dissolved the conscious connection between feminism, social reform, and peace protest that was a political given for the postsuffrage peace activists. That link had already been undermined by the 1920s red scare that targeted all progressive women's organizations in the interwar period, but it was driven from historical memory in the 1950s by McCarthyism, the rise of the cult of domesticity, and the low priority given by the communist left to what it perceived of as bourgeois feminists' demands for women's rights at the expense of class rights. Thus the link between Left feminism and peace activism was severed, not to be joined together again until January 15, 1968, when the radical feminists, who were part of the coalition that organized the Jeannette Rankin Brigade in opposition to the Vietnam War and poverty at home, declared that neither peace nor social justice could be achieved if women remained economically and politically powerless.

> *A new generation of women sense the boredom and bitterness of their mothers.*
> *They do not want to be confined to the same roles.*
> *— Heather Booth, "Towards a Radical Movement," 1968*

"What makes a rebel?" asks Zane, the heroine of Alix Kates Schulman's 1978 feminist novel, *Burning Questions*. Born before World War II and raised in Babylon, Indiana, Zane restlessly passes her childhood digging holes to China in her backyard. In adolescence, she chafes against the shallow conformity and empty materialism of her middle-class suburban family. A misfit and nonconformist who devours biographies of revolutionaries and plays chess, Zane eventually escapes in the late fifties to MacDougal Street, where she throws herself into the underground Beat culture of Greenwich Village. Soon disillusioned, Zane marries, bears three children in short order, and rapidly descends into domestic drudgery. From the window of her Washington Square apartment, an envious Zane watches a slightly younger generation march for civil rights, demonstrate against the Vietnam War, and float to a new consciousness on the free drugs and sex of an exuberant counterculture. At the end of the novel, Zane joins a women's group, where, for the first time, she feels free to explore the "burning questions" of a lifetime.[1]

As Zane's generation came of age, social critics observed a "generation gap" that separated the "sixties generation" from their parents. What they—and future historians—did not notice was that *two* generation gaps existed, side by side, each with its own gender-specific fears, dreams, and solutions. This is the story of that *female* generation gap—the wide gulf that separated daughters of the fifties from the world of their mothers—the ways in which it differed from young men's alienation, and how it shaped the emergence of the women's movement.

Several microgenerations forged the American women's movement in the 1960s. People like Betty Friedan, already wives and mothers and workers in the 1950s, formed the adult feminist core of women who, in their forties and fifties, rejected the Feminine Mystique. Zane's generation—born before and during World War II—played an especially influential role in igniting the younger side of the women's movement. With one foot firmly planted in the fifties, these daughters viscerally understood the contradictions and hypocrisies experienced by adult women. A few flirted with the Beats; some went south as civil rights workers or helped found the student movement in the North; many married in the early sixties. Some became the most articulate leaders of the early women's liberation movement.[2] A good number did all of the above.[3] As Zane put it, "I was fortunate enough and young enough to pass from one generation to another at the appropriate moment by a timely change of style. From Silent to Beat to Revolutionary."[4]

These women, along with the elders of the baby boom (born between 1946 and 1952), formed the shock troops of the women's liberation movement, stamping the political culture of the movement with their spirit. By the late sixties and early seventies, they found themselves confronting the glaring contradiction between their aspirations and the reality of their subordinate status with men, in movement and in jobs.

The younger baby boomers—those born after 1952—were still in school when feminist ideas began reverberating through the culture. They grew up in an atmosphere saturated with media images of protest, the sexual revolution, the counterculture, and the sense that American society was pliable, boisterous, and unstable. Still, most remembered the assassination of John F. Kennedy, which for many activists, became *the* symbol of the generational divide. These women reached adulthood when the women's movement was a rising tide. They took for granted freedoms and responsibilities that, just a few years earlier, had emblazoned their older sisters' banners. They did not launch the movement (though many spawned women's groups in their high schools), but many became pioneers of a different sort: they were the first women to shape adult lives amid the new opportunities and burdens created by feminism. Some became dedicated feminists; others adopted a more complicated attitude, later dubbed, oversimply, "post-feminist."

Whatever their ages, the young women—mostly white, college-educated, and middle-class—who created and joined the women's liberation movement had personal acquaintance with the power of the Feminine Mystique—sometimes in the person of their mother, but most often with the fifties' cultural symbol of motherhood. The invisible ghost haunting their youth wore an apron and lived vicariously through the lives of her husband and children. Against her, the women's liberation movement was forged.

Zane's question, "What makes a rebel?" has never received an adequate feminist response, partly because the female generation gap has remained invisible to social critics and scholars. Thoughtful generalizations about the generation gap have been proposed by many observers of sixties' movements.[5] Richard Flacks, for example, has argued that protesters frequently grew up in egalitarian, liberal families that stressed self-regulation and expected their children to live up to intellectual, aesthetic, political, and religious ideals. Young rebels, he argued, did not simply reject the world of their parents; on the contrary, they tried to live out parents' ideals that had been compromised by the chilling atmosphere of McCarthyism, political disillusionment, or the material comforts of success. In the name of their parents' values, they rebelled against the world of their parents. For many "red-diaper babies"—children born of parents who had been members or fellow travelers of the Communist Party—this was particularly true.[6]

Kenneth Keniston, in another study of New Left activists, similarly observed how profoundly parents influenced the ideals of "committed youth." "One of the most striking findings of this study," he noted, "is the great similarity in the families of alienated students. Both parents seem to have been frustrated and dissatisfied. The mother's talents and emotionality found little expression within her marriage; the father's idealism and youthful dreams were crushed by the realities of his adult life."[7]

Although both Flacks and Keniston included young women among the activists they studied, their analyses and conclusions were based largely on the male experience. Whatever created a male rebel, they reasoned, also molded his female counterpart. Neither analyzed the different roots of female rebellion.

They were partly right. Young men and women in the civil rights and New Left movements alike criticized the excessive materialism and shallow conformity of their culture, feared the madness of nuclear deterrence, and denounced the anticommunist hysteria that squelched dissent and led to proxy wars like Vietnam. Both expressed shock and indignation at America's pervasive poverty and racism; both loathed the hypocrisy of a democratic society that daily violated its own ideals. Both young men and women expressed contempt for the military and economic "establishment," vowed to change "the system," and favored direct action over the stodgy, hierarchical, bureaucratic ways of the adult world.

So female and male radicals seemed quite similar on the surface. But there were important differences that never fully surfaced until women aired them in consciousness-raising groups or in movement pamphlets. Even then, feminists became so engrossed with the discovery of hidden injuries, so exhilarated by the possibility of transforming society, that the history of their specific alienation quickly became lost, never fully entering public consciousness. As a result, critics and scholars discovered and then debated the meaning of the generation gap without noticing that *two* overlapping generation gaps existed and that young women faced a different set of obstacles and opportunities.

How could the generation gap not have meant different things to young men and women? After all, if Flacks and Keniston are right, each had to reject different worlds and play out different aspirations. When a son lived out his father's values within a movement context, he might reject the breadwinner ethic but not his future as a father. Instead of becoming a lawyer, banker, teacher, or bureaucrat, a son might join the Peace Corps, work in a poverty program, enter the ranks of social workers, even become a professional movement organizer. Whatever his unconventional politics or way of life, his choices did not foreclose future relations with women and children. Whether he married or cohabited, or adopted the late sixties mandate to "smash monogamy," he never felt required to reject a future as a parent. One could combine a life as a movement organizer with fatherhood. Many did.

For daughters, the generation gap was more complicated. What did it mean to a daughter to reject the world of her mother—or to live out her dreams? Many mothers, as Betty Friedan discovered, had lost a sense of their identity and lived vicariously through the lives of their mates and children. Usurped by the exigencies of family life or political work, many had forfeited careers or political ideals for the comforts of suburbia. Some mothers had dared not even dream.

However their mothers' lives had turned out, many daughters of the fifties early recognized that *they* needed an independent identity, one that challenged the Feminine Mystique's emphasis on marriage and motherhood. Fear of becoming an "ordinary housewife"—in the words of one sixties feminist writer—is what fueled the female generation gap.[8]

Could women in their twenties mate and bear children without descending to the domestic drudgery they had witnessed in the fifties? They did not know. And if daughters rejected the marriage-and-motherhood world of their (actual or symbolic) mothers, what would give meaning to their lives? To live out the suppressed ambitions of their mothers, they would have to achieve an identity based on something outside of marriage and motherhood. And for that, there were precious few female models.

Rejecting the world of their mothers not only invited social stigma, but also potentially posed serious psychological risks. Nancy Chodorow, Jean Baker Miller, and other feminist theorists and clinicians have argued that female development follows a different path than that of males. Unlike boys, who early separate from their mothers to "earn" their identity as males, girls appear to grow up in a state of "merged attachment" to their mothers, grounding their very identity in connection to others. Only in adolescence do girls begin separating from their mothers, and then with considerable guilt and confusion. To reject the world of the mother, by refusing marriage and motherhood, could intensify an already guilt-ridden and difficult psychological struggle.[9]

Liberal egalitarian families—as well as post–Sputnik America—further confused daughters by encouraging them to imagine nontraditional futures. Expected to attend college, these daughters early learned to take their intellectual achievements seriously. Some fantasized following in the footsteps of their father. But like their male counterparts, they also rejected the social conformity expected by suburban life and corporations, and the compromises associated with their fathers' lives. Many activists and countercultural enthusiasts also regarded professionals as "sell outs." So, for a variety of reasons—including the fact that society still denied them a legitimate claim to "male" occupations—patterning themselves after adult men was simply not a viable solution.

As fifties daughters began rejecting the world of their mothers—and often their fathers as well—they faced a collective identity crisis for which there seemed to be no female-specific answers. One solution many young women tried was to model themselves after the young men of their generation, a temporary solution fraught with contradictions and complications. For those who postponed marriage and childbearing, successive identities could be found in teen culture, in youth culture and college life, perhaps in "the movement," and eventually in the women's movement itself. Within these peer worlds, young women could fashion themselves as autonomous individuals. Movement culture even offered a surrogate family life in which young women's nurturing and need for "connectedness" was valued as comradely solidarity.

Identifying with men was no more than a provisional solution, however. Assuming the garb of a male rebel simply postponed the day when young women would have to figure out whether and how to mate and bear children while still creating an independent identity. This is one reason the American women's movement became so profoundly engrossed with the question of female identity. As future feminists tried to escape the Feminine Mystique, they discovered solutions that suited men but not themselves. This conundrum became the very existential core of American feminism.

All societies try to prepare their children for adult roles. In the twentieth century, that task became increasingly complicated as each generation of daughters encountered broader educational, economic, and social opportunities than their mothers had enjoyed. By the late fifties and sixties, the differences separating mothers and daughters had widened into an unpassable gulf. The Feminine Mystique, which ruled so many middle-class white mothers' lives, was about to crumble under the weight of social and economic change. As Barbara Berg has noted, "Surely this was not the first time in American history that daughters yearned to live lives different from their mothers, to forge new paths, to go in new directions. What was unique to us—the generation coming of age in the sixties and seventies—however, was that we had the *opportunity* to act on these dreams and inspiration and to make them a reality."[10]

Many daughters viscerally understood their mother's disappointments years before Betty Friedan published her revelations. However much they enjoyed their families and homes, fifties mothers also seethed with quiet resentment; from an early age, daughters sensed it. As one fifties daughter explained, "We learned that many of our mothers chafed against their restricted spheres; we learned that underneath the busy dailyness of their lives, there was a deep and stagnant well of frustration and sorrow."[11] Occasionally, mothers openly discussed their unhappiness with their daughters.[12] But nonverbal messages—sighing, psychosomatic complaints, unexplained weeping, episodes of domestic violence—communicated what a conspiracy of silence forbade: the expression of profound disappointment.

Many fifties mothers clearly wanted something better for their daughters. In a 1962 Gallup poll, only 10 percent of surveyed mothers wanted their daughters to repeat their lives.[13] In letters to Betty Friedan, after the publication of *The Feminine Mystique* in 1963, women around the country described their hopes for their daughters. One woman urged other mothers "to help their daughters to avoid the traps in which they have already fallen. . . . Their daughters can still change their course." Another reader of Friedan's book described herself as a "drop-out from Oberlin College" who became "a victim of the Feminine Mystique . . . the mother of five." More than anything, she hoped her daughter would never experience the "servile feeling" she had felt as a housewife. "How can we help our daughters to avoid making the mistake of following the crowd into early marriage. . . . I would be heart-broken to see any of them make the mistakes I've made."[14]

Being mothers, they also wanted to ensure their daughters' security. So mothers often preached conflicting lessons. They encouraged daughters to imagine new futures even as they pushed them to achieve economic security and respectability through marriage and motherhood. "Be like me, but don't be like me": this was the confusing message a good many daughters imbibed along with their milk and cookies.

The cumulative impact was extraordinary. Raised in the fifties, many of these daughters grew up feeling, as one feminist explained, "a pervasive sense of ambivalence" about the future.[15] Daughters of the fifties grew up fearful of repeating—or failing to repeat—the lives of their mothers or the cultural image of the fifties mother.[16] In her research on middle- and working-class daughters of the fifties, Kathleen Gerson found that 79 percent of their families stressed the primacy of a domestic future over all other interests. Yet 45 percent of these women early developed an aversion to a traditional domestic life and "looked on marriage and children with either indifference or disdain as children. Instead, they had given central importance to work." Simply put, their mothers' lives frightened them. Though adult opportunities and experiences sometimes altered their attitudes, the more significant fact is that so many of these women emphasized "the dangers of domesticity instead of its joys."[17]

WATCHING MOTHER

Each generation of daughters is finely attuned to what has caused their mothers' unhappiness. Many daughters of sixties feminists, for example, have privatized what they learned from their mothers but resist calling themselves feminists. As one daughter explained, "All I think of is how unhappy it made all of you, all the trials and sorrows you experienced. I don't want any part of it."[18]

Her revulsion is understandable. Just as she associates our adult problems with the women's movement, feminists in the late sixties instinctively blamed the Feminine Mystique for their mothers' compromises and miseries. Just as she wants no part of "movement stuff," young feminists, too, sought to avoid their mother's "domestic stuff." "As we grew older," explained Barbara Berg, "we saw our mothers—our role models, the women we were to become— thwarted in their efforts toward self-realization and expression. A deep and bitter lesson, this one—and one we couldn't take lightly. It reverberated through the core of our being, and we resolved not to let it happen to us; we resolved to be different."[19]

Many daughters, of course, became "different" without a fuss. They simply slid into different lives, without declaring a generational war or joining any movements at all. They quietly embraced new opportunities for higher education, pursued higher-status careers, married, juggled work and children, or decided to forego marriage and children altogether. Those young women who became feminists, however, politicized their rejection of the Feminine Mystique. Why they became feminists and others did not is impossible to say with any certainty. One obvious reason is that their involvement in other social movements politicized their understanding of social and personal problems.

Even before that, however, many young women rebelled against the constraints of the fifties and, like Zane, harbored fantasies of rebellion. Some felt that their parents' political or cultural values, though compromised in their own lives, ignited their own intolerance for injustice and inequality. In other cases, intellectual ambition or artistic temperament collided with conventional expectations of femininity and sparked a lifelong search for an unconventional life. Some unknown number of young women found a political language for their alienation when they encountered red-diaper babies during their youth. Many talented young women, especially those of Zane's generation, married and bore children early, only to find themselves mindlessly repeating the drudgery of their mothers' lives, stuck between the dreams of their youth and the constraints of the present. Zane's question—"What makes a rebel?"—has thousands of individual answers, many patterns, but no definitive answer.

As they look back upon their youth, many feminists who launched the women's liberation movement fit the profiles described by Gerson, Flacks, and Keniston. Early on, they observed their mothers' lives and, although they often admired them, they decided they wanted no part of their domestic roles. Interviews with early leaders and participants of the women's movement reveal a self-conscious rejection of domestic life.[20]

Naomi Weisstein, for example, one of the movement's major theorists and activists, describes herself as a "polka dot diaper" baby, the daughter of a mother who "had grown up in a Bolshevik family and had become the kind of feminist you could be in the 1920s, not sufficient to pursue her career [as well as] have kids." Before having children, Weisstein's mother had been a concert pianist; afterward, she stopped her career. As a teenager, her daughter recalls, "I vowed to myself I would never get married and that I would never have kids. I was sure it ruined her life. And I still think so."[21] Perhaps to live out her mother's unfinished dream, Weisstein, a well-known physiological psychologist, later founded the Chicago Women's Liberation Rock and Roll Band.

Barbara Ehrenreich, a widely published feminist writer and activist, remembers how "you had to steel yourself as a girl if you didn't want to follow a prescribed role." Her mother's expectations ran low. "Even at a young age, I could understand that the only good thing you could do as a woman was to be a housewife, but you would never have any respect that way. Because I don't think my father respected my mother. . . . She was a full-time housewife, and that's what I did not want to be."[22]

Middle-class girls were not alone in rejecting the Feminine Mystique, as Gerson's research revealed. Irene Peslikis, a feminist activist and artist, grew up in a Greek working-class family in Queens, New York. Her mother frequently worked outside the home—as a hatcheck girl, at Macy's, at making hats, in a paper flower factory—to help the family stay afloat. By the time she reached adolescence, Peslikis had decided "I wasn't going to be a housewife." The more her parents tried to become Americans, the more she found herself rebelling against the marriage that awaited her. "I didn't think too much about marriage, and when I did I would cringe at it.[23]

Fearful of repeating their mothers' lives or succumbing to the Feminine Mystique, many young feminists saw domesticity as a trap.[24] Whether or not they ended up as mothers, some future feminists early developed an aversion to child rearing. Paula Weideger, a feminist who never had children, reveals with exceptional clarity why so many young future feminists badmouthed motherhood during the early years of the movement:

> The desire to have children, along with good feelings about motherhood, were buried because women were so scared. They were afraid they would turn out like their own mothers, most of whom were housewives and housewives only. Women like me who grew up in the 1950's had been made edgy and claustrophobic by the narrowness of the life laid out for them from birth. To give mother-feeling any place in your heart might mean being lost to mothering forever—or at least "till the kids are grown."[25]

Anna Quindlen, a *New York Times* columnist who has frequently written about her children and family life, felt the same way: "When I was growing up, motherhood was a kind of cage. . . . You stayed home and felt your mind turn to the stuff that you put in little bowls and tried to spoon into little mouths and eventually wound up wiping off of little floors. . . . By the time I was a grown-up, the answer, if you were strong and smart and wanted to be somebody, was not to be a mom. I certainly didn't want to be one."[26]

Not all young feminists felt that way. Many already had children or wanted large families. Even so, they were determined to avoid the plight of the housewife—somehow. Those who politicized their rejection of what Friedan had dubbed "the happy housewife" understood that their survival as an autonomous individual required separation from the world of their mothers.

TELL ME WHAT'S WRONG

Alienated sons and daughters commonly described their parents' lives as empty, hypocritical, frustrated, and unreal.[27] Why should a sense of the unreal have plagued a generation of educated young Americans during the late fifties and early sixties?

As they came of age, the young of the fifties contemplated a society whose values were shifting rapidly, perhaps faster than many could assimilate. There were good reasons for young people to wonder where reality resided. The consumer culture accelerated so fast in the post–World War II years that reality and illusion often seemed to blur, leaving the "self" more than ever a hollow vessel to be "filled and refilled according to the expectations of others and the needs of the moment."[28] The consumer culture glorified personal fulfillment, challenging traditional obligations to family and community. Affluence, however modest, sheltered bright young people from the nasty underside of life. A fractured culture idealized sentimental and chaste love but increasingly exploited sex as an adjunct to consumption. (As young people, moreover, war babies and baby boomers could not see that their collective energy and economic clout only accelerated the sexualization of the culture.) Much of this generation reached their early teens before they watched television. The discrepancy between their own experience and television's idealized families probably helped contribute to a sense of the "unreal." Political menace—communism, the Korean War—was supposed to be acute but was, despite the efforts of Senator Joseph R. McCarthy and coinquisitors, remote and therefore eerie. Corporate culture, gobbling up small businesses, rewarded teamwork and conformity in a society that still worshiped individual initiative: more eeriness. And over all of this hung the threat that the cold war might turn hot, that the Bomb, in the flash of an instant, might incinerate reality beyond recognition.

At such moments, the disenchanted young often search for intellectual, cultural, and political mentors. Unfortunately, much of what educators offered only deepened youth's sense of the "unreal." With few notable exceptions, both popular and scholarly commentators exuded an upbeat intellectual consensus that celebrated American greatness and unanimity.[29] Here and there, dissenting notes invaded the celebration. Forceful critics dissected conformity, analyzed power relations, and exposed rampant inequality, racial injustice, and the preparations for war. Critics red-baited them, denounced them as fellow travelers or bleeding heart liberals, and, in the spirit of the decade, dismissed them as "eggheads."[30] But a dissenting tradition survived and affirmed young people's inchoate sense that something was profoundly wrong in America. Many of these readers, as it turned out, would later become leaders of the New Left.[31]

The disenchanted sons and daughters of the fifties had a growing body of dissident literature to help them articulate and comprehend their growing sense of alienation. But most of the literature, written by men, failed to address young women's specific identity needs. From the French existentialists, especially Jean Paul Sartre and Albert Camus, they learned that there was dignity in the absurdity of many situations, that meaninglessness could be transcended through political commitment. From David Riesman's *The Lonely Crowd* (1950) they learned how American men had forsaken authentic selves, evolving into "outer-directed" persons who learned to match their inner needs to external expectations. C. Wright Mills, the great intellectual iconoclast on a motorcycle, lamented in *White Collar* (1951) the sales mentality of the new middle class and in *The Power Elite* (1956) that self-perpetuating ruling groups managed and manipulated the nation irresponsibly. William Whyte's *The Organization Man* (1956) deepened young men's fears of ending up as dispensable cogs in the corporate machinery. Kenneth Galbraith's *The Affluent Society* (1958) indicted the starvation of public services. Paul Goodman, in *Growing Up Absurd* (1956), confirmed young men's suspicions that they had inherited an empty world. Vance Packard, in *The Hidden Persuaders* (1957), exposed Madison Avenue's efforts to manipulate American consumers. Ironically, Daniel Bell proclaimed the "exhaustion" of political ideas in *The End of Ideology* (1961), just as Michael Harrington's *The Other America* (1962) and Rachel Carson's *Silent Spring* (1962) began providing intellectual ammunition for the future war on poverty and the ecology movement.[32]

For alienated sons, popular as well as oppositional culture began to offer up models of male rebellion. Few could forget Holden Caulfield, J. D. Salinger's hero in *Catcher in the Rye* (1956). From his psychiatric captivity, the sensitive Holden condemned a society held hostage to materialism. Searching for an authentic self, Holden dreamed of catching little children as they ran off a cliff. To the elders of the baby boom generation, Allen Ginsberg's shrieking poem *Howl* (1956) against Moloch, America's God of materialism, resonated deeply; Jack Kerouac's *On the Road* (1957) fired fantasies of sex, drugs, and adventures. On the road, cut loose from crabgrass and family responsibilities, a man took what he needed, indulged his appetite, and freed himself from the responsibilities of conventional marriage and fatherhood.

Playboy, first published in 1953, offered yet another alternative to familial responsibility. Hugh Hefner's "playboy philosophy" encouraged bachelors— for the first time in American history—to enjoy a satisfying sexual life without supporting a wife, children, and home. For the upscale single man, an elaborately appointed apartment—complete with revolving bed, rotating lovers, and reflecting mirrors—furnished all the sex but none of the burdens of family. In *Death of a Salesman* (1949), Willy Loman had to live a Sisyphean life as a salesman in order to support a nagging wife and unappreciative children. In the film *Rebel Without a Cause* (1955), James Dean popularized the sensitive and brooding young man who, taking the comforts of suburban life for granted, inarticulately searches for something "real," even if the search results in tragedy.[33]

Male freedom, then, meant cutting loose from women and children—hardly a new theme in American culture. As Leslie Fiedler has observed in *Love and Death in the American Novel* (1960), American men have always equated freedom with escape from the drab duties of home and community. For young men determined to avoid the world of their fathers, freedom meant avoiding the ties that bind. True, only a tiny number of American men followed the Beats into coffeehouses or onto the road, and even fewer had the guts or money to imitate Hugh Hefner's sybaritic bachelor lifestyle. Still, as the alienated sons of the fifties entered the sixties, they had before them personal models of revolt, intellectual analyses of their alienation, prophetic mentors, and fantasies of a way out, if only they dared.

Young alienated women also searched for mentors. They read the same criticism, saw the same films, and danced to the same music. Like their male counterparts, they embraced jazz or rock and roll—both derived from black music—in defiance of their parents' loyalties to the blandness of American pop music. Like educated women before them, however, they lived in a dual culture, experiencing life as women but learning to interpret the world as men. They read critiques of the dominant culture through men's eyes, learned to view society's failures through men's needs, and avoided acting like the nagging domestic women free-spirited men condemned.

In the short run, men's social criticism and models of rebellion short-circuited young women's need to confront their own cultural matriphobia and their specific existential need to develop autonomous female identities. Many years later, feminists wondered how they had ever missed the blatant misogyny expressed by these male mentors. Still, men's critique of conformity and family life had a powerful and positive long-term impact on young women. However inappropriate or inadequate, the fifties literary and cultural tradition taught dissident young women vital lessons. They inspired dreams of freedom, unleashed a critical distrust of authority, and encouraged a taste for the unconventional—all of which created the necessary consciousness for a feminism that would question all received wisdom. This criticism was indispensable. Applying it to their own situation would take place later, after they had discovered—and created—feminist critiques of their own condition.

In the meantime, as educated women living in a dual culture, they learned to see their freedom and justice through men's eyes. When the solution did not exactly fit, they learned to blame themselves for insufficient daring, insufficient learning, insufficient radicalism.

Where could young women look for answers? For many middle-class women, college provided the first real opportunity for intellectual exploration.[34] The percentage of women aged twenty-five to twenty-nine who had completed high school rose from 55 percent in 1950 to 82 percent in 1975. In 1950, 102,631 women earned bachelor's degrees and 643 graduated with doctorates. Ten years later, the respective numbers were 138,677 and 1,028. By 1970, 341,276 women graduated with bachelor's degrees and 3,976 earned doctorates.[35]

Growing affluence and changing cultural mores allowed an increasing number of young women to leave their families and experience the greater sexual and social freedoms offered by campus life. Equally important, college provided young women with opportunities to take their minds seriously. No matter how condescending the professors, no matter how mocking the male students, university life provided greater freedom and equality than marriage or entry into the labor force. College offered the leisure to reflect on the culture's sins, to embrace new artistic and political ideas, and to experiment with sex. "Probably never before in human history," Richard Flacks reflected, "has a society brought together such a large number of potential dissidents . . . under conditions that so greatly facilitated their mutual influence."[36] Such relative equality, as Gloria Steinem later noted, made organizing college women very difficult. Unlike men, educated women frequently grew more radical with age. It was when they married or entered the labor force that young women confronted the truth of their sexual subordination.[37] In college, they also gained a sense of entitlement—to be taken seriously, to be respected, to be treated as equals, which, for many young women, had both a class and a gender dimension.

Later, the media would describe all feminists as white middle-class women. They were not wholly wrong. But the media's perception was only partial; appearances sometimes deceive. The movement naturally grew from this educated and privileged constituency. After all, this constituency was primarily addressing and articulating problems as white middle-class women experienced them. But I am also convinced, from my own experience and from interviews with so many participants in the women's movement, that some unknowable but large percentage of feminists who joined the early women's liberation movement in fact grew up in white working-class homes, many of them second-generation immigrants.[38] Often they were the first children in their families to enter college. As they mingled with middle-class students, they soon acquired the social confidence, verbal skills, and appearance to mask their working-class background. With these changes came a growing sense that they were entitled to the equality commensurate with their middle-class status.

Such well-known feminist leaders and writers as Betty Friedan, Ellen Willis, Marge Piercy, Susan Griffin, Alta, and Alix Kate Shulman, to name but a few, grew up in working-class homes but developed their talents and sense of injustice through higher education. As one feminist recalled, she entered college concerned above all with achieving middle-class status. As soon as she gained that security, however, it was only a matter of time before she was struck by her subordinate status as a woman.[39] By the time the women's movement erupted in the late sixties, many feminists spoke, wrote, dressed, and otherwise acted like middle-class women. They first crossed class lines, gained a sense of middle-class entitlement from their education, and only afterward turned their attention to the "woman question."

THE SEXUAL END RUN: THE BEATS AND SWINGING SINGLES

During and after college, a small number of future feminists found in the Beats a tantalizing revolt against the Feminine Mystique. Allen Ginsberg's shrieking incantation against Moloch and Kerouac's seductive tales of life on the road titillated young women along with young men. Here was the alternative to life with an apron or, for that matter, an attaché case. The Beats provided no map to transcendent experience; this was precisely their attraction. Instead, the Beats romanticized spontaneous unpredictability.

In 1959 Marilyn Coffey, who later became a sixties activist, was twenty-two years old, an aspiring writer juggling headlines for the society page of the *Evening Journal* in Lincoln, Nebraska, a city she regarded as "the epitome of hypocrisy and sterile living: I was a member of the so-called Silent Generation and silent many of us were, back in the fifties, in the aftermath of Joe McCarthy and the Korean war. Speechless. A strange condition for a woman who aspired to be a writer." Then, Jack Kerouac's *On the Road* somehow fell into her hands:

> I didn't understand half what I was reading, but something of the life being described was comprehensive to me, foreign as it was to the young woman who'd been born and bred in the conservative Midwest. . . . The words shot through me like a fusillade of bullets. I was undone, a changed person. I bought myself a straw-covered bottle of Chianti, a candle, and a pad of paper . . . began to write by candlelight, scribbling words onto paper as fast as my hand could compose, following instinctively Kerouac's model of Spontaneous Prose. . . . The novel liberated me as it did many others of my generation. There was that instantaneous recognition of self. For the first

time since I began writing . . . I felt free to say anything I wanted. . . . For I, in those blissfully naive pre-feminist days, felt the equal of any man."

Coffey fled to Denver, "where, in the Greyhound Bus Depot, I twirled a girlfriend, eyes closed, arm extended, in front of a gigantic map of the United States. She pointed and we set off."[40]

For some future feminists, the Beats proved irresistible. Especially on both coasts, adventuresome young women made open breaks with family and community. Throughout the late fifties and early sixties, thousands of black-attired high school and college-aged young women descended upon New York's Greenwich Village and San Francisco's North Beach in search of "meaningful" poetry, folk music and art, and, not unimportantly, sexual adventures.[41]

The Beats did not attract most future feminists: most were too young or too old. Many more future feminists spent their high school and college years cheering football teams, joining sororities, and planning their domestic futures. But for those born before and during the war, as well as the elders of the baby boom, bohemian life created the first opportunity to cast oneself as a misfit, to revel in social disapproval, to elevate a subculture over the dominant culture—all of which proved invaluable assets to female activists in later movements. As one sixties feminist later wrote: "Our adult lives began born out of these fragments of stolen consciousness. The basic awareness grew that truth, whatever it was, was something we had all our lives been protected from. Reality had been kept in quarantine so we could not become contaminated."[42] By living a bohemian existence, some daughters of the fifties voluntarily chose to end that quarantine.

While some young women imitated the Beats through fashion and unconventional behavior, a few women actually broke into the inner sacred circle. In a critical and thoughtful memoir of her experience as Jack Kerouac's girlfriend, Joyce Johnson described herself and other female Beats as "minor characters" on a stage reserved mainly for men. Already at age sixteen, the talented and intellectually ambitious Johnson observed that "just as girls guarded their virginity, the boys guarded something less tangible which they called Themselves. They seemed to believe they had a mission in life, from which they could easily be deflected by being exposed to too much emotion."[43]

After she became Kerouac's lover, Johnson observed the same pattern among Kerouac and his pals. She represented the anchorage he needed, when he wanted it, but with no strings attached. Kerouac, whose life alternated between the open road and his mother's home, dropped in on Johnson for short reunions. She rarely demanded more; hip culture ridiculed commitment as uncool. Men defined freedom and if women wanted more, they had to drop their "bourgeois hangups." Between their adventures, the men survived by "scuffling"—living off others—and working only when absolutely necessary. Their great accomplishment, remembers Johnson, "was to avoid actual employment for as long as possible and by whatever means. But it was all right for women to go out and earn wages, since they had no important creative endeavors to be distracted from. The women didn't mind, or, if they did, they never said—not until years later."

What attracted Johnson to Kerouac and his friends were their spiritual adventures, "some pursuit of the heightened moment, intensity for its own sake." This, she disappointingly learned, was "something they apparently find only when they're with each other." Some, like Ginsberg, proclaimed the joy of homosexual love, and some just preferred male buddyship to heterosexual romance. Looking back, Johnson could no longer ignore the truth that women and drugs were necessary for the heightened moment, but not for full partnership. Viewed as spoilsports, women symbolized commercial materialism, the chains that bind. For men who created the world of the Beats, concluded Johnson, "I think it was about the right to remain children."[44]

True enough. But Johnson also faithfully records the many freedoms that "minor characters" enjoyed as well. The absence of men's economic and emotional commitment also freed women from daily subordination to male authority. Because the men "scuffled," women like Johnson early achieved a sense of social and economic independence. Moreover, female Beats did gain partial entry into an intellectual fellowship mostly reserved for men. No other cultural niche permitted a woman to enjoy such unconventional intellectual and sexual experiences—academic women needed to appear asexual; Hollywood sex symbols had to appear stupid. Within the limits of a male-defined aesthetic of freedom, women like Joyce Johnson revitalized a bohemian ideal of female sexual independence, which, spread by the mid-sixties sexual revolution, infused the counterculture as well as the New Left.

Most young college women, of course, never took up the unconventional life of the Beats; they married. But another noticeable minority began carving out a less exotic alternative lifestyle as singles working in large cities. By the late fifties and early sixties, a growing number of college-educated women began migrating to large urban areas. Lured by the promise of adventure and excitement, they worked as airline stewardesses, teachers, social workers, editorial assistants, or office workers, filling the thousands of new clerical and secretarial office jobs created by expanding corporate and state bureaucracies. After a few years of adventure, most young women probably expected to marry. In the meantime, they survived by sharing apartments with other single women and socialized in the singles subculture that their very numbers created.

Single women had worked in cities for two centuries. What distinguished these young women was that they lived neither at home nor in boarding-houses, the rules governing their social life being those of self-preservation. Just as important, working women's wages had achieved a greater purchasing power. Some moved casually from one sexual encounter to another, without anyone's disapproval, indeed, often without anyone's knowledge. As the authors of *Re-Making Love* have argued, "for young, single heterosexual women in the fifties and sixties, the city held forth an entirely new vision of female sexual possibility—and the first setting for a sexual revolution."[45]

Unlike the exotic enclaves of the Beats, the embryonic "swinging singles" subculture at first captured little public attention. When Helen Gurley Brown published her controversial *Sex and the Single Girl* in 1962, however, Americans got their first peek at a trend already in the making: the sexually liberated world of single working women. Without much fanfare, single working women had gradually changed their sexual behavior and no longer regarded premarital sex as taboo.

Brown's lighthearted advocacy of the single life became a national best-seller. Like Betty Friedan, whose *Feminine Mystique* appeared a year later, Brown addressed realities that had been kept under wraps during the fifties. Unlike Friedan, who encouraged married women to combine motherhood with a career, Brown urged single women to postpone or skip marriage altogether and still enjoy a fulfilling sexual life.

Brown's ideas mirrored Hugh Hefner's playboy philosophy by trying to legitimize sex for unmarried women. Few single women in the early sixties may have preferred the swinging single life to marriage. But while they waited, Brown gave them permission to enjoy themselves. In large cities, she contended, "there is something else a girl can say and frequently does when a man 'insists' and that is 'yes.' . . . Nice girls *do* have affairs, and they do not necessarily die of them." Married couples could keep their diapers and crabgrass. For the single man or woman, Hefner and Brown promised a sybaritic and hedonistic lifestyle.[46]

Like women attached to the Beats, swinging singles made a temporary end run around the Feminine Mystique by not marrying. But they too discovered that a fundamental gender inequality undercut their seemingly liberated lifestyle. Affairs with married men often brought loneliness and disappointment. Since they earned less than men, single women had trouble supporting their lifestyle. Unlike single men, unmarried women's value depreciated as they aged. If they waited too long, they risked ending up with no husband at all. And if they wanted children, they ran up against a biological clock that only infrequently influenced men's decisions. Without perfect contraception or legal abortions, women literally risked their lives if they became pregnant.

Despite these difficulties and disappointments, single working women accelerated and expanded women's social freedom, not by politicizing their behavior, but simply by living and asserting their right to enjoy sex.[47]

The lifestyles of both female Beats and urban singles emphasized sexual emancipation rather than a redefinition of marriage and motherhood. Growing numbers of unmarried women began to stake out their right to enjoy sex for pleasure rather than for procreation. In 1960, when the U.S. government approved the use of the birth control pill, the sexual revolution shifted into high gear. As some women later discovered, sex without commitment could lead to unbridled sexual exploitation. For now, though, those who rebelled defined their liberty in terms of sexual experimentation, happy to explore the pleasures of the body, thrilled to leave behind fears of pregnancy, tantalized by the belief that "free love" could destroy the Feminine Mystique.

Yet however much single women rebelled, the Feminine Mystique, seemingly engraved in concrete, still governed life *after* marriage. As growing numbers of young women privately bridled against a domestic future, many felt inarticulate, devoid of a language with which to express their inchoate yearnings. The fifties provided no vision of what constituted freedom for an adult married woman.

BEYOND THE SEXUAL SOLUTION

Where could they look for answers? Before Betty Friedan or Helen Gurley Brown, there was only Simone de Beauvoir. Her classic study of *The Second Sex*, published in France in 1949, made its way across the Atlantic by 1953 and quickly gained national attention.[48] As Jean Paul Sartre's lifelong but unmarried companion, de Beauvoir had already generated considerable curiosity, if only for the café-bohemian life she and Sartre popularized in postwar Paris. Her refusal to marry and her decision to remain childless provoked controversy but also appealed to young women wary of domesticity.

In retrospect, *The Second Sex* was an astonishingly subversive piece of writing. At a time when the world's industrial societies still assumed that women belonged at home, de Beauvoir countered that woman's fate was created, not inherent. Without apology, she attacked the myth of blissful domesticity, describing marriage as servitude and housework as unrelenting drudgery "comparable to the punishment of Sisyphus." Criticizing the cult of sentimental motherhood, de Beauvoir argued that pregnancy and maternity were often as enslaving as they were enriching. Maternal devotion, she wrote, "may be lived out in perfect authenticity, but this is rarely so."[49]

A central paradox wove itself through *The Second Sex*. To document female subordination, de Beauvoir relentlessly described the range of economic, social, and psychological obstacles that ground women down. At the same time, she insisted upon woman's freedom to create her own destiny. How did she reconcile this apparent contradiction? She did not. The very nature of existentialist philosophy stood in her way. Existentialism enshrined individual choice, not collective action. Born with no predetermined position, each individual faced the terrifying aloneness of his or her existence as well as the responsibility of freedom. Women were free, therefore, to create their own destiny; if they avoided making choices, they collaborated in their loss of freedom and were guilty of "bad faith." For herself, de Beauvoir chose a life freed of the usual domestic burdens. But practically, she offered no solution to women in general. She presumed that as women grew enlightened about their situation, they would gain the capacity to make choices about their freedom.

De Beauvoir was too politically astute to let individual choice suffice. At the end of her book, she lamely argued that socialism would free women. With the collectivization of housework and child care, women would gain the economic freedom to create their own fate. Later, when she declared herself a feminist in 1972 and became an enthusiastic supporter of the French women's movement, de Beauvoir reconsidered her conclusion and asserted that socialism without feminism would not transform women's subordination.

Though many women admit that they never finished de Beauvoir's weighty tome, *The Second Sex* had a profound and lasting influence on many of its readers. Alice Schwarzer, a West German writer who later interviewed de Beauvoir, speaks for many women of her generation: "In the darkness of the Fifties and Sixties before the new women's movement dawned, *The Second Sex* was like a secret code that we emerging women used to send messages to each other."[50]

A professor of philosophy at Ohio Weslyan University first introduced Mary King, a future civil rights activist and feminist, to de Beauvoir's thought. In 1963 King and Casey Hayden, two of the most prominent white women in the Student Nonviolent Coordinating Committee, worked as organizers in southwestern Atlanta. They spent evenings reading and discussing Doris Lessing's *The Golden Notebook* (1962) and de Beauvoir's *The Second Sex*. In her memoir, Mary King recalled: "Casey and I had an insatiable appetite for these two authors and especially for de Beauvoir's global perspective." What especially influenced them was the "fundamental existential belief that the human race is responsible for its own destiny," an idea that deepened and reinforced their tireless efforts for civil rights. But de Beauvoir's influence went even further. From her philosophy and novels, Hayden and King—central figures in starting the women's movement—gained startling revelations about their position as women. "Our copy of Beauvoir's *The Second Sex*," wrote King, "was underlined, creased, marked up, and finally coverless from our study of it." Eager to spread the message, they began circulating the exhilarating idea that women could define themselves.[51]

When *The Second Sex* was published in the United States in 1953, anticommunism and antifeminism were at a peak. Nevertheless, educated women quickly discovered the book and passed it on to friends; gradually de Beauvoir's ideas trickled into the margins of American intellectual life. For some women, de Beauvoir's work represented pure heresy, properly banned by papal authority. To others, the emphasis on French women's experiences seemed too remote and irrelevant to American women's lives. But dedicated thousands felt that they had been struck by the truth and dated their transformed consciousness to the discovery of this one book. As feminist writer Susan Griffin explained, "I read de Beauvoir in 1961 and was never the same. Every time I think we have discovered some new idea, I go back and find that de Beauvoir saw it first, that we often are reinventing what she first revealed."[52]

De Beauvoir was not the first person to write of women's subordination; ever since antiquity women have been writing about the woman question. She was the first, however, to address modern women's dilemma—the fact that they possess basic political rights but suffer extreme cultural, social, and economic marginality; and she was the first to provide a theoretical foundation for the marginality that modern women still experience.

Her work was not without flaws. She made universal claims based on the experience of French (and, as it turns out, her perception of American) girls and women. She wistfully predicted that socialism by itself would end female oppression. Her insistence on existential freedom, a luxury of the privileged, ignored the powerful constraints of class and race, as well as those of religion and global politics. Her emphasis on individual choice ignored a movement's needs for solidarity and collective advancement. She failed to see that women do in fact have a history, thereby ignoring women's historic efforts to transcend their condition, as well as the world around them.[53] By describing woman as the Other, she reified woman's role as victim and failed to imagine her as activist. And, as younger feminists and later biographies would discover, she underemphasized the inequalities in her alliance with Sartre.[54]

Despite such limitations and imperfections, de Beauvoir had issued a brilliant and daring analysis of women's condition: "One is not born, but rather one becomes, a woman: no biological, psychological or economic fate determines the figure that the human female presents in society."[55] With these few words, de Beauvoir elegantly challenged received traditional ideas about woman's nature and exposed the artificial construction of gender. She encouraged women to see themselves and their world through their own eyes. Her detailed description of women's socialization, as well as the example she set in her own life, made personal life the setting for high drama. Through her writing and personal example, she taught a generation of young admirers the political implications of seemingly private matters. For young intellectual women, she combined a bohemian sexual freedom with serious intellectual commitment. Though she frequently gave inadequate answers, she asked the right questions, creating a formidable intellectual agenda for a new generation of feminists.

VOICES OF INSPIRATION

Only a small and elite group of young women read de Beauvoir during the fifties and early sixties. The voices that most influenced the alienated daughters of the fifties were not those who challenged women's place, but those who questioned the danger of the Bomb and race relations.

As they matured, Zane's generation and the baby boom elders began to make peace a pressing issue. Here was an important symbol of the generational divide. For most parents, the atomic bomb had mercifully ended a ghastly war. To their children, it had ushered in the threat of planetary holocaust. For this generation, raised in the aftermath of Hiroshima and Nagasaki, the mushroom cloud cast a long shadow on childhood and adolescence.[56]

Daughters of the fifties first learned about peace protest from adult women. Many recall their mothers or other women protesting the danger of strontium 90—a by-product of nuclear testing—poisoning their children's milk. As a radioactive cloud from a Russian nuclear test hung over the United States, fear of nuclear fallout intensified some citizens' desire for a test-ban treaty. Suddenly, seemingly out of nowhere, an estimated fifty thousand women in over sixty cities walked out of their homes in a one-day nationwide strike on November 1, 1961. The group had been organized by five women who had met in the Committee for a Sane Nuclear Policy (SANE) but had grown weary of what they judged to be that group's ineffective bureaucratic and lobbying tactics. They determined to take direct action against the nuclear threat, called themselves Women Strike for Peace, and, in the process, created an example of protest for younger women.[57]

The civil rights movement also profoundly influenced daughters of the fifties. Little Rock, Selma, Montgomery, the Freedom Rides, Greensboro—all these battles dramatized a young generation of brave activists challenging the country to live up to its ideals. As they came of age, future feminists admired the courage of those who fought desegregation. Even more, they learned that race relations, once regarded as "natural," could, through collective protest, be fundamentally altered.[58]

But neither the peace nor the civil rights movement resolved the female generation gap. As they entered the sixties, daughters of the fifties had no clear vision of their future and frequently felt caught in contradictory expectations. Permissive parents and higher education raised their expectations, but the Feminine Mystique still haunted many daughters' desires for an emancipated life. An increasingly sexualized culture promoted the illusory hope that sexual freedom might snatch them from the jaws of suburban marriage. In cities, bohemian enclaves and the new singles culture offered intellectual and sexual adventures. But this temporary respite from marriage and domesticity also required women to forfeit claims for love and commitment. None of these solutions, moreover, showed young women how to create a life as an independent woman who also bore children.

The resurrection of a peace movement, the moral drama of the civil rights movement, and the rediscovery of poverty gave new legitimacy to questioning authority and challenging adults' interpretation of the world. As liberal Americans began redirecting their attention toward problems neglected for more than a decade, they helped inflate the idealistic expectations of a generation just coming of age. Immersion in the student and New Left movements politicized young women's lives but still did not reveal how to create a self that could survive family life.

What they lacked was knowledge, a feminist awareness of their own situation. As Gerda Lerner has argued in *The Creation of Feminist Consciousness*, it is women's lack of education, especially their knowledge of women's history, that has led them to reinvent feminism over and over again.[59] Such was the case with the daughters of the fifties. Without a feminist consciousness, daughters of the fifties mostly learned dissent from others. The critical literature of the fifties furnished them with a fresh critique of conformity and materialism, but not with a feminist analysis of their own condition.

Still young at the dawn of the sixties, future feminists carried their unarticulated and unresolved cultural matriphobia into college, bohemian adventures, love affairs, marriage, the civil rights movement, antiwar activities, and the New Left. Haunted by their own private demons, they lived a parallel generation gap until the second half of the sixties, when their female generation gap, fueled by a decade of social activism and a reinvented analysis of women's condition, turned into the contemporary feminist movement.

CHAPTER 15 : THE MAKING OF

BLACK WOMEN IN AMERICA: AN HISTORICAL ENCYCLOPEDIA

DARLENE CLARK HINE

*B*lack Women in America: An Historical Encyclopedia (1993), which I
edited in collaboration with Elsa Barkley Brown and Rosalyn
Terborg-Penn, is 1,530 pages long. Its two volumes contain 640
biographical entries and 143 topical essays. In creating the *Encyclopedia*, my coeditors and I brought into existence a wide-ranging body of
research and reference materials. These provide the essential elements of our
quest for the acceptance of black women's history as a legitimate area of
scholarly study. The *Encyclopedia*'s existence challenges contemporary historians of every field and has profound implications for the future research,
writing, and analysis of women's history, of African American history, and of
American history in general. This essay lays out the evolution of my thinking
as editor and emphasizes what I believe are some of the broader ramifications
of this project. I share the belief Gerda Lerner articulated in her major works
on the creation of patriarchy and the rise of feminist consciousness: when
women control their past they will control their future.

To make an encyclopedia is to claim a historiographical moment. An
encyclopedia of black women not only exposes the state of black women's
history, it also suggests the issues, themes, and individuals still in need of
exploration and analysis. Twenty years ago, for example, few people wrote
about the role of black women in the civil rights movement. Only now are Ella

Baker, Fannie Lou Hamer, and Jo Ann Gibson Robinson receiving biographical treatment. Twenty years ago it would have been impossible to write an extended essay on the slavery experience of black women. Today several scholars are working on books on the subject. A virtual revolution had to take place in African American history, in women's history, and in the new social history before black women historians could claim the voice and space for their subjects who warrant a hearing at the bar of history.

This is the revolution in which the *Encyclopedia* participates. When Ralph Carlson, president of Carlson Publishing, first approached me with the suggestion that I edit an encyclopedia on the history of black women, I turned him down. I had gone down that road before. Back in 1980, Shirley Herd, an Indianapolis public school teacher and president of the Indianapolis section of the National Council of Negro Women (NCNW), had asked me to write a history of black women in Indiana for her organization. When I told Herd that I knew nothing about black women's history and had never taken any courses on the subject, she was nonplussed. "You are a black woman? You are a historian?" she rejoined. "You mean to tell me that you can't put those two things together and write us a history of black women in Indiana?"

Herd's questions disconcerted me and eventually prompted me to connect my biography with my profession, to forge an integrated identity that equally emphasized my race, gender, and work. My immediate response to her challenge was to write *When the Truth Is Told: A History of Black Women's Culture and Community in Indiana, 1875-1950* (1981). The long-term impact of our relationship and my ensuing work with literally hundreds of community black women was to raise my consciousness and forever to transform my scholarship to focus more specifically on issues of the intersection of race, gender, and class.

After completing *When the Truth Is Told*, I suffered pangs of conscience due to the fact that all the primary documents—the letters, diaries, club minutes, institutional records, and photographs that Herd and the members of the NCNW Indianapolis section had so painstakingly collected—were returned to their original donors. These records had enabled me to write the book, but now they were dispersed and difficult to retrieve. Many future historians would not have the benefit of this material; the lives, deeds, and contributions of black women in Indiana might never find a way into future constructions of the state's history.

To promote the regional study of black women's history, I launched the Black Women in the Middle West archival creation project, securing a $150,000 grant from the National Endowment for the Humanities (NEH). I will always remember how difficult it was to persuade NEH to fund this effort in the face of reviewers' objections. At least one reviewer asserted that black women had never done anything; if they had, they would already be in the history books. Their absence demonstrated that they had done nothing worthy of historical note. As Shirley Herd, Patrick Bidelman, a white male historian colleague at Purdue University, and I wrestled with these simpleminded reservations, I began to question the meaning of history. Fortunately, James Early, a black male program officer, strongly supported the project and eventually prevailed upon NEH officers to grant us a portion of the funds we requested.

Two years of intense work with the 1,200 participants in the Black Women in the Middle West Project aggravated my discomfort with American history. The very process of reclaiming the past records and documents of ignored, excluded, distorted, and stereotyped black women in Indiana and Illinois taught me valuable lessons about the power of history and the politics of historical construction. I had asked, for the first time, who decided what events or individuals are important in history, worthy of consideration and investigation? By the same token, I wondered about the psychological and political damage done to those destined never to see their lives or contributions reflected in official chronicles of America's past. I fretted long and hard over the effects and processes of historical black disfranchisement or disempowerment.

By the time Carlson called, a decade after Herd's call, I had written a book on the history of black women in the nursing profession. I had completed the Black Women in the Middle West Project and successfully gathered and created archives. I was catching my breath from editing a sixteen-volume series that contained 248 articles and essays, 5 previously unpublished dissertations, and a collection of conference papers on black women in the civil rights movement, which Carlson had just published.

Do not get me wrong. I was in no way sanguine about the status and progress of black women's history. It still rankled when some white women and black male historians routinely failed to include discussion of black women in their articles, monographs, and surveys, rationalizing that appropriate and accessible material did not exist to allow them to do so. Although black women historians had published several noteworthy books and biographies, they remained, with a few exceptions, uncited and ignored. In fact, I and other black women historians still witness too many slightly raised eyebrows in the profession when we admit that our concern is black women's history. The feeling lingers that black women's experiences and lives scarcely warrant distinct and separate treatment. Many believe that black women's history is more appropriately subsumed either under black history or women's history. Much intellectual and political work remains to be done before this area of study approaches maturity. I share a sense of the urgency that grips all of us who are engaged in its pursuits and who embrace the power of history.

For six months Ralph Carlson kept after me until finally I agreed to take on the encyclopedia. I had refused for so long, less because I doubted the importance or value of the project than because the idea of editing an encyclopedia of this magnitude and complexity was downright intimidating. To produce an encyclopedia is to create a system of meaning. Having been a veteran of earlier projects in black women's history, I feared that the sheer intellectual scope, physical labor, and endless judgment calls would eventually overwhelm me.

Gradually, through conversations with Carlson, I formed a vision of the *Encyclopedia*. I knew that it had to be as inclusive as possible. We had to pay attention to regionality, class, and individual differences while simultaneously educating the general public as to the culture of struggle and resistance that sustains all black women in America. It would not be enough to underscore the victimization of black women. Such emphasis was indeed warranted: the reality of race, class, and sexual oppression and exploitation daily dog the lives of too many black women. Yet this three-hundred-year-long history, full of good solid drama, achievement, and transcendent truths, should also empower those who take the time to study the past and generate appropriate respect for the lives and worth of black women.

Initially, because I was so utterly daunted by the challenge of an encyclopedia on black women, I questioned Ralph Carlson's motivations and persistence. What, beyond profit, could motivate a white male publisher's interest in and willingness to tackle such a monumental project? Whatever the answer, and frankly I do not believe it was purely for profit, I doubt that Carlson imagined the magnitude of the financial and personnel resources it would require. He remained convinced that the sixteen-volume series had only heightened the need for a major reference work on black women, a source that would contain accurate, accessible information about the lives and contributions of hundreds of nationally and locally known black women. Carlson also confided that he had always wanted to show his support of the women's movement and now he could do so by publishing this work. When I pressed him, he added, "They deserve it." Perhaps he had undergone his own intellectual odyssey. Of course, I shared Carlson's conviction that a truly comprehensive, compellingly written, accessible historical encyclopedia of black women replete with hundreds of biographical and topical essays and with stunning photographs would energize my colleagues and suggest enough potential dissertation topics to sustain several generations of researchers and scholars. I had drawn considerable inspiration and intellectual sustenance from Gerda Lerner's documentary volume, *Black Women in White America* (1972), when I began working in the field.

Before describing the actual process of developing the *Encyclopedia*, I would like to reflect on the problematics of black women's history and open up some of the lessons I had learned from a decade of working in the area. Black women's unique experiences and distinct angle of vision enabled them collectively and individually to fashion a worldview, to create their own meaning systems and estimations of what constituted beauty, culture, and respectability. Over the years, black women had assembled an arsenal of womanist strategies ranging from a "culture of dissemblance" to a deep spiritualism that enabled them to reject at least some of the prevalent self-damaging notions of black inferiority. These internal strengths aided their determination to shatter demeaning stereotypes that limited their access to educational and employment opportunities. The determination to reimagine themselves was a serious, unrelenting battle that continues to this day.

Mobility is another critical dimension of black women's lives that warrants much greater attention than it has yet received. Both during and after slavery black women dared to flee situations that dehumanized them. Many of the early free black women inhabitants of the Middle West, for example, were escaped slaves or daughters of women who had risked their lives to secure freedom for them. After emancipation, black women, in numbers that increased with each passing decade, left their southern homes with and without families to escape rape, the threat of rape, and domestic violence, and to secure better education and jobs. Indeed, it was the plight of poor, single, migrating black women who landed on the inhospitable streets of Detroit, Cleveland, Chicago, Philadelphia, New York, and other northern and middle western cities that motivated settled black matrons to open working girls' homes, training schools in domestic arts, and other agencies to rescue them from sexual exploitation and prostitution. The processes of migration and urbanization required that black women redouble their efforts to create and sustain the separate parallel institutional infrastructure that they had established in the South in the decades following emancipation and the entrenchment of segregation. Black women, in sum, brought a whole lot more with them on their trek north than their bodies. They carried with them the knowledge of how to organize and build community.

New knowledge has led black women historians to become increasingly attentive to questions about the inner lives of black women and the ways in which interior consciousness intersects with and is shaped by external community needs. Three questions guide current research: What is the relationship between black women and the black community? What is the relationship between black women and the institutions in the community that ensures the survival and progress of black people? How have these relationships changed over time as reflected in differing gender roles and expectations?

Apparently to protect their interior lives, to maintain self-esteem and dignity, black women sought refuge in myriad ways. At pivotal moments in history, they withdrew behind their men, or they joined with women relatives, friends, and club members or submerged themselves into their communities. When forced to encounter whites most black women, with significant exceptions such as Ida Wells Barnett, adhered to the "culture of dissemblance." By dissemblance I mean the behavior and attitudes of black women that created the appearance of openness and disclosure but actually shielded the truth of their inner lives and selves from their oppressors. In other words, while some black women struggled to acquire and project their voice, the majority converted invisibility into a survival strategy.

Institution building, as well as their interior struggles to reconstruct and redefine self, demanded the development of a distinct consciousness. Thus, consciousness and activism were another kind of refuge. Black women internalized and institutionalized the idea of and commitment to resistance. Their consciousness of struggle transcended participation in the established political order. Struggle for black women pivoted on a Harriet Tubman–like obsession to carry on, regardless. I owe a debt to Elsa Barkley Brown's analysis of the connection between theory or consciousness and activism. She warns against assuming that theory "is found only in carefully articulated position statements." Brown posits that the clearest articulation of Maggie Lena Walker's theoretical perspectives on the power of black women lay not in her public statements but in her activities, especially the organization and institution she helped to create: "Her theory and her action are not distinct and separable parts of some whole: they are often synonymous and it is only through her actions that we clearly hear her theory." Brown concludes, and I concur, "The same is true for the lives of many other Black women who had limited time and resources and maintained a holistic view of life and struggle."[1]

The *Encyclopedia* shatters black women's self-imposed invisibility and lifts the veil of affected ignorance and indifference in the larger society. Its existence portends transformations in both black and white women historians and eventually will affect all who write American history. The incremental approach of adding one or two black women to discussions of suffrage, reform, the professions, domesticity, and religious work, for example, is rendered inadequate and unsophisticated in face of the impressive number of women engaged in these activities, as chronicled in the *Encyclopedia*. No longer will excuses or complaints of insufficient evidence be persuasive responses to black women's exclusion from scholarly texts. The *Encyclopedia* maps new spaces, directing a glaring spotlight on omissions while turning up the volume on silences. This black woman's encyclopedia effectively challenges the claims to capaciousness of general surveys about American history that exclude black women. In seizing the historiographical moment of giving black women the space and place to create a meaning system of their own lives, the *Encyclopedia* helps to shape the future of the history of women and of black people in America.

As I contemplated the logistics of the project, Ralph Carlson assured me that there would be an even division of labor and that he would employ whatever staff was necessary to handle most of the production details. The more we talked, the more comfortable I became until I was convinced that it was indeed possible to produce, in a timely fashion, a high-quality, intellectually sound, and aesthetically pleasing reference work on black women's history. Without a doubt, a smoothly functioning administrative structure, a host of talented people, and a secure organizational base were key factors. Within a matter of weeks, Carlson and I had hammered out a general blueprint of the project. Like most publishers, Carlson was overly optimistic in estimating that the *Encyclopedia* would take about a year to complete. It actually took almost three years. Nevertheless, given the comprehensive nature of the finished volumes, three years was an incredibly short time frame.

During the period between Summer 1990 and Fall 1992, I do not recall a day's passing when I did not think about or work on the *Encyclopedia*. I had anticipated that the project would be all consuming and therefore was not surprised. Excluding the conceptualization phase, the actual work was neatly divided into at least four stages: inviting associate editors and advisory editors to participate, developing a list of entries, making assignments and editing the manuscript, and fund-raising.

The first stage was definitely the easiest and most delightful, for it entailed persuading some of the most talented scholars in black women's history to join me. I assured them that this would be fun and would not unduly tax their time. I asked historians Elsa Barkley Brown of the University of Michigan and Rosalyn Terborg-Penn of Morgan State University to serve as associate editors responsible for general oversight of the project. They readily agreed to do so.

I had worked with Brown on the earlier sixteen-volume series and had acquired enormous respect for the subtlety and range of her intellect and the depth of her commitment to black women's history. She is meticulous and exacting. Elsa made it clear that she intended to avoid the three diseases common to encyclopedias: inaccuracies, datedness, and arcane prose. I knew that Brown, herself a relentless researcher and engaging writer, would hold us to the highest possible standards.

Similarly, I had enjoyed working on numerous projects with Rosalyn

Terborg-Penn, beginning with the founding of the Association of Black Women Historians in 1979. Terborg-Penn and I had collaborated on a program funded by the Fund for the Improvement of Post-Secondary Education that Gerda Lerner initiated during her presidency of the Organization of American Historians. The aim of that project was to increase the participation of black women in the historical profession. Terborg-Penn's own pathbreaking scholarship in black women's history has earned her "founding mother" status. Moreover, her knowledge of who is doing what and where they are located is in itself encyclopedic. True to expectations, Elsa and Rosalyn proved essential to the success of the project. Once they were on board, we developed a list of individuals who might serve as members of the advisory editorial board. Meanwhile, Ralph Carlson began interviewing candidates to manage the project from his office and launched a search for freelance staff editors.

Inviting people to be on the advisory board was itself a significant gesture. Black women scholars are rarely asked to serve on editorial boards of mainstream publishing or media projects. To this day, not one black woman has ever coauthored a general undergraduate textbook in American history. It is difficult to acquire visibility in the historical profession regardless of what you study or who you are, but it is even more so for young black women historians. Thus, in spite of demonstrated ability to do good work, black women historians still, with a few laudable exceptions, inhabit the periphery of the profession. The production of scholarship is one side of the challenge. The other side is to win recognition for the contribution. Indeed, one of my unshakable principles is to give credit for the work that others do on any project that I administer. I remain convinced that black women in particular rarely receive the recognition or the salaries that they deserve for the work they do. Nowhere is this more graphically illustrated than in higher education. Undoubtedly, as more of us acquire prominence and greater access, the publishing and editing opportunities in the mainstream will increase.

Meanwhile, we must create our own opportunities. Accordingly, I aimed to involve a large number of black women scholars in the development of the *Encyclopedia* for both intellectual and political reasons. I anticipated that for the junior black women historians, service on the advisory board would be an important item on their curriculum vitae. The experience of advising, editing, writing, and reviewing entries would expand knowledge, enhance careers, and cement networks.

With suggestions from Terborg-Penn, Brown, and Carlson, I extended invitations to senior scholars Mary Francis Berry, Nell Irvin Painter, and Nellie McKay. Authors and editors of key monographs, dissertations, essays, anthologies, and works in progress in black women's history invited to join also included Paula Giddings, Sharon Harley, Evelyn Brooks Higginbotham, Jacqueline Jones, Wilma King, Cynthia Neverdon-Morton, Tiffany R. L. Patterson, Linda Reed, Gwendolyn Keita Robinson, Jacqueline Rouse, Stephanie Shaw, Janet Sims-Wood, Deborah Gray White, and Lillian S. Williams.

We agreed on the importance of involving scholars who, like Nellie McKay, possessed expertise in cultural studies. It is impossible to imagine how the *Encyclopedia* would have achieved its "astounding" breadth without the critical advice and contributions of Kariamu Welsh Asante on dance, Elizabeth Brown-Guillory on literature, Daphne Duval Harrison on music, and Kathy Perkins on film. With the exception of Catherine Clinton and Jacqueline Jones, all of the members of the advisory board were black women. To be sure, many of the essays and biographical entries were written by white women and by black and white male scholars. Catherine Clinton engaged an entire seminar at Harvard in the preparation of numerous essays for the *Encyclopedia*. Thus, to a noticeable degree this project reflects the greatest collaboration within the academy across race and gender lines that I have witnessed.

Brown, Terborg-Penn, and I met with Carlson in May 1991 to discuss the preliminary list of topics for the essays and the women to receive biographical treatment. We also nominated people to write the entries. We agreed to circulate a basic topical and biographical list to all members of the advisory board. Gradually over a few months, we hammered out the final list, all the while soliciting comments and recommendations from select black librarians and archivists. Not surprisingly, the index to the sixteen-volume series served as our major guide for the names of historical black women.

In compiling the list of topical essays and of biographical entries we were guided by the desire to represent the broadest possible spectrum of black women. Black women's history is different from white women's history in many telling ways. Most glaringly is our lack of knowledge and information about the lives of exemplary women in local communities. We were not satisfied simply to identify the top one hundred or *even* the five hundred most prominent black women nationally and internationally. This reference and research tool was not intended to be merely about the notable black woman, the *colored* counterparts of outstanding American *white* women or a *Who's Who* companion. We needed not only to know the average black woman but also to define "average." An exclusive orientation would scarcely capture the rich diversity and nuance of black women's lives and experiences on American soil.

For over two years a great part of my direct work on the *Encyclopedia* involved searching for both average and exemplary black women and for the people interested in writing about them. I would make mental notes of the various topics or unusual lives I heard discussed or mentioned wherever I was invited to lecture. I amassed names and collected business cards as I traveled across the country attending conferences of every stripe. Religiously, I wrote notes directly to individuals or dispatched brief missives to Carlson or to Christine Lunardini, the project's office editor, urging that a formal invitation be sent to a particular person. This became a standard operating procedure that allowed me to uncover the scores of locally known representative black women. Their inclusion gives the *Encyclopedia* a truly national flavor.

My earlier experiences with black community women made me acutely sensitive to the imperative to include biographical and topical essays about women and groups of women who had devoted their lives to serving others and building community. These are the lives that capture best the millions of black women who contributed and endured, who built human bridges and whose backs carried many of us to better lives, but who never dreamed of seeing their names in any history book.

The *Encyclopedia* had to include certain individuals. To have left out Phillis Wheatley, Harriet Tubman, and Sojourner Truth, for example, would be unthinkable and inexcusable. Yet this work also had to make a place for retired pediatrician Dr. Helen Nash of St. Louis, Missouri, Creole folk artist Clementine Hunter (1886–1988), nurse Anna De Costa Banks (1869–1930) of Charleston, South Carolina, and Hawaiian schoolteacher Carlotta Stewart-Lai (1881–1952), along with the millions of women who had worked as domestic servants earning the meager sums that saved families from starvation. The 143 historical essays reclaim the lives of the obscure and anonymous by focusing on a wide spectrum of subjects such as slavery, civil rights, domestic service, religion, and military service.

It is possible to exaggerate the mechanical nature of the process of encyclopedia construction. In several cases serendipity, or just plain luck, account for the inclusion of some of the topical and biographical entries. For example, at a reception on my campus I just happened to mention to a colleague in the Department of Communications, Lawrence Redd, that I would love to have someone prepare an entry on black women in radio for the *Encyclopedia*. It turned out that this topic was one of his research interests, and he willingly accepted the assignment. A similar conversation at a conference in Galveston, Texas, with Anne Hudson Jones of the Institute for the Medical Humanities of the University of Texas revealed our mutual admiration of Clementine Hunter. Jones subsequently wrote the entry on Hunter. Even more frequently, individual scholars volunteered to write entries in their area of expertise. Many of my friends and colleagues at educational institutions in every region insisted that I include their favorite deserving local woman in the *Encyclopedia*. Had not historian Albert S. Broussard sent me a reprint of an article he had written on

Carlotta Stewart-Lai, it is doubtful that the *Encyclopedia* would contain an entry on this schoolteacher who had migrated to Hawaii around the turn of the century.

Black women historians are active in various professional associations, and this proved invaluable as work on the *Encyclopedia* progressed. Prior to annual meetings of professional historical associations, the project staff would circulate topical and biographical lists to members of the advisory group. We scheduled breakfast gatherings or luncheons at the meetings. The largest collection of black women historians usually meets in the fall in conjunction with the Association for the Study of Afro-American Life and History (ASALH). The Association of Black Women Historians (ABWH) enjoys a mutually respectful affiliation with ASALH and has for the past fourteen years hosted a luncheon during that organization's annual convention. The ASALH convention proved an ideal event at which to meet with advisory editors and to deliver periodic updates as a way of maintaining general interest in the project. Late developments were announced and invitations issued for others to recommend additional entries to the *Encyclopedia*. The ABWH/ASALH conferences had the added advantage of providing a good opportunity to go to panels to find out who was doing research on new topics, and to make contacts for further essay assignments.

We continued to circulate lists among advisory board members until each entry had a name assigned to it. If, after approximately five circulations, there was no one willing or able to write a particular entry, then it was dropped from the list. On occasion, Brown, Terborg-Penn, or I had to prepare essays when the person was someone whom we simply could not omit. Time was a constant goad and foe. The longer the project took, the more expensive it became and the more worn was the patience of those upon whom we relied to advise, to review, and to write for free.

The large editorial staff Carlson retained reviewed each entry and reshaped, refocused, or shortened it when necessary. Brown, Terborg-Penn, and I read entries for historical accuracy and interpretive analysis. Mary Wyer did a superb job of editing for readability and style. At the outset we all agreed that this *Encyclopedia* would be free of jargon and would be accessible to the general reader. Yet it was important that the work be a useful reference and research tool. Toward this end all entries are signed, and virtually all include a short bibliography. Actually, the bibliographies vary in length from one or two items to two columns, depending on the topic and the individual authors.

Authors maintained the right to review and to question all changes made on their manuscripts. On occasion, essays were returned several times, and in a few instances frustrated authors withdrew their own submissions. It required great patience and diplomacy not to offend the host of writers and scholars who contributed. But when difficult decisions had to be made about quality and relevance, I simply thought about what was best for the *Encyclopedia*. Regrettably, I am sure that I incurred the wrath of some whose work was rejected. For the most part, however, the contributors appeared to be pleased with the amount of attention accorded each submission.

I encountered my biggest trauma in the fourth, or fund-raising, stage of the enterprise. Although I maintained almost daily—sometimes hourly—contact with Ralph Carlson about every major and minor aspect of the project, it was nevertheless a shock to receive a letter from him in June 1992 asking for my help to raise $100,000 in order to pay the printers. Specifically, we had to find ten people who would put up $10,000 each. In return, we promised to acknowledge their sponsorship in the *Encyclopedia*; moreover, Carlson would pay 15 percent interest on the loan. It is difficult indeed to ask friends and colleagues to give up their time and forego financial remuneration to serve as associate and advisory editors and then to ask them to write essential biographical entries and analytical essays. But my nerves threatened to abandon me completely when I had to help locate the funds to pay the printers. I was petrified to ask my friends to trust me and invest their hard-earned money in the project. With the *Encyclopedia*, unlike previous undertakings in black women's history, I placed my good name—and, in the end, my personal savings—on the line.

That I was thankful that some of my friends had discretionary funds and a lot of faith is a gigantic understatement. Once they had put up their money, however, failure was simply out of the question. In retrospect, I shudder at the risk I had invited Delores Aldridge, Carolyn Dorsey, Wilma King, Nell Irvin Painter, and Arvarh Strickland to share. Ralph Carlson was able to persuade Randall K. Burkett, David Garrow, Betty Gubert, and Richard Newman to also become sponsors of the project. Had Carlson and I been willing to delay the launching of the *Encyclopedia*, we might well have secured a grant from the National Endowment for the Humanities or some other funding agency. But neither of us relished the prospect of becoming mired in bureaucratic paperwork, so we stubbornly decided to go it alone. We also doubted whether NEH would be interested enough or willing to fund a project on black women. Nevertheless, my advice to anyone contemplating the production of an encyclopedia or other research or reference tool is to secure adequate funding at the outset. It reduces anxiety.

Clearly, Carlson made the greatest economic investment in the *Encyclopedia*. After the June 1992 letter in which he informed me of his economic woes, I remember calling to ask him precisely when he had decided to throw financial caution to the wind and to go for broke. He confided that the decision had been made fairly early in the project. Only then did I recall how, when presented with a choice, I had invariably selected expensive type, paper, and cover design. I considered the book's esthetics to be of paramount importance. Simply put, the *Encyclopedia* had to be beautiful. To his credit, Carlson could not have found more effective and committed people. He hired the full-time services of two pivotal women, Christine A. Lunardini, office editorial director, and Mary Wyer, editor-in-chief; retained a sixteen-member editorial staff; and employed four additional persons to work on production and to do research for photographs.

Salaries, production, design, and promotional brochures made this a very costly project. A conservative estimate would put the price tag in the half-million-dollar range. My fund-raising efforts netted loans of seventy thousand dollars. Instead of cash, each contributing author received a set of the *Encyclopedia*, more as a token of our appreciation than as any pretense of adequate compensation. To have promised contributors even modest financial compensation would have been prohibitive. Additional costs accumulated in the closing months of the project. When you are counting on over four hundred people to write entries, invariably a few individuals will fail to deliver on their commitment. With backs up against the wall and some important entries long overdue, Carlson and I surveyed our options. We thus paid Chicago-based freelance writer Kathleen Thompson to prepare several important essays, including the entry on sexual harassment.

The enthusiastic media reception of and individual responses to the *Encyclopedia* have fully justified our efforts. Everyone seems to have gotten the point. While a few reviewers questioned the amount of space accorded one black woman versus another or mused about who was missing, they all concluded that the *Encyclopedia* is an "astounding" achievement. Columbia University law professor Patricia Williams, in an insightful review in *Ms.* magazine (May/June 1993), declared that the existence of the *Encyclopedia* renders all the standard references and histories of America suspect and inadequate. She and others have reasoned that we are now in a position to judge and to assess earlier and future historical scholarship in quite different ways. *Black Women in America: An Historical Encyclopedia* has ushered in a new meaning system grounded in the intersectional analysis of the historical constructions of race, gender, and class. At a minimum, the historical profession must now take action to end the exclusion, distortion, and marginalization of black women.

NOTES

Introduction

1. "Placing Women in History: Definitions and Challenges," in *The Majority Finds Its Past: Placing Women in History*, by Gerda Lerner (New York: Oxford University Press, 1979).

2. Edward T. James, Janet Wilson James, and Paul S. Boyer, eds., *Notable American Women: A Biographical Dictionary*, 3 vols. (Cambridge: Harvard University Press, 1971); Barbara Sicherman and Carol Hurd Green, eds., *Notable American Women: The Modern Period* (Cambridge: Harvard University Press, 1980); Darlene Clark Hine, Elsa Barkley Brown, and Rosalyn Terborg-Penn, eds., *Black Women in America: An Historical Encyclopedia* (Brooklyn, N.Y.: Carlson Publishing, Inc., 1993).

3. Alice Kessler-Harris, "A New Agenda for American Labor History: A Gendered Analysis and the Question of Class," in *Perspectives on American Labor History: The Problems of Synthesis*, edited by J. Carroll Moody and Alice Kessler-Harris (DeKalb: Northern Illinois University Press, 1989), p. 226.

4. "The American Revolution: Revisions in Need of Revising," *William and Mary Quarterly*, 3d ser., 14 (1957): 3–15.

5. Michel Foucault, "Two Lectures," in *Power/Knowledge: Selected Interviews and Other Writings, 1972–1977*, edited by Colin Gordon (New York: Pantheon Books, 1980), p. 82.

6. Gerda Lerner, *The Creation of Feminist Consciousness: From the Middle Ages to Eighteen-seventy* (New York: Oxford University Press, 1993), p. 281.

CHAPTER 1. A Constitutional Right to Be Treated Like American Ladies

This essay emerges from my book in progress, "A Right to Be Ladies: American Women and the Obligations of Citizenship." I am particularly grateful to the University of California–Berkeley for inviting me to offer the 1989 Jefferson Lectures, where this work began; the John Simon Guggenheim Foundation, the National Endowment for the Humanities, and the National Humanities Center for fellowship support; the Rockefeller Foundation for a residency at Bellagio; and the University of Iowa's Center for Advanced Studies.

1. Hearings on Military Posture and H.R. 6495 before the Subcommittee on Military Personnel of the House Committee on Armed Services, 96th Cong., 2d sess. (1980), pp. 135 (President Carter), 105 (Teague).

2. Glendon, *Rights Talk: The Impoverishment of Political Discourse* (New York: Free Press, 1991). See the suggestive analysis of Gwendolyn Mink, "The Lady and the Tramp: Gender, Race, and the Origins of the American Welfare State," in *Women, the State, and Welfare*, edited by Linda Gordon (Madison: University of Wisconsin Press, 1990), pp. 92–122. In his classic essay, "Citizenship and Social Class," T. H. Marshall offers a tripartite concept of citizenship. Civil citizenship "is composed of the rights

necessary for individual freedom"; political citizenship involves "the right to partici-pate in the exercise of political power." Social citizenship, Marshall thought, should involve a wide range of rights not yet widely acknowledged, "from the right to a modicum of economic welfare and security to the right to share to the full in the social heritage . . . [of] the society," including the right to work, to a range of health and welfare supports, and to education. T. H. Marshall, *Class, Citizenship, and Social Democracy*, edited by Seymour Martin Lipset (Garden City, N.Y.: Doubleday, 1964), pp. 71–72. In a paper presented at the June 1993 Berkshire Conference in Women's History, Vassar College, Lizabeth Cohen suggests that increasingly citizenship is understood primarily as a matter of entitlement.

3. In this and what immediately follows, I am leaning on the shrewd work of Rogers M. Smith, "Rights," in *A Companion to American Thought*, edited by Richard Wightman Fox and James Kloppenberg (Oxford and Boston: Blackwell's, forthcoming), and on my own essay in that volume, "Obligation."

4. But Magna Carta was prepared in a feudal context, in which hierarchy and obligation were already strong; lords owed military service to their king, vassals owed military service to lords.

5. Edmund S. Morgan, *Inventing the People: The Rise of Popular Sovereignty in England and America* (New York: Norton, 1988), p. 153. The term *imagined community* is Benedict Anderson's in his *Imagined Communities: Reflections on the Origin and Spread of Nationalism* (London: Verso, 1983).

6. Michael Warner, *The Letters of the Republic: Publication and the Public Sphere in Eighteenth Century America* (Cambridge: Harvard University Press, 1990), pp. 98–99, 102, 109.

7. Carole Pateman, *The Sexual Contract* (Stanford: Stanford University Press, 1988), pp. 48–49 and passim.

8. I have developed this argument at greater length in "The Paradox of Women's Citizenship in the Early Republic: The Case of *Martin v. Commonwealth*, 1805," *American Historical Review* 97 (1992): 349–78.

9. Tapping Reeve, *The Law of Baron and Feme, Parent and Child, Guardian and Ward, Master and Servant, and of the Powers of the Courts of Chancery* (1816; reprint, Burlington: Chauncey Goodrich, 1846).

10. Ibid., chap. 8.

11. Ibid., chaps. 3, 6.

12. Ibid., chap. 8, pp. 98–99.

13. George Blake, in *Martin v. Commonwealth*, cited in Kerber, "The Paradox of Women's Citizenship," p. 370.

14. For an insightful summary history of women and citizenship, see Rogers M. Smith, " 'One United People': Second-Class Female Citizenship and the American Quest for Community," *Yale Journal of Law and the Humanities* 1 (1989): 229–93.

15. Deep into the twentieth century, courts sustained the understanding that hus-bands retained property rights in their wives' bodies and fathers retained property rights in the services of their daughters; see Rogers Smith's shrewd comments here in " 'One United People,' " p. 269, citing *Tinker v. Colwell*, 193 U.S. 473 (1904), and *In re Freche*, 109 F. 620 (D.N.J. 1901).

16. "Statue of Liberty or Statue of Sham?," in box 46, folder 455, Dorothy Kenyon Papers, Sophia Smith Collection, Smith College, Northampton, Mass.

17. Martha C. Howell brilliantly describes the continental European antecedents of this pattern. So long as feudal patterns of authority persisted and the family was "the consistent unit" of political organization, women "actively belonged" to the citizenry; in the late medieval period, though subordinate to male heads of households, women were counted as citizens and shared in some civic responsibility. Howell links the exclusion of women from civic roles to the "shift from the family to the individual as the constituent civic unit" and the reservation of "political authority for individual men (rather than for families) in the interests of civic peace, unity and independence." She locates this shift in the early modern period; it was solidly in place by the seventeenth century. Howell, "Citizenship and Gender: Women's Political Status in Northern Medieval Cities," in *Women and Power in the Middle Ages*, edited by Mary Erler and Maryanne Kowaleski (Athens: University of Georgia Press, 1988), pp. 37–60 (quotations, pp. 51–54). It is against this pattern that the republican theorists of the era of the democratic revolution located themselves.

18. Carroll Smith-Rosenberg, "Dis-Covering the Subject of the 'Great Constitutional Discussion,' 1786–1789," *Journal of American History* 79 (December 1992): 841–73; Susan Juster, "Patriarchy Reborn: The Gendering of Authority in the Evangelical Church in Revolutionary New England," *Gender and History* 6 (1994): 58–81 (quotations, p. 76).

19. This argument required that they attack the claim that women's desires for luxury goods and for leisure undermined the new and fragile middle class. See Smith-Rosenberg, "'Great Constitutional Discussion,'" esp. pp. 857–61. Wollstonecraft went on the offensive, sneering at standing armies, likening uniformed soldiers who were admired for their status and attire to frivolous women who were brought up to be deferential and to please their superiors.

20. I have discussed this ideology in a number of places, especially in "The Republican Mother—Women and the Enlightenment: An American Perspective," *American Quarterly* 28 (1976): 187–205, and *Women of the Republic: Intellect and Ideology in Revolutionary America* (Chapel Hill: University of North Carolina Press, 1980).

21. Elizabeth Blackmar, *Manhattan for Rent, 1785–1850* (Ithaca, N.Y.: Cornell University Press, 1989), p. 117 and passim.

22. For the power of this attack at its most virulent, see Kenneth Lockridge, *On the Sources of Patriarchal Rage: The Commonplace Books of William Byrd and Thomas Jefferson and the Gendering of Power in the Eighteenth Century* (New York: New York University Press, 1992). I have commented on this theme in *Women of the Republic*, pp. 198–99.

23. See my more extended comments on this point in "The Republican Ideology of the Revolutionary Generation," *American Quarterly* 37 (1985): 482–85.

24. Ellen Carol DuBois, "Taking the Law into Our Own Hands: *Bradwell, Minor* and Suffrage Militance in the 1870s," in *Visible Women: Essays in American Activism*, edited by Nancy Hewitt and Suzanne Lebsock (Urbana: University of Illinois Press, 1993), p. 34.

25. For the continuing vitality of the old law of domestic relations, see James Schouler, *A Treatise on the Law of the Domestic Relations: Embracing Husband and Wife,*

Parent and Child, Guardian and Ward, Infancy, and Master and Servant (Boston: Little, Brown, 1870), and its many subsequent editions.

26. Carl Degler quotes Corbin in his brilliant chapter, "The Suffrage Fight: The Last Step Was Really the First," in Degler, *At Odds: Women and the Family in America from the Revolution to the Present* (New York: Oxford University Press, 1980), p. 354.

27. Ibid., p. 358.

28. Ibid., p. 357. Ellen DuBois points out, however, that "the larger spirit of militant direct action resurfaced in a spectacular way in the last decade of the American suffrage movement" ("Taking the Law into Our Own Hands," p. 34), and that much of the egalitarian vigor of the New Departure years was injected into the campaign at its end; see DuBois, "Working Women, Class Relations, and Suffrage Militance: Harriot Stanton Blatch and the New York Woman Suffrage Movement, 1894–1909," *Journal of American History* 74 (1987): 24–58.

29. As late as 1940, Degler reminds us, "a quarter of the states did not permit a wife to make a contract." Degler, *At Odds*, p. 333. See also North Carolina Governor's Commission on the Status of Women, *The Many Lives of North Carolina Women* (N.p.: North Carolina Governor's Commission on the Status of Women, 1964) and comments on it by Jane Sherron De Hart, "The New Feminism and the Dynamics of Social Change," in *Women's America: Refocusing the Past*, edited by Linda K. Kerber and Jane Sherron De Hart, 3d ed. (New York: Oxford University Press, 1991), p. 504. The Report of the U.S. President's Commission on the Status of Women documented an extensive list of disparities in the legal standing of men and women—in eligibility for jury service, in ownership and control of property, in civil capacity, in inheritance rights, in a woman's right to choose her domicile, in the age at which marriage could be contracted, in eligibility for unemployment compensation. In 1965 three states still completely excluded women from jury service, four states required court approval before a married woman could operate an independent business, and thirty-eight states refused unemployment compensation to pregnant women who considered themselves available for work. U.S. President's Commission on the Status of Women, *American Women* (New York: Scribner, 1965), pp. 136–57, 230–47.

30. Argument of George Blake, in *Martin v. Commonwealth*, pp. 362–63, in Kerber, "The Paradox of Women's Citizenship," p. 369. See also the argument of Richard Stockton in *Kempe's Lessee v. Kennedy et al.*, 5 Cranch (U.S.) 175–78 (1809), to the effect that a *feme covert* "cannot properly be called an inhabitant of a state. The husband is the inhabitant." The point is discussed in Kerber, *Women of the Republic*, pp. 131–32, and Smith, "'One United People,'" pp. 248–49.

31. This was the practice as early as the Revolution. Since wives were understood to owe allegiance above all to their husbands, the Revolutionary government took the position that the wives of Tories could not have freely consented to the loyalist position and protected their dower rights and the property they held outright even when seizing their husbands' property. See Kerber, "The Paradox of Women's Citizenship."

32. *Mackenzie v. Hare*, 239 U.S. 229 (1915). Candice Dawn Bredbenner, "Toward Independent Citizenship: Married Women's Nationality Rights in the United States, 1855–1937" (Ph.D. diss., University of Virginia, 1990), is the most complete examina-

tion of this subject. See also Sophonisba Breckinridge, *Marriage and the Civic Rights of Women: Separate Domicile and Independent Citizenship* (Chicago: University of Chicago Press, 1931); Virginia Sapiro, "Women, Citizenship, and Nationality: Immigration and Naturalization Policies in the United States," *Politics and Society* 13 (1984): 1–26; Smith, "'One United People,'" pp. 254–55; and Nancy Cott, "Giving Character to Our Whole Civil Polity," chap. 5, this volume.

33. In a classic essay on the subject, Blanche Crozier argued that the precedent for a woman's loss of citizenship when she married an alien man was established by the Code Napoleon, but that many people justified the practice as a "primitive" custom. She pointed out that "primitive" peoples were likely to be matrilocal; that ancient practice was more likely to involve the husband joining the wife's kin or tribe. Crozier, "The Changing Basis of Women's Nationality," *Boston University Law Review* 14 (1934): 129–53.

34. Bredbenner, "Toward Independent Citizenship," p. 289.

35. For example, after the original passage of the Cable Act of 1922, "American women who married foreigners and left the country had to seek reentry into the country as *aliens* not citizens. As immigration law became more restrictive, it became increasingly difficult—sometimes impossible—for female expatriates to return to the United States." The Cable Act made "a married woman's chances of becoming or remaining an American dependent on her husband's potential as a citizen; if a woman remained abroad for as little as two years with her alien husband, she lost her United States citizenship; if an American woman married a man ineligible for naturalization, she automatically forfeited her citizenship and could not seek naturalization until the marriage ended." Ibid., pp. 153, 155. See also Smith, "'One United People,'" p. 277.

36. Matthews, "The Woman without a Country," quoted in Bredbenner, "Toward Independent Citizenship," p. 298.

37. Bredbenner has rich evidence on this matter; see chap. 9, ibid. American-born women married to alien men had difficulty negotiating the restrictions of the immigration act; amid the virulent anti-Semitism of the interwar years, these difficulties bore extraordinary risks for Jewish women, who could not bring their husbands from Poland or elsewhere. For the persistence of the issue deep into the 1950s, see my comments at the end of "The Paradox of Women's Citizenship."

38. An odd exception to this point was publicized in 1937, when, deciding *Breedlove v. Suttles*, 302 U.S. 277, the U.S. Supreme Court sustained a Georgia law exempting women who did not register to vote from the obligation to pay poll taxes "in view of the burdens necessarily borne by them for the preservation of the race." Once again, motherhood was used to trump civic obligation, although, as Rogers Smith points out, "the law obviously rewarded women for not voting and gave husbands an incentive to discourage their wives' political interests." Smith, "'One United People,'" p. 280.

39. Carolyn C. Jones, "Split Income and Separate Spheres: Tax Law and Gender Roles in the 1940s," *Law and History Review* 6 (1988): 273–74. Jones's essay is a rich resource on this point; see also pp. 270–72 and nn. 66–67, p. 301.

40. Ibid., pp. 290–91.

41. *Newsweek*, October 13, 1947, pp. 64–65; quoted in Jones, "Split Income," p. 270.

42. Jones, "Split Income," p. 295.

43. Elizabeth Cady Stanton and Susan B. Anthony, Centennial Address, 1876: "the women of this nation have never been allowed a jury of their peers." E. C. Stanton, S. B. Anthony, and M. J. Gage, eds., *History of Woman Suffrage* (Rochester, N.Y.: Susan B. Anthony, 1886), 3:33.

44. Gladys Harrison, "Re-Fighting an Old Battle," *New York Herald Tribune Magazine*, Sunday, February 4, 1930, in pt. III, ser. A, *Papers of the League of Women Voters* (Frederick, Md.: University Publications of America, 1985) (hereafter cited as LWV Papers), reel 18, pp. 493–97.

45. *New York Laws*, 1939, pp. 1491–91, par. 720.

46. George Wickersham to Belle Sherwin, president, National LWV, February 18, 1930, pt. III, ser. A, LWV Papers, reel 18, p. 374.

47. Jennie Loitman Barron, *Jury Service for Women* (Washington, D.C.: League of Women Voters, 1924), p. 11. Indeed, she argued, "Homemaking is something more than housekeeping. Many homes are hurt by the trivialities and lack of interest of mothers in the affairs of life" (p. 9).

48. *Hoyt v. Florida*, 368 U.S. 57 (1961). The tape recording of the oral argument is in the National Archives.

49. The *New York Times* featured Justice Harlan's phrase, "woman is the center of home and family life" as the Quotation of the Day when the *Hoyt* decision was reported. Among the people most dismayed by the decision, and by the rhetoric that supported it, was Dorothy Kenyon, a New York attorney and political activist who had written the *amicus* brief that the American Civil Liberties Union had filed. She would never forgive Harlan for that phrase, quoting it acerbically every chance she got until her death ten years later. Throughout her long career, which began with her graduation from the New York University School of Law in 1917, Kenyon framed women's rights issues squarely as matters of contested citizenship. She also understood the tension over women's rights as resulting from contested relations between men and women; the implications of equality were that men did indeed stand to lose both services and deference. Kenyon consistently sought to place her arguments in historical context. Writing as she did just before the explosion of work in women's history that accompanied second-wave feminism, Kenyon constructed a narrative that stressed the power men used to keep women from political and civic authority. In developing this narrative, she had few authorities on whom to lean. All were women who understood their work as historians to be integral to their duties as social critics: Mary Beard, Caroline Ware, and Eleanor Flexner. And, at the very end of her life, in 1971, writing one of the last pieces of her work, Kenyon found Gerda Lerner, early in her own career as a professional historian. "One of the things that has puzzled me most in women's and men's behaviour towards one another," Kenyon wrote, "has been the indifference of most intelligent men towards womens' problems. Indifference and boredom seem the usual attitude as revealed by a large yawn. Others have commented on it too. A historian (Professor Gerda Lerner at Sarah Lawrence College) observes that 'until very recently American historians have paid scant, almost absent minded attention to the history of women. The field has, for many decades, been left to amateurs, feminist enthusiasts, writers and scholars from the social sciences. . . . The sources available to the historians in the field have long been

neglected and have, in turn, served to limit the scope and range of scholarship.'" Dorothy Kenyon, "Women's Place Is in the Home: Men and Women—Boredom, Violence, and Political Power," typescript, post–May 1971, box 23, folder 241, Kenyon Papers. The citation from Lerner is from "The Woman in American History," *American Scholar* 40 (1971): 235.

50. Roosevelt to Hamlin Garland, July 19, 1903, in *The Letters of Theodore Roosevelt*, edited by Elting E. Morison (Cambridge: Harvard University Press, 1951), pp. 520–21. For the antiquity of this argument, see Nancy Huston, "The Matrix of War: Mothers and Heroes," *Poetics Today* 6 (1985): 153–70.

51. Hearings on Military Posture and H.R. 6495, p. 104ff.

52. The literature in the popular press is vast; it can be followed in *Newsweek*, including September 10, November 12, 1990, February 11, 1991, and subsequent issues.

53. Cynthia H. Enloe has remarked that peace activists find "the issue of women in the military . . . ideologically awkward." Enloe, *The Morning After: Sexual Politics at the End of the Cold War* (Berkeley: University of California Press, 1993), p. 210.

54. Ibid., pp. 210–11.

55. For thoughtful reflections on the associations of race, sex, and violence, see George L. Mosse, *Nationalism and Sexuality: Middle-Class Morality and Sexual Norms in Modern Europe* (Madison: University of Wisconsin Press, 1985), and Kenneth Karst, "The Pursuit of Manhood and the Desegregation of the Armed Forces," *UCLA Law Review* 38 (1991): 499–581.

56. Thus some of the most forceful Supreme Court decisions maintaining the power of husbands over wives well into the twentieth century—*Mackenzie v. Hare* (1907), which removed citizenship from American-born women who married aliens; *Thompson v. Thompson* (1910), which denied a wife damages against violent beating; *Breedlove v. Settles* (1937), which rewarded women for not voting—do not appear in the otherwise admirable standard histories. As late as 1992, in *Planned Parenthood of Southeastern Pennsylvania v. Casey* (1992), 112 Sup. Ct. 2791, the Supreme Court evaluated, and overturned, a statutory requirement that no physician perform an abortion on a married woman unless she had provided a statement that she had notified her spouse. The Court declared that "the common-law principle that 'a woman had no legal existence separate from her husband . . . [io] no longer consistent with our understanding of the family, the individual, or the Constitution."

57. For elegant contemplation of this problem, see Sara M. Evans, "Women's History and Political Theory: Toward a Feminist Approach to Public Life," in *Visible Women: Essays in American Activism*, edited by Nancy Hewitt and Suzanne Lebsock (Urbana: University of Illinois Press, 1993), pp. 119–39.

CHAPTER 2. Two Political Cultures in the Progressive Era

I am grateful to Alice Kessler-Harris and Linda Kerber for their comments on earlier drafts of this essay, and to Kathleen Babbitt for invaluable research assistance.

Unless otherwise identified as reel 61 or 62, all correspondence and documents pertaining to the American Association for Labor Legislation can be found in chronological order in the microfilm edition of the AALL Papers. Originals reside at the Institute for Labor Relations, Cornell University, but due to their fragility are not available to researchers.

1. New York City directories offer an extensive guide to the inhabitants of the Charities Building in the Progressive Era.

2. "Meeting of Council, March 16, 1906," reel 61, AALL Papers; Josephine Goldmark, *Impatient Crusader: Florence Kelley's Life Story* (Urbana: University of Illinois Press, 1953; Greenwood, 1976), p. 69.

3. Paula Baker, "The Domestication of Politics: Women and American Political Society, 1780–1920," *American Historical Review* 89 (June 1984): 620–47; Maureen A. Flanagan, "Gender and Urban Political Reform: The City Club and the Woman's City Club of Chicago in the Progressive Era" *American Historical Review* 95 (October 1990): 1032–75; Theda Skocpol, *Protecting Soldiers and Mothers: The Political Origins of Social Policy in the United States* (Cambridge: Harvard University Press, 1992).

4. See Linda Gordon, *Pitied but Not Entitled: Single Mothers and the History of Welfare* (New York: Free Press, 1994).

5. See Kathryn Kish Sklar, "The Historical Foundations of Women's Power in the Creation of the American Welfare State, 1830–1930," in *Mothers of a New World: Maternalist Politics and the Origins of Welfare States,* edited by Seth Koven and Sonya Michel (New York: Routledge, 1993), pp. 43–93.

6. For this definition of the welfare state, see James Leiby, *A History of Social Welfare and Social Work in the United States* (New York: Columbia University Press, 1978), p. 141.

7. See, for example, the AALL report on "The Spring Meeting of the General Administrative Council," Saturday, April 10, 1909, reel 61, AALL Papers.

8. *New York Times,* October 10, 1888, cited in Dorothy Rose Blumberg, *Florence Kelley: The Making of a Social Pioneer* (New York: Augustus M. Kelley, 1966), p. 102. The goals of the Working Women's Society were described in its 1892 *Annual Report:* "to found trades organizations in trades where they do not exist, and to encourage and assist existing labor organizations to the end of increasing wages and shortening hours." Quoted in Blumberg, *Florence Kelley,* p. 102. The New York Working Women's Society evolved into the New York Women's Trade Union League. See Nancy Schrom Dye, *As Equals and As Sisters: Feminism, Unionism, and the Women's Trade Union League of New York* (Columbia: University of Missouri Press, 1980), pp. 10–11. For more on Huntington and this meeting, see Clyde Griffin, "Christian Socialism Instructed by Gompers," *Labor History* 12, no. 2 (Spring 1971): 195–213.

9. *New York Times,* October 10, 1888.

10. Maud Nathan, *The Story of an Epoch-Making Movement* (New York: Doubleday, 1926), pp. 23, 25–30. The London league's statement of purpose is reprinted in ibid., pp. 130–31. Interestingly enough, the London league, which collapsed soon after its formation, did not emphasize a female constituency as strongly as the NCL did. For example, its statement of purpose used the male pronoun: "No buyer has time to find out for himself what the conditions actually are under which those things which he purchases are made."

11. Nathan, *Story,* p. 132.

12. Florence Kelley (hereafter cited as FK), "Aims and Principles of the Consumers' League," *American Journal of Sociology* 5, no. 3 (November 1899): 289–304.

13. Ibid., p. 290.

14. Ibid., pp. 289–304 (quotation, p. 290; FK's emphasis).

15. Ibid., pp. 290, 294–95.

16. Ibid., p. 294.

17. Ibid., p. 298.

18. "Secretary's Report," NCL, *Second Annual Report*, Year Ending March 6, 1901 (New York: NCL, 1901), p. 14; "The Consumers' League of Ann Arbor," in NCL, *Fourth Annual Report*, Year Ending March 4, 1903 (New York: NCL, 1903), pp. 46–47; NCL, *Seventh Annual Report*, Year Ending March 1, 1906 (New York: NCL, 1906), p. 14.

19. "Consumers' League of Massachusetts," in NCL, *Fourth Annual Report*, pp. 37–39.

20. NCL, *Fourth Annual Report*, p. 7. Maud Nathan exemplified the leadership of Jewish women in Consumers' Leagues. "Secretary's Report," NCL, *Fourth Annual Report*, pp. 6–7. See also sermon preached by Cardinal Gibbons at the cathedral, Sunday, December 6, 1903, "Am I My Brother's Keeper?" ("G-3, Publications, 1899–1915," Consumers' League of Maryland, Baltimore, in NCL Papers, Library of Congress, Washington, D.C. [hereafter cited as NCL Papers]), which concluded: "All [wage earners] demand is to obtain living wages for the work they perform. They appeal to you and to the public for compassion and consideration. They are our own flesh and blood."

21. NCL, *Third Annual Report*, Year Ending March 4, 1902 (New York: NCL, 1902), p. 44.

22. NCL, *Fourth Annual Report*, p. 45.

23. NCL, *Third Annual Report*, p. 39.

24. NCL, *Fourth Annual Report*, p. 49.

25. Nathan, *Story*, p. 26.

26. See Daniel Robinson Ernst, "The Lawyers and the Labor Trust: A History of the American Anti-Boycott Association, 1902–1919" (Ph.D. diss., Princeton University, 1989), pp. 11–46. Nathan (*Story*, p. 45) noted: "The printing of all these White Lists constituted a great expense, especially as black listing was illegal, and therefore we were not allowed by law to draw a line through a name already on our list. So, if we were to be compelled to drop a firm, we were obliged to destroy all the old lists and print new ones, leaving out the delinquent firm."

27. NCL, *Third Annual Report*, p. 7.

28. See, for example, the questions posed in Mary I. Wood, *The History of the General Federation of Women's Clubs* (New York: General Federation of Women's Clubs, 1912), p. 147.

29. James Weber Linn, *Jane Addams: A Biography* (New York: Appleton-Century, 1938), pp. 138–39. Linn was Jane Addams's nephew.

30. See Louise Wade, "Florence Kelley," *Notable American Women, 1607–1950: A Biographical Dictionary*, 3 vols., edited by Edward T. James, Janet Wilson James, and Paul S. Boyer (Cambridge: Harvard University Press, 1971); Blumberg, *Florence Kelley*; and

Kathryn Kish Sklar, *Florence Kelley and the Nation's Work: The Rise of Women's Political Culture, 1830–1900* (New Haven: Yale University Press, 1995).

31. Wood, *History of the General Federation*, pp. 131–32.

32. NCL, *Second Annual Report*, p. 15.

33. Ibid.

34. Ibid.; Wood, *History of the General Federation*, pp. 139, 173.

35. Wood, *History of the General Federation*, pp. 145–46.

36. Ibid., p. 178.

37. NCL, *Fourth Annual Report*, pp. 20–21

38. FK, *Some Ethical Gains through Legislation* (New York: Macmillan, 1905; New York: Arno, 1969), p. 162.

39. Samuel Gompers, *Seventy Years of Life and Labor* (New York: Dutton), 1:194. The best treatment of the case that changed Gompers's mind about legislative action, *In re Jacobs* (98 N.Y. 98, 1885), can be found in Eileen Boris, *Home to Work: Motherhood and the Politics of Industrial Homework in the United States* (New York: Cambridge University Press, 1994). Gerald Friedman, in "Worker Militancy and Its Consequences: Political Responses to Labor Unrest in the United States, 1877–1914," *International Labor and Working-Class History*, no. 40 (Fall 1991): 5–17, analyzed the political conditions that limited the AFL's options: at the national level the hegemony of the Republican Party from 1894 to 1910 allowed the party to rule without labor's support, at the local level the consolidation of Tammany in New York and other Democratic political machines in other urban areas could compel "concessions to the machine's upper-class allies" while still mobilizing majorities among poorer voters, and registration rules led to a sharp drop in voter turnout after 1896. The correlation between strong courts and a weak labor movement is analyzed in Victoria C. Hattam, *Labor Visions and State Power: The Origins of Business Unionism in the United States* (Princeton: Princeton University Press, 1993). See also Eileen Boris, "A Man's Dwelling House Is His Castle: Tenement House Cigarmaking and the Judicial Imperative," in *Work Engendered: Towards a New History of American Labor*, edited by Ava Baron (Ithaca: Cornell University Press, 1991), pp. 114–41; *A Verbatim Report of the Discussion on the Political Programme, at the Denver Convention of the American Federation of Labor, 1894* (New York: Freytag Press, 1895); Howard H. Quint, *The Forging of American Socialism* (Columbia: University of South Carolina Press, 1953), pp. 32–71; Leon Fink, "Labor, Liberty, and the Law: Trade Unionism and the Problem of the American Constitutional Order," *Journal of American History* 74 (December 1987): 904–25; Gerald Friedman, "The Working Class and the Welfare State: Working-Class Militancy and Its Consequences: Political Response to Labor Unrest in the United States, 1877–1914," *International Labor and Working-Class History* 40 (Fall 1991): 5–17; and Benjamin R. Twiss, *Lawyers and the Constitution: How Laissez-Faire Came to the Supreme Court* (Princeton: Princeton University Press, 1942), pp. 93–109.

40. See Sklar, "Historical Foundations," pp. 58–60.

41. Elizabeth Landes, "The Effect of State Maximum Hours Laws on the Employment of Women in 1920," *Journal of Political Economy* 88, no. 31 (1980): 476–94.

42. See, for example, a report on the NCL's work, "Watchmen on the Walls of Labor," *The Survey* 38 (May 5, 1917): 122–23.

43. Appendix, "Constitution of the American Association for Labor Legislation," 1906, reel 61, AALL Papers. The international also organized the International Labor Office, which published a periodical bulletin of labor laws in all countries. See Carol Riegelman Lubin and Anne Winslow, *Social Justice for Women: The International Labor Organization and Women* (Durham: Duke University Press, 1990).

44. Carroll Wright to Dr. Adna F. Weber, Worcester, Mass., March 12, 1906, AALL Papers.

45. Florence Kelley was among those listed on the "American Association for Labor Legislation Committee on Constitutional Convention," [1906], reel 61, AALL Papers, but a line was drawn through her name on the membership list of 1908. Her relationship with the AALL in general and with John Andrews's leadership in particular was stormy. Charter members at the 1906 meeting included thirteen men and eight women. Their occupations reflected the range of professionals interested in labor legislation at this mature stage in the development of Progressive reform. Among the men were Richard T. Ely, professor of economics at the University of Wisconsin; Edward T. Devine, editor of *Charities and the Commons*; Owen Lovejoy, head of the New York Child Labor Committee; Henry W. Farnam, professor of economics at Yale University; and Adna F. Weber, secretary of the New York State Department of Labor. The women included Helen Marot, executive secretary of the Women's Trade Union League of New York; Mary Van Kleeck, who was conducting research on child labor in tenements and later was employed by the Russell Sage Foundation; and Mary K. Simkovitch, head of the Greenwich House Settlement.

46. Richard Ely to Adna Weber, Madison, Wis., February 26, 1907, AALL Papers. See also Ely to Weber, Quadrangle Club, Chicago, April 5, 1907. During the AALL's early years Florence Kelley was a member of the AALL Executive Committee (along with Jane Addams). See "Meeting of the Council," April 18, 1907, reel 61, AALL. Kelley was included on the "tentative program for the first annual meeting of the Association to be held in Madison, Wisconsin," in 1907, scheduled to speak on "The Working Conditions of Stokers on Transatlantic Steamers" (reel 61). In November 1907 the AALL's position "on working hours in the clothing trades" was "submitted to Mrs. Florence Kelley for criticism and suggestions" (reel 61).

47. Born in 1880, John B. Andrews (JBA) was twenty years younger than Florence Kelley. He had grown up on his family's farm in Wisconsin and graduated from the University of Wisconsin, where he pursued doctoral studies in history and economics. For Irene Osgood's unpaid status, see John Commons to Henry Farnam, [Madison], December 25, 1909. Irene Osgood and John Andrews married in 1910, forming a partnership that greatly benefited the AALL. The AALL did not include its finances in its annual report or in the Council or Executive Committee minutes, but for a typical list of contributions, see Irene Osgood to Henry Farnam, [Madison], December 24, 1908, reel 61, AALL Papers. There Farnam himself and V. Everett Macy are listed as the biggest 1908 donors with contributions of $200.

48. Richard Ely hoped for "a large appropriation, in fact, $15,000 a year, from the Russell Sage Foundation." Ely to H. B. Favill, [Madison], February 17, 1908. Although Ely's prediction did not prove true, in 1911 the Russell Sage Foundation did provide the AALL with $8,500. See John M. Glenn, Lilian Brandt, and F. Emerson Andrews,

Russell Sage Foundation, 1907–1946, 2 vols. (New York: Russell Sage Foundation, 1947), pp. 161, 229–30, 689. John Commons remembered that Henry Farnam told him, "I am so enthusiastic about this first year's work [of the AALL] that I will give $5,000 a year to bring Andrews to New York and set up there the headquarters of the Association." Commons, *Myself: The Autobiography of John Commons* (Madison: University of Wisconsin Press, 1964), p. 139.

49. "Organization," *American Labor Legislation Review* 4 (1914): 511–13.

50. [Richard Ely], "The Nature and Work of the American Association for Labor Legislation," p. 2, reel 61, AALL Papers; "Organization," *American Labor Legislation Review*, p. 517.

51. AALL, "Leaflet No. 3," 1909, reel 61, AALL Papers; letterhead motto of the Massachusetts Association for Labor Legislation, Henry Holcombe to JBA, Cambridge, Mass., January 25, 1912.

52. Jane Addams to Richard T. Ely, Hull House, March 26, 1908, and Irene Osgood to Jane Addams, [Madison], October 21, 1908, AALL Papers.

53. Irene Osgood to John Martin, [Madison], November 14, 1908, AALL Papers.

54. John Commons to Henry Farnam, Madison, December 25, 1909, AALL Papers. The process of phasing out AALL locals began with the Executive Committee meeting of December 19, 1912, when the committee voted to end the New York local, reel 61, AALL Papers.

55. Commons to Farnam, December 25, 1909.

56. Ibid. For a summary of the AALL agenda on industrial disease, industrial accidents, workmen's compensation, vocational rehabilitation, health insurance, and unemployment, see Lloyd F. Pierce, "The Activities of the American Association for Labor Legislation in Behalf of Social Security and Protective Labor Legislation" (Ph.D. diss., University of Wisconsin, 1953), pp. 156, 166. See also Daniel Nelson, *Unemployment Insurance: The American Experience, 1915–1935* (Madison: University of Wisconsin Press, 1969), pp. 13–43; Udo Sautter, *Three Cheers for the Unemployed: Government and Unemployment before the New Deal* (Cambridge: Cambridge University Press, 1991), pp. 26–31.

57. Arthur N. Holcombe to JBA, Cambridge, Mass., January 2, 1912, AALL Papers.

58. Holcombe to JBA, Cambridge, Mass., November 28, 1911, AALL Papers.

59. Henry Seager to Seth Low, New York, February 1, 1912, AALL Papers.

60. Henry Farnam to JBA, March 27, 1909, New Haven, and JBA to Henry Farnam, March 30, 1909, AALL Papers.

61. See John R. Commons to Henry W. Farnam, [Madison], January 23, 1909, AALL Papers; and Glenn, Brandt, and Andrews, *Russell Sage Foundation*, pp. 230, 688.

62. JBA to John Commons, New York, February 15, 1910, AALL Papers.

63. JBA to Commons, [New York], December 10, 1910, AALL Papers.

64. Henry Farnam to JBA, New Haven, March 27, 1909, AALL Papers.

65. For the national's view of the Massachusetts local as a financial liability, see AALL president Henry Seager to Edwin F. Gay, New York, October 21, 1912, AALL Papers: "Since the Massachusetts Association was organized we have drawn almost no revenue from the state except the two-thirds of the dues of old members."

66. See scattered reports in reel 61, AALL Papers.

67. Arthur Holcombe to JBA, Cambridge, Mass., January 25, 1912, AALL Papers.

68. See JBA to Henry W. Farnam, New York, October 25, 1911, AALL Papers, for Andrews's diary of telephone calls received and letters written one day in October. In the first volume of the *ALLR* John and Irene Andrews coauthored an article on "Scientific Standards in Labor Legislation." There they demonstrated how the precise wording of labor legislation determined whether it was enforceable and effective or unenforceable and ineffective. A well-written factory inspector law might reduce the possibility of disputes between employers and inspectors and thereby make employers more willing to support such legislation.

69. Crystal Eastman, *Work-Accidents and the Law* (New York: Russell Sage Foundation, 1910). The date of Eastman's appointment can be inferred from Glenn, Brandt, and Andrews, *Russell Sage Foundation*, p. 688.

70. Irene Andrews to Leonard W. Hatch, [New York], May 21, 1910, AALL Papers.

71. Pierce, "Activities of the American Association for Labor Legislation," pp. 156, 166.

72. Marguerite Green, *The National Civic Federation and the American Labor Movement, 1900–1925* (Washington, D.C.: Catholic University of America Press), pp. 3, 245, 248.

73. Ibid., pp. 257, 245–67.

74. JBA to John R. Commons, [New York], October 11, 1911; JBA to JRC, [New York], October 18, 1911; and JBA to JRC, [New York], October 18, 1911—all in AALL Papers.

75. JBA to John R. Commons, New York, October 16, 1911, AALL Papers. Officials caught in the middle of this conflict tried to devise a division of labor. For example, Edgar Davies, chief factory inspector of Illinois, suggested to the NCF that it allow the AALL "to carry on the work of the occupational disease question, and for the Federation to confine itself to the Model Safety Act, although I fear and am convinced that they have gone too far to drop their uniform accident blank." Edgar Davies to Irene Osgood Andrews, Chicago, December 16, 1911, AALL Papers. The fact that there was a small but distinct membership overlap in the two organizations apparently did nothing to help resolve this conflict.

76. Morris Hillquit to JBA, New York, June 29, 1911, and JBA to William Coshman, [New York], January 5, 1915, AALL Papers.

77. See n. 39 above.

78. Milton Fairchild to Henry Seager, Washington, D.C. [June 1915], and Samuel Gompers to JBA, January 3, 1913, AALL Papers. Seager replied for the AALL to the AFL's ongoing opposition to hours and wage legislation for men in "American Labor Legislation," *American Labor Legislation Review* 6, no. 1 (March 1916): 87–98.

79. H. S. Millis, "Some Aspects of the Minimum Wage," *Journal of Political Economy* 22 (1914): 132–33.

80. See Sklar, *Florence Kelley*, chaps. 9–10, and FK, "Minimum Wage Boards," reprinted from *Proceedings of the National Conference of Charities and Correction, June 1911* as an NCL pamphlet, box G-2, "Clippings from Magazines and Leaflets, 1902–1924," NCL Papers, and reprinted in *American Journal of Sociology* 17 (November 1911): 303–14.

81. Sidney Webb and Beatrice Webb, *Industrial Democracy* (1897; reprint, London:

Longmans, Green, 1920), p. 751. See "Parasitic Trades" and "The National Minimum," pp. 749–84.

82. For a telling gendered comparison between British and American wage legislation, see Vivien Hart, *Bound by Our Constitution: Women, Workers, and Minimum Wage Laws in the United States and Britain* (Princeton: Princeton University Press, 1994).

83. FK, "Aims and Principles of the Consumers' League," p. 298.

84. *Première Conférence Internationale des Ligues Sociales d'Acheteurs, Genève, September 1908* (Fribourg, Switzerland: N.p., 1909), pp. 449–55.

85. For Mary Dewson, see James T. Patterson, "Mary Dewson and the American Minimum Wage Movement," *Labor History* 5, no. 2 (Spring 1964): 134–52. Elizabeth Glendower Evans's relationship with Kelley began in 1903, when Evans declared: "It is a thorough pleasure and satisfaction . . . to me to have dealings of any kind with you, because I like you and your ways right through to the backbone." Evans to FK, December 6, 1903, William D. Kelley Papers, Historical Society of Pennsylvania. At first Evans represented both the NCL and the AALL in her minimum-wage activity. AALL, "Minutes Executive Committee Meeting," February 8, 1911, reel 61, AALL Papers. For an example of the way Evans sold the idea of minimum wage to middle-class women, see "Address by Mrs. Glendower Evans," City Club of Philadelphia, *City Club Bulletin* 6 (January 27, 1913): 203–5.

86. For the campaign generally, see NCL *Annual Reports*, 1910, 1911, and 1912. For the centrality of the Oregon and Washington Consumers' Leagues in the passage of those states' minimum wage laws, see Edwin V. O'Hara, *A Living Wage by Legislation* (New York: Paulist Press, 1916), pp. 203–4, and George M. Piper to Edwin V. O'Hara, Olympia, January 12, 1913, "The Minimum Wage Law: Scrapbook of Edwin V. O'Hara," Oregon Historical Society, Portland. For the NCL's leadership in Wisconsin, where the American Federation of Labor opposed minimum wage laws, see Gordon M. Haferbecker, *Wisconsin Labor Laws* (Madison: University of Wisconsin Press, 1958), pp. 98–100. For the NCL's work with the Minnesota AFL on minimum wage, see W. E. McEwen to JBA, Duluth, February 1, 1913, AALL Papers. In Massachusetts and Minnesota the committee's work was especially strongly supported by organized labor. For the importance of regional considerations on this and other social legislation, see Edward Berkowitz and Kim McQuaid, *Creating the Welfare State: The Political Economy of Twentieth-Century Reform* (New York: Praeger, 1980), pp. 30–33.

87. Not all trade union women endorsed minimum wage legislation for women. In 1912 the Executive Committee of the New York WTUL voted not to endorse the New York bill, and it failed to pass. In New York and elsewhere women who earned more than the projected minimum and thus did not stand to gain from wage legislation sometimes opposed it. Some shared Gompers's fears that state-mandated minimums would become maximum wages. Some WTUL members opposed state setting of wages based on sex. On the whole, however, women trade unionists supported wage legislation for women, and even where they did not, they acknowledged that it improved the wages of most women workers. On the latter point, see Rebecca J. Mead, "Trade Unionism and Political Activity among San Francisco Wage-Earning Women, 1900–1922" (master's thesis, San Francisco State University, 1991), p. 200; and U.S. Department of Labor, Women's Bureau, *The Effects of Labor Legislation on the Employ-*

ment Opportunities of Women, Women's Bureau Bulletin 65 (Washington, D.C.: GPO, 1928), pp. 43–49. For the WTUL, see Elizabeth Anne Payne, *Reform, Labor, and Feminism: Margaret Dreier Robins and the Women's Trade Union League* (Urbana: University of Illinois Press, 1988), pp. 106, 129–30, and Dye, *As Equals and As Sisters*, pp. 146–47. Kelley sympathized with labor's opposition:

> The hostility of certain labor unions to the whole idea of statutory minimum wages arises, doubtless, from their cruel past experience with American courts in relation to labor laws, and their suspicion in relation to these boards seems to me to have as much justification as this: that the few wage boards statutes hitherto enacted in this country have eliminated those democratic features of the Australian and English laws which best safeguard the interest of the workers, namely, the inclusion of men under the statutes, and the election of the boards by the persons most closely concerned—the employers and employees.
>
> There is, in my opinion, reason to fear that these boards, on their present undemocratic basis, may become sources of injury to the workers, when the present inflamed interest in the relation of poverty to vice dies down, and the boards fall into the hands of politicians, as they are obviously destined to do wherever the governor appoints the commission, and the commission appoints the boards, and the wage earners and employers have no deciding vote in the matter.
>
> In other words, I believe that our task is only begun in all such states, and that our laws will have to be amended in the direction of the English and Australian legislation before the workingman can reasonably be expected to give them support.

FK to Edwin V. O'Hara, New York, March 20, 1913, "The Minimum Wage Law: Scrapbook of Edwin V. O'Hara," Oregon Historical Society.

88. FK, "Minimum Wage Boards"; FK, "Married Women in Industry," *Proceedings of the Academy of Political Science in the City of New York* (New York: Academy of Political Science, 1910), pp. 90–97. Kelley's wage campaign ignored the circumstances of African American women, since most young black women did not have access to the occupations she sought to protect, and since about a third of married black women were wage earners (compared to about 5 percent of married white women) in 1910. See Lynn Weiner, *From Working Girl to Working Mother: The Female Labor Force in the United States, 1820–1980* (Chapel Hill: University of North Carolina Press, 1985), p. 89. Kelley understood that the chronic low wages of African American men accounted for this difference but did not explicitly address the problem.

89. FK, "Ten Years from Now," *Survey*, March 26, 1910, pp. 978–81; FK, "Minimum Wage Boards," *Proceedings of the National Conference of Charities and Correction* (Fort Wayne, Ind.: NCCC, 1911), pp. 148–56 (quotation, p. 152).

90. Joanne J. Meyerowitz, *Women Adrift: Independent Wage Earners in Chicago, 1880–1930* (Chicago: University of Chicago Press, 1988), pp. 3–6.

91. FK, "Minimum Wage Laws," *Journal of Political Economy* 20 (December 1912): 1007.

92. FK, "Minimum Wage Boards," p. 398. Yet Kelley often had to accept half a loaf in this regard. See n. 87 above. The AALL's and John Commons's position on wage boards was shaped by their commitment to state industrial commissions rather than

statutes as the means for advancing labor legislation. In an unpublished 1911 report on the prospects for minimum wage legislation in the United States, Mary Van Kleeck noted that Commons doubted that such legislation met "the constitutional restrictions against discrimination and taking property without due process of law." With the creation of the Wisconsin Industrial Commission in 1911, Commons gained what he thought were the means by which minimum wages could be imposed—by experts. John B. Andrews thought that the establishment of the Wisconsin Industrial Commission was "the most significant labor law of the year," because it established "the first thorough-going attempt to . . . give our labor law greater elasticity through the work of experts clothed with the power of issuing orders." JBA to Mary Dreier, [New York], December 14, 1911, AALL Papers.

93. Elizabeth Glendower Evans, quoted in FK to Edwin V. O'Hara, October 28, 1912, "The Minimum Wage Law: Scrapbook of Edwin V. O'Hara," Oregon Historical Society.

94. FK, "The Present Status of Minimum Wage Legislation," *National Conference of Charities and Correction, Proceedings, July 1913* (Fort Wayne, Ind: NCCC, 1913), p. 7.

95. For a penetrating analysis of the gendered aspects of this process of wage determination, see Alice Kessler-Harris, *A Woman's Wage: Historical Meanings and Social Consequences* (Lexington: University Press of Kentucky, 1990).

96. JBA to Erich Stern, New York, December 14, 1910, AALL Papers.

97. Arthur Holcombe to JBA, Cambridge, Mass., January 2, 1912, AALL Papers.

98. Henry R. Seager to Seth Low, New York City, February 1, 1912, AALL Papers. The AALL's summary of its achievements during its first five years focused entirely on occupational safety standards, disease, and injury.

99. Irene Osgood Andrews, "The Relation of Irregular Employment to the Living Wage for Women," *American Labor Legislation Review* 5, no. 2 (1915): 287–418.

100. JBA to Miss Caroline Straughan, New York, December 11, 1918, AALL Papers.

101. For the FLSA, see Boris, *Home to Work*, pp. 273–301.

CHAPTER 3. Putting Children First

1. The first epigraph is from Emma Duke, Director, Industrial Division, Children's Bureau, to Rev. J. C. Cunningham of Buffalo, S.C., July 12, 1919, folder 13-1-4, box 152, Children's Bureau Records, National Archives, Washington, D.C. The second is quoted in Clarke A. Chambers, *Seedtime for Reform: American Social Service and Social Action, 1918–1933* (Minneapolis: University of Minnesota Press, 1963), p. 56.

2. See Theda Skocpol, *Protecting Soldiers and Mothers: The Political Origins of Social Policy in the United States* (Cambridge: Harvard University Press, 1992); Seth Koven and Sonya Michel, eds., *Gender and the Origins of Welfare States in Western Europe and North America* (Boston: Routledge, 1992); Linda Gordon and Theda Skocpol, "Gender, State, and Society: A Debate," *Contention* 2, no. 3 (Spring 1993): 139–89; "Maternalism as a Paradigm," a symposium in *Journal of Women's History* 5, no. 2 (Fall 1993): 95–131; Karen Offen, "Defining Feminism: A Comparative Historical Approach," *Signs* 14 (Autumn 1988): 119–57; Eileen Yeo, "Social Motherhood and the Sexual Communion

of Labor in British Social Science, 1850–1950," *Women's History Review* 1, no. 1 (1992): 63–87. Another critique of the consequences of maternalist policies is in Mary Frances Berry, *The Politics of Parenthood: Child Care, Women's Rights, and the Myth of the Good Mother* (New York: Viking, 1993).

3. Poverty rates for 1990 are from the *1992 Green Book* (Washington, D.C.: GPO, 1992), p. 1275, table 3.

4. Barbara Wolfe, "The Deteriorating Economic Circumstances of Children," in *Essays on the Economics of Discrimination*, edited by Emily Hoffman (Kalamazoo, Mich.: Upjohn Institute, 1991).

5. This periodization is based mainly although not exclusively on evidence about white and relatively prosperous women, but it offers a promising start.

6. Lori D. Ginzburg, " 'Moral Suasion Is Moral Balderdash': Women, Politics, and Social Activism in the 1850s," *Journal of American History* 73, no. 3 (December 1986): 601–22.

7. Aileen Kraditor, *The Ideas of the Woman Suffrage Movement, 1890–1920* (New York: Columbia University Press, 1965); Ellen Carol DuBois, ed., *Elizabeth Cady Stanton, Susan B. Anthony: Correspondence, Writings, Speeches* (New York: Schocken, 1981).

8. Anne Firor Scott, "Women's Voluntary Associations: From Charity to Reform," in *Lady Bountiful Revisited: Women, Philanthropy, and Power*, edited by Kathleen D. McCarthy (New Brunswick, N.J.: Rutgers University Press, 1990), pp. 35–49.

9. I am aware that some historians argue to restrict *feminist* to apply to a new, early-twentieth-century perspective, and to a time when the word was used by women activists themselves. However, I think there is a need for a generic word that identifies continuities across longer historical time—say, from the eighteenth century on—among women activists who explicitly sought to raise the status of women, and I know no other term.

10. Wendy Sarvasy, "Beyond the Difference versus Equality Policy Debate: Post-suffrage Feminism, Citizenship, and the Quest for a Feminist Welfare State," *Signs* 17, no. 2 (Winter 1992): 329–62.

11. Michael Grossberg, *Governing the Hearth: Law and the Family in Nineteenth-Century America* (Chapel Hill: University of North Carolina Press, 1985), chap. 7.

12. *Wenham v. State*, 65 Nebraska 394, 1902, quoted in Elizabeth Faulkner Baker, *Protective Labor Legislation, with Special Reference to Women in the State of New York*, Studies in History, Economics, and Public Law 116, no. 2 (New York: Columbia University Press, 1925), p. 62.

13. Quoted in Edward MacGaffey, "A Pattern for Progress: The Minnesota Children's Code," *Minnesota History* 41, no. 5 (Spring 1969): 231–32.

14. Maureen Fitzgerald, "Saints, Seduction, and Social Control: Irish-Catholic Nuns in New York City, 1845–1900" (Ph.D. diss., University of Wisconsin, 1993).

15. The term *single mother* was not used at the time and the laws were mainly intended for widows, although in many states mothers who were alone due to marital separation or desertion were also entitled to stipends, and some states even accepted unmarried mothers.

16. Louis J. Covotsos, "Child Welfare and Social Progress: A History of the United States Children's Bureau, 1912–1935" (Ph.D. diss., University of Chicago, 1976), p. 53.

This historian saw the Children's Bureau's constant extragovernmental consultation as a sign of its weakness, but the record suggests otherwise.

17. It is important to bear in mind, however, that the social-work tradition was by no means exclusively female. Men retained a majority of top positions in charity and social-work establishments; many men joined settlements and worked as caseworkers.

18. Linda Gordon, "Social Insurance and Public Assistance: The Influence of Gender in Welfare Thought in the United States, 1890–1935," *American Historical Review* 97, no. 1 (February 1992): 19–54, and *Pitied but Not Entitled: Single Mothers and the History of Welfare* (New York: Free Press, 1994).

19. Linda Gordon, "Black and White Visions of Welfare: Women's Welfare Activism, 1890–1945," *Journal of American History* (September 1991): 559–90, and *Pitied.*

20. Edith Howe, "Our Right to the Lives of Babies," *Delineator* 73, no. 3 (March 1909): 400–402, 480.

21. Harriot Stanton Blatch, "Voluntary Motherhood," in *Up from the Pedestal: Selected Writings in the History of American Feminism,* edited by Aileen S. Kraditor (Chicago: Quadrangle, 1968), pp. 167–75. This hereditarian thought, which became a full-fledged eugenics program by the early twentieth century, was to one degree or another characteristic of nearly all reformers at this time. It was based on the belief in the inheritability of acquired characteristics. For a discussion of this perspective, see Linda Gordon, *Woman's Body, Woman's Right: Birth Control in America,* 2d ed. (New York: Viking, 1990), chap. 6.

22. Gordon, *Woman's Body, Woman's Right,* chap. 6.

23. Mrs. Carrie W. Clifford, Ohio Federation of Colored Women's Clubs, 1915, quoted in Eileen Boris, "The Power of Motherhood: Black and White Activist Women Redefine the 'Political,'" *Yale Journal of Law and Feminism* 2, no. 1 (Fall 1989): 25.

24. The relationship between Americanization and the reconstruction of family life is discussed in Linda Gordon, *Heroes of Their Own Lives: The Politics and History of Family Violence, Boston, 1880–1960* (New York: Viking, 1988).

25. For an excellent discussion of these racial goals in reform, see Gwendolyn Mink, "The Lady and the Tramp: Gender, Race, and the Origins of the American Welfare State," in *Women, the State, and Welfare,* edited by Linda Gordon (Madison: University of Wisconsin Press, 1990).

26. Paula Baker, "The Domestication of Politics: Women and American Political Society, 1780–1920," in *Women, the State, and Welfare.*

27. Linda K. Kerber, *Women of the Republic: Intellect and Ideology in Revolutionary America* (Chapel Hill: University of North Carolina Press, 1980), p. 284.

28. Kathryn Kish Sklar, *Catharine Beecher: A Study in Domesticity* (New Haven: Yale University Press, 1973).

29. Andrea Friedman, "Prurient Interests: Gender and Religion in Anti-Obscenity Campaigns in New York City, 1909–1945" (Ph.D. diss., University of Wisconsin, forthcoming).

30. Emma Duke to Rev. J. C. Cunningham, July 12, 1919.

31. Ellen Fitzpatrick, *Endless Crusade: Women Social Scientists and Progressive Reform* (New York: Oxford University Press, 1990), p. 169.

32. The organizing committee also included Zona Gale, Frieda Kirchwey, Norman

Thomas, Eduard Lindeman, and David Starr Jordan. Proposal dated February 24, 1928, folder 132, box 14, United Neighborhood Houses Papers, Social Welfare Historical Archives, University of Minnesota, Minneapolis. On the issue of using children as a wedge for further welfare development, see also Martha Minow, "Rights for the Next Generation: A Feminist Approach to Children's Rights," *Harvard Women's Law Journal* 9 (1986): 1–24.

33. Chambers, *Seedtime for Reform*, p. 56.

34. Gordon, "Social Insurance and Public Assistance" and *Pitied*.

35. The following discussion is taken from material in my *Heroes of Their Own Lives*.

36. I do not use *patriarchy* here as a synonym for male supremacy or *sexism*. Rather I refer to an earlier, historical, and more specific sense of patriarchy as a family form in which fathers had control over all other family members—children, women, and servants. In this sense of patriarchy, fathers' control flowed from the fathers' monopolization of economic resources. The patriarchal family presupposed a family mode of production, as among peasants, artisans, or farmers, in which individuals did not work individually as wage laborers. That historical patriarchy defined a set of parent-child relations as much as relations between the sexes. The claim of an organization such as an SPCC to speak on behalf of children's rights, its claim to the license to intervene on behalf of children who were mistreated by their parents, was an attack on patriarchal power.

37. From very early on in the history of the SPCCs, the major sources of complaints were family members themselves, primarily women and secondarily children.

38. The story of how women maneuvered to force child-protection agencies to become involved in wife-beating cases is told in Gordon, *Heroes of Their Own Lives*.

39. On social-work efforts against family violence, see Linda Gordon, "The Frustrations of Family Violence Social Work: An Historical Critique," *Journal of Sociology and Social Welfare* 15, no. 4 (December 1988): 139–60.

40. Despite many reform efforts, contemporary foster care remains inadequate to a degree that is distinctly abusive to children. For one recent discussion, see J. C. Barden, "Foster Care System Reeling, Despite Law Meant to Help," *New York Times*, September 21, 1990, p. 1.

41. The following discussion is taken from Gordon, *Pitied*.

42. The argument that our welfare system has two unequal tracks has been widespread, and recently several scholars have pointed out the gendered as well as the racialized nature of these programs. See Barbara Nelson, "The Origins of the Two-Channel Welfare State: Workmen's Compensation and Mothers' Aid," and Diana Pearce, "Welfare Is Not *for* Women," both in Gordon, ed., *Women, the State, and Welfare*; and Linda Gordon, "What Does Welfare Regulate?" *Social Research* 55, no. 4 (Winter 1988): 609–30.

43. Edith Abbott, "Abolish the Pauper Laws," *Social Service Review* 8, no. 1 (March 1934): 1–16.

44. For example, see Grace Abbott's 1938 essay, "Mothers' Aid and Public Assistance," in *From Relief to Social Security*, edited by Grace Abbott (New York: Russell and Russell, 1941), pp. 275–76; Grace Abbott, "What about Mothers' Pensions Now?" *Survey* 70, no. 3 (March 19, 1934): 80–81.

45. Several of the designers of the Social Security Act later reported that this had been a mistake, but it was a conscious decision among the Children's Bureau women.

46. For example, Mary Dewson after the fact continually defended ADC as a program for children, never women; see her series of speeches in Chairman of the Board group, folder 062.2, box 39, Social Security Papers, National Archives, Washington, D.C.

47. Katherine Ward Fisher, "Suggestions for Child Security," typed memo submitted to Committee on Economic Security, Witte box 200, n.d. [probably 1934], ibid.

48. Grace Abbott, memo to Committee on Economic Security, July 1934, Committee on Economic Security, box 20, Social Security Papers, National Archives, Washington, D.C.

49. I have discussed elsewhere the complex ways in which these views expressed and constructed the women's own class and race position. See Gordon, "Black and White Visions" and *Pitied.*

50. Jane Addams, *Twenty Years at Hull-House* (New York: Macmillan, 1910), p. 169; Addams, *My Friend Julia Lathrop* (New York: Macmillan, 1935), p. 171 (Lillian Wald's view); Emily D. Cahan, *Past Caring: A History of U.S. Preschool Care and Education for the Poor, 1820–1965* (New York: National Center for Children in Poverty, School of Public Health, Columbia University, 1989).

51. Grace Abbott, *The Child and the State* (Chicago: University of Chicago Press, 1938), p. 230.

52. The authors of the ADC Title of Social Security did not ask for such low stipends, but it was harder for them to prevent the low maximums because of the fiction that the money was only for children, not their parents.

53. Although the suitable home provision was not in the federal law, it was in the model law drawn up and proposed to the states.

54. This invasive investigative practice began being curtailed in the 1960s, as welfare recipients and lawyers supporting them won court challenges.

55. "The Reminiscences of Katharine Lenroot," in Columbia University Oral History Collection, p. 26.

56. Abbott, "Mothers' Aid and Public Assistance."

57. Only one attempt has been made to involve the child recipient in the contract, and that is the "learnfare" program recently tried in Wisconsin and now widely condemned as a failure.

58. The Children's Bureau designers of ADC believed that the program would provide better support for single-mother families because they expected greater federal authority over the local programs. Through this authority they thought that they would be able to insist upon civil-service (i.e., nonpatronage) administration by professionally trained social workers doing casework for each recipient. In these hopes they were disappointed by two separate but related defeats at the hands of Congress. First, the proviso for federal supervision of and standards for local ADC programs was amended out of the act by a southern-led states'-rights voting bloc. Its motives derived from both class and race interests, as it wanted to retain the ability of state and local governments to exclude from assistance programs those who customarily performed low-wage work; see Jill Quadagno, "From Old Age Assistance to

Supplemental Security Income," in *The Politics of Social Policy in the United States*, edited by Margaret Weir, Ann Shola Orloff, and Theda Skocpol (Princeton: Princeton University Press, 1988), pp. 235–63. Second, for related reasons a similar bloc prevented ADC and other assistance programs from being administered by the Children's Bureau, whose personnel would have insisted on greater equity and higher standards in awarding stipends.

59. Controlled by Southern Democrats, the congressional leadership threatened to block any federal welfare provision that would include African Americans and thereby subvert their absolute dependence on low-wage labor. This is discussed at length in Gordon, *Pitied*.

60. On the incidence of single-mother families, see Linda Gordon and Sara McLanahan, "Single Parenthood in 1900," Institute for Research on Poverty Discussion Paper no. 919–90, University of Wisconsin-Madison, 1990, and *Journal of Family History* 16, no. 2 (1991): 97–116.

CHAPTER 4. Designing Women and Old Fools

My thanks to Eileen Boris and my coeditors, Linda Kerber and Kitty Sklar, for insightful readings; and to perceptive and stimulating audiences at the German Historical Institute, Wichita State University, Kansas, and Stetson University, where I presented versions of this essay. Special thanks to Stephen Robertson for invaluable research assistance.

1. The epigraph is from Mary W. Dewson, "What the Social Security Act Means to Women," typescript of an address for the National Radio Forum, broadcast October 11, 1937, file entitled "Speeches and Addresses, 1937," box 9, Mary W. Dewson Papers, Franklin Delano Roosevelt Library, Hyde Park, N.Y. (hereafter cited as Dewson Papers).

2. *Weinberger v. Wiesenfeld*, 420 U.S. 636 (1975), 652.

3. *Califano v. Goldfarb*, 97 S.Ct. 1021 (1977).

4. *Califano v. Webster*, 430 U.S. 313 (1977).

5. *Califano v. Goldfarb*, 1022.

6. Federal Advisory Council Minutes, February 19, 1938, afternoon session, p. 18, file 025, box 12, Chairman's Files, RG 47, Social Security Administration Papers, National Archives, Washington, D.C. (hereafter cited as Advisory Council Minutes).

7. Ibid. The actuary was William Williamson.

8. Ibid.

9. Ibid., April 29, 1938, 2d half of morning session, pp. 5–6. Mary Dewson followed up Brown's comment, not by questioning the explicit stereotypes in his statement but by reaffirming that the "single woman who has earned enough can get just as high an annuity as a single man." No one else on the Advisory Council challenged the image of the aged woman.

10. Gosta Esping-Anderson, *The Three Worlds of Welfare Capitalism* (Princeton: Princeton University Press, 1990), p. 23.

11. Edwin Amenta and Theda Skocpol, "States and Social Policies," *Annual Review of*

Sociology 12 (1986): 131–57; Theda Skocpol and Gretchen Ritter, "Gender and the Origins of Modern Social Policies in Britain and the United States," *Studies in American Political Development* 5 (Spring 1991): 36–93.

12. Ann Shola Orloff, "Gender and the Social Rights of Citizenship: The Comparative Analysis of Gender Relations and Welfare States," *American Sociological Review* 58 (June 1993): 303–28; Theda Skocpol, *Protecting Soldiers and Mothers: The Political Origins of Social Policy in the United States* (Cambridge: Harvard University Press, 1992).

13. Fred Block, *Revising State Theory: Essays in Politics and Postindustrialism* (Philadelphia: Temple University Press, 1988), chap. 1. For the same reason, I have moved away from the interpretations of Nicos Poulantzas and Jill Quadagno, both of whom see the state as a mediating body that, in Quadagno's words, "weighs priorities, filters information given, and, because of its autonomy from any given class or faction, integrates contradictory measures into state policy." Jill S. Quadagno, "Welfare Capitalism and the Social Security Act of 1935," *American Sociological Review* 49 (October 1984): 634. See also Nicos Poulantzas, *State, Power, Socialism* (London: New Left Books, 1978).

14. A large literature is now beginning to open up the role of gender in constructing social policy. It includes Mimi Abramovitz, *Regulating the Lives of Women: Social Welfare Policy from Colonial Times to the Present* (Boston: Southend Press, 1988); Linda Gordon, ed., *Women, the State, and Welfare* (Madison: University of Wisconsin Press, 1990); Eileen Boris and Peter Bardaglio, "The Transformation of Patriarchy: The Historic Role of the State," in *Families, Politics, and Public Policy: A Feminist Dialogue on Women and the State*, edited by Irene Diamond (New York: Longman, 1983).

15. Conservatives resented the restrictions the act imposed on individual autonomy and derided its premise that the well-being of citizens required government intervention. Liberals continue to take it to task for its persistent deficiencies, including its sexually and racially discriminatory outcomes and its failure to redistribute income. For some of this history, see esp., Andrew Achenbaum, "Reconstructing the History of Federal Policies toward the Aged since 1920," in *Federal Social Policy: The Historical Dimension*, by Donald W. Critchlow and Ellis W. Hawley (University Park: Pennsylvania State University Press, 1988); Jill S. Quadagno, *The Transformation of Old Age Security: Class and Politics in the American Welfare State* (Chicago: University of Chicago Press, 1988), chap. 5. See also Richard Burkhauser and Karen Holden, *A Challenge to Social Security: The Changing Roles of Women in American Society* (New York: Academic Press, 1982), and Roy Lubove, *The Struggle for Social Security* (Cambridge: Harvard University Press, 1968).

16. Robert M. Ball, "The 1939 Amendments to the Social Security Act and What Followed," in *Report of the Committee on Economic Security and Other Basic Documents*, edited by Wilbur Cohen (Washington, D.C.: National Conference on Social Welfare, 1985), p. 165.

17. Unemployment compensation, like the relief programs in the legislation, was run separately by each state in conformity with federal rules and with contributions from the federal government. Tracking the legislative history of Social Security is best accomplished through the memoirs of those who participated in constructing the system, esp. Arthur J. Altmeyer, *The Formative Years of Social Security* (Milwaukee: Univer-

sity of Wisconsin Press, 1966); Edwin Witte, *The Development of the Social Security Act* (Madison: University of Wisconsin Press, 1963); and Eveline M. Burns, *Toward Social Security: An Explanation of the Social Security Act and a Survey of the Larger Issues* (New York: Whittlesey House, 1936).

18. Witte, *Development of the Social Security Act*, p. 119.

19. Paul Douglas, *Social Security in the United States* (New York: Whittlesey House, 1936), p. 100. Jill Quadagno, "Welfare Capitalism and the Social Security Act of 1935," *American Sociological Review* 50 (August 1985): 643, offers another explanation, namely that high OAA payments would disrupt the economic dependency that ensured an available black workforce.

20. Some observers have argued that adequacy governs women's programs and equity those of men. See, e.g., Barbara Nelson, "The Origins of the Two-Channel Welfare State: Workmen's Compensation and Mother's Aid," in *Women, the State, and Welfare*, pp. 123–51. A fully gendered perspective demonstrates the need for a more complicated interpretation.

21. Witte, *Development of the Social Security Act*, pp. 85, 95–96; Quadagno, *Transformation of Old Age Security*, p. 72. Quadagno (pp. 108–9) notes the pressures of the Townsend plan—a politically popular proposal making its way through the states that would provide minimum government pensions to every person over sixty-five without individual contribution and regardless of need—on the initial Social Security Act. The state-based OAA programs permitted payments of up to $30 per month to individuals, male or female, compared to the $17.50 per month that an average worker might expect under Social Security's OAI program. See Quadagno, pp. 119–21, and "The New Pension Scale," *New York Times*, April 1, 1939, p. 18.

22. Advisory Council Minutes, February 18, 1938, morning session, p. 33. Forty percent of employed *women* worked in covered industries at the start. Ewan Clague, then assistant director of research for the Social Security Board, claimed that though more than 21 million workers were excluded—12 million self-employed and 9 million in uncovered occupations—many of these would ultimately be included in the system because they would occasionally work in covered jobs. But the assertion directly contradicts the assumptions of Williamson and others that the costs of the system would be reduced by the contributions of those who were not eligible for benefits. See "The Problem of Extending Old Age Insurance to Cover Classes Now Excluded," typescript, file entitled "December 1937," box 20, J. Douglas Brown Papers, Mudd Manuscript Library, Princeton University (hereafter cited as Brown Papers).

23. Unemployment provisions also disadvantaged women whose job histories tended to be intermittent and who were frequently falsely assumed to be unavailable for jobs. Pregnancy was prima facie evidence of ineligibility for unemployment insurance.

24. The labor representatives were G. M. Bugniazet, secretary, International Brotherhood of Electrical Workers; Harvey Fremming, president of the Oil Field, Gas Well, and Refinery Workers International Union; John Frey, president, Metal Trades Department, American Federation of Labor; Sidney Hillman, president, Amalgamated Clothing Workers of America; Philip Murray, vice president, United Mine Workers of America; and Mathew Woll, International Photo Engravers Union of North America.

Brown frequently expressed concern at the lack of labor participation. For example, when Brown surveyed the council members in February 1938, not a single labor representative responded. See untitled chart, folder 1, box 19, Brown Papers.

25. Linda Gordon, "Social Insurance and Public Assistance: The Influence of Gender in Welfare Thought in the United States, 1890–1935," *American Historical Review* 97 (1992): 19–54.

26. "Social Security Advisory Council Is Appointed," typescript of press release, May 10, 1937, file 025, box 10, Chairman's Files, RG 47, Social Security Administration Papers, National Archives, Washington, D.C. (hereafter cited as Chairman's Files).

27. I. S. Falk to the Advisory Council, November 5, 1937, "Benefits for Disabled Persons and Survivors, and Supplemental Allowances for Dependents," typescript, file entitled "November, 1937," box 20, Brown Papers.

28. House Committee on Ways and Means, *Hearings on H.R. 5710: Amendments to the Social Security Act,* 76th Cong., 1st sess., March 3, 1939, p. 1217 (hereafter cited as House Committee on Ways and Means, *Hearings*).

29. See, e.g., Abraham Epstein, *Insecurity: A Challenge to America: A Study of Social Insurance in the United States and Abroad,* 2d ed. (New York: Random House, 1938), pt. 9; Joanne Goodwin, "Gender, Politics, and Welfare Reform: Mothers' Pensions in Chicago, 1900–1930" (Ph.D. diss., University of Michigan, 1991); and Skocpol, *Protecting Soldiers and Mothers,* chap. 8.

30. Altmeyer, House Committee on Ways and Means, *Hearings*, p. 2263, estimated that 43 percent of the children then being helped by ADC had deceased fathers and another 25 percent disabled fathers. Covering these by survivors insurance would leave 32 percent on ADC.

31. Advisory Council on Social Security, *Final Report,* 76th Cong., 1st sess., December 10, 1938, S. Doc. 4 (Washington, D.C.: GPO, 1939), pp. 17–18.

32. Ibid. p. 218. At least early on, Brown seems to have been ambivalent about this idea. On February 25, 1938, he wrote to Gerald Morgan suggesting that it might be better to include aged widows first and then slowly phase in younger widows. File entitled "February, 1938," box 22, Brown Papers.

33. Advisory Council Minutes, April 29, 1939, morning session, pp. 8–10ff. That it was the role, and not the woman being rewarded, emerged clearly in the discussion on February 18 (morning session, p. 51) around the question of whether the wife's allowance should be given to "a single person who has a sister or mother who is acting in lieu of spouse and taking care of the household for that person." The Advisory Council provided a rather elaborate defense of this decision to the House Ways and Means Committee, arguing that middle-aged widows were "likely to have more savings than younger widows and many of them have children who are grown and able to help them until they reach 65 years of age," that any other age selected would seem arbitrary, and, finally, that the retirement age for women in general could not be lowered without discriminating against men. See House Committee on Ways and Means, *Hearings,* February 1, 1939, p. 6.

34. Advisory Council Minutes, April 29, 1938, 2d half of morning session, p. 9. A. L. Mowbray, University of California, Berkeley, is the council member quoted.

35. Ibid., pp. 3, 40. The following discussion suggests that, on the one hand, the

Advisory Council distrusted widows, who they thought were likely to spend their death benefits all at once; on the other hand, they acknowledged the real need of widows with children. My sense is that this ambivalence led to their consensus that a widow's benefits should be based on need, thus justifying their removal if she remarried. Falk pointed out the discrepancy when he acquiesced in the council's decision: "I think we should recognize that there are two quite separate provisions written there, one following from a banking principle and the other from a social insurance principle, and then to give some income to persons who need it."

36. Advisory Council, *Final Report*, p. 17.

37. Advisory Council Minutes, April 29, 1st half of morning session, pp. 37–38. This restriction seemed lacking in rigor to research director Falk, who protested that the council had opened the door to "deathbed marriages," which would entitle a woman to a widow's pension when she reached age sixty-five (2d half of morning session, p. 3).

38. Wilbur Cohen, untitled memo of October 4, 1937, p. 1, file 025, box 10, Chairman's Files. But the proposal could not have come as a surprise. See House Committee on Ways and Means, *Hearings*, March 1939, p. 1022. See also Falk to the Advisory Council, "Benefits for Disabled Persons and Survivors." Falk included widowers and husbands in his recommendations—the only time I have seen them mentioned as possible beneficiaries.

39. Advisory Council Minutes, December 11, 1937, morning session, p. 37. The quotations in the following discussion come from pp. 37–39.

40. Dewson indicated her desire to resign on June 10, 1938, but her formal resignation is dated six months later, on December 10, 1938. She was replaced by Ellen Woodward, director of the Works Progress Administration, on December 21. Dewson to Arthur Altmeyer, June 10, 1938, carton 8, Dewson Papers. Susan Ware, *Partner and I: Molly Dewson, Feminism, and New Deal Politics* (New Haven: Yale University Press, 1987), p. 238, comments that Dewson used the excuse of her health "to extricate herself from a job that no longer offered satisfaction." The evidence here raises questions about maternalist interpretations of the development of the welfare state such as are found in Skocpol, *Protecting Soldiers and Mothers*, and in Seth Koven and Sonya Michel, *Mothers of a New World: Maternalist Politics and the Origins of Welfare States* (New York: Routledge, 1993).

41. Dewson began an October 1937 speech, entitled "What the Social Security Act Means to Women," by proclaiming her lack of enthusiasm about the subject that had been assigned to her. Box 9, entitled "Speeches and Addresses, 1937," Dewson Papers. In the course of the council debate, she published several speeches and an article, none of which mentioned the issue embroiling the council. See esp. "Next Steps in Social Security Legislation," *Social Service Review* 12 (March 1938): 21–33. Other women reformers do not seem to have been particularly concerned with the issue. For example, Sophonisba Breckinridge's October 24, 1937, lecture, entitled "Social Security and Public Welfare: A Comprehensive Program" (pamphlet in carton 8, Dewson Papers), does not mention wives, farmers, and domestics.

42. Gordon, "Social Insurance and Public Assistance."

43. See, e.g., Grace Abbott to Mary Dewson, February 3, 1938, carton 1, Dewson

Papers, where Abbott emphasizes the importance of paying special attention to men over forty-five as well as to integrating unemployment compensation and "invalidity" assistance with grants for relief. In the same period, Dewson also seems to have been profoundly interested in what she called an "integrated system" for men. Dewson to Ed Dewson, April 25, 1938, carton 8, Dewson Papers. There is some evidence that these concerns survived the depression. On August 24, 1946, Clara Beyer (who, according to Eileen Boris, was an early supporter of gender-neutral labor legislation) wrote to Mary Dewson with regard to the Women's Bureau's continuing efforts to promote special legislation for women: "My feelings on the subject rather correspond with yours. I can't get excited any more about separate legislation for women and believe we are losing a lot of the push for real improvement of conditions by the emphasis on sex." Box 1, Dewson Papers.

44. On the influence of southern politicians on the OAA portion of the Social Security Act, see Quadagno, *Transformation of Old Age Security*, chap. 6.

45. Ibid., p. 39.

46. "Suggested Amendments to the Social Security Act," typescript, file 025, box 10, Chairman's Files, contains Swope's language. Dewson clearly did not pick up the potential implications of earnings sharing. Her laconic response to Swope's proposed amendments including earnings sharing was simply: "The Swope plan seems to be the absolute opposite of the Senator Harrison plan. Thanks for sending it to me." Dewson to Altmeyer, November 19, 1937, ibid. For Brown's introduction of the suggestion to the Advisory Council, see Advisory Council Minutes, December 11, 1937, 11:30 A.M.–12:30 P.M., p. 10.

47. Advisory Council Minutes, February 18, 1938, morning session, p. 66. See also Brown's summary of the February 19 morning session, p. 2: "After some discussion, the alternatives of course being the enhancement of the individual benefit or the adding of an arrangement for wives, the statement worked out was that the enhancement of early benefits be attained by the method of paying allowances to aged wives." The Social Security Board's final language was even stronger. In a typescript headed "Strictly Confidential" (22 October 1938, file 025A, box 138, Executive Director's Files, RG 47, Social Security Administration Papers, National Archives, Washington, D.C. [hereafter cited as Executive Director's Files]), the SSB proposed that "the enhancement of early old-age benefits under the system be attained, not by increasing the amount of benefit now payable to an individual, but by the method of paying to a married annuitant on behalf of an aged wife a supplementary allowance equivalent to fifty percent of the husband's own benefit."

48. Advisory Council Minutes, February 18, 1938, morning session, p. 43.

49. Ibid., pp. 6–7. See also "Description of Proposed Plan AC-12," typescript, file 025B, box 138, p. 1, Executive Director's Files: "A male annuitant will be eligible to receive at age 65 an additional 50% of his basic annuity on behalf of a wife age 60 or over."

50. *New York Times*, June 8, 1939, p. 24.

51. Jay Iglauer, Advisory Council Minutes, February 18, 1938, morning session, p. 14; "Description of Proposed Plan AC-12," p. 6.

52. Walter Fuller, Advisory Council Minutes, February 19, 1938, afternoon session, pp. 11–12. Fuller was president of the Curtis Publishing Company of Philadelphia.

53. Douglas Brown, ibid., p. 11.

54. Ibid., April 29, 1938, morning session, p. 25.

55. Brown, ibid., February 19, 1938, afternoon session, p. 13.

56. Brown, ibid., April 29, 1938, morning session, p. 27.

57. Ibid., February 19, 1938, afternoon session, pp. 11–12, and April 29, 1938, morning session, p. 23; Advisory Council, *Final Report*. The failure to give men extra benefits unless their wives were also sixty-five came under harsh attack in the Senate debate on the proposal. *Congressional Record*, 76th Cong., 1st sess., July 13, 1939, p. 9011.

58. Advisory Council Minutes, April 29, 1938, pp. 32–33.

59. Ibid., 2d half of morning session, pp. 1–2.

60. Brown, ibid., February 18, 1938, morning session, p. 14.

61. House Committee on Ways and Means, *Hearings*, p. 1218.

62. The debate on this issue occurred within the Advisory Council on February 18–19, 1938. See esp. Advisory Council Minutes, February 18, morning session, pp. 15, 33, and February 19, afternoon session, p. 19.

63. Ibid., February 18, 1938, morning session, p. 33. Fuller is the council member quoted.

64. Ibid., February 18, 1938, afternoon session, p. 46.

65. See, e.g., the comments of Theresa McMahon, ibid., February 18, 1938, morning session, p. 8.

66. Ibid., afternoon session, p. 46.

67. *New York Times*, June 8, 1939, p. 24. An earlier editorial (December 19, 1938, p. 22) had noted that some of the increased costs would be covered by "tax contributions from persons not now included."

68. For example, when the council recommended eliminating the guaranteed return to those who had paid too little to receive benefits, it suggested that these contributions (most of them from poor and temporary workers) simply be absorbed by the system. These implications did not pass by at least some members of Congress. See *Congressional Record*, 76th Cong., 1st sess., July 13, 1939. See also House Committee on Ways and Means, *Hearings*, p. 2176.

69. Paul Douglas, Advisory Council Minutes, February 19, 1938, afternoon session, p. 20.

70. The staff of the Social Security Board summed up its problems with including the excluded groups in a memo presented to the Advisory Council on November 5, 1937. "The Problem of Extending Old-Age Insurance to Cover Classes Now Excluded," file 025, box 9, Chairman's Files. Its reasoning affirmed and extended that of its chair, Arthur Altmeyer. See Altmeyer to Miss E. Pangle, February 25, 1937, and Wilbur Cohen to Thomas C. Blaisdell, March 9, 1937, both in file 720, box 237, Central Files, RG 47, Social Security Administration Papers, National Archives, Washington, D.C. (hereafter cited as Central Files). Altmeyer raised the administrative objections to including these groups while indicating that the SSB was "on record as favoring the extension of the benefits of the Social Security Act as rapidly as administrative experience is developed." Cohen reported the difficulty of adopting a "stamp system" as opposed to a payroll deduction system. The 5 million figure comes from his memo and excludes unpaid family labor. Dewson presented their position to the Advisory

Council: "I think that the Board feels it is only fair as fast as we feel we can administer the law that we should take in every one of these excluded groups. The difficulty is in administering the law with domestic workers and with agricultural labor." Advisory Council Minutes, December 11, 1937, morning session, p. 21. For additional discussion, see ibid., February 19, 1938, afternoon session, pp. 19–25, and Wilbur Cohen to George Bigge, October 17, 1938, file 025A, box 138, Executive Director's Files, which forwards a proposal for a stamp system of collecting taxes on low-wage workers. In testimony before the House Ways and Means Committee, Altmeyer conceded that these administrative problems were not insuperable. House Committee on Ways and Means, *Hearings*, p. 2264.

71. Louis Resnick to Altmeyer, March 23, 1937, file 720, box 237, Central Files.

72. Adam Clayton Powell Jr. to John G. Winant, February 23, 1937, file 721, box 238, ibid.

73. Roy Wilkins to FDR, August 30, 1988, file 011.1, box 133, Executive Director's Files.

74. "Description of Proposed Plan AC-12," p. 1. See also Advisory Council, *Final Report*, p. 15.

75. Quoted in Robert B. Stevens, ed., *Statutory History of the United States: Income Security* (New York: McGraw-Hill, 1970), from Social Security Act Amendments of 1939, 76th Cong., 1st sess., May 14, 1939, H. Doc. 728, p. 232.

76. House Committee on Ways and Means, *Hearings*, p. 1217. See also "Press Conference Releasing Report," December 10, 1938, typescript, p. 21, in file entitled "December 10, 1938," box 26, Brown Papers, where Brown ducked the issue as to whether this was not the first time that wives' unpaid services were compensated to remark that "the source of protection of the family is precisely from the head of the family" and defended the concept of family protection "because you want your widow protected not merely while the children are small but after the children are grown and she herself becomes old."

77. Dewson, "What the Social Security Act Means to Women," p. 2.

CHAPTER 5. Giving Character to Our Whole Civil Polity

I am very grateful to Ellen DuBois, Eric Foner, Linda Gordon, Hendrik Hartog, Linda Kerber, Alice Kessler-Harris, Carole Pateman, and Carol Weisbrod for their helpful comments on earlier versions of this essay.

1. Deprivations suffered by homosexual couples who wish to marry but cannot are summarized by Martha Minow in "The Free Exercise of Families," *University of Illinois Law Review* 1191, no. 4 (1992): 940. While unmarried heterosexual couples also suffer these lacks, they have the option to marry. On one issue—property and support settlements upon divorce—courts have recently moved in the direction of treating established but unmarried heterosexual couples as though they were legally married.

2. The literature of family history in which treatment of marriage is embedded is too large to review here, but some examples worthy of note are John Demos, *A Little Commonwealth: Family Life in Plymouth Colony* (New York: Oxford University Press,

1970); Lawrence Stone, *The Family, Sex, and Marriage in England, 1500–1800* (New York: Harper and Row, 1977); John R. Gillis, *For Better, For Worse: British Marriages, 1600 to the Present* (New York: Oxford University Press, 1985); Christiane Klapisch-Zuber, *Women, Family, and Ritual in Renaissance Italy*, trans. Lydia Cochranie (Chicago: University of Chicago Press, 1985); and Leonore Davidoff and Catherine Hall, *Family Fortunes: Men and Women of the English Middle Class, 1780–1850* (Chicago: University of Chicago Press, 1987). Stronger emphasis on marriage as a public institution is visible in more recent works such as Susan Staves, *Married Women's Separate Property in England, 1660–1833* (Cambridge: Harvard University Press, 1990), a source of inspiration for my work, and Sarah Hanley, "Engendering the State: Family Formation and State Building in Early Modern France," *French Historical Studies* 16, no. 1 (1989): 4–27. Recent work in U.S. history that connects marriage to public order includes Michael Grossberg's pioneering effort to cross legal history with social history and to map domestic relations law, *Governing the Hearth: Law and the Family in Nineteenth-Century America* (Chapel Hill: University of North Carolina Press, 1985), a book to which I owe a great deal despite my differences with it, and Amy Dru Stanley's dissertation, "Contract Rights in the Age of Emancipation: Wage Labor and Marriage after the Civil War" (Ph.D. diss., Yale University, 1990), and article, "Conjugal Bonds and Wage Labor: Rights of Contract in the Age of Emancipation," *Journal of American History (JAH)* 75, no. 2 (September 1988): 471–500. Lee Teitlebaum, "Family History and Family Law," *Wisconsin Law Review* (1985): 1135–81, which I discovered after drafting this essay, takes an approach consistent with mine.

3. At the Council of Trent in 1563 the church decreed that marriages were valid only when celebrated by a priest before two witnesses, after posting of banns, whereas consent and consummation had earlier been accepted as constituting a valid (although not approved) marriage. The doctrine of indissolubility of marriage bonds was not formally included in canon law by the church, nor was marriage declared a sacrament, until the sixteenth century. Roderick Phillips, *Putting Asunder: A History of Divorce in Western Society* (Cambridge: Cambridge University Press, 1988), pp. 25–27, 34–35.

4. See Phillips, *Putting Asunder*, pp. 194–206; Ramon Gutierrez, *When Jesus Came, the Corn Mothers Went Away* (Stanford: Stanford University Press, 1991), pp. 315–17; Gillis, *For Better*, pp. 139–41.

5. On the contractualists, see Linda J. Nicholson, *Gender and History: The Limits of Social Theory in the Age of the Family* (New York: Columbia University Press, 1986), esp. pp. 134–38; Carole Pateman, *The Sexual Contract* (Stanford: Stanford University Press, 1988), esp. pp. 91–96, and Teresa Brennan and Carole Pateman, " 'Mere Auxiliaries to the Commonwealth': Women and the Origins of Liberalism," *Political Studies* 27 (June 1979): 183–200.

6. Francis Lieber, a German immigrant who became a very influential political philosopher in mid-nineteenth-century America, directly linked marriage and property, declaiming that monogamy "is one of the primordial elements out of which all law proceeds, or which the law steps in to recognize and to protect. Wedlock, that is, the being locked of one man in wedding to one woman, stands in this respect on a level with property"—i.e., in being antecedent to law. In a footnote he continued: "The attention of the philosopher cannot help being arrested by the fact that at all times

property and marriage have stood or fallen together. Wherever fanatics, Protestants, Catholics, and even Mahometans, have attacked the one, they have attacked the other." "The Mormons: Shall Utah Be Admitted into the Union?" *Putnam's Monthly* 5 (March 1855): 234. This unsigned article was brought to my attention by Carol Weisbrod and Pamela Sheingorn, "Reynolds v. United States: Nineteenth-Century Forms of Marriage and the Status of Women," *Connecticut Law Review* 10, no. 4 (Summer 1978): 828–58, where (p. 835) Lieber is identified as the author; and indeed, in the footnote I quote, the reader is referred to Lieber's *Essays on Labor and Property* for fuller discussion.

7. Raymond Williams, *Keywords: A Vocabulary of Culture and Society* (New York: Oxford University Press, 1976), pp. 203–4.

8. See Demos, *Little Commonwealth*; Nancy F. Cott, "Eighteenth-Century Family and Social Life Revealed in Massachusetts Divorce Records," *Journal of Social History* 10 (Fall 1976): 20–43; Carole Shammas, "The Domestic Environment in Early Modern England and America," *Journal of Social History* 14 (1980): 3–24.

9. For further elaboration, see my entry on "Privacy" in *A Companion to American Thought*, edited by Richard W. Fox and James Kloppenberg (Cambridge: Basil Blackwell, forthcoming), from which this discussion is drawn; see also entry on "Domesticity."

10. Cf. Frances E. Olsen's complex analysis of these divisions in "The Family and the Market: A Study of Ideology and Legal Reform," *Harvard Law Review* 96 (May 1983): 1497–1578; Stanley I. Benn and Gerald F. Gaus, eds., *Public and Private in Social Life* (London: Croom and Helm, 1983); and Morton Horwitz, "The History of the Public/Private Distinction," *University of Pennsylvania Law Review* 130, no. 6 (June 1982): 1423–28.

11. Robert Gordon eloquently sums the insight of critical legal studies into the way that the legal system (partially) constitutes common consciousness: "The power exerted by a legal regime consists less in the force that it can bring to bear against violators of its rules than in its capacity to persuade people that the world described in its images and categories is the only attainable world in which a sane person would want to live. . . . One never has more power than when one has so successfully appropriated the symbols of authority that one's actions are not seen as exercises of power at all, but simply as expressions of sound pragmatic common sense." Gordon, "Critical Legal Histories," *Stanford Law Review* 57 (1984): 57–125 (quotations, pp. 109, 112).

12. Martha Albertson Fineman, "Intimacy Outside of the Natural Family: The Limits of Privacy," *Connecticut Law Review* 23 (Summer 1991): 955–72.

13. See, for example, Susan Moller Okin, *Women in Western Political Thought* (Princeton: Princeton University Press, 1979); Pateman, *Sexual Contract*.

14. Joan Gunderson, "Independence, Citizenship, and the American Revolution," *Signs* 13, no. 1 (Autumn 1987): 59–77 (Thomas Jefferson to Edmund Pendleton, August 26, 1776, p. 64). See also Linda K. Kerber, *Women of the Republic: Intellect and Ideology in Revolutionary America* (Chapel Hill: University of North Carolina Press, 1980), esp. pp. 13–32, 137–56.

15. I adopt the phrase *gender formation* from Mariana Valverde's "Comment" in

"Dialogue: Gender History/Women's History: Is Feminist Scholarship Losing Its Critical Edge?," *Journal of Women's History* 5 (Spring 1993): 123; she chooses it in preference to *gender structure* for its more dynamic sense; she parallels this to the use of *class formation* rather than *class structure*, declaring, "We want to analyze how the two genders are formed and reformed, renegotiated, contested." Cf. Michael Omi and Howard Winant's concept of "racial formation" in *Racial Formation in the United States from the 1960s to the 1980s* (New York: Routledge, 1986).

16. Indentured servants in the seventeenth and eighteenth century were also generally forbidden to contract marriage, but that was a temporary deprivation of civil rights. As Margaret Burnham points out in "An Impossible Marriage: Slave Law and Family Law," *Law and Inequality* 5 (1987): 207, n. 84, the denial of slave marriage was judicially defined rather than legislated. See Grossberg, *Governing*, pp. 130–32, on southern courts' views of slave marriages. Grossberg includes discussion of a Pennsylvania decision, *Commonwealth v. Clements*, 6 Binney 206, which denied the rights of coverture to the husband of an escaped slave from Maryland, declaring that the reclaiming master's rights trumped the husband's. The postbellum U.S. Supreme Court confirmed that "an inflexible rule of the law of African slavery, wherever it existed, [was] that the slave was incapable of entering into any contract, not excepting the contract of marriage." *Hall v. U.S.* 92 U.S. 27 (1875), quoted in Grossberg, *Governing*, p. 135. Slaveholders, of course, knew what they were doing: viz. minister and slaveholder C. C. Jones's reflection that "the divine institution of marriage depends . . . largely upon the protection given it by the law of the land." Quoted in Herbert Gutman, *The Black Family in Slavery and Freedom, 1750–1925* (New York: Random House, 1976), p. 295.

17. See Leon F. Litwack, *Been in the Storm So Long: The Aftermath of Slavery* (New York: Random House, 1979), pp. 240–41; Gutman, *Black Family*, pp. 18, 412–17, 425–29.

18. *Murphy v. Ramsey*, 114 U.S. 15, 43, 45 (1884). This was a unanimous decision.

19. Grossberg, *Governing*, pp. 120–21. In early modern England, bigamy was an offense against church law; in 1604 Parliament made it a criminal offense as well. Phillips, *Putting Asunder*, p. 203. Blackstone said bigamy was a felony, and not simply an ecclesiastical offense, "by reason of its being so great a violation of the public economy and decency of a well ordered state." Quoted from *Commentaries* (1765) by David Flaherty, "Privacy in Early America," in *Law in American History*, edited by Donald Fleming and Bernard Bailyn (Boston: Little, Brown, 1971), p. 56. On the frequency of bigamy in antebellum America, see Norma Basch, "Relief in the Premises: Divorce as a Woman's Remedy in New York and Indiana, 1815–1870," *Law and History Review* 8, no. 1 (Spring 1990): 1–24; Timothy J. Gilfoyle, "The Hearts of Nineteenth-Century Men: Bigamy and Working-Class Marriage in New York City, 1800–1870" (paper presented at the Barnard Conference on Men and Masculinity, New York, January 1988), in my possession; and Hendrik Hartog, "Marital Exits and Marital Expectations in Nineteenth-Century America," *Georgetown Law Journal* 80, no. 1 (October 1991): 122–26.

20. *In re McLaughlin's Estate*, 4 Wash. 570, 591 (1892), quoted in Grossberg, *Governing*, p. 85.

21. The medieval Catholic Church's view that consent and consummation con-

stituted marriage migrated to Protestantism and to Protestant states, although the accompanying Catholic dogma that marriage was a sacrament was rejected.

22. William Bradford, governor of Plymouth during most of the period 1621–56, wrote that marriage was "a civill thing, upon which many questions aboute inheritances doe depende"—quoted in Phillips, *Putting Asunder*, pp. 134–35, 159. See also David Flaherty, "Law and the Enforcement of Morals in Early America," in *American Law and the Constitutional Order*, edited by Lawrence M. Friedman and Harry N. Scheiber (Cambridge: Harvard University Press, 1978). As the colonies developed, in many denominations church discipline was instituted to parallel secular authority, but not to replace it—except in Maryland, where during the Revolutionary period civil ceremonies were not allowed and marriages (of white couples) had to be performed by a Protestant minister, Catholic priest, or Quaker ceremony. See Frank Gaylord Cook, "The Marriage Celebration in the Colonies," *Atlantic Monthly*, March 1888, pp. 355–56. Blackstone, the most important legal authority in early America, put marriage within the grasp of secular rather than ecclesiastical law and emphasized that it was a civil contract—see Grossberg, *Governing*, p. 66; Norma Basch, "Invisible Women: The Legal Fiction of Marital Unity in Nineteenth-Century America," *Feminist Studies* 5, no. 2 (Summer 1979): 363, n. 21.

23. See Kermit Hall, *The Magic Mirror: Law in American History* (New York: Oxford University Press, 1991), pp. 153–55; Grossberg, *Governing*, pp. 69–102; Otto E. Koegel, *Common Law Marriage and Its Development in the United States* (Washington: John Byrne, 1922); John E. Semonche, "Common Law Marriage in North Carolina: A Study in Legal History," *American Journal of Legal History* 9 (1965): 324–41; Maxwell Bloomfield, *American Lawyers in a Changing Society, 1779–1876* (Cambridge: Harvard University Press, 1976), pp. 106–8; Basch, "Relief in the Premises."

24. Building on insights of the legal realists in the 1920s and 1930s, critical legal studies scholars emphasize that it is a fiction that contracts are in a private realm apart from the state. Since the courts enforce contracts—since the threat of legal coercion is a condition of their functioning—contracts are inherently participant in the public legal order. Betty Mensch, in "Freedom of Contract as Ideology," *Stanford Law Review* 83 (1981): 764, insists "that the state was not implicated in the outcomes of free market bargaining was *never* true" not only because legal coercion is implicit in the enforcement of contracts, but also because "ownership is a function of legal entitlement, [so] every bargain (and, taken collectively, the 'natural' market price) is a function of the legal order." Not cited by Mensch are the pathbreaking articles by Robert Hale, "Coercion and Distribution in a Supposedly Non-coercive State," *Political Science Quarterly* 38 (1923), and Morris R. Cohen, "Property and Sovereignty," *Cornell Law Quarterly* 13 (1927), which preceded and to a certain extent precipitated the core of the critical legal studies approach as summarized by Gordon, "Critical Legal Histories," pp. 297–99, i.e., the contention that one cannot divide law from society, because "any set of 'basic' social practices" cannot be adequately described without showing "the legal relations among the people involved." Conceding the "fundamentally constitutive character of legal relations in social life," this amounts to collapsing the public/private divide on which liberalism is premised. My approach to marriage in this essay is consistent with such a perspective and must have been influenced by it in general ways although I discovered the specific congruities after I had outlined my own approach.

25. Justice Story's remarks and the decisions quoted in the next paragraph—*Adams v. Palmer*, 51 Maine 481, 483 (1866); *Noel v. Ewing*, 9 Indiana 37 (1857)—are taken from quotations in the U.S. Supreme Court decision, *Maynard v. Hill*, 125 U.S. 190, 210–13 (1888). Amy Stanley discusses lawyers' and treatise writers' awareness of marriage as a contract sui generis in the 1870s in "Contract Rights in the Age of Emancipation," pp. 254–56, and the similarity seen between the marriage contract and other civil contracts during the congressional debate over the 1866 Civil Rights Act in "Conjugal Bonds," pp. 471–81. For recent feminist perceptions of the paradox of marriage as a contract and a status, see Carole Pateman, "The Shape of the Marriage Contract," in *Women's Views of the Political World of Men*, edited by Judith H. Stiehm (Dobbs Ferry, N.Y.: Transnational Publications, 1984), p. 77.

26. Charles W. McCurdy, "Justice Field and the Jurisprudence of Government-Business Relations: Some Parameters of Laissez-Faire Constitutionalism, 1863–1897," *JAH* 61, no. 4 (March 1975): 970–1003.

27. See, for example, David Montgomery, *Beyond Equality: Labor and the Radical Republicans, 1862–1872* (Urbana: University of Illinois Press, 1981); William E. Forbath, "The Ambiguities of Free Labor: Labor and the Law in the Gilded Age," *Wisconsin Law Review* (1985): 767–817; Eric Foner, *Reconstruction: America's Unfinished Revolution, 1863–77* (New York: Harper and Row, 1988), p. 364ff.; Terence McDonald, "The Burdens of Urban History," *Studies in American Political Development* 3 (1989): esp. 26–29; Ellen DuBois, "Outgrowing the Compact of the Fathers: Equal Rights, Woman Suffrage, and the U.S. Constitution, 1820–1878," *JAH* 74, no. 3 (December 1987): 836–62.

28. The question in *Munn v. Illinois* was whether the state of Illinois could regulate rates of the Chicago grain elevators that had come to hold a practical monopoly of the area's business. A majority of the Supreme Court upheld the regulation, claiming, in Chief Justice Morrison R. Waite's language, that although the warehousers had a private business, it was "affected with a public interest." After this decision the chief justice wrote to a friend: "The great difficulty in the future will be to establish the boundary between that which is private and that in which the public has an interest. The Elevators furnished an extreme case, and there was no difficulty in determining on which side of the line they properly belonged"—this last despite the fact that two of Waite's colleagues, including the eminent and influential Justice Stephen Field, strongly felt that the elevators belonged on the other side of the public/private divide. Waite, March 30, 1877, quoted in Harry Scheiber, "The Road to *Munn*: Eminent Domain and the Concept of Public Purpose in the State Courts," in *Law in American History*, edited by Donald Fleming and Bernard Bailyn (Boston: Little, Brown, 1971), pp. 329–402. See also Andrew Rutten, "*Munn v. Illinois* and the Search for an Economic Constitution, 1877–1897," paper dated May 1992 in my possession, and McCurdy, "Justice Field," pp. 996–99.

29. See Stephen Skowronek, *Building a New American State: The Expansion of National Administrative Capacities, 1877–1920* (Cambridge: Cambridge University Press, 1982), in which the nineteenth-century United States is described as a state of "courts and parties."

30. Cf. Duncan Kennedy's humorous and insightful "The Stages of the Decline of

the Public/Private Distinction," *University of Pennsylvania Law Review* 130 (1982): 1349–58.

31. *Loan Association v. Topeka*, 87 U.S. (20 Wall), 655, 662–64 (1875), quoted in William E. Nelson, *The Fourteenth Amendment: From Political Principle to Judicial Doctrine* (Cambridge: Harvard University Press, 1988), pp. 169–70.

32. For the argument that the Oneida experiment and women's rights agitation affected the court's decision in *Reynolds v. United States* (to be discussed later), see Weisbrod and Sheingorn, "Reynolds v. United States."

33. See Grossberg, *Governing*, pp. 83–95, and, as examples of reformers' publicity, Frank Gaylord Cook, "The Marriage Celebration in the United States," *Atlantic Monthly*, April 1888, pp. 520–32, and "Reform in the Celebration of Marriage," *Atlantic Monthly*, May 1888, pp. 680–90; Samuel W. Dike, "The Statistics of Marriage and Divorce," *Political Science Quarterly* 4 (December 1889): 592–614, and "The Theory of the Marriage Tie," *Andover Review* 17 (November 1893): 672–80.

34. *Meister v. Moore*, 96 U.S. 76, 83, 81 (October 1877). The decision is all the more interesting because the union in question was between a white man and an Indian woman.

35. *Sapp v. Newsom*, 27 Tex. 537, 540, quoted in Hans W. Baade, "The Form of Marriage in Spanish North America," *Cornell Law Review* 61 (November 1975): 78. See Grossberg, *Governing*, pp. 65–83.

36. *Maryland v. Baldwin*, 112 U.S. 490, 494–95 (1884).

37. See Grossberg, *Governing*, pp. 121–24, for a brief summary of the anti-Mormon campaign; see also Edwin Brown Firmage and Richard Collin Mangrum, *Zion in the Courts: A Legal History of the Church of Jesus Christ of Latter-Day Saints, 1830–1900* (Urbana: University of Illinois Press, 1988).

38. The sensitivity of Republican leaders to polygamy during the Civil War was probably heightened by their antislavery discourse, which put the sexually exploitative aspects of the slave system—white masters' access to a "harem" of black female slaves—at center stage. The greatest crime of slavery in many Northerners' minds was its destruction of the monogamous family (both black and white), its degradation of monogamy through the hypocrisy that allowed white men to hold black women in a sort of forced prostitution. The Republican platform of 1856 linked and denounced slavery and polygamy as the "twin relics of barbarism," a phrase suggested by Massachusetts radical Republican E. Rockwood Hoar. On congressional discourse in the 1850s and 1860s linking slavery to prostitution and polygamy, see Neal Kumar Katyal, "Men Who Own Women: A Thirteenth Amendment Critique of Forced Prostitution," *Yale Law Journal* 103 (December 1993): 796–805; on Hoar, see Foner, *Free Soil, Free Labor, Free Men* (New York: Oxford University Press, 1970), pp. 121–22, 130.

39. *Reynolds v. United States*, 98 U.S. 145 (1879). I am greatly indebted to Weisbrod and Sheingorn's "Reynolds v. United States" for inspiration and guidance.

40. *Reynolds v. United States*, 98 U.S. 145, 164, 165–66 (1879). Waite cited Francis Lieber (see n. 6 above) in associating polygamy with "patriarchalism" and "stationary despotism" and finding only monogamy consistent with principles of democratic government. Lieber waxed poetic in "The Mormons," p. 234, declaring monogamy "'a law written in the heart' of our race. . . . one of the elementary distinctions—

historical and actual—between European and Asiatic humanity. It is one of the frames of our thoughts, and moulds [*sic*] of our feelings; it is a psychological condition of our jural consciousness, of our liberty, of our literature, of our aspirations, of our religious convictions, and of our domestic being and family relation, the foundation of all that is called polity."

41. *Reynolds v. United States*, 98 U.S. 164, 166–67. Subsequent Supreme Court decisions confirmed acts of Congress during the 1880s disfranchising polygamists (as mentioned earlier) and dissolving the corporation of the Church of Jesus Christ of the Latter-Day Saints and taking its property. See *Murphy v. Ramsey*, 114 U.S. 15 (1884); *Davis v. Beason*, 133 U.S. 33 (1889); *Mormon Church v. United States*, 136 U.S. 1 (1889).

42. Sidney Kansas, *U.S. Immigration Exclusion and Deportation and Citizenship of the United States of America*, 2d ed. (Albany: Matthew Bender, 1940), pp. 4–6; Edward P. Hutchinson, *Legislative History of American Immigration Policy, 1798–1965* (Philadelphia: University of Pennsylvania Press, 1981), pp. 422–23, 452. In 1930 foreigners filing declarations of intention to obtain U.S. citizenship not only had to state their bona fide intentions to renounce all other national allegiances but also had to aver that they were neither anarchists nor polygamists. Sophonisba Breckinridge, *Marriage and the Civic Rights of Women* (Chicago: University of Chicago Press, 1931), pp. 21–22.

43. *Maynard v. Hill*, 125 U.S. 190 (1888).

44. Ronald Takaki asserts, however, that during the sixteenth-century English colonization of Ireland, English were forbidden to marry Irish "savages." See "*The Tempest* in the Wilderness: The Racialization of Savagery," *JAH* 79, no. 3 (December 1992): 894, and James Muldoon, "The Indian as Irishman," *Essex Institute Historical Collections* 3 (October 1975): 284. According to Gutierrez, *When Jesus Came*, p. 302, Spanish church and state officials in the New World in the seventeenth and eighteenth centuries assumed that interracial sex took the form of concubinage.

45. David H. Fowler, *Northern Attitudes towards Interracial Marriage: Legislation and Public Opinion in the Middle Atlantic and the States of the Old Northwest, 1780–1930* (New York: Garland, 1987), pp. 34–44 (Maryland statute, pp. 41–42), 236 (*West Chester and Philadelphia Railroad Co. v. Miles*, 55 Pa. 213–14 [1867]). Fowler contends (p. xi) that laws prohibiting interracial marriage were "vital" to the creation of "an American version of a caste system."

The first statute in the American colonies that made a racial distinction marking the cohering system of lifelong hereditary bondage was an act by the Virginia assembly in 1662 imposing double punishment on the "Christian" who committed fornication with a "negro." It is worth noting that these early acts dealt with race definition through questions of sex/reproduction. The act also stipulated that children fathered by Englishmen and borne by Negro women would take the status of their mothers. The Virginia, not the Maryland, statute augured the future regarding the fate of the offspring of interracial couplings: i.e., children would take the status (bond or free) of their mothers. Both statutes were passed in colonies in which the sex ratio among blacks was even more skewed (toward males) than it was among whites, and in which white female indentured servants interacted with black male slaves/servants. The Maryland statute (dictating that offspring followed the status of their *fathers*) caused the scandalous phenomenon of masters fostering unions between their white female indentured servants and their black male slaves in order to enslave the wives and create another generation of slaves in the children. In 1681 the Maryland assembly dealt with this by placing a very high penalty (10,000 pounds of tobacco) on anyone who performed a marriage between a white woman and a Negro man, and likewise fining a master or mistress who permitted or encouraged such a marriage; the white woman and her issue would remain free if the master or mistress had cooperated in the marriage. See, in addition to Fowler, George M. Frederickson, *White Supremacy: A Comparative Study in American and South African History* (New York: Oxford University Press, 1981), pp. 101–4; Karen Getman, "Sexual Control in the Slaveholding South: The Implementation and Maintenance of a Racial Caste System," *Harvard Women's Law Journal* 7 (1984): 124–29; A. Leon Higginbotham Jr. and Barbara K. Kopytoff, "Racial Purity and Interracial Sex in the Law of Colonial and Antebellum Virginia," *Georgetown Law Journal* 77 (1989): 1989–2007.

46. Fowler, *Northern Attitudes*, pp. 38–39, 62–74, 78–79. Fowler argues persuasively that the factor precipitating marriage prohibition in southern colonies was the presence of substantial numbers of white female indentured servants mixing with enslaved male Africans. South Carolina, which had no proscription, had a more strictly African labor force. By the World War I era, when almost two-thirds of the states and territories still prohibited interracial marriage, "more statutes banned miscegenation than any other form of racially related conduct," in the words of Hall, *Magic Mirror*, p. 157. See also Grossberg, *Governing*, pp. 136–40, and "Guarding the Altar: Physiological Restrictions and the Rise of State Intervention in Matrimony," *American Journal of Legal History* 26, no. 3 (July 1982): 200–203.

Laws in twenty states also criminalized sexual relations, bastardy, cohabitation, or concubinage between a white and a nonwhite partner—but laws voiding and criminalizing mixed-race marriages were more likely to be enforced: an official is required to perform a legal marriage (and most of these laws penalized the official who would perform an interracial marriage). Second, marriage often involved property transmission, which in any contest would have to enter the domain of the courts and subject the marriage itself to scrutiny.

47. My point is analogous to (and was stimulated by) Gisela Bock's analysis of Nazi family policy as not simply pronatalist, because it prevented some groups from reproducing. See her essay, "Racism and Sexism in Nazi Germany: Motherhood, Compulsory Sterilization, and the State," *Signs* 8, no. 3 (Spring 1983): 400–421. I use the phrase "marriage across the color line" in emulation of Martha Elizabeth Hodes, "Sex across the Color Line: White Women and Black Men in the Nineteenth-Century American South" (Ph.D. diss., Princeton University, 1991). As Hodes emphasizes, "interracial" is not really the correct term, because race is a constructed category and because the marriages prohibited were always between whites and another group, never between two other racial groups. The word *miscegenation* also carries heavy freight: it was a neologism invented during the Civil War era by enemies of the Republican Party to name the crime or sin of "species-mixing." The word's logic derived from the theory of polygenesis put forward by an American school of ethnology, which claimed that the races had been separately (and unequally) created and had distinct and permanent physical and mental characteristics. See George M. Fredrick-

son, *The Black Image in the White Mind: The Debate on Afro-American Character and Destiny, 1817–1914* (New York: Harper and Row, 1971), pp. 74–90, 171–74.

48. See Tessie Liu's illuminating discussion of the indebtedness of racial thinking to notions of biological kin, in "Race and Gender in the Politics of Group Formation: A Comment on Notions of Multiculturalism," *Frontiers* 12, no. 2 (1991): 155–65.

49. The states that passed such laws for the first time were Alabama, Arizona, Colorado, Idaho, Mississippi, Nevada, Ohio, Oregon, South Carolina, and West Virginia. Fowler, *Northern Attitudes*, pp. 265–55 and appendix. In South Carolina, marriage between whites and persons of color was declared illegal and void by an 1865 act; this was repealed in the 1868 constitution, so intermarriage was then legal until the Redeemer legislature passed a new statute in 1879 declaring whites' marriages to Indians, Negroes, mulattoes, or mestizos null and void.

50. Fowler, *Northern Attitudes*, p. 234 and app.; Harvey Applebaum, "Miscegenation Statutes," *Georgetown Law Journal* 53 (1964), esp. pp. 56–57; Grossberg, "Crossing Boundaries: Nineteenth-Century Domestic Relations Law and the Merger of Family and Legal History," *American Bar Foundation Research Journal* 1985, no. 4 (1985): 823; Nelson, *Fourteenth Amendment*, p. 152. See also Mary Frances Berry, "Judging Morality: Sexual Behavior and Legal Consequences in the Late Nineteenth-Century South," *JAH* 78, no. 3 (December 1991): 839–40. Fowler says that challenges occurred in eight states, but I count nine including the cases mentioned by Applebaum and Nelson. These include appellate cases brought in federal courts as well as in state courts. More cases went in the same direction in the twentieth century.

During Reconstruction two state supreme courts struck down bans of marriage between whites and blacks on the ground that marriage was a contract as defined in the Civil Rights Act. In Alabama, *Burns v. State*, 48 Ala. 195 (1872), was quickly overruled by the Redeemer court in *Ford v. State*, 53 Ala. 150 (1875), and definitively in *Green v. State*, 58 Ala. 190 (1877). The most successful challenge was in Louisiana in *Hart v. Hoss and Elder*, 26 La. Ann 90 (1874), for the Louisiana legislature had repealed the prohibition on racial intermarriage in 1870 and did not reinstate it until 1894, so interracial marriage was legal in Louisiana from 1870 to 1894.

51. *Maynard v. Hill*, 125 U.S. 190, 211 (emphasis added).

52. *Plessy v. Ferguson*, 163 U.S. 537 (1896); Fowler, *Northern Attitudes*, p. 257. In the Dred Scott decision a half century earlier, the Taney court had referred to laws banning interracial marriage as a stigma. *Dred Scott v. Sandford*, 60 U.S. 393, 409 (1857). The closest the Supreme Court came to judging an antimiscegenation law during the nineteenth century was in *Pace v. Alabama*, 106 U.S. 583 (1883), a decision also written by Field, which left standing an Alabama law that penalized interracial cohabitation more harshly than cohabitation between people of the same race. That decision was repudiated in *McLaughlin v. Florida*, 379 U.S. 184 (1964), three years before the high court definitively declared antimiscegenation laws unconstitutional in *Loving v. Virginia*, 388 U.S. 1 (1967).

53. See Grossberg, *Governing*, pp. 75–78, on the promarriage policies of the early nineteenth century.

54. Carol Weisbrod, "Family, Church, and State: An Essay on Constitutionalism and Religious Authority," *Journal of Family Law* 26, no. 4 (1987–88): 741–70.

55. *Mormon Church v. United States*, 136 U.S. 49; *Kinney v. Commonwealth*, 71 Va. (30 Graft.) 284, 285 (1878). The general proposition regarding interracial marriage laws was that since God had made the races look different, they should not mix: "He intends," a Pennsylvania Supreme Court justice in 1867 knew, "that they shall not overstep the natural boundaries He has assigned them." *West Chester and Philadelphia Railroad Co. v. Miles*, 55 Pa. 209 (1867). On views of civilization vs. barbarism in this period, see Joan Brumberg, "Zenanas and Girlless Villages: The Ethnology of American Evangelical Women, 1870–1910," *JAH* (1982): 347–71, and Gail Bederman, "'Civilization,' the Decline of Middle-Manliness, and Ida B. Wells' Antilynching Campaign (1892–94)," *Radical History Review* 52 (1992): 5–30.

56. There were ideological limits, however, to states' definitions of common-law marriages. For instance, "free lovers" E. C. Walker and Lillian Harman, who carried out a unique and private ceremony of "autonomistic" marriage in which they abjured the usual marital duties and prerogatives, were indicted, convicted, and jailed under a Kansas statute that stipulated forms and required a license for marriage, and the Kansas Supreme Court upheld the actions against them despite accepting common-law marriage. *State v. Walker*, 36 Kans. 297 (1887). On states' increasingly "hands-on" policies in the late nineteenth century, see Grossberg, "Guarding the Altar" and *Governing*, pp. 103–52.

CHAPTER 6. Soul Murder and Slavery

Thanks to Carole Beal, Jean Layzer, Glenn Shafer, Constance and Preston Williams, and Elaine Wise for suggestions, encouragement, and assistance.

1. See Paul E. Johnson and Sean Wilentz, *The Kingdom of Matthias: A Story of Sex and Salvation in Nineteenth-Century America* (New York: Oxford University Press, 1994); [Olive Gilbert, Frances Titus], *Narrative of Sojourner Truth: A Bondswoman of Olden Time . . . [with] Her Book of Life*, [2d ed.], (1878; reprint, New York: Schomburg Collection, 1990), pp. 87–96.

2. Philip Greven is exceptional among historians in investigating child abuse carefully. See Philip Greven, *The Protestant Temperament: Patterns of Child-rearing, Religious Experience, and the Self in Early America* (New York: Knopf, 1977) and *Spare the Child: The Religious Roots of Punishment and the Psychological Impact of Physical Abuse* (New York: Knopf, 1991).

3. Daniel Paul Schreber, *Memoirs of My Nervous Illness*, translated and edited by Ida Macalpine and Richard A. Hunter, with a new introduction by Samuel M. Weber (Cambridge: Harvard University Press, 1988), pp. xii–xiii. See also Sigmund Freud, "Psycho-Analytic Notes on an Autobiographical Account of a Case of Paranoia (Dementia Paranoides)" [1911], in *The Standard Edition of the Complete Psychological Works of Sigmund Freud*, edited and translated by James Strachey (London: Hogarth Press, 1958), pp. 9–82; Jacques Lacan, "On a Question Preliminary to any Possible Treatment of Psychosis" [1955–56], in *Ecrits*, translated by Alan Sheridan (New York: Norton, 1977); and Leonard Shengold, *Halo in the Sky* (New York: Guilford, 1988). The great legal reformer Anselm von Feuerbach was the father of philosopher Ludwig

Feuerbach. My thanks to Ulrich Struve for help in sorting out the story of Kaspar Hauser.

4. Leonard Shengold, *Soul Murder: The Effects of Childhood Abuse and Deprivation* (New Haven: Yale University Press, 1989), pp. 1–5; James A. Chu, "The Repetition Compulsion Revisited: Reliving Dissociated Trauma" (paper presented at the International Conference on Multiple Personality and Dissociative States, November 6, 1987), p. 1. I am grateful to Becky Thompson for bringing this paper to my attention.

5. Ian Hacking, "Memoro-politics: Trauma and the Soul" (Davis Center Seminar Paper, Princeton University, September 25, 1992; used with the permission of the author), and "The Making and Molding of Child Abuse," *Critical Inquiry* 17 (Winter 1991): 253–88; Carol Tavris, "Beware the Incest-Survivor Machine," *New York Times Book Review*, January 3, 1993.

6. See Louis Althusser, "A Letter on Art," in *Lenin and Philosophy and Other Essays*, translated by Ben Brewster (New York: Monthly Review Press, 1971), pp. 221–27, and Pierre Macherey, *A Theory of Literary Production* (1966), translated by Geoffrey Wall (London: Routledge and Kegan Paul, 1978), esp. pp. 82–97; Judith Lewis Herman, *Trauma and Recovery: The Aftermath of Violence—From Domestic Abuse to Political Terror* (New York: Basic Books, 1992) and *Father-Daughter Incest* (Cambridge: Harvard University Press, 1981).

7. Elkins, *Slavery*, pp. 1, 122–23 (Elkins's emphasis). See also Ann J. Lane, ed., *The Debate over Slavery: Stanley Elkins and His Critics* (Urbana: University of Illinois Press, 1971); Peter Kolchin, *American Slavery: 1619–1877* (New York: Hill and Wang, 1993), pp. 135–39; and Peter J. Parish, *Slavery: History and Historians* (New York: Harper and Row, 1989), pp. 7, 67–70.

8. Herbert Gutman, *The Black Family in Slavery and Freedom, 1750–1925* (New York: Oxford University Press, 1976).

9. Karl Marx and Frederick Engels, "Feuerbach: Opposition of the Materialist and Idealist Outlook," in *The German Ideology, Part One* [written 1845–46], edited by C. J. Arthur (New York: International Publishers, 1947, 1970), pp. 47–49 (emphasis in the original).

10. Alexis de Tocqueville, *Democracy in America*, edited by J. P. Mayer (Garden City, N.Y.: Doubleday, 1969), pp. 345, 375–76, 585–88.

11. Althusser sees the family one of the potent "ideological state apparatuses" that silently inculcate ideology alongside whatever coercion the state may employ. Lacan speaks of the "paternal metaphor" and "the name of the father" as means by which children are initiated into the conventions and power relations of social life. Althusser, "Ideology and Ideological State Apparatuses" and "Freud and Lacan," in *Lenin and Philosophy*, pp. 143–45, 150–58, 189–220; Jacques Lacan, *Ecrits*, pp. 65–73, 142–43, 196–97, 201–20, 252.

12. Quoted in Brenda Stevenson, "Distress and Discord in Virginia Slave Families, 1830–1860," in *In Joy and in Sorrow: Women, Family, and Marriage in the Victorian South, 1830–1900*, edited by Carol Bleser (New York: Oxford University Press, 1991), p. 111.

13. Kenneth Stampp, *The Peculiar Institution: Slavery in the Ante-Bellum South* (New York: Knopf, 1959, Vintage ed.), p. 141.

14. William Wells Brown, *Narrative*, quoted in John Blassingame, *The Slave Commu-*

nity: Plantation Life in the Antebellum South, rev. ed. (New York: Oxford University Press, 1979), p. 186; [Olive Gilbert], *Narrative of Sojourner Truth*, p. 73.

15. Theodore Rosengarten, *All God's Dangers: The Life of Nate Shaw* (New York: Knopf, 1974), pp. 6–11.

16. Stampp, *Peculiar Institution*, p. 144 (irregular capitalization in original); Alice Miller, *For Your Own Good: Hidden Cruelty in Child-Rearing and the Roots of Violence* (New York: Farrar, Straus, Giroux, 1983, 1990), pp. 58, 65, 88.

17. Concerning attachment, the three-volume work of John Bowlby is crucial: *Attachment* (London: Tavistock Institute of Human Relations, 1969; reprint, New York: Basic Books, 1982), *Separation: Anxiety and Anger* (New York: Basic Books, 1973), and *Loss: Sadness and Depression* (New York: Basic Books, 1980).

18. Parish, *Slavery*, p. 86; Kolchin, *American Slavery*, pp. 96–98, 125–39. The dust jacket of Kolchin's book shows a slave auction in which a black mother on her knees reaches vainly for her baby, whom the auctioneer holds up for sale by one arm and on whom a gentleman bids. In the lower right corner, a soon to be sundered slave family huddles in tears.

19. Harriet A. Jacobs, *Incidents in the Life of a Slave Girl, Written by Herself*, edited by Jean Fagan Yellin (Cambridge: Harvard University Press, 1987), pp. 27–28, 33.

20. Mary Chesnut quoted in Lee Ann Whites, "The Civil War as a Crisis in Gender," in *Divided Houses: Gender and the Civil War*, edited by Catherine Clinton and Nina Silber (New York: Oxford University Press, 1992), p. 6.

21. Gayle Rubin, "The Traffic in Women: Notes on the 'Political Economy' of Sex," in *Toward an Anthropology of Women*, edited by Rayna R. Reiter (New York: Monthly Review Press, 1975), pp. 157–210.

22. Andrew Jackson, *Narrative and Writings of Andrew Jackson of Kentucky* (Syracuse: Daily and Weekly Star, 1847), p. 24. I thank Walter Johnson for bringing this anecdote to my attention.

23. Herman, *Father-Daughter Incest*, pp. 81–83, and *Trauma and Recovery*, p. 106.

24. Catharine A. MacKinnon, *Sexual Harassment of Working Women: A Case of Sex Discrimination* (New Haven: Yale University Press, 1979), pp. 29, 40, 45. MacKinnon also notes that "racism is deeply involved in sexual harassment" (p. 31).

25. David Finkelhor with Sharon Araji, Larry Baron, Angela Browne, Stefanie Doyle Peters, and Gail Elizabeth Wyatt, *A Sourcebook on Child Sexual Abuse* (Newbury Park, Calif.: Sage Publications, 1986), pp. 152–64.

26. Benjamin Mays, *The Negro's God as Reflected in His Literature* (Boston: Chapman and Grimes, 1938), pp. 22, 87.

27. John Hope Franklin, "Slavery and Personality: A Fresh Look," *Massachusetts Review* 2 (Autumn 1960), and Earl E. Thorpe, "Chattel Slavery and Concentration Camps," *Negro History Bulletin* 25 (May 1962), both quoted in August Meier and Elliott Rudwick, *Black History and the Historical Profession, 1915–1980* (Urbana: University of Illinois Press), pp. 140, 248.

28. Unfortunately, due to the state of the historiography, I cannot elaborate on the cultural and psychological situation of the millions of slaves who lived outside black communities, for this, like much in studies of the psychology of households that included whites and blacks, remains to be investigated. Historical scholarship on

nonplantation southern blacks is virtually nonexistent. Historians writing on northern slavery have tended to examine those slaves' conditions of life rather than their lives. One exception to this rule is Shane White, *Somewhat More Independent: The End of Slavery in New York City, 1770–1810* (Athens: University of Georgia Press, 1991). The first two chapters of my biography of Sojourner Truth, *Sojourner Truth: A Life, a Symbol* (New York: Norton, forthcoming), deal with the personal experience of slaves in New York State.

29. Blassingame, *Slave Community*, p. 191; Deborah Gray White, *Ar'n't I a Woman? Female Slaves in the Plantation South* (New York: Norton, 1985), pp. 119–41.

30. Gail Elizabeth Wyatt and M. Ray Mickey, "The Support by Parents and Others as It Mediates the Effects of Child Sexual Abuse: An Exploratory Study," in *Lasting Effects of Child Sexual Abuse*, edited by Gail Elizabeth Wyatt and Gloria Johnson Powell (Newbury Park, Calif.: Sage Publications, 1988), pp. 211–25.

31. Albert Raboteau, *Slave Religion: The "Invisible Institution" in the Antebellum South* (New York: Oxford University Press, 1978); Gayraud S. Wilmore, *Last Things First* (Philadelphia: Westminster Press, 1982), pp. 42, 77; James H. Cone, *God of the Oppressed* (San Francisco: Harper San Francisco, 1975), pp. 32, 57, 175.

32. Arthur A. Stone, Lynn Helder, and Mark S. Schneider, "Coping with Stressful Events: Coping Dimensions and Issues," in *Life Events and Psychological Functioning: Theoretical and Methodological Issues*, edited by Lawrence H. Cohen (Newbury Park, Calif.: Sage Publications, 1988), pp. 187–88.

33. Catherine Clinton, *The Plantation Mistress: Woman's World in the Old South* (New York: Panthcon, 1982), p. 165.

34. Elizabeth Fox-Genovese notes that the family "figured as a central metaphor for southern society as a whole." "Family and Female Identity in the Antebellum South: Sarah Gayle and Her Family," in *In Joy and in Sorrow*, p. 19.

35. On white women in the fields, see Stephanie McCurry, "The Politics of Yeoman Households in South Carolina," in *Divided Houses*, pp. 28–31.

36. [Theodore Dwight Weld], *American Slavery as It Is: Testimony of a Thousand Witnesses* (New York: American Anti-Slavery Society, 1839), pp. 51–52.

37. Elizabeth Fox-Genovese, *Within the Plantation Household: Black and White Women in the Antebellum South* (Chapel Hill: University of North Carolina Press, 1988), pp. 24, 97, 308–14.

38. Quoted in [Weld], *American Slavery*, pp. 54–55 (emphasis in the original).

39. Thomas Jefferson, *Notes on the State of Virginia* (1787; reprint, New York: Norton, 1972), p. 162. Similarly, an advice manual for slave-owning mothers published in 1830, *Letters on Female Character*, noted that slave owning encouraged "all the most malignant vices of his nature" in the child. Quoted in Clinton, *Plantation Mistress*, p. 91.

40. Philip G. Ney, "Triangles of Abuse: A Model of Maltreatment," *Child Abuse & Neglect* 12 (1988): 363–73.

41. See Virginia Walcott Beauchamp, ed., *A Private War: Letters and Diaries of Madge Preston, 1862–1867* (New Brunswick, N.J.: Rutgers University Press, 1987).

42. Stephanie McCurry, "In Defense of Their World: Gender, Class, and the Yeomanry of the South Carolina Low Country, 1820–1860" (Ph.D. diss., State University of New York at Binghamton, 1988), pp. 98–101.

43. A. Leon Higginbotham Jr., *In the Matter of Color: Race and the American Legal Process: The Colonial Period* (New York: Oxford University Press, 1978), pp. 40–47; Peter Bardaglio, "Families, Sex, and the Law: The Legal Transformation of the Nineteenth-Century Southern Household" (Ph.D. diss., Stanford University, 1987), pp. 107–66.

44. Daniel Blake Smith, *Inside the Great House: Planter Family Life in Eighteenth-Century Chesapeake Society* (Ithaca, N.Y.: Cornell University Press, 1980).

45. Carol Lawson, "Violence at Home: 'They Don't Want Anyone to Know,' " *New York Times*, 6 August 1992.

46. Ronald C. Summit, "Hidden Victims, Hidden Pain: Societal Avoidance of Child Sexual Abuse," in *Lasting Effects of Child Sexual Abuse*, p. 40.

47. Jeffrey Moussaieff Masson, *The Assault on Truth: Freud's Suppression of the Seduction Theory* (New York: HarperCollins, 1984, 1992).

48. Richard L. Bushman, *The Refinement of America: Persons, Houses, Cities* (New York: Knopf, 1992), pp. xiv, 55, 288; Jay Fliegelman, *Declaring Independence: Jefferson, Natural Language, and the Culture of Performance* (Stanford: Stanford University Press, 1993), pp. 79–129, 189–200.

49. Lillian Smith, *Killers of the Dream*, rev. ed. (New York: Norton, 1961), pp. 83–89, 121–24.

CHAPTER 7. Gendered Expectations

I want to thank many people for their help and encouragement in my Mary Mallon project, of which this essay is a part. John Duffy and Daniel Fox, both of whom have written on public health in New York, were most generous in discussing resources with me. Joel Howell and David Rosner offered helpful suggestions along the way. Joan Jacobs Brumberg, Susan Stanford Friedman, Linda Gordon, and John Harley Warner read drafts of earlier versions of the work and provided essential insights. R. Alta Charo, Hendrik Hartog, and Leslie Reagan gave needed advice with the legal sources. Research assistance by Dawn Corley and Sarah Leavitt was crucial to the completion of my first paper on the project, in time for its earliest presentation at Yale University in February 1990. Lewis Leavitt offered consultation on the medical issues and critical judgments throughout. I also wish to thank Lian Partlow, Sarah Pfatteicher, and Jennifer Munger for their help with research. I am grateful for all the suggestions and questions I received from my colleagues at the University of Wisconsin, Yale University, Harvard University, the University of Washington, and the Canadian Association for Medical History when I presented various versions of my work on Mary Mallon.

Since writing this essay, I have been fortunate to meet and to interview three people whose insights into Mary Mallon's situation have already proved very helpful to me. Even though I was unable to incorporate their wisdom into this chapter, I will be calling upon it in future writing. I would like here to acknowledge and to thank Ida Peters Hoffman, Dr. John Marr, and Emma Sherman for their gracious cooperation and support.

1. My favorite recent example of how adding women's perspectives to traditional history totally transforms it is Laurel Thatcher Ulrich, *A Midwife's Tale: The Life of Martha Ballard, Based on Her Diary, 1785–1812* (New York: Knopf, 1992), in which men's medicine is shown to be at best only half of late-eighteenth-century medicine. Ulrich's brilliant exposure of the full range of medical practice was built on the work of women's historians over the past twenty-five years, led so well by the woman we honor in this volume, Gerda Lerner.

2. Judith Walzer Leavitt, " 'Typhoid Mary' Strikes Back: Bacteriological Theory and Practice in Early-Twentieth-Century Public Health," *Isis* 83 (December 1992): 608–29. My book in progress (tentatively titled, *"Typhoid Mary": Personal Liberty versus the Public's Health in the Twentieth Century*, to be published by Beacon Press) addresses these and other factors that are part of the full story of Mallon's experiences.

3. Many historians have described the narrowing of public health work in the early twentieth century. See, e.g., Paul Starr, *The Social Transformation of American Medicine* (New York: Basic Books, 1982), in which he writes: "The limitations on public health in the twentieth century were . . . profound. The early public health reformers of the nineteenth century, for all their moralism, were concerned with social welfare in a broad sense. Their twentieth-century successors adopted a more narrow and technical view of their calling" (p. 196). Recent historians, however, have altered this view and have called attention to the broad social concerns that continued to influence public health practices. For the latter, see esp. Nancy Tomes, "The Private Side of Public Health: Sanitary Science, Domestic Hygiene, and the Germ Theory, 1870–1900," *Bulletin of the History of Medicine* 64 (1990): 509–39, and "The Wages of Dirt Were Death: Women and Domestic Hygiene, 1870–1930" (paper presented at the Annual Meeting of the Organization of American Historians, Louisville, 1991); Allan M. Brandt, *No Magic Bullet: A Social History of Venereal Disease in the United States since 1880* (New York: Oxford University Press, 1985); John Ettling, *The Germ of Laziness: Rockefeller Philanthropy and Public Health in the New South* (Cambridge: Harvard University Press, 1981); and my article in *Isis* (see n. 2).

4. Abram S. Beneson, ed., *Control of Communicable Diseases in Man*, 14th ed. (Washington, D.C.: American Public Health Association, 1985), pp. 420–24.

5. See, e.g., George A. Johnson, "The Typhoid Toll," *Journal of the American Water Works Association* 3 (1916): 249–326, and Eric Ashby, "Reflections on the Costs and Benefits of Environmental Pollution," *Perspectives in Biology and Medicine* 23 (1979): 7–24.

6. On single working domestics, see Susan Strasser, *Never Done: A History of American Housework* (New York: Pantheon Books, 1982), chap. 9; Barbara Mayer Wertheimer, *We Were There: The Story of Working Women in America* (New York: Pantheon Books, 1977); Rosalyn Baxandall, Linda Gordon, and Susan Reverby, comps. and eds., *America's Working Women* (New York: Vintage Books, 1976); David M. Katzman, *Seven Days a Week: Women and Domestic Service in Industrializing America* (New York: Oxford University Press, 1978); Faye E. Dudden, *Serving Women: Household Service in Nineteenth-Century America* (Middletown, Conn.: Wesleyan University Press, 1983); Daniel E. Sutherland, *Americans and Their Servants: Domestic Service in the United States, 1800 to 1920* (Baton Rouge: Louisiana State University Press, 1981); and Phyllis Palmer, *Domesticity and Dirt: House-*

wives and Domestic Servants in the United States, 1920–1945 (Philadelphia: Temple University Press, 1989).

7. The first published account linking Mallon with typhoid fever was George A. Soper, "The Work of a Chronic Typhoid Germ Distributor," *Journal of the American Medical Association* 48 (1907): 2019–22. See also Soper's "The Curious Career of Typhoid Mary," *Bulletin of the New York Academy of Medicine* 15 (October 1939): 698–712, and his "Typhoid Mary," *Military Surgeon* 45 (July 1919): 1–15.

8. Soper, "Curious Career," p. 704.

9. S. Josephine Baker, *Fighting for Life* (New York: Macmillan, 1939), p. 73.

10. Ibid., pp. 74–75.

11. See, e.g., " 'Typhoid Mary' Has Reappeared: Human Culture Tube, Herself Immune, Spreads the Disease Wherever She Goes," *New York Times*, April 4, 1915, sec. 5, pp. 3–4.

12. William H. Park, "Typhoid Bacilli Carriers," *JAMA* 51 (1908): 981.

13. C.-E. A. Winslow, *The Life of Hermann M. Biggs, M.D., D.Sc., LL.D.: Physician and Statesman of the Public Health* (Philadelphia: Lea and Fabiger, 1929), p. 199.

14. The first newspaper account of Mallon appeared in the *New York American* on April 2, 1907, fifteen days following her initial incarceration, and identified her as "Mary Ilverson"—knowing it was a pseudonym. The 1907 and 1908 accounts, and the medical accounts from those years, refer to her as an Irish cook but do not name her. During the discussion of Park's paper (see n. 12), in June 1908, M. J. Rosenau used the term "typhoid Mary" (small *t*). George Whipple's 1908 book referred to her as "Typhoid Mary." George C. Whipple, *Typhoid Fever: Its Causation, Transmission, and Prevention* (New York: John Wiley and Sons, 1908), p. 20. The major news coverage using her name did not begin until an *American* article of June 20, 1909.

15. The writ of habeas corpus and all accompanying documentation can be found in the county courthouse in New York City.

16. *New York American*, June 30, 1909, p. 3. See also *New York Times*, July 1, 1909, p. 8.

17. *New York Times*, July 17, 1909, p. 3. The decision was filed on July 22.

18. The undated letter is filed with the writ in the county courthouse (irregular spelling and capitalization in original). It had been addressed to the editor of the *American*, but this was crossed out, and George Francis O'Neill's name was penned in its place.

19. Quoted in *New York Times*, February 21, 1910, p. 18.

20. *New York American*, February 21, 1910, p. 6.

21. An account of the hospital outbreak, without naming Mallon, is M. L. Ogan, "Immunization in a Typhoid Outbreak in the Sloane Hospital for Women," *New York Medical Journal* 101 (March 27, 1915): 610–12. See *New York Times*, March 28, 1915, sec. 2, p. 1, and March 31, 1915, p. 8; *New York American*, March 28, 1915, p. 1; and *New York Tribune*, March 28, 1915, p. 7.

22. See the death and funeral accounts in all New York newspapers. Soper claims that the date of Mallon's stroke was Christmas 1932, and all commentators since have followed his lead. I am more convinced by two pieces of evidence suggesting the October 1933 date. First is a news article of December 1933 indicating that she suffered a stroke "two months ago," which would be in October, and the second is my

informant Emma Goldberg Sherman, who says she was the person who found Mallon after her stroke. Sherman remembers the day as quite warm; she went looking for Mallon after she did not show up for work. She also believes that 1933, a date five years before Mallon's death, is closer to the right date. She is unable to remember more specifically. She knows that she never worked on Christmas Day or other holidays. See "I Wonder What's Become of—Typhoid Mary," Sunday *Mirror* magazine sec., *New York Daily Mirror*, December 17, 1933, p. 19, and Emma Sherman to author, December 1993.

On the number of cases traced to Mallon, see my forthcoming book. I have been able to account for forty-seven, with possibly two additional ones, whereas the official listing is fifty-three. Soper seems to have miscounted his own evidence.

23. Soper, "Typhoid Mary," p. 13. The *New York Tribune* editorialized similarly; "The sympathy which would naturally be granted Mary Mallon is largely modified for this reason: The chance was given to her five years ago to live in freedom, and . . . she deliberately elected to throw it away. . . . It is impossible to feel much commiseration for her" (March 29, 1915, p. 8).

24. Quoted in *New York Times*, April 4, 1915, sec. 5, p. 3.

25. The key case in making this argument was *Jacobson v. Massachusetts* (1905), 197 U.S. 11. I have written about this decision in " 'Be Safe, Be Sure': New York City's Experience with Smallpox," in *Hives of Sickness*, edited by David Rosner (New Brunswick, N.J.: Rutgers University Press, forthcoming).

26. Some vaccination rules, too, were in effect only during epidemics.

27. Quoted in *New York Times*, April 4, 1915, sec. 5, p. 4.

28. The efficacy of quarantines through history needs more examination than it has thus far received, especially in light of recent suggestions about quarantining people infected with the HIV virus. For a good treatment of the issue of quarantines historically as relevant to AIDS, see David Musto, "Quarantine and the Problem of AIDS," *Milbank Quarterly* 64, supp. 1 (1986): 97–117. See also a longer discussion of the importance of isolation in this specific instance in my forthcoming book.

29. I examine fully the medical aspects of Mallon's case in " 'Typhoid Mary' Strikes Back."

30. *Medical Record* 71 (June 1, 1907): 924.

31. New York City Department of Health, *Annual Report*, 1916, p. 56.

32. *New York Times*, March 14, 1924, p. 19.

33. Ibid.; *New York Times*, March 15, 1924, p. 13 (quotations).

34. *New York Tribune*, March 29, 1915, p. 8.

35. Baker, *Fighting for Life*, p. 75. A California study of healthy typhoid fever carriers revealed that in that state a full 25 percent of identified carriers did not cooperate with authorities. See M. Dorthy Beck and Arthur C. Hollister, *Typhoid Fever Cases and Carriers: An Analysis of Records of the California State Department of Public Health from 1910 through 1959* (Berkeley: State of California Department of Public Health, 1962).

36. Soper, "Curious Career," pp. 704–5.

37. New York City Department of Health, *Annual Report*, 1916, p. 56 (emphasis added).

38. Soper, "Typhoid Mary," p. 11.

39. On the status of single working domestics, see Strasser, *Never Done*; Wertheimer, *We Were There*; Baxandall, Gordon, and Reverby, *America's Working Women*; Katzman, *Seven Days*; Dudden, *Serving Women*; Sutherland, *Americans and Their Servants*; and Palmer, *Domesticity and Dirt*.

40. See, for example, "Typhoid Mary," *Scientific American* 112 (May 8, 1915): 428. See my forthcoming book for more discussion of ethnicity as a factor in Mary Mallon's case.

41. Educational level also seems to have been of interest to health officers. Josephine Baker, in her effort to explain why Mallon would not cooperate during her arrest, had described her as "uneducated"; yet Mallon's clear handwriting in the letter cited above refutes that claim. Religion may also have been a factor working against Mallon. These points need to be examined elsewhere.

42. *New York American*, April 2, 1907, p. 2.

43. A 1916 Minnesota study found that 25 of 30 identified carriers were women. The investigators noted that because women cooked for their families and friends, as well as took many low-paying jobs in food-handling occupations, it was natural to find more women than men among healthy carriers. Men were less likely to be discovered, and also less likely to become public health hazards, because their daily tasks and their occupations did not center upon food preparation. A. J. Chesley, H. A. Burns, W. P. Greene, and E. M. Wade, "Three Years' Experience in the Search for Typhoid Carriers in Minnesota," *JAMA* 68 (1917): 1882–1885 (this finding, p. 1884). A Boston study similarly concluded that "we have a preponderance of women on our carrier list, this is largely because they handle food more frequently and are therefore more frequently discovered in connection with outbreaks." George H. Bigelow and Gaylord W. Anderson, "Cures of Typhoid Carriers," *JAMA* 101 (1933): 348–52. It was not until the 1940s that studies began to document more women carriers in the population at large, not just among those found in food-handling jobs transmitting the disease. In a New York State study published in 1943, the investigators concluded that "the rate of development of the carrier state at all ages is almost twice as high for females as for males." The most striking sex difference found in that study occurred in the 40–49 age group, in which 16 percent of female cases and only 3.5 percent of male cases resulted in the chronic carrier state. Wendell R. Ames and Morton Robins, "Age and Sex as Factors in the Development of the Typhoid Carrier State, and a Method for Estimating Carrier Prevalence," *American Journal of Public Health* 33 (1943): 223. Medical science in the 1990s acknowledged similar differentials. I want to thank Dennis Maki, head of the Section of Infectious Diseases, Department of Medicine, University of Wisconsin, and Herbert Dupont, chief of Infectious Diseases, University of Texas, Houston, for generously consulting with me on this issue.

44. Soper is quoted in *New York Times*, April 4, 1915, sec. 5, p. 3.

45. New York City Department of Health, *Annual Report*, 1922, p. 92. See also *New York Times*, October 13, 1922, and January 21, 1923.

46. It was common practice to allow breadwinners greater latitude in public health restrictions. See, e.g., a national study of laws and regulations controlling infectious diseases in which researchers noted that "exceptions in favor of breadwinners . . . may be made by local health authorities." J. W. Kerr and A. A. Moll, "Communicable

Diseases: An Analysis of the Laws and Regulations for the Control Thereof in the United States," *Public Health Bulletin #62*, July 1913 (Washington, D.C.: GPO, 1914), pp. 66–67.

The health department did ultimately retrain Mallon, years after her second incarceration, when she began to work in the hospital laboratory. This occurred probably in the mid-1920s and did not result in her release.

47. See, e.g., *New York Times*, March 30, 1913, and Herman F. Senftner and Frank E. Coughlin, "Typhoid Carriers in New York State with Special Reference to Gall Bladder Operations," *American Journal of Hygiene* 17 (1933): 711–23.

48. Soper, "Curious Career," p. 698.

49. *Medical Record* 71 (May 18, 1907): 818.

50. *New York World-Telegram*, November 12, 1938, p. 26.

51. *The People ex. rel. Jennie Barmore v. John Dill Robertson et al. Respondents* (1922), 302 Ill. 422. All of the papers in this case are in the Archives of the Supreme Court of Illinois, Springfield, RG 901, microfilm roll 30-1807. The final opinion can be found in *Reports and Cases at Law and in Chancery*, Supreme Court of Illinois, vol. 302 (Bloomington, Ill., 1922), pp. 422–36. At Iroquois Hospital Ruth Moore, nurse, and Leonea Letourneau, clerk, collected the specimens and delivered them to the laboratory. Their testimony is recorded on pp. 177–80.

52. The Chicago newspapers reported Barmore's story, although not often or fully. See, e.g., *Chicago Tribune*, November 24, 1920, sec. 2, p. 1; June 19, 1921, p. 14; and *Chicago Herald and Examiner*, November 24, 1920, p. 2. The health department recognized her extremely briefly in its publications. The legal record is most complete. The writ, return, traverse to the return, stipulations, briefs and arguments, typescript of all testimony, and opinions in the case are located in the Archives of the Supreme Court of Illinois, Springfield (hereafter cited as Illinois Supreme Court Archives). It is primarily through these records that I have reconstructed Barmore's story and can examine its meanings.

53. The placard was introduced as part of the stipulation (that part not disputed by either side) on December 9, 1921, p. 7, Illinois Supreme Court Archives.

54. Bundesen testimony in the printed Abstract of Record, pp. 55–56, ibid..

55. Brief and argument for relatrix, p. 65, ibid.

56. Bundesen testimony is in the printed brief and argument for the relatrix, p. 24, ibid.

57. The case centered on due process, although during the examination of expert witnesses, Darrow tried (and to some extent succeeded) to make the physicians sound inept. His challenge to science in this case stands in stark contrast to his defense of science in the Scopes trial a few years later.

58. Judge Sabath's opinion, pp. 210, 214, Illinois Supreme Court Archives.

59. Sabath's opinion, p. 214, ibid.

60. Typescript of witness testimony, p. 198, ibid.

61. Quotations in this paragraph are from the court discussion about when the briefs would be filed and appear on pp. 200–201 of the printed testimony, ibid.

62. Application for Rehearing, pp. 1, 4, ibid.

63. Ibid., pp. 4, 9.

64. Darrow's autobiography does not mention this case, nor do various biographies of him. See Clarence Darrow, *The Story of My Life* (New York: Scribner's, 1932); Kevin Tierney, *Darrow: A Biography* (New York: Thomas Y. Crowell, 1979); Geoffrey Cowan, *The People versus Clarence Darrow* (New York: Random House, 1993).

65. Brief and argument for respondents, p. 57, Illinois Supreme Court Archives.

66. *Chicago Tribune*, April 15, 1922, sec. 2, p. 17; *Report of the Department of Health of the City of Chicago for the Years 1919, 1920, and 1921* (Chicago, 1923), p. 189. In 1923 twelve women filed for release, in 1924 fifteen; in 1925 five women used the courts to attempt to get their release: "in every instance the defendants were remanded and ordered detained by the Commissioner of Health until such time as, in his opinion, they were no longer a menace to the public." *Report of the Department of Health of the City of Chicago for the Years 1923, 1924, and 1925* (Chicago, 1926), p. 32. I am grateful to Bonnie Ellen Blustein for helping me locate these reports and to Patricia Spain Ward for alerting me to health department activity in this area and for sharing her views about Herman Bundesen.

CHAPTER 8. Separatism Revisited

I would like to thank Mary Felstiner, Linda Gordon, Susan Krieger, Susan Lynn, Peggy Pascoe, Kim Philips, Mary Louise Roberts, and Kathryn Kish Sklar for their stimulating comments on drafts of this essay.

1. Journal of Miriam Van Waters, vol. 7, November 1, 1945, Miriam Van Waters Papers, Schlesinger Library, Radcliffe College, Cambridge, Mass. (hereafter cited as MVW Papers).

2. Lori D. Ginzberg, *Women and the Work of Benevolence: Morality, Politics, and Class in the Nineteenth-Century United States* (New Haven: Yale University Press, 1990); Cynthia Neverdon-Morton, *Afro-American Women of the South and the Advancement of the Race* (Knoxville: University of Tennessee Press, 1989); Paula Baker, "The Domestication of Politics: Women and American Political Society, 1780–1920," *American Historical Review* 89 (June 1984): 620–47; Kathryn Kish Sklar, "The Historical Foundations of Women's Power in the Creation of the American Welfare State, 1830–1930," in *Mothers of a New World: Maternalist Politics and the Origins of Welfare States*, edited by Seth Koven and Sonya Michel (New York: Routledge, 1993); Seth Koven and Sonya Michel, "Womanly Duties: Maternalist Politics and the Origins of Welfare States in France, Germany, Great Britain, and the United States, 1880–1920," *American Historical Review* (October 1990): 1076–1108; Linda Gordon, "The New Feminist Scholarship on the Welfare State," in *Women, the State, and Welfare*, edited by Linda Gordon (Madison: University of Wisconsin Press, 1990), pp. 9–35; Kathleen D. McCarthy, ed., *Lady Bountiful Revisited: Women, Philanthropy, and Power* (New Brunswick, N.J.: Rutgers University Press, 1990).

3. On clubs, see Sheila Rothman, *Woman's Proper Place: A History of Changing Ideals and Practices, 1870 to the Present* (New York: Basic Books, 1978), pp. 186–87, and Karen Blair, "The Limits of Sisterhood: Its Decline among Clubwomen, 1890–1930" (paper presented at the Annual Meeting of the American Historical Association, Los An-

geles, December 1981). Peggy Pascoe describes the decline of rescue homes in *Relations of Rescue: The Search for Female Moral Authority in the American West, 1874–1939* (New York: Oxford University Press, 1990). On social workers, see Clarke A. Chambers, "Women in the Creation of the Profession of Social Work," *Social Service Review* (March 1986): 23, and Nancy Cott, *The Grounding of Modern Feminism* (New Haven: Yale University Press, 1987), p. 224.

4. Robin Muncy, *Creating a Female Dominion in American Reform, 1890–1935* (New York: Oxford University Press, 1991); Baker, "The Domestication of Politics," p. 647. Even historians who stress continuity between progressivism and the New Deal note a contraction of women's authority during the late 1920s: J. Stanley Lemons, in *The Woman Citizen: Social Feminism in the 1920s* (Urbana: University of Illinois Press, 1973), sees an ebb in reform activism between 1925 and 1933, and Muncy states that reform contracted after 1924 (p. xvii). Clarke Chambers's important early argument for continuity, *Seedtime for Reform: American Social Service and Social Action, 1918–1933* (Minneapolis: University of Minnesota Press, 1963), refers to reform as "quiescent" rather than "dead" (p. xi). See also Sarah Deutsch, "Learning to Talk More Like a Man: Boston Women's Class-Bridging Organizations, 1870–1940," *American Historical Review* (April 1992): 379–404. For the emergence of historical challenges to the interpretation of a decline in women's politics after suffrage, see my review essay, "The New Woman: Changing Views of Women in the 1920s," *Journal of American History* 61 (September 1974): 372–93.

5. The title of this chapter, "Separatism Revisited," refers to my essay "Separatism as Strategy: Female Institution Building and American Feminism, 1870–1930" (*Feminist Studies* [Fall 1979]: 512–29), in which I proposed that "a major strength of American feminism prior to 1920 was the separate female community that helped sustain women's participation in both social reform and political activism." I argued that "the self-consciously female community began to disintegrate in the 1920s" as women attempted to integrate as equals into male politics and social life.

6. Nancy Cott provides a useful summary of the literature that attempts to clarify the definitions of feminism and the women's movement in "What's in a Name? The Limits of 'Social Feminism'; or, Expanding the Vocabulary of Women's History," *Journal of American History* 76 (December 1989): 809–29.

7. Elsa Barkley Brown, "Womanist Consciousness: Maggie Lena Walker and the Independent Order of Saint Luke," *Signs* 14 (Spring 1989): 610–33; Neverdon-Morton, *Afro-American Women of the South*; Darlene Clark Hine, *Black Women in the Middle West: The Michigan Experience* (Ann Arbor: Historical Society of Michigan, 1990), pp. 15–17, 20–23, and " 'We Specialize in the Wholly Impossible': The Philanthropic Work of Black Women," in *Lady Bountiful Revisited*, pp. 70–95; Jacqueline Anne Rouse, *Lugenia Burns Hope: Black Southern Reformer* (Athens: University of Georgia Press, 1989); Kim Philips, " 'Heaven Bound': Black Migration, Community, and Working-Class Activism in Cleveland, 1915–1945" (Ph.D. diss., Yale University, 1992), esp. chap. 5; Dorothy Salem, *To Better Our World: Black Women in Organized Reform, 1890–1920* (New York: Carlson Publishing, Inc., 1990), chap. 8. On black women who did become more politically active after suffrage, see Evelyn Brooks Higginbotham, "In Politics to Stay: Black Women Leaders and Party Politics in the 1920s," in *Women, Politics, and Change*,

edited by Louise Tilly and Patricia Gurin (New York: Russell Sage Foundation, 1990), pp. 199–220. On black women's organizations, see also Anne Firor Scott, "Most Invisible of All: Black Women's Voluntary Associations," *Journal of Southern History* (February 1990): 3–22; Paula Giddings, *In Search of Sisterhood: Delta Sigma Theta and the Challenge of the Black Sorority Movement* (New York: William Morrow, 1988); Linda Gordon, "Black and White Visions of Welfare: Women's Welfare Activism, 1890–1945," *Journal of American History* 78 (September 1991): 559–90; and Debra Gray White, "The Cost of Club Work, the Price of Black Feminism," in *Visible Women: New Essays on American Activism*, edited by Nancy Hewitt and Suzanne Lebsock (Urbana: University of Illinois Press, 1993), pp. 247–70.

8. Felice Gordon distinguishes between two groups of postsuffrage activists: "moral prodders"—who sought, for example, goals once labeled "social feminist," such as protective labor legislation and temperance—and "equal righters"—who were committed to expanding on the political victory of suffrage through their support of an Equal Rights Amendment. Felice Gordon, *After Winning: The Legacy of the New Jersey Suffragists, 1920–1947* (New Brunswick, N.J.: Rutgers University Press, 1986). See also Cott, *Grounding of Modern Feminism*, chap. 3.

9. Hine, " 'We Specialize in the Wholly Impossible,' " pp. 83–84; Susan Ware, *Beyond Suffrage: Women in the New Deal* (Cambridge: Harvard University Press, 1981) and *Partner and I: Molly Dewson, Feminism, and New Deal Politics* (New Haven: Yale University Press, 1987); Muncy, *Female Dominion*; Leila J. Rupp, "The Women's Community in the National Woman's Party, 1945 to the 1960s," *Signs* (Summer 1985): 715–40, and Rupp and Verta Taylor, *Survival in the Doldrums: The American Women's Rights Movement, 1945 to the 1960s* (New York: Oxford University Press, 1987).

10. Dorothy Sue Cobble, "Rethinking Troubled Relations between Women and Unions: Craft Unionism and Female Activism," *Feminist Studies* 16, no. 3 (Fall 1990): 521, 529, and *Dishing It Out: Waitresses and Their Unions in the Twentieth Century* (Urbana: University of Illinois Press, 1991); Vicki L. Ruiz, *Cannery Women, Cannery Lives: Mexican Women, Unionization, and the California Food Processing Industry, 1930–1950* (Albuquerque: University of New Mexico Press, 1987).

11. Jodi Vandenberg-Daves, "The Manly Pursuit of a Partnership between the Sexes: The Debate over YMCA Programs for Women and Girls, 1914–1933," *Journal of American History* 78 (March 1992): 1324–46; Frances Taylor, "On the Edge of Tomorrow: The Southern Student YWCA and Race, 1920–1944" (Ph.D. diss., Stanford University, 1984); Susan Lynn, *Progressive Women in Conservative Times: Racial Justice, Peace, and Feminism, 1945 to the 1960s* (New Brunswick, N.J.: Rutgers University Press, 1992).

12. Carroll Smith-Rosenberg, "The Female World of Love and Ritual: Relations between Women in Nineteenth-Century America," *Signs* (Autumn 1975): 1–29; Nancy Sahli, "Smashing: Women's Relationships before the Fall," *Chrysalis* (Summer 1979): 17–27; Lillian Faderman, *Surpassing the Love of Men: Romantic Friendship and Love between Women from the Renaissance to the Present* (New York: William Morrow, 1981).

13. Leila J. Rupp, "Imagine My Surprise: Women's Relationships in Historical Perspective," *Frontiers* (Fall 1980): 61–70; Ware, *Partner and I*; Eric Garber, " 'T'ain't Nobody's Bizness': Homosexuality in 1920s Harlem," in *Black Men / White Men*, edited

by Michael J. Smith (San Francisco: Gay Sunshine Press, 1983); Allan Berube, *Coming Out under Fire: The History of Gay Men and Women in World War Two* (New York: Free Press, 1990); Madeline Davis and Elizabeth Lapovsky Kennedy, "Oral History and the Study of Sexuality in the Lesbian Community: Buffalo, New York, 1940–1960," *Feminist Studies* (Spring 1986): 7–26, and *Boots of Leather, Slippers of Gold: The History of a Lesbian Community* (New York: Routledge, 1993); Linda Gordon, "Black and White Visions of Welfare," pp. 574–75. See also the essays by Esther Newton, Eric Garber, and John D'Emilio in *Hidden from History: Reclaiming the Gay and Lesbian Past*, edited by Martin Bauml Duberman, Martha Vicinus, and George Chauncey Jr. (New York: New American Library, 1989), and Lillian Faderman, *Odd Girls and Twilight Lovers: A History of Lesbian Life in Twentieth-Century America* (New York: Columbia University Press, 1991).

14. On the women's peace movement, see Barbara Steinson, " 'The Mother Half of Humanity': American Women in the Peace and Preparedness Movements in World War I," in *Women, War, and Revolution*, edited by Carol R. Berkin and Clara M. Lovett (New York: Holmes and Meier, 1980), pp. 259–81, and Linda Schott, "The Woman's Peace Party and the Moral Basis for Women's Pacifism," *Frontiers* 8, no. 2 (1985): 18–25. On antilynching, see Jacquelyn Dowd Hall, *Revolt against Chivalry: Jessie Daniel Ames and the Women's Campaign against Lynching* (New York: Columbia University Press, 1979).

15. I am currently writing a biography of Van Waters that uses her life as a window on several themes in U.S. women's history, including women and higher education during the Progressive Era, the politics of the juvenile court movement, Van Waters's complex family and personal relationships, the treatment of women criminals, and the post–World War II reaction to female authority.

16. "Coeds and the Franchise," *University of Oregon Monthly*, vol. 11, 1907–8, p. 42, in Special Collections, University of Oregon Library, Eugene.

17. Henry D. Sheldon, *History of the University of Oregon* (Portland: Binfords and Mort, 1940), pp. 79, 177.

18. On early women social scientists, see Rosalind Rosenberg, *Beyond Separate Spheres: Intellectual Roots of Modern Feminism* (New Haven: Yale University Press, 1982), pp. 239–40, and Ellen Fitzpatrick, *Endless Crusade: Women Social Scientists and Progressive Reform* (New York: Oxford University Press, 1990). Van Waters spoke of her quest for constructive work in letters to her parents on February 7, 1911 (file 40), April 15, 1911 (file 41), and October 23, 1912 (file 42), MVW Papers.

19. Mary Ellen Odem, "Delinquent Daughters: The Sexual Regulation of Female Minors in the United States, 1880–1920" (Ph.D. diss., University of California, Berkeley, 1989), chap. 1, p. 2.

20. Van Waters, "Where Girls Go Right," *Survey Graphic* (May 27, 1922): 361–76, *Youth in Conflict* (New York: Republic Publishing Co., 1925), and *Parents on Probation* (New York: Republic Publishing Co., 1927).

21. Van Waters used the term in a letter to her mother to describe the historic step of Orfa Jean Shontz running for political office. July 28, 1918, file 46, MVW Papers.

22. Van Waters to parents, September 2, 1917 (file 35), March 23, 1919 (file 47), and April 8, 1925 (file 53), ibid.

23. Van Waters, untitled and undated memoir, typescript, pp. 14–18, file 508, ibid.

24. Margaret van Wagenen, interview by author, Ashland, Mass., July 31, 1989.

25. Van Waters, untitled book proposal, n.d. (ca. 1957), file 508, MVW Papers.

26. Journal, vol. 2, August 11, 1934, ibid.

27. Journal, vol. 4, June 13, 1936, ibid.

28. Janis Howe, "Framingham Report," September 21, 1946, p. 8, file 247, ibid.

29. Mrs. Hazel Rubbitt to State Auditor, May 21, 1947, file 193, ibid.

30. Report of Mrs. O'Keefe, Massachusetts League of Women Voters, June 20, 1947, file 247, ibid.

31. Mrs. M. H. [Willa W.] Brown to Miriam Van Waters, February 10, 1949, file 203, ibid.

32. On the Society of the Companions of the Holy Cross, see Mary Sudman Donovan, *A Different Call: Women's Ministries in the Episcopal Church, 1850–1920* (Wilton, Conn.: Morehouse-Barlow, 1986), and Vida Scudder, *On Journey* (New York: E. P. Dutton, 1937).

33. Felice Gordon, *After Winning*, pp. 55–56, 78, 97; Meline Karakashian, "The Great Lady of Brookdale," in *A Triangle of Land: A History of the Site and the Founding of Brookdale Community College*, by Northern Monmouth Country Branch of the American Association of University Women (Lincroft, N.J.: Brookdale Community College, 1978), pp. 62–96.

34. Journal, vol. 2, May 11, 1934, MVW Papers.

35. Geraldine Thompson to Eleanor Roosevelt, February 10, 1945, file 191, ibid.

36. All letters on March 11–12, 1949, file 206, box 18, ibid.

37. *Boston Daily Record*, July 29, 31, 1957; Massachusetts Legislature, Report of the Special Committee on the Reorganization of the Correctional System, April 29, 1958, House Document 3015 (1958).

38. Anne Firor Scott, *Natural Allies: Women's Associations in American History* (Urbana: University of Illinois Press, 1993).

39. For capsule biographies of most of these women, see *Notable American Women: The Modern Period*, edited by Barbara Sicherman and Carol Hurd Green (Cambridge: Belknap Press, 1980). On Esther Peterson, see Joan Hoff, *Law, Gender, and Injustice: A Legal History of U.S. Women* (New York: New York University Press, 1991), pp. 231–33; Mary Q. Hawkes, *Excellent Effect: The Edna Mason Story* (Arlington, Va.: American Correctional Association, 1994).

40. On the persistence of middle-class female "devoted companions," see Faderman, *Odd Girls*, chap. 1. Linda Gordon suggests that such relationships were much rarer among black women reformers. Gordon, "Black and White Visions of Welfare."

41. Cf. the veiled threats of lesbianism used to discredit Judge Marion Harron, cited by Leila J. Rupp in "Imagine My Surprise," rev., in *Hidden from History*, p. 407.

42. *Notable American Women*; Dorothy M. Brown, *Mabel Walker Willebrandt: A Study of Power, Loyalty, and Law* (Knoxville: University of Tennessee Press, 1984).

43. Anne Firor Scott, *Making the Invisible Woman Visible* (Urbana: University of Illinois Press, 1984), p. xiv. On the League of Women Voters, see also Susan Ware, "American Women in the 1950s: Nonpartisan Politics and Women's Politicization," in *Women, Politics, and Change*, pp. 281–99. For arguments about the persistence of

women's reform after 1950, see Lynn, *Progressive Women*, and Joanne Meyerowitz, ed., *Not June Cleaver: Women and Gender in Postwar America, 1945–1960* (Philadelphia: Temple University Press, 1994).

44. Cott, *Grounding*, pp. 96, 276–83.

45. Journal, June 12, 1945, vol. 7, and Van Waters to Hon. Paul Doyle, September 20, 1948, file 197, MVW Papers.

46. Susan Hartmann, *The Home Front and Beyond: American Women in the 1940s* (Boston: Twayne Publishers, 1982), pp. 150–51. These and other women in Congress, Hartmann notes, sponsored legislation to advance women's opportunities. On postwar women's formal politics, see Cynthia Harrison, *On Account of Sex: The Politics of Women's Issues, 1945–1968* (Berkeley: University of California Press, 1988).

47. Sara Evans, *Born for Liberty: A History of Women in America* (New York: Free Press, 1989), pp. 256–60. See also John D'Emilio, *Sexual Politics / Sexual Communities: The Making of a Homosexual Minority in the United States, 1940–1970* (Chicago: University of Chicago Press, 1983), and David J. Garrow, ed., *The Montgomery Bus Boycott and the Women Who Started It: The Memoir of Jo Ann Gibson Robinson* (Knoxville: University of Tennessee Press, 1987).

48. Barbara Steinson provides a good example of separate women's organizations taking different political positions, in this case mobilizing for and against World War I. Steinson, " 'The Mother Half of Humanity.' " Conservative women's organizations often began as auxiliaries or adjuncts to right wing male movements (e.g., the Women's Ku Klux Klan). See Kathleen M. Blee, "Women in the 1920s' Ku Klux Klan Movement," *Feminist Studies* (Spring 1991): 57–77.

CHAPTER 9. The Personal and the Political

1. Sara Evans, *Personal Politics: The Origins of Women's Liberation in the Civil Rights Movement* (New York: Harper and Row, 1979).

2. On the impact of the modern feminist movement, see Evans, *Personal Politics*; Winifred Wandersee, *On the Move: American Women in the 1970s* (New York: Twayne, 1992); Alice Echols, *Daring to Be Bad: Radical Feminism in America, 1967–1975* (Minneapolis: University of Minnesota Press, 1989); Rosalind Rosenberg, *Divided Lives: American Women in the Twentieth Century* (New York: Hill and Wang, 1992); and William II. Chafe, *The Paradox of Change: American Women in the Twentieth Century* (New York: Oxford University Press, 1991).

3. Blanche Wiesen Cook, *Eleanor Roosevelt: Volume One, 1884–1933* (New York: Viking, 1992). Cook's is the first full-scale biography since Joseph Lash's two-volume study, *Eleanor and Franklin* (New York: Norton, 1971) and *Eleanor: The Years Alone* (New York: Norton, 1978). Lash was the chosen family biographer. Due to his own deep and intimate relationship with Mrs. Roosevelt, as well as his ties to the family, he evidently chose not to deal with certain personal issues that Cook has investigated more thoroughly and explicitly. Doris Faber initiated some of the discussion about those issues in her book, *The Life of Lorena Hickok: ER's Friend* (New York: William Morrow, 1980). Subsequent books and articles have taken up the personal themes, but never with the thoroughness or detail of Cook's work. Joseph Lash became more

candid about his own relationship with Roosevelt in his volume, *A World of Love: Eleanor Roosevelt and Her Friends, 1943–1962* (Garden City: Doubleday, 1984). I wrote a lengthy biographical sketch of Roosevelt on the occasion of her centenary. It drew on primary research in the Eleanor Roosevelt Papers, as well as on Lash and Faber, and dealt to some extent with the personal and political issues, arguing among other things that Roosevelt's public activism could be traced in a direct line to her experience with Mme. Souvestre at Allenwood and her settlement house work at the turn of the century. The material presented here draws primarily on that essay (William H. Chafe, "A Biographical Sketch," in *Without Precedent: The Life and Career of Eleanor Roosevelt*, edited by Joan Hoff-Wilson and Marjorie Lightmen, [Bloomington: Indiana University Press, 1984]) and on the much more comprehensive work of Blanche Wiesen Cook.

4. Chafe, "Biographical Sketch," p. 4.

5. Ibid.

6. Ibid., p. 5.

7. Ibid.

8. Ibid.

9. Ibid., pp. 6–7.

10. Ibid., p. 7.

11. Ibid., pp. 12–13.

12. Chafe, *Paradox of Change*, p. 39.

13. Chafe, "Biographical Sketch," pp. 10–11.

14. Ibid., p. 15.

15. Ibid.

16. Doris Faber, in *Lorena Hickok*, was the first person to focus on the Hickok/Roosevelt association. Blanche Cook has explored the relationship much more fully in *Eleanor Roosevelt: Volume One, 1884–1933*, but that book ends prior to the emergence of some of the strains in the friendship that occurred after 1933 and that are illustrated here in Roosevelt's letters to Hickok.

17. Cook, *Eleanor Roosevelt*, p. 479.

18. Chafe, "Biographical Sketch," pp. 20–21.

19. Ibid., p. 23.

20. Joseph Lash writes about some of these relationships, including his own, in his 1984 volume, *A World of Love*.

21. This entire section is based on my biography of Lowenstein, which in turn is grounded in extensive archival work in the Allard Lowenstein Papers at the Southern Historical Collection, University of North Carolina, Chapel Hill, as well as approximately 150 interviews. See William H. Chafe, *Never Stop Running: Allard Lowenstein and the Struggle to Save American Liberalism* (New York: Basic Books, 1993). Other books on Lowenstein include Richard Cummings, *The Pied Piper* (New York: Grove Press, 1986), and David Harris, *Dreams Die Hard* (New York: St. Martin's Press, 1982).

22. The best history of the gay experience in America during the postwar years is John D'Emilio, *Sexual Politics, Sexual Communities: The Making of a Homosexual Minority in the United States, 1940–1970* (Chicago: University of Chicago Press, 1983). Martin Duberman has also written vividly of what is was like to grow up with homosexual urges in a

New York Jewish home in the 1930s; see his *Cures: A Gay Man's Odyssey* (New York: Dutton, 1991). Another excellent book on the same subject is Paul Monette, *Becoming a Man* (New York: Harcourt, Brace, Jovanovich, 1992).

CHAPTER 10. Rights and Representation

I am indebted to many individuals for their contributions to this essay. Ruth Mandel, Elizabeth Perry, Glenna Matthews, and Cynthia Harrison read a paper presented to the Organization of American Historians on which portions are based. Linda Gordon, Hugh Graham, Otis Graham, Linda Kerber, Alice Kessler-Harris, and Barbara Lindemann offered helpful comments on drafts of the much-expanded essay. Valery Garrett, Daniel Gomes, and Jennifer Lettierei provided assistance at various stages of the research, while Stacey Robertson and other members of my graduate seminar in women's history helped me develop a label for "the politics of realism."

1. I am aware of the distinction between formal equality of rights and gender equity. ERA activists and women politicians did not usually make that distinction, desiring both equal rights and various measures designed to ensure parity or equity. I use the term *equality* broadly to describe their goal.

2. See Jane Sherron De Hart, "Gender on the Right: Meanings behind the Existential Scream," *Gender and History* 3 (1991): 246–67, and Donald Mathews and De Hart, *Sex, Gender, and the Politics of ERA: A State and the Nation* (New York: Oxford University Press, 1990). Other works focusing on the response of women on the right to feminism and abortion rights include Rebecca Klatch, *Women on the Right* (Philadelphia: Temple University Press, 1989). There is no single study of the political behavior of right-wing women that seeks to do what this essay attempts for their ideological counterparts. Also underresearched is the political activism of poor and minority women.

3. For a detailed analysis of the ratification effort, see Mathews and De Hart, *Sex, Gender, and the Politics of ERA*; Jane J. Mansbridge, *Why We Lost the ERA* (Chicago: University of Chicago Press, 1986); and Mary Frances Berry, *Why ERA Failed: Politics, Women's Rights, and the Amending of the Constitution* (Bloomington: Indiana University Press, 1986).

4. For a profile of ERA activists, see Theodore S. Arrington and Patricia A. Kyle, "Equal Rights Activists in North Carolina," *Signs* 3 (1978): 666–80; Carol Mueller and Thomas Dimierei, "The Structure of Belief Systems among Contending ERA Activists," *Social Forces* 60 (1982): 657–73; Kent L. Tedin, "Religious Preference and Pro/Anti Activism on the Equal Rights Amendment Issue," *Pacific Sociological Review* 21 (1978): 55–67; and Iva Deutchman and Sandra Prince-Embury, "Political Ideology of Pro- and Anti-ERA Women," *Women and Politics* 2 (1982): 39–55.

5. Much of the research on the ratification struggle that is cited below was originally done for *Sex, Gender, and the Politics of ERA*. I am indebted to my coauthor for his initial insights concerning ratificationists' political behavior.

Unless otherwise noted, the following discussion is based on participant observation of the ratification struggle in North Carolina, 1972–82; interviews with activists in Washington-based headquarters of ERAmerica and NOW; extensive interviews with North Carolina activists and legislators who supported ERA, as well as broadsides, folders, information sheets, newsletters, and other materials used and disseminated by ratificationist groups; and extensive records of the North Carolina ratification coalition (which included the North Carolina Women's Political Caucus, North Carolina Conference of NOW, League of Women Voters, BPW, AAUW, YWCA, North Carolina Chapter of the Women's International League for Peace and Freedom, Federally Employed Women in North Carolina, North Carolina Federation of Women's Clubs, North Carolina Nurses Association, Board of Managers of Church Women United of North Carolina, North Carolina Association of Women Deans and Counselors, North Carolina Association of Educators, Professional Women's Caucus, and others).

Interviews are in the possession of De Hart and Mathews. To allow for a degree of anonymity, quotations from interviews are not always cited. For a full list of interviews, see Mathews and De Hart, *Sex, Gender, and the Politics of ERA*, app. 4. Other materials either in my possession or on loan to me from Maria Bliss, Wilma Davidson, Nancy Dawson-Sauser (formerly Drum), Bobette Eckland, Florence Glasser, Tennala Gross, Patricia S. Hunt, Betty R. McCain, Elisabeth Petersen, and Miriam Slifkin have been recently deposited at the University of North Carolina at Greensboro. Other papers include the NOW Papers at the Schlesinger Library, Radcliffe College, Cambridge, Mass.

6. For an analysis of the rational basis of antiratificationist charges, see De Hart, "Gender on the Right," pp. 246–66.

7. Quotations are from "Fact Sheet on the Equal Rights Amendment" and "Cool Facts for the Hot-Headed Opposition (League of Women Voters, n.d., n.p.), and Betty Gordon Becton and Betty Belk Morehead, "At Ease with ERA" (American Association of University Women, 1980), in my possession.

8. Although none of the studies cited in n. 4 speak to the low proportion of black activists, my own interviews with ratificationists and black women in North Carolina suggest that many of the former, while eager in principle to include the latter, never made their recruitment a top priority. Although a few politically active black women were part of the coalition, most felt that ratification was a white women's cause and that other issues took precedence. Class barriers proved even more difficult to bridge. National surveys of ERA sentiment indicated that, among white women, support for ERA was associated with educational level and professional status. In North Carolina, working-class women overwhelmingly opposed the amendment. My own observation of numerous rallies and legislative hearings generating large crowds of ratificationists and antiratificationists confirms survey findings with respect to the absence of working-class women among ratification activists. See Val Burris, "Who Opposed the ERA?: An Analysis of the Social Basis of Antifeminism," *Social Science Quarterly* 64 (1983): 305–17; Joan Huber, Cynthia Rexroat, and Glenna Spitze, "A Crucible of Opinion on Women's Status: ERA in Illinois," *Social Forces* 57 (1978): 549–65; Institute for Research in the Social Sciences at the University of North Carolina at Chapel Hill, "Survey of North Carolina Women," 1978.

9. For a sympathetic account of actions in Illinois, see Berenice Carroll, "Direct

Action and Constitutional Rights: The Case of the ERA," in *Rights of Passage: The Past and Future of ERA*, edited by Joan Hoff-Wilson (Bloomington: Indiana University Press, 1986), pp. 63–75.

10. This particular ratificationist had subsequently joined Teen Democrats, YDC, College YDC, Democratic Women, and the Democratic Party in North Carolina.

11. Christopher Matthews, *Hardball: How Politics Is Played—Told by One Who Knows the Game* (New York: Summit Books, 1988), p. 11.

12. Patricia Stanford Hunt, a former member of the North Carolina legislature, was particularly adamant about playing "hardball." To the extent that female legislators were socialized in predominantly female organizations in which the orientation to power differs, some found it difficult to do so. Other factors may have contributed more directly. On the difficulties facing female legislators in the 1970s, see Irene Diamond, *Sex Roles in the State House* (New Haven: Yale University Press, 1977), chaps. 4–5; and Jeane J. Kirkpatrick, *Political Woman* (New York: Basic Books, 1974), chaps. 6–7. For a congressional study, see Irvin N. Gertzog, *Congressional Women: Their Recruitment, Treatment, and Behavior* (New York: Praeger, 1984).

13. Felice D. Gordon, *After Winning: The Legacy of the New Jersey Suffragists, 1920–1947* (New Brunswick, N.J.: Rutgers University Press, 1986), pp. 38–39 (quotations).

14. Eleanor Smeal, interview by author, Washington, D.C., April 1, 1987. On the growing political efficacy of anti-ERA women in the critical three unratified states, see Joan S. Carver, "The Equal Rights Amendment and the Florida Legislature," *Florida Historical Quarterly* 60 (1982): 455–81; Judson H. Jones, "The Effect of Pro- and Anti-ERA Campaign Contributions on the ERA Voting Behavior of the 80th Illinois House of Representatives," *Women and Politics* 2 (Spring 1982): 84; and Mathews and De Hart, *Sex, Gender, and the Politics of ERA*, chaps. 3–4.

15. Janet K. Bowles, "Building Support for the ERA: A Case of 'Too Much Too Late,'" *PS* 15 (1982): 576. NOW's membership, which had risen by the fall of 1982 to 220,000, plunged below 130,000 for the next several years; it surged again in the wake of the *Webster* decision and the Senate hearings on the nomination of Clarence Thomas to the Supreme Court, generating a parallel trend in resources.

16. A primary goal of the National Women's Political Caucus and the Women's Campaign Fund since the early 1970s, the election of feminist-oriented candidates did not become a priority of other organizations until the ratification struggle. Accordingly NOW, which had virtually ignored partisan politics during the first ten years of its existence, formed its first PAC in 1975. For a fuller discussion of the shift, see Mary Fainsod Katzenstein, "Feminism and the Meaning of the Vote," *Signs* 10 (1984): 4–26. For a discussion of the relationship between feminism and the two major parties, see Jo Freeman, "Whom You Know versus Whom You Represent: Feminist Influence in the Democratic and Republican Parties," in *The Women's Movements of the United States and Western Europe: Consciousness, Political Opportunity, and Public Policy*, edited by Mary Fainsod Katzenstein and Carol McClurg Mueller (Philadelphia: Temple University Press, 1987), pp. 215–43.

The possibilities that the Voting Rights Act created for nonminority women candidates sensitive to minority interests were pointed out to me by Blandina Cardenas-Ramirez. In Texas, for example, the Latino vote would prove especially important to the election victories of Ann Richards, Annette Strauss, and Kathryn Whitmire, among others.

17. On the precise meaning of the gender gap, see Keith T. Poole and L. Harmon Ziegler, *Women, Public Opinion, and Politics: The Changing Political Attitudes of American Women* (New York: Longmans, 1985), chap. 2; Carol M. Mueller, ed., *The Politics of the Gender Gap: The Social Construction of Political Influence* (Newberry Park, Calif.: Sage Publications, 1988); and Mueller, "The Gender Gap and Women's Political Influence," *Annals* 515 (1991): 23–37. That the linkage between the gender gap and an electoral strategy was evident to strategists in the early 1980s is clear, although initially the political potential of the gender gap was assumed to lie in the additional clout it provided for lobbyists who could now point to distinct "women's interests." The readiness of activists to maximize its potential and extend its meaning is evident from quotations in Anne N. Costain and Douglas Costain, "Strategy and Tactics of the Women's Movement in the United States: The Role of the Political Parties," in *The Women's Movements*, pp. 205–7.

18. On the relationship between the increasing number of women running for office and women politicians' support for feminist/women's issues, see Carol McClurg Mueller, "Collective Consciousness, Identity Transformation, and the Rise of Women in Public Office in the United States," in *The Women's Movements*, pp. 89–108. The assumption that women politicians would stand up for women's interests received support from a few political scientists in the late 1970s. See, e.g., Susan Gluck Mezey, "Support for Women's Rights Policy: An Analysis of Local Politicians," *American Politics Quarterly* (1978): 485–97, and Shelah Gilbert Leader, "The Policy Impact of Elected Women Officials," in *The Impact of the Electoral Process*, edited by Louise Maisel and Joseph Cooper (Beverly Hills, Calif.: Sage Publications, 1977). For a more definitive study, see Kathy A. Stanwick and Katherine E. Kleeman, *Women Make a Difference: Report* (New Brunswick, N.J.: Center for the American Woman and Politics, 1983).

Candidates themselves were often forthcoming about their interests in women's issues, although not all were as direct or as committed as U.S. Senator Barbara Mikulski. "You can bet I'm going to pay special attention to women," the Maryland Democrat had replied during her 1976 congressional campaign, "because if I don't, who will?" Quoted in Susan J. Carroll and Barbara Geiger-Parker, *Women Appointed in the Carter Administration: A Comparison with Men* (New Brunswick, N.J.: Center for the American Woman and Politics, 1983).

19. For an extensive discussion of the attack on equality as principle and policy during this period, see Jane Sherron De Hart, "Equality Challenged: Equal Rights and Sexual Difference," *Journal of Policy History* 6 (1994): 40–72.

20. Much of the early discussion of problems facing politically ambitious women focused on socialization and situational and structural constraints. The extent to which women are disadvantaged in terms of family roles, the recruitment process, and party and voter bias has also been extensively explored. See, e.g., Emily Stoper, "Wife and Politician: Role Strain among Women in Public Office," and Virginia Currey, "Campaign Theory and Practice—The Gender Variable," both in *A Portrait of Marginality: The Political Behavior of the American Woman*, edited by Marianne Githens and Jewel L. Prestage (New York: D. McKay Co., 1977); Kirkpatrick, *Political Woman*;

Diamond, *Sex Roles in the State House*; Susan Tolchin and Martin Tolchin, *Clout: Womanpower and Politics* (New York: Coward, Mc Cann, and Geoghagan, 1974); and Ruth B. Mandel, *In the Running: The New Woman Candidate* (New Haven: Ticknor and Fields, 1981). For a more recent view, see R. Darcy, Susan Welch, and Janet Clark, *Women, Elections, and Representation* (New York: Longman, 1987). Johnson's actual words were: "Every politician should have been born an orphan and remain a bachelor." See Carolyn Warner, *The Last Word: A Treasury of Women's Quotes* (Englewood Cliffs, N.J.: Prentice Hall, 1992), p. 234.

For minority women, the problems of money and discrimination are compounded. See Susan J. Carroll and Wendy S. Strimling, *Women's Routes to Elective Office: A Comparison with Men's* (New Brunswick, N.J.: Center for the American Woman and Politics, 1983), chaps. 7–12, and Irene Natividad, "Women of Color and the Campaign Trail," in *The American Woman, 1992–1993: A Status Report*, edited by Paula Ries and Anne J. Stone (New York: Norton, 1992), pp. 127–48.

21. Although poll data indicated greater acceptance of women in public life during the 1980s, voter bias continued to exist. See the report of the survey commissioned by the NWPC in the *New York Times*, August 13, 1987, sec. A, p. 14, and also October 3, 1986, sec. A, p. 14.

Money and image remained critical problems, as is evident from their abundant press coverage in the 1990 and 1992 campaigns. See, e.g., *New York Times*, August 8, 1989, sec. 1, p. 12, April 22, 1990, sec. 1, p. 30, and *Los Angeles Times*, March 11, 1990, sec. M, p. 4, April 12, 1990, sec. A, p. 1, June 19, 1990, sec. A, p. 5. Manipulation of gender stereotypes was a primary focus of many journal articles as well. See esp. Margaret Carlson, "It's Our Turn," *Time*, Fall 1990, pp. 16–18, and Eleanor Clift, "Battle of the Sexes," *Newsweek*, April 30, 1990, p. 22.

For a scholarly treatment of media bias and gender stereotyping, see Kim Fridkin Kahn, "The Distorted Mirror: Press Coverage of Women Candidates" (paper presented at the Annual Meeting of the American Political Science Association, Washington, D.C., 1991). See also Leonie Huddy and Nayda Terkildsen, "The Acceptability of Female Political Candidates: Contrasting Stereotypes of Women and the 'Ideal Politician'" (paper presented at the Annual Meeting of the Midwest Political Science Association, Chicago, 1991). On the Richards race in particular, see Sue Tolleson Rinehart and Jeanie R. Stanley, "Claytie and the Lady in The 1990 Texas Gubernatorial Race from the Perspective of the Campaign and the Citizens" (paper presented at the Annual Meeting of the American Political Science Association, Washington, D.C., 1991). The conflict among Richards's close male advisers about her feminism is related in Celia Morris, *Storming the Statehouse: Running for Governor with Ann Richards and Dianne Feinstein* (New York: Scribner, 1992), pp. 77–78.

22. Natividad, "Women of Color and the Campaign Trail." The quotation on voter preference with respect to age and sexuality is in Clift, "Battle of the Sexes," p. 22. Since public space is sexual space, women challenging gender and spatial boundaries have long found themselves subjected to charges of sexual misconduct. See Mary P. Ryan, *Women in Public: Between Banners and Ballots, 1825–1889* (Baltimore: Johns Hopkins University Press, 1989), and Glenna Matthews, *The Rise of Public Woman: Woman's Power and Woman's Place in the United States* (New York: Oxford University Press, 1992). A

recent example involving a political candidate is provided by Ferraro, who was accused during her campaign for the vice presidency of being a lesbian—a charge also leveled in her 1978 campaign. See Geraldine A. Ferraro, *Ferraro: My Story* (New York: Bantam Books, 1985), pp. 33, 208, 214–15. Such charges were also made in the 1990 gubernatorial races against Barbara Roberts (Oregon) and Ann Richards (Texas). See Morris, *Storming the Statehouse*, pp. 25, 124–25. For the quotation from the Texas mayor, I am indebted to Glenna Matthews. That sexuality is still used to discredit women in politics is made abundantly clear in a 1993 handbook for female candidates. See Joanne Rajoppi, *Women in Office: Getting There and Staying There* (Westport, Conn.: Bergin and Garvey, 1993), pp. 31, 42.

23. For a list of PACs operative in 1990 that either gave money predominantly to women candidates or had predominantly female donors, see "Women's PACs in 1990: Continuing to Make a Difference" and "Women's PACs in 1990" in *CAWP News and Notes* 8 (1991): 10–12. The designation CAWP refers to the Center for the American Woman and Politics. All sources so designated in this and subsequent notes are based on data from the National Information Bank on Women in Public Office, Eagleton Institute for Politics, Rutgers University, New Brunswick, N.J.

24. Information on the NCWESG is based on an interview with one of its founders, Jane Smith Patterson, Chapel Hill, N.C., February 15, 1991. On the greater cohesion and strength of a women's policy network, see David Knoke, "Mobilization of Members in Women's Associations," in *Women, Politics, and Change*, edited by Louise A. Tilly and Patricia Gurin (New York: Russell Sage Foundation, 1990), pp. 383–410, and Kay Lehman Schlozman, "Representing Women in Washington: Sisterhood and Pressure Politics," in *Women, Politics, and Change*, pp. 339–82. On CAWP research initiatives, see Susan Carroll, "Remarks at the Plenary Session 'Reshaping the Agenda: The Impact of Women in Public Office'" (CAWP Forum for Women State Legislators, San Diego, Calif., November 15, 1991).

25. Margery Tabankin, executive director of the Hollywood Women's Political Committee, is quoted in "Climbing Up the Ladder," *Newsweek*, February 26, 1990, p. 45. On the Ferraro factor, see Ferraro, *My Story*, chaps. 10–11, 13, and Susan Faludi, *Backlash: The Undeclared War against American Women* (New York: Crown, 1991), chap. 10. That successful candidates simply refused to see obstacles as obstacles is made clear by psychologists who interviewed twenty-five high-level women politicians, many of them members of Congress. See Dorothy W. Cantor and Toni Bernay with Jean Stoess, *Women in Power: The Secrets of Leadership* (Boston: Houghton Mifflin, 1992), pp. 4–5. For one woman's account of the successful clearing of these hurdles, see Madeleine M. Kunin, *Living a Political Life* (New York: Knopf, 1994).

26. On the Texas mayors, see Molly Ivins, "The Women Who Run Texas," *McCalls*, August 1990, p. 96ff, and Lisa Belkin, "Lace Over Steel: The Women Mayors of Texas," *New York Times Magazine*, March 20, 1988, p. 41ff.

27. Richards quoted in "The Titan of Texas," *Vogue*, August 1991, p. 247. Biographical information in this and the next paragraph is taken from *Current Biography* (1991): 42–46. For the Carpenter quote and a discussion of the building of that female network, see Morris, *Storming the Statehouse*, pp. 42–47, 147–57, 148.

28. "Climbing Up the Ladder," *Newsweek*, February 26, 1990, p. 45 (quotations). See

also Sidney Blumenthal, "A Woman of Independent Means," *New Republic*, August 13, 1990, pp. 23–26; "Snow White's Biggest Test," *U.S. News & World Report*, June 18, 1990, pp. 20–21; *Los Angeles Times*, October 7, 1991, sec. A, p. 1ff, November, 10, 1990, sec. A, p. 28; and *Christian Science Monitor*, February 15, 1991, p. 10.

29. Schroeder quoted in *New York Times*, April 22, 1990, sec. A, p. 30. California pollster Mervin Field was one of those predicting that 1990 would be not just the year but the decade of women in politics; Field is quoted in "It's Our Turn," *Time*, Fall 1990, p. 16. For a small sample of the articles in which these explanations are offered, see "Women in Power," *Ms*, April 1988, p. 79; Clift, "Battle of the Sexes," *Newsweek*, April 30, 1990, pp. 20–22; Steven V. Roberts, "Will 1992 Be the Year of the Women?," *U.S. News & World Report*, April 27, 1992, pp. 37–39; Celia Morris, "Waiting for Ms. President," *Harper's Bazaar*, July 1992, pp. 87–88, 118; *Washington Post*, June 10, 1990, sec. A, p. 1; *New York Times*, April 30, 1992, sec. A, p. 10, May 29, 1992, sec. A, pp. 1, 11; and *Christian Science Monitor*, May 1, 1992, p. 20.

30. The impact of the Thomas hearings and the role of Hill in generating both candidacies and funds are abundantly documented in virtually every newspaper and magazine article on women and politics in 1992. See, e.g., *New York Times*, April 29, sec. A, pp. 1, 10; April 30, sec. A, p. 10; May 24, sec. 4, pp. 1, 4; August 31, sec. A, pp. 1, 10.

31. *Washington Post*, June 10, 1990, sec. A, pp. 1, 16; *New York Times*, April 22, 1990, sec. 1, p. 30; *Los Angeles Times*, March 11, 1990, sec. M, p. 4, November 17, 1991, sec. A, p. 3; Paula Dryer, "The 'Year of the Woman'? Well, Maybe," *Business Week*, October 1, 1990, p. 170ff; Roberts, "Will 1992 Be the Year of the Women?"

For an excellent scholarly discussion of the gender gap in the 1980 and 1984 elections that makes the point that the gap is about issues rather than the sex of candidates, see Ethel Klein, "The Gender Gap: Different Issues, Different Answers," *Brookings Review* (1985): 33–37. According to a Roper poll, those people who cited abortion as one of the most (or as one of the two most) important issues to them had voted Republican in the 1988 election. See "Public Opinion and Demographic Report," *American Enterprise* 1, no. 2 (January/February 1993): 102.

32. Dallas columnist Molly Ivins's characterization of Richards's toughness is quoted in the *Washington Post*, October 22, 1990, sec. B, p. 1ff. See also *Chicago Tribune*, November 25, 1990, sec. 6, p. 2; *Los Angeles Times*, November 8, 1990, sec. A, p. 24, November 10, 1990, sec. B, p. 7ff; and "1990 Elections: A Year of Wins for Women!," *Women's Political Times*, 1990/1991, p. 1ff. Typical of Clayton Williams's sexist remarks was his comment comparing bad weather to rape. "If it is inevitable," he said, "just relax and enjoy it." Quoted in Marci McDonald, "Thorns among the Roses," *Maclean's*, November 5, 1990, pp. 30–31. For a close look at both campaigns, see Morris, *Storming the Statehouse*.

Although prochoice Democrats such as Richards benefited from prochoice Republican crossovers, voters citing abortion as critical to how they voted continued to vote Republican in 1992. See "Public Opinion and Demographic Report," *American Enterprise Institute* 4, no. 1 (January/February 1993): 102–3.

33. For the characterization of the new women in Congress as "the Anita Hill class," see "Who's In, Who's Out in the New Congress," *Newsweek*, November/December 1992, p. 17. On election results, see "Candidates and Winners in 1992," CAWP Fact

Sheet. The sixth woman in the Senate was veteran Republican Nancy Kassebaum of Kansas. Among the House members in the 103d Congress, 35 were Democrats and 12 Republican.

34. "Women in Elective Office, 1991," "Women Candidates and Winners in 1992," and "Women in Elective Office, 1993," all CAWP Fact Sheets. In 1993, according to the CAWP, women held 72 (22.2 percent) of the 324 statewide elective executive offices (3 governors, 8 lieutenant governors, 8 attorneys general, 11 secretaries of state, 17 treasurers, and 47 other positions). Among 1,517 female state legislators, women of color, most of them Democrats, made gains. At the local level, women held 1,653 (8.9 percent) seats on county governing boards. While women mayors in cities with a population of over 100,000 numbered 19 according to CAWP figures, the U.S. Conference of Mayors put the figure at 18, according to Doug Baj, U.S. Conference of Mayors, Washington, D.C., telephone interview by author, 27 July 1993.

35. "1990 Women Candidates," "Women in Elective Office, 1991," "Women Candidates and Winners in 1992," and "Women in Elective Office, 1993," all CAWP Fact Sheets. A more precise breakdown put the number of African American women in state legislatures in 1993 at 151, Asian/Pacific American women at 18, and Latinas at 17. Native American women held 6 seats. In addition to Washington's Sharon Pratt Dixon, Carrie Saxon Perry of Hartford, Connecticut, was the only other African American woman serving as mayor in a city with a population of over 100,000. About 50 to 60 percent of Democratic Party state officials were also African American women, according to Natividad, whose figures were provided by the Joint Center for Political Studies. See Natividad, "Women of Color and the Campaign Trail," in *The American Woman: 1992–93*, p. 129.

36. See "Post-Election Wrap Up," *CAWP News and Notes* 8 (1991): 10–11, 4–5, and Lucy Baruch and Katheryne McCormick, "Women's PACs Dramatically Increase Their Support in 1992: An Overview," *CAWP News and Notes* 9 (1993): 10–11. According to the CAWP, the total amount contributed by women's PACs in 1990 is not available since only 26 of the 35 questioned provided information on the amount contributed to candidates. Those 26 reported contributions amounting to $2,695,354. On the impact of the Hill-Thomas hearings on fund-raising in 1992, see *New York Times*, May 24, 1992, sec. 4, pp. 1, 4; Barbara Ehrenreich, "What Do Women Have to Celebrate?," *Time*, November 16, 1992, p. 62. On the Hollywood Women's Political Committee, see "The Power of Glitz," *Mirabella*, November 1992, p. 66. Mikulski's characterization of women campaign volunteers is quoted in "Nancy Kassebaum and Barbara Mikulski," *Ms*, September 1988, p. 59.

37. West Coast fund-raiser Beverly Thomas is quoted in *Los Angeles Times*, April 12, 1990, sec. A, p. 1. Schlafly is quoted in Ehrenreich, "What Do Women Have to Celebrate?" On the gender gap, see "Post-Election Wrap Up," *CAWP News and Notes* 8 (1991): 4–5, and "1992 Post-Election Wrap Up," *CAWP News and Notes* 9 (1993): 6–9. The women whose voting patterns created the gender gap were, for the most part, younger, better educated, and employed. According to Sue Tolleson Rinehart, they tended to be "egalitarian" and "gender-identified"; hence my use of the term *feminist*. Pamela Johnston Conover, who examines the gender gap in public opinion rather than voting behavior, also finds a feminist identity to be key. See Rinehart, *Gender Conscious-*

ness and Politics (New York: Routledge, 1992), p. 156, and Conover, "Feminists and the Gender Gap," *Journal of Politics* 50 (1988): 965–1010. On the gains of antifeminist candidates in the Christian Right in 1992, see *New York Times*, November 21, 1992, sec. A, pp. 1, 8.

38. For a summary of the findings of the CAWP study, see Susan J. Carroll, Debra L. Dodson, and Ruth B. Mandel, *The Impact of Women in Public Office: An Overview* (New Brunswick, N.J.: Center for the American Woman and Politics, 1991). See, e.g., Michelle A. Saint-Germain, "Does Their Difference Make a Difference? The Impact of Women on Public Policy in the Arizona Legislature," *Social Science Quarterly* 70 (1989): 965–68; also Iva Ellen Deutchman and Mark Considine, "Sex and Representation: A Comparison of American and Australian State Legislators" (paper presented at the Annual Meeting of the American Political Science Association, Chicago, 1992).

In a talk in Santa Barbara, Calif., on April 30, 1994, Boxer provided various examples. With respect to the health care debate, she pointed to the insistence of female senators that menopause begins at different ages in women and that the average age of onset should not be used as the determinant for establishing coverage of mammograms, as was being advocated by a male expert.

39. On the relationship between the number of women in office and their ability to reshape policy agendas, see Janet Flammang, "Female Officials in the Feminist Capital: The Case of Santa Clara County," *Western Political Quarterly* 38 (1985): 94–118; Sue Thomas, "The Impact of Women on State Legislative Policies," *Journal of Politics* 53 (1991): 958–76; Sue Thomas and Susan Welch, "The Impact of Gender on Activities and Priorities of State Legislators," *Western Political Quarterly* 44 (1991): 445–56; Susan Gluck Mezey, "Increasing the Number of Women in Office: Does It Matter?," in *The Year of the Woman: Myths and Realities*, edited by Elizabeth Adell Cook, Sue Thomas, and Clyde Wilcox (Boulder, Colo.: Westview Press, 1994), p. 266.

For projections, see "Post-Election Wrap Up," *CAWP News and Notes*, p. 3; also chart on "Projected Dates When Women Will Achieve Equity in Elected Office, Based on Current Rates of Increase," in Mary Thom's "Elections: Southern Women Hold the Key," *Ms*, February 1988, p. 22.

40. For quotations of legislators, see Iva Ellen Deutchman, "Ungendered but Equal: Male Attitudes toward Women in State Legislatures," *Polity* 24 (1992): 429. Salaries reflected the difference in the relative power of mayors in Houston and Dallas. Houston's Kathryn Whitmire, who had power to appoint, reject, and decide, earned $130,000 a year. Dallas's Annette Strauss had one vote on an 11-member city council and was paid $50 per council meeting. Political styles differed as well and reflected the different routes by which the two women came to office. See Ivins, "The Women Who Run Texas," and Belkin, "Lace Over Steel."

The other nine states with a high percentage of women legislators were Arizona, Colorado, Idaho, Kansas, Maine, South Dakota, Vermont, and Washington. Washington moved to the forefront in the 1992 elections as the percentage of women legislators reached almost 40 percent. See CAWP, Fact Sheet on "Preliminary Information about [1992] State Legislative Races." Generally, the least professional state legislatures have the highest percentage of women. See Deutchman and Considine, "Sex and Representation." The number of women in state legislatures is also affected by structure. Women, both Anglo and black, do better if they are running in multi-member rather than single-member districts. (There is of yet no discernible pattern with respect to Hispanic women.) See Wilma Rule, "Multimember Legislative Districts: Minority and Anglo Women's and Men's Recruitment Opportunity," in *United States Electoral Systems: Their Impact on Women and Minorities*, edited by Wilma Rule and Joseph F. Zimmerman (New York: Greenwood Press, 1992), pp. 57–72. On Pennsylvania, see Sandra A. Featherman, "Barriers to Representing Women and Blacks in Pennsylvania: The Impacts of Demography, Culture, and Structure," also in *United States Electoral Systems*, pp. 73–85.

41. Martha McKay, interview by author, Raleigh, N.C., February 8, 1991. On changing behavior of women legislators at the state level, see Sue Thomas, *How Women Legislate* (New York: Oxford Unversity Press, 1994), pp. 50–52. My discussion of ambivalence about power derives in part from my interview with Martha McKay. McKay's preoccupation with the difficulties many women have dealing with power grew out of her efforts in the 1970s to recruit female employees of AT&T for management positions. Before and since that work, McKay was involved with politics, although not as a candidate. Her concerns are shared by psychologists Dorothy Cantor and Toni Bernay, to whom I am indebted for the quotation by Congresswoman Nancy Johnson of Connecticut. Johnson was by no means the only congresswoman who expressed ambivalence. Other high-level women politicians talked less of ambivalence than of their desire to redefine power, also a priority of the authors. See Cantor and Bernay, *Women in Power*, esp. pp. 35–64. Ruth Mandel, director of the Center for the American Woman and Politics, reports that discomfort with power is less apparent among women politicians in the 1990s. Conversation with author, June 12, 1993.

42. CAWP Forum for Women State Legislators, November 14–17, 1991, *Program* (New Brunswick, N.J.: Center for the American Woman and Politics, 1991). For discussion of the critical mass of female legislators required with respect to policy goals, see Susan J. Carroll and Ella Taylor, "Gender Differences in the Committee Assignments of State Legislators: Preferences or Discrimination?" (paper presented at the Midwest Political Science Association, Chicago, 1989); also Thomas, *How Women Legislate*, p. 154.

43. "Women Left, Right and Centre," *Economist* 318 (March 23, 1991): 56.

44. I am grateful to Mary Berry, who heightened my awareness of the importance of women knowing how to empower positions to which little power is attached. For an excellent discussion of women officeholders' desire to achieve policy and procedural change and the institutional context and constraints within which they must work, see Thomas, *How Women Legislate*, esp. chaps. 4–5, 7.

On the glass ceiling, see *New York Times*, July 1, 1990, sec. 1, p. 14, as well as CAWP, Fact Sheets on "Women in State Legislatures, 1991" and "Women in the U.S. Congress, 1991." Currently the only woman who is part of the congressional leadership is Barbara Kennelly (D-Conn.), who is chief deputy whip in the House, a position created in order to introduce more diversity into the leadership.

With respect to gender parity, the issue proved to be a hot one in California in 1990 when it was endorsed by Dianne Feinstein during her gubernatorial campaign. Vehemently attacked for advocating quotas, Feinstein subsequently insisted that no time-table should be attached. Bills mandating parity were then being considered in ten other states. See *New York Times*, August 21, 1990, sec. A, p. 18.

45. NWPC president Kathy Wilson's characterization of politics is quoted in the *Raleigh News and Observer*, October 10, 1982, sec. A, p. 10; U.S. senator Barbara Mikulski's (D-Md.) appears in Warner, *The Last Word*, p. 237.

46. Judy Goldsmith, who as NOW president was active in promoting both the Ferraro candidacy and an insider role for the organization, was ousted from her position in 1985 by Eleanor Smeal, who, with her successor Molly Yard, effectively determined style and strategy for NOW throughout the 1980s and early 1990s. Whether the new president, Patricia Ireland, a former corporate lawyer, would modify NOW's outsider stance remained to be seen. See *New York Times*, July 1, 1990, sec. 1, p. 14, January 12, 1991, sec. 1, p. 11. See also Jane Gross, "Patricia Ireland, President of NOW: Does She Speak for Today's Women?," *New York Times Magazine*, March 1, 1992, p. 17ff.

47. Kunin and others are quoted in "Talk of the Town," *The New Yorker*, August 3, 1992, p. 24. Feinstein's comment was made at a May 9, 1992, fund-raiser in Santa Barbara that I attended. A slight variation is quoted in the *New York Times*, May 25, 1992, sec. 1, p. 9. The need for a comprehensive family leave policy still exists despite passage of recent legislation. The current family leave act benefits only those families that conform to the archetypal nuclear family and that have the financial resources to support themselves during an unpaid leave.

48. The definition of gender consciousness quoted is that of Rinehart, *Gender Consciousness and Politics*, p. 32. Analyzing data from 1972 through 1988 from the quadrennial American National Election Studies, Rinehart provides the most comprehensive study yet of the relationship between gender consciousness and political behavior. On gender consciousness among women on the political right, see De Hart, "Gender on the Right."

49. On the importance of a weak party system in the United States, which contrasts with Great Britain, where party discipline mitigates against such bipartisan efforts as the Congressional Caucus on Women's Issues, see Joyce Gelb, *Feminism and Politics: A Comparative Perspective* (Berkeley: University of California Press, 1989), chaps. 3–4. On the persistent barriers to greater representation of women in Congress, see Wilma Rule and Pippa Norris, "Anglo and Minority Women's Underrepresentation in Congress: Is the Electoral System the Culprit?," in *United States Electoral Systems*, pp. 41–54.

50. Hutchinson was denied support by the Hollywood Women's Political Committee and NARAL PAC but received backing from the Republican PAC WISH List. She was also endorsed by the Christian Coalition. With respect to abortion, she supported choice through the first trimester but at the same time approved of state legislation limiting access. See Clyde Wilcox, "Why Was 1992 the 'Year of the Woman'? Explaining Women's Gains in 1992," in Cook, Thomas, and Wilcox, *Year of the Woman*, chap. 1. For a fuller discussion of the problem of representation, see Virginia Sapiro, "When Are Interests Interesting? The Problem of Political Representation of Women," and Irene Diamond and Nancy Hartsock, "Beyond Interests in Politics: A Comment on Virginia Sapiro's 'When Are Interests Interesting? The Problem of the Political Repre-

sentation of Women,'" *American Political Science Review* 75 (1981): 701–21. Sapiro makes several important points. First, that the issue is not whether my representative looks like me (descriptive representation)—it is whether my interests are being represented (substantive representation). Second, that in talking about women's interests, one is not talking about an interest group in a narrow sense, but rather interests that derive from women's different social position. Third, that it is not necessary for *all* women to be conscious of these differences or to define themselves as having interests radically different from other groups. What is necessary is that enough women conceive of themselves as having group interests and place demands on the system.

51. For a fuller discussion of the present and potential impact of women officeholders, see Thomas, *How Women Legislate*, pp. 125–53. On the gains of the Religious Right, see *New York Times*, November 21, 1992, sec. A, pp. 1, 8; July 18, 1994, sec. A, p. 6; July 22, 1994, sec. A, pp. 1, 9.

52. The need for effective articulation of women's issues by voters is essential. As California congressman Michael Huffington tellingly observed in conversation with me during his 1990 campaign, "I have talked to thousands of women in this district over the past months. Except for abortion, I haven't heard them even mention 'women's issues.'" He then noted one exception, the women who sat on the endorsement committee of a feminist political PAC. Even if the term served to confuse, his point is well taken. Effective articulation of women's issues by female voters and an opponent candidate can require even a previously indifferent politician to address those issues in a tight race, although that did not happen in this particular contest.

53. The speech by Jill Ruckelshaus is reprinted on the caucus's 1990 calendar. I am grateful to former NWPC president Sharon Rodine, who called the calendar to my attention.

CHAPTER 11. Reading *Little Women*

I thank Joan Jacobs Brumberg, Marlene Fisher, Linda K. Kerber, Alice Kessler-Harris, Elizabeth Young, and members of my writing group—Ann duCille, Joan Hedrick, Gertrude Hughes, Indira Karemcheti, and Laura Wexler—for reading earlier drafts of this essay; Ann Morrissey and Janet Murphy for research assistance; the Watkinson Library, Patricia Bunker, and Mary Curry for reference and interlibrary loan assistance; Trinity College for a sabbatical leave; and the William R. Kenan Jr. Professorship of American Institutions and Values for research funds. Joan Hedrick, who read several versions, deserves special mention. Citations from the Little, Brown and Co. Papers (*87M-113) and the Alcott Family Papers (bMS Am 1130.8 and bMS Am 800.23) are by permission of the Houghton Library, Harvard University.

1. Addams to Vallie Beck, March 16, 1876, *The Jane Addams Papers*, edited by Mary Lynn McCree Bryan (Ann Arbor: University Microfilms International, 1984) (hereafter cited as *Addams Papers*), reel 1.

2. Frank Luther Mott, *Golden Multitudes: The Story of Best Sellers in the United States* (New York: Macmillan, 1947), p. 102; *Books in Print, 1992–93*.

3. May 1868, *The Journals of Louisa May Alcott*, edited by Joel Myerson and Daniel

Shealy, associate ed. Madeleine B. Stern (Boston: Little, Brown, 1989), pp. 165–66 (hereafter cited as *Journals*). On rereading this entry in later years, Alcott quipped: "Good joke." Niles first requested a girls' book in 1867; Alcott says she "[b]egan at once . . . but didn't like" it. September [1867], *Journals*, p. 158.

4. June [1868], *Journals*, p. 166.

5. Niles to Alcott, June 16, 1868 (#1) and July 25, 1868 (#2), bMS Am 1130.8, Alcott Family Papers, Houghton Library, Harvard University (all citations from Niles's letters are from this collection). On Alcott's publishing history, see Raymond L. Kilgour, *Messrs. Roberts Brothers Publishers* (Ann Arbor: University of Michigan Press, 1952), and Daniel Lester Shealy, "The Author-Publisher Relationships of Louisa May Alcott" (Ph.D. diss., University of South Carolina, 1985). I am grateful to Michael Winship for the last reference.

6. August 26 [1868], *Journals*, p. 166. According to most sources, Niles tested the manuscript on his niece, whose age is variously given.

7. For an account of Alcott's sales through 1909, by which time nearly 598,000 copies of *Little Women* had been printed by Roberts Brothers, see Joel Myerson and Daniel Shealy, "The Sales of Louisa May Alcott's Books," *Harvard Library Bulletin*, n.s., 1 (Spring 1990), esp. pp. 69–71, 86. I am grateful to Michael Winship for this reference. See also Roberts Brothers Cost Book D, [i], *87M-113, Little, Brown and Co. Papers, Houghton Library, Harvard University (hereafter cited as Little, Brown Papers). These figures do not include foreign sales. Although *Little Women* was not published in a single volume until 1880, I will refer to it in the singular except when one volume is specifically intended.

Sales figures are unreliable for the twentieth century, in part because of foreign sales and the proliferation of editions after the expiration of copyright. Dorothea Lawrence Mann, "When the Alcott Books Were New," *Publishers' Weekly* 116 (September 28, 1929): 1619, claimed sales of nearly three million. According to an account published three years later, Little, Brown and Co., which had absorbed Roberts Brothers, reported that over 1.5 million copies of *Little Women* had been sold in the United States. "Louisa M. Alcott Centenary Year," *Publishers' Weekly* 122 (July 2, 1932): 23–24. Charles A. Madison, *Book Publishing in America* (New York: McGraw-Hill, 1966), p. 134, cites sales of 3 million but gives no sources.

Sales, of course, are only part of the story: library use was high at the outset and remained so. Niles to Alcott (#18), undated fragment [1870? but probably about August 1869] and "Popularity of 'Little Women,' " December 22, 1912, "Press [illegible] Albany," in bMS Am 800.23 (newspaper clippings, reviews, and articles about Louisa May Alcott and her family), Alcott Family Papers.

8. Mann, "When the Alcott Books Were New."

9. " 'Little Women' Leads Poll," *New York Times*, March 22, 1927, p. 7, reprinted in Madeleine B. Stern, ed., *Critical Essays on Louisa May Alcott* (Boston: G. K. Hall, 1984), p. 84.

10. See Gloria T. Delamar, *Louisa May Alcott and 'Little Women': Biography, Critique, Publications, Poems, Songs, and Contemporary Relevance* (Jefferson, N.C.: McFarland and Co., 1990), p. 167 and passim. I am grateful to Joan Jacobs Brumberg for this reference.

11. For an intriguing analysis of well-loved texts that takes *Little Women* as a point of departure, see Catharine R. Stimpson, "Reading for Love: Canons, Paracanons, and Whistling Jo March," *New Literary History* 21 (Autumn 1990): 957–76.

12. "Spells, Wishes, Goldfish, Old School Hurts," *New York Times Book Review*, January 31, 1982, p. 24.

13. The classic biography is still Madeleine B. Stern, *Louisa May Alcott* (Norman: University of Oklahoma Press, 1950), which should be supplemented by Stern's extensive criticism on Alcott. See also Sarah Elbert, *A Hunger for Home: Louisa May Alcott and "Little Women"* (Philadelphia: Temple University Press, 1984), and Martha Saxton, *Louisa May: A Modern Biography of Louisa May Alcott* (New York: Avon Books, 1978).

14. Richard H. Brodhead, "Starting Out in the 1860s: Alcott, Authorship, and the Postbellum Literary Field," chap. 3 in *Cultures of Letters: Scenes of Reading and Writing in Nineteenth-Century America* (Chicago: University of Chicago Press, 1993), p. 89.

15. On cultural work, see Jane Tompkins, *Sensational Designs: The Cultural Work of American Fiction, 1790–1860* (New York: Oxford University Press, 1985). Two theoretically sophisticated, historically based studies of readers are Janice A. Radway, *Reading the Romance: Women, Patriarchy, and Popular Literature* (1984; reprint, with a new introduction by the author, Chapel Hill: University of North Carolina Press, 1991), and Roger Chartier, "Texts, Printing, Readings," in *The New Cultural History*, edited by Lynn Hunt (Berkeley: University of California Press, 1989), pp. 154–75.

16. The critical literature on *Little Women* is immense and growing. Useful starting points are Stern, *Critical Essays*; Alma J. Payne, *Louisa May Alcott: A Reference Guide* (Boston: G. K. Hall, 1980); and Judith C. Ullom, *Louisa May Alcott: A Centennial for Little Women: An Annotated Selected Bibliography* (Washington, D.C.: Library of Congress, 1969).

17. For nineteenth- and early twentieth-century reviews, mainly in newspapers, see bMS Am 800.23, Alcott Family Papers, and Janet S. Zehr, "The Response of Nineteenth-Century Audiences to Louisa May Alcott's Fiction," *American Transcendental Quarterly*, n.s., 1 (December 1987): 323–42, which draws on this mostly undated collection.

18. For Foucauldian approaches, see Steven Mailloux, "The Rhetorical Use and Abuse of Fiction: Eating Books in Late Nineteenth-Century America," *boundary 2* 17 (Spring 1990): 133–57, and Brodhead, "Starting Out in the 1860s," pp. 69–106.

19. Elizabeth Janeway, "Meg, Jo, Beth, Amy and Louisa," *New York Times Book Review*, September 29, 1968, p. 42; Angela M. Estes and Kathleen Margaret Lant, "Dismembering the Text: The Horror of Louisa May Alcott's *Little Women*," *Children's Literature* 17 (1989): 98–123. See also Judith Fetterley, "*Little Women*: Alcott's Civil War," *Feminist Studies* 5 (Summer 1979): 369--83, and Linda K. Kerber, "Can a Woman Be an Individual?: The Limits of Puritan Tradition in the Early Republic," *Texas Studies in Literature and Language* 25 (Spring 1983): 165–78.

20. Madelon Bedell, "Introduction," *Little Women* (New York: Modern Library, 1983), p. xi, and Elaine Showalter, "*Little Women*: The American Female Myth," chap. 3 in *Sister's Choice: Tradition and Change in Women's Writing* (Oxford: Clarendon Press, 1991), p. 42. All quotations from *Little Women* are from the Modern Library edition, which is taken from 1869 printings of parts one and two.

21. Dorothy Richardson, *The Long Day: The Story of a New York Working Girl as Told by Herself* (1905; reprint, New York: Quadrangle Books, 1972), pp. 84–85. Alcott's juvenile fiction did not appear in the story papers most likely to be found in working-class homes; nor was it available in the Sunday school libraries to which some poor children had access. The latter might encounter Alcott in middle-class sites. In the late 1880s, for example, she was one of the three most popular authors at the reading room for "deprived" girls run by the United Workers and Woman's Exchange in Hartford; the others were Mrs. A. D. T. Whitney and Edgar Allen Poe. *Annual Report* 1 (1888): 8.

22. Lerner, *The Creation of Feminist Consciousness: From the Middle Ages to Eighteen-seventy* (New York: Oxford University Press, 1993).

23. Lewis M. Terman and Margaret Lima, *Children's Reading: A Guide for Parents and Teachers*, 2d ed. (New York: Appleton, 1931), pp. 68–84, found that "at every age girls read more than boys" (p. 68) and read more fiction. Half the adult female respondents in one study named *Little Women* as one of ten books read in childhood that they could recall most easily. Men's choices were far more varied.

24. By reading communities, I adopt the definition proposed by Janice Radway for those who, without necessarily constituting a formal group, "share certain assumptions about reading as well as preferences for reading material" based on their social location or, I would add, the position to which they aspired. "Interpretive Communities and Variable Literacies: The Functions of Romance Reading," *Daedalus* 113 (Summer 1984): 54. This essay builds on my earlier work on the interpretive conventions of specific reading communities in "Sense and Sensibility: A Case Study of Women's Reading in Late Victorian America," in *Reading in America: Literature and Social History*, edited by Cathy N. Davidson (Baltimore: Johns Hopkins University Press, 1989), pp. 201–25, and "Reading and Ambition: M. Carey Thomas and Female Heroism," *American Quarterly* 45 (March 1993): 73–103.

25. Carolyn G. Heilbrun emphasizes the lack of autonomous female models in literature and the exceptional nature of Jo in *Reinventing Womanhood* (New York: Norton, 1979), pp. 190–91, 212. See also Heilbrun, *Writing a Woman's Life* (New York: Norton, 1988).

26. June [1868], *Journals*, p. 166.

27. Niles told Alcott that her royalties were higher than any other Roberts Brothers author, including Harriet Beecher Stowe, whom he considered the American writer who could command the highest fees (Alcott possibly excepted). Niles to Alcott, June 7, 1871 (#25), February 17, 1873 (#39). Whether or not this was the case, Alcott was the firm's best-selling author, an awareness registered in a poem she wrote and sent Niles entitled "The Lay of a Golden Goose." Myerson and Shealy, "The Sales of Louisa May Alcott's Books," p. 67, settle on $103,375 as the most accurate estimate of Alcott's earnings with Roberts Brothers between 1868 and 1886; this figure does not include foreign sales or magazine earnings.

28. Other "juvenile" classics that appeared about the same time were *Hans Brinker; or, The Silver Skates* (1865) by Mary Mapes Dodge and *The Story of a Bad Boy* (1869) by Thomas Bailey Aldrich. A 1947 source claims that these titles, along with *Little Women*, "initiated the modern juvenile." *One Hundred Influential American Books Printed before 1900: Catalogue and Addresses: Exhibition at The Grolier Club* (New York: The Grolier

Club, 1947), p. 106. Also of the period, though less highly esteemed, were *Elsie Dinsmore* (1867) by Martha Finley and Horatio Alger Jr.'s *Ragged Dick* (1868).

29. See Richard L. Darling, *The Rise of Children's Book Reviewing in America, 1865–1881* (New York: Bowker, 1968). Though he compared Alcott as a satirist to William Makepeace Thackeray and Anthony Trollope and thought her "extremely clever," James took her to task for her "rather vulgar prose" and her "private understanding with the youngsters she depicts, at the expense of their pastors and masters." *Nation*, October 14, 1875, pp. 250–51, reprinted in Stern, *Critical Essays*, pp. 165–66.

30. Elizabeth Segel, "'As the Twig Is Bent...': Gender and Childhood Reading," in *Gender and Reading: Essays on Readers, Texts, and Contexts*, edited by Elizabeth A. Flynn and Patrocinio P. Schweickart (Baltimore: Johns Hopkins University Press, 1986), pp. 165–86, is a useful brief analysis. See also Daniel T. Rodgers, *The Work Ethic in Industrial America, 1850–1920* (Chicago: University of Chicago Press, 1978), pp. 125–52, and R. Gordon Kelly, ed., *Children's Periodicals of the United States* (Westport, Conn.: Greenwood Press, 1984).

31. See Edward G. Salmon, "What Girls Read," *Nineteenth Century* 20 (October 1886): 515–29, and the ad for a series of "Books for Girls" whose intended audience was those "between eight and eighteen.... for growing-up girls, the mothers of the next generation." *American Literary Gazette and Publishers' Circular* (*ALG*) 17 (June 1, 1871): 88.

32. Niles to Alcott, July 25, 1868 (#2).

33. *Little Women*, p. 290.

34. November 1, [1868], *Journals*, p. 167; Alcott to Elizabeth Powell, March 20, [1869], in *The Selected Letters of Louisa May Alcott*, edited by Joel Myerson and Daniel Shealy, associate ed. Madeleine B. Stern (Boston: Little, Brown, 1987), p. 125 (hereafter cited as *SL*). Erin Graham, "Books That Girls Have Loved," *Lippincott's Monthly Magazine*, September 1897, pp. 428–32, makes much of Bhaer's foreignness and ungainliness. The author recalls reading Alcott after the age of thirteen, when more "lachrymose" heroines had "palled" and she and her friends "did not take kindly to the romantic passion."

35. Jo's standing as a tomboy was recognized—and even respected; an ad for *Little Men* noted that "when a girl, [Jo] was half a boy herself." *ALG* 17 (May 15, 1871): 49. For girls in early adolescence and/or for lesbian readers, the young Jo may have been the primary romantic interest.

36. A conversation with Dolores Kreisman contributed to this analysis.

37. See Rachel Blau DuPlessis, *Writing beyond the Ending: Narrative Strategies of Twentieth-Century Women Writers* (Bloomington: Indiana University Press, 1985).

38. *Harper's New Monthly Magazine*, August 1869, pp. 455–56, reprinted in Stern, *Critical Essays*, p. 83.

39. For an analysis of changes in girls' stories as the heterosexual imperative became stronger, see Martha Vicinus, "What Makes a Heroine?: Nineteenth-Century Girls' Biographies," *Genre* 20 (Summer 1987): 171–87.

40. Frank Preston Stearns, *Sketches from Concord and Appledore* (New York: Putnam, 1895), p. 82.

41. Niles to Alcott, April 14, 1869 (#4). On advertising techniques of the era, see

Susan Geary, "The Domestic Novel as a Commercial Commodity: Making a Best Seller in the 1850s," *Papers of the Bibliographical Society of America* 70 (1976): 365–93.

42. "Roberts Brothers, Boston," *ALG* 17 (July 1, 1871): 118. Led by *Little Women*, *An Old-Fashioned Girl*, and *Little Men*, Alcott's fiction for younger readers continued to sell. Her adult books, including *Hospital Sketches* which received excellent reviews, did not do as well. In general, sales fell off in the late 1870s but picked up again in the 1880s with the repackaging of *Little Women* as a single volume and publication of eight titles in a "'Little Women' Series." Roberts Brothers Cost Books, including summary in Cost Book D [i], *87M-113, Little, Brown Papers, and Myerson and Shealy, "The Sales of Louisa May Alcott's Books."

43. An early ad called *Little Women* a "history of actual life" (*Boston Evening Transcript*, September 30, 1868, p. 3), while an undated source claimed: "It was known to friends and acknowledged by Miss Alcott herself that 'Little Women' is the transcript, more or less literal, of her own and her sisters['] girlhood" (torn clipping, probably an obituary, bMS Am 800.23, Alcott Family Papers). See also [Franklin B. Sanborn], "The Author of 'Little Women,'" *Hearth and Home*, July 16, 1870.

44. Letter in *St. Nicholas*, February 1878, p. 300.

45. "Little Things," at first handwritten, then typeset on a small press, was part of a national phenomenon. See Paula Petrik, "The Youngest Fourth Estate: The Novelty Toy Printing Press and Adolescence, 1870–1886," in *Small Worlds: Children and Adolescents in America, 1850–1950*, edited by Elliott West and Paula Petrik (Lawrence: University Press of Kansas, 1992), pp. 125–42. Alcott's correspondence with the Lukens sisters, which extended over fourteen years, is reprinted in *SL*; it was published earlier in the *Ladies' Home Journal*, April 1896, pp. 1–2. The Alcott sisters had their own Pickwick Club in 1849.

46. Niles to Alcott, August 30, 1870 (#16), August 14, 1871 (#29). Unfortunately, only a few letters from Alcott's fans survive.

47. Letter from "Nelly," dated March 12, 1870, reproduced in Delamar, *Louisa May Alcott*, p. 146.

48. Alcott to the Lukens Sisters, October 2, 1874, *SL*, pp. 185–86. Readers' disappointment with her appearance is a recurrent subject in Alcott's letters. Alice Stone Blackwell, who knew the writer, found her "positively unpleasant looking." See Marlene Deahl Merrill, ed., *Growing Up in Boston's Gilded Age: The Journal of Alice Stone Blackwell, 1872–1874* (New Haven: Yale University Press, 1990), p. 174.

49. April [1869], *Journals*, p. 171.

50. Louisa May Alcott to Amos Bronson Alcott, [October 18, 1875], *SL*, p. 198; see also September–October 1875, *Journals*, pp. 196–97. It is an interesting commentary on changing sex and gender expectations that Alcott had the kind of fan appeal for teenage girls that in the twentieth century has been reserved for male pop singers.

51. "Jo's Last Scrape," pp. 45–65.

52. See, however, Richard H. Brodhead's stimulating discussion of Alcott's professional options in "Starting Out in the 1860s." An earlier, more amateur mode of "starting out" is analyzed by Joan D. Hedrick, "Parlor Literature: Harriet Beecher Stowe and the Question of 'Great Women Artists,'" *Signs* 17 (Winter 1992): 275–303. For an analysis of efforts to make "high culture" a safe space for men, see Hedrick,

Harriet Beecher Stowe: A Life (New York: Oxford University Press, 1994); on the literary marketplace, see Susan Coultrap-McQuin, *Doing Literary Business: American Women Writers in the Nineteenth Century* (Chapel Hill: University of North Carolina Press, 1990).

53. "American Literature," [1878–79], *Addams Papers*, reel 27, frames 239–95.

54. Undated review of *Little Men* ("Capital" penciled in), bMS Am 800.23, Alcott Family Papers.

55. Stearns, *Sketches from Concord and Appledore*, p. 84. Nina Baym claims that Alcott and Stowe were the only women included in the American literary canon at the end of the century. Baym, *Woman's Fiction: A Guide to Novels by and about Women in America, 1820–1870* (Ithaca: Cornell University Press, 1978), p. 23.

56. See, e.g., Louise Chandler Moulton, "Louisa May Alcott," *Our Famous Women* (1883; reprint, Hartford: A. D. Worthington, 1884), pp. 29–52, which was prepared with Alcott's assistance. Reports of Alcott's financial success appeared frequently in the press. An obituary estimated her earnings for *Little Women* alone at $200,000. "Death of Miss Alcott," *Ladies' Home Journal*, May 1888, p. 3. The figure is high, but it attests to belief in her success.

57. In this sense, *Little Women* may be considered a book that extends readers' "horizons of expectations," to use Hans Robert Jauss's term. Jauss, "Literary History as a Challenge to Literary Theory," *New Directions in Literary History*, edited by Ralph Cohen (Baltimore: Johns Hopkins University Press), pp. 11–41.

58. It is a sign of the changing times that the Elsie books were banned from some libraries on the grounds that they were commonplace and not true to life. Esther Jane Carrier, *Fiction in Public Libraries, 1876–1900* (New York: Scarecrow Press, 1965), pp. 356–60.

59. For comparisons of the two authors, see the review of *An Old-Fashioned Girl* in *Nation*, July 14, 1870, p. 30, and Niles to Alcott, January 13, 1871 (#20). Niles reported that Stowe wanted to know why Alcott's books were "so much more popular" than Mrs. Whitney's, which she considered "equally as good." *Faith Gartney's Girlhood* had a long run in the Sunday school libraries.

60. *The Ladies' Repository* ([December 1868], p. 472), while finding *Little Women* "very readable," pointedly observed that it was "not a Christian book. It is religion without spirituality, and salvation without Christ."

61. Alcott's depiction of home theatricals drew the wrath of some evangelicals. Niles to Alcott, October 26, 1868 (#3). *The Christian Union*, edited by Henry Ward Beecher, evidently did not include her books on its Sunday school list, to Niles's great irritation. Lawrence F. Abbott to Roberts Brothers, June 6, 1882, with appended note by Niles to Alcott (#128).

62. On tomboys, see Sharon O'Brien, "Tomboyism and Adolescent Conflict: Three Nineteenth-Century Case Studies," in *Woman's Being, Woman's Place: Female Identity and Vocation in American History*, edited by Mary Kelley (Boston: G. K. Hall, 1979), pp. 351–72, which includes a section on Alcott, and Alfred Habegger, "Funny Tomboys," in *Gender, Fantasy, and Realism in American Literature* (New York: Columbia University Press, 1982), pp. 172–83. Habegger claims that although remembered today only in the figure of Jo March, the tomboy became a major literary type in the 1860s (pp. 172–73).

63. The Katy books of "Susan Coolidge," pen name of Sarah Chauncey Woolsey,

another Roberts Brothers author, are perhaps closest to Alcott's. But even Katy Carr, who begins as another Jo, an ambitious, harumscarum, and fun-loving girl, is severely punished for disobedience; only after suffering a broken back and several years of invalidism does she emerge as a thoughtful girl who will grow into "true womanhood."

64. By the early twentieth century Franklin B. Sanborn, a New England writer and reformer, claimed that Alcott was more widely read than any other of the " 'Concord Authors,' so-called." Sanborn, *Recollections of Seventy Years* (Boston: Richard G. Badger, 1909), 2:342, 338. He had earlier deemed her very American in "her humor, her tastes, her aspirations, her piety." [Sanborn], "The Author of 'Little Women.' " English reviews emphasized Alcott's Americanness.

65. Roosevelt, *An Autobiography* (1913; reprint, New York: De Capo Press, 1985), p. 17.

66. Gilman, *The Living of Charlotte Perkins Gilman* (1935; reprint, New York: Harper and Row, 1975), p. 35.

67. Baker, *Fighting for Life* (New York: Macmillan, 1939), pp. 17, 9.

68. Franklin Whitall Smith to Thomas, February 20, 1870, *The Papers of M. Carey Thomas in the Bryn Mawr College Archives*, edited by Lucy Fisher West (Woodbridge, Conn.: Research Publications, 1982) (hereafter cited as MCTP), reel 58. Thomas's reading is analyzed more fully in Sicherman, "Reading and Ambition"; on *Little Women*, see pp. 80–83.

69. M. Carey Thomas Journal, June 20, 1870, MCTP, reel 1.

70. Elizabeth King Ellicott to Thomas, November 23, [1879], MCTP, reel 39.

71. See Marjorie Housepian Dobkin, ed., *The Making of a Feminist: Early Journals and Letters of M. Carey Thomas* (N.p.: Kent State University Press, 1979), pp. 66–67 and passim.

72. These remarks draw on Sicherman, "Reading and Ambition," pp. 82–83.

73. *Little Women*, pp. 328–29.

74. See Nina Auerbach, *Communities of Women: An Idea in Fiction* (Cambridge: Harvard University Press, 1978), pp. 55–73.

75. On this subject, see Lee Virginia Chambers-Schiller, *Liberty, a Better Husband: Single Women in America: The Generations of 1780–1840* (New Haven: Yale University Press, 1984). In her next book, *An Old-Fashioned Girl*, Alcott ventures much further in envisioning a life of singlehood and lovingly depicts a community of self-supporting women artists.

76. Simone de Beauvoir, *Memoirs of a Dutiful Daughter*, translated by James Kirkup (1949; reprint, Cleveland: World Publishing Co., 1959), pp. 94–95. Despite differences in culture and religion, de Beauvoir found many parallels between the March family and her own, in particular the belief "that a cultivated mind and moral righteousness were better than money" (p. 94). According to Deirdre Bair, de Beauvoir had read *Little Women* by the time she was ten. Bair, *Simone de Beauvoir: A Biography* (New York: Summit Books, 1990), pp. 68–71.

77. Bair, *Simone de Beauvoir*, p. 69. Shirley Abbott, who grew up in Arkansas in the 1940s and 1950s, was also dismayed by Jo's rejection of Laurie: "I took a page in my notebook and began: / JO AND LAURIE / by Louisa May Abbott"; she literally rewrote the ending to suit herself. Shirley Abbott, *The Bookmaker's Daughter: A Memory Unbound* (New York: Ticknor and Fields, 1991), pp. 133–34.

78. These conclusions emerge from my reading and from discussions of *Little Women* with more than a dozen women. They were highly educated for the most part and mainly over fifty, but some women under thirty also felt passionately about the book. Most of my informants were white, but see n. 81 below.

79. On the relation of class and education to cultural preferences, see Pierre Bourdieu, *Distinction: A Social Critique of the Judgement of Taste*, translated by Richard Nice (Cambridge: Harvard University Press, 1984). There was greater overlap in cultural tastes in the nineteenth-century United States than Bourdieu's analysis of late-twentieth-century France allows.

80. Mary Church Terrell, *A Colored Woman in a White World* (1940; reprint, New York: Arno Press, 1980), p. 26; Alfreda M. Duster, ed., *Crusade for Justice: The Autobiography of Ida B. Wells* (Chicago: University of Chicago Press, 1970), pp. 7, 21–22. Wells observed that in her early years, she "never read a Negro book or anything about Negroes."

81. *The Middletown Press*, June 1, 1994, p. B1, and Ann Petry to author, letter postmarked July 23, 1994; I am grateful to Farah Jasmine Griffin for the *Middletown Press* reference. *Little Women* continues to play an important role in the lives of some young black women. A high school student in Jamaica, for example, rewrote the story to fit a local setting. And a young, African American academic felt so strongly about *Little Women* that, on learning about my project, she contended with some heat that Aunt March was unfair in taking Amy rather than Jo to Europe; she seemed to be picking up a conversation she had just left off. Comments like these and Petry's suggest the need for research on the interaction between race and class in African American women's reading practices. A conversation with James A. Miller was helpful on this point.

82. Edith Wharton, *A Backward Glance* (New York: Appleton-Century, 1934), p. 51. Annie Nathan Meyer, a member of New York's German-Jewish elite who describes the authors in the family library as "impeccable," claims that Alcott was the only writer of children's books she could "endure." Meyer, *It's Been Fun: An Autobiography* (New York: Henry Schuman, 1951), pp. 32–33.

83. Richardson, *The Long Day*, pp. 75–86 (quotation, p. 86); I am grateful to Michael Denning for pointing out this episode. *The Long Day*, which purports to be the story of an educated woman forced by circumstances to do manual labor, must be used with caution. It was initially published anonymously, and many scenes read like sensational fiction. Leonora O'Reilly, a feminist trade unionist, was so outraged at the book's condescension and its insinuations that working-class women were immoral that she drafted a blazing indictment. Leonora O'Reilly Papers, edited by Edward T. James, *Papers of the Women's Trade Union League and Its Principal Leaders* (Woodbridge, Conn.: Research Publications, 1981), reel 9.

84. Michael Denning, *Mechanic Accents: Dime Novels and Working-Class Culture in America* (London: Verso, 1987), pp. 197–200, analyzes *Little Rosebud's Lovers* as a "Cinderella tale." He suggests that stories read by the middle class tended to depict working-class women as victims (of seduction and poverty) rather than as triumphant. Joyce Shaw Peterson, "Working Girls and Millionaires: The Melodramatic Romances of Laura Jean Libbey," *American Studies* 24 (Spring 1983): 19–35, also views Libbey's

stories as a "success myth for women." There were other sorts of female working-class traditions than the one suggested here, particularly among the politically aware. These included reading circles, some with a particular political or philosophical slant, and various efforts at "self-improvement." See, e.g., n. 83.

85. I have discussed Jewish immigrants at some length because of the abundance of evidence, not because I view them as the only model for an alternative reading of *Little Women*.

86. *My Mother and I* (New York: Macmillan, 1917) is a problematic book. Some contemporaries reviewed it as autobiographical fiction, but recent critics have tended to view it as autobiography. Theodore Roosevelt must have considered it the latter when he lauded it as a "really noteworthy story" of Americanization in the foreword. (A shorter version appeared in the *Ladies' Home Journal*, October 1916, as "My Mother and I: The Story of How I Became an American Woman, with an Appreciation by Theodore Roosevelt, to Whom the Manuscript Was Sent.") Moreover, the facts Stern gave out about her early life—including her status as an Eastern European Jewish immigrant—correspond with the narrator's history. Stern's older son, however, maintains that his mother was native born and Protestant and claimed her Jewish foster parents as her biological parents to hide her out-of-wedlock birth. T[homas] Noel Stern, *Secret Family* (South Dartmouth, Mass.: T. Noel Stern, 1988). Ellen M. Umansky, who generously shared her research materials with me, concludes in "Representations of Jewish Women in the Works and Life of Elizabeth Stern," *Modern Judaism* 13 (1993): 165–76: "[I]t may be difficult if not impossible to ever determine which of Stern's literary self representations reflected her own experiences" (p. 174). Sources that appear to substantiate Elizabeth Stern's foreign and Jewish birth are the U.S. Census for 1900 and for 1910, which both list her birthplace as Russia; the certificate of her marriage, which was performed by a prominent Orthodox rabbi in Pittsburgh; and Aaron Levin's will, which lists Stern as his oldest child.

Despite its contested status, I have drawn on *My Mother and I* because Stern's choice of *Little Women* as a critical marker of American aspirations is consistent with other evidence. The narrative's emphasis on the differences between immigrant and American culture comports with representations in less problematic works by Jewish immigrant writers. Moreover, whatever the facts of Stern's birth, she lived with the Jewish Levin family for many years.

87. *My Mother and I*, pp. 69–71.

88. Ibid., pp. 71–72.

89. Leo Lerman, "Little Women: Who's in Love with Miss Louisa May Alcott? I Am," *Mademoiselle*, December 1973, reprinted in Stern, *Critical Essays*, p. 113. See also Stephan F. Brumberg, *Going to America, Going to School: The Jewish Immigrant Public School Encounter in Turn-of-the-Century New York City* (New York: Praeger, 1986), pp. 121–22, 141.

90. See, e.g., *The Louisa Alcott Reader: A Supplementary Reader for the Fourth Year of School* (1885; reprint, Boston: Little, Brown, 1910) and Fanny E. Coe, ed., *The Louisa Alcott Story Book* (Boston: Little, Brown, 1910). The former included fairy tales, the latter, more realistic stories, with the moral printed beneath the title in the table of contents, e.g. "Kindness to horses" and "Wilfulness is punished." In Philadelphia in the 1930s, *Little Women* was on a list from which seventh graders could choose books for reports.

91. Rose Cohen, *Out of the Shadow* (New York: Doran, 1918), p. 253.

92. "'Zelda' on Books," English Department, *Jewish Daily News* (New York), August 4, 1903; see also "Just Between Ourselves, Girls," ibid., July 12, 1903. Stokes also recommended the novels of Charles Dickens, George Eliot, Charlotte Brontë, and Grace Aguilar, an English Jewish writer, as well as Jewish and general history. I am grateful to Harriet Sigerman for the references.

93. Mary Antin, *The Promised Land* (Boston: Houghton Mifflin, 1912), pp. 257, 258–59.

94. Showalter, *"Little Women,"* pp. 55–56; Madeleine B. Stern to author, July 31, 1993. The English edition continued to be published in two volumes, the second under the title *Good Wives*.

95. Paradoxically, in view of the sanctity of Victorian motherhood, *Little Women* is one of the few books of its era (adult or juvenile) that depicts a strong maternal figure; mothers are often dead, ill, or powerless. See Baym, *Woman's Fiction*. The female-dominated March household and the figure of Marmee may, in consequence, have had a special appeal to Alcott's early readers.

96. Elizabeth Young, "Embodied Politics: Fictions of the American Civil War" (Ph.D. diss., University of California, Berkeley, 1993), reading *Little Women* in conjunction with *Hospital Sketches*, views it as a "war novel" (p. 108).

CHAPTER 12. Between Culture and Politics

I would like to thank the editors of this volume for their insightful comments. Special thanks are also due Kathy Spray, archivist at the American Jewish Archives in Cincinnati, and members of the Brandeis University Faculty Seminar and Graduate Seminar in Jewish women's history and theory. Paul Buhle, Morris U. Schappes, and Rose Raynes provided a helpful context about the organization and the Jewish immigrant left.

1. Louis Levine, *The Women's Garment Workers* (New York: B. W. Huebsch, 1923), p. 154.

2. According to Morris U. Schappes, Feigenbaum used his knowledge of the Bible and Jewish tradition to promote socialist ideas. Among other works, he translated August Bebel's *Women and Socialism* and *Yiddishkeit and Sozialismus* (Jewishness and Socialism) into Yiddish. See Schappes, "Clara Lemlich Shavelson," *Jewish Currents* 36 (November 1982): 11.

3. Clara Lemlich Shavelson, "Remembering the Waistmakers General Strike, 1909," *Jewish Currents* 36 (November 1982): 11; also recounted in Paula Scheier, "Clara Lemlich Shavelson: Heroine of the Garment Strike of 1909," *Morgen Freiheit*, September 17, 1982. See also Scheier, "Clara Lemlich Shavelson: Fifty Years in Labor's Front Line," *Jewish Life* (November 1954): 7–11; Arthur Zipser, "A Labor Heroine," *Daily Worker*, August 13, 1982; Miriam Silver, "Clara Shavelson—Heroine of Labor," and tape of Memorial Meeting for Shavelson, October 24, 1982, both in the Papers of the Emma Lazarus Federation of Jewish Women's Clubs, American Jewish Archives, Cincinnati (hereafter cited as ELF Papers). Shavelson's biography is drawn from these

sources and from one of the few scholarly histories to treat Shavelson's mature activities, Annalise Orleck, "Common Sense and a Little Fire: Working-Class Women's Activism in the Twentieth-Century United States" (Ph.D. diss., New York University, 1990).

4. On the strike, see Meredith Tax, *The Rising of the Women: Feminist Solidarity and Class Conflict, 1880–1917* (New York: Monthly Review Press, 1980), pp. 205–40, and Ann Schofield, "The Uprising of the 20,000: The Making of a Labor Legend," in *A Needle, a Bobbin, a Strike: Women Needleworkers in America*, edited by Joan M. Jensen and Sue Davidson (Philadelphia: Temple University Press, 1984), pp. 167–82. On Jewish women radicals, see Alice Kessler-Harris, "Organizing the Unorganizable: Three Jewish Women and Their Union," *Labor History* 17 (Winter 1976): 5–23. Also of interest are Ruth A. Frager, *Sweatshop Strife: Class, Ethnicity, and Gender in the Jewish Labour Movement of Toronto, 1900–1939* (Toronto: University of Toronto Press, 1992), and Naomi Shepherd, *A Price below Rubies: Jewish Women as Rebels and Radicals* (Cambridge: Harvard University Press, 1993), which, with a few exceptions, concentrates on European women. On radical women generally, see Mari Jo Buhle, *Women and American Socialism, 1870–1920* (Urbana: University of Illinois Press, 1981), and Robert Schaffer, "Women and the Communist Party, USA, 1930–1940," *Socialist Review* 9 (May–June 1979): 73–118.

5. Among major studies in American Jewish women's history, see the pioneering volume by Charlotte Baum, Paula Hyman, and Sonya Michel, *The Jewish Woman in America* (New York: New American Library, 1975); Jacob Rader Marcus, *The American Jewish Woman, 1654–1980,* (New York: KTAV Publishing House, 1981); June Sochen, *Consecrate Every Day: The Public Lives of Jewish American Women, 1880–1980* (Albany: State University of New York Press, 1981); Sydney Stahl Weinberg, *The World of Our Mothers: The Lives of Jewish Immigrant Women* (Chapel Hill: University of North Carolina Press, 1988); Susan A. Glenn, *Daughters of the Shtetl: Life and Labor in the Immigrant Generation* (Ithaca, N.Y.: Cornell University Press, 1990); Linda Kuzmack, *Woman's Cause: The Jewish Woman's Movement in England and the United States, 1881–1933* (Columbus: Ohio State University Press, 1990); and Faith Rogow, *Gone to Another Meeting: The National Council of Jewish Women* (Tuscaloosa: University of Alabama Press, 1993.)

6. See Arthur Hertzberg, *The Jews in America: Four Centuries of an Uneasy Encounter: A History* (New York: Simon and Schuster, 1989), and Edward S. Shapiro, *A Time for Healing: American Jewry since World War II* (Baltimore: Johns Hopkins University Press, 1992). Deborah Dash Moore's study of the children of immigrants, *At Home in America: Second-Generation New York Jews* (New York: Columbia University Press, 1981), offers a different argument. On the question of immigrant generations, see Peter Kivisto and Dag Blanck, eds., *American Immigrants and Their Generations: Studies and Commentaries on the Hansen Thesis after Fifty Years* (Urbana: University of Illinois Press, 1990).

7. On an earlier protest by Jewish housewives, see Paula Hyman, "Immigrant Women and Consumer Protest: The New York Kosher Meat Boycott of 1902," *American Jewish History* 70 (September 1980): 91–105. For an account of the housewives' movement in the Great Depression, see Annalise Orleck, "'We Are That Mythical Thing Called the Public': Militant Housewives during the Great Depression," *Feminist Studies* 19 (Spring 1993): 147–72. See also Mark Naison, *Communists in*

Harlem during the Great Depression (New York: Grove Press, 1983), pp. 149–50, for an account of the 1935 meat boycott led by Shavelson and Rose Nelson [Raynes].

8. Tape of Memorial Meeting for Clara Lemlich Shavelson, October 1982, ELF Papers.

9. See, e.g., "Class Struggle in Fraternal Organizations," *Daily Worker*, July 18, 1930, IWO Papers, Tamiment Library, New York University (hereafter cited as IWO Papers).

10. Mark Naison, "Remaking America: Communists and Liberals in the Popular Front," in *New Studies in the Politics and Culture of U.S. Communism*, edited by Michael E. Brown, Randy Martin, Frank Rosengarten, and George Snedeker (New York: Monthly Review Press, 1993), pp. 58–59; Arthur Leibman, *Jews and the Left* (New York: John Wiley and Sons, 1978), pp. 59, 350–51.

11. "Straight from the Shoulder Fraternalism," JPFO Bulletin, IWO Papers. On the IWO, see Arthur J. Sabin, *Red Scare in Court: New York versus the International Workers Order* (Philadelphia: University of Pennsylvania Press, 1993), pp. 10–23; Rose Raynes, Gertrude Decker, Morris U. Schappes, and Annette Rosenthal, interviews by author, February–March 1993. On Jews and American communism, see Paul Buhle, "Jews and American Communism: The Cultural Question," *Radical History Review* 23 (Spring 1980): 9–33; Leibman, *Jews and the Left*; and David Leviatin, *Followers of the Trail: Jewish Working-Class Radicals in America* (New Haven: Yale University Press, 1969).

12. Morris U. Schappes, ed., *Emma Lazarus: Selections from Her Poetry and Prose* (New York: Cooperative Book League, Jewish-American Section, IWO, 1944); the ELF sponsored new editions of the volume in 1978 and 1982. Schappes also wrote an introduction and notes to *An Epistle to the Hebrews by Emma Lazarus*, centennial ed. (New York: Jewish Historical Society of New York, 1987), and he edited, with an introduction, *The Letters of Emma Lazarus, 1868–1885* (New York: New York Public Library, 1949).

13. Founding documents, ELF Papers.

14. Ibid.; Rose Raynes, interview by author, February 1993.

15. Rose Raynes, interview by Paul Buhle, March 21, 1979, Oral History Interviews of the Left, Tamiment Library, New York University.

16. In his book about the case, law professor Arthur J. Sabin describes the prosecution as without parallel in American law and concludes that the IWO had been destroyed for political reasons. See Sabin, *Red Scare in Court*. For further information, see IWO Papers, including "Report of the Officers," IWO, February 3–4, 1951.

17. See, e.g., Leah Nelson, "They Shall Not Die," *The Lamp* 1, no. 3 (November–December 1952): 4–5.

18. Robert Meeropol, interview by author, May 1993.

19. "Resume of a Discussion by the Executive Committee of the Emma Lazarus Federation on the Destruction of Jewish Culture and Unjust Execution of Jewish Cultural and Civic Leadership," July 10, 1956, ELF Papers; Rose Raynes and Gertrude Decker, interviews by author. See also the discussion of the ELF and the Soviet Jewish question in *Israel Horizons and Labour Israel* 21 (January–February 1974): 2, 28–30.

20. *Proceedings of the Third Convention*, February 6–8, 1959, ELF Papers.

21. On postwar Jewry, see Moore, *At Home in America*; Shapiro, *A Time for Healing*;

and Marshall Sklare and J. Greenblum, *Jewish Identity on the Suburban Frontier* (New York: Basic Books, 1967).

22. The Jewish Cultural Clubs and Societies, like the Yiddisher Kultur Farband, supported such institutions as the *Morgen Freiheit* newspaper, *Yiddishe Kultur* magazine, and Camp Kinderland and worked to publish Yiddish books.

23. Cited in ELF Papers—see Eve Merriam, *Woman with a Torch* (New York: Citadel Press, 1957).

24. Study outline on Emma Lazarus, ELF Papers.

25. Schappes, *Epistle to the Hebrews*, p. 30.

26. Lazarus, "The Jewish Problem," reprinted in Schappes, *Emma Lazarus: Selections from Her Poetry and Prose*, p. 78.

27. ELF constitution and by laws, January 20–21, 1951, ELF Papers.

28. Cited in Ernestine Rose study guide, ELF Papers, from Yuri Suhl, *Ernestine L. Rose and the Battle for Human Rights* (New York: Reynal, 1959).

29. Study guide on Ernestine Rose, ELF Papers.

30. Discussion outline, "Women, Heroines of the Warsaw Ghetto," 1951, ELF Papers.

31. Report of June Gordon, Executive Director of the Third National Convention, *Proceedings of the Third Convention*

32. See, e.g., Miriam Silver, Cultural Report, December 4, 1976, ELF Papers.

33. Report of Ida Sper to the Second National Convention, October 23, 1955, ELF Papers.

34. *The Lamp* 1, no. 1 (May 1952): 6.

35. Ibid., pp. 6–7.

36. In 1959, for example, under the auspices of the Brooklyn Emma Lazarus clubs, hundreds of blacks and Jews attended a brotherhood meeting at the Eastern Parkway Jewish Center cosponsored by local affiliates of the American Jewish Congress, the NAACP, and the Brownsville Neighborhood Health Council. A new Brooklyn Emma Lazarus club, made up of young mothers, rejected the lecture/meeting format and organized a brotherhood puppet show about changing neighborhoods attended by 1,400 black and white children.

37. See, e.g., address of Leah Nudell, Vice President of the ELF and President of the Los Angeles club, to the Seventh National Convention, November 14–16, 1975, ELF Papers.

38. Speakers Guide, "Racism, Enemy of the Jewish People," ELF Papers.

39. To the Emmas, genocide not only was "actually killing" but also was caused by poverty, starvation, malnutrition, and the social ills that "killed people's spirit." See Miriam Silver, "Helping to Shape a Brighter Future for Our New Generation," 1969, and remarks of Rose Raynes, April 9, 1989, ELF Papers.

40. Report of Eva Mamber, Boston ELF, to the Fifth National Convention, 1964, ELF Papers.

41. Report of the Fifth National Convention, ibid.

42. Rose Raynes, keynote address, Seventh National Convention, November 14–16, 1975, ELF Papers.

43. Press release, August 18, 1967, ELF Papers.

44. *The Lamp* 1, no. 6 (May–June 1960): 6.

45. In 1959, for example, the ELF sponsored a mass meeting in Union Square that attracted 8,000 Americans who protested a swastika outbreak in West Germany and the United States. At the same time the Brooklyn chapter called a mass meeting with twelve other organizations at which Jackie Robinson spoke. Thus was the fight against anti-Semitism joined, they said, "with the Negro people's struggle for equality." Mollie Ilson, "As I See It," *The Lamp* 6, no. 12, ELF Papers.

46. Rose Raynes, Gertrude Decker, and Morris U. Schappes, interviews by author.

47. At the urging of the Emma Lazarus Committee in Los Angeles (which included 15 member clubs), WILPF called a conference of Jewish women's organizations. ELF Papers.

48. Quotation from the Third National Convention, *Proceedings of the Third Convention.*

49. Local branches also supported regional issues: the Los Angeles group, for example, started a cooperative nursery school for Mexican American, Filipino, and Jewish children.

50. When some members of the Jewish community criticized the ELF for a member's anti-Israel statement, leadership disassociated the federation from the member, noting that its firm support for Israel had long been a matter of public record. See letters from Rose Raynes and Morris U. Schappes discussing the incident in *Israel Horizons and Labour Israel* 21 (January–February 1974): 2, 28-30.

51. Undated typescript, ELF Papers.

52. Leah Nelson, President's Report, *Proceedings of the Third Convention.*

53. Shirley Bolton, Newark, N.J., Second National Convention, October 1955, ELF Papers.

54. Helen Lewis, Second National Convention, ibid.

55. See letter of Rose Raynes in *Israel Horizons and Labour Israel* 21 (January–February 1974): 30.

56. IWO press release, November 13, 1947, IWO Papers. See also photos of Louise W. Wise and June Croll Gordon embracing on the stage of Assembly Hall, Hunter College, ELF Papers.

57. Abzug spoke on October 25, 1970, at the ELF's 50th anniversary celebration of woman suffrage; on December 14, 1974, she spoke at its celebration of Emma Lazarus's 125th birthday. Holtzman, described as a "twentieth century disciple of Ernestine Rose," was the guest of honor at a March 25, 1974, celebration of Rose.

58. June Gordon, Fifth National Convention, 1964, ELF Papers.

59. Ida Good, "Why I Joined the E.L. Club," *The Lamp* 4, no. 8 (October 1958): 4.

60. Scheier, "Clara Lemlich Shavelson: Fifty Years in Labor's Front Line," p. 11; Schappes, "Clara Lemlich Shavelson," p. 11.

61. Rose Raynes, interview by Buhle.

62. Leah Nelson, address at the Fourth National Convention, November 3–5, 1961, ELF Papers.

63. ELF constitition and by-laws, January 20–21, 1951, ELF Papers.

64. For example, on the problem of class/gender paradigms in women's history, see Nancy A. Hewitt, "Beyond the Search for Sisterhood: American Women's History in

the 1980s," reprinted in *Unequal Sisters: A Multicultural Reader in U.S. Women's History*, edited by Ellen Carol DuBois and Vicki L. Ruiz (New York: Routledge, 1990), pp. 1–14.

65. Biddy Martin and Chandra Talpade Mahanty, "Feminist Politics: What's Home Got to Do with It?," in *Feminist Studies: Critical Studies*, edited by Teresa de Lauretis (Bloomington: Indiana University Press, 1986), p. 192.

66. The term is used by Nancy Fraser in "Rethinking the Public Sphere: A Contribution to the Critique of Actually Existing Democracy," in *Habermas and the Public Sphere*, edited by Craig Calhoun (Cambridge: MIT Press, 1992), p. 118.

67. Address (unsigned) of Leah Nelson to the Sixth National Convention, 1971, ELF Papers.

68. Scheier, "Clara Lemlich Shavelson: Fifty Years in Labor's Front Line," p. 8.

69. Miriam Silver, "Report on Culture: Anti-Semitism and Resurgence of Nazism," ca. 1978, ELF Papers.

70. James Clifford, *The Predicament of Culture: Twentieth-Century Ethnography* (Cambridge: Harvard University Press, 1988), pp. 341–42, 344.

71. Gloria Anzaldúa, "La conciencia de la mestiza: Towards a New Consciousness," in *Borderlands / La Frontera: The New Mestiza* (San Francisco: Spinster/Aunt Lute Books, 1987), p. 79. On feminist consciousness and "otherness," see esp. Martin and Mahanty, "Feminist Politics"; Teresa de Lauretis, "Eccentric Subjects: Feminist Theory and Historical Consciousness," *Feminist Studies* 16 (Spring 1990): 115–50; Trinh T. Minh-Ha, *Woman Native Other: Writing Postcoloniality and Feminism* (Bloomington: Indiana University Press, 1989); and Shane Phelan, "(Be)Coming Out: Lesbian Identity and Politics," *Signs* 18 (1993): 765–90. Also useful are Barbara Smith, ed., *Home Girls: A Black Feminist Anthology* (New York: Kitchen Table/Women of Color Press, 1983), and Elly Bulkin, Minnie Bruce Pratt, and Barbara Smith, eds., *Yours in Struggle: Three Feminist Perspectives on Anti-Semitism and Racism* (Brooklyn, N.Y.: Long Haul Press, 1984).

72. Kurt H. Wolff, ed., *The Sociology of Georg Simmel*, (New York: Free Press, 1950), p. 408; Daniel Boyarin and Jonathan Boyarin, "Diaspora: Generation and the Ground of Jewish Identity," *Critical Inquiry* 19 (Summer 1993): 721.

CHAPTER 13. The Congress of American Women

1. Amy Swerdlow, *Women Strike for Peace: Traditional Motherhood and Radical Politics in the 1960s* (Chicago: University of Chicago Press, 1993).

2. A 1949 officers' report, prepared by Gene Weltfish, Muriel Draper, Betty Millard, Helen Wortis, Helen Phillips, and Stella Allen, states that WIDF had, by 1949, "grown to be the most tremendous women's organization that the world has ever seen," with 80 million members in 57 countries. CAW, Officers' Report, First National Constitutional Convention, New York City, May 6–8, 1949, p. 1, box 2, folder 20A, Smith College Communist Collection, Northampton, Mass. I am indebted to Kate Weigand for this reference.

3. According to Virginia Warner Brodine's unpublished manuscript, "Millions of Women: The Story of the Women's International Democratic Federation and the Congress of American Women" (lent to me by Gerda Lerner), Muriel Draper headed

the delegation. The others were WAC Sergeant Anne M. Bradford, anthropologist Dr. Gene Weltfish, former first lady of Pennsylvania Mrs. Gifford Pinchot, writer Henrietta Buckmaster, and actress Florence Eldridge March. Three African American women were in the group: Dr. Charlotte Hawkins Brown, Thelma Dale, and Vivian Carter Mason. Eleanor T. Vaughan, Jeannette Stern Turner, and Elizabeth Gurley Flynn completed the delegation. This list adds up only to twelve, but Gerda Lerner informed me that Dr. Beryl Parker was also a delegate.

4. CAW, First National Constitutional Convention, New York City, May 6–8, 1949, p. 1, box 2, folder 20, WIDF Papers, Sophia Smith Collection, Smith College, Northampton, Mass.; Brodine, "Millions of Women"; CAW, *American Women in Pictures, Souvenir Journal, Congress of American Women* (New York: CAW, n.d. [1949, as indicated by photo captions]), p. 5.

5. *What Is the Congress of American Women?* (New York: CAW, n.d.), p. 3.

6. Ellen C. DuBois, "Eleanor Flexner and the History of American Feminism," *Gender and History* 3 (Spring 1991): 84.

7. *New York Times*, February 22, 1948. Abby Scher has suggested that a tendency to greater political activism on the part of ordinary middle-class women in the postwar period may have come about as a response to successive national emergencies in which women as well as men were mobilized to support federal governmental solutions to local problems. "During World War II, for instance," she argues, "local women's groups developed more extensive networks and new organizing skills to serve the war effort, and developed an interest in international affairs and patriotism." This influence on women and politics was suggested by Anna Lord Strauss, president of the League of Women Voters from 1944 to 1950. See Anna Lord Strauss, interview by Kitty Gellhorn, Columbia Oral History Project, November 8, 1971, pp. 153–54, cited in Abby Scher, "The Political Incorporation of Women during the Second Red Scare" (paper presented at the Social Science History Association Conference, Baltimore, Md., November 1993), p. 12.

8. Elaine Tyler May, "Explosive Issues: Sex, Women, and the Bomb," in *Recasting America: Culture and Politics in the Age of the Cold War*, edited by Lary May (Chicago: University of Chicago Press, 1989), pp. 159–70. For a fuller discussion of the relationship of family values to the cold war, see May, *Homeward Bound: American Families in the Cold War Era* (New York: Basic Books, 1988).

9. Gerald Horne records that the CPUSA's *Daily Worker* reported in February 1943, only three years before the founding of CAW, that blacks were joining the party in "growing numbers." Doxey Wilkerson, in an article in the *New Masses*, claimed that "nearly 5,000 Negroes joined the party [nationally] during the 1943 spring recruiting drive alone." Horne, "The Red and the Black: The Communist Party and African Americans in Historical Perspective," in *New Studies in the Politics and Culture of U.S. Communism*, edited by Michael E. Brown, Randy Martin, Frank Rosengarten, and George Snedeker (New York: Monthly Review Press, 1993), p. 215. See also Doxey Wilkerson, "The Negro in the War," *New Masses* 49 (December 14, 1943): 8–19; *Daily Worker*, September 6, 1943.

10. Claudia Jones, in a report on the CAW constitutional convention, claimed that "a highlight of the convention was the tremendous participation of Negro women

trade unionists, one of whom was elected to one of the three highest posts in the Congress of American Women." Some of the other black women who played "an outstanding role" were Ada P. Jackson, Pearl Lawes, and Heloise Moorhead. Jones, "Peace Is a Woman's Business," *Daily Worker Magazine*, May 1949, p. 3.

11. In a "Call for the World Congress of Women!" WIDF stated clearly: "To make our full contribution as mothers, workers and citizens to the creation of a better life, we must possess complete political, economic and social rights. That is why in the countries where these rights have not been granted women are demanding both the possession of their rights and the means of exercising them." First among the slogans for the conference was "For the Winning and Defence of our Rights," followed by "For the Protection of Our Children and Homes," and "For a Peaceful World." *For Their Rights as Mothers, Workers & Citizens* (Berlin [East]: WIDF, n.d.), pp. 60, 62.

12. A. Landy, *Marxism and the Woman Question* (New York: Workers Library Publishers, 1943), p. 7.

13. *Daily Worker*, July 29, 1942, cited in Kathleen A. Weigand, "The Woman Question and the Communist Mystique: Propaganda and Practice in the Communist Party, 1941–1945" (paper presented at the Duquesne History Forum, 24th Annual Meeting, Duquesne University, Pittsburgh, Pa., October 1990), p. 24.

14. *Daily Worker*, July 30, 1943. I have emphasized the word *citizen* because appealing to women's citizenship as their basis for political activism is far different and more feminist than the call of Women Strike for Peace for powerless women to influence public policy as mothers defending their children.

15. Weigand, "The Woman Question and the Communist Mystique," p. 3; Robert Schaffer, "Women in the Communist Party, USA, 1930–1940," *Socialist Review* 45 (May 1978): 73–118; Elsa Dixler, "The Woman Question: Women and the American Communist Party, 1929–1941" (Ph.D. diss., Yale University, 1974). Kate Weigand, who is studying the contributions of the Old Left to the women's movement of the 1960s, argues that in the postwar period the CPUSA sustained a radical tradition of women's activism. It fought male supremacy, or male chauvinism as it was called in the party, and encouraged women's economic and political struggles, keeping alive women's political activism in a decade distinguished by the glorification of women's passivity and conformity. Weigand, "Vanguards of Women's Liberation: The Contributions of the Old Left to the Women's Movement of the 1960s" (paper presented at the "Toward a History of the 1960s" Conference, State Historical Society of Wisconsin, Madison, April 29, 1993).

16. Techniques for grassroots organizing may have been learned from the party cadre in CAW. According to Van Gosse, who has examined the gender politics of American Communists between the wars, the party turned to a focus on family and community issues in the 1930s in response to the depression. CPUSA activities— included canvassing and home visits, cultivating all possible allies in the community, and embedding the party in the minutiae of working-class life—depended on a substantial cadre of neighborhood women. "Yet," Van Gosse contends, "the CPUSA still lacked a program and a rhetoric that explicitly addressed the need for women's liberation and the duty of men to recognize themselves as oppressors in the home, on the job, and even in the Party." Van Gosse, " 'To Organize in Every Neighborhood, in

Every Home': The Gender Politics of American Communists between the Wars," *Radical History Review* 50 (1991): 113, 134.

17. Theodore Draper, "The Life of the Party," *New York Review*, January 13, 1994, p. 46.

18. Margaret Cowl, "Women's Struggle for Equality," *Political Affairs* 53 (May 1974): 44, cited in Susan Ware, *Holding Their Own: American Women in the 1930s* (Boston: Twayne Publishers, 1982), p. 122.

19. Obituary, *New York Times*, March 16, 1950.

20. Robin D. G. Kelley, "Claudia Jones," *Encyclopedia of the Left*, pp. 394–95.

21. *Time*, June 5, 1950; September 8, 1952, p. 28.

22. Peace historian Merle Curti estimates that in 1936 NCCCW included, by affiliation, one-fifth of the adult women in the United States. Curti, *Peace or War: The American Struggle, 1636–1936* (New York: Norton, 1936), p. 272. The organizations involved in the NCCCW were the American Association of University Women, Council of Women for Home Missions, Board of Foreign Missions of North America, General Federation of Women's Clubs, National Board of the YWCA, National Council of Jewish Women, National League of Women Voters, Women's Christian Temperance Union, Women's Trade Union League, and National Federation of Business and Professional Women's Clubs. See Jacqueline Van Voris, *Carrie Chapman Catt: A Public Life* (New York: Feminist Press at the City University of New York, 1987).

23. CAW, Officers' Report, First National Constitutional Convention, p. 12.

24. *Ten Women Anywhere Can Start Anything* (New York: CAW, n.d.), p. 3. For information on rising prices in this period, see William Chafe, *The Paradox of Change: American Women in the Twentieth Century* (New York: Oxford University Press, 1992), p. 167.

25. CAW, Digest of Minutes, Enlarged National Executive Board, Chicago, May 22–23, 1948.

26. CAW, "Report of the Commission on the Status of Women," submitted by Susan B. Anthony, chairman of Working Conference, May 25, 1946, MS in possession of author, pp. 1–10.

27. Ibid., p. 21.

28. See Dolores Hayden, *The Grand Domestic Revolution: A History of Feminist Designs for American Homes, Neighborhoods, and Cities* (Cambridge: MIT Press, 1981), chap. 4.

29. *What Is the Congress of American Women?*

30. *Information Bulletin, Women's International Democratic Federation*, p. 14.

31. CAW declared: "Today the Women's Party plays a reactionary role: it is interested chiefly in passing the so-called Equal Rights Amendment, which would wipe out all protective legislation for women." Not only did the CPUSA take that position, but many trade unions did so as well, including the noncommunist United Auto Workers.

32. CAW, Officers' Report, First National Constitutional Convention, p. 22.

33. CAW, *American Women in Pictures*, p. 4.

34. "Preamble, Constitution," *Congress of American Women* (New York: CAW, n.d.), p. 3.

35. Gerda Lerner, "The Lady and the Mill Girl: Changes in the Status of Women in the Age of Jackson," *American Studies Quarterly* 10 (Spring 1969): 5–15; Eleanor Flex-

ner, *Century of Struggle: The Woman's Rights Movement in the United States* (Cambridge: Harvard University Press, 1959). Gerda Lerner represented CAW at the Budapest congress of the WIDF in 1948. An article in the Los Angeles CAW bulletin, headed "Los Angeles to Hear Story of World's Women, Gerda Lerner, Jan. 27," reported that Lerner, "a mother of two children and a talented writer . . . still found time to be active in the Los Angeles Chapter of CAW since its formation in 1946 and was Educational Chairman until her departure for Europe in August, 1948." "Women in Action: Bulletin of the Los Angeles Congress of American Women," January 1949, p. 1.

Eleanor Flexner was present at an Executive Board meeting of CAW on April 13, 1948. A discussion of a Mother's Day Parade to take place in Harlem was led by Audley Moore, of the Civil Rights Congress (CRC), who urged CAW to participate in the parade with the CRC and the National Federation of Colored Women on an equal basis. Eleanor Flexner volunteered to serve on the parade committee. Minutes of Executive Board Meeting, CAW, April 13, 1948, mimeographed, p. 1, in possession of author.

36. "Women in Action: Bulletin of the Los Angeles Congress of American Women," September–October 1949, p. 1. This example of race consciousness parallels that of the CPUSA. Los Angeles Communist Party leader Dorothy Healey recalls that the party paid special attention to all conscious and unconscious ways in which whites in a racially divided society could display attitudes of racial superiority. "I think it was to the Party's lasting credit," Healey asserts, "that it was never complacent about those issues and as a result came closer than anyone else on the Left before or since, to building a genuinely interracial movement." Dorothy Ray Healey and Maurice Isserman, *California Red: A Life in the American Communist Party* (Urbana: University of Illinois Press, 1993), p. 126.

37. Ibid.

38. The entry on Brown in *Notable American Women: The Modern Period* (Cambridge: Belknap Press of Harvard University Press, 1980), pp. 111–13, makes no mention of her role in the CAW.

39. CAW, *Around the World: Bulletin of the Congress of American Women*, March 1949, p. 3.

40. *California [Los Angeles] Eagle*, June 2, 1949.

41. According to the recollection of Gerda Lerner, who worked with CAW on the grassroots level in Los Angeles, white and black women worked together on the neighborhood projects, and black women who were prominent church and community leaders were also leaders of "Congress."

42. Elizabeth Moos was a Communist peace activist who represented CAW at a WIDF executive committee meeting in Paris in 1949, while she was working in Paris with W. E. B. Du Bois as the executive secretary of the Peace Information Center.

43. Stella Allen, Harriet Magil, Abe Magil, and Betty Millard, interview by Katherine Moos Campbell, transcript, February 17, 1981, p. 12.

44. CAW, Officers' Report, First National Constitutional Convention, p. 2.

45. Stella Allen, Harriet Magil, Abe Magil, and Betty Millard, interview by Katherine Moos Campbell, transcript, February 17, 1981, p. 16.

46. *Paris Herald Tribune*, December 7, 1948.

47. *New York Times*, November 20, 1949.

48. *Christian Science Monitor*, January 26, 1949.

49. HUAC, *Report on the Congress of American Women*, 81st Cong., 1st sess., October 23, 1949 (Washington, D.C.: GPO, 1949), p. 1.

50. See Joan Jensen, "All Pink Sisters: The War Department and the Feminist Movement," in *Decades of Discontent: The Woman Movement, 1920–1940*, edited by Lois Scharf and Joan M. Jensen (Westport, Conn.: Greenwood Press, 1983), pp. 190–222. See also John M. Craig, "Redbaiting, Pacifism, and Free Speech: Lucia Ames Mead and Her 1926 Lecture Tour in Atlanta and the Southeast," *Georgia Historical Review* 71 (Winter 1987): 601–22.

51. Leila Rupp, *Survival in the Doldrums: The American Women's Rights Movement, 1945 to the 1960s* (New York: Oxford University Press, 1987), p. 138.

52. HUAC, *Report on the Congress of American Women*, p. 102.

53. CAW, *Around the World: A Publication of the Congress of American Women*, July–August 1948, p. 1.

54. Rupp, *Survival in the Doldrums*, p. 102. It should be noted that in 1946 Nora Stanton Barney wrote a pamphlet, *Women as Human Beings*, that endorsed the Equal Rights Amendment and chastised those who took the CAW position that "an amendment calling for equal rights, and therefore, equal protection would destroy all benefits that the mass of protective laws have built up in the name of health, welfare and morals in the last forty years." Apparently Barney ignored CAW's opposition to the ERA, and CAW ignored her support of what they saw as a reactionary program. Barney, *Women as Human Beings* (Greenwich, Conn.: Nora Stanton Barney, 1946), p. 6.

55. *The Spirit of Houston: The First National Women's Conference: An Official Report to the President, the Congress, and the People of the United States* (Washington, D.C.: National Commission on the Observance of International Women's Year, 1978), p. 148.

56. *Newsweek*, January 16, 1950, p. 21.

57. Statement by Stella Allen in interview by Katherine Campbell with Allen, Harriet Magil, Abe Magil, and Betty Millard, February 17, 1981, p. 17.

58. Katherine Campbell to Amy Swerdlow, May 18, 1981.

59. Ibid.

CHAPTER 14. The Female Generation Gap

Beyond the collective dedication of this volume, I want to personally dedicate this essay to Gerda Lerner. Although she was not my teacher when I was young, she has become a mentor and friend in recent years. She has encouraged my sense of the absurd, tutored me in boldness, and shared her bountiful wisdom and warm friendship with me. For all this, I am deeply grateful. I am also indebted to Kitty Sklar for her excellent criticism, thoughtful editing, and enduring friendship.

The epigraph is from a 1968 position paper in the Women's Liberation File, Social Action Collection, Bancroft Library, University of California, Berkeley.

1. Alix Kates Shulman, *Burning Questions* (New York: Bantam, 1978), p. 3.

2. Susan Bassnett, *Feminist Experience: The Women's Movement in Four Countries* (London: Allen and Unwin, 1986), p. 6.

3. This profile comes from over one hundred interviews I conducted during the 1980s for a book I am writing on the women's movement. The question of what constitutes the baby boom generation has many answers. The standard demographic response is that those born between 1946 and 1964 are the baby boom generation. But in fact, there are important generational differences that showed up in movement culture and politics. The birthrate began rising before 1946, moreover, and the 1964 baby bust did not necessarily make babies born in that year feel generational solidarity with those born in 1946. For demographic data, see Andrew J. Cherlin *Marriage, Divorce, Remarriage* (Cambridge: Harvard University Press, 1981). For an overview of the baby boom generation and its impact on American culture, see Landon Y. Jones, *Great Expectations: America and the Baby Boom Generation* (New York: Ballantine Books, 1980).

4. Jones, *Great Expectations*, preface, p. xx.

5. See, for example, the classic study by Kenneth Keniston, *Young Radicals: Notes on Committed Youth* (New York: Harcourt Brace, 1968), especially the appendix.

6. See Richard Flacks, "The Liberated Generation: An Explanation of the Roots of Student Protest," in *Conformity Resistance and Self-Determination*, edited by Richard Flacks (Boston: Little, Brown, 1973).

7. Keniston, *Young Radicals*, p. 337.

8. Susan Griffin, panel discussion on the women's movement, Berkeley, Calif., October 1988.

9. See Nancy Chodorow, *The Reproduction of Mothering: The Psychoanalysis and the Sociology of Gender* (Berkeley: University of California Press, 1978), and Jean Baker Miller, ed. *Psychoanalysis and Women* (New York: Vintage, 1978).

10. Barbara Berg, *The Crisis of the Working Mother: Resolving the Conflict between Family and Work* (New York: Summit, 1986), p. 40.

11. Ibid., p. 34.

12. See Elizabeth Stone, "Mothers and Daughters," *New York Times Magazine*, May 13, 1979, p. 91.

13. George Gallup and Evan Hill, "The American Woman," *Saturday Evening Post*, December 22, 1962.

14. Letters dated May 17, 1963, from Irvine, Tex., and March 13, 1963, from Ridgewood, N.J., Betty Friedan Papers, Schlesinger Library, Radcliffe College, Cambridge, Mass.

15. Isabel Marcus, feminist law professor at the State University of New York at Buffalo, used this term in an interview with me on March 3, 1988. Wini Breines's study of girls in the fifties also documents this profound undercurrent of ambivalence, especially through fiction and popular culture. Breines, *Young, White, and Miserable: Growing Up Female in the Sixties* (Boston: Beacon Press, 1992).

16. Here I draw upon dozens of interviews with women who became leaders of the younger branch of the women's movement. A longer version of this essay, a chapter in my book, will include excerpts from those interviews. See also Kathleen Gerson, *Hard Choices: How Women Decide about Work, Career, and Motherhood* (Berkeley: University of California Press, 1985), whose study supports my thesis.

17. Gerson, *Hard Choices*, p. 55. Gerson's book, in general, documents the ambivalence I found in my interviews of daughters of the fifties.

18. Isabel Marcus and her daughter Erica, interview by author, Buffalo, N.Y., March 3, 1988. See also Rose Glickman's *Daughters of Feminists: Young Women with Feminist Mothers Talk about Their Lives* (New York: St. Martin's, 1993), an oral history of daughters of feminists that confirms this perspective.

19. Berg, *The Crisis of the Working Mother*, p. 38.

20. This part of the study is based particularly on interviews with Naomi Weisstein, Alix Kate Shulman, Barbara Ehrenreich, Vivian Gornick, Ellen Willis, Charlotte Bunch, Susan Griffin, Ti-Grace Atkinson, Barbara Haber, Valerie Miner, Irene Peslikis, and dozens of other less well-known feminists.

21. Naomi Weisstein, interview by author, New York City, April 7, 1987, transcript, p. 40.

22. Barbara Ehrenreich, interview by author, New York City, April 6, 1987.

23. Irene Peslikis, interview by author, New York City, April 4, 1987.

24. Ellen Willis and Ti-Grace Atkinson, interviews by author, New York City, April 16, 1987. Writings by Molly Haskell and several dozen other interviews confirm this fear of replicating one's mother's life.

25. Paula Weideger, "Womb Worship," *Ms.*, February 1988, p. 54.

26. Anna Quindlen, "Mother's Choice," *Ms.*, February 1988, p. 55.

27. See especially Keniston, *Young Radicals*. T. Jackson Lears described a similar ennui or malady that afflicted young people at the turn of the twentieth century, during the beginning years of the consumer society. He describes this "dread of unreality" as part of the confusion the young, educated members of the bourgeoisie experienced as they entered a period of rapid change in values. See Lears, "From Salvation to Self-Realization," in *The Culture of Consumption: Critical Essays in American History, 1880–1980*, edited by Richard Wightman Fox and T. Jackson Lears (New York: Pantheon, 1983).

28. Fox and Lears, *Culture of Consumption*, p. 5.

29. In history, for example, "consensus" was celebrated and "conflict" was diminished; in sociology, functionalism helped rationalize the status quo.

30. Douglas T. Miller and Marion Novak, *The Fifties: The Way We Really Were* (New York: Doubleday, 1975), p. 236.

31. This is revealed in the memoirs of at least two major New Left leaders, but it is also evident in the position papers of SDS writers in general. See Todd Gitlin, *The Sixties: Years of Hope, Days of Rage* (New York: Bantam, 1987), and Tom Hayden, *Reunion: A Memoir* (New York: Random House, 1988).

32. Gitlin points out the centrality of this dissident literature to the New Left in *The Sixties*, p. 19.

33. For a fuller discussion of the impact of these "underground channels," as Gitlin called them, see the chapter by that name in *The Sixties*. The larger argument of the ways in which men first rebelled against conformity is made in Barbara Ehrenreich, *The Hearts of Men: American Dreams and the Flight from Commitment* (New York: Doubleday, 1983).

34. Valerie Miner, Susan Griffin, Mary Waters, Barbara Haber, Irene Peslikis, Alex Kate Shulman, and Vivian Gornick, interviews by author, New York City and Berkeley, Calif., 1987–88. Many others substantiate this observation.

35. U.S. Department of Commerce, *Social Indicators* (Washington, D.C.: GPO, 1973),

pp. 106–7. Figures based on Office of Education, National Center for Education Statistics, *Projection of Educational Institutions* (Washington, D.C., 1972), and *Digest of Educational Statistics* (Washington, D.C., 1971); *Earned Degrees Conferred on Higher Educational Institutions*, 1949–50, 1959–60.

36. Flacks, "The Liberated Generation," p. 105.

37. Gloria Steinem, *Outrageous Acts and Everyday Rebellions* (New York: Holt, 1983), pp. 111–18.

38. More than half of the women in my consciousness-raising group in 1967, for example, came from working-class homes. Their college education, however, had given them a sense of entitlement that they expressed in the group. As one of the first such groups, it seemed to be filled with aspiring writers and professionals. But their appearance masked their actual experience. This group was brought together largely through a note tacked onto a university bulletin board.

39. Ann Schofield, interview by author, Berkeley, Calif., April 1986; also Mary Waters, Valerie Miner, Pat Cody, Betty Friedan, and many others, interviews by author, 1988.

40. Marilyn Coffey, "Those Beats," in *Sixties without Apology*, edited by Sonya Sayres, Anders Stephenson, Stanley Aronowitz, and Frederic Jameson (Minneapolis: University of Minnesota Press, 1984), pp. 238–40.

41. Many of the feminists who were born before and during World War II described this foray into bohemia. Particularly revealing are the author's interviews with Barbara Ehrenreich and Susan Griffin. For a description of young women's forays into bohemian culture as part of their search for something "real," see Breines, *Young, White, and Miserable*.

42. Ellen Maslow, "Storybook Lives," in *Liberation Now*, edited by Deborah Babcox and Madeleine Belkin (New York: Dell, 1971), p. 175.

43. Joyce Johnson, *Minor Characters* (Boston: Houghton Mifflin, 1983), p. 56.

44. Ibid., pp. 151, 171, 207, 260.

45. Barbara Ehrenreich, Elizabeth Hess, and Gloria Jacobs, *Re-Making Love: The Feminization of Sex* (New York: Anchor, 1986).

46. Helen Gurley Brown, *Sex and the Single Girl* (New York: Pocket Books, 1962), p. 206.

47. Part of this line of reasoning is persuasively argued in Ehrenreich, Hess, and Jacobs, *Re-Making Love*. The twentieth century is filled with examples of young women asserting their social freedom and expanding their personal autonomy—without any political theory or movement for women's rights. Women who began dancing in public, entering bars, and so forth are part of the nonpolitical history of women's emancipation in twentieth-century America.

48. For a good analysis of how different generations of women responded to de Beauvoir's classic work, see Judith Okely, *Simone de Beauvoir* (New York: Pantheon, 1986).

49. Simone de Beauvoir, *The Second Sex* (New York: Harmondsworth, 1953).

50. Alice Schwarzer, *After the Second Sex: Conversations with Simone de Beauvoir* (New York: Pantheon, 1984), p. 13, quoted in Okely, *Simone de Beauvoir*, p. 2. See also the description by Judith Okely, a British biographer of de Beauvoir, of her fascination

with this bohemian life and critique of family and motherhood. Rachel Brownstein, an American literary critic, was similarly influenced by de Beauvoir. See Brownstein, *Becoming a Heroine* (New York: Harmondsworth, 1984), p. 18.

51. King, *Freedom Song*, p. 76.

52. Susan Griffin, "Eco-Feminism," talk at panel on feminism and ecology, San Francisco, April 10, 1988.

53. It is worth noting that the translation that was published in the United States omitted her discussion of women in history, but her view of woman as "other" still did not provide a full understanding of women's agency in history.

54. One recent work that provides a good overview of her life is Deidre Bair's *Simone De Beauvoir: A Biography* (New York: Summit, 1990). A film titled *Daughters of de Beauvoir*, directed by Imogen Sutton, explores her influence on the women's movement. A brilliant essay by Mary Felstiner early assessed feminism's second-wave relationship to de Beauvoir. See Felstiner, "Seeing the Second Sex through the Second Wave," *Feminist Studies* 6 (Winter 1986): 247–76.

55. De Beauvoir, *The Second Sex*, p. 295.

56. For a broader discussion of this generational divide, see Gitlin, *The Sixties*, p. 23ff.

57. See Amy Swerdlow, "Ladies' Day at the Capitol: Women Strike for Peace versus HUAC," *Feminist Studies* 2 (Fall 1982): 493–521, and her "Pure Milk, Not Poison: Women Strike for Peace and the Test Ban Treaty of 1963" (paper presented at the Berkshire Conference on Women's History, Wellesley College, Mass., June 1988).

58. The impact of the civil rights movement on future New Leftists, as well as future feminists, has been amply documented by all historians of the New Left. My interviews confirm this observation. See, e.g., Gitlin, *The Sixties*.

59. Gerda Lerner, *The Creation of Patriarchy* (New York: Oxford University Press, 1986).

CHAPTER 15. The Making of *Black Women in America*

1. Elsa Barkley Brown, "Womanist Consciousness: Maggie Lena Walker and the Independent Order of St. Luke," *Signs* 14 (Spring 1989): 631.

BIBLIOGRAPHY OF THE
WRITINGS OF GERDA LERNER

COMPILED BY THOMAS DUBLIN

Fiction, Poetry, Autobiographical Writings, and Drama

"The Prisoners." *The Clipper* 2, no. 7 (September 1941): 19–22.

"The Russian Campaign." *Story: The Magazine of the Short Story* 23, no. 103 (September–October 1943): 59–66.

With Eve Merriam. *Singing of Women: A Dramatic Review*. Performed off-Broadway, 1951.

No Farewell. New York: Associated Authors, 1955.

Black Like Me (screenplay). New York: Walter Reade Distributors, 1964.

A Death of One's Own. New York: Simon and Schuster, 1978. Reprint, Madison: University of Wisconsin Press, 1985. German edition: *Ein Eigener Tod*. Dusseldorf: Boehme und Erb Verlag, 1979. Reprint, Frankfurt: Campus Verlag, 1993. Dutch edition: *Een Eigen Dood*. Amsterdam: Wereldbibliotheek, 1978.

"On Keeping House at the Edge of the Volcano" (poem). *Ms* magazine, July 1979, p. 22.

"Dreaming" (poem). *Women's Studies Quarterly* 11, no. 4 (Winter 1983): 26.

"Reflections: In the Footsteps of the Cathars." *The Progressive* 58, no. 3 (March 1994): 18–22.

Interviews

Interviews of Gerda Lerner. In a series of interviews of women historians, Columbia University Oral History Research Office, New York City, 1978, 1981.

"Gerda Lerner on the Future of Our Past." Interview by Catharine R. Stimpson, *Ms* magazine, September 1981, p. 50.

Interview. *Columns* 5, no. 1 (February–March 1984): 4–6.

Historical Writings

BOOKS

The Grimké Sisters from South Carolina: Rebels against Slavery. Boston: Houghton Mifflin, 1967. Paperback reprint, Schocken Books, 1971.

The Woman in American History. Reading, Mass.: Addison-Wesley, 1971.

Ed. *Black Women in White America: A Documentary History*. New York: Pantheon Books, 1972. Reprint, New York: Vintage, 1992. French edition: *De L'esclavage à la Segregation: Les Femmes Noires dans L'Amerique des Blancs*. Paris: Denoel/Gonthier, 1975.

Ed. *The Female Experience: An American Documentary*. Indianapolis, Ind.: Bobbs-Merrill, 1976. Reprint, New York: Oxford University Press, 1992.

The Majority Finds Its Past: Placing Women in History. New York: Oxford University
Press, 1979.
Teaching Women's History. Washington, D.C.: American Historical Association, 1981.
The Creation of Patriarchy. New York: Oxford University Press, 1986. Vol. 1 of *Women
and History.* Spanish edition: *La Creacion del Patriarcado.* Barcelona: Editorial
Crítica, 1990. German edition: *Die Entstehung des Patriarchats.* Frankfurt: Campus
Verlag, 1991.
The Creation of Feminist Consciousness: From the Middle Ages to Eighteen Seventy. Vol. 2 of
Women and History. New York: Oxford University Press, 1993. German edition:
Frauen und Geschichte. Frankfurt: Campus Verlag, 1993.

ARTICLES, PAMPHLETS, AND REPORTS

"The Grimké Sisters and the Struggle against Race Prejudice." *Journal of Negro
History* 26 (October 1963): 277–91
"The Lady and the Mill Girl: Changes in the Status of Women in the Age of
Jackson." *Midcontinent American Studies Journal* 10 (Spring 1969): 5–15
"New Approaches for the Study of Women in American History." *Journal of Social
History* 3 (Fall 1969): 53–62. Reprinted in *Liberating Women's History: Theoretical and
Critical Essays,* edited by Berenice A. Carroll. Urbana: University of Illinois Press,
1976.
"The Feminists: A Second Look." *Columbia Forum* 13 (Fall 1970): 24–30.
"Sarah Mapps Douglass." In *Notable American Women, 1607–1950: A Biographical
Dictionary,* edited by Edward T. James, Janet Wilson James, and Paul S. Boyer, pp.
811–13. Cambridge: Harvard University Press, 1971.
"Women's Rights and American Feminism." *American Scholar* 40 (Spring 1971): 235–
48.
"Lost Women: Quiz on History of American Women." *Ms* magazine, September
1972, p. 32.
"Sarah and Angelina Grimké." In *Encyclopedia of American Biography,* edited by John A.
Garraty, pp. 458–60. New York: Harper and Row, 1974.
"Early Community Work of Black Club Women." *Journal of Negro History* 59 (April
1974): 158–67.
"Placing Women in History: Definitions and Challenges." *Feminist Studies* 3 (Fall
1975): 5–14. Reprinted in *Liberating Women's History: Theoretical and Critical Essays,*
pp. 357–68, edited by Berenice A. Carroll (Urbana: University of Illinois Press,
1976), and *Major Problems in American Women's History: Documents and Essays,* pp. 2–
9, edited by Mary Beth Norton (Lexington, Mass.: D.C. Heath, 1989).
"Sarah M. Grimké, 'Sisters of Charity.' " *Signs: Journal of Women in Culture and Society* 1
(Winter 1975): 246–56.
"Black and White Women in Interaction and Confrontation." In *Prospects: An Annual
of American Cultural Studies,* edited by Jack Salzman, 2:193–208. N.p.: Burt Franklin,
1976.
"Teaching Women's History." *American Historical Association Newsletter,* May 1976, pp.
3–6.
"Lost from the 'Official' Record." *Ms* magazine, December 1979, pp. 109–10.

With Ellen DuBois, Mari Jo Buhle, Temma Kaplan, and Carroll Smith-Rosenberg. "Politics and Culture in Women's History: A Symposium." *Feminist Studies* 6 (Spring 1980): 49–54.

Foreword to *Elizabeth Cady Stanton and Susan B. Anthony: Correspondence, Writings, Speeches*, edited by Ellen Carol DuBois. New York: Schocken, 1981. A volume in the Schocken series "Studies in the Life of Women," Gerda Lerner, general editor.

"The Challenges of Women's History." In *Liberal Education and the New Scholarship on Women*, a report of the Wingspread Conference, October 1981, sponsored by the Association of American Colleges, pp. 39–47.

"The Necessity of History and the Professional Historian." *Journal of American History* 69 (June 1982): 7–20.

"Non-violent Resistance—The History of an Idea in Theory and Practice." Harvey Wish Memorial Lecture, Case Western Reserve University, Cleveland, Ohio, 1983.

"Women and Slavery." *Slavery and Abolition: A Journal of Comparative Studies* 4 (December 1983): 173–98.

"The Rise of Feminist Consciousness." In *All of Us Are Present: The Stephens College Symposium*, pp. 33–50. Columbia, Mo.: Women's Education, 1984.

Ed., with Marie Laberge. *Women Are History: A Bibliography in the History of American Women*. 4th rev. ed. Madison: Graduate Program in Women's History, University of Wisconsin-Madison, 1986. Earlier editions published by Sarah Lawrence College as *Bibliography in the History of American Women*.

"The Origins of Prostitution in Ancient Mesopotamia." *Signs: Journal of Women in Culture and Society* 11 (Winter 1986): 236–54.

"Women and History." In *Critical Essays on Simone de Beauvoir*, edited by Elaine Marks, pp. 154–68. Boston: G. K. Hall, 1987.

Coauthor with Kathryn Kish Sklar. *Graduate Training in U.S. Women's History: A Conference Report*. N.p., 1989.

"A View from the Women's Side." In "Radical Historians and the Crisis in American History: 1959–1980." *Journal of American History* 76 (September 1989): 446–56.

"Blick auf das Jahr 2000." In *Vor der Jahrtausendwende: Berichte zur Lage der Zukunft*, edited by Peter Sloterdijk, 1:292–308. Frankfurt: Edition Suhrkamp, 1990.

"Another View." In "A Round Table: The Living and Reliving of World War II." *Journal of American History* 77 (September 1990): 588–89.

"Reconceptualizing Differences among Women." *Journal of Women's History* 1 (Winter 1990): 106–22.

Introduction to *High Tea at Halekulani: Feminist Theory and American Club Women*, by Margit Misangyi Watts. Brooklyn, N.Y.: Carlson, 1993. A volume in the Carlson series "Scholarship in Women's History: Rediscovered and New," Gerda Lerner, general editor.

"Sarah Douglass." In *Black Women in America: An Historical Encyclopedia*, edited by Darlene Clark Hine, 1:351–53. Brooklyn, N.Y.: Carlson, 1993.

CONTRIBUTORS

Joyce Antler teaches American Studies at Brandeis University, where she directed the Women's Studies Program for many years. In addition to a biography of Lucy Sprague Mitchell and works on the history of women's education, she has written on feminist biography and Jewish women's history. She is the editor of a volume of short stories by American Jewish women writers and one on the cultural representation of Jewish women, which contains a wonderful autobiographical essay by Gerda Lerner. She is currently writing a book entitled *Journey Home: A History of Twentieth-Century American Jewish Women and the Struggle for Identity*.

William H. Chafe is Alice Mary Baldwin Professor of American History at Duke University. For ten years he was Academic Director of the Duke-UNC Center for Research on Women. He is also a founding member of the Duke University Center for Documentary Studies. He is the author of numerous books, including *The American Woman* (1972), *Women and Equality* (1977), *Civilities and Civil Rights* (1980), *The Unfinished Journey* (1986), and *The Paradox of Change* (1991). His most recent book is *Never Stop Running: Allard Lowenstein and the Struggle to Save American Liberalism* (1993).

Nancy F. Cott is Woodward Professor of History and American Studies at Yale University, where she has taught since 1975. She is the author of *The Bonds of Womanhood: "Woman's Sphere" in New England, 1780–1835* (1977), *The Grounding of Modern Feminism* (1987), and other studies in women's history. Her most recent book, *A Woman Making History: Mary Ritter Beard through Her Letters* (1991), owes much of its inspiration to Gerda Lerner's account of her own relation to Beard's work.

Jane Sherron De Hart is professor of History at the University of California, Santa Barbara. She first encountered Gerda Lerner in the early 1970s at a meeting of the American Historical Association. Lerner's formidable courage and authority continued to prod and inspire as her younger colleague shifted her own examination of cultural conflict, politics, and policy to the field of women's history. Coauthor of the prize-winning *Sex, Gender, and the Politics of ERA*, De Hart is at work on a collection of essays on feminism, antifeminism, and the state.

Thomas Dublin is professor of History at the State University of New York at Binghamton. He taught women's history for twelve years at the University of California, San Diego, where he drew repeatedly on the writings of Gerda Lerner. He is author of *Women at Work: The Transformation of Work and Community in Lowell, Massachusetts, 1826–1860* (1979) and *Transforming Women's Work: New England Lives in the Industrial Revolution* (1994). He is editor of *From Farm to Factory: Women's Letters, 1830–1860* (1981) and *Immigrant Voices: New Lives in America, 1773–1986* (1993), and coeditor of *Women and Power in American History* (2 vols., 1991).

Estelle B. Freedman is Professor of History at Stanford University and Chair of the Program in Feminist Studies. Her books include *Their Sisters' Keepers: Women's Prison Reform in America, 1830–1930* and, with John D'Emilio, *Intimate Matters: A History of Sexuality in America* (1988). Her biography, *Maternal Justice: Miriam Van Waters and the Female Reform Tradition*, will be published in 1996.

Linda Gordon is Florence Kelley Professor of History at the University of Wisconsin-Madison, where she has had the privilege of being Gerda Lerner's colleague since 1984. She received her Ph.D. from Yale in Russian history. She is the author of *Woman's Body, Woman's Right: A History of Birth Control in America* (1976; 2d ed., 1990), *Heroes of Their Own Lives: The Politics and History of Family Violence* (1988), and *Pitied but Not Entitled: Single Mothers and the History of Welfare* (1994) and the editor of *America's Working Women: A Documentary History* (1976) and *Women, the State, and Welfare* (1990).

Darlene Clark Hine is John A. Hannah Professor of American History at Michigan State University. Following in the tradition of black women's reclamation history as reflected in Gerda Lerner's *Black Women in White America: A Documentary History* (1972), she launched the Black Women in the Middle West project (1982) in order to create a black women's archive. And playing off the title of Lerner's work, she was the author of *Black Women in White: Racial Conflict and Cooperation in the Nursing Profession, 1890–1950* (1989).

Linda K. Kerber is May Brodbeck Professor in the Liberal Arts and Professor of History at the University of Iowa. She has served as President of the American Studies Association and, in 1996–97, will be President of the Organization of American Historians. She is the author of *Federalists in Dissent: Imagery and Ideology in Jeffersonian America* (1970) and *Women of the Republic: Intellect and Ideology in Revolutionary America* (1980) and the coeditor, with Jane Sherron De Hart, of *Women's America: Refocusing the Past* (4th ed., 1995). She is completing a book entitled *A Right to Be Ladies: American Women and the Obligations of Citizenship.*

Alice Kessler-Harris is Professor of History at Rutgers University, where she served as Director of the Women's Studies Program from 1990 to 1995. After working with Gerda Lerner for two years in the exciting young days of the Women's History Program at Sarah Lawrence College, she sought to thread together the then disparate fields of labor and women's history. The results appear in several books, including *Women Have Always Worked: A Historical Overview* (1981), *Out to Work: A History of Wage-Earning Women in the United States* (1982), and *A Woman's Wage: Historical Meanings and Social Consequences* (1992).

Judith Walzer Leavitt is Professor of the History of Medicine and History of Science and Evjue-Bascom Professor of Women's Studies at the University of Wisconsin-Madison, where she also participates in the Graduate Program in Women's History. She is the author of *The Healthiest City: Milwaukee and the Politics of Health Reform* (1982) and *Brought to Bed: Childbearing in America, 1750–1950* (1986). She is the editor of *Women and Health in America: Historical Readings* (1984) and, with Ronald L. Numbers, *Sickness and Health in America: Readings in the History of Medicine and Public Health* (1985). She is finishing a manuscript tentatively entitled *"Typhoid Mary" Remembered: Personal Liberty versus the Public's Health in the Twentieth Century.*

Nell Irvin Painter is Edwards Professor of American History at Princeton University. She met Gerda Lerner in the mid-1970s, after she had completed her graduate work at Harvard but still had everything to learn. Still learning, she is finishing a biography of Sojourner Truth, entitled *Sojourner Truth: A Life, A Symbol*, and will soon turn to a study of sexuality and families in the nineteenth- and twentieth-century South. The author of three books in the 1970s and 1980s, she has received numerous awards and fellowships, most recently from the National Endowment for the Humanities for her work on Sojourner Truth.

Ruth Rosen is Professor of History at the University of California, Davis. She is the editor of *The Maimie Papers* (1978) and the author of *The Lost Sisterhood* (1982). She is currently writing a history of the contemporary women's movement in the United States, entitled *The Second Wave*, and is a regular contributor to the op-ed page of the *Los Angeles Times*.

Barbara Sicherman is William R. Kenan Jr Professor of American Institutions and Values at Trinity College in Hartford. When she taught her first women's history course in 1970, she relied heavily on Gerda Lerner's syllabus and has counted on her ever since. She is the coeditor of *Notable American Women: The Modern Period* (1980) and the author of *The Quest for Mental Health in America, 1880–1917* (1980) and *Alice Hamilton: A Life in Letters* (1984). She is currently working on a book entitled *Gender and the Culture of Reading in Late-Victorian America*.

Kathryn Kish Sklar is Distinguished Professor of History at the State University of New York at Binghamton. She has served as president of the Society of Historians of the Gilded Age and Progressive Era and of the Pacific Coast Branch of the American Historical Association. In 1988 she had the pleasure of organizing with Gerda Lerner a national conference on graduate training in U.S. women's history. Her books include *Catharine Beecher: A Study in American Domesticity* (1973) and *Florence Kelley and the Nation's Work: The Rise of Women's Political Culture, 1830–1900* (1995). She is the editor of *The Autobiography of Florence Kelley: Notes of Sixty Years* (1986) and the coeditor of *Women and Power in American History* (2 vols., 1991), *The Social Survey Movement in Historical Perspective* (1992), and *A Transatlantic Dialogue: Women and Social Reform in Germany and the United States, 1880–1930* (forthcoming, 1996).

Amy Swerdlow is Professor of History and Director of the Women's Studies Program *Emerita* at Sarah Lawrence College, a post she "inherited" from Gerda Lerner, who introduced her to U.S. women's history and encouraged her to dig into the field. Swerdlow's recent article, "Abolition's Conservative Sisters: The Ladies' New York City Anti-Slavery Societies, 1834–1840," which appears in *The Abolitionist Sisterhood* (edited by Jean Fagan Yellin and John C. Van Horne, 1994), comes directly from her work with Gerda Lerner. Lerner's original analysis of female culture and women's movements for social transformation helped to shape Swerdlow's conceptualization of *Women Strike for Peace: Traditional Motherhood and Radical Politics in the 1960s* (1993), as well as the essay that appears in this volume.

250; career as writer, 250, 255, 417 (n. 27), 419 (n. 52); royalties of, 250, 417 (n. 27), 420 (n. 56); *Little Men*, 252, 254, 256; *An Old-Fashioned Girl*, 252, 256; juvenile fiction of, 252, 417 (n. 21), 419 (n. 42); autobiography of, 252, 419 (n. 42); *Hospital Sketches and Camp and Fireside Stories*, 252, 419 (n. 42); *Comic Tragedies*, 253; European travel of, 253; *Shawl-Straps*, 253; appearance of, 253, 419 (n. 48); celebrity of, 253–54, 255, 419 (n. 50); *Work*, 258; biographies of, 263, 416 (n. 13); pedagogical use of, 263, 423 (n. 90); publishing history of, 415 (nn. 5, 6); literary reputation of, 420 (n. 55), 421 (n. 64). See also *Little Women*

Aleichem, Sholom, 279

Alger, Horatio, Jr., 418 (n. 28)

Alienation: in postwar culture, 321–24, 333

Allen, Stella, 308, 311

All God's Dangers (Rosengarten), 133

Althusser, Louis, 132, 387 (n. 11)

Altmeyer, Arthur, 93, 375 (n. 70)

American Association for Labor Legislation (AALL), 36–37, 62, 358 (n. 43); founding of, 51–52; goals of, 52, 53–54, 360 (n. 56); women in, 53; local branches of, 53–55, 360 (n. 54); Massachusetts local of, 54, 55, 59, 360 (n. 65); and workman's compensation, 56; policy making by, 57; and minimum wage campaign, 60–61, 361 (n. 78), 363 (n. 92); charter members of, 359 (n. 45); contributors to, 359 (nn. 47, 48); achievements of, 364 (n. 98)

American Association of University Women (AAUW), 217, 432 (n. 22)

American Civil Liberties Union (ACLU), 354 (n. 49)

American Federation of Labor (AFL),

50; and workman's compensation, 56; and minimum wage, 59, 362 (n. 86)

American Jewish Congress, 301–2, 427 (n. 36)

American Labor Legislation Review (quarterly), 55, 61

American League to Abolish Capital Punishment, 170

American Medical Liberty League, 165

American Nazi Party, 284

American ORT (Organization for Rehabilitation and Training), 302

American Revolution: and slavery, 23; and status of women, 23, 24–25; women's property rights during, 352 (n. 31); marriage during, 380 (n. 22)

Anderson, Mary, 196

Andrews, Irene Osgood: in AALL, 52, 53, 359 (n. 47); and minimum wage, 61

Andrews, John B., 39; as secretary of AALL, 52, 53; and AALL locals, 54–55; publishing activities of, 55; and NCF, 56; and trade unions, 57; and minimum wage campaign, 60–61; and Florence Kelley, 359 (n. 45); early life of, 359 (n. 47); on labor legislation, 360 (n. 68)

Anthony, Susan B., 277, 306

Anthony, Susan B., II, 298; on Commission on the Status of Women, 304; in Congress of American Women (CAW), 305, 310; and House Un-American Activities Committee, 308, 309, 311

Anticommunism, 332. *See also* Communist Party of the United States of America; McCarthyism

Antin, Mary, 264

Antinuclear movement, 333, 334

Anti-Semitism: ELF's work against, 270, 273, 277, 280–86, 291, 294–95, 428 (n. 45); Ernestine Rose's stance against, 278; by African Americans,

Cohen, Lizabeth, 18, 350 (n. 2)
Cohen, Rose, 263, 264
Cohen, Wilbur, 95, 375 (n. 70)
Collins, Barbara-Rose, 230
Colored Women's Federation, 177
Comic Tragedies (Alcott), 253
Comins, Lizbeth B., 246
Commission on Civil Rights, 225
Commission on the Status of Women
   (1961), 201, 304
Committee for a Sane Nuclear Policy
   (SANE), 285, 333
Committee for World Development
   and World Disarmament, 285
Committee on Economic Security, 102
Commons, John R., 36; and AALL, 52,
   53–55, 359 (n. 48); and NCF, 56; and
   Advisory Council on Social Security,
   93; on wage boards, 363 (n. 92)
Commonwealth v. Clements, 379 (n. 16)
Communes, nineteenth-century, 126
Communist Party of the United States
   of America (CPUSA), 296; Clara
   Shavelson in, 271, 272; Jewish immi-
   grant women in, 273; attacks against,
   274; racial agenda of, 300; support of
   women's movement, 300; Women's
   Commission of, 301; influence on
   CAW, 301, 302, 308, 310; gender
   issues in, 305–6, 431 (n. 16); African
   Americans in, 430 (n. 9); women
   activists in, 431 (n. 15); programs for
   working women, 431 (n. 16)
Community: women as builders of, 3;
   imagined, 20, 350 (n. 5); of African
   American women, 139–40, 344
Community property systems, 29
Concubinage, 384 (n. 46)
Cone, James, 140
Conformity: in postwar era, 322–24,
   334, 436 (n. 33)
Confrontation, politics of, 220, 221
Congress, U.S.: on polygamy, 117; and
   ERA, 216; women in, 230, 231–33,

238, 409 (n. 33); and ADC, 368
   (n. 58)
Congressional Caucus on Women's
   Issues, 241, 413 (n. 49)
Congress of American Women (CAW),
   12, 296; work for social justice, 297;
   goals of, 297, 304–5; support of
   Soviet policies, 297, 308, 309; and
   postwar conservatism, 299; African
   American women in, 299, 300,
   306–8, 430 (n. 9), 433 (n. 41); constituency of, 299, 301–2; disbanding
   of, 299, 312; class consciousness of,
   300; tactics of, 300; influence of
   Communist Party on, 301, 302, 310;
   Communist members of, 302, 308;
   coalition-building of, 303; local chapters of, 303–4, 311; foreshadowing of
   contemporary feminism, 304; and
   earlier women's movements, 305, 306,
   310; opposition to ERA, 305, 432
   (n. 31), 434 (n. 54); awareness of
   women's history, 305–6; peace efforts
   of, 308; racial inclusiveness of, 310;
   effect of McCarthyism on, 310–11,
   312
Conover, Pamela Johnston, 410 (n. 37)
Consciousness: common, 378 (n. 11);
   gender, 413 (n. 48). *See also* Class consciousness
Consciousness, feminist, 4, 125, 292,
   429 (n. 71); and patriarchy, 13; CAW's
   role in, 296, 301; of 1960s, 334; rise
   of, 335; of African American women,
   340
Consciousness raising, 189–90, 316, 324
Consent theory, 20–21
Conservatism: of child welfare movement, 70; of 1980s, 225–26; of postwar era, 299; in construction of Social
   Security Act, 370 (n. 15); women's
   organizations in, 401 (n. 48), 413 (n.
   48)
Constitution, U.S.: Fourteenth Amend-

ment, 18, 19–20, 216, 218; obligation in, 19–20; as social contract, 20, 21; First Amendment, 117; Fifth Amendment, 216

Consumerism, 43; effect on production, 44–45; women's power in, 46; of postwar era, 321–22

Consumers' League movement, 43–44, 58; middle-class women in, 49; Jewish women in, 357 (n. 20); and minimum wage campaign, 362 (n. 85). *See also* National Consumers' League

Consumer's White Label, 46, 49, 58

Continental Congress, 20

Contraception, 68

Contracts: by married women, 22; in U.S. law, 113; by slaves, 379 (n. 16); and the state, 380 (n. 24). *See also* Marriage; Property

Cook, Blanche Wiesen, 199, 401 (n. 3), 402 (n. 16)

Cook, Nancy, 197, 199

Corbin, Caroline, 26

Cotils, Alphonse, 157; social condition of, 158, 159

Cott, Nancy, 9, 186, 365 (n. 2), 397 (n. 6)

Council of Jewish Women (Los Angeles), 177

Council of Trent, 377 (n. 3)

Council of Women for Home Missions, 432 (n. 22)

Coverture, 20, 22, 112, 352 (n. 30); and exemption from obligation, 27; and second-wave feminism, 32; ending of, 34; Supreme Court decisions on, 355 (n. 56)

Cowl, Margaret, 301

CPUSA. *See* Communist Party of the United States of America

Creation of Feminist Consciousness, The (Lerner), 4, 125, 334

Creation of Patriarchy, The (Lerner), 4

Crozier, Blanche, 353 (n. 33)

Cultural pluralism, 275

Curti, Merle, 432 (n. 22)

Dale, Thelma, 307, 430 (n. 3)

Darrow, Clarence: defense of Jennie Barmore, 147, 165–66, 395 (n. 57); autobiography of, 396 (n. 64)

Daughters of de Beauvoir (film), 438 (n. 53)

Davies, Edgar, 361 (n. 75)

Davis, Angela, 281

Daycare: opposition to, 82; CAW's support for, 304, 309

Dean, James, 324

Death of a Salesman (Miller), 323

De Beauvoir, Simone, 330–33, 438 (n. 50); and *Little Women*, 259–60, 421 (n. 76); women's history in, 438 (n. 53)

Debs, Eugene, 204

Decker, Gertrude, 284–85, 286

Degler, Carl, 26–27, 352 (nn. 26, 29)

De Hart, Jane, 8–9

De Lauro, Rosa, 230

Democratic Party, 358 (n. 39); feminists in, 225; Southern, 369 (n. 59); women officials in, 410 (n. 34)

Devine, Edward T., 359 (n. 45)

Dewson, Mary W., 59, 174, 362 (n. 85), 369 (n. 9); on Social Security Advisory Council, 93, 96, 97, 105, 374 (n. 46); and Eleanor Roosevelt, 196, 197, 201; resignation from Advisory Council, 373 (n. 40); and Social Security, 373 (n. 41), 374 (n. 43), 375 (n. 70)

Dickerman, Marian, 197

Disease, communicable: germ theory of, 149–50; responsibility of middle-class women for, 150, 160. *See also* Public health; Typhoid fever

Disease carriers, 150–51, 154–58, 161–62, 166–69; women as, 160, 394 (nn. 43, 46); noncooperating, 393

92–93, 96, 371 (n. 24); and family
benefits, 94–102; and domestic workers, 102, 103; report to Congress,
104. *See also* Social Security Act (1939
amendments to)
Feigenbaum, Benjamin, 267, 424 (n. 2)
Feinstein, Dianne, 230, 233, 413 (n. 47);
gubernatorial campaign of, 238, 412
(n. 44); Senate race of, 240
Female Experience, The, (Lerner), 3
Feme covert. See Coverture
Feminine Mystique, 314, 315; and
motherhood, 316; rejection of, 317,
318–21; and Beats, 326; marriage in,
329–30
Feminism: consciousness of, 4, 125,
292, 429 (n. 71); of nineteenth century, 67, 365 (n. 2); political styles of,
216–24; and class consciousness, 296,
301; and women's movements, 296,
309, 312; Left, 309, 316; media perceptions of, 325, 407 (n. 21); and
working-class women, 325–26, 437
(n. 38); definitions of, 397 (n. 6); and
conservative women, 403 (n. 2); and
party politics, 405 (n. 16); and gender
gap, 410 (n. 37); impact of civil rights
movement on, 438 (n. 58). *See also*
Women's liberation movement
(1960s); Women's rights movements
Ferenczi, Sandor, 145–46
Ferraro, Geraldine, 226, 227; campaign
for vice president, 229, 408 (n. 22)
Feuerbach, Anselm von, 128, 386
(n. 3)
Fiedler, Leslie, 324
Field, Mervin, 409 (n. 29)
Field, Stephen, 118, 119, 381 (n. 28)
Fifth Amendment, 216
Finley, Martha, 255, 418 (n. 28)
First Amendment: and polygamy, 117
Fisher, Katherine Ward, 82
Fisher, Sara, 177
Flacks, Richard, 315, 316, 320, 325

Flanagan, Maureen, 41
Flexner, Eleanor, 1–2, 306, 354 (n. 49),
433 (n. 35)
Fliegelman, Jay, 146
Flynn, Elizabeth Gurley, 300, 302, 430
(n. 3)
Foster care, 80, 367 (n. 40)
Foucault, Michel, 11, 12
Fourteenth Amendment, 18, 19–20,
216, 218
Fox-Genovese, Elizabeth, 142, 389
(n. 34)
Framingham Women's Prison (Massa-
chusetts), 170, 171; Eleanor Roo-
sevelt's support for, 172; Miriam Van
Waters at, 175, 178–83; staff of, 179,
180; club support for, 180; criticism
of, 182, 183
Franklin, John Hope, 139
Freedom: in antebellum society, 10; in
postwar era, 324; for postwar women,
330, 437 (n. 47)
Freedom Rides, 281, 333
"Freedom Summer" (1964), 207, 281
"Freedom Vote" campaign (Missis-
sippi), 206–7
Free love, 115
Freud, Sigmund, 128, 145–46
Friedan, Betty, 311, 326; and women's
liberation movement, 314; on moth-
erhood, 316, 318. *See also* Feminine
Mystique
Friedman, Sanford, 204
Fulbright, William, 282
Fuller, Margaret, 258
Fund for the Improvement of Post-
Secondary Education, 342

Gaines, Irene McCoy, 307
Galbraith, Kenneth, 323
Garment worker' strike (1909), 267;
mural of, 279
Gay rights movement, 210, 242
Gender: teaching of issues in, 5; social

construction of, 6, 37, 332, 347; and construction of power, 7, 9, 189, 214, 236, 237, 240–42; and citizenship, 8, 14, 18, 23–26, 214; and entitlements, 9, 18, 92; in generation gap, 13; role in constitutional rights, 18, 403 (n. 1); and aggression, 34, 355 (n. 55); and social reform, 37, 62; in construction of public policy, 42, 89, 237–38; and minimum wage legislation, 59–60, 364 (n. 98); and division of labor, 68, 111, 174, 287; nineteenth-century concept of, 68; role in Social Security benefits, 84, 87–89, 101–2; role in welfare state, 90, 239, 367 (n. 42); effect on social policy, 90, 370 (n. 14); and Old Age Insurance, 92, 94, 104, 106; and attitude towards slavery, 142–43; role in public health decisions, 159–63, 167–69; as source of authority, 186; role in politics, 214, 223, 240–42; and equality before law, 218–19; and equal representation, 224–25; in juvenile fiction, 250; role in Jewish culture, 291; ELF's view of, 292; CAW's ideology of, 300; formation of, 378 (n. 15); and spatial boundaries, 407 (n. 22)

Gender gap (voting), 225, 231, 234, 239; in candidate preference, 240; and electoral strategy, 406 (n. 17); role of issues in, 409 (n. 31); demography of, 410 (n. 37)

Gender relations: history of, 3; in mainstream history, 6, 14; and state formation, 8; and social change, 14; and race relations, 89

Gender roles, 8; and taxation, 28–29; and public health, 147–49, 159–63, 167–69; stereotyping of, 190, 227, 407 (n. 21); in *Little Women*, 264; of African American women, 339

General Federation of Women's Clubs (GFWC), 48, 432 (n. 22)

Generation gap, 313; gender in, 13; female, 314, 316, 334; causes of, 315

Genocide Convention, 282, 290

Georgieff, George, 31

Germ theory, 149–50

Gerson, Kathleen, 319, 330

Gibbons, Cardinal James, 45, 357 (n. 20)

Gilman, Charlotte Perkins, 256

Gimbel, Elinor, 299

Ginsberg, Allen, 323, 326

Ginsburg, Ruth Bader, 87

Ginzburg, Lori, 67

Girls, adolescent: and *Little Women*, 249, 252–55; ideals of, 255, 420 (n. 63); psychological development of, 317; reading habits of, 417 (n. 23). *See also* Juvenile fiction for girls

Glass ceiling, 230, 238

Glendon, Mary Ann, 18

Goldberg, Arthur, 282

Golden Notebook, The, (Lessing), 331

Goldman, Emma, 136

Goldsmith, Judy, 413 (n. 46)

Goldwater, S. S., 154

Gompers, Samuel, 50; and AALL, 57; and legislative action, 358 (n. 39), 362 (n. 87)

Goodman, Paul, 323

Gordon, Eugene, 281

Gordon, Felice, 398 (n. 8)

Gordon, June Croll, 283; and ELF, 273, 280; human rights activities of, 280, 281; on outreach programs, 289

Gordon, Linda, 9, 41

Gordon, Robert, 378 (n. 11)

Governors, women, 231, 233, 410 (n. 34)

Graham, Frank Porter, 208

Grandparents, old age benefits for, 88, 95

Gratz, Rebecca, 278

Great Awakening, 128

Great Depression (1930s): and welfare state, 80; CPUSA activities during, 431 (n. 16)

Greven, Philip, 386 (n. 2)
Griffin, Susan, 326, 332
Grimké, Angelina, 142
Grimké sisters, 2, 3
Growing Up Absurd (Goodman), 323
Gulf War (1991), 33; women in, 34
Gurewitsch, David, 201
Gutman, Herbert, 131

Hacking, Ian, 130
Hall, G. Stanley, 176
Hamer, Fannie Lou, 336
Hannah (slave), 137
Hansen, Alvin, 93
Harlan, John Marshall, 31, 354 (n. 49)
Harman, Lillian, 386 (n. 56)
Harper, Mary Ellen, 279
Harrison, Gladys, 30
Hart, Gary, 211
Hartmann, Susan, 187
Hauser, Kaspar, 127
Hawthorne, Nathaniel, 248, 254
Hayden, Casey, 331
Healey, Dorothy, 301, 433 (n. 36)
Hefner, Hugh, 323, 324, 329
Heilbrun, Carolyn G., 417 (n. 25)
Henry Street Settlement Adult Council,
    303
Herd, Shirley, 336, 337
Heredity, 74, 366 (n. 21)
Herman, Judith, 130, 137
Hickok, Lorena, 198–99, 201, 213, 402
    (n. 16)
Hidden Persuaders, The, (Packard), 323
Higginbotham, A. Leon, 145
Hill, Anita, 231, 409 (n. 30)
Hillquit, Morris, 57, 204, 361 (n. 76)
Hine, Darlene Clark, 3, 13
Historians, women, 1–2, 391 (n. 1);
    African American, 339, 342–43, 345.
    See also Women's history
History, normative, 14; and women's
    history, 6–7, 337; and African Ameri-
    can women's history, 340, 342

Hoar, E. Rockwood, 382 (n. 38)
Hobbes, Thomas, 20
Hobby, Oveta Culp, 229
Hobby, William P., Jr., 229
Hodes, Martha Elizabeth, 384 (n. 47)
Holcombe, Arthur, 55, 58; and mini-
    mum wage campaign, 61
Hollywood Women's Political Commit-
    tee, 228, 234, 410 (n. 36), 413 (n. 50)
Holocaust: effect on Jewish women's
    culture, 273, 292
Holtzman, Elizabeth, 288
Home theatricals, 255, 420 (n. 61)
Homosexuality, 402 (n. 22); taboo
    against, 204, 208; and exclusion from
    marriage, 376 (n. 1)
Hoover, Herbert, 177
Hoover, J. Edgar, 274
Horn, Joan Kelly, 230
Horne, Gerald, 430 (n. 7)
*Hospital Sketches and Camp and Fireside
    Stories* (Alcott), 252, 419 (n. 42)
House Un-American Activities Com-
    mittee (HUAC), 302; attack on CAW,
    296, 308, 309–11
House Ways and Means Committee:
    and Social Security benefits, 100, 105,
    372 (n. 33)
Housewives Leagues, 173
Housework, criticism of, 32, 321, 330,
    331, 354 (n. 47)
Howe, Edith, 69, 74
Howl (Ginsberg), 323
Hoyt, Gwendolyn, 31–32
Hull House, 47, 48; as model for Fram-
    ingham, 178
Human rights: ELF's work in, 280–87
Hunt, Patricia Stanford, 405 (n. 12)
Hunter, Clementine, 344
Huntington, James Otis, 43
Hutchinson, Anne, 279, 306
Hutchinson, Kay Bailey, 241, 413
    (n. 50)

Immigrants: Jewish, 12, 271, 423 (n. 85); cultural absorption of, 75; child protection for, 78; polygamy among, 117; to Israel, 285; ELF's support for, 286

Immigrants, women: assimilation of, 262–64, 275, 276, 295; Jewish, 270, 272. *See also* Women, Jewish

Incest, 144–45

Incidents in the Life of a Slave Girl (Jacobs), 135

Indentured servants, 383 (n. 45), 384 (n. 46)

Individualism: of women, 25–26; role in welfare state, 66; and child abuse, 80; and child welfare programs, 85, and privacy, 109; and marriage, 111; in postwar era, 322; and political authority, 351 (n. 17)

Industrial injuries, 54, 55, 56, 360 (n. 56), 361 (n. 75)

Industrialization: and social reform, 37, 40, 42; effect on women, 48

Infant mortality, 66, 69

Institute for Women Leaders, 5

Institution building, 173; separatism in, 174, 184, 187

International Association for Labor Legislation, 51

International Conference of Consumers' Leagues (First, Geneva), 58

International Labor Office, 358 (n. 43)

International Ladies' Garment Workers Union (ILGWU), 270

International Woman's Day (1946), 297

International Women's Congress against War and Fascism, 271

International Women's Day celebrations (ELF), 286

International Workers Order (IWO), 272, 303; liquidation of, 274, 426 (n. 16)

Interracial Mothers' Association, 281

Ireland, Patricia, 413 (n. 46)

Israel: Emma Lazarus's support for, 277; ELF's work for, 285–87, 428 (n. 50)

Jackson, Ada B., 307, 431 (n. 10)

Jackson, Andrew (slave), 137

Jackson, Ida, 45

Jacobs, Harriet, 135, 137

Jacobson v. Massachusetts, 394 (n. 25)

Jacoby, Johann, 277

Jealous mistresses (slave owners), 135–37, 142

Jeannette Rankin Brigade, 312

Jefferson, Thomas: on suffrage, 111; and slavery, 143–44

Jewish Cultural Clubs and Societies, 274, 275, 427 (n. 22)

Jewish fraternal organizations, 272, 275–76

Jewishness, cultural, 269, 290–95; of postwar era, 275

Jewish People's Fraternal Order (JPFO), 272, 292

Jim Crow laws, 205

Johnson, Joyce, 327–28

Johnson, Lady Bird, 226, 407 (n. 20)

Johnson, Lyndon, 202; Vietnam policy of, 207

Jones, Anne Hudson, 344

Jones, Carolyn C., 28–29

Jones, Claudia, 302, 308, 430 (n. 10)

Jordan, Barbara, 241

Judiciary, U.S.: effect on labor movement, 50; and child abuse, 80; on women's role in family, 88; on marriage contract, 113–14; power of, 114, 381 (n. 29); on public/private sphere, 114–15; on common-law marriage, 116, 386 (n. 56); and minimum wage campaigns, 363 (n. 87); on interracial marriage, 385 (n. 49). *See also* Supreme Court, U.S.

Jury service, 352 (n. 29); as obligation, 27, 29–32; permissive, 30, 31; and suffrage, 353 (n. 43)

Juster, Susan, 24

Juvenile fiction: gender in, 250; classics of, 417 (n. 28)

Juvenile fiction for girls, 247–48, 252, 418 (n. 39); Alcott's contributions to, 250, 254–55; marketing of, 255; consumption by Jewish girls, 262–63. *See also* Girls, adolescent

Kelley, Florence, 38; leadership of NCL, 36, 37, 43–45, 48; role in consumer movement, 45, 48–49; early life of, 47; social activism of, 47–49; and women's labor legislation, 48, 49–50, 57; and minimum wage campaigns, 58–60, 362 (n. 87), 363 (nn. 88, 92); and E. G. Evans, 59, 362 (n. 85); socialism of, 72; and child welfare, 76; and John Andrews, 359 (n. 45); in AALL, 359 (nn. 45, 46)

Kelley, William Darrah, 47

Kellogg-Briand Pact, 303

Kellor, Frances, 185

Keniston, Kenneth, 315, 316, 320

Kennedy, Edward, 210

Kennedy, John F., 314

Kennelly, Barbara, 412 (n. 44)

Kenyon, Dorothy, 185, 354 (n. 49)

Kerber, Linda, 8, 75–76

Kerouac, Jack, 323, 326, 327–28

Kerr, Florence, 196

Kessler-Harris, Alice, 6, 11

Key, Ellen, 76

Khrushchev, Nikita, 274

King, Bessie, 256, 257

King, Mary, 331–32

Knowledge: effect of gender on, 7; in state formation, 11; role in policy making, 11–12; subjugated, 12; relationship to power, 13; effect on consumerism, 45, 46

Ku Klux Klan, 284; Women's, 401 (n. 48)

Kunin, Madeleine, 240

Labor: unrest in nineteenth century, 40, 41; gender division of, 68, 111, 174, 287

Labor legislation, 42; NCL's role in, 46, 47, 48; Florence Kelley's role in, 48, 49–50; for women, 48, 49–51, 57, 76; scientific basis of, 53, 54, 56; minimum wage campaigns in, 57–61; Supreme Court decisions on, 61; effectiveness of, 361 (n. 68)

Lacan, Jacques, 128; on patriarchy, 143

Ladies Catholic Benevolent Association, 45

"Lady and the Mill Girl, The" (Lerner), 306

La Leche League, 75

Lamp, The (ELF publication), 281, 288

Landy, A., 300

Lape, Esther, 197

Lash, Joseph: biography of Eleanor Roosevelt, 192, 195, 401–2 (n. 3); friendship with Eleanor Roosevelt, 200, 201

Lassalle, Ferdinand, 277

Lathrop, Julia, 71; and child welfare, 76, 77

Lawes, Pearl, 431 (n. 10)

Lazarus, Emma, 271; publication of works, 272; biography of, 276, 277; on anti-Semitism, 284

League of Women Voters, 173, 239; and professionalization of reform, 185; female legislators in, 187; Eleanor Roosevelt in, 196, 197; and ERA campaign, 217, 218

League of Working Women's Clubs, 49

Learnfare programs, 368 (n. 57)

Lears, T. Jackson, 436 (n. 27)

Leavitt, Judith Walzer, 11

Lederle, Ernst J., 154

Left, political: women leaders of, 296, 297. *See also* New Left

Legislators, women, 229–30; and women's issues, 187, 224–25, 241–42, 406 (n. 18), 414 (n. 50); and ERA ratification, 222, 223, 405 (n. 12); public opinion on, 230–31; and Anita Hill case, 231, 232; number of, 233, 235–36, 237, 410 (n. 34), 411 (nn. 39, 40), 412 (n. 42); priorities of, 235; effectiveness of, 236; stereotypes of, 237; constraints on leadership, 238, 412 (n. 44); in state legislatures, 410 (n. 34), 411 (n. 40), 412 (n. 41); minority, 410 (n. 35); power of, 412 (n. 41); gender parity for, 412 (n. 44); impact of, 414 (n. 51); as outsiders, 414 (n. 51). *See also* Political candidates, women; Politics, electoral

Lemlich, Clara. *See* Shavelson, Clara Lemlich

Lenroot, Katharine, 83

Lerner, Carl, 2

Lerner, Gerda, 1, 12, 14, 125, 334; publications of, 2–4; *The Female Experience*, 3; *Black Women in White America*, 3, 125, 338; *The Creation of Patriarchy*, 4; *The Creation of Feminist Consciousness*, 4, 125, 334; and marginalization of women, 12, 13; and second-wave feminism, 127; and access to learning, 249; poetry of, 285; "The Lady and the Mill Girl," 306; in CAW, 306, 433 (nn. 35, 41); and creation of patriarchy, 335; in Organization of American Historians, 342; and Dorothy Kenyan, 354 (n. 49)

Lesbianism, 174, 175, 400 (n. 41); at Framingham Women's Prison, 175; social networks of, 185, 187; and women candidates, 408 (n. 22)

Lessing, Doris, 331

Letourneau, Leonea, 395 (n. 51)

Levin, Aaron, 423 (n. 86)

Libbey, Laura Jean, 261, 264, 422 (n. 84)

Liberty Lobby, 284

Lieber, Francis, 377 (n. 6), 382 (n. 40)

Lincoln, Abraham, 278; melancholia of, 211

Linton, Albert, 93, 95–96; on flat entitlements, 97; and equity for men, 98, 99

Littlefield, Jennifer, 203

Little Men (Alcott), 252, 254, 256

Little Rosebud's Lovers (Libbey), 261, 422 (n. 84)

Little Women (Alcott): as social text, 11; commissioning of, 245–48; popularity of, 246–49, 255, 265–66, 417 (n. 23); and cultural work, 247, 416 (n. 15); readers' response to, 247–48, 249, 250–53, 260–61, 265, 422 (n. 78); feminist readings of, 248; marketing of, 248, 255–56; critical reception of, 248, 416 (nn. 16, 17); as quest story, 249, 251, 252, 253, 257, 265; and working-class women, 249, 261–62, 417 (n. 21); as middle-class model, 249, 262–64; composition of, 249–50; marriage in, 251–52, 258, 259, 260; autobiographical aspects of, 252–53; religious viewpoint of, 255, 420 (n. 60); as bildungsroman, 257; selfhood in, 259; African American readers of, 260, 422 (n. 81); and Jewish immigrant women, 262–64; gender roles in, 264; motherhood in, 265, 424 (n. 95); Civil War in, 266; library use of, 415 (n. 7); literary influence of, 416 (n. 11); lesbian readers of, 418 (n. 35); royalties of, 420 (n. 56). *See also* Alcott, Louisa May

Little Women, Part Second (Alcott), 246, 248, 250, 251; publication of, 252, 253

Lobbying, legislative: for ERA, 174, 219, 220; by feminists, 225

Locke, John, 19

nies, 113, 380 (n. 22), 383 (n. 45); as civil contract, 113–14, 115, 352 (n. 29), 380 (n. 22); public/private aspects of, 114–15; "complex," 115; common-law, 115, 116, 382 (n. 34), 386 (n. 56); restrictions on, 118–19, 120, 383–84 (nn. 44, 47); and segregation, 119; "Boston," 197; in *Little Women*, 251–52, 258, 259, 260; and women's liberation movement (1960s), 316, 319; and Feminine Mystique, 316, 329–30; rejection of, 329–30, 334; in de Beauvoir, 330; exclusions from, 376 (n. 1); as sexual contract, 377 (n. 5); in Civil Rights Act (1866), 381 (n. 25); interracial, 383–84 (nn. 45, 47), 385 (nn. 49, 50, 52), 386 (n. 55). *See also* Contracts; Property

Marshall, T. H., 349 (n. 2)
Marshall Plan, 308
Martin, Lynn, 230
Marx, Karl, 132, 277
Mason, Lucy Randolph, 93
Mason, Vivian Carter, 307, 430 (n. 3)
Massachusetts: ERA campaign in, 216
Massachusetts Association for Labor Legislation, 54, 55, 59, 360 (n. 65)
Massachusetts Consumers' League, 45, 59
Massachusetts Society for Social Hygiene, 182
Massachusetts State Federation of Women's Clubs, 182
Masson, Jeffrey, 146
Materialism, 334; and New Left movement, 315; in postwar culture, 323
Maternalism (women's reform), 41, 42, 65; strategy of, 66, 68; and development of social work, 69, 70–71; and child protection movements, 79–80; and family wage, 82; and AFDC, 85; in postsuffrage era, 173; in peace movement, 296; consequences of,

365 (n. 2); and welfare state, 373 (n. 40). *See also* Activism; Reformers, women

Matthews, Burnita Shelton, 28
Matthews, Robert, 126
May, Elaine Tyler, 299
Mayors, women, 233, 235, 408 (n. 26), 410 (n. 34); salaries of, 411 (n. 40)
Mays, Benjamin, 138
Means testing: for ADC, 83; in Social Security Act, 90, 91, 105
Meeropol, Ann, 274
Melish, Mary Jane, 308
Men: as normative, 6; social insurance programs for, 81; equity under Social Security, 95–100; civil status of, 111
Men, married: rights of, 21–23
Mensch, Betty, 380 (n. 24)
Mercer, Lucy, 195–96, 197, 201
Merriam, Eve, 2, 276
Meyer, Annie Nathan, 422 (n. 82)
Mezey, Susan Gluck, 235
Michigan Consumers' League, 46
Mickey, M. Ray, 140
Middle class, American: and children's rights, 9; during nineteenth century, 40. *See also* Women, middle-class
Middle East, peace in, 286–87
Mikulski, Barbara, 233, 234, 406 (n. 18)
Military service, obligatory, 17, 18, 19, 27, 32–35
Millard, Betty, 304, 308
Miller, Alice, 133–34
Miller, Earl, 197–98, 199, 201
Miller, Samuel, 115
Mills, C. Wright, 323
Minimum wage campaigns, 57–61, 362 (nn. 85, 86, 87); Florence Kelley in, 58–60; of AALL, 60–61; of CAW, 304. *See also* Family wage; Wages
Mink, Patsy, 227
Minor v. Happersett, 18–19
Miscegenation, 384 (nn. 45, 46, 47), 385 (nn. 52, 55)

(n. 38), 388 (n. 18); Jefferson's view
of, 143–44; escape from, 339; and
bigamy, 382 (n. 38); status of children
in, 384 (n. 45); northern, 389 (n. 28)
Slavery (Elkins), 130–31, 138–39
Slaves: marriage of, 111–12, 379 (n. 16);
sexual abuse of, 130, 134–39, 140,
142; internalization of attitudes, 130–
31; anger among, 133–34, 138; victimization of, 137, 338; in plantation
communities, 139; isolated, 139, 388
(n. 28); religion of, 139–40; powerlessness of, 140
Smeal, Eleanor, 239, 413 (n. 46)
Smith, Hilda, 196
Smith, Lillian, 146, 185
Smith, Margaret Chase, 187
Smith, Rogers, 353 (n. 38)
Smith-Rosenberg, Carroll, 24
Snelling, Paula, 185
Social contract, 19; Constitution as, 20,
21; and law of domestic relations,
21–23; for women, 23; and labor
standards, 61; of ADC, 83; legal rela-
tions in, 380 (n. 24)
Social insurance paradigm (of social
work), 71, 72
Social insurance programs: of New
Deal, 80; for men, 81; in Social Secu-
rity amendments, 90. *See also* Social
Security
Socialism: of Florence Kelley, 72; of
Jane Addams, 72; of Gabriel Lowen-
stein, 204; Jewish-based, 272, 277, 424
(n. 2); in de Beauvoir, 331
Socialist Party, 72
Social justice, role of CAW in, 297
Social policy: role of knowledge in, 12;
effect of gender on, 90, 370 (n. 14)
Social processes: evaluation of, 7;
women's influence in, 10, 14
Social reform: during Progressive Era,
36–37, 41, 61–62; role of gender in,
37, 62; role of women in, 41, 65, 66,

68, 79–80, 82, 170–71; in antebellum
period, 67, 171; and child welfare
movements, 76–77; and religious
values, 185; professionalization of,
185, 186; and women's separatism,
187–88, 397 (n. 5); racial goals in, 366
(n. 25)
Social scientists, women, 176, 399
(n. 18)
Social Security Act (1935), 80; opposition to, 90, 102; components of,
90–91
Social Security Act (1939 amendments
to), 11, 89; impact on women, 12,
102, 104–5; family in, 94–102. *See also*
Federal Advisory Council on Social
Security
Social Security benefits, 12; for children,
65, 82; for widowers, 87–88, 373
(n. 38); for widows, 88, 91–92, 94–96,
101, 103; exclusions from, 92, 103,
371 (n. 22), 375 (n. 70); for married
women, 94–102; adequacy in, 95,
96, 98, 104; integrated system of, 97,
374 (n. 43); caps on, 101; universal,
102–3; for African Americans, 103,
369 (n. 59); legislative history of, 370
(n. 17)
Social Security Board (SSB), 92, 93; on
exclusions, 103, 375 (n. 70)
Social work: casework paradigm of, 42,
72, 82; women in, 63–67, 170,
183–84, 366 (n. 17); role of maternalism in, 69, 70–71; social insurance
paradigm of, 71, 72; child-centered,
71, 77; as cause of poverty, 72; in
New Deal programs, 80; view of
family life, 82; professionalization of,
170, 171, 183; male domination of,
171
Societies for the Prevention of Cruelty
to Children (SPCCs), 77–79, 367
(n. 36)
Sojourners for Truth and Justice, 281

Soper, George: theory of typhoid transmission, 151; and Mary Mallon case, 155–56, 159, 160, 161, 392 (n. 7)

Soul murder, 128, 146; definition of, 127

South, antebellum: freedom in, 10; social reform in, 67, 171; family life in, 136–37, 141–42, 146, 382 (n. 38), 389 (n. 34); divorce in, 144; abuse of women in, 144–46

South, postsuffrage era in, 173

South Africa, U.N. delegation to, 206

Souvestre, Marie, 193–94, 201; influence on Eleanor Roosevelt, 196, 197, 402 (n. 3)

Soviet Union: ELF's stance toward, 274, 284–85, 295; expansion into Eastern Europe, 299; CAW's support for, 308, 309

SPCC. See Societies for the Prevention of Cruelty to Children

Spruill, Julia Cherry, 2

Stampp, Kenneth, 133

Stanley, Amy, 381 (n. 25)

Stanton, Elizabeth Cady, 25–26, 34, 306; at Seneca Falls, 310

State: role in domestic relations, 9; power over women, 18; rights of citizens in, 19; role of duty in, 20; strong state-weak state paradigm, 41; protection of children by, 69, 78; control over family, 69, 105, 387 (n. 11); contract theory of, 108; and institution of marriage, 108–9, 110, 118, 378 (n. 11); autonomy of, 370 (n. 13); contracts in, 380 (n. 24)

State formation: role of women in, 7, 8; power in, 11; during nineteenth century, 40; role of child custody in, 69–70; role of marriage in, 117

Steinem, Gloria, 311, 325

Steinson, Barbara, 401 (n. 48)

Stern, Elizabeth G., 262–63, 283, 423 (n. 86)

Stern, Madeleine B., 416 (n. 13)

Stevenson, Adlai, 282

Stewart-Lai, Carlotta, 344, 345

Stokes, Rose Pastor, 264, 424 (n. 92)

Story, Joseph, 113, 381 (n. 25)

Stowe, Harriet Beecher, 306, 417 (n. 27), 420 (nn. 55, 59)

Strauss, Anna Lord, 430 (n. 7)

Student movement, 205, 334; women in, 314

Student Nonviolent Coordinating Committee, 206, 331

Suffrage: universal, 26; and taxation, 28–29, 353 (n. 38); Thomas Jefferson on, 111; and marriage, 112–13

Suffrage, women's, 10, 23; as constitutional right, 18–19; opposition to, 26–27; and domestic relationships, 26–27, 352 (n. 28); and jury service, 29–32, 353 (n. 43); and child welfare, 74; and decline in women's reform movements, 170, 171, 173, 397 (n. 4); militancy in, 220; Clara Shavelson's work in, 270; ELF's celebration of, 286

Suhl, Yuri, 277

Supreme Court, U.S.: on women's citizenship, 28; and women's jury service, 30, 31; labor decisions of, 51, 61; on widow's benefits, 87; on suffrage qualifications, 112–13; on public/private sphere, 114–15, 381 (n. 28); on marriage, 116; on polygamy, 116–17; on divorce, 117–18, 119; on abortion, 231, 239; and taxation of women, 353 (n. 38); on coverture, 355 (n. 56); on slave marriages, 379 (n. 16); on marriage, 381 (n. 25); on monogamy, 382 (n. 40); on miscegenation, 385 (n. 52). See also Judiciary, U.S.

Survey (reform periodical), 36

Survivor's insurance (Social Security), 94, 372 (nn. 30, 33)

Sweatshops, 43, 58, 279, 292

373 (n. 35); Old Age Insurance for, 91–92. *See also* Women, married
Wiesenfeld, Stephen, 87, 88
Wife beating, 77, 79, 367 (n. 38)
Wilkerson, Doxey, 430 (n. 9)
Wilkins, Roy, 103
Willebrandt, Mabel Walker, 185
Williams, Clayton, 409 (n. 32)
Williamson, William, 93, 101, 369 (n. 7), 371 (n. 22)
Willis, Ellen, 326
Wilmore, Gayraud S., 140
Wischnewetzky, Lazare, 47
Wisconsin Consumer's League, 45–46
Wisconsin Industrial Commission, 363 (n. 92)
Wise, Louise Waterman, 288
Wisner, Elizabeth, 93, 96
Witches, 1
Witte, Edwin, 93
Wives. *See* Women, married
Wolfson, Theresa, 184
Wollstonecraft, Mary, 24, 277, 351 (n. 19); and motherhood, 75
Womanhood, Christian, 186
Women: as caregivers, 1; ritual status of, 1; role in public culture, 2, 41, 42; as community builders, 3, 344; subordination of, 4, 331, 332; historical agency of, 6, 7, 8, 214, 438 (n. 53); constitutional rights of, 8, 17; political strategies of, 8–9, 216–24, 242; political history of, 9, 215; marginalization of, 12, 13, 223, 224, 332; impact of Social Security amendments on, 12, 102, 104–5; in military service, 17, 18, 19, 32–35, 355 (n. 52); relationship to state, 18; property rights of, 21–23, 352 (n. 29); civic identity of, 21–27, 351 (n. 17), 354 (n. 49); citizenship of, 23, 27–28, 111, 350 (n. 14), 352 (n. 31), 354 (n. 49), 431 (n. 14); as "other," 24, 429 (n. 71), 438 (n. 53); capability of, 24–

25; role in American republic, 24–25; individualism of, 25–26; as jurors, 30–32, 304, 354 (n. 49); role in consumer movement, 43–46; Catholic, 45; effect of industrialization on, 48; labor legislation for, 48, 49–51, 57, 76; role in child welfare, 63; philanthropic work of, 67; physiological differences with men, 68; "new," 76; victimization of, 79, 332, 338; exclusions from Social Security, 92, 371 (n. 22); sexual harassment of, 134–39; as property, 136; obedience of, 141; treatment in public health issues, 148, 149, 160; institution building by, 173; as social scientists, 176, 399 (n. 18); political authority of, 183–87; public authority of, 184, 186; maternal health care for, 186; antifeminist, 242; as authors, 254–55; creativity of, 257–58; career opportunities for, 258–59, 318–19; psychological development of, 317; alienated, 322, 324; sexual liberation for, 329; legal status of, 352 (n. 29); conservative, 401 (n. 48), 403 (n. 2)
Women, African American: history of, 5, 13, 335–37, 343–44; activism among, 67, 69, 75, 171; as mothers, 74–75; after suffrage, 173; in public office, 226, 227, 234, 235; reading habits of, 260–61; ELF's support for, 282; in CAW, 299, 300, 306–8, 430 (nn. 9, 10), 433 (n. 41); mobility of, 339; worldview of, 339; survival strategies of, 339–40; community-building of, 344; organizations of, 345; marginalization of, 347; in state legislatures, 410 (n. 35). *See also* African Americans
Women, immigrant: citizenship of, 28, 353 (n. 37)
Women, Jewish, 12, 70; in NCL, 45; workplace culture of, 174; and *Little*

GENDER & AMERICAN CULTURE

Within the Plantation Household: Black and White Women of the Old South,
   by Elizabeth Fox-Genovese (1988)

The Limits of Sisterhood: The Beecher Sisters on Women's Rights
   and Woman's Sphere,
   by Jeanne Boydston, Mary Kelley, and Anne Margolis (1988)